Foundations

of Library and Information Science

2ND EDITION

RICHARD E. RUBIN

Neal-Schuman Publishers, Inc.
New York   London

Published by Neal-Schuman Publishers, Inc.
100 William Street, Suite 2004
New York, NY 10038

Printed and bound in the United States of America.

The paper used in this publication meets the minimum requirements of American Standard for Information Sciences—Permanence of Paper for Printed Materials. ANSI 239.48–1992. ∞

Library of Congress Cataloging-in-Publication Data

Rubin, Richard, 1949–
   Foundations of library and information science / Richard E. Rubin.— 2nd ed.
       p. cm.
   Includes bibliographical references and index.
   ISBN 1–55570–518–9 (alk. paper)
   1. Library science—United States. 2. Information Science—United States.   I. Title.
   Z665.2.U6R83 2004
   020'-0973—dc22   2004046010

Table of Contents

List of Figures

Foreword

Since the first edition of *Foundations of Library and Information Science* in 2000, the current American political landscape is placing librarians at the forefront of debates about equal access to information, free speech, and privacy issues in the wake of recent court decisions and legislative actions. Internet access and Web-filtering debates were already emerging in 2000, but the 2003 Supreme Court decision that the Children's Internet Protection Act (CIPA) was constitutional means that equal access to information can no longer be assumed to take place in public libraries. Similarly, the USA Patriot Act was thrust upon the profession as painfully as the events of September 11, 2001—which inspired the hastily written, nearly impenetrable legislation. As of this writing, there is movement to eliminate the severe library provisions, but only because the American Library Association joined in a lawsuit to obtain information about how many times the government sought library records.

Libraries continue to survive, and sometimes even thrive, amidst this charged landscape. One need only read the annual April architecture issue in *American Libraries* to see resourceful renovations and splendid new public, special, and academic library buildings. This is the architecture of reassurance, to appropriate the title of a recent exhibition about Disney Theme Parks.[1] One of the premises of the exhibit was that after World War II, people were drawn to the ideal of American life that the Disney theme parks represented. Libraries, too, represent an American ideal, and library buildings themselves often attract visitors. Library use is on the rise, and although fewer users are checking out books, use of library computers to access the Internet is escalating.

Challenges to library services and programming abound. Funding for library construction or for wiring libraries is often easier to obtain than the ongoing support that is required to sustain or improve services. Internet access is available in about 95 percent of American public libraries,[2] yet these libraries often lack the resources required for staffing and technical support. In many parts of the country, state aid to libraries has been cut dramatically.[3] At the same time, however, federal aid under the Library Services and Technology Act has increased significantly.

How can one make sense of the complex landscape of librarianship today?

Luckily, we have Richard Rubin to help us understand the political, social, and economic dynamics that help shape libraries. He tackles the issues in three ways: by looking at the library as a cultural institution, by examining the major national information policies that affect libraries, and by considering the profession of librarianship.

The multiple lenses with which Dr. Rubin views the profession make this book invaluable. The historical background helps to establish the traditions and values of librarianship. The chapters on policy provide us with the crucial context for the environment in which we work. The ethics and standards chapter addresses the challenges inherent in all service professions. Throughout the book, Dr. Rubin makes it possible to understand the values—and sometimes the challenge—of librarianship in a democratic society.

Dr. Rubin has delineated a foundation that amply supports further study while encouraging action. It should be the undertaking of everyone who reads this book to build on this foundation to create new and flexible library structures.

Michèle V. Cloonan
Dean, Simmons College Graduate School of Library and Information Science

NOTES

1. *The Architecture of Reassurance: Designing the Disney Theme Park* (Montreal: The Canadian Centre for Architecture, 1997).
2. Cited in "News," *Library Journal* 129 (April 1, 2004): 16.
3. A Library Funding page now exists on the American Library Association website: *http://www.ala.org/ala/news/libraryfunding/libraryfunding.htm*

Preface

Back in the ancient days of early 2000, the first edition of *Foundations of Library and Information Science* began with the sentence: "These are not quiet times for anyone involved with library and information services." In hindsight, that was a vast understatement. The scope and rapidity of change within our profession has never been as great as it is now. Socially our world has changed—the digital divide, information architecture, knowledge management. Legally our world has changed—the Digital Millennium Copyright Act, Uniform Computer Information Transactions Act (UCITA), the No Child Left Behind Act, the USA Patriot Act. Technologically our world has changed—Open Source, XML, metadata, Google. These changes have made our lives more interesting, our institutions more diverse and complex, our profession more essential, and our education more important. Information professionals need to respond to the changes in our world with adaptability, creativity, flexibility, and resolve. An appropriate response to these changes must be rooted in an understanding of our profession, practice, and progression.

In response to the many changes occurring in the field and the society, this second edition of *Foundations of Library and Information Science* preserves much of the content and organization of its predecessor, but introduces new discussion of issues important to the profession. In addition to the legal and technological changes mentioned above, this new edition covers (1) the ever-increasing impact of the Internet and the World Wide Web on library and information science, the nature of information, and society in general; (2) evolving fields and aspects of information science, such as competitive intelligence; (3) new issues affecting intellectual freedom, such as filtering and the impact of homeland security activities; (4) the evolving impact of digital libraries and metadata; and (5) the changing environment of library and information science education. Important revisions have also been made—important because ours is a profession that is anything but static. The information throughout the text has been updated, including discussions of the information infrastructure, intellectual freedom, current issues in the organization of information (MARC 21, Dublin Core, metadata), and copyright issues (including digital rights management and file sharing). This edition also takes on the changes facing academic, public, school, and special libraries, including scholarly publishing, access to government documents, censorship, diversity, preservation, information literacy, and the information commons.

Not so very long ago a basic library and information text would simply have been about libraries and librarians. A discussion of the history of libraries, a review of the basic services provided by them, some observations on organizational structure, and a review of library classification systems would have sufficed. This is no longer a possibility. The library is now embedded in a complex and dynamic society, in which, according to some, information is the ultimate commodity. For librarians and information professionals, the value of information is nothing new, though the emphasis on information creation, organization, and access places an incredible responsibility on our profession and our practice.

PURPOSE

The primary purpose of *Foundations of Library and Information Science* remains: to explain the current information environment to students of library and information science and to practitioners who are grappling with these issues, so that further study and practice will be informed by a realistic picture of the still-developing information society. Without such a context, it is impossible to grasp the challenges that the profession faces.

There is ongoing debate as to whether library science and information science are separate disciplines. There is also argument about what constitutes the domain of each. *Foundations of Library and Information Science* is focused on the complementary nature of these two disciplines using Boyd Rayward's 1983 description of the relationship between library and information science as "a disciplinary continuum . . . with no easily identifiable boundary separating them, though the difference between the extreme ends of the continuum are clear and even dramatic" (p. 344). This book assumes that the areas can be discussed jointly in a manner that is fruitful to all those entering the profession: it emphasizes the points of convergence and the interrelationships.

Bearing this emphasis in mind, *Foundations of Library and Information Science* is designed to accomplish six objectives:

1. To provide an introduction to the field for individuals intending to work in libraries or "library-like" institutions, related settings, or the information field in general. Reference will also be made to other institutions that share the mission of libraries or information centers.

2. To identify and discuss major topics and issues in library and information science that are current in the United States and which will continue to affect the profession for years to come. Library and information science is changing rapidly, and this book provides a summary of some of the issues that are likely to have the greatest impact.

3. To provide librarians and information professionals with an opportunity to refresh their knowledge through a systematic review of major issues and topics that have changed the field. As the profession progresses, it is useful to look back at its development and heritage, which informs and structures how we act and practice today and in the future.

4. To introduce the profession to interested individuals or those undecided about entering the library and information science field, and to show its multifaceted character and possibility. There is ample evidence that many individuals will be needed to create, organize, and disseminate information—not only librarians, but also many individuals who will not be called "librarians" but will perform similar functions.

5. To place librarianship in a larger social, economic, and political context. It is too easy to view the work of librarians purely within the institutional setting, noting only those topics that deal directly in the day-to-day affairs of librarianship. Increasingly librarianship must interact with a variety of political, economic, technological, and social forces.

6. To invite the interested reader to explore further topics raised in this discussion, such as the history of library science; reference, cataloging, and computer science; and the many facets of library and information science that continue to have an impact on librarianship and on our society. This is not a closed discussion, but rather one that encourages further reading, research and exchange.

ORGANIZATION

Foundations of Library and Information Science discusses the field's broader, contextual issues first; the focus then narrows in on libraries and librarianship.

Chapter 1, "The Information Infrastructure: Libraries in Context,"

presents a context for library and information science by placing libraries and librarians within the broader perspective of the information infrastructure. To grasp the role of libraries today, it is necessary to examine the vast array of societal information components and channels and
to understand how these information channels are used or misused.

Chapter 2, "Information Science: A Service Perspective," concentrates
on information science, calling special attention to those aspects of the
discipline that inform the work of librarians and information center personnel.

Chapter 3, "Redefining the Library: The Impacts and Implications
of Technological Change," deals with one of the biggest areas of change
in our field, the growth of information technologies, especially those
that have affected the organization and delivery of information in libraries. Information technologies have changed the way information
providers in all types of organizations interact with their users. Issues
arising out of these changes are addressed.

Chapters 4 and 5, "Information Policy: Stakeholders and Agendas,"
and "Information Policy as Library Policy: Intellectual Freedom" respectively, define and examine information policy. Government, business
and industry, public institutions, librarians, and citizens all are stakeholders trying to shape how information will be disseminated and who
will disseminate it. Chapter 4 discusses the more general aspects of information policy; in Chapter 5 the focus shifts to libraries in particular,
including those information policies (for example, intellectual freedom
and equitable access to information) that govern library use.

Chapter 6, "Information Organization: Issues and Techniques," discusses one of the truly remarkable aspects of libraries and other information providers—their organization of information. In spite of the vast
amounts of disparate knowledge stored in them, refined use of classification systems, subject headings, thesauri, databases, and powerful catalogs enables libraries to offer information retrieval on demand. Organization is still key to our practice and deserves careful examination.

Chapter 7, "From Past to Present: The Library's Mission and Its Values," reviews the historic mission of libraries and reveals the underlying values that help define the role of libraries today. Many of the field's
contemporary values have their roots in the ideals of the past. This discussion also provides a foundation for Chapter 8, "Ethics and Standards:
Professional Practices in Library and Information Science," which deals
with the ethical aspects of library and information science. The relationship between information provider and information seeker must be one

of trust and honesty, and the provider must have a strong sense of professional obligation. This chapter discusses areas of ethical concern to information providers, especially the competing interests that are involved in making ethical judgments. The subjects of these two chapters (mission, values, ethics and standards) are still very much a living part of library and information science—concerns that are changing and reshaping our profession every day.

Chapter 9, "The Library as Institution: An Organizational View," examines the various types of libraries, their internal functions, and the major organizational issues that they face. An understanding of this institutional infrastructure is necessary for all information professionals.

Chapter 10, "Librarianship: An Evolving Profession," reviews the evolution and development of the library profession. The contemporary American librarian is a product of more than a hundred years of professional evolution. Understanding the development of librarianship will help contemporary librarians place the current professional tensions and demands in perspective.

To allow an examination of the same topic from different vantage points, *Foundations of Library and Information Science* tackles most topics solely in one chapter, but some are raised anew in a different context in a different chapter. For example, censorship and intellectual freedom issues are found in the chapters on information policy (Chapters 4 and 5) and library organization (Chapter 9). The Internet and Web, because they undergird most information transmission today, are covered in many chapters.

A revised list of highly selected readings follows Chapter 10. These selections not only provide sources of further information, but should also stimulate thought on the basic issues raised in this text. Of course readers must understand that continuous consultation with the most recently published material is essential if one is to stay current.

Appendices are included to provide supporting information. They include a fully updated, selected listing of library and information science periodicals, indexes, encyclopedias, and dictionaries that may be helpful to those who are interested in the profession; a revised list of major library and information-related organizations; and a list of accredited graduate programs of library and information studies.

No librarian can function unless he or she understands the importance of information, how libraries are organized intellectually and administratively, the effects of information policies, and the values and ethics of libraries and the profession. The challenge for all professionals is to stay current in a world in flux. The library is a special place, librarianship a special profession. The roles of the former and latter, as well as the broader forces that shape those roles, constitute the major focus of *Foundations of Library and Information Science*. Its goal is to be a necessary resource for those entering the profession and those who have already taken their place within it.

REFERENCE

Rayward, Boyd. "Library and Information Sciences." In *The Study of Information: Interdisciplinary Messages*. Edited by Fritz Machlup and Una Mansfield. New York: Wiley, 1983, 343–363.

Acknowledgments

The second edition of this book would not have been possible without the considerable help and support of many individuals. Thanks go to Carolyn Brodie, Greg Byerly, William Caynon, Thomas Froehlich, Meghan Harper, Jason Holmes, Mary Stansbury, Donald Wicks, Yin Zhang, and Marcia Zeng for contributing their thoughts and carefully reviewing and commenting on drafts of various chapters. Thanks also to graduate assistants Jennifer Greene, Megan Bushong Lyon, and Lyndsay Martinko, who provided invaluable assistance locating, verifying, and preparing information collected for the book. Thanks must also go to the outside readers of the manuscript whose valuable criticisms improved the work substantially. Special thanks to my wife, Marcia, and daughter, Rachel, for their incredible patience.

1

The Information Infrastructure: Libraries in Context

As the amount of information grows, so does the challenge of providing information to those who need it. No group is more aware of this than librarians, who have been trying to collect, organize, and disseminate recorded knowledge for centuries. Information once obtained primarily through books, periodicals, and other print materials is now available in additional formats, such as videocassettes, audiocassettes, microfilm, laser discs, DVDs, and the World Wide Web. Librarians, as well as the public, often feel uneasy with the tremendous growth of information. This uneasiness is evidenced by the way we talk about such growth. Consider some of the expressions that are used to describe it:[1]

Information *explosion*. This common expression reflects many of our concerns. An explosion is dangerous, terrifying, and unanticipated; it suggests a world out of control. To come near it is to risk being destroyed; to ignore it does not mean it does not exist or that its effects can be avoided.

The *flood* of information. A flood is another symbol of catastrophe. It conveys an image of being overwhelmed and of victims helplessly being swept away. As with an explosion, there is lack of control over the raging tide of information. In its wake are left ruins.

Bombarded by information. Yet another image of destruction, this time by repetitive bursts, is that of information crashing in on the heads of its

1

victims and destroying them. It is descriptive of warfare with an enemy that produces a firestorm of chaos.

Information *overload*. This image is an electronic one conveying the sense that the amount of information is so great that it short circuits our brains, causing us to malfunction and break down. It conveys the discomforting notion that we need information to live, just as a machine needs electricity to function, but too much information coming in at an unregulated pace is destructive.

All of these images suggest fear and trepidation. One seldom hears an optimistic phrase like "cornucopia of information," reflecting pleasure at its abundance, although "wealth of information" is sometimes heard. Are we in an age of information anxiety? If so, it is the librarian who can help reduce this anxiety. Few professions have been so devoted to helping people find their way among the bewildering variety of information sources.

If the librarian is to continue to collect, organize, and disseminate information on demand, it is vital that the way information flows in our society be understood. Only then can librarians exploit the ever-expanding information resources and channels and serve the information needs of library users. Today, such an understanding comes, in part, from the realization that the library is a member of a much larger structure: the "information infrastructure." An infrastructure is both a foundation and a framework, much the same as the infrastructure of a house includes its foundation and frame. Without such a structure the house would collapse. Societies have a variety of infrastructures. For example, the United States has a transportation infrastructure that is necessary for efficient travel. This includes highways, train tracks, air routes, and waterways. It also includes the governmental agencies that regulate transportation. An information infrastructure is in many ways like a transportation infrastructure, except that the "traffic" is information rather than modes of transportation. An information infrastructure makes it possible for information to be created and disseminated. Information infrastructures vary greatly in their sophistication: some are very primitive and inefficient, others are highly advanced and efficient. As might be expected, the U.S. information infrastructure is advanced and complex, and libraries are but one part of it. This is not to diminish the role of libraries. On the contrary, as we will see in subsequent chapters, the values and traditions of libraries make them a vital part of that infrastructure. But if libraries are to thrive within it, they must become increasingly aware of how they fit in.

How can we understand the components of the information infrastructure and the place of the library? One way is to consider this structure in terms of the process that begins with the creation of information and ends with its use. This process is sometimes referred to as the information cycle. The traditional information cycle can be characterized as shown in Figure 1.1.

From the traditional perspective of the information cycle, the information infrastructure consists of institutions and individuals involved in a linear process by which information is created, disseminated, and used in the society. At the foundation of such a cycle are the creators of information, and here, information should be seen very broadly as any message to be conveyed. So writers, researchers, artists, musicians, and database producers can be seen as creators of information. Generally, creators of information embody their ideas in a product or physical form—traditionally a book, an article, a painting, or sheet music, more recently a multimedia presentation, a database, or a Web site. In general, the products are made available by someone other than the creator—a distributor could be a publisher or a vendor (who makes the products of many creators available). Databases are often distributed by database vendors. In turn, many agencies perform the function of disseminator. This is a function similar to wholesaling in that disseminators acquire significant volumes of materials from distributors and disseminate the materials to individual users. In the information world,

Figure 1.1
Information Infrastructure Viewed as
Part of the Information Cycle

Creators	Products	Distributors	Disseminators	Users
Authors	Books	Publishers	Schools	Individuals
Artists/Musicians	Magazines	Vendors	Libraries	Researchers
Database	CD-ROMs	Internet	Universities	Students
producers	Databases	providers	Museums	Employers
	Web pages		Businesses	Employees
			Governmental	
			agencies	

Source: Adapted from Science Applications International Corporation (SAIC). *Information Warfare: Legal, Regulatory, Policy and Organizational Considerations for Assurance*. Washington, D.C.: Joint Staff, 1995.

many of these entities are part of the public as well as the private sector and include schools, universities, governmental agencies, bookstores, and libraries. Finally, there are the users, those who consume and use the information. The user may be the average citizen or business person who visits the local bookstore or library, a student visiting the school library, or a researcher using a special research collection at a governmental research center or academic institution.

Overall, the library can be viewed as an institution involved in the dissemination of information—it is an intermediary between the user and the information that has been created. The character of library collections is affected by the creators of information. Librarians must organize the various products provided, they must negotiate with vendors, and they must deal with library users.

This traditional view, however, has been changed by the Web, which has dramatically altered the relationships between creators, products, distributors, disseminators and users. In the past, participants in the cycle had a distinct, linear relationship. By contrast, in the Web environment, authorship and the functions of authorship have changed. This dynamic relationship is characterized in Figure 1.2.

In the new characterization, who becomes an author and the role of authors in publication and distribution have broadened. The traditional aspects of the information cycle remain (the periphery of the circle), but within this circle is a dynamic relationship in which such agencies as publishers, schools, and libraries also can become authors (for example, through individual Web pages). Similarly, authors may no longer rely on individual publishers and distributors to produce and disseminate their work, but publish and distribute themselves. Hence, a novelist might write a novel, put it on the Web, and distribute it directly to the readership, albeit for a fee. Similarly, a musician might create, distribute, and disseminate musical works directly to musical consumers. The impact of this new dimension to the information cycle on authors, distributors, and disseminators will no doubt continue to be considerable.

Another way to look at the infrastructure is to examine the various networks that serve as major channels for the transmission of information, such as telephones and telephone lines, online services, cable television, and the Internet (see Figure 1.3).

Viewing the infrastructure from this perspective reveals the extent to which the library is part of a much larger system or network that makes broad dissemination of information possible. Libraries are deeply interested in information networks because of the large amounts of in-

Figure 1.2
New Information Cycle

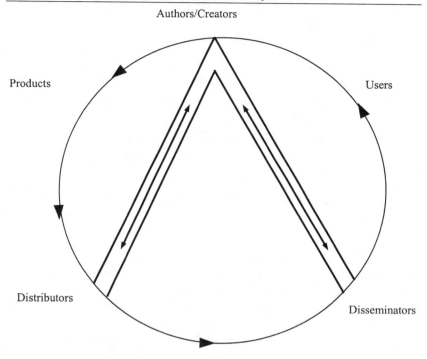

Authors/Creators

Products

Users

Distributors

Disseminators

Figure 1.3
Typical Information Infrastructure Networks and Services

Internet
Public Switched Telephone Network
Public Data Networks
Cellular Networks
Commercial Satellite Networks
Broadcast Radio Networks
Cable TV Networks
Direct Broadcast Satellite

Online Services
Publishing Services
Entertainment Services
Financial Networks and
    Services
Power Networks
Broadcast TV Networks
Transportation Networks
Public Safety Networks

Source: Adapted from Science Applications International Corporation (SAIC).
*Information Warfare: Legal, Regulatory, Policy and Organizational Considerations for
Assurance.* Washington, D.C.: Joint Staff, 1995.

Figure 1.4
Typical Information Infrastructure Components

Scanners	Cable
Keyboards	Wire
Telephones	Satellite
Fax machines	Optical fiber
Computers	Microwave
Switches	Televisions
Compact disks	Monitors
Video- and audiotapes	Printers
Facilities	Cameras
Radios	

Source: Adapted from Science Applications International Corporation (SAIC). *Information Warfare: Legal, Regulatory, Policy and Organizational Considerations for Assurance.* Washington, D.C.: Joint Staff, 1995.

formation that can be accessed by many of them. The promise for libraries is greatest with the Internet and the Web because of the capacity to connect many information networks on a national and international scale. Such networks are, however, a double-edged sword. On the one hand, they provide access to vast amounts of information; on the other hand, as more and more information is created and transmitted in electronic form, there may be greater and greater reliance on the electronic components of this infrastructure and less reliance on traditional disseminators of information, such as libraries.

Librarians also interact with the information infrastructure in other ways. For example, they must be familiar with the numerous media that make effective information transmission possible (see Figure 1.4).

One is struck by the variety of media and equipment and the multitude of information channels implied by the variety. The dominance of electronic and computer technologies is obvious. If librarians are to continue to make substantial contributions as information disseminators, they will have to understand and exploit these resources. The increasingly sophisticated electronic information technologies have great promise for increasing the dissemination of information, but they also provoke concern over the cost of purchasing and maintaining such equipment. Again, there is concern over the effect of electronic transmission of information on the use of traditional materials, such as books and periodicals.

USES OF THE INFORMATION INFRASTRUCTURE IN THE UNITED STATES

Understanding the composition of the information infrastructure gives the librarian a good idea of what it is, but it does not tell us about the extent and nature of its use. Because libraries serve primarily as disseminators, it is useful also to examine more closely which media people use and what trends have developed concerning their use (see Figure 1.5).

As can be seen from Figure 1.5 a variety of overall patterns have emerged regarding the consumption of various media. The total number of hours an individual uses one medium or another continues to increase: individual media consumption has increased nearly 9 percent from 1997 to 2002, and is expected to increase another 8 percent by 2007. Additional patterns of media consumption include the following:

1. The time spent watching television has increased by 10 percent from 1997 to 2002 and is expected to increase through 2007.
2. The time spent watching broadcast television networks is steadily declining, dropping nearly 15 percent from 1997 to 2002. It is expected to drop an additional 3 percent from the 1997 levels by 2007.
3. The time spent watching cable and satellite networks has risen 47 percent since 1997, and is expected to increase an additional 18 percent over the 1997 levels by 2007.
4. The time spent listening to the radio is increasing slowly; listening has grown 6 percent from 1997 to 2002. It is expected to grow an additional 11 percent from 1997 to 2007.
5. Attendance at movie theaters represents a very small proportion of total media consumption (1 percent in 2002) and is not expected to increase.
6. Viewing home videos and DVDs is steadily growing, and by 2007 is expected to double when compared to use in 1997. A similar pattern is expected for video games.
7. Internet consumption is, predictably, increasing faster than any other category of media, growing nearly 500 percent from 1997 to 2002, and is expected to grow an additional 238 percent by 2007.
8. Newspapers, books, and magazines use is slowly declining (5 percent, 6 percent, and 8 percent respectively from 1997 to 2002). Similar declining rates are expected at least until 2007 (Veronis, Suhler, Stevenson 2003).

Additional patterns regarding media use provide useful information for the librarian or other information professional. The following sections provide more specific analysis of different sources of information.

Figure 1.5
Hours Per Person Per Year Using Consumer Media

Year	Network-Affiliated Stations	Independent Stations	Total Broadcast Television	Basic Cable & Satellite Networks	Premium Cable & Satellite Services	Total Cable& Satellite TV	Total TV	Radio[†]
1997*	752	174	926	521	101	622	1,548	941
1998	710	174	884	565	101	667	1,551	911
1999	706	162	867	617	103	720	1,588	939
2000[†]	805	61	865	638	137	774	1,640	945
2001	766	62	828	697	147	844	1,672	953
2002	724	62	786	758	156	914	1,701	994
2003	715	62	778	789	159	949	1,726	1,013
2004	711	62	773	812	164	976	1,749	1,046
2005	709	63	772	830	168	999	1,770	1,068
2006	693	63	756	834	173	1,007	1,763	1,074
2007	697	63	759	845	180	1,026	1,785	1,098

Sources: Veronis Suhler Stevenson, PQ Media LLC, Adams Media Research, Anderson & Associates, AOL Time Warner, Arbitron, Audit Bureau of Circulations, Book Industry Study Group, *Daily Variety*, Datamonitor, *Editor & Publisher*, *The Financial Post*, The Gallup Organization, Interactive Digital Software Association, Kagan World Media, Kinetic Strategies, Magazine Publishers of America, Motion Picture Association of America, National Cable & Telecommunications Association, Newspaper Association of America, Nielsen Media Research, NPDFunworld, Online Publishers Association, Recording Industry Association of America, Scarborough Research, U.S. Bureau of the Census, Video Software Dealers Association, Yankee Group

Note: Estimates for time spent were derived using rating data for television, cable & satellite television and radio survey research and consumer purchase data (units, admissions, access) for book, home video, Internet, interactive television, magazines, movies in theaters, newspapers, recorded music and video games. Adults 18 and older were the basis for estimates for television, cable & satellite television, daily newspapers, consumer books, consumer magazines, home video and interactive television. Persons 12 and older were the basis for estimates for radio, recorded music, movies In theaters, video games and consumer Internet.

Box Office	Home Video[†ʃ]	Interactive TV[ʃ]	Recorded Music[‡]	Video Games[‡]	Consumer Internet	Daily Newspapers[‡]	Consumer Books[‡]	Consumer Magazines[‡]	Total[#]
12	49	—	264	34	26	186	116	136	3,311
13	52	—	275	45	54	186	118	134	3,339
13	55	1	281	53	80	183	119	134	3,444
12	57	2	258	59	107	180	109	135	3,505
13	60	2	229	60	136	177	106	128	3,534
14	58	2	201	67	154	176	109	125	3,599
13	67	2	188	75	169	173	110	123	3,660
13	73	3	179	84	182	171	107	122	3,732
14	83	4	166	90	193	171	109	122	3,789
14	91	4	163	98	205	169	109	121	3,811
14	98	5	152	109	216	168	108	119	3,874

*From 997 to 1999, UPN, WB and PAX affiliates are included in independent stations, superstations are included in independent stations and pay-per-view is included in basic cable.

†Since 2000, UPN, WB and PAX affiliates have moved to network-affiliated stations, superstations have moved to basic cable and pay-per-view has moved to premium services.

‡Does not include Internet-related use of traditional media. Examples of traditional media being used on the Internet include: listening to downloaded music directly on the computer or from a burned disc on an MP3 player, reading a downloaded e-book, listening to a radio station transmitted by a Windows media player, reading a Web-based newspaper article, taking a Web-based magazine survey, gathering product information also found in the printed version, or playing an Internet single- or multiplayer video game. All the examples listed are included in the time spent data under consumer Internet, although the media content was originally provided on a traditional medium.

ʃPlayback of prerecorded VHS cassettes and DVDs only.

ʃʃVideo-on-demand (VOD) only. Personal video recorders (PVR) included in total TV.

#Can include media multitasking, such as using the Internet and television simultaneously.

The Print Industry

Records have been around since the invention of written language (on stone, clay, vellum, papyrus) and print materials have been around since printing. Printing in China predates printing in the West. After the printing press was developed in the West in Germany in the mid–1400s, the influence of print materials vastly increased. (Martin Luther used the printing press quite effectively in stimulating what was to become the Protestant Reformation.) Despite predictions that print materials will disappear in the onslaught of electronic access, the numbers do not suggest this. Book sales, for example, have grown from 16 billion in sales in 1992 to more than 26 billion in 2001, with compounded growth rates of about 5 percent per year. U.S. publishers printed more than 141,000 titles in 2001 compared to 119,000 in 1999 (Bowker 2003). The time spent reading books remains at around 100 to 120 hours per person per year between 1997 and 2002 and is expected to remain within this range through 2007 (Veronis, Suhler, Stevenson 2003).

It is worth noting that the electronic equivalent of the book, the e-book, is also beginning to establish itself after a slow start, and is becoming a significant force in the electronic publishing industry. The term e-book is not precise. It can be described simply as the electronic contents of a print book that is converted into electronic format, or it can be construed more broadly as any monograph or document that is available electronically. Certainly, as the e-book market expands and grows more sophisticated, it is likely that it will move beyond the conversion of already-published books into electronic formats, to works that are produced originally and exclusively in an electronic medium. Connaway (2001) has identified five "key trends" that are promoting demand for e-books. They are:

1. The e-book market is growing.
2. There is a growing commitment among publishers to provide e-book content.
3. There is an increasing demand for access to electronic "knowledge that matters."
4. There is an increasing number of remote/distributed learning programs and a need for the electronic resources to support this type of teaching and learning.
5. There is a growing demand for increased functionality and more advanced technology for utilizing electronic content. (p. 27)

Large companies such as Amazon.com, AOL Time Warner Book Group, Barnes and Noble, Dell, HarperCollins, Houghton Mifflin, and Simon & Schuster are all involved in either the publication or distribution of e-books. Total U.S. retail sales of e-books exceeded 660,000 *in the first half* of 2002, an increase of 40 percent over the same period in 2001. Sales revenues approached $5 million in the first half of 2002 compared to $3.8 million in the same period in 2001 (Econtentmag.com 2003). Perhaps the most notable use of the e-book was the publication of Stephen King's novella, *Riding the Bullet*, which is available only through the Internet. The book sold for only $2 and more than a half-million individuals attempted to download it in the first week (Ormes 2003). Although the economics of e-book publication is still unclear, there is considerable potential for such books to be cost effective for libraries. Savings might be derived from lower costs per title, immediate access to titles, no necessity to repair or replace them, and no storage costs. All of these could be substantial benefits to libraries (Ormes 2003). Of course, one of the major challenges is the cost of display. E-books require readers. They can be readers specifically dedicated to e-book display, or they can be multipurpose devices (such as PDAs) or PC-based e-book software (Roush 2003). Much of e-books' potential success will rely on such reading being easy to use, inexpensive, and commonplace.

Periodicals are also a healthy part of the information marketplace. There are approximately a million periodical articles published every year in the United States. Consumer periodical circulation spending rose about 1 percent in 2002, although the number of subscriptions remains steady and the number of individual-issue purchases has declined slightly. Still, new periodicals continue to be introduced, with 290 appearing in 2002 (Veronis, Suhler, Stevenson 2003). The periodical marketplace is widely diversified, with more than 80,000 scientific journals alone. There are more than 9,600 periodical titles available at newsstands. Despite the dynamism of the periodical publishing industry, as noted above, time spent reading periodicals is trending slowly downward.

Historically the newspaper has been a popular source of print information. Consumer spending on newspapers has risen from $10 billion in 1997 to $11.4 billion in 2002. Circulation, however, continues to decline slowly, and individuals spend less time reading the newspaper each year. Individuals spent an average of 186 hours reading the paper in 1997 and 176 hours in 2002 (Veronis, Suhler, Stevenson 2003). Reasons for this decline might be that other sources of information, such as TV, are more interesting, more timely, and more appealing to a visually-oriented culture. The combination of well-edited pictures and sound are strong competitors to the more sedate quality of the written word. Nonetheless, newspapers are launching competitive efforts by producing their newspapers on the Web and exploiting the new visual technologies, such as the Tablet PC, to attract a new generation of individuals who function comfortably in the Web environment. Certainly e-newspapers are growing in number and have developed considerable market penetration. Despite these efforts, the intense competition of such news services as CNN and MSNBC will make survival difficult.

Telephones

The importance of the telephone cannot be underestimated in the history of communications and in the contemporary world. More than 94 percent of all households in the United States have telephones. The amount of information transmitted from one individual to another is undoubtedly great, and the growth of conference calls merely increases this volume of information. In addition, what makes telephone access even more important today is that the telephone lines are now used for telecommunication with computers and databases. Over these lines are transmitted e-mail, Web sites, and interactions with computer databases for search purposes. The telephone and its infrastructure still represents crucial underpinnings for the computer information revolution (U.S. Bureau of the Census 2002).

Radio

More than 98 million people in the United States have radios, accounting for 99 percent of American households. The average household has more than five radios. Today, there is not only the traditional news broadcast on commercial and educational radio stations, there is the ever-present radio talk show, spanning the political spectrum, sometimes stimulating us and sometimes infuriating us. There are also distinct radio programs that educate us about issues in the community and the nation. The ubiquitous radio not only sits on our bedside and coffee tables at home, it is plugged into our ears when we walk, run, and drive. It is broadcast in restaurants and other public places, copyright violations notwithstanding. The number of radio stations has also increased, especially FM stations. The number of FM stations has increased from about 3,200 in 1980 to 5,900 in 2000, an increase of 84 percent (U.S Bureau of the Census 2002). In terms of actual use, an average individual listens to the radio nearly 1,000 hours per year, which is second only to TV in hours of use (Veronis, Suhler, Stevenson 2003).

Television

One cannot avoid the omnipresent television. The number of households owning televisions is only slightly fewer than those with radios. One hundred and one million households have 245 million television sets, which accounts for more than 98 percent of all households. The average home owns 2.4 sets. (U.S. Bureau of the Census 2002).

Television, like radio, provides information in many different formats including traditional news programs, special informational programming, and talk shows. One might debate the quality of content in many of these sources, but one cannot ignore that Americans draw much information from the television. For example, in 2000–2001, the average U.S. household had the TV on 7 hours and 35 minutes a day; more than 50 hours a week. One should not assume that it is the kids watching the TV. In 2000, women were the heaviest users watching the television 4 hours and 46 minutes a day; men watched 4 hours and 11 minutes. Contrary to what might be popular belief, teens and children consistently watch the TV less than adults, around 3 hours a day. This is not to trivialize young people's exposure to TV; their viewing habits run directly parallel to those of their parents (*International Television and Video Almanac* 2003).

In addition, the television marketplace is growing in diversity when it comes to delivery. For example, in the 1960s the concept of cable television stations was new and not well received. By 1980 only 15 million households (20 percent) had cable television, but in the last decade this has changed dramatically. By 2000, 69 million households had cable television, accounting for 68 percent of all households in the U.S. Each cable user was expected to watch approximately 914 hours of cable TV/satellite broadcasting in 2002. Similarly, the number of television stations is expected to increase, especially commercial stations, which rose from 734 in 1980 to 1,288 in 2000. This is a 75 percent increase. The number of cable systems also is increasing steadily. In 1980 there were 4,225 such systems serving 17.7 million households. By 2000 there were more than 10,000 such systems serving more than 69 million households. Overall, while viewing of network TV stations has dropped, consumption of basic cable has increased substantially (U.S. Bureau of the Census 2003).

Perhaps even more fascinating is how U.S. citizens are turning their homes into satellite reception areas. Those umbrella-shaped antennae once thought to be the domain of radio astronomers at observatories and universities now adorn the roofs and yards of many American homes. There were no home satellite stations in 1980, but by 1997 there were more than ten million satellite subscribers (*International Television and Video Almanac* 2003).

Broadcast television is also being affected by the transformation of its signal from analog to digital, which has been mandated by Congress to be completed by 2006. The development of "high-definition" TV however has been slowed by a variety of issues including developing the means to prevent piracy. To date, fewer than 1 percent of U.S. homes are actually viewing high-density programs (*International Television and Video Almanac* 2003). Nonetheless, substantial increases in the use of digital signals for TV should be anticipated.

The development of the videocassette and DVD has also meant that the TV is being used in a new way for information (as well as entertainment). In 1980 only one million households owned a VCR (videocassette recorder). By 2000, 86 million households had them, accounting for more than 85 percent of all households (U.S. Bureau of the Census 2002). Despite the growth in the use of the videocassette, it is rapidly being supplanted by the DVD. The number of DVD video titles has risen from 600 in 1997 to 13,000 in 2001. Less than a half million units were in use in 1997; in 2002 there were more than 39 million units in use. DVD spending on rentals reached $2.9 billion in 2002, and total DVD sales reached $8.7 billion (*International Television and Video Almanac* 2003; Video Trade Association 2003). There can be little doubt that home video and DVD consumer use, including on-demand video, will continue to grow, which will put constant pressure on the use of movie theaters. Indeed, unless movie theaters can convert their images into digital rather than analog formats (an expensive conversion), the temptation to view high-definition images on the television will keep viewers at home.

The Database Industry

Over the last decade, access to electronically stored information in computers has been increasing regularly. An excellent summary of the character and growth of the database industry is provided by Williams (2003) in the *Gale Directory of Databases*. Unless otherwise noted, the following data in this section have been taken from this source.

Figure 1.6
Growth of the Database Industry

	1975	1991	1993	1995	1997	1998	1999	2002
Databases	301	7,637	8,261	9,207	10,338	11,339	11,681	16,417
Producers	200	2,372	2,744	2,860	3,216	3,686	3,674	4,042
Vendors	105	933	1,629	1,810	2,115	2,459	2,454	4,060
Records (in millions)	52	4,060	5,572	8,160	11,270	12,050	12,860	18,550

Compiled from data provided in Williams, Martha. "The State of Databases Today: 2003." *Gale Directory of Databases*. Detroit: Gale, 2003.

As might be expected, the number of database producers continues to increase (see Figure 1.6). In 1975 there were 200 database producers, compared to 4,042 in 2002. Similarly, the number of vendors has risen from 105 in 1975 to 4,060 in 2002. Predictably, as the amount of information increases, and the number of vendors and producers remains high, the number of electronically stored records has increased greatly. The number of such records has increased from 52 million in 1975 to 18.6 billion in 2002.

Most of the databases are business oriented (23 percent); followed by science, technology, and engineering (20 percent); general (19 percent); life sciences (13 percent); law (11 percent); humanities (8 percent); multidiscliplinary (8 percent); social sciences (5 percent); and news (4 percent). Reflecting the evolution of electronic information access from governmental to commercial, the percent of commercial/industrial databases has risen steadily over the years until 2004—90 percent of all databases now fall into this category. In 1977 only 22 percent of databases were commercial in nature. In contrast, the percentage of governmental databases has dropped from 56 percent in 1977 to 6 percent in 2002. Only 3 percent are not-for-profit (mostly academic) databases. A significant majority of databases (62 percent) are produced in the U.S. although a substantial percentage (33 percent) are also produced in Western Europe.

In terms of the types of databases available, Williams reports that most (74 percent) are word-oriented databases (bibliographic or full text), far fewer are number-oriented (10 percent), and even fewer are image-

or audio-oriented (12 percent and 2 percent respectively). The trend is toward full-text databases, that is, those in which the entire text is available for viewing, not just the abstract or bibliographic citation. In 2002 there were 12,610 word-oriented databases, 58 percent of which were full text, compared to only 42 percent in 1990. Bibliographic databases, on the other hand, have dropped from 32 percent in 1990 to 19 percent in 2002. This shift is testimony to the fact that computer databases as information channels are improving substantially in the extensiveness of the information available. With the increasing sophistication of digitization and the ubiquity of the Web, full-text and image-based databases are bound to grow.

With the rapid expansion of personal computers, access to electronic information has become commonplace. There can be little doubt that, at least for millions of Americans, access to vast amounts of information will increase. However, access to great amounts of information does not necessarily mean that Americans will get the *right* information. In fact, one can easily foresee that most citizens, awash in information, will drown in it, or at the least lose their bearings. Perhaps that is why the term "navigation" has become so popular in attempting to assist people along the information highway. Nonetheless, one cannot consider the information context in which libraries are placed without recognizing the importance of computerized access to electronic data. It is not unreasonable to presume that librarians will become expert navigators for future information seekers.

The Internet and the World Wide Web

The development of the Internet and the World Wide Web has had a profound effect on the way we communicate. Data provided by the U.S. Department of Commerce (2002) suggest that the role of these resources is dramatic and wide ranging and that there continues to be an important "digital divide" (see Figure 1.7).

In 2001 there were nearly 143 million Internet users in the United States with 2 million more being added each month (only Norway has more users as a percent of its population!). More than half (54 percent) of the United States was online in 2001, compared to 22 percent of the population in 1997. In addition, Internet use is increasing for people regardless of income, education, age, race, ethnicity, or gender. Since 1997, for example, use of the Internet has grown for African-Americans from 13 percent to 40 percent; for individuals with an income less than

Figure 1.7
Internet Use from Any Location by Individuals Age 3 and Older

	Oct. 1997 (thousands)		Dec. 1998 (thousands)		Aug. 2000 (thousands)		Sept. 2001 (thousands)		Internet Use (percent)			
	Internet Users	Total	Internet Users	Total	Internet Users	Total	Internet Users	Total	Oct. 1997	Dec. 1998	Aug. 2000	Sept. 2001
Total Population	56,774	255,689	84,587	258,453	116,480	262,620	142,823	265,180	22.2	32.7	44.4	53.9
Gender												
Male	30,311	124,590	43,033	125,932	56,962	127,844	69,580	129,152	24.3	34.2	44.6	53.9
Female	26,464	131,099	41,555	132,521	59,518	134,776	73,243	136,028	20.2	31.4	44.2	53.8
Race/Origin												
White	46,678	184,295	69,470	184,980	93,714	186,439	111,942	186,793	25.3	37.6	50.3	59.9
Black	4,197	31,786	6,111	32,123	9,624	32,850	13,237	33,305	13.2	19.0	29.3	39.8
Asian Amer. & Pac. Isl.	2,432	9,225	3,467	9,688	5,095	10,324	6,452	10,674	26.4	35.8	49.4	60.4
Hispanic	3,101	28,233	4,897	29,452	7,325	30,918	10,141	32,146	11.0	16.6	23.7	31.6
Employment Status												
Employed	37,254	130,857	56,539	133,119	76,971	136,044	88,396	135,089	28.5	42.5	56.6	65.4
Not Employed	9,012	72,911	14,261	73,891	21,321	73,891	28,531	77,268	12.4	19.5	28.9	36.9
Family Income												
Less than $15,000	4,069	44,284	5,170	37,864	6,057	32,096	7,848	31,354	9.2	13.7	18.9	25.0
$15,000–$24,999	3,760	32,423	5,623	30,581	7,063	27,727	8,893	26,650	11.6	18.4	25.5	33.4
$25,000–$34,999	5,666	33,178	8,050	31,836	11,054	31,001	12,591	28,571	17.1	25.3	35.7	44.1

Figure 1.7
(continued)

	Oct. 1997 (thousands)		Dec. 1998 (thousands)		Aug. 2000 (thousands)		Sept. 2001 (thousands)		Internet Use (percent)			
	Internet Users	Total	Internet Users	Total	Internet Users	Total	Internet Users	Total	Oct. 1997	Dec. 1998	Aug. 2000	Sept. 2001
$35,000–$49,999	8,824	38,776	13,528	39,026	16,690	35,867	20,587	36,044	22.8	34.7	46.5	57.1
$50,000–$74,999	13,552	41,910	19,902	43,776	25,059	43,451	30,071	44,692	32.3	45.5	57.7	67.3
$75,000 & above	16,276	36,572	24,861	42,221	36,564	52,189	44,547	56,446	44.5	58.9	70.1	78.9
Educational Attainment												
Less Than High School	516	29,114	1,228	29,039	2,482	28,254	3,506	27,484	1.8	4.2	8.8	12.8
High School												
Diploma/GED	5,589	57,487	10,961	57,103	17,425	56,889	22,847	57,386	9.7	19.2	30.6	39.8
Some College	10,548	42,544	16,603	43,038	24,201	44,628	28,321	45,420	24.8	38.6	54.2	62.4
Bachelors Degree	11,503	27,795	16,937	28,990	21,978	30,329	24,726	30,588	41.4	58.4	72.5	808
Beyond Bachelors	7,195	13,863	9,635	14,518	12,104	15,426	13,633	16,283	51.9	68.4	78.5	83.7
Age Group (and Labor Force)												
Age 3–8	1,748	24,445	2,680	24,282	3,671	23,962	6,637	23,763	7.2	11.0	15.3	27.9
Age 9–17	11,791	35,469	15,396	35,821	19,579	36,673	25,480	37,118	33.2	43.0	53.4	68.6
Age 18–24	7,884	24,973	11,356	25,662	15,039	26,458	17,673	27,137	31.6	44.3	56.8	65.0
Age 25–49	27,639	101,853	41,694	101,836	56,433	101,946	65,138	101,890	27.1	40.9	55.4	63.9

Figure 1.7
(continued)

	Oct. 1997 (thousands)		Dec. 1998 (thousands)		Aug. 2000 (thousands)		Sept. 2001 (thousands)		Internet Use (percent)			
	Internet Users	Total	Internet Users	Total	Internet Users	Total	Internet Users	Total	Oct. 1997	Dec. 1998	Aug. 2000	Sept. 2001
Male	14,679	50,177	20,889	50,054	27,078	50,034	30,891	50,020	29.3	41.7	54.1	61.8
Female	12,960	51,676	20,806	51,781	29,356	51,913	34,247	51,871	25.1	40.2	56.5	66.0
Age 50 +	7,712	68,949	13,669	70,852	21,758	73,580	27,895	75,272	11.2	19.3	29.6	37.1
Male	4,560	31,252	7,356	32,248	10,989	33,561	13,757	34,438	14.6	22.8	32.7	39.9
Female	3,152	37,697	6,313	38,604	10,769	40,019	14,138	40,834	8.4	16.4	26.9	34.6
Geographic Location of Household In Which the Individual Lives												
Rural	n/a	n/a	19,274	65,828	28,889	67,980	35,751	67,642	n/a	29.3	42.5	52.9
Urban	n/a	n/a	65,313	192,625	87,591	194,640	107,072	97,537	n/a	33.9	45.0	54.2
Urban Not Central City	n/a	n/a	41,881	116,091	56,773	118,641	69,342	120,724	n/a	36.1	47.9	57.4
Urban Central City	n/a	n/a	23,432	76,534	30,818	75,999	37,730	76,813	30.6	40.6	49.1	

Source: U. S. Department of Commerce. *A Nation Online: How Americans Are Expanding Their Use of the Internet.* Washington, D.C.: Department of Commerce, February 2002.

$15,000 from 9 percent to 25 percent; for individuals with less than a high school education from 2 percent to 13 percent.

Despite these increases, other data reveal the realities of a "digital divide." For example, as incomes rise so does Internet use, and the differences are dramatic. Internet use is only 25 percent among those with the lowest levels of income (less than $15,000), while 67 percent of those with incomes exceeding $75,000 use the Internet. When race or ethnicity is examined, it is clear that Whites (60 percent) and Asian Americans (60 percent) use the Internet more than African Americans (40 percent) or Hispanics (32 percent).

Not surprisingly, young people are heavy users of the Internet. Sixty-nine percent of children ages 9 to 17 use the Internet. From 1998 to 2001 children between the ages of 10 and 13 have increased their use from 39 percent to 65 percent; between 14 and 17 from 51 percent to 76 percent. As might be expected based on the data above, children from homes of higher income are more likely to use the Internet than children from lower income homes. In addition, there are revealing patterns when one examines where use occurs. Although children exhibit heavy use of the Internet at home, school also is a vital location for use. For example, 45 percent of children between 10 and 13 use the Internet at school and 55 percent between the ages of 14 and 17. In addition, children from lower income homes, African Americans, and Hispanics are more likely to use the Internet at school exclusively. Adults are also heavy users. Between the ages of 18 and 50, use of the Internet exceeds 64 percent; but use drops precipitously after 50, with only 37 percent of adults over 50 using the Internet. Men and women use the Internet in equal proportions.

The reasons for using the Internet are various (see Figure 1.8). For example, 84 percent employ it for e-mail; 67 percent for product or services information; 62 percent for news, weather, or sports information; 42 percent play games; 39 percent use it to purchase products; and 35 percent search for health information or practices. Men are somewhat more likely to use the Internet to search for news (67 percent to 57 percent); women are more likely to search for health information (40 percent to 30 percent). Men are also more likely than women to trade stocks, play games, or watch television or movies online. Older individuals were more likely to search for health information while online shopping was a favorite of those between 25 and 44. African Americans and Hispanics were less likely than Whites or Asian Americans to use the Internet for e-mail, product/services information, news, or purchasing products.

Figure 1.8
Activities of Individuals Online, 2001,
as a Percentage of Internet Users Age 3 and Older

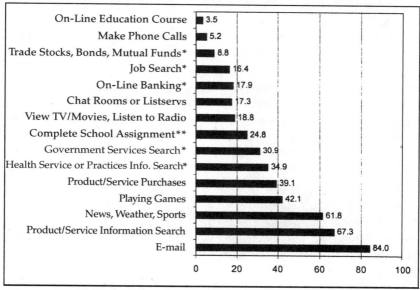

*These online activities surveyed individuals age 15 and over only. **This activity was asked of all respondents. If the response was restricted to individuals enrolled in school, the percentage of Internet users completing school assignments would increase to 77.5 percent
Source: NTIA and ESA, U.S. Department of Commerce, using U.S. Census Bureau Current Population Survey Supplements.

Although the primary technique to connect to the Internet from home is "dial-up" (80 percent), broadband access through cable or DSL is growing (12.9 percent and 6.6 percent respectively). Use of these higher-speed connections doubled in one year from 2000 to 2001. Of course, not all connections are made from the home. Although 44 percent of Internet use is from the home, 20 percent is from work, 12 percent from school, and 5 percent from public libraries. In 2001, nearly 42 percent of Internet users accessed the Internet from their work, compared to 26 percent in 2000.

More detailed data concerning use of computers in public libraries are particularly revealing and suggest that public libraries may play a significant role in addressing the problem of the digital divide. For example, only 9 percent of Whites who are Internet users use the public library for Internet access, while 19 percent of African Americans and 14 percent of Hispanics use the public library for this purpose. In addition, Internet access at public libraries is used more heavily by people with lower incomes than by those with higher ones. Fourteen percent of users with incomes under $15,000 use the public library for access compared to 7 percent of those with incomes of $75,000 or more.

The digital divide is also noticeable for individuals with disabilities. In general, among individuals ages 25 to 60 with disabilities who have computers in their homes, between 56 percent and 68 percent also access the Internet. Among the population who have computers at home but no disabilities, 75 percent use the Internet.

It is also useful to identify the characteristics of individuals who do *not* use the Internet. Those least likely to use it are individuals with low incomes, with low levels of formal education, and who are either African American or Hispanic. Not surprisingly, cost is the most common factor for non-use, and is also a primary factor in the discontinuation of Internet use. This strongly suggests that the digital divide may persist at the very least due to economic disparities. Although the digital divide may be with us for some time, the Department of Commerce (2002) analysis also suggests that "whether measured against income, education, family type, or race/Hispanic origin, the distribution of Internet use at home has moved in the direction of lower inequality" (p. 87). In other words, the gap is closing. This trend contrasts with earlier research in the late 1990s that indicated a widening gap. It is also clear that schools and public libraries contribute to the closing of this gap7.

Mossberger, Tolbert, and Stansbury (2003) report that the digital divide must be understood as more than unequal access, but should also be understood as a skills gap. Among their findings are that 22 percent of adults still need assistance using a mouse and keyboard, 31 percent need help using e-mail, and 52 percent need assistance with word-processing or spreadsheet programs. Those who are mostly likely to need assistance are the elderly and less educated, individuals of low income, African Americans, and Latinos. Interestingly, the public library may be an excellent place to redress this gap because Latinos, African Americans, and individuals of low income are most likely to view the public library as a "community gathering place" (Mossberger, Tolbert, and Stansbury 2003, p. 51).

Despite the ubiquity of Internet use, the most recent data collected in the spring of 2002 and reported by Lenhart (2003) of the Pew Internet and American Life Project suggest that the growth in overall use may finally be abating. Lenhart suggests that Internet use has been hovering between 57 percent and 61 percent of the population since October 2001 and is not showing the steady increases of the past. Of course, there are still new users, but the number of "drop-outs" may be off-setting their numbers. In addition, Lenhart reports that Internet use by many is fluid, in that use and non-use varies over time based on such factors as economic conditions, availability of technology, and level of interest. In fact, between 27 percent and 44 percent of users report that they have gone offline for extended periods, only to return later.

Interestingly, Pew makes some subtle distinctions concerning non-users that are revealing. She divides them into three groups:

Net evaders:	Individuals (approximately 20 percent of non-users) who rely on a person with whom they reside to use the Internet for them. Many of these individuals are parents whose children are online users.
Net dropouts:	Individual (approximately 17 percent) who were Internet users, but are no longer. The reasons for dropping out may often be economic or technological. Some simply found the Web unhelpful, some lost use of a computer. Many are young, have low incomes, or are from minority groups.
Truly disconnected:	Individuals (approximately 24 percent) who have no direct or indirect experience with the Internet. Many are older, have lower incomes, and lower levels of formal education.

As a rule, the Pew data support the findings above from the Department of Commerce concerning the nature of the digital divide (see Figure 1.9).

Use is more common among individuals who are younger, have higher incomes, are employed, are white, and live in urban or suburban areas in contrast to rural ones. Pew also found that individuals who are socially content, feel they have control over their lives, and use other media such as newspapers, radio, and television are also more likely to

Figure 1.9
Users and Non-Users of the Internet

This table reports the share of the Internet population that comes from each group. For example, reading the first line of the table: 50% of all Internet users are men; 46% of non-users are men; 48% of the overall U.S. population are men.

	Internet Users	Non-Users	All Americans
Men	50%	46%	48%
Women	50%	54%	52%
Race/Ethnicity			
Whites	77%	71%	75%
Blacks	8%	14%	11%
Hispanics	9%	10%	10%
Age			
18–29	29%	14%	23%
30–49	47%	32%	42%
50–64	18%	22%	20%
65+	4%	28%	15%
Household Income			
Less than $30,000	18%	41%	28%
$30,000–$49,999	23%	17%	21%
$50,000–$75,000	18%	9%	14%
More than $75,000	26%	6%	18%
Educational Attainment			
Not high school graduate	5%	25%	14%
High School grad	23%	41%	35%
Some college	34%	21%	25%
Colege and graduate school degree	37%	11%	26%
Community Type			
Rural	21%	31%	26%
Suburban	52%	42%	48%
Urban	26%	26%	26%

Source: Pew Internet & American Life Project Tracking Survey, March-May 2002. N=3,553. Margin of error is ±2% for All Americans and Internet Users and ±3% for Non-Users. Numbers in columns do not always add to 100% due to participant non-response.

use the Internet. Among the primary reasons for non-use are cost, concern about identity theft, lack of time, and complexity of the technology. Many non-users assert simply that they do not want or need the Internet.

Lenhart (2003, p.5) also confirmed that the disabled are victims of the digital divide reporting that: "The disabled have among the lowest levels of Internet access in America." Only 38 percent go online compared to 58 percent of individuals who are not disabled. Twenty-eight percent of disabled non-users say their disability makes it very difficult or impossible to go online.

Taking an even broader perspective, Horrigan (2003) reporting for the Pew Internet & American Life Project concluded that there is a technology elite in the United States who are described as "high-end technology adopters." These adopters are consistent users of the Web, cell phones, digital videodisc players, and personal digital assistants (PDAs), and they primarily are composed of the following groups: (1) "young tech elites," usually males in their early 20s; (2) "older wired baby boomers," usually males in their mid–50s; (3) "wired generation Xer's" who use the Web and cell phones heavily; and (4) "wired senior men" who are wealthy and average 70 years old. As a group these adopters constitute less than one-third of the U.S. population, but have a disproportionate impact and influence on the information goods and services used and produced in the United States.

Libraries

The information infrastructure is a complex and dynamic environment. The role of libraries within this context is also dynamic. Traditionally libraries were part of this infrastructure long before electronic information technologies were even conceived. They have been a constant source of information in the United States since the settlement of America, although the number and sophistication of these libraries were quite limited until the nineteenth century. Today, there are more than 117,000 libraries in the United States: 9,445 are public libraries, 3,480 are academic, 10,452 are special, and 94,342 are school or media center libraries (*American Library Directory* 2002; *Digest of Education Statistics* 2002). Their many and varied purposes will be discussed later. Suffice it to say here that libraries have played a role in the infrastructure largely by providing institutional support to individuals or small groups through the provision of services and materials for educational, informational, and recreational purposes. Historically, libraries have been an especially important channel of exposure to books, promotion of reading, literacy, and self-development within the population.

In addition, the contemporary library integrates many other information channels in its continuing mission to meet the needs of its users. Most libraries are actively engaged in developing electronic information links and introducing electronic information technologies to their users. In this sense, they are evolving, becoming part of the larger national information infrastructure.

The complex interrelationships among the various components of the information infrastructure present many challenges that libraries must meet if they are to prosper. Some have predicted that libraries may be coming to an end, that their electronic competitors will render them obsolete. It is an intriguing prediction, but do the data support it? Figure 1.10 shows a retrospective look at the number of libraries as reported by the *American Library Directory* since 1980.

From this perspective, the prediction seems unconvincing. One might predict that with the development of electronic access, libraries will become even more popular as information seekers look to libraries and librarians as important sources of expertise and assistance in an ever more complex information environment. Only time will tell.

SUMMARY

Library and information science is a discipline oriented to providing access to vast amounts of accumulated knowledge and information. In many ways the growth of information technologies and the expansion of knowledge is an exciting prospect, but it also raises many crucial questions. Certainly, the library and the librarian must address these questions if they are to survive and prosper, and by addressing these questions, they must also reexamine their own values and mission.

Information providers must realize that developments in electronic information technologies have led to the emergence of many powerful stakeholders in the development of the information infrastructure. Business and industry, the communications industry (cable and telephone companies), electronic database producers, the federal government, the military, libraries, researchers, academic institutions, and citizens all are eager to influence developments related to the infrastructure.

In addition, information consumers are developing new expectations in the digital environment. De Rosa, Dempsey, and Wilson (2004)

Figure 1.10
Number of Public, Academic, Government, and Special Libraries, 1980–2003 (Excludes Branches and Junior Colleges)

Year	Public	Academic	Government	Special	Total
1980	8,717	4,618	1,260	8,609	28,665
1981	8,782	4,796	1,615	8,571	29,278
1982	8,768	4,924	1,565	8,453	28,949
1983	8,822	4,900	1,591	8,387	29,044
1984	8,796	4,989	1,551	8,574	29,465
1985	8,849	5,034	1,574	8,955	29,843
1986	8,865	5,592	1,237	9,704	32,995
1987–88	9,170	4,824	1,760	9,147	31,524
1989–90	9,068	4,607	1,676	8,990	30,751
1990–91	9,060	4,593	1,735	9,051	30,761
1991–92	9,075	4,613	1,773	9,348	31,127
1992–93	9,076	4,620	1,776	9,811	31,850
1993–94	9,097	4,619	1,871	10,149	32,414
1994–95	9,101	4,684	1,864	11,280	32,441
1995–96	9,165	4,730	1,875	11,340	32,666
1997–1998	9,767	4,707	1,837	11,044	33,004
1999–2000	9,837	4,723	1,874	10,808	32,852
2000-2001	9,480	3,491	1,411	9,993	31,628
2001-2002	9,415	3,406	1,376	11,017	31,392
2002-2003	9,445	3,480	1,326	10,452	30,903

Source: *American Library Directory.* New Providence, N.J.: R.R. Bowker, 1978–2003.

suggest, for example, that such consumers expect to exercise more self-sufficiency in locating information, and they expect a seamless environment in which various technologies (for example, music, television, computers, Internet) all are easily integrated into one "infosphere."

Among the many issues that must be addressed are open access to information; copyright protection, and, at the same time, protection of citizens' right to access copyrighted information; appropriate security for information; individual privacy; and the cost of information access. Given these important and often competing interests, it becomes increasingly important that libraries, as institutions that often reflect the public interest rather than personal gain, play critical roles in influencing the policies that affect information dissemination. It is a tremendous responsibility, and it becomes increasingly ponderous as the world of information and the social and technological environment grow in complexity.

Among the questions that librarians must address are:

- What are the role and mission of the library and librarian in our society?
- Where do libraries fit in the developing information infrastructure?
- What are our citizens' rights to information and how do we protect those rights?
- What are the barriers citizens face in getting information?
- What ethical responsibilities and dilemmas do information providers face in providing information?
- How can we ensure that our libraries survive and prosper?
- How does the growth of information in electronic formats change the way information providers develop adequate collections and services for their patrons?
- What will happen to the library as a physical place as more and more access is electronic?
- What kinds of library and information professionals do we need for the future?

There is no one answer to these questions. It is hoped that the remainder of this book will improve the reader's understanding of the issues.

ENDNOTE

1. I wish to acknowledge Dr. Brett Sutton, who first proposed the use of such metaphors to understand how the growth of information is understood. This is not to say that he would necessarily interpret the significance of these metaphors in the same way.

REFERENCES

American Library Directory. New York: R.R. Bowker, various editions.

The Bowker Annual: Library and Book Trade Almanac. 42nd ed. Medford, N.J.: Information Today, 2003.

Connaway, Lynn Silipigni. "E-book Trends in Public Libraries." *Public Libraries Supplement* (2001): 27–29.

De Rosa, Cathy, Lorcan Dempsey, and Alane Wilson. *The 2003 OCLC Environmental Scan: Pattern Recognition: A Report to the OCLC Membership*. Dublin, Ohio: OCLC, 2004.

Digest of Education Statistics 2002. Washington D.C.: U.S. DOE, 2002.

Econtentmag.com. "OeBF Releases eBook Sales Statistics." [Online] Available at *www.econtentmag.com/?ArticleID=5495.*

Horrigan, John B. *Consumption of Information Goods and Services in the United States.* Washington, D.C.: Pew Internet and American Life Project, November 2003.

International Television and Video Almanac. 48th ed. Edited by Tracey Stevens. New York: Quigley, 2003.

Lenhart, Amanda. *The Ever-Shifting Internet Population.* Washington, D.C.: Pew Internet and American Life Project, April 2003.

Mossberger, Karen, Caroline J. Tolbert, and Mary Stansbury. *Virtual Inequality: Beyond the Digital Divide.* Washington, D.C.: Georgetown University, 2003.

Ormes, Sarah. "An E-Book Primer." [Online] Available at *www.ukoln.ac.uk/ public/earl/issuepapers/ebook.htm.* (Accessed September 2, 2003.)

Roush, Wade. "Ebook Basics: eBook Primer." [Online] Available at *http:// 12.108.175.91/ebookweb/primer?print-friendly=true.* (Accessed September 2, 2003.)

U.S. Bureau of the Census. *Statistical Abstract of the United States 2002.* Washington, D.C.: GPO, 2002.

U.S. Department of Commerce. *A Nation Online: How Americans Are Expanding Their Use of the Internet.* Washington, D.C.: Department of Commerce, February 2002.

Veronis, Suhler & Associates. *Communications Industry Forecast.* New York: Veronis, Suhler, Stevenson, 2003.

Video Trade Association. "Video Trade Association Releases Comprehensive Report on DVD, VHS, and Video Game Sales and Rentals." [Online] Available at *http:quicstart.clari.net/qs_se/webnews/wed/ay/Bea-vsda.RoVw_Da5.html.*

Williams, Martha E. "The State of Databases Today: 2003." In *Gale Directory of Databases.* Detroit: Gale, 2003.

2

Information Science: A Service Perspective

Familiarity with the issues to which the field of information science is devoted provides an enriched understanding for the work of librarians and other information professionals. Definitions of information science abound, but the first definition was proposed in the early 1960s and will suffice for the general discussion that ensues.

Information Science:

> the science that investigates the properties and behavior of information, the forces governing the flow of information, and the means of processing information for optimum accessibility and usability. The processes include the origination, dissemination, collection, organization, storage, retrieval, interpretation, and use of information. The field is derived from or related to mathematics, logic, linguistics, psychology, computer technology, operations research, the graphic arts, communications, library science, management, and some other fields. (Taylor 1966, p. 19)

Several features of this definition stand out: (1) The focus of information science is on the phenomenon of information. Information science deals with information regardless of the package (for example, a book or a database) or context (such as government, business, or personal). Sometimes libraries are not seen within this more general focus because they are viewed as "document-based." (2) Information science deals with the entire information cycle, from creation to use. (3) The field is clearly interdisciplinary, drawing from scientific, social scientific, and psychological fields. (4) Although the definition is not institution-based (that is, it does not mention libraries or information organizations per se), it does emphasize a central purpose of libraries—accessibility and usability of information. This notion has usually been preserved in subsequent definitions and is an edifying aspect for the librarian for it demonstrates a substantial similarity in objectives.

To the librarian, the importance of information science lies not so much in *what* is done as in *why* it is done. The goal of information science is the resolution of human problems. Information science's emphasis on usability and accessibility comports very closely with one of the major objectives of librarians and reveals the substantial instrumental value of the field for librarianship. It is no wonder that information science has sometimes been characterized as deinstitutionalized library science; it is the library without walls, the entire world of information is the "collection," and the librarian or information scientist is the agent who acquires, organizes, and disseminates that information. The librarian or information scientist facilitates the dissemination of information to people to meet their needs. This could be seen as the defining character of library and information science if one wants to see it as a single discipline: it focuses on the transmission of information to meet human needs, be they practical, theoretical, religious, or aesthetic. As Brittain (1980) has observed: "it may be that information science is a different way of looking at many of the problems and tasks that have confronted librarians for many decades" (p. 37).

If one accepts that information is a critical aspect of our lives and our society as a whole, then librarians and other information specialists must develop information systems that can acquire, organize, maintain, and disseminate information with minimum effort and cost to users. In information science there are countless areas that have direct and indirect application to the work of libraries and librarians. Clearly if librarians are to respond to the changing information environment and provide the best service, they must integrate information science into their professional outlook.

The growth of information technologies and studies of the information-seeking behavior and information needs of the population suggest that the traditional perspectives of the librarian may require a substantial shift, if not in values, then in librarians' expectations of user needs and what is required of them. Our current concept of information provision has been historically conditioned by a traditional preoccupation with the collection rather than people. It may well be that the conceptualization of library collections and services is woefully inadequate to meet the information needs of the citizenry, and as information becomes increasingly available from other sources, the library will need to decide what role it will play and how it will synthesize these new sources. If librarianship is to focus on truly serving its users, it must understand how and why they use information.

From a historical perspective, the definition of information science provided above suggests that information science in some form has been around for a very long time, although it may not have been called by that name. Libraries, librarianship, and bibliography, for example, are part of the foundation of information science. The history of libraries and librarianship is primarily one of collecting, organizing, and disseminating materials, largely of the print variety. One could go back to the organization of library materials beginning nearly 5,000 years ago in Sumeria and find early attempts to organize information, at that time impressed in clay tablets. Similarly, over the centuries there have been many attempts to organize the available literature through the compilation of bibliographies, and there have been systematic attempts to organize published knowledge through the development of classification systems such as the Dewey Decimal System. Each of these attempts to organize information and to make it available and usable is part of the important foundation on which the field of information science is constructed (Shera and Cleveland 1977).

Capturing the contemporary spirit of information science, however, requires us also to look to more recent antecedents, especially those in the first half of the twentieth century. These developments represent additional layers in the foundation. Among these developments was a shift in emphasis, *away from the book to information itself.* For years the book played the central role in the dissemination of information, and certainly was central to librarianship. With the significant proliferation of scientific and technical information in the twentieth century, considerable interest had grown in the theoretical and practical aspects of how to organize it and improve access. This information was often stored in media other than books: in periodicals, documents, research reports, and microfilm. It was clear that the package in which the information was contained was far less important than locating specific information stored within these media. This was substantially different from the way libraries had traditionally satisfied information needs—by providing a physical item (usually a book)—and presented significantly different, although still related, challenges. As it became clear that scientific and technical information was distributed in a variety of formats, and that it was the information not the format that was of special interest, a new field developed outside the traditional discipline of librarianship. This emerging field was systematically developed first in Europe and was known originally as "documentalism." The focus of documentalism was on the creation, organization, and dissemination of information in all formats. Important organizations were developed to promote these techniques, most notably the Federation Internationale de Documentation (FID) and its U.S. counterpart, the American Documentation Institute, which continues today as the American Society of Information Science and Technology (ASIST). It might be said, then, that central change in the way information was accessed in the twentieth century was a shift in emphasis away from the item that held the information to an emphasis on accessing the content of the information. Taken together, documentalism and librarianship, including bibliography, constitute the critical foundation of information science.

The foundation of information science has at least one additional and critical component on which it rests: the development of computers. One can immediately see how, with the strong interest in organizing and retrieving scientific and technical information, computer technologies would have a magnetic attraction. Early articles on the information potential of computers following World War II predicted great things. Vannevar Bush's (1945) article "As We May Think" in which he projected "Memex," a machine for the storage and retrieval of documents, was certainly a prominent exemplar of the hopes raised by computerized information technologies and is recognized as a seminal work in the field. It was only five years after Bush's article that the phrase "information retrieval" was first used in this context (Wellisch 1972, p. 161). Computers, of course, significantly increase the capacity to store information without the need for a physical document. Therefore it was logical to exploit the computer for information retrieval. Interestingly, despite the importance of the computer to information science, definitions of the field seldom mention computers directly. However, they have given information science much greater prominence and have provided for much of the subsequent research and development in the field to the present day. With the integration of the computer, information science took on its current cast, which emphasizes electronic information: its creation, storage, retrieval, and use.

THE FEATURES OF INFORMATION SCIENCE

Although the debate about the nature and definition of information science will not be resolved here, it is useful to identify briefly some of the areas of activity in the field of information science that directly contribute to our understanding of how information can be created, organized, and disseminated to meet human information needs. The breadth and variety of fields explored by information science can be seen at a glance by looking at the categories of information science as identified by *Information Science Abstracts* (see Figure 2.1).

Librarianship is only one of the eleven major categories. Obviously, electronic information technologies are very important to information science, but there are also other issues that the field addresses, including socioeconomic, educational, psychological, international, national, and legal aspects. Below is a more detailed summary of some of the major issues addressed by information science that directly affect libraries. Information technology and information policy are discussed in Chapters 3 and 4 respectively.

Area 1: Examination of Information Needs, Information Seeking, Information Use, and Information Users

One major area of study is how users of information systems solve information problems. Allen (1996) observes that user-centered approaches are especially useful in the information professions which are intended, in large part, to resolve the information problems of their clients. Such approaches focus "on the ways that information systems meet the information needs of users" (p. 14). Allen suggests that understanding the nature of information needs and their resolution is extremely complex and requires clarity on a variety of levels. For example, one must distinguish information *devices*, which include individual things such as books and electronic databases, from *information systems*, which are composed of information devices that are linked or otherwise related for the purpose of informing the user. Sometimes, there are collections of information systems designed to help users resolve their information problems; these are referred to as *information services* (for example, a reference department). Information services may be grouped to serve a particular clientele or variety of client groups to form *information institutions*, such as libraries. In a user-centered approach, a significant part of designing

---

Figure 2.1
Information Science Abstracts Classification Scheme

INFORMATION SCIENCE RESEARCH

1.1	Basic Concepts, Definitions, Theories, Methodologies, and Applications
1.2	Properties, Needs, Quality, and Value of Information
1.3	Statistics, Measurements
1.4	Information Retrieval Research
1.5	User Behavior and Uses of Information Systems
1.6	Human-Computer Interface
1.7	Communication
1.8	Operations Research/Mathematics
1.9	History of Information Science, Biographies

KNOWLEDGE ORGANIZATION

2.1	Thesauri, Authority Lists
2.2	Cataloging and Classification
2.3	Abstracting, Indexing, Reviewing
2.4	Standards and Protocols

THE INFORMATION PROFESSION

3.1	Information Professionals
3.2	Organization and Societies

SOCIETAL ISSUES

4.1	Information Ethics, Plagiarism, Credibility
4.2	Information Literacy, Lifelong Learning
4.3	The Information Society

THE INFORMATION INDUSTRY

5.1	Information and Knowledge Management
5.2	Markets and Players
5.3	Economics and Pricing
5.4	Marketing, E-Commerce

PUBLISHING AND DISTRIBUTION

6.1	Print
6.2	Electronic
6.3	Secondary Publishing
6.4	Scholarly Communication

INFORMATION TECHNOLOGIES

7.1	Internet
7.2	Intranets (Private), Web Conferencing
7.3	Software
7.4	Hardware

7.5   Multimedia
7.6   Document Management
7.7   AI, Expert Systems, Intelligent Agents
7.8   Telecommunications
7.9   Security, Access Control, Authentication, Encryption
7.10   Other

ELECTRONIC INFORMATION SYSTEMS AND SERVICES

8.1   Information Searching and Retrieval Systems and Services
8.2   Customized Information Systems, Alerting, Current Awareness
8.3   Document Delivery Systems and Services
8.4   Geographic Information Systems

SUBJECT-SPECIFIC SOURCES AND APPLICATIONS

9.1   Physical Sciences
9.2   Life Sciences
9.3   Social Sciences, Humanities, History, Linguistics
9.4   Business
9.5   Law, Political Science, Government
9.6   News
9.7   Education, Library and Information Science, Ready Reference
9.8   Other/Multidisciplinary

LIBRARIES AND LIBRARY SERVICES

10.1   Library Descriptions and Types
10.2   Library Services
10.3   Library Automation, Operations, and Strategic Planning
10.4   Library Consortia and Networks, Coalitions, Cooperatives
10.5   Digital and Virtual Libraries, Hybrid Libraries
10.6   Education and Training

GOVERNMENT AND LEGAL INFORMATION AND ISSUES

11.1   Intellectual Property Protection
11.2   Legislation, Laws, and Regulations (Except Copyright)
11.3   Contracts and Licensing
11.4   Liability issues
11.5   Sources of Public Information
11.6   Information Policies and Studies
11.7   Systems and Infrastructure

Source: *Information Science & Technology Abstracts* (EBSCO Publishing) and Hawkins, Donald T.; Larson Signe E.; and Bari Q. Caton. "Information Science Abstracts: Tracking the Literature of Information Science. Part 2: A New Taxonomy for Information Science." *Journal of the American Society for Information Science and Technology* 54 (2003): 771-781.
Reprinted with permission Information Science & Technology Abstracts (EBSCO Publishing) and Donald Hawkins.

and evaluating how user needs are met requires an understanding of user characteristics and needs on all levels.

The approaches to studying information needs vary considerably. Some focus on individuals, others on institutions, often libraries; still others focus specifically on the information needs of various disciplines, such as business executives, scientists, nurses, and engineers. Information systems cannot be well designed without a clear understanding of what the intended users want or need to know, how they seek information, and how they evaluate the information that they receive.

The concept of an information need can be understood very generally; *it is when an uncertainty arises in the individual which the individual believes* can be satisfied by information (Krikelas 1983). But the concept can also be separated into information wants (or desires) and information needs. An information want is a *desire* for information to satisfy an uncertainty; an information need is the *condition*, whether recognized by the individual or not in which information is required to resolve a problem. Such a distinction is especially important for librarians if they intend to satisfy both their patrons' wants and needs. Merely answering a patron's question may not be enough. The person may want a particular piece of information, only to discover that something else is needed after all. If librarians are to perform their jobs well, they must find out what is wanted and needed.

Seeking and gathering information is a highly complex process that requires much explanation and refinement. How someone seeks information may vary by age, level of education, intelligence, and discipline. Many models for how people seek information have been advanced. Scientists, for example, rely heavily on informal communications with their colleagues, information gleaned at conferences, journal references and articles, and electronic sources of information, while humanities scholars rely more heavily on references in books, the library's subject catalog, and printed indexes and bibliographies (Broadbent 1986; Van Styvendaele 1977; Meadows 1974). Of course, these differences might diminish somewhat as more and more information is digitized and made available on the Web. Nonetheless, scientists tend to have a greater need for currency than humanities scholars, while humanities researchers seem to have a greater need to browse information. These differences have been confirmed in the online environment. Humanities scholars' search strategies when conducting online searches are significantly different from those used by scientists. Humanities scholars use more named individuals, geographical terms, chronological terms, and discipline terms (Bates, Wilde, and Siegfried 1993). As Durrance (1989) has observed: "What people *do* drives their need for information" (p. 161).

Effectively assessing individuals' information wants and needs requires knowledge of how patrons search for information and how they learn, as well as how to interview effectively, how to evaluate the patron's need, and how to evaluate the degree to which the information has satisfied the need. It also requires that the librarian possess thorough and current knowledge of the available electronic, print, and human resources and know how to access these sources. This approach places a very serious responsibility on the librarian, one beyond that of merely getting pieces of information requested by the patron.

Interestingly, despite the unique character of some groups' information needs, there is also great commonality when one considers the general population. Chen and Hernon (1982), for example, found that among the general population, the primary reason for seeking information was personal. That is, more than half the subjects they studied (52 percent) sought information to solve day-to-day problems and nearly three-quarters (73 percent) described their information need as personal. Among the information of greatest interest were the following: (1) job-related issues such as performing specific tasks or establishing businesses, getting or changing jobs, advancing careers, or obtaining promotions; (2) consumer issues relating to the quality or availability of a product or obtaining product information; (3) housing and household maintenance issues relating to dealings with landlords, obtaining loans and mortgages, performing do-it-yourself repairs on the car or home; (4) education and schooling issues relating to information on adult education, parenting, and obtaining support for education. Certainly, these findings are of great value to libraries, especially public ones, in building their library collections and services.

There are many other studies concerning information seeking that provide a useful context for librarians and other information professionals. Following is a highly selected summary of findings from these studies that can be useful in understanding and designing information services.

THERE IS A DIFFERENCE BETWEEN INFORMATION SEEKING AND INFORMATION GATHERING.

The notion of information seeking is a broad one. Krikelas (1983) has suggested that there may be two different basic activities: information seeking and information gathering. Information *seeking* is "an attempt to satisfy an immediate need by searching for relevant information." Information *gathering* is "an attempt to satisfy a deferred need by searching for relevant information" (p. 8). In information gathering there is no immediate need for the information, but the search is expected to yield useful information for future use.

For libraries, these differences may have a profound effect on how a library is used. An information seeker may be looking for a specific item, ask the reference librarian a specific query, or have a specific time requirement. An information gatherer may browse a collection in a specific area without need for specific information or time requirement. Newspaper and magazine collections may be best suited, although not exclusively, for information gatherers, while reference materials may be best suited for information seekers.

PEOPLE USUALLY SEARCH FOR INFORMATION IN SOME TYPE OF CONTEXT.

As Donald Case (2002) has noted, "Information needs do not arise in a vacuum, but rather owe their existence to some history, purpose, and influence" (p. 226). People seldom seek information as an end in itself; they usually seek it within a particular context or "problem environment" (Durrance 1989, p. 162). The individual is usually trying to solve a particular problem or make a particular decision. A scientist may be trying to locate information on a procedure, an English teacher trying to locate an essay, a neighbor trying to repair a refrigerator, or a minister seeking quotations for a sermon.

The fact is that people ask questions for a purpose, and this has considerable implications for the librarian. Traditionally, reference librarians have been taught not to probe "why" a particular question is asked, for fear that this would violate the patron's privacy. There is a fear that such a query could deter an information seeker from using the library. But this is not consistent with what we know about information seeking. The seeker enters the library with a problem that needs to be solved, and it seems logical that the objective of the librarian is to help solve the problem. This harkens back to distinguishing between information wants and information needs. As Durrance (1989) has observed, the issue is not only "What do you want to know?" but "How and why is the information needed? How is it likely to help? What does the user know already? What is expected? What are the parameters of the problem?" (p. 163). This is not to suggest that the librarian is to probe into the personal lives of patrons, but it does suggest that merely answering the questions asked without understanding the real issues can be problematic. Ironically, despite the librarian's ethical obligation to provide the highest quality of service, restrictiveness in questioning tends to be preferred. Wilson (1986) suggests a middle ground which he calls the "face value rule," which emphasizes question clarification rather than inquiry into the purposes of the questions (p. 469). Nonetheless, information-seeking research suggests that we should not be too restrictive if we are actually to deal with why individuals come to ask their questions, the traditional prohibitions of the library profession notwithstanding.

People Prefer Personal Rather Than Institutional Sources to Satisfy Their Information Needs.

There is little doubt that individuals are very likely to consult the most convenient human sources before they appeal to an institutional one. When an information need arises, one's memory is most likely to be checked first before seeking other sources for information; in other words, we look inward to see if we can answer the question. If this fails, we might attempt to answer the question by using our own powers of observation, if practical (Krikelas 1983). Failing this, individuals attempt to seek the information from external sources, human or institutional. When faced with an information need, people are more likely first to seek individuals rather than institutions (Chen and Hernon 1982). This means that individuals are more likely to contact their doctors, clergy, coworkers, or neighbors before coming to the library. The quality of the information may or may not be as good, but people are the preferred sources of information.

People Seldom See Librarians as a Source of Information.

There is discouraging evidence that when individuals have an information need, they do not think of libraries or librarians as a primary source of information. Chen and Hernon (1982), in a large study of information seekers in New England, for example, found that only 3 percent of the individuals with a recent information need identified the library as a possible source for resolving that need. Durrance (1989), reporting on reference user studies, noted that even library users themselves do not wish to trouble staff with questions and think of reference service as only for simple questions.

These findings may have some disturbing implications for librarians. Durrance (1989) suggests, pessimistically and consistent with Chen's observations, that people perceive the library as the solver of their problems rather than librarians. She notes that we speak of "library users" rather than the "librarian's clients" (p. 165). Indeed, the librarian often appears to be transparent, with the patron perceiving the library as a collection of books and materials, not a source of information specialists. Ironically, the impersonality of the library may be aggravated by the new networked technologies that give the appearance of requiring even less human mediation. This is something we need to think about—how do we make ourselves more visible? This lack of visibility may encourage people to continue to underestimate the importance of the librarian in the information transfer process. In addition, if people really prefer human rather than institutional sources of information, emphasizing the librarian rather than the library might increase individual use of the library. In other words, "humanizing" the library may well reduce resistance to its use.

INFORMATION SEEKING IS A DYNAMIC PROCESS.

The search for information generally goes through a variety of phases beginning with an undefined notion that there is a need for information, which is referred to as an "anomalous state of knowledge (ASK)" (Belkin, Brooks, and Oddy 1982, p. 62). Generally, as the process proceeds, the search becomes more and more defined and the area to be explored narrows. The search strategy will vary depending on the nature of the inquiry itself, and as the query becomes narrowed the strategy and type of information sought will vary (Rouse 1984). Bates (1989) has described the model by which people search as "berrypicking." Berries, the author notes, are usually scattered on bushes; not found in one clump. For the information seeker, the information that may be needed may also be scattered. The information need itself is dynamic, and there are many stages of the information search process. As the search for information evolves, the individual pursues a variety of strategies, locating references and individual pieces of information at each stage of the search process.

Kuhlthau (1991) has proposed that an information seeker generally goes through a six-stage process, which she refers to as the Information Search Process (ISP). The stages are explained in an abbreviated fashion below.

Stage 1, Initiation: This stage is characterized by uncertainty as the information seeker realizes that he or she has a need for some knowledge or understanding. The need is still unfocused; the individual has not yet defined the topic or the approach to be taken and may discuss possible courses of action with others.

Stage 2, Selection: The information seeker begins to focus on a particular topic and begins to explore the best approaches for meeting the information need. Some tentative attempts to gather information on the topic begin.

Stage 3, Exploration: The information seeker begins serious exploration of the topic, gathering information to provide orientation. The information seeker may still have a considerable sense of confusion or doubt because the information may appear to be contradictory. At this point, the information seeker may still not be able to articulate precisely the type of information required to meet the information need.

Stage 4, Formulation: This stage is critical as the seeker begins to establish a clear focus for the exploration, and feelings of uncertainty begin to diminish. Rather than just collecting information, the seeker begins to evaluate critically the information obtained, accepting some information and discarding information that appears to be irrelevant. The information seeker becomes more confident in the search and the search process.

Stage 5, Collection: The focus is now clear, and the information seeker collects only information related to the defined topic. The seeker is able to articulate clearly the type of information needed, the search process becomes more effective, uncertainty is reduced, and the seeker's confidence is increased further.

Stage 6, Presentation: The search for information is now complete, although the success of the search may vary depending on factors such as the availability of information, the effectiveness of the information system used, and the skills of the searcher. At this late stage, some of the information obtained may turn out to duplicate previous information. Attention is turned to summary, synthesis, and reporting of the information gathered.

Information search processes, like the one proposed above, reveal the essentially personal, as well as dynamic, nature of information seeking. The problem context in which people search for information provides its own frame of reference, and the meaning and relevance of the information is largely dictated by this frame of reference rather than some objective measure. Analysis of information needs within this personal context is sometimes referred to as a sense-making approach to information seeking (Dervin 1983). Such an approach suggests that developers of information systems understand not only the internal aspects of an information system, but the importance of responding to the particular problem environment that the user brings to the system. Indeed, if the relevance of a piece of information can be determined only by the user, evaluating information systems requires that the user constantly be consulted to determine if the information retrieved will satisfy the patron's needs. The dynamic nature of information seeking has led some libraries, especially academic ones, to design "information commons" that strive to provide a more flexible environment for information seeking. The information commons is discussed in more detail in Chapter 9.

INDIVIDUALS HAVE SIGNIFICANTLY DIFFERENT ABILITIES IN SEEKING INFORMATION.

It should come as no surprise that some people are very good at seeking information and others are a good deal less skillful. Obviously, there are significant differences in intelligence, analytical ability, and manual dexterity. This has a substantial effect on the capacity of individuals to seek information effectively and can also have a substantial effect on the shaping of library services. Generally speaking, the more varied the users' abilities, the more flexible the information system must be to accommodate these variations. Hence, in a specialized library, where the users might be highly educated and familiar with the organization of the literature and the technologies to search it, the system need not be very flexible. But, in a public library, where the patrons range from highly educated individuals to those who are barely literate, the library needs to be highly flexible.

Not only do individuals vary in abilities, but different groups of individuals use different information strategies. This has led to studies of how specific groups such as the elderly or the economically disadvantaged seek information. For example, they have found that the information-seeking ability improves with age. For those of us who are aging, this seems quite promising, if a bit surprising. But unfortunately, although these skills improve with age, our ability to process information tends to decline with age. In other words, we can find the information, but we can't understand it! Chatman (1996) has found that the information poor often weigh the risks of seeking information. For example, an individual, in order to get information, might have to provide information on income, family problems, or health condition. In these circumstances, some may find the risk greater than the potential benefit, hence not seek information at all.

PEOPLE WILL USE THE LEAST EFFORT IN SEEKING INFORMATION.

Sometimes referred to as the "Principle of Least Effort," this finding suggests that people will seek the most convenient source to meet their information need, even when they realize that this source may produce information of lower quality than other sources. Such a finding, although not surprising, can be unnerving when considering the roles of libraries and librarians. There is little doubt that many view libraries as complicated places. Often finding information in libraries *is* a complicated process. It is certainly more convenient to ask one's neighbor or friend than to drive to the library. The problem is exacerbated when one considers that even if a library is used, varying quality of the information makes it critical that the best sources of information also be the most convenient. Libraries need to design their collections and services so that convenience and quality are one and the same for the user (Mann 1993).

In addition to the findings noted above, information scientists have investigated a variety of factors that impair or prevent information seeking. These barriers include the following:

Physical aspects: It is known that the location of a library has an impact on its use. Libraries that are geographically remote or difficult to reach are bound to create significant problems for those seeking information. Similarly, libraries that are difficult to enter or negotiate, especially for those with physical disabilities, will have restricted use. No doubt, collections with a poor physical arrangement or poor signage will also exacerbate the problems of information access. One wonders, as the Web becomes ubiquitous and a great deal of information becomes accessible in the home only "a few steps away," whether declining use of libraries will be an inevitable result.

Policy and procedural aspects: Often libraries create rules, regulations, and procedures that inhibit the use of materials and services. Sometimes there are very good reasons for these rules, but they can have undesired effects. Restrictive circulation or reference policies; inadequate operating hours; limited use of meeting rooms; restricted use because of age, poor training, or poor scheduling of library staff; inadequate or inappropriate allocation of fiscal resources—all can be impediments to information seeking.

Economic/financial aspects: The ability of the library to afford the latest and best information technology and other information resources has a direct impact on the ability of information seekers to find what they need. Even when such resources are available, library economics have sometimes significantly altered the direction of library services to a "fee-for-service" perspective. As the costs of electronic access increase, this problem is bound to increase, and those with minimal financial resources may well receive a lower quality of service. In addition, the financial status of users has a bearing on their familiarity with and knowledge of electronic information technologies. Wealthier individuals are more likely to own computers or to attend schools where computers are common and up-to-date. Such individuals will likely find using libraries now and in the future easier and more satisfying. This is a troubling trend if one assumes that access to information should not be dependent on one's financial resources.

Legal aspects: Laws and regulations governing the flow of information, such as copyright law, inevitably affect the dissemination of information. Similarly, laws governing the restriction of certain types of information or images, such as those governing access to sexually explicit or violent materials to children and adults, limit the types of information that can be made available. This situation is likely to worsen because there is growing concern over the accessibility of such information on the Web.

Social aspects: A troubling but common finding in studies of library users is that those most likely to use libraries have more formal education, tend to have higher incomes, and are white. There may be many reasons for this phenomenon, but some reasons may relate to the way members of minority groups perceive the library or are treated by library staff. If libraries are perceived as aristocratic, authoritarian institutions, unfriendly and unresponsive to minorities, then these groups are bound to have diminished enthusiasm for libraries as sources of information.

Similarly, there are now many social pressures placed on libraries to restrict access to some of the information within them. Organized groups, especially those with a religious agenda, have attempted to influence not only the availability of specific materials, but also library policies (for further discussion see Chapter 5).

In addition, information technologies tend to be "less friendly" to older individuals. The extent to which generational characteristics affect access to such technologies needs to be addressed if access is to be effected.

PEOPLE'S WEB SEARCH BEHAVIOR VARIES WIDELY.

As the Web increasingly becomes a dominant force in satisfying information needs, research on how the Web is searched has grown as well. The Web is a very different search tool from most traditional tools. Bilal (2002) identifies at least three differences: (1) it is an extraordinarily large system that often produces information overload and disorientation, (2) it is constantly changing, and (3) it is unindexed. Not surprisingly, many searches conducted on the Web are not successful (approximately 30 percent find no hits) and it is frequently the case that Web searchers do not go beyond the first page of "hits" in trying to find the information they want. Similarly, much searching is done on a "spoke and hub" pattern in which the searcher begins at a certain point, searches, returns to the original point, and starts the search again. This searching style accounts for the very heavy use of "Back" buttons in searching, sometimes called, "Backtracking" (Slone 2002). Because it is easy to lose one's place on the Web, returning to an original point provides a stable point of reference.

Among the individual characteristics that may affect Web searching are cognitive style, level of anxiety related to searching, age (children versus adults), experience with Web searching, gender, and domain expertise. Research on adults reveals that many adults depend on hyperlinks to find documents, seldom use Boolean search strategies, rely heavily on keyword searching, limit their explorations to specific sections within a site, use a few pages frequently, and spend much time scrolling, reading Web pages, and waiting for Web pages to load (Hsieh-Yee 2001). Searchers familiar with a field (domain expertise) will have significantly greater search success and take less time to complete the search (Lazonder, Biemans, and Wopereis 2000). When it comes to experience on the Web, less experienced users (novices) are more prone to make search errors, retrieve irrelevant hits, avoid the use of advanced features, or quickly become frustrated and stop the search (Slone 2002).

The Web search behavior of children has also been studied. Hsieh-Yee (2001, 2002), on reviewing the literature found that children's information needs are different from those of adults, and they have fewer problem-solving and mechanical skills as well as less developed cognitive abilities. Hsieh-Yee also found that children prefer to browse the Web and do not search it systematically. They have difficulty evaluating the quality of Web sites, developing search strategies, using correct search syntax, typing in the proper search terms, and locating relevant hits. At the same time, ironically, children feel confident about their Web searches.

Research on gender also reveals some significant differences in Web search success. Women, for example, tend to encounter more difficulty, believe they are less competent in searching, use the Internet less frequently, and use fewer Internet applications (Hsieh-Yee 2001). There is some evidence that the gap between men and women's use has narrowed over the years.

Area 2: Information Storage and Retrieval

A central area for research and development in information science is the issue of information storage and retrieval and the systems that support it. Harter (1986) defines an information retrieval system as "a device interposed between a potential end-user of an information collection and the information collection itself. For a given information program, the purpose of the system is to capture wanted items and filter out unwanted items from the information collection" (p. 2). This definition highlights a central concept of information retrieval: relevance. This concept can be difficult to understand, and much has been written on the subject (Saracevic 1975). There are at least two aspects of relevance: relevant to the user and relevant to the topic. In the former, it is clear that the user defines the context for relevance. An item retrieved from an information system is relevant if the user believes that it helps to meet his or her information need. In the latter case, an item is relevant if it can be shown that it is about the subject, regardless of a given user (Pao 1989). Relevance forms the basis of much evaluation of information systems. Systems that retrieve relevant items and avoid the retrieval of irrelevant items (sometimes referred to as "false hits" or "false drops") naturally are considered more effective.

It was the information retrieval research in the 1960s that constituted the "first flowering of information science as a science" (Rayward 1983, p. 353). Certainly, this is a critical area for libraries. With the increasing number of information technologies employed by libraries, the effectiveness of these technologies in retrieving the desired information is significant. Systems without computers can also be considered information storage and retrieval systems—libraries, for example, can be conceived as just such systems. But generally, the focus in information science is on computerized information systems. Areas studied in information storage and retrieval are discussed in the following sections.

EVALUATION OF INFORMATION RETRIEVAL SYSTEMS

Evaluating an information retrieval system is a very complex task. By what criteria are such systems to be evaluated? Two basic concepts are *recall* and *precision*. Within any given system, it is critical to know if all the available items relevant to a particular search were found; the degree to which this is accomplished is a measure of *recall*. With poor recall, many items that might have been useful were not located. On the other hand, it is also important to know if *only* the relevant items were found. Sometimes, many irrelevant items are found. This is difficult and time consuming for the searcher, who must then review all of the items—including those that were not relevant—to find the relevant ones. The degree to which the system finds only the relevant items is a measure of *precision*. The formula for each is noted below:

$$\text{Recall} = \frac{\text{Number of relevant documents retrieved}}{\text{Total number of relevant documents in the file}}$$

$$\text{Precision} = \frac{\text{Number of relevant documents retrieved}}{\text{Total number of documents retrieved in the file}}$$

However, these measures are somewhat controversial. They emphasize quantitative, not qualitative aspects, and there are many ambiguities associated with what one might define as "relevant." As Froehlich (1994) observes, relevance judgements are made dynamically, and often involve the application of multiple criteria rather than a single criterion. More recent approaches have emphasized the responsiveness of the system to the user's needs and psychological characteristics. This type of evaluation places greater emphasis on the searcher's knowledge, cognitive process, and problem to be solved. It will be discussed further below.

SEARCH RETRIEVAL MODELS

An information storage and retrieval system is not useful unless there are search strategies that permit information to be quickly and effectively retrieved. The search models in use vary considerably. The most common search strategy in library settings is the *Boolean logic* model. In the Boolean model, an individual can search a database by combining terms with a variety of logical operators including *and*, *or*, or *not*. With this method, multiple terms can be included in the search simultaneously; this permits highly flexible search strategies compared to manual searching operations. Other operators can also be employed to further limit searches. For example, retrieval models may permit searching by author, title, year of publication, and journal title. Such models play a crucial role in the discipline and will continue to demand time and attention. Unless effective searches can be performed, information cannot be extracted from an information system.

DATABASE AND FILE STRUCTURE

Database design, the structure of the information, and how it is presented to the user all have a significant effect on the user's ability to retrieve the information. For example, how is the information represented to the user? What types of information are available (numerical, textual, video, audio), and what vocabulary is used? Are the words used in the search process highly restricted, or is the language relatively open? What fields and subfields are searchable, and how are the records searched (for example, by author? by title or keyword? by subject?)? Can the search be narrowed by date, language, or publisher? Do the records contain abstracts, full text, or images? The usefulness of the database for any given user depends on the answers to these questions. Further discussion of this issue can be found in Chapter 6.

HUMAN-COMPUTER INTERFACE

Information systems, and certainly systems for libraries, are designed to satisfy human information needs. The point of contact between the human and the computer is called the *human-computer interface* (HCI). In the early development of computers, little attention was paid to this area; only a small number of individuals used computers and they tended to be very knowledgeable with the technical languages of computer systems. As computer use became more widespread, especially when the personal computer became commonplace, it became necessary to pay more attention to creating successful searches for the average citizen. Today, the human-computer interface is considered a vital aspect in the success or failure of a computer system (Shaw 1991).

For an information system to function effectively, it must make the user comfortable and make the process of searching as easy as possible. This means that designers of information storage and retrieval systems must understand the way that humans approach computers and how they search for information. This understanding permits computer designers to create, or strive to create, "user-friendly front-ends," which allow users to sit down in front of the computer screen and satisfy their information needs with a minimum of jargon, confusion, or technical knowledge. Some of the issues in exploring human-computer interfaces include screen display features such as color and windows, speed of response, interaction functions such as commands and menus, post-processing functions such as downloading, help systems and messages, graphics capabilities, training time required, user satisfaction, and error rates when using the system (Shaw 1991).

One important area in the exploration of human-computer interfaces is *cognitive research*, which explores how the user's knowledge and the knowledge contained within the information systems can be matched effectively. Knowledge, on a variety of levels, affects the use of information systems. Allen (1991) has identified four such levels:

- **World knowledge**: The user's world knowledge may affect the information they search for and their search strategies. Factors such as ethnicity, gender, and nationality have all been shown to influence the use of information systems.
- **Systems knowledge**: The extent and type of knowledge that users possess about information systems and their expectations of the systems affect their ability and manner of use.
- **Task knowledge**: The users' particular information goals or needs affect their use of the systems. How users define the information problem to be resolved and the process by which information problems are defined, refined, and resolved have a direct impact on the use of the information systems.
- **Domain knowledge**: the users' familiarity with the actual subject will affect their use of the systems. Experts are bound to use information systems differently from the way naive users do. In addition, cognitive research explores how a user's problem-solving techniques are applied to information systems, how the user proceeds with the information search process, how users judge the relevance of information, how memory affects information users, and how users learn to use information systems, and the relationship between cognitive ability and the ability to use an information system (Allen 1991).

Exploring these cognitive areas provides some guidance in how to design the information systems themselves. Understanding how people think, what they know, and how they approach information problems can help designers create knowledge models within their systems that more closely match the methods and data by which users can meet their needs. This understanding helps designers create what is commonly referred to as "user-friendly" systems or effective "gateways" for information access.

Closely related is the issue of how the user communicates with the computer. For this issue, information science draws upon the field of linguistics. A crucial area of study is *natural language processing* (NLP), which attempts to develop user interfaces that allow users to employ their "natural" language to have their queries answered. In other words, using NLP they should be able to ask a computer a question in the same way they would ask another person, or reference librarian, a question. This capability eliminates the need for the user to use the "right" term selected by the database developers. Lee and Olsgaard (1989) observe that use of NLP requires that at least four areas be addressed: (1) Speech recognition: the computer should be able to hear and understand a question being asked of it through a voice recognition system. (2) Command recognition: the computer should be able to understand the command without use of an artificial language or vocabulary. (3) Content analysis and representation: the computer should be able to understand the actual meaning of a document. This process involves understanding the context in which the language is used. Given the subtleties and ambiguities of language, content analysis represents a major challenge in NLP. (4) System interaction: the system has to be able to take the natural language query and relate it to the database so that correct information can be retrieved.

Artificial Intelligence (AI) and Expert Systems

Artificial intelligence is an extremely broad field, and much of the research and application lie outside the realm of librarianship or even of information retrieval in general. Among the many fields of artificial intelligence are machine translation, robotics, expert systems, natural language interfaces, speech understanding, knowledge acquisition and representation, and pattern matching. One of the most intriguing areas of information storage and retrieval lies in the continuing attempt to develop machines that think like people—or even better than people. There is little doubt that the concept of an actual "thinking machine" has been an attractive concept for years, as any decent survey of science fiction would attest. How many times have we witnessed on a movie screen a computer ready to take over the world, a computer that knows everything and responds in a friendly, mellifluous voice, or an android that even looks much like us and mimics our thoughts and actions. Work in artificial intelligence is intended, at least in part, to create computers that mimic human thought processes, judgments, and sometimes human actions in the hope that computers can provide invaluable information, perform valuable services, and even render judgments that would assist humans. These activities might be in industrial production (robotics for manufacturing), in game playing (chess programs), or even in assisting medical diagnosis or legal practice. Sometimes these systems possess considerable power and are referred to as *expert systems*. Expert systems are "computer programs which inform, make recommendations, or solve problems in a manner and at a level of performance comparable to that displayed by a human expert in the field" (Vedder 1990, p. 4).

In libraries, artificial intelligence might be applied to reference functions such as identification and retrieval of documents or data, cataloguing and authority control, and library instruction through computer assisted instruction (CAI) (Smith 1987). In addition, work in developing "expert search intermediaries" would assist users in searching online systems without the need for human intermediaries (Smith, p. 55).

Area 3: Defining the Nature of Information and Its Value

There are many theoretical and practical discussions in information science concerning the fundamental object of the field—information. Perhaps the most conspicuous debate deals with distinguishing among at least three basic constructs: data, information, and knowledge. A fourth construct—wisdom—is also added from time to time. This debate will not be settled here; rather, one perspective, albeit a conventional one, will be advanced in abbreviated form to provide a basic understanding of the distinctions among these concepts. Although such discussions may seem unnecessarily abstract, a critical examination of these concepts can lead to a deeper understanding of the purposes of institutions like libraries.

DATA

The term *data* is sometimes used synonymously with information, but it also has a more characteristic use, as the building blocks of information and knowledge. It refers to the material out of which information is created. In this sense, data are commonly seen as numbers, letters, or symbols, which may or may not be processible by a computer. The term often implies that meaning is as yet absent, or unassigned, as in *raw data*. Hence, the numbers stored in a computer file are referred to as a data set.

INFORMATION

Attempting to understand the meaning of the term *information* is more complex, perhaps in part because the term has had a very long etymological history. There are many definitions that persist today, including highly technical ones in the telecommunications industry, law, and genetics, as when DNA is described as passing on genetic information. These more abstract, technical, or metaphorical uses are not addressed in this discussion, but it is important to know that they are part of this definitional milieu.

Many of the historical uses of information have found their way into common usage or are suggestive of current usage. Early senses of the term, for example, suggested that information involved a "forming" or "moulding of the mind" (*Oxford English Dictionary* 1989, p. 944). In this early sense, the soul might be "informed." Although this is not a current usage, it is suggestive of our current concern with the power of information. One hears the phrase "information is power," and certainly many are concerned that the information our citizenry receives from television and other media is a critical component in the shaping of our attitudes. Other senses of the term information are more directly accepted by contemporary society. For example, information can be seen as an activity, namely, "the action of informing" or the "communication of the knowledge or 'news' of some fact or occurrence" (*Oxford English Dictionary*, p. 944). This is what is meant by the phrase "for your information." Information can also be seen as that which is being communicated. It is the "knowledge communicated concerning some particular fact, subject, or event; that which one is apprised of or told; intelligence, news" (*Oxford English Dictionary*, p. 944). To say that the library or information center is in the information business plays on both these latter senses of the term. Libraries both inform their users and provide them with information.

Although the terms information and data are often used synonymously, a greater understanding of information science can be gained by noting their distinctive characteristics. Commonly, library and information science sees information as, at the least, an aggregation, organization, or classification of data, and perhaps more importantly, as *meaning* that is assigned to data. In other words, information possesses meaning (data being its "raw" state), and this seems also to imply that some type of human understanding and processing has occurred. Somewhat more restrictive definitions of information hold that information must not only contain meaning, but that meaning must be previously unknown to the recipient of the information; in other words, it is something new. Some definitions suggest that the information must also be true or accurate, or that it must be conveyed (that is, communicated) from one person to another. Clearly libraries and information centers are constructed for humans, and one can see them as possessing data which are then processed either by staff or patrons—in this sense meaning arises within the walls of the library or information center.

KNOWLEDGE, WISDOM, AND COGNITIVE AUTHORITY

Knowledge is sometimes used synonymously with information, but it is also defined as a *cohesive* body of information, or information that is *integrated* into a larger body of knowledge. That is, it is a body of interrelated information. Knowledge is applied or potentially applicable to some end. From a library perspective, one presumes that knowledge as well as information is gained through libraries—that users gain an understanding of the interrelationship of the information obtained and its applicability to a particular setting. Such a view recognizes the obligation of libraries and librarians to make connections whenever possible so that information becomes knowledge to the user.

Although not always part of the discussion, wisdom is also an important notion. One way of understanding wisdom is as knowledge applied to human ends to benefit the world. In this sense, wisdom is the only one of the above terms that is laden with the values of human progress. One can apply knowledge to immoral ends, but wisdom is wisdom because there is a beneficial end to its application. The goals of libraries as a social institution are to benefit the members of society and the society as a whole.

In summary, there appears to be a conceptual ladder: data are raw and unprocessed, information is processed data from which meaning arises and is communicated, and knowledge is further processed information that is organized and interrelated and more broadly understood and applied. Wisdom is knowledge applied to the benefit of humanity. Despite the seeming simplicity of this hierarchy, one should accept these distinctions with great caution. Notably, for libraries, the question of what constitutes knowledge is a very important one, for libraries rely on bodies of knowledge, or knowledgeable works, to perform many of their question-answering functions. That is, although libraries are full of information, when librarians attempt to respond to a query, the knowledgeable or authoritative work is the one that is preferred. In this sense, librarians rely on a canon of authoritative literature to provide the most dependable responses.

This is a thorny question; after all, how does something come to be accepted as knowledge in our society, knowledge that we may end up putting on our shelf to refer to and transmit to others? Wilson (1983) has observed that most of the "knowledge" we acquire does not come from direct experience (first-hand knowledge), but from what he refers to as "second-hand" knowledge: "We mostly depend on others for ideas, as well as for information about things outside the range of direct experience. . . . Much of what we think about the world is what we have second hand from others . . . " (p. 10). That which makes one infer that one item is knowledge and another mere information or speculation is referred to as *cognitive authority*. We believe those sources we think are cognitive authorities—others we reject. What sources have the greatest cognitive authority for librarians? Are they those prepared by famous publishers like Harvard University Press or the *New England Journal of Medicine*? Are librarians censoring materials because they regard some authors or publishers as low in cognitive authority (although other groups may not regard them as such)? Are there new cognitive authorities on the Web? Can we assess the cognitive authority of a Web site in the same way we do other publications? Although librarians often characterize themselves as objective information providers, their attitudes toward what constitutes knowledge has a profound effect on their ability to serve the entire citizenry.

Value of Information and Value-Added Processes

Part of understanding the nature of information is trying to understand its value. Although information has had value over the centuries, attempts to determine its monetary value have arisen as its critical value has become more prominent. With the industrial society evolving into an information-based society, the concept of information as a product, a commodity with its own value, has emerged. The increasing complexity of the society and its reliance on information have only made the concept of information as a commodity more prevalent. As a consequence those people, organizations, and countries that possess the highest quality information are likely to prosper economically, socially, and politically.

For the field of information science, the attention to the value of information has spawned a variety of investigations into the economics of information; the costs of information and information services; the effects of information on decision making; the savings from effective information acquisition; the effects of information on productivity, sometimes referred to as "downstream productivity"; and the effects of specific information agencies (such as corporate, technical, or medical libraries) on the productivity of organizations. Obviously many of these areas overlap, but it is clear that information has taken on a life of its own, outside the media in which it is contained. Information has become a recognized entity to be measured, evaluated, and priced.

Another sense of value that is critical to library and information science is the notion of value-added functions. Value-added functions are those performed by librarians and information scientists to increase the value of the information by making it more accessible. Much of the important work in this area has been developed by Robert Taylor (1986). Taylor sees libraries as document-based systems, which are simply one part of the broader rubric of information systems. He identifies a variety of functions that librarians or information scientists perform to enhance the value of information by increasing its accessibility. A condensation of some of the processes that relate both to information systems in general and to libraries in particular include the following:

Access processes: Processes that help narrow the search for information. These processes include the classification system, indexes, and subject headings. In addition, there are processes that reduce larger amounts of information into manageable quantities for summary and review; these include abstracts, summaries, and graphs.

Accuracy processes: Processes that decrease the possibility of error in the data or information provided. These processes include the employment of standards to ensure consistency, completeness, and accuracy of bibliographic records; the use of high-quality sources to select materials; and the employment of weeding processes to remove inaccurate materials.

Browsing processes: Processes that permit the user to browse a "neighborhood" of information. Such processes include classification systems that group items of a similar subject or author together (see Chapter 6). Library classification systems accomplish this purpose, as does the system of subject headings that permits grouping catalog records by subject. Physical book arrangement can also foster browsing, as do book displays or special exhibitions of materials. These processes permit serendipitous discovery of related information.

Currency processes: Processes that ensure that the materials or data provided are up-to-date. Among these processes are those that continuously review materials (weeding) and order later editions. They also include processes that employ the most recent indexing terms, abstracting terms, and subject headings to reflect current thinking.

Flexibility (adaptability) processes: Processes that adapt to the needs and abilities of the user, that provide a variety of methods or techniques to find information. Processes that assist the patron in analyzing, interpreting, and evaluating information fall within this scope as well because such activities provide means of maximizing the usefulness of the information search and the information itself. Obviously human intermediaries, such as librarians, play a vital role in this process as they assist information seekers with various search strategies and as they provide information on those sources that are considered reliable as well as those that are less so.

Formatting processes: Processes that affect the physical arrangement and presentation of information. This function often focuses on the arrangement of a particular electronic record on a computer screen. It can also have an institutional context as well, that is, how the institution provides for guidance to the arrangement of its information. In libraries this process would include the use of signs and graphics to guide patrons to the appropriate information or services.

Interfacing processes: Processes that provide assistance to the user in understanding and using the system. Computer-based systems have screens and navigation systems that facilitate users' access to information contained in them. In libraries, the fundamental interpreter of the system is the librarian. Also known as information intermediaries, librarians perform reference interviews and help dispel the "mystery" of libraries through their knowledge and guidance. Interface processes also include special services that the library staff provide, such as orientations, story hours, and summer reading clubs.

Ordering processes: Processes that provide basic organization to the collection. These processes include those dividing the collection by subject area, format, or type of user and those separating types of materials, such as encyclopedias and other reference works, from the rest of the collection.

Physical access processes: Processes that improve physical access to library collections or computer databases including circulation systems, check-out desks, study areas, shelving and shelf-reading, and computers that permit searching remote databases and other library collections throughout the nation and world.

Taylor (1986) identifies many other value-added processes that could be applied in institutional settings such as libraries, and it is obvious that many of these processes overlap conceptually. For example, ordering processes can also be seen as flexibility processes. Despite the fact that these value-added services play a critical role in locating information, the systems that provide these services, including libraries, are often underestimated in terms of their importance. The reason may well be, at least in part, that by making the information search easier, these processes are transparent. The user doesn't necessarily struggle to find the information (perhaps they simply ask the librarian) and, therefore, they underestimate the complex design of the information system that makes that search so easy. To the extent that such functions are invisible to the information seeker, librarians and other information providers need to find ways to increase the user's understanding of the importance of these processes. Perhaps the status of information professionals would increase if these value-added processes were made more prominent.

Area 4: Bibliometrics and Citation Analysis

Wallace (1989) defines bibliometrics as "the application of quantitative methods to the study of information resources" (p. 10). Such a field explores patterns in the production of knowledge as well as the patterns of its use. Examples of the direct use of bibliometric approaches for libraries include: (1) Explorations concerning the use or circulation of library materials. Studies of which items circulate or fail to circulate can provide valuable information to the library regarding future purchases or reveal deficiencies in the library's organization or practices. (2) Studies of how materials are used *inside* libraries can provide valuable insights into the information-seeking behavior of patrons and the use of reference materials. (3) Studies of the obsolescence (aging) of library materials can reveal the currency of library collections and the patterns that govern the use of aging materials. (4) Studies of collection overlap, which often involve comparing the collections of two or more libraries to reveal duplications, can help in planning cooperative collection development, revealing unique features of different library collections, and reducing unnecessary expenditures for materials.

Bibliometric studies can also provide a broader understanding of entire disciplines, revealing which authors are most productive within a discipline and which countries or languages produce greater amounts of material within a field. Sometimes consistencies are so great that bibliometric "laws" can be established. Among the most common is Lotka's Law, named after Alfred Lotka. Lotka (1926) observed that with a body of literature, there are a few authors who contribute a large number of publications, a larger number of authors who contribute a smaller group of publications, and then many authors who contribute a few or only one publication. This relationship was expressed as $1/n^2$, where n is the number of contributions. Hence, the number of authors making three contributions in a field would be one-ninth $(1/3^2)$ of the total number of authors. The number of authors making four contributions would be one-sixteenth $(1/4^2)$. The pattern quickly becomes obvious; far fewer authors will be contributing a large number of contributions. Unlike actual physical laws, Lotka's law is not a perfect description of how authors and publications are related within a discipline, but generally it is a good estimate.

Another law that is frequently mentioned is Bradford's Law or the Bradford distribution, based on the work of Samuel Bradford (1934). Bradford's law deals with the concept of "scatter," which describes in a quantitative manner how articles within a particular field are distributed among periodical titles. Bradford found that given a body of journal literature in a particular area (such as engineering), the distribution throughout the various journals is not even, nor is the literature consulted equally. Although the distribution is not even, it *is* predictable. Most notably, he found that the spread of journal articles could be placed into three zones. The first zone was the nucleus of the field in which most articles appeared in a relatively small number of journal titles. A second zone contained the same number of articles spread out in a substantially larger number of journals. A third zone contained the same number of articles but scattered among even more titles. This relation was expressed as $1{:}n{:}n^2$. That is, if there were a total of 1,500 articles, the first 500 might be found in ten journals (Zone 1); the next 500 might be found in 50 journals (Zone 2). This produces a ratio of Zone 1 to Zone 2 of 1:5. The next 500 articles should therefore be of a ratio of $1{:}5^2$ or 1:25. This means that Bradford's law would predict that the 500 articles of Zone 3 would be scattered among (10x25) or 250 journal titles. This regularity suggests that there is a predictable scatter, and such regularity can have a significant impact on the selection and development of library collections. Obviously, in selecting materials for library collections, the crucial selections would be those found in the nucleus, or Zone 1, of a discipline. As with Lotka's law, this regularity has its exceptions, but nonetheless it holds for many disciplines and represents an important bibliometric finding.

A related area of bibliometrics is citation analysis. Citation analysis deals with the frequency and pattern of citations (for example, references cited in articles and books). There are various ways to analyze the patterns of citations. Among them are direct citation, bibliographic coupling, and cocitation. Direct citation analyzes the items cited by authors. Bibliographic coupling and cocitation are closely related but distinct concepts. As Smith (1981) has observed:

> Two documents are bibliographically coupled if their reference lists share one or more of the same cited documents. Two documents are cocited when they are jointly cited in one or more subsequently published documents. Thus in cocitation earlier documents become linked because they are later cited together; in bibliographic coupling later documents become linked because they cite the same earlier documents. The difference is that bibliographic coupling is an association intrinsic to the documents (static) while cocitation is a linkage extrinsic to the documents, and one that is valid only so long as they continue to be cocited (dynamic). (p. 85)

Among the information that can be revealed by citation studies is identification of which works and which authors are most often cited within a given discipline and why items are cited. For collection development or selection in libraries this procedure can be very useful in that it identifies works that may well be influential. Works that are cited frequently are likely to be requested by those reading the article in which the citations appear. Frequently cited authors may be individuals whose works the library may wish to include. The same might be said for frequently cited journal titles. As with other bibliometric practices, citation analysis may be useful beyond the instrumental uses of libraries. It may, for example, help explain which ideas and thinkers tend to influence the conceptual development within a discipline. It also has been used to identify which disciplines appear to be active and whose work is playing a central role in that discipline.

Area 5: Management and Administrative Issues

The growth of information technologies has placed additional burdens on the managers of libraries and other information organizations. Given the initial and continuing expenses of these technologies, making the wrong decisions can be expensive in terms of time, money, productivity, and human resources. As information services play a more central role, demands for accountability will grow. This accountability will require increasing levels of sophistication in measuring library services. Among the issues that information scientists have addressed in trying to cope with these managerial burdens are the following:

IDENTIFYING AND SELECTING INFORMATION TECHNOLOGIES

It is often assumed that the introduction of information technologies always results in increased productivity—this cannot be assumed. Administrators must be able to determine which processes lend themselves to effective computerization and which do not. Once the processes to be computerized are identified, the appropriate technology must be identified and installed. The essential steps are: (1) identify appropriate computer vendors, (2) develop criteria and establish decision-making structures for comparing and evaluating vendors, (3) develop timetables for implementing automation, (4) plan on-site visits and demonstrations, (5) develop and implement training and orientation on automated systems for staff, and (6) conduct post-implementation evaluation to determine if the technologies are performing effectively.

DEALING WITH HUMAN FACTORS IN TECHNOLOGY

While information science sometimes focuses on the technology itself, the application of most technologies requires human participation. Over the last two decades, it has become increasingly obvious that how people deal with computers can have a significant effect on how useful they are. Similarly, it has become clear that technologies can have significant influences on the people who use them. For this reason, information science explores how technologies can be effectively implemented, what factors generate resistance or acceptance of technologies, and what aspects of technologies have the potential to create physical problems for people. This latter area has spawned a field called ergonomics, which explores the fit between people and machines. Ergonomics will be discussed further in the next chapter.

Developing Management Information Systems/Information Resources Management (IRM)/Records Management

Organizations increasingly rely on information to perform their functions. Managing information inside organizations has many purposes: for record maintenance and oversight (which has spawned an entire subfield referred to as records management), for decision making, and for strategic and tactical planning. The nature of the information can be extremely varied: data, text, images, sound, or multimedia. Making the best management decisions relies, in part, on an organization's ability to acquire, access, and evaluate information in a timely fashion. As organizations have become increasingly complex and their reliance on rapid access to high-quality information has grown, the field known as information resources management (IRM) or information management has emerged. Managing information has become a task with the same significance as managing the fiscal and human resources of an organization.

IRM is much more than file maintenance. It requires that one view information as the life blood of the organization. As such, each aspect of the organization needs to be considered in terms of how it produces, organizes, selects, and disseminates information for use by its members. Among the major objectives of IRM are: (1) ensuring that the relevant documents are made available for decision making; (2) developing and implementing a cost/benefit analysis of information provision; (3) creating an environment in which IRM and the information manager are perceived by management and administration as a major contributor to the organization; (4) assisting in the evaluation and implementation of information management technologies; (5) defining responsibility and accountability for information management, preservation, and disposal; (6) creating an environment in which the corporate managers recognize properly organized and accessible information as vital for critical corporate decisions (Levitan, 1982).

From these objectives it is clear that IRM has many aspects and responsibilities. The need to ensure that the correct information is provided in a timely manner and the acquisition of appropriate, cost-effective information systems are basic to this activity. In addition, there are political and educational components, including getting organizational leaders and staff to recognize the importance of information and the value of the individual who organizes that information and then training staff in the creation and use of information. The growth of new positions, such as chief information officers (CIOs), is testimony to the increasing recognition of how important IRM is to the survival of organizations. IRM has also contributed to the development of a new, somewhat broader, field, "knowledge management" which will be discussed below.

MEASURING AND EVALUATING LIBRARY AND INFORMATION SERVICES

Most information services take place within an organizational context, and administrators and managers need the means to determine whether their organizations are, in fact, accomplishing what they set out to do. Such information is critical not only in evaluating current activities, but also in planning for staffing, planning future services, and determining the direction of collection development. It also provides political and economic justification for budget requests. To this end, information science is concerned with how to measure and evaluate information services.

Some typical targets of measurement and evaluation include collections; services, including reference and document delivery; programs; and staff. Among the most common measures for evaluating information services are *user* and *use* studies. These studies are usually conducted through questionnaires, focus groups, interviews, or analysis of available data such as circulation or interlibrary loan data. The focus of these studies is usually on some aspect of the collection or services provided and the satisfaction of the user with those collections and services. Although user and use studies may appear the same and are interrelated, they focus on different aspects. A user study focuses on the individual or group of individuals. It might examine demographic features, such as age, income, sex, and level of education, and analyze them in relation to library use. It might focus on the reasons individuals use an information service or where they sought information before coming. Such studies attempt to answer the question: who is using the library and why? An offshoot of user studies is nonuser studies. Nonusers can provide vital information in evaluating a library for they can reveal organizational inadequacies that prevent full use of library services. Perhaps individuals or groups of individuals do not know that there are library services to help them; perhaps they consider the library unfriendly, or as not having the materials or services they need.

Use studies on the other hand, focus on what is used. They might look at the subjects consulted (for example, fiction/nonfiction, specialized subject areas), the number of items used, where they were used (for example, in-house or checked out), the types of materials used (such as AV, print, computer disks), types of services used (such as reference, children's, the Web), the types of programming used, or whether a librarian was consulted. Such information can provide valuable planning information. As might be expected, because of the close connection between users and uses of libraries, it is common that both are studied and cross-analyzed. Hence, libraries might look not only at which parts of a collection are used most, but also, who uses that collection.

There are many ways to measure library services and different ways to measure them. Perhaps the best known measures of library performance are found in the public library world. These are measures developed by the Public Library Association (PLA, a division of American Library Association [ALA]), referred to as the "output measures" for public libraries (PLA 1987). The measures are intended to provide guidance on measuring public library performance and to suggest methods of data collection (see Chapter 9). As an extension of these general output measures, PLA worked with the Young Adult Library Services Association (YALSA) to create output measures specifically designed for young adults (Walter 1995), and with the Association for Library Service to Children to create output measures for children's services (Walter 1992).

Some types of libraries have an easier time than others in measuring and evaluating their services using these measures. The more generalized the activities and purposes of a library, the more difficult it is to measure its effectiveness. As a rule, public libraries are more difficult to assess, notwithstanding the output measures, than special libraries because the purposes and activities are not as clearly defined. This difficulty is especially apparent when trying to measure productivity and cost-effectiveness or develop cost-benefit ratios (Koenig 1990).

EMERGING FIELDS: INFORMATION ARCHITECTURE, KNOWLEDGE MANAGEMENT, USABILITY ENGINEERING, COMPETITIVE INTELLIGENCE

Information Architecture (IA)

As Web sites have proliferated and their applicability has extended to nearly every aspect of our lives, it has become clear that how information is organized and presented on a Web site has substantial impact on our ability to get the information that we need. Designing information systems, whether paper or electronic, has been around a long time, but the Internet has dramatically changed our information environment; today, "post-Web information system design" has spawned new fields, including knowledge management, experience design, content management, interaction design, information design, customer relationship management, and information architecture (Rosenfeld 2002).

Although it comes as no surprise to information professionals that information organization and presentation is a critical component to information access, the developing field of "information architecture" (IA) is increasing in prominence. Certainly, well-designed Web sites are important. Significant costs are incurred in their creation, maintenance, and updating, and additional costs arise if the information they provide is not easily located. Web sites that have poor graphics, are confusing, or are overly complex to use fail in their fundamental objective of providing the information intended.

There is no one definition of "information architecture." Froehlich (2003) defines it as

> the art and science of organizing information and interfaces to help information seekers solve their information needs efficiently and effectively. . . . The information architect designs and implements a specific system and interface, based on organizational requirements and aesthetic and functional considerations, similar to the ways an architect deploys a building in physical space, focusing on aesthetic, functional and use goals.

Rosenfeld and Morville (2002) separate the field into four components:

1. The combination of organization, labeling, and navigation schemes within an information system.
2. The structural design of an information space to facilitate task completion and intuitive access to content.

3. The art and science of structuring and classifying Web sites and intranets to help people find and manage information.
4. An emerging discipline and community of practice focused on bringing principles of design and architecture to the digital landscape. (p. 4)

IA focuses on two distinct but closely related areas: the use of graphic or multimedia design to facilitate communication, and the use of intellectual technologies, such as site and content organization, needs analysis, usability studies, metadata application, and programming, to make an information interface or source easy to locate, comprehend, navigate, and use (Froehlich, 2003). Attention is paid both to the mission of the site and the anticipated needs of those who use it.

Farnum (2002, p. 34) describes information architects as those who "help build Web sites by organizing them to make it easier for people to find what they want . . . much like an architect for physical buildings, information architects design *information* spaces by considering the ways they will be used and then create blueprints and detailed plans for that use" (34). He identifies four components of the field:

1. *Visual design*: concerned with the graphic design and layout of the information on the site.
2. *Interaction design*: designing the dynamic components of the sites.
3. *User experience design*: tailoring the site to the users needs.
4. *Usability*: evaluating the site to make sure it can be used easily, efficiently, and effectively.

Because of the newness of the field, the precise disciplinary content of information architecture is still unclear. The same is true of the tasks that information architects perform. Rosenfeld and Morville (1998) identify four roles for the information architect:

1. Clarifies the mission and vision for the site, balancing the needs of its sponsoring organization and the needs of its audiences.
2. Determines what content and functionality the site will contain.
3. Specifies how users will find information in the site by defining its organization, navigation, labeling, and searching systems.
4. Maps out how the site will accommodate change and growth over time. (p. 11)

Information architects should not be confused with graphic designers who focus only on the graphical aspects of the Web site. Certain aesthetic concerns are important to the information architect as well, but information architects also emphasize the underlying structure of the site.

Information architects address many complex and varied issues and identifying some of them also helps to elucidate the nature and scope of the field. Among the major issues are the following:

1. Effective navigation techniques, so that users can move easily throughout the site (e.g., menus, hyperlinks, guided tours, site maps and indexes).
2. Effective orientation for users within the site.
3. Making the site usable in terms of language and terminology employed.
4. Developing an aesthetically pleasing site.
5. Maintaining "portability": maintaining a consistent look and feel of a site across different platforms, different browsers, and different screen resolutions.
6. Developing effective search systems, e.g. Boolean, natural language.
7. Developing a logical Web site structure that is easily understood by the user.
8. Developing effective hyperlinks that anticipate user information needs.
9. Effective labeling (links, terms in indexes, choices in dropdown lists, product names) for improved information access.
10. Effective linking to related information on other Web sites.
11. Developing personalization or customization processes that permit users to set their own preferences for a site, or which provide filters for site contents.
12. Using metadata effectively to improve access to the site.
13. Ensuring that the Web site is "scaleable"—that it can grow and retain its effectiveness and usability.

With the increasing reliance on Web sites for education, business, and government, their effective design is critical. For this reason, it is expected that the field will continue to grow and represent an important new aspect of organizational life.

Knowledge Management (KM)

Organizations contain a wealth of knowledge. Locating knowledge in a usable form and in a timely manner when decisions need to be made is another matter. The organizational environment is a complex one and the willingness to share knowledge may vary from individual to individual, department to department. There may be political, economic, or even social barriers to sharing knowledge. There may be structural or procedural barriers as well. In some cases, critical knowledge to resolve a particular problem may be stored in only one of many databases, and that database may be unknown to the decision maker, or the search tools may be inadequate to extract the needed knowledge from it. In some cases, needed knowledge may be possessed by only one or a few individuals who may or may not be involved in the immediate decision-making process. Even when involved, these individuals for personal or professional reasons may not be willing to share their knowledge. The consequences in each case is that much important knowledge in organizations remains lost, or is discovered only after decisions are made. When this potential knowledge, sometimes referred to as "tacit knowledge," remains unused, it degrades the decision process, reduces decision quality, and impairs organizational effectiveness.

Similarly, organizations rely on inventiveness and innovation to survive and prosper. This means that they rely on their employees' knowledge, skills, and ideas (sometimes referred to as "human capital," one of the main components of the "intellectual capital" of the organization) to create new services and products. Often, innovation and inventive thinking require collaboration and the sharing of information, and a work environment that encourages both activities on a formal and informal level. From the latter perspective, individuals engaged in similar work or dealing with similar problems form "communities of practice." These communities define authority and work goals within them based on the expertise of the participants rather than formal assignments. Organizations structured to facilitate collaborative activities, information sharing, and communities of practice are likely to progress more quickly and leverage the talents of their people effectively.

At the same time, there is a certain elusiveness to knowledge in organizations. Knowledge, McInerney (2002) observes, is dynamic because it is dependent on human experience. It changes based on personal interactions; it is active and has a social dimension. Knowledge evolves as it is influenced by the thoughts, feelings, and experience of others. Some knowledge can be "explicit," such as knowledge contained within a database or in a document; but, as noted above, much other knowledge is "tacit" and consists of the values, beliefs, and perspectives of individuals within an organization that create the context for the explicit knowledge. Organizations themselves may have values, history, "unwritten laws," and ways of doing things, which also serve as "tacit knowledge" and shape how explicit knowledge is created and used. Understanding and managing both the explicit and tacit knowledge in an organization is likely to achieve the best results. Similarly, much knowledge is communicated in informal as well as formal organizational environments. It may be equally important to provide an environment in which casual conversations are encouraged as well as communications in meetings.

To help diminish the impact of poor use of knowledge within organizations, the field of "knowledge management" (KM) has emerged. This field focuses specifically on understanding and structuring the organization so that the knowledge contained within it can be best exploited. Although much attention in organizations is often focused on *information* with its attendant emphasis on information technologies, KM places considerable emphasis on people. As Blair (2002) notes, "knowledge management is largely the management and support of expertise . . . it is primarily the management of individuals with specific abilities, rather than the management of repositories of data and information" (p. 1022). For Blair, people are the "repositories" of the knowledge. Davenport, De Long, and Beers (1997) identify four objectives to KM: creating knowledge repositories, improving knowledge access, enhancing the knowledge environment, and managing knowledge as an asset. Overall, KM is concerned with planning, capturing, organizing, interconnecting, and providing access to organizational knowledge through both intellectual and information technologies. It is an interdisciplinary field drawing from a variety of disciplines including psychology, sociology, business, economics, information science, and computer science. It focuses on the human aspects of the organization as much as the structural and technological aspects.

Given the broad role that knowledge plays within the organization, the concerns of KM are many and various. A possible way of viewing these concerns is to consider them as they relate to two contexts: concerns with managing the individuals who have knowledge, and concerns with managing the knowledge itself. Such an approach, albeit simplistic, provides a framework for viewing some of the major activities of KM.

Managing the People Who Have Knowledge

1. Create an environment to stimulate knowledge growth, and identify barriers to knowledge creation.
2. Create an organizational culture that facilitates the sharing of knowledge and collaborative processes, both formal and informal.
3. Develop and manage people as knowledge assets.
4. Ensure that useful (tacit) knowledge is accessible when decisions are being made.
5. Create a corporate culture and values that encourage knowledge building and sharing.
6. Identify, develop, and use effectively the expertise of staff (human capital).
7. Develop competent individuals who manage and supervise the knowledge processes and expertise of the organization.

8. Develop and maintain processes that enable the knowledge of individuals to be used effectively.

MANAGING THE KNOWLEDGE ITSELF

1. Organize knowledge so that it can be accessed and used through effective search and document management.
2. Represent knowledge in ways that improve its use (documents, databases).
3. Facilitate use of knowledge from outside sources.
4. Facilitate processes that develop and exploit the intellectual capital and assets of the organization, including individual expertise, corporate memory, and organizational research.
5. Develop effective document management techniques throughout the life cycle of a document, i.e., from authorship to archiving and disposal.
6. Identify the nature of the knowledge stored and where it is stored in the organization so that it can be exploited.
7. Evaluate, maintain, and improve the information technology (IT) infrastructure to encourage knowledge building and sharing.
8. Develop effective techniques for competitive intelligence.
9. Facilitate effective publishing and dissemination of information, e.g. through e-mail or word-processing.

Given the tremendous range of functions involved in managing knowledge in organizations it is obvious that how knowledge is dealt with must be a conscious part of the culture and the organizational life of the institution. McInerney (2002) suggests that organizations might spend less time trying to extract knowledge from workers to create specific "knowledge artifacts," and spend more time developing a "knowledge culture" in which opportunities for knowledge creation are optimized and there is encouragement for learning and sharing knowledge.

Usability Engineering

From the perspective of libraries and information centers, it is vital that Web sites meet the information needs of their users. Libraries rely heavily on such sites to serve their patrons, and the library's own Web site may serve as a critical portal for library users. Energy must be devoted to ensure that these sites perform the functions for which they were designed.

Evaluation of a Web site's effectiveness can be conducted in many ways, but one critical perspective comes from the Web site user, and the field devoted to this perspective is called "usability engineering," which has foundations in the established field of human-computer interface. The usability engineering field addresses the question: "To what extent is a particular Web site usable by the individuals who were intended to use it?" The International Standards Organization (ISO, 1998) defines usability as "the extent to which a product can be used by specified users to achieve specified goals with effectiveness, efficiency and satisfaction in a specified context of use" (p. 2). Usability engineering generally requires a research process designed to assess satisfaction with, and efficiency and effectiveness of a Web site from the user's perspective.

Generally, usability engineering involves usability testing: giving individuals a set of tasks while trained observers collect information on how the site is used. A variety of research methods are employed, including the common techniques of questionnaires, surveys, interviews, focus groups, and intrusive and unobstrusive observation. In addition, more novel techniques are sometimes employed. One example is the "think aloud" protocol. In this case, as a user is observed addressing a particular task, the user also is asked to "talk aloud" expressing his or her feelings, thoughts, opinions, and strategies. The responses of the user are usually audiotaped and sometimes videotaped for subsequent analysis. Another technique employs a "question-asking" protocol. In this case, the researcher asks questions of the user to get feedback while he or she is using a Web site (Norlin and Winters 2002). Software packages, including site usage logs, that collect information on the search strategies employed and sites consulted are also helpful in evaluating Web site use. Of course usability testing is not perfect; findings are often based on small samples and the users may or may not be representative of the many types of users who might be exposed to the Web site.

Various criteria are employed in evaluating use of a site. These include the following:

Effectiveness. Does the site satisfy the needs of the user? Is it accurate and complete for the intended use? Can users readily find and navigate to the needed information?

Efficiency. To what extent are the resources readily used to meet the need?

Satisfaction. What are the feelings of the user toward the site? Is there freedom from discomfort in using the site? Does the user have a positive attitude toward its use?

Learnability. How easy is it to learn how to use the site?

As the number of Web sites proliferates and information organizations increase their reliance on them, usability testing will increasingly play an important role in ensuring that users are prominent participants in their design, maintenance, and improvement.

Competitive Intelligence

Competitive intelligence has experienced a marked growth in interest since the early 1990s. As the economic marketplace becomes increasingly competitive and reliant on computers and networks, the need and possibilities for competitive intelligence (CI) has grown. Certainly, the need for current, complete, and accurate information in order to compete is widely accepted as necessary for success. It is a relatively old principle in organizational management that in order to survive, the organization must know the threats and opportunities in the environment. For some years environmental scanning and information resources management have been accepted practices to try to cope with this dynamic and uncertain world.

CI is a subunit of the total practices of information management within an organization. Often seen as a subset of "business intelligence" or "social intelligence," CI serves as the "scout" to determine where the threats and opportunities are, their nature and magnitude. The Society of Competitive Intelligence Professionals defines CI as "a systematic and ethical program for gathering, analyzing, and managing external information that can affect your company's plans, decisions, and operations. . . . It is the legal collection and analysis of information regarding the capabilities, vulnerabilities, and intentions of business competitors . . . " (Society of Competitive Intelligence Professionals [SCIP] 2003). Miller identifies the goal of CI as "actionable intelligence that will provide a competitive edge." CI is proactive rather than reactive (Miller 2003). It is estimated that the market value of business intelligence is $2 billion a year and companies large and small have undertaken formal CI programs (SCIP 2003). The value of CI has been well documented. CI companies tend to outperform their competitors when comparing average sales, market share, and profitability (Cappel 1995). Another function of CI is counterintelligence, which involves developing systems that prevent access to organizational information that could threaten the organization's competitiveness.

Competitive intelligence is not the same as industrial espionage, which involves unlawful and unethical tactics and actions; CI is governed by ethical standards and generally relies on sources that are open to inspection. The "SCIP Code of Ethics for CI Professionals" promulgated by the Society of Competitive Intelligence Professionals explicitly identifies such responsibilities as complying with all laws and disclosing truthfully one's identity prior to seeking information [see Appendix E]. Intelligence gathering may occur in various sectors, including information on specific competitors, new technologies or scientific discoveries, new products or services, new or proposed legislation or regulations, potential mergers or acquisitions, or information on or from customers, suppliers, industry experts, or partners. Similarly information can be gathered from the Web or mass media, trade shows, or conferences, or by tracking patents.

Bergeron and Hiller (2002) break down the CI process into four phases: planning/identifying CI needs, data collection, organization and analysis, and dissemination. The analysis stage is a particularly important aspect of CI, and a variety of techniques have been employed to interpret the information that is collected. These techniques include SWOT analysis (Strength/Weaknesses/Opportunities/Threats), benchmarking, environmental analysis, scenario planning, patent analysis, and bibliometrics (Bergeron and Hiller 2002).

SUMMARY

The field of information science has much to offer when one is considering how to improve information services. The growth of new information technologies has provided a considerable impetus to research in information science, and the efforts of information scientists have contributed much to our understanding of how information is generated, organized, disseminated, and used. Librarians can make good use of much of this research and also contribute to it.

A central value underlying this field is the desire to study how to make information accessible and usable. Information science is designed in large part to satisfy individuals' information needs. As such it has much in common with the purposes of libraries and librarianship. An understanding of how to define information needs and wants, how individuals behave when they search for information, and how information systems can best be designed and used to satisfy information needs is critical if librarians are to continue to perform their jobs effectively in the future. To a large extent, librarians must rely on information scientists as a source for this understanding. As the field of information science grows, so should the librarian's interest in it. A strong partnership can only benefit those who use library services.

REFERENCES

Allen, Bryce L. "Cognitive Research in Information Science: Implications for Design." *Annual Review of Information Science and Technology (ARIST)* 26 (1991): 3–37.

Allen, Bryce L. *Information Tasks: Toward a User-Centered Approach to Information Systems.* New York: Academic, 1996.

Association of College and Research Libraries. "Standards for College Libraries, 1986." *College and Research Libraries* 47 (March 1986): 189–200.

Bates, Marcia J. "The Design of Browsing and Berrypicking Techniques for the Online Search Interface." *Online Review* 13 (October 1989): 407–424.

Bates, Marcia J., Deborah N. Wilde, and Susan Siegfried. "An Analysis of Search Terminology Used by Humanities Scholars: The Getty Online Searching Project Report Number 1." *Library Quarterly* 63 (January 1993): 1–39.

Belkin, Nicholas J., Helen M. Brooks, and Robert N. Oddy. "ASK for Information Retrieval." *Journal of Documentation* 38 (1982): 61–71.

Bergeron, Pierrette, and Christine A. Hiller. "Competitive Intelligence." In *Annual Review of Information Science and Technology.* Vol. 36. Edited by Blaise Cronin, Medford N.J.: Information Today, 2002, 353–390.

Bilal, Dania. "Children's Use of the Yahooligans! Web Search Engine." *Journal of the American Society for Information Science and Technology* 53 (2002): 1170–1183.

Blair, David C. "Knowledge Management: Hype, Hope, or Help?" *Journal of the American Society of Information Science and Technology* 53 (2002): 1019–1028

Bradford, Samuel C. "Sources of Information on Specific Subjects." *Engineering* (1934): 85–86.

Brittain, J. M. "The Distinctive Characteristics of Information Science." In *Theory and Application of Information Research: Proceedings of the Second International Research Forum on Information Science.* Edited by Ole Harbo and Leif Kajberg. London: Mansell, 1980.

Broadbent, Elaine. "A Study of Humanities Faculty Library Information Seeking Behavior." *Cataloguing and Classification Quarterly* 6 (spring 1986): 23–37.

Bush, Vannevar. "As We May Think." *Atlantic Monthly* 176 (July 1945): 101–108.

Cappel, James J., and Jeffrey P. Boone. "A Look at the Link Between Competitive Intelligence and Performance." *Competitive Intelligence Review* 6 (summer 1995): 15–23.

Case, Donald O. *Looking for Information: A Survey of Research on Information Seeking, Needs, and Behavior.* San Diego: Academic, 2002.

Chatman, Elfreda A. "The Impoverished Life-World of Outsiders." *Journal of the American Society for Information Science* 47 (1996): 193–206.

Chen, Ching-Chih, and Peter Hernon. *Information Seeking: Assessing and Anticipating User Needs*. New York: Neal-Schuman, 1982.

Davenport, Thomas, David De Long, and Michael Beers. *Building Successful Knowledge Management Projects.*" Center for Business Innovation Working Paper, Ernst & Young, 1997.

Debons, Anthony. *The Information Professional: Survey of an Emerging Field*. New York: Dekker, 1981.

Dervin, Brenda. "An Overview of Sense-Making: Concepts, Methods, and Results to Date." Paper presented at the International Communication Association Annual Meeting, May 1983, Dallas, Texas.

Durrance, Joan C. "Information Needs: Old Song, New Tune." In *Rethinking the Library*. Washington, D.C.: GPO, 1989, 159–178.

Farnum, Chris. "Information Architecture: Five Things Information Managers Need to Know." *The Information Management Journal* (September/October 2002): 33–40.

Froehlich, Thomas. PowerPoint Presentation on Information Architecture, Kent State University, 2003.

Froehlich, Thomas J. "Relevance Reconsidered—Towards an Agenda for the 21st Century." *Journal of the American Society of Information Science* 45 (April 1994): 124–134.

Harter, Stephen. *Online Information Retrieval*. Orlando, Fla.: Academic Press, 1986.

Hsieh-Yee, Ingrid. "Research on Web Search Behavior." *Library and Information Science Research* 53 (2001): 167–185

ISO 9241–11: *Ergonomic Requirements for Office Work with Visual Display Terminals (VDTs) —Part 11: Guidance on Usability*. London: International Standards Organization, 1998.

Koenig, Michael E. D. "Information Services and Downstream Productivity." *Annual Review of Information Science and Technology* 25 (1990): 74–76.

Krikelas, James. "Information-Seeking Behavior: Patterns and Concepts." *Drexel Library Quarterly* 19 (spring 1983): 5–20.

Kuhlthau, Carol C. "Inside the Search Process: Information Seeking from the User's Perspective." *Journal of the American Society of Information Science* (1991): 361–371.

Lazonder, Ard W., Harm J.A. Biemans, and Iwans G.J.H. Wopereis. "Differences Between Novice and Experienced Users in Searching Information on the World Wide Web." *Journal of the American Society for Information Science* 51 (2000): 576–581.

Lee, Chingkwei Adrienne, and John N. Olsgaard. "Linguistics and Information Science." In *Principles and Applications of Information Science for Library Professionals*. Edited by John N. Olsgaard. Chicago: ALA, 1989, 27–36.

Levitan, Karen B. "Information Resources Management." *Annual Review of Information Science and Technology (ARIST)* 17 (1982): 227–266.

Lotka, Alfred J. "The Frequency Distribution of Scientific Productivity." *Journal of the Washington Academy of Sciences* 16 (1926): 317–323.

Machlup, Fritz, and Una Mansfield, eds. *The Study of Information: Interdisciplinary Messages*. New York: Wiley, 1983.

Mann, Thomas. "The Principle of Least Effort." In *Library Research Models: A*

Guide to Classification, Cataloging, and Computers. New York: Oxford University, 1993, 91–101.

McInerney, Claire. "Knowledge Management and the Dynamic Nature of Knowledge." *Journal of the American Society for Information Science and Technology* 53 (2002): 1009–1018.

Meadows, A.J. *Communication in Science*. London: Butterworths, 1974.

Miller, Stephen H. "Competitive Intelligence—An Overview." [Online] Available at *www.scip.org/ Library/overview.pdf*. (Accessed July 21, 2003.)

Norlin, Elaina, and C.M. Winters. *Usability Testing for Library Web Sites: A Hands-On Guide*. Chicago: ALA, 2002

Oxford English Dictionary, 2d ed. Oxford: Clarendon Press, 1989.

Pao, Miranda Lee. *Concepts of Information Retrieval*. Englewood, Colo.: Libraries Unlimited, 1989, 54–55.

Public Library Association. *Output Measures for Public Libraries*. 2nd ed. Chicago: ALA, 1987.

Rayward, Boyd. "Library and Information Sciences." In *The Study of Information: Interdisciplinary Messages*. Edited by Fritz Machlup and Una Mansfield. New York: Wiley, 1983, 343–363.

Rosenfeld, Louis. "Information Architecture: Looking Ahead." *Journal of the American Society for Information Science and Technology* 53 (2002): 874–876.

Rosenfeld, Louis, and Peter Morville. *Information Architecture for the World Wide Web*. Sebastopol, Calif.: O'Reilly, 1998, 2002.

Rouse, William B. "Human Information Seeking and Design of Information Systems." *Information Processing and Management* 20 (1984).

Saracevic, T. "Relevance: A Review of and a Framework for the Thinking on the Notion in Information Science." *Journal of the American Society for Information Science* 26 (1975): 321–343.

Shaw, Debora. "The Human-Computer Interface for Information Retrieval." *Annual Review of Information Science and Technology (ARIST)* 26 (1991): 155–195.

Shera, Jesse H., and Donald B. Cleveland. "History and Foundations of Information Science." In *Annual Review of Information Science and Technology*. Vol. 12. Edited by Martha E. Williams. Knowledge Industry, 1977, 249.

Slone, Debra J. "The Influence of Mental Models and Goals on Search Patterns During Web Interaction." *Journal of the American Society for Information Science and Technology* 53 (2002): 1152–1169

Smith, Linda C. "Artificial Intelligence and Information Retrieval." *Annual Review of Information Science and Technology (ARIST)* 22 (1987): 41–77.

———. "Citation Analysis." *Library Trends* 30 (summer 1981): 83–106.

Society for Competitive Intelligence Professionals. [Online] Available at *www.scip.org/*. (Accessed July 21, 2003.)

Taylor, Robert S. "Professional Aspects of Information Science and Technology." In *Annual Review of Information Science and Technology*. Vol. 1. Edited by Carlos A. Cuadra. New York: Wiley, 1966, 15–40.

———. "Question–Negotiation and Information Seeking in Libraries." *College and Research Libraries* 29 (May 1968): 178–194.

———. *Value-Added Processes in Information Systems*. Norwood, N.J.: Ablex, 1986.

Van Styvendaele, J. H. "University Scientists as Seekers of Information: Sources of References to Periodical Literature," *Journal of Librarianship* 9 (October 1977): 270–277.

Vedder, Richard G. "An Overview of Expert Systems." In *Expert Systems in Libraries*. Edited by Rao Aluri and Donald E. Riggs. Norwood, N.J.: Ablex, 1990.

Wallace, Danny P. "Bibliometrics and Citation Analysis." In *Principles and Applications of Information Science for Library Professionals*. Edited by John N. Olsgaard. Chicago: ALA, 1989, 10–26.

Walter, Virginia A. *Output Measures and More: Planning and Evaluating Public Library Services for Young Adults*. Chicago: ALA, 1995.

———. *Output Measures for Public Library Services to Children: A Manual of Standardized Procedures*. Chicago: ALA, 1992.

Wellisch, Hans. "From Information Science to Informatics: A Terminological Investigation." *Journal of Librarianship* 4 (July 1972): 157–187.

Wilson, Patrick., "The Face Value Rule in Reference Work." *RQ* 25 (summer 1986): 468–475.

———. *Second-Hand Knowledge*. Westport, Conn.: Greenwood, 1983, 10.

3

Redefining the Library: The Impacts and Implications of Technological Change

Obtaining current and accurate information is central to our economic, political, and social well-being, as well as to our ability to compete in the global marketplace. Because libraries have been a major source of information for centuries, they have held a special place in the life of the community. The growth of electronic information technologies has challenged this role and resulted in considerable instability and uncertainty among librarians. The introduction of new technologies has caused librarians to redefine and restructure library services, and in the process, the library itself. New information technologies have revolutionized information access, reducing the distinction between the physical library collection and the information stored beyond its walls. What has emerged is a hybrid of physical and digital library. Will the physical library ultimately disappear as the digital library increases in use? Only time will tell.

There is no doubt, however, that the increasingly critical need for information and its increasingly electronic nature has produced competitors and alternatives to traditional library practice. These competitors also recognize that information is a valued commodity and that both profit and power can be acquired if its dissemination can be controlled. Electronic information technologies stimulate and promote intense competition in the information marketplace, and as such, libraries must understand their capacities and limitations.

It is very tempting to accept uncritically the belief that new information technologies inevitably lead to progress. Librarians are no more immune than others to this belief. After all, the excitement generated by such technologies is often considerable, and one is often made to feel "behind the times" when doubts are raised. Perhaps librarians have additional reasons to be accepting. They may embrace technology because they think it will raise their status and image and put them on the cutting edge of change. As a consequence, librarians sometimes fail to demand evidence that the technologies adopted actually have an overall beneficial effect on library service (Bushman 1990). The alternative to this uncritical acceptance is not to become a Luddite, however, lamenting all new technologies and pining for the old days of print materials and card catalogs. Rather, we must all remind ourselves that technological developments need to be evaluated objectively and critically, in the same manner that other new techniques or devices are evaluated. Technological developments produce both positive and negative changes. The fact that the consequences of new technologies can be both good and bad is not to say that their use should be discouraged; only that they should be applied appropriately and their negative as well as positive effects anticipated and, when necessary, ameliorated.

INFORMATION TECHNOLOGIES IN THE TWENTIETH CENTURY

The term *technology* has very broad application and can be defined in many ways. For the purposes of this discussion, *Webster's* (1970) provides a sound working definition: "a technical method of achieving a practical purpose." As such, the term can be applied to nonelectronic tools as well as electronic ones. Given this definition, it is clear that technologies have been around in libraries for many years. A prime example is the card catalog of the nineteenth century. This technology allowed us to consult a significant body of knowledge by systematically scanning physical representations of books and other materials, that is, the catalog cards, albeit with varying success. Some would maintain that even today the manual card catalog has some distinct advantages over electronic ones (Baker 1994). In addition, the nineteenth century also saw the introduction of the electric light in library stacks, an addition that undoubtedly helped many locate materials without burning down the library. It also saw the development of important intellectual technologies such as the Dewey Decimal Classification System, which is discussed in greater detail in Chapter 6.

The following historical overview is a thumbnail sketch from 1900 forward and is intended to provide a basic outline of these developments and to provide a framework for discussing the issues that are now facing our field.

Developments in Microphotography: 1900–1960

The first half of the twentieth century was a very fruitful period for technological development. Major improvements in communications and transportation were especially notable. Changes included the growth and expansion of telephone services, the development of photo technologies, improvements to airplanes and automobiles, development of the cathode ray tube, diode, triode, and photoelectric cell. It also saw the development of "punch cards" that could be used for mechanical sorting—the forerunner of computer technologies (Buckland 1996).

In terms of their effects on libraries, perhaps the most notable developments in the first half of the century related to the new photographic technologies, especially microphotography. This technology permitted the reproduction of print documents (reprography) onto film (microforms). The physical format was usually a roll of film, the microfilm, or a rectangular card, the microcard. As an alternative to paper, microphotography had many advantages: it could provide much more information in a more compact medium and it was lighter and easier to store. In addition, it proved to be an exceptional medium for the preservation of materials that were likely to deteriorate over time, such as newspapers, magazines, and documents. By the 1920s, there were tremendous successes in reducing print to microform as well as in developing equipment to read the microforms. The potential of microphotography for the library led at least one enthusiast to suggest that the actual book be photographed and attached to the back of the catalog card. Hence, once the user found the right catalog card, the item was literally on the back of the card (Rider 1944)!

Reprography saw additional advances in the 1960s with the development of duplicating machines, most notably the photocopier. This was a tremendous addition to the arsenal of reprographic devices, yet unless one reflects on it, the effect that photocopying equipment has on society is easily lost. The ability to make multiple copies of individual pages had a profound effect on the ability to provide documents over considerable distances and to allow many more individuals to possess the intellectual content of a document simultaneously. (And resulted probably in a great increase in paper consumption as well!) Although not as dramatic as the invention of the printing press, photocopying certainly revolutionized communications for libraries because it permitted them much greater flexibility in the distribution of published materials. In essence, as De Gennaro (1989) observed, "Libraries became publishers of single copies on demand" (p. 42). Interestingly, photocopying may also have reduced the amount of time spent in libraries by patrons who no longer needed to sit for long periods and copy by hand material out of texts.

First Application of Computers to Libraries: The 1960s

Our contemporary sense of technology deals with electronic devices, especially computers. Although the notion of computers has been around more than a hundred years, their application to libraries did not begin in earnest until the 1960s. It is during this time that one encounters the term library automation, although it was first known as "library mechanization." Bierman (1991) defines library automation as "the application of computer and communication technologies to traditional library processes and services" (p. 67).

The 1960s was largely a period of big mainframe computers, punch cards, and mechanical sorting machines. The rationale for the application of computers to library processes was simple: computerization would increase efficiency of library services, produce costs savings, and reduce the size of staff. The most significant library application of technology during this period was the creation of a standardized bibliographic format that could be read and manipulated by a computer. Machine Readable Cataloging, or MARC, created by the Library of Congress, became a standard for the creation of bibliographic records. MARC allowed bibliographic data to be entered, stored, and disseminated electronically on computer tapes. (See Chapter 6 for further discussion of the MARC format.) Once records were centralized in this fashion, the first major use of the tapes was to generate catalog cards. The uses of these computer-generated tapes, however, quickly expanded as its potentialities were grasped by support agencies linked to libraries known as bibliographic utilities.

The development of the MARC format led to the creation of the Ohio College Library Center (OCLC), incorporated as a not-for-profit corporation in 1967. OCLC offered access to the MARC database, which was supplemented by the cataloging efforts of the OCLC member libraries. OCLC loaded the MARC tapes and made these records available to member libraries. The libraries could locate and examine the bibliographic record, make changes for their local institutions as needed, and then electronically order catalog cards to their specifications from OCLC. In a short time the cards would arrive at the library, ready for filing. In turn, their bibliographic records would be entered into the OCLC database. In effect, this created an online shared cataloging network. The advantages of OCLC quickly became clear to many libraries, and in 1972, OCLC opened its membership to nonacademic libraries as well (Grosch, 1995). This led to tremendous growth in membership and increased cooperation among different types of libraries and among regional library networks. Consequently, in 1981 OCLC changed its name to the Online Computing Library Center.

Over the decades, OCLC services grew, offering interlibrary loan and document delivery, acquisition systems, serials control, electronic publishing, and access to electronic databases. But its early contribution was primarily in the area of shared cataloging. Other bibliographic utilities appeared. For example, major research libraries formed a group called the Research Libraries Group (RLG). This group created the Research Libraries Information Network (RLIN), offering access to a tremendous bibliographic database and thousands of research records. Today, it is difficult to imagine the major changes that were created by these utilities. The impact on cataloging departments, for example, was substantial, resulting in a reduction in the number of catalogers.

The first applications of online information retrieval developed in the early 1960s. These were prototype systems, usually consisting of a small database and one terminal. One of the major developers of early online systems during this time was the System Development Corporation (SDC) in California, which produced some of the earliest computers for simple full-text searching and document retrieval (Hahn 1996). There was also another major commercial competitor, the Lockheed Missiles and Space Company, which made major contributions to computerized information retrieval. Working primarily with government agencies such as NASA, Lockheed developed the DIALOG system around 1964. By the early 1970s Lockheed realized the commercial potential of an online search service and in 1972 created the Lockheed Retrieval Service. This commercial service was also known as "DIALOG."

While libraries were introducing these changes, other developments were occurring, such as the computerizing of specialized bodies of knowledge for scientific and medical purposes. The National Library of Medicine (NLM), one of the great special libraries in the world, was confronted with a common problem in the sciences—the rapid expansion of scientific and technical knowledge. For years NLM had been indexing the medical literature manually, but this was becoming extremely cumbersome and costly. The decision to input bibliographic citations on computer tapes led to a computerized version of its medical index, *Index Medicus*. At first, the computer tapes were used to produce a paper copy of the index, but it was not long before it became obvious that the tapes themselves could be searched, creating a searchable database that is one of the great achievements of the decade.

Other events occurring in the 1960s would have even greater impact for the future. In 1969 the Defense Advanced Research Projects Research Agency (DARPA) within the Department of Defense developed a computer network called ARPANET at the University of California at Los Angeles. The network was developed to improve government-sponsored research by electronically linking organizations at different sites and allowing them to share research and data (Tenner 1994). One of the fundamental innovations of this system was the first practical use of a new technology to break information messages into discrete packets, which could be sent independently of one another across "packet-switching" networks. These packets could be reassembled at the receiving computer. Such a method increased reliability and speed. This process substantially improved transmission of research data and analysis. Although ARPANET membership was restricted to institutions with defense-related contracts, this network was the genesis of what would become the Internet, and it advanced development of key features such as file transfer, remote access of data, and electronic mail (Bishop 1990).

These advances had little effect on libraries in the 1960s. Library automation at that time focused primarily on the creation of computerized bibliographic records for catalog card production. Some attention was paid to automating basic maintenance functions including the creation of book catalogs and generating purchase orders, but there remained considerable skepticism on the part of librarians that automation could be applied practically to most library functions and services

(Grosch 1995). The knowledge base, however, was expanding and the application of computers was inevitable.

Use of Online Information Technologies for Reference: The 1970s

The increasing sophistication of computer technologies, including the development of the minicomputer, made online interactive capabilities a reality (Grosch 1995). The application of online computer access for information retrieval, replacing card files and print indexes, represents one of the most significant breaks from the past. Major information-dependent institutions, such as the military and business and industry, quickly recognized the potential for these capabilities. Consequently, commercial vendors developed a variety of databases and made them available through telephone lines. Thus, a library in Chicago could access databases that were created and made available by a vendor like DIALOG from Palo Alto, California. Although these vendors did not necessarily design their services for libraries, it was clear that libraries would be substantial users of the systems.

Libraries began to create their own internal online services for library patrons. Most early online services were developed in academic libraries, primarily because the databases generally available from the major vendors at that time were scientific and technical in nature. Because of the cost and sophistication of these early systems, academic libraries created specifically-designed services, often with their own separate facilities or space and a special, trained staff to conduct online searches. Most online searches were mediated by a trained librarian or an information specialist because the cost of a search depended in large part on how long it took to perform the search. Even then, libraries often had to pass on at least part of the costs to the individual patron—a practice that runs counter to the normal practice of libraries in providing free services, and which caused consternation.

The development of online access also necessitated the creation of search strategies that could exploit the unique flexibility of computerized access to information. Perhaps the most prominent development in this area was Boolean searching, based on the logical theory of George Boole in the nineteenth century. Its application in the online environment permits one to search a database using logical connectors such as *and, or,* or *not*. Such logical techniques permitted very sophisticated searching by narrowing the search and obtaining more precise access to large bodies of knowledge in a much shorter period of time. Another strategy involved keyword searching. The computer searched for a particular word or phrase anywhere in the bibliographic record, including an abstract. This strategy was very different from searches that required certain subject terms or searches that were limited to titles or authors.

In addition to the use of computers for reference purposes, the 1970s also saw the beginning of early attempts to automate library circulation, serials control, cataloging, and acquisition systems. These systems were a lot more complex than anticipated, and they did not reach maturity until a decade later.

The Growth of the CD-ROM and Integrated Library Systems: The 1980s

The CD-ROM

The 1980s saw a remarkable revolution in information access with the development of the Compact Disk—Read Only Memory (CD-ROM). One small, 4 1/2" disk could contain all, or a great percentage, of the contents of standard reference tools, such as the *Reader's Guide to Periodical Literature*. The disks, along with updates, were sent to the library by an information vendor. They were operated on computer equipment that ran on software also provided by the vendor. CD-ROMs had several distinct advantages over online searching. First, the CD-ROM was locally held; for all practical purposes the computer databases were in the library. There was no need for a telephone line; all the user had to do was come to the library. Second, the disks could hold a tremendous amount of information, which could be consulted at one time. Third, CD-ROMs had the flexibility of Boolean searching. The material could be searched by author, title, and subject, and by one term or multiple terms, similar to online access. Fourth, CD-ROMs provided the computing power of online searching at a fixed cost. This was very helpful in the financial management of libraries. Costs for online searching were indeterminate, depending on the frequency of use and length of time per search, and so budgeting for these services was difficult. CD-ROMs, on the other hand, had known annual subscription costs.

Integrated Library Systems

In addition to radical changes in information access, the 1980s saw substantial developments in coordinating and automating internal processes such as online catalogs, circulation systems, and acquisitions systems.

The result of performing so many basic library functions by computer was the growth of what is called "integrated library systems" (ILS). Such a system consists of the computerized integration of six key library functions: acquisitions, serials, cataloging, online catalog, circulation, and collection management. Among the companies that developed such systems were Data Research Associates (DRA), Geac Computers, VTLS, and Innovative Interface. ILS allowed the library to reduce duplication of effort and coordinate and share information more efficiently through the departments that process and use library materials. Integrated library systems would not have been possible without developments in the following areas:

THE DEVELOPMENT OF ONLINE PUBLIC ACCESS CATALOGS (OPACS)

Online Public Access Catalogs (OPACs) can be seen as a very early example of the first "end-user" search systems. For years, librarians had access to bibliographic information which was searchable by many approaches; with the OPAC, the user could accomplish the same tasks with little or no mediation on the part of the librarian. OPACs permitted access to the bibliographic records of the library, similar to the manual card catalog, but with much more flexible search capabilities. The system could be searched by author, title, subject, keywords, and sometimes combinations of these terms. In addition, some systems could be searched by specialized numbers, such as call numbers or ISBNs. There was no longer any need to buy catalog cards or hire individuals to file them. The introduction of OPACs meant the eventual removal of the card catalog, the opportunity for remote access, and a change in the physical environment of the library. It also meant major investments in hardware, software, and computer maintenance.

THE MATURATION OF ONLINE CIRCULATION SYSTEMS

Once the materials of the library could be accessed electronically, it seemed a logical step to create a system that would control the circulation of these materials. Although the 1970s saw early developments in this area, it was in the 1980s that commercial vendors developed automated circulation systems in earnest. These circulation systems, referred to as "turn-key" systems, were introduced with little modification from one library to another. These systems were relatively inexpensive, and although supposedly one could simply "turn the key and start the system," it was seldom that smooth. In addition, there were costs associated with the time it took staff to prepare the materials for the system, such as barcoding books and converting the library's records into machine-readable format. Staff needed additional time to weed the collection, as well, since there was little reason to spend money to input old, unused materials.

For the most part, automated circulation systems were designed so that staff could check out the materials for the patron. During the 1980s, however, some academic libraries implemented systems that enabled patrons to check out their own books. These systems were known as "self-initiated services." They could also track overdue items, send out recall notices, and produce reports on the circulation of library materials. Such systems helped in analyzing how the library collection was being used and, therefore, in planning.

Automated Acquisitions and Serials Systems

The 1980s also saw the burgeoning of systems designed to help libraries acquire materials. Some of the larger book vendors, such as Blackwell North America and Baker and Taylor, were quite active in developing these systems. In addition, early automation vendors such as Innovative Interface developed acquisitions systems for serials. The acquisition systems were directly connected to the vendors. The library would order its materials through terminals in the library, and the materials would be sent to the library. The acquisition system could monitor budgets, setting limits so that a particular department could not exceed its budget, and produce reports for analysis and evaluation. It might also include a serials check-in system so that the cumbersome tasks of checking in magazines and other periodicals could be performed without labor-intensive activity. In addition, an automated acquisition system permitted the library to create an electronic profile of its needs, and the vendor could automatically send materials that matched the profile without the library ordering each item. This saved time for the library and for the vendor, who did not have to process so many individual orders.

The Linked System Project/Linked Systems Protocol

As online catalogs proliferated, it became obvious that there would be a great advantage if the computers of various libraries and other information organizations could be made to "talk" to each other. Because various developers had created systems that were incompatible with each other, this had proved an elusive goal. The incompatibility problem led to the creation of the Linked System Project. The participants in this project included the American Library Association, OCLC, the Research Libraries Information Network, the Western Library Network, and the Library of Congress with funding from the Council on Library Resources. Their efforts produced the linked systems protocol (LSP), otherwise known as the Z39.50 standard (National Information Standards Organization 1994).

The protocol is a national standard for bibliographic information retrieval that sets standards so that different automated systems can be linked together electronically. With the development of this protocol, authorized users could consult not only their own online catalogs, but the online catalogs of countless other libraries and information organizations (Buckland and Lynch 1987, 1988). Although there was much concerted effort toward the development of this protocol in the 1980s, it wasn't until the 1990s that the protocol, in conjunction with major improvements in telecommunications technologies, made significant gains in linking online bibliographic systems.

The Growth of the Internet and the World Wide Web: The 1990s

The Internet is a term applied to an electronic network that permits access to thousands of other computer networks. Developed in the 1960s, and available in a very limited fashion in the 1970s and 1980s, its use was restricted primarily to researchers and academics. It was only in the 1990s that use of the Internet became commonplace with the development of the Web. The Internet is the product of a marriage between the technology perfected by the Department of Defense's ARPANET and the National Science Foundation (NSF). In 1984 NSF was establishing national supercomputing centers to provide high-speed computing for research purposes at major research sites, including several universities. These supercomputing centers could perform some of the most advanced research in the world. Given the importance of these centers, there was a need to facilitate communication among them. Consequently, NSF needed a "high-speed telecommunications backbone." At the same time, funding from the Department of Defense for ARPANET was beginning to decline. An agreement was reached wherein NSF would establish a civilian network (NSFNET) using the ARPANET technology. This electronic backbone now serves as one of the essential components of the Internet. The NSF also played an important role in increasing participants by encouraging faculty and students at universities to participate and by inviting universities to join the network for a flat, reasonable fee.

As computing power became more and more important for research, there was a need to develop faster and faster means of electronic communication. The issue became a popular political one in the 1990s as the importance of research and computer technologies for national productivity and international competitiveness became a matter of public discussion in the political arena. The George H. W. Bush administration (with strong support from then Democratic Senator Al Gore) introduced legislation—the National High Performance Computing Act of 1991—to develop an "information highway" that could drastically increase the amount of transmittable information. The goal of this legislation was not only to maintain and further develop an extremely efficient electronic highway for the transmission of information, but it also mandated the creation of the National Research and Education Network (NREN). NREN's purpose was to provide electronic links and access to federal agencies, industry and business, libraries, and educational institutions. This linking provided access not only to the institutions themselves, but to the information resources contained within them. In essence, what was being proposed was a virtual library, where resources could be consulted from countless sources at a tremendous speed—the speed that only electronic access could provide. The research and educational implications of such a network are manifest.

Although the early development of the Internet was funded by the government, the 1990s witnessed increased participation by those with a significant stake in its development and use. With the shift in political attitudes in the 1990s toward greater privatization and less reliance on government support, the Clinton administration emphasized more corporate participation in the Internet's development, with the government providing limited financial assistance and some regulatory relief (Gomery 1994). It is likely that participants such as the telecommunications industry (e.g. telephone, television, and cable industries) and private enterprise will continue to be the primary developers in the future.

FEATURES OF THE INTERNET

The Internet is, in essence, a network of many networks. These computer networks are able to "talk" to each other using standardized practices referred to as communication protocols (Tennant 1992, p. 1). The protocol used on the Internet is referred to as the Transmission Control Protocol/Internet Protocol (TCP/IP), which was originally developed by ARPANET. Every computer on the Internet (known as a host) is given a numeric address (for example, 121.123.46.22) based on the Internet Protocol (IP). Because most users are better at remembering names than numbers, a service called DNS (Domain Name Service) is used to translate between names of computers, (for example, www.slis.kent.edu) and the numeric version required in IP addresses.

In the 1990s the Internet offered a variety of basic services. Among the most notable were electronic mail, remote login, and file transfer.

Electronic mail (e-mail) permits an Internet user to communicate electronically with individuals or organizations. Messages can be sent locally or worldwide. The benefits for both personal and professional communication are immense, as ideas can be easily and quickly exchanged. The potential for collaboration among scientists and other researchers is clear. Electronic mail can also be employed to communicate with multiple individuals simultaneously. There are different models for multiple individuals accessing messages sent on e-mail. For example, information can be centralized by posting a message on a bulletin board, which individuals can access as needed. Another model is a listserv. Listservs usually deal with a particular topic or area of interest, and interested individuals can subscribe. (In some cases, membership to a listserv is restricted.) There is usually an administrator who handles the membership and other administrative functions. Listservs permit individuals to receive messages from and send messages to all subscribers. As messages are sent to the listserv they are also distributed to all the subscribers on the mailing list. Thus, a common message can be distributed to thousands of individuals, providing information and often promoting further discussion and responses from listserv members.

Remote login allows an individual to access thousands of computer systems located anywhere in the world. A user can search an electronic database or library catalog anywhere in the world by following the necessary standardized protocols referred to as *telnet*. IP addresses are established for each remote computer system and through telnet a user can connect with a remote computer. Today, remote login is also frequently accomplished by Web access. Tennant (1992) identifies the significant advantage of remote login:

> What makes this application truly remarkable is that ease and speed of access are not dependent upon proximity. An Internet user can connect to a system on the other side of the globe as easily as . . . he can connect to a system in the next building. In addition, since many Internet users are not at present charged for their network use by their institutions, or at least are not charged by the level of their use, cost is often not a significant inhibitor of usage. Therefore the barriers of distance, time and costs, which are often significant when using other forms of electronic communication, can be reduced in the Internet environment. (p. 2)

The last feature of the Internet is *file transfer*. A logical feature of such a system is the ability to transfer files from one computer to another. Consider the many types of information that could be usefully transmitted: reports, numerical data, sounds, and images. To this end, a protocol referred to as the File Transfer Protocol (FTP) has been developed to allow users to copy electronic files. Such transfers can occur from one computer to another or make large numbers of electronic files, sometimes referred to as "archives," available for anyone to access or download whenever convenient.

These services are still offered today, but are often incorporated into other more sophisticated services.

The World Wide Web

The vastness of the Internet is intimidating and its lack of organization, coupled with the quantity of information available, can be overwhelming. The Web is not the same as the Internet. Rather, it is an interface and navigation tool that provides a means of structuring Internet documents and relating them to other documents so that maximum use can be made of Internet resources (December and Randall 1995).

Originally, the Web provided a hypertext environment in which to transmit scientific information among researchers. Subsequently, the types of information and applications expanded markedly and became extremely useful for business, industry, students, and the general population. In a hypertext environment, documents have visible links to other documents. The links are highlighted or otherwise identified in the text of the document and are referred to as "hypertext links." This means that publications on the Internet can be linked by highlighting ideas within the texts of these publications. In this way, a user can move from one part of a publication to another, or from one publication to another, through multiple links within the document merely by moving the computer mouse to the highlighted term. In addition, a hypermedia environment is created. That is, traditionally Internet resources are transmitted as written text; in the hypermedia environment, sound, video, graphics, and illustrations can also be transmitted. Hence, individuals who prepare Internet documents can integrate sound, motion, and graphics into their materials, and users can download these documents, including the images and sound. To allow interaction with the Web its developers created a special protocol known as HTTP (HyperText Transfer Protocol). In addition, a special language HTML (HyperText Markup Language) was created to prepare documents for use on the Web. With HTML a document is divided into various elements, such as headings, titles, lists, addresses, and paragraphs. Each element has a special HTML tag. A particular document is then coded appropriately (for example, the beginning of the document is identified by a heading tag, the title of the document by a title tag). A document usually has at least tags for the head, body, and paragraphs (NCSA 1997).

Navigation on the Web is provided by graphical Web browsers. Examples of such browsers are Netscape and Internet Explorer. The purpose of such browsers is to display Web documents and allow the user to use the hyperlinks (December and Randall 1995).

Searching the Web is accomplished primarily by search engines. Search engines play a vital role in effective information retrieval on the Web. A basic definition of a search engine is: "a software program that searches a database and gathers and reports information that contains or is related to specified terms" (American Heritage Dictionary 2003). Fielden and Kuntz (2002) describe a search engine as "an automated software that matches a searcher's topic terms (keywords) with an indexed list of documents found on the Web . . . arranges that list according to some order of relevancy, and provides hyperlinks to those documents so that they may be visited" (p. 13). Search engines do not search the entire Web, but rather a specific collection of documents. This collection, or database, can be composed of millions of Web sites and documents. Google, for example, indexes more than 3 billion Web documents. Search engines compile this collection of sites by sending out what are called "spiders," "robots," "bots," or "crawlers" to locate as many seemingly relevant databases as possible. Crawlers may scan entire Web documents, or just scan the title and certain parts of the documents. Documents that are located are read by "indexer" software which creates an index based on the keywords in each document. When a specific query is made, the search engine then attempts to relate the search terms to the index and produce a list of relevant documents. Each search engine is different and therefore the results returned may vary substantially. There is some evidence that there is an approximately 60 percent overlap in search engines (University of South Carolina at Beaufort Library 2003). Some search engines rank the contents from most relevant to least relevant. Ranking may be influenced by the "tags" assigned to a particular Web document, or the frequency of keywords or phrases contained in various parts of the document.

Web computer users have a wide variety of search engines to choose from including Google, Yahoo, AOL, and MSN. In terms of total searches conducted, Google accounts for about a third of all searches, Yahoo! nearly one-fourth, and AOL and MSN, each about one-fifth. These data include internal searches of particular sites such as a Yahoo! search of "Yahoo Sports." When only overall Web searches are included, Google dominates heavily, accounting for 76 percent of all searches. This is because Google actually provides results to search engines such as Yahoo! and AOL. MSN accounts for an additional 17 percent (Media Metric 2003).

Librarians quickly recognized the advantages of the Web. With access more manageable, the great stores of information on the Internet become a more practical source for assisting patrons. In 2003–2004, for example, more than 96 percent of all public libraries now have access to electronic services and the Internet (NCES 2003). At the same time, the proliferation of Web sites and the popularity of the Web for both library practitioners and the public at large has highlighted some serious concerns. Of particular concern is the quality, or lack thereof, of the information contained on the Web. Traditionally, librarians select the materials for their collections using criteria that help establish the authority and accuracy of the material. This practice is especially true of reference materials. When patrons enter a library, they can generally have confidence that the information materials that they consult have been reviewed for authority and accuracy. This is not the case, however, with Web sites, which substantially increases the chance that patrons may access incomplete or inadequate information. Librarians have begun to address this issue by establishing their own Web pages for their libraries, which guide the patron to specific electronic sites that have been examined in a manner similar to other materials selected by the library. This is not necessarily to say that access to other sites is prohibited, although that may be the case. Rather, it demonstrates the traditional concern of information professionals to guide the patron to information that is timely and accurate.

Trying to establish some consistency on the Web has been a strong desire of its early developers. For this reason the World Wide Web Consortium (W3C) was created in 1994. Its creation was intended to develop common protocols that would maintain and promote its growth. The goals of W3C are three-fold: to make the Web available to all, to develop software that permits users to make the best use of the Web, and to provide guidance in the Web's development, taking into account the many economic, legal, and social forces that affect and are affected by this new technology (World Wide Web Consortium 2003). Many of its member organizations contribute the expertise of engineers and researchers usually operating in W3C working groups. Products include technical reports and open source software. W3C promotes standardization by making recommendations regarding the architecture of the Web; features that affect interaction with Web users; social, legal, and public policy concerns; and accessibility issues related to usability for people with disabilities.

The Rise of the Digital Library and Web Portal: 2000 and Beyond

THE DIGITAL LIBRARY

The rise of electronic resources, the Web, and the ability to digitize print, sound, and visual information have revolutionized the concept of the library. All digital data have the same underlying structure, the binary digit or "bit." Digital images are structured by "pixels" which are composed of dots on the computer screen or on paper. Such images can be black and white, or color. Nearly all types of information can be represented in this manner, including objects in a virtual 3-dimensional space. In the digital environment, objects can be manipulated, transmitted, and combined in endless ways that would be impossible if they were physical objects (Deegan and Tanner 2002).

Libraries are now combinations of physical objects accessed in physical space, and electronic objects that exist in electronic space and are accessible from almost any place. Today's libraries are a combination of resources that include traditional print materials, but also e–books and e-journals, remote databases, and electronic collections provided by outside vendors or developed internally. Such a library is somewhere between the traditional print-based library and the purely electronic library, and is sometimes referred to as a "hybrid" library. Pinfield et al. (1998) describe the hybrid library as "on the continuum between the conventional and digital library, where electronic and paper-based information sources are used alongside each other. The challenge associated with the management of the hybrid library is to encourage end-user resource discovery and information use, in a variety of formats and from a number of local and remote sources, in a seamlessly integrated way."

Hybrid libraries are now commonplace and likely to persist for many years. Nonetheless, it is important to gain an understanding of digital libraries as they become more and more prevalent. Digital libraries are historically founded on the developments of information retrieval systems, including automated indexing and search systems of the 1960s, the hypertext systems of the 1980s, and early research and experimentation largely by the National Science Foundation in the 1990s. They have also arisen because of the development of distance learning, especially at the university level, which requires students to be able to access an electronic library in the absence of proximity to a local one (Fox and Urs 2002; Wright 2002). There are many possible ways to define such libraries. Arms (2000) describes them as "a managed collection of information, with associated services, where the information is stored in digital formats and accessible over a network" (p. 2). The Digital Libraries Initiative (2003) characterizes them as libraries that "basically store materials in electronic format and manipulate large collections of those materials effectively." Sun Microsystems defines a digital library "as the electronic extension of functions users typically perform and the resources they access in a traditional library" (Wright 2003, p. 3). The manipulation of the electronic resources may be electronic or intermediated by an information professional, but a key concept is that they are "managed," not simply a static collection of data. Overall, digital libraries share the fact that they are organized on computers, accessible over a network, and maintain procedures to select, organize, make available, and archive the information (Arms, 2000).

Greenstein (2000) has observed that digital libraries create a "'digital library service environment," that is, a networked online information space in which users can discover, locate, acquire access to and, increasingly, use information" (pp. 290–291). Since the environment is electronic, the formats themselves (such as e-books, e-journals, and videos) are relatively unimportant. The content of virtual libraries extends well beyond text, including graphic, video, audio, images, data sets, and software (Fox and Urs 2002). Much of the information in digital libraries was originally created in nondigital format and converted, but more and more digital information is being created as digital from the start. As increasing amounts of information begin as digital, their integration into digital libraries becomes easy and natural and digital libraries become a natural outgrowth of this transformation of "publication."

In a world of ever-expanding digital information, digital libraries define an electronic space designed to serve its own clientele and organizational objectives. This digital space has some distinct advantages. For example, although some information is still stored as print materials (for example, some manuscript collections) large amounts of scholarly information available worldwide in digital formats can be consulted without the need to visit a physical library. In addition, digital information can be shared by multiple users simultaneously, can be updated quickly, and can be available 24 hours a day. Many constituencies benefit from digital libraries. These include government employees and political leaders, teachers, archivists, librarians, researchers and developers, commercial enterprises, multilingual communities, and homebound citizens. With the increasing capacities and portability of computers and the growth of high-speed networks, the digital library is becoming commonplace, and may well be affecting the frequency and nature of traditional library use (Fox and Urs 2000; Arms 2000; Wright 2003). Of course, the vast amount of information stored in a digital library requires that various value-added services be provided, including searching, user profiling, authentification services, and user interfaces.

THE WEB PORTAL

As the number of Web pages proliferate, it becomes increasingly difficult to narrow searches to find exactly what the user wants. To some extent, search engines like Google attempt to solve this problem, but although they may appear to be easy to use, they often locate incorrect or inaccurate sites, or find many more sites than are needed. Nonetheless, the Web is a significant competitor to libraries due to its apparent ease and convenience, and libraries must be prepared to compete by providing ease, convenience, and high-quality information (Jackson 2002).

Recently, the unruliness of the Web has spawned a new concept: the "Web portal." There is no one definition for "portal." Suffice it to say that a portal assembles a variety of information resources, including Web sites, catalogs, online journals, and digitized resources, and links them to library-like services, such as online reference and interlibrary loan. Rather than randomly searching the Web, a portal permits the user to go to one location, perform high-quality searches of high-quality electronic resources, and receive other value-added services as well. As Jackson (2002) observes about the ideal portal:

> Imagine one web site that can combine the powerful searching of web resources with the searching of local catalogs, online journals, or locally digitized resources. Add to this the ability to initiate a reference question, submit an interlibrary loan (ILL) request, and transfer into course management systems a citation or portion of a journal article, all without leaving that web site. (p. 36)

Although the potential of portals has been emphasized in the scholarly work environment and academic libraries, the concept of the portal has wide-ranging applications:

1. Portals can be personalized to limit the resources that are consulted. Limitations can be by many factors, including date, journal title, and whether a source is full text. They can also be configured to display results in certain formats and possibly to rank results by relevancy.
2. Portals can offer access to both generally accessible and restricted sites.
3. Portals can provide value-added delivery services by providing full-text material or interlibrary loan access.
4. Portals can provide online reference services which may require contact with a human intermediary or interaction with an online reference tool.
5. Portals can provide alert services. Once the portal is personalized, the system may notify the user when pertinent material has been added to the portal. (Schottlaender and Jackson, pp. 281–283)

For libraries, portals can offer opportunities for patrons to go well beyond the concept of the library "home page." With a portal the library provides an electronic gateway which not only identifies a wide variety of resources, but also, through use of a variety of search tools can conduct a single search of multiple resources. In addition, the sources could be linked to delivery systems such as interlibrary loan (ILL), as well as online reference services. Both local and remote sources can be provided, including e-books and e-journals, licensed databases, abstracting and indexing services, local and remote online catalogs, and other Web resources. In essence, the portal becomes an extremely muscular integrated library system. The advantage is obvious for libraries: if the library can provide easy one-stop access to the world of information, it can remain competitive with a World Wide Web that remains unorganized and unselective.

INTERNET2

The Internet, although originally conceived as a network for research and development, was quickly diverted to popular and commercial purposes. Although this change has served the general public's needs, the original Internet goals were subjugated to these forces. It was clear, especially to the academic and research sector, that the original research and development purposes remained critical and that energies needed to be redirected to these ends. In addition, the Internet was not originally designed to serve millions and perhaps billions of users, nor did it originally anticipate multimedia or real-time interactions of the type currently in use. Consequently, the Internet2 consortium, led by more than 2,000 universities and supported by corporate, governmental, and other institutional partners, was formed to create an advanced network devoted to research, education, and development. The goal is not to replace the Internet but to enhance and improve it, and share new developments with others in the educational community. Although membership in Internet2 may be prohibitively expensive for some academic institutions, it is also expected that the discoveries of Internet2 will quickly be transferred to nonmembers of academic institutions and to the K–12 educational community. Nearly $80 million had been devoted to this effort by the university and corporate community by the end of 2003 (Internet2 2003).

Today, the Internet2 consortium has approximately 60 corporate members and 40 international partners. More than 500 four-year colleges and 550 community colleges now have access to the Internet2 backbone called Abilene (Olsen 2003). The speed of this backbone is remarkable: data that would take 30 minutes to transfer over a T–1 line takes about one second on Abilene (Mutch and Ventura 2003). The goal of the consortium is to develop and implement leading-edge network applications and technologies that can be effectively and quickly transferred and applied by the Internet community. The consortium has working groups focused on such areas as network infrastructure, middleware (software that provides such intermediate functions as authentification, authorization, and security), engineering, and applications (for example, digital libraries, digital video, virtual laboratories). In addition to working groups, the consortium also has sponsored interest groups (SIGs), which are informal discussion groups centered around a particular topic area, and advisory groups, which provide expertise to various working groups (Internet2 2003).

Already the developments of Internet2 have transformed higher education, permitting much larger amounts of data to be transferred quickly. Similarly, the growth of videoconferencing and distance education has been significantly advanced due to this network. At the same time colleges and universities have come to the realization that the costs of Internet2 membership, as well as the costs of upgrading their technological infrastructure to take advantage of Internet2, are great (Olsen 2003). Of course, Internet2 can provide significant benefits to libraries by opening these new communication channels to library users. Teleconferencing, videoconferencing, and distance education can be equally useful for providing information to library patrons as it is to the classroom: indeed, the library can become more and more a classroom and educational programmer.

TECHNOLOGY AND THE TWENTY-FIRST CENTURY LIBRARY

> The last decade of the twentieth century, and the initial years of the twenty-first have seen the most dramatic changes in libraries in their many centuries of evolution. While political walls have fallen, statues tumbled, the currencies of great nations given up for a common new unit, and the globe has been enwrapped in an electronic web, libraries too have been subjected to economic, social, technological, and other transformative forces that have brought constant, consuming change. (Billings 2002, p. 1)

There is little doubt that the rise of electronic information technologies and the digital age are having a transformative effect in the twenty-first century. Rutenbeck (2000) has observed that the digital age is recreating attitudes toward information that were originally formed when the printing press first created a stable publishing environment. He identifies "five great challenges of the digital age":

1. *Malleability*—Information, rather than being stable in print form, invites constant change and manipulation.
2. *Selectivity*—Those who have grown up in the digital environment may soon consider predigital forms of information, e.g. print books and articles, as "prehistoric" and not worth using. The result may be excluding important knowledge.
3. *Exclusivity*—The digital age is likely to create a new class of haves and

have-nots. Digital literacy will require new skills as well as traditional skills, e.g. typing.

4. *Vulnerability*—The digital environment will increasingly be susceptible to viruses, security violations, unscrupulous e-commerce transactions, e-mail attacks, and scams. In addition, as artificial intelligence improves, people may become increasingly dependent on systems that are not human and are difficult if not impossible to "understand."

5. *Superficiality*—The ability to network with many more people and to access so much more information does not mean that the relationships established or information obtained are particularly substantive or reliable. In fact, we may be more inclined to make our judgements quickly, less reflectively, and superficially.

Similarly, De Rosa, Dempsey, and Wilson (2004) suggest that the rise of the Web creates an entirely new search environment that may become a major competitor to the library itself. They note:

> The library itself has long been a metaphor for order and rationality. The process of searching for information within a library is done within highly structured systems and information is exposed and knowledge gained as a result of successfully navigating these preexisting structures. Because this is a complicated process, the librarian helps guide and navigate a system where every piece of content has a preordained place. Contrast this world with the anarchy of the Web. The Web is free-associating, unrestricted and disorderly. Searching is secondary to finding and the process by which things are found is unimportant. "Collections" are temporary and subjective where a blog entry may be as valuable to the individual as an "unpublished" paper. . . . The individual searches alone without expert help and, not knowing what is undiscovered, is satisfied. (p. ix)

Although this environment may be foreign to traditional library users, it may still be perceived as more convenient and cost effective to them; in addition, to the young, the Web environment is the "normal" one and may well be the preferred situation in which searching for information is accomplished.

On the other hand, D'Elia, Jorgensen, and Woelfel (2002) have argued that use of the Internet and the public library are, in fact, complementary. Based on a national sample, they point out that "75% of Internet users are public library users and 60% of public library users are Internet users" (p. 818). In addition, they note that the frequency of use of the Internet does not affect frequency of use of public libraries.

Even if we do not consider the Web to be an imminent threat to libraries, the impact of information technologies on libraries cannot be overestimated. The means of information production, organization, and dissemination have undergone a major transformation in recent years, with computer technologies emerging as a dominating force. The significance for libraries of these transformations are broad and deep, and it is important to reflect on some of the more profound effects.

Impact on the Library's Physical Environment and on the Library as a Physical Place

New technologies have forced a major redesign of the library's physical environment. The card catalog has been removed, as well as some tables, chairs, and shelving in most libraries, and in its place are online public access catalog terminals (OPACs) providing access to the local collection, ILL services, reference service, and the Web. The new technologies have completely different physical requirements: they may not only be placed in a centralized area but also dispersed throughout the library.

Because of the electronic character of these technologies, their implementation has led to significant alterations in the wiring of libraries and the placement of electrical outlets and lighting. It can be quite expensive and complicated to redesign the electrical systems of buildings that were built 50 or 100 years ago, and many libraries have made an uneasy accommodation. In some libraries major changes in wiring and even asbestos removal have resulted. Similarly, these technologies have also led to new furniture with significantly different design because of health concerns that may arise among those who use these devices over long periods of time. In all, the library from the outside may appear quite similar as a physical structure, but inside there has been substantial redesign and the costs have been considerable. As these technologies increase, more changes will follow.

From a different perspective, there are also important implications for the library as a *physical place*. As Whitney and Glogoff (1994) observed:

> Over the past few years, library automation has undergone a shift in its direction. Attention has changed from in-house processing of traditional tasks to the use of computing and telecommunications tools to develop the "library without walls" . . . using technologies to expand services, resources, and relationships between libraries and resources around the world. (p. 321)

The notion of a library without walls is an exciting prospect for many in that it conjures an image of breaking physical barriers to permit total freedom of access to all information throughout the world. It would seem that computers can be a suitable means for removing these walls. As more and more information is accessed remotely or provided by organizations that exist to provide information through telecommunication lines and electronic databases, the obsolescence of the library is considered a possibility—even a desired end for some (Birdsall 1994). Does this presage the end of the library as a physical place to be visited? Is it to be replaced by the virtual library?

To some extent, the answer to these questions depends on how we perceive the purpose of libraries, a subject that will be covered in more detail in Chapter 8. Birdsall (1994) has noted that those who envision the end of physical libraries rely more on a research and academic model than on the traditional service model prevalent throughout the history of American libraries and represented more by the public library than the academic one.

There is a significant political advantage to emphasizing the electronic aspects of information access. These networks seem to resolve some of the basic political liabilities that libraries as places have often had, for example, duplication in collections or unequal access due to wealth of particular communities. In addition, politicians and community leaders are as much taken by the "bells and whistles" of technology as anyone else. By the same token, much activity goes on in a library as a place—story hours, adult programming, collaboration with librarians in the research process, and access to print and audiovisual materials. Libraries have often been perceived as community centers—as centers of education. Their presence has served as a material symbol of cultural and educational values for many years. It is unclear how electronic networks could serve in this social capacity. No doubt, the tension between increasing remote access to information and access to physical objects or electronic files in a physical place will remain a dynamic one for a long time to come.

The Impact of Networks, the Web, and the Digital Library on Service

One of the most profound impacts of technology is the ability of libraries to reach beyond their walls to access information remotely and to act cooperatively with other libraries in an electronic environment. Even if one were to set aside the most recent developments, such as the Web and digital libraries, the potential of electronic networking has been exploited in many ways. Examples include various libraries sharing online catalog information, coordinating collection development, coordinating the circulation of materials from other libraries, providing and using cooperative reference services. Such networks are often semi-independent organizational entities. Networks have not only improved access to information, they have reduced some costs by reducing duplication of materials and human resources. Interestingly, networks have also led to some organizational changes, including the appointment of new staff, such as network liaisons and more interlibrary loan and document-delivery personnel—even the creation of new departments. In addition, the networks as semi-independent units need their own administrative policies and procedures, which often affect the internal policies, practices, and staffing of libraries that are members of the network. For example, in many public and academic libraries, the staffing of cataloging departments has changed, reducing the number of professional catalogers and increasing reliance on support staff.

Of course, the greatest impact on libraries has come with the creation of the Web and the digital library. Consider some of the major consequences of these developments:

THE ONLINE CATALOG

The term "online catalog" is probably no longer accurate for the catalog has become the portal to a universe of information far beyond the walls of the library. With the development and maturation of Web-based access to information, the online catalog has become a "one-stop" shop for many important aspects of information access. Certainly, through the online catalog one still has access to the physical holdings of the library itself, as well as information on whether an item is currently unavailable. Such a catalog typically provides the patron with the ability to "reserve" such an item as well, and in some cases can result in the physical delivery of an item. But much more is now available. The catalog can link the user directly to the Web for broad-based access to publicly available Web sites, and also can provide special access to Web sites and databases that are not accessible to the general public. Such Web sites might provide access to literally thousands of periodicals, including fulltext access. The catalog might also provide access to Web sites "selected" by the library on topics of special interest, and provide direct electronic access to specialists in various fields, to interlibrary loan, and to reference librarians. The online catalog has become the doorway to the world of information.

DIGITAL REFERENCE SERVICE

It is important to understand how reference services change as the library collection evolves from reliance on physical items in the collection to remote access to information, whether in print or electronic. This change requires a new way of looking at service: the key is relating the user to the entire world of information rather than to items in the local collection. It requires librarians to master an entirely new domain of knowledge and to structure their reference services to conform to the wide-ranging capacity of the digital world. This transition does not mean that local library collections are ignored; user needs will require libraries to maintain substantial local collections of physical items. But it does require increasing recognition that something has dramatically changed, and that library services must change as well. Unless they do change, individuals will likely seek out the information they need without the librarian's assistance. This is a justifiable fear, particularly in academic libraries, which often find that student use of the reference desk is steadily declining.

Digital reference service is not simply adding another service to traditional reference activities. It is a transformative activity. The traditional reference desk model implies that information sources are concentrated in a specific geographic area. The reference librarian, at least theoretically, is able to master a manageable collection of these sources. But in the digital environment, the reference librarian no longer is matching the information needs of a particular patron with the library collection; rather, he or she is matching the information needs of the library user with a vast world of information (Lankes 2000). Because the physical library collection is only one of many potential resources open to the reference librarian for consultation, there is a greater need to evaluate the quality of outside resources at the point a query is made. Indeed the resources being consulted might be themselves human, such as an "Ask an Expert" Web site. Lankes (2000) argues that this new model makes the reference librarian more of an information broker than an information intermediary who simply places a library user in contact with an information resource. Certainly the reference interview, the physical reference desk, and hours of service are all susceptible to substantial reconsideration.

Similarly, the reference patron is no longer constrained by geography or hours. Service that relies on digital access to information can be provided from many locations and at any time, and the individuals asking for service may also come from anywhere. A "24/7" reference service is now a reality. Traditional library service is reserved almost entirely to members of a defined geographic community; but the model of digital reference does not require this limitation. In addition, typical reference service is usually offered during the day or early evening; but digital reference could permit, even encourage, the concept of a graveyard shift for reference service. Similarly, traditional reference service is primarily synchronous, that is, the question is asked and answered at the same time. In a digital environment, a substantial amount of reference can be asynchronous, permitting a patron to ask a question at any time and receive an answer later. As libraries attempt to manage such services, it is likely that joint and cooperative efforts (collaborative digital reference services) will be forthcoming so that service at off hours could be provided through networks. Such services could be regional, national, or even global. One thing is for certain: the tide of digital reference will not be restrained. As McClure has observed "Digital reference can no longer be considered the future of librarianship. Digital reference is *now*" (Lankes, Collins, and Kasowitz 2000, p. xiii).

Of course, there are many issues facing the development of digital reference services including cost, management, evaluation, and such legal issues as copyright concerns. Nonetheless, there is little doubt that digital reference service will be an essential complement to traditional reference service for years to come.

Impact of Technology on the Library Collection

No doubt one of the major challenges of electronic access to information is the need to define what the library collection is. Traditionally, that task has been fairly easy. The library collection was the group of physical objects either available for consultation by staff and patrons inside the library or available for circulation outside the library. From time to time one might borrow materials on interlibrary loan, but interlibrary loan represented a very tiny proportion of the library's service and was not enough to confound the basic notion of what the collection was.

Today, a vast amount of available information is remote, residing in computer databases or on the Web. Presuming that libraries will remain as sources of information, the very concept of the library collection has been transformed. In this new environment, the library collection consists of at least two parts: items and information contained within the library (stored as physical objects or electronically), and information stored electronically (and sometimes physically) outside the library either as data or documents. This reconceptualization of the library collection raises many issues which can only be briefly mentioned:

FINANCIAL IMPLICATIONS

Libraries must confront the increasing costs of making digital information available to library users. Information vendors, for example, are providing access to vast amounts of information, including data from statistical databases, and articles from hundreds of periodicals in full text. This access is sometimes provided to networks as well as individual libraries based on a negotiated contract. The costs to individual libraries for such access may be considerable. Similarly, if a library chooses to offer digital reference services, there may be a significant increase in staffing costs, overhead, and costs for additional computer hardware and software. There may also be costs for contracting with outside reference firms who may be willing to provide "backup" reference services at times when the library is typically closed.

Information obtained electronically from outside the library may also involve new or increased costs of telecommunications, access to databases, downloading, and compensation concerning copyright, as well as the costs of the hardware and software to access these external sources of information. This model requires new perspectives on the allocation of resources and new attitudes toward which items will be collected locally and which will be remotely accessed. Dugan (2002) has identified a "costs structure model" to assist libraries in assessing the overall fiscal burden that a new technology can create for libraries. The eight components of the model include the following:

Investigation. Researching what is needed by the users and is available on the marketplace to meet these needs.
Negotiation. Leveraging the institution's or consortium's economic and legal advantages into an agreement to acquire or lease.
Acquisition. Turning the negotiation into a purchase or lease; this component may require approval from other parts of a hierarchy.
Installation. Preparing the library and/or acquisition (purchase or lease) for use.
Training. Making the acquisition usable by staff and users.
Maintenance. Keeping the acquisition usable.
Evaluation. Determining and then recommending whether the acquisition as maintained continues to serve a purpose.

Upgrade, Migrate, Replace, or Abandon. Implementing the evaluative
recommendation (p. 240).

But there is also good news from a fiscal perspective. As networks
are created for the benefit of libraries, a much broader access to materials may be available at very reasonable costs. Some statewide networks,
such as OhioLINK, which serves the academic libraries in Ohio, and the
Ohio Public Library Information Network (OPLIN), which serves the
public libraries in Ohio, have negotiated with vendors like EBSCO to
provide access to thousands of periodicals, including full-text access.
These costs are borne significantly by the state rather than by local libraries. Because periodical subscriptions represent a substantial cost to
libraries, access to so many periodicals is a significant fiscal advantage.
Similarly, networks have revolutionized the concept of resource sharing. Traditionally, interlibrary loan was a relatively cumbersome, time-
consuming, and staff-intensive process. Networks such as OhioLINK
provide highly effective resource sharing of materials. Under these circumstances, libraries may limit their own purchases because their users
can obtain the desired copies quickly. The result is a salutary effect on
monograph budgets which have been under considerable pressure for
years.

Impact on Selection and Acquisitions of Information Resources for the Library Collection

As noted above, traditionally library collections have consisted of physical items that were provided by vendors and publishers or producers of
books, audio-visual materials (AV), or serials. Collection development
involved the selection and acquisition of materials through these publishers and vendors. At its most basic level, electronic technologies have
changed the way that these traditional print materials are identified and
ordered. Vendors have created electronic systems that permit selectors
to access their databases and identify items, consult tables of contents,
and read reviews. These systems also permit placing orders and downloading essential bibliographic material for cataloging purposes. These
electronic processes not only streamline acquisition and selection processes, but they can also provide fiscal control and financial reports. Integrated library systems can also reveal which items or subject areas are
circulating and which are out on interlibrary loan. These data can also
be used for collection development and planning. In addition, electronic

technologies have increased the number of information resources for selectors; for example, e-mail and listservs provide advice and information on material selection.

Perhaps even more significant in the long run is the effect on the collection. As noted above, significant and positive effects can arise as libraries no longer need to order and physically maintain as many periodicals as they have in the past, and, in many cases this may also be true for some books and monographs that now can be easily borrowed.

But the most important reconceptualization arises as we try to conceive of what is meant by the "library collection" when much of the texts, sights, and sounds become available on the Web. Where does the library collection begin and end, and how does the library effectively exercise control of such a collection? Given that information on the Web is available for consultation and downloading at the local library, then this information becomes, for all intents and purposes, part of the library collection. But to what extent can the library apply its traditional notions of selection? Certainly, as a rule, it cannot change the content and organization of Web sites. If the library is unable to apply its traditional controls, then it must address additional questions, such as the following:

- What are the "selection criteria" for libraries and information centers for information available on the Web?
- To what extent does the library staff control access to the content of the Web? What policies are needed to balance intellectual freedom issues with protection of vulnerable clientele such as children?
- To what extent does the library staff create interfaces that guide patrons to particular Web sites?
- How does the library staff decide if a particular information resource should be made accessible in print, AV, or electronic format? When should the same information be available in multiple formats?
- What responsibility does the library staff have to make available only information that they feel is accurate or reliable?
- To what extent are librarians responsible for evaluating information for the patron?
- To what extent should libraries or information centers warn patrons that the information available may be inaccurate, biased, or incomplete?
- Under what conditions does a library decide to order a physical item, even when it can be obtained from another library easily?

Similarly, the library has the opportunity not just to offer individual Web sites, but to build substantial electronic collections. Kovacs (2000) suggests that the building of such e-libraries can save the time of users, create an organized environment of accurate and credible resources, and increase access to new users. Kovacs also reveals that the potential range of such collections are considerable, including core reference materials, and collections on business, health, law, social and physical sciences, and education.

In addition, remote access to electronic information creates entirely new issues regarding collection evaluation. It is no longer enough to examine the local collection to determine if it is meeting users' needs. Rather, there will be much greater attention to whether the library can provide adequate access to the needed information. As De Gennaro (1989) presciently observed more than a decade ago, "In the future, the size of a library's collection of conventional materials will matter far less than it does now. The question is no longer how many volumes a library has, but how effectively the library can deliver needed resources from a wide variety of sources to users via the new technology" (p. 42).

PRESERVATION

Preservation seems a relatively easy concept when considering print materials. Among the measures to be implemented include encouraging the purchase of materials printed on acid-free paper; maintaining proper humidity, temperature, and other environmental controls; ensuring the use of preservation-quality materials for binding, repair, and storage of materials; and applying such technologies as mass and individual deacidification techniques to deteriorating items of importance. In the last decade, digitization has also become a method of preservation. Certainly digitization would seem to be a tempting alternative. As Smith (1999) has observed, digitization on first glance is often as a means of reducing costs while providing greatly expanded access. She suggests, however, that at least today, digitization is expensive and it does not have the permanence of microfilm. Digitization may provide greatly expanded access to large numbers of images, but access and preservation are related but distinct activities. In our rush to provide access, we must also remember that the media we use to preserve must be stable. In addition, the content preserved must be authentic. The ease with which digital material can be altered raises serious questions about its capacity to serve as a preservation technique.

Electronic media raise important new issues. Ironically, Smith (1999) has also observed that "The next century's major preservation challenge will be to cope with the fragile media of the present [twentieth] century from magnetic tape to digital files. The record of the twentieth century exists on many media that are far more fragile than paper" (p. 13). For example, there is the issue of *fixity*. That is, print materials are considered to have some permanence, but electronic text is impermanent. In fact, that is part of its attractiveness: it is a characteristic of the media that the text can be changed, edited, and manipulated often with considerable ease. In many instances modifications or damage can be done inadvertently as well as intentionally. But with so many possible iterations, which versions are to be preserved and how? Similarly, much electronic information is vulnerable to damage, tampering, and deterioration over time. For more than a decade, some information has been stored on CD-ROMS. As they become outdated as an information storage format, what do we do with valuable information that has been stored in that format? How can we migrate that material onto more contemporary media? As more and more information appears on Web sites, how do we preserve them? Electronic information has also been stored on floppy or zip disks. Such data will need to be refreshed or transferred to a different medium; otherwise, the data may be corrupted. Given the vast amount of information stored on such disks, how can it be effectively preserved? Preservation of electronic media implies that equipment on which it is preserved also be preserved. Retaining CD-ROMs or floppy disks is of little use if the software and hardware to use the medium is not available.

The issue becomes even more difficult when one considers the information on the Web. It is likely that much of the information on the Web will not exist a year or two from now. Already it is common to search for a Web site and see the familiar message: "File Not Found." If the marketplace determines what is preserved, then probably only material of commercial value will remain (Coyle 1994). Obviously this is not the traditional basis for preservation of library materials. Who will take responsibility for determining what will be preserved and how it will be preserved? The implications can well be substantial. If for example the e-mail of government officials are not preserved, much of the historical evidence could disappear through deletion of files. These are just a few of the challenges that will face the preservation officers of today and tomorrow, as their electronic collections increase in proportion to their traditional print holdings.

Impact of Technology on Human Resources Issues

During the 1960s and 1970s, when automation was introduced into libraries, little attention was paid to the effect on staff. Indeed, a major argument regarding the desirability of its implementation was that it would reduce dependence on library staff. However, the experiences of the last two decades have made it clear that the reaction of staff to the introduction and implementation of automation plays an important role in its effective use and the retention of valued employees.

In fact, the introduction of new technologies has generated considerable perturbation in the workplace and especially in regard to human resources. It can be examined from two perspectives: effects of technology on the organizational structure and human responses to the introduction of technologies.

IMPACT ON THE POSITIONS AND ORGANIZATIONAL STRUCTURE

Whenever new technologies are introduced in an organization, they often bring the need to hire new people with different knowledge and skills. Hiring such individuals raises a variety of issues and problems. For example, as computer technologies are integrated into library functions, libraries have hired systems and network experts to maintain and enhance the system, to train others in the use of the system, report on the system's operation, and make recommendations for new systems as needed. Depending on the size of the library and the sophistication of the system, additional systems staff have been retained. The individuals hired for these positions are often quite different from library staff both in terms of knowledge and disposition. The organizational culture from which they come may also be different. The result is potential estrangement of certain staff or conflict within the organization, which in turn may affect organizational productivity.

In addition, the introduction of these new positions with special technical expertise has often required the creation of new job descriptions and new job classifications that have unique relationships to the traditional organizational structure. New reporting lines have been established, which can lead to resentment or concern. For example, the head of a systems department might report directly to the library director or other high-level administrative position. These seemingly privileged lines of communication may make other managers uneasy and suspicious. Similarly, compensation for new technically-oriented classifications is problematic. The marketplace for individuals with computer expertise is often substantially more lucrative than the marketplace for librarians. To recruit and retain talented individuals with computer expertise, it may be necessary to pay these individuals more than librarians. Such a distortion of the traditional pay structure can affect the morale of other staff. Similarly, a variety of new competencies have been suggested for current information professionals in this dynamic situation, including knowledge of new information technologies, substantial adaptability and flexibility, creativity, ability to manage change, willingness to take risks, increased ability to plan and supervise, increased skills in determining the information needs of users, ability to create and maintain information systems, strong interpersonal skills, leadership, and vision (Bailey 1991; Tees 1991). No doubt, there will be significant organizational challenges as qualified individuals must be identified, hired, and retained.

Support staff are also experiencing changes in their work. They, like librarians, must also be adaptable and flexible and be able to learn new things quickly. Support staff may well be providing basic reference services using electronic technologies or developing strong skills in desktop publishing or information management systems. As support staff acquire new, complex, technical skills, they are also likely to demand greater status and pay and want to be treated in a collaborative manner rather than in the context of the traditional superior/subordinate relationship. The result is that many support/professional staff tensions have been magnified as these technologies have been introduced. The recognition of the significant contributions of support staff and the responsibility of motivating and rewarding these workers constitute fundamental management challenges for library administrators and staff.

Libraries as organizations are changing in other ways as well. Some of the activities that have traditionally been performed by libraries are now being outsourced to other organizations. For example, automated acquisitions have permitted vendors to supply some materials already processed and cataloged, and even re-bound to specification. This outsourcing effectively reduces the need for library departments devoted to these activities. The extent to which outsourcing will become an integral part of library processes is yet to be seen.

Finally, the organization is changing as some of the duties performed by employees will be performed by the users themselves. For example, technology makes certain functions much easier for the patron to perform, essentially eliminating the need for librarians as intermediaries in some cases. These are sometimes referred to as patron-initiated service systems. Examples include self-checkout of local materials, direct inter-library loan and document delivery, and electronic systems that permit renewal, recalls, and holds on materials or access to databases or the Web.

IMPACT OF TECHNOLOGIES ON THE PHYSICAL AND PSYCHOLOGICAL CONDITION OF WORKERS

The effect of technologies on people can be profound, and because new technologies are introduced regularly, it is important to understand the many potential reactions to their presence in the workplace. One concern is the physical impact of electronic technologies. Experience with employees working with computers has revealed that a variety of physical symptoms, some quite serious, can arise: carpal tunnel syndrome, repetitive motion disorders, headaches, neck aches, vision problems, joint pain, numbness in limbs, and fatigue. These problems have highlighted the field of ergonomics, which devotes itself to studying the fit between people and machines. Ergonomic studies have revealed the need for carefully redesigning workspaces so that lighting is appropriate for video display terminals; chairs provide proper support for arms, legs, neck, and back; and keyboards and desks are designed and placed at appropriate heights to minimize injury to hands and arms. In addition, employers are discovering that employees working all day on computers need frequent breaks to maintain their productivity.

Similarly, employers are concerned with the negative psychological reactions from employees when new technologies are introduced. Their reactions are sometimes described as technostress or resistance to change. Technostress is "a condition resulting from the inability of an individual or organization to adapt to the introduction and operation of new technology" (Brod 1984, p. 30). The introduction of new technologies sometimes creates irrational fears, but many of the fears are perfectly rational and need to be anticipated and dealt with. There are, for example, natural fears of job loss, of being unable to master new training, of technical jargon, and of physical harm, as well as fear that computers will be used to inappropriately monitor work. Such fears often produce symptoms of technostress.

Regrettably, the symptoms of technostress are not uncommon and can be quite serious. They include mental fatigue, combativeness, depression, increased errors and bad judgments, panic, resistance to change, and feelings of helplessness. These undesirable responses can cause loss of productivity and morale not only among the particular workers experiencing the problem, but also among those who work with or rely on the work of those employees. The causes of technostress are many and varied and include poorly designed or inadequate computer hardware and software, poor lighting or wiring, noisy equipment, poor training, poor organizational communication, and existing feelings of job insecurity and fragmentation. Dealing with these factors can diminish the unproductive responses of workers encountering new technologies.

Experience has revealed that there are a variety of steps libraries can take to alleviate negative psychological responses to change. These include the following:

1. Involving staff from the beginning in the planning and acquisition of new technologies. Keeping secrets only leads to the proliferation of rumors and a feeling of being left out. Ideas should emerge from the staff itself, which increases commitment and reduces the feeling that the technology is being imposed.
2. Demonstrating to the employees that there are direct beneficial consequences from the change. After all, self-interest is a strong motivator: if the change helps the employees do their needed work, it is more likely to be greeted positively.
3. Communicating to staff the progress of technological changes and providing time to adjust. This should include plenty of time for learning how to operate and use new technologies, opportunities to make mistakes without penalties, and chances to receive and provide feedback on the effectiveness of or any problems with new systems. For technological change to work well, there must be open communications in both directions.
4. Refraining from ridiculing critics. There are bound to be people who will resist technological change. Although they sometimes can be difficult, they also can serve a vital purpose: they can reveal inadequacies that should be remedied. Criticizing these individuals may simply build resentment and fear on the part of others.
5. Ensuring staff they will not lose their job or be reduced in rank or pay following the change. After all, resistance is bound to arise if one feels that one's interests are being threatened.

IMPACT OF TECHNOLOGY ON THE TRADITIONAL MISSION OF LIBRARIES

It has been the traditional mission of public, academic, and school libraries to serve all their constituents' information needs, regardless of their background or economic standing. Does the introduction of electronic technologies alter that mission? It is a common belief that technologies themselves are value-neutral, that it is the uses to which technology is put that dictate the values. But there are those who argue that this is not so, that technologies have significant social, political, and economic impact, and their development and use is promoted by select groups to serve their own purposes. This concern has been reflected professionally with the creation of the Progressive Librarians Guild (PLG) in 1990, an affiliate of the Social Responsibilities Round Table of ALA. Among the PLG's stated concerns is "our profession's rapid drift into dubious alliances with business and the information industry, and into complacent acceptance of service to the political, economic, and cultural status quo (Progressive Librarians Guild 1998, p. 1). As John Bushman (1990) has observed, "the implementation of technologies is not democratically controlled; it serves the interests of the people who control them" (p. 1029). It is hard not to argue that the computer revolution has been developed and exploited for economic purposes, and that many of the electronic resources developed are designed for business and industry. Certainly, access to electronic information is not equally distributed; the digital divide is a persistent and unfortunate reality. It is important, therefore, to reexamine regularly whether the social mission of libraries is also being accomplished as it employs its technologies.

SUMMARY

As new information technologies provide increasingly greater access to information, libraries will undoubtedly continue to acquire them. Continuous change will be an inherent part of this process. In such a dynamic environment, many questions need to be answered:

- How will new technologies affect the future mission of libraries?
- How will electronic publications and information be evaluated and selected?
- How will access to electronic information be provided, controlled, and paid for?
- How does technology affect the employees of the organization, and how can it be implemented for maximum productivity?

There is no doubt that the concept of the library is changing—some say it is in transition from "collection to connection." The extent to which this transition will actually occur and its impact on library services is yet to be fully determined. There is no doubt that libraries of the future will be looking for new skills and abilities among its employees and will be continually emphasizing retraining and continuing education as new technologies are introduced. The new technological environment is one in which professional and support staff each need significant skills, and there are many types of professionals (for example, systems operators and librarians) working to provide information services. There are many unknowns regarding the future of libraries and how they will be affected by technology. What we do know is that change will be a natural and continuous part of that world.

REFERENCES

American Council of Learned Societies. *Scholars and Research: Academic Libraries in the 21st Century*. ACLIS Occasional Paper, No. 14. New York: ACLS, 1990.

American Heritage Dictionary. "Search Engine." [Online] Available at *www.bartleby.com/61/32/S0193256.html*. (Accessed November 3, 2003.)

Arms, William Y. *Digital Libraries*. Cambridge, Mass.: MIT, 2000.

Bailey, Martha J. "Characteristics of the Successful Information Professionals of the Future: Branch Libraries/Information Centers." In *Future Competencies of the Information Professional*. SLA Occasional Papers Series, Number One. Washington, D.C.: SLA, 1991.

Baker, Nicholson. "Discards." *New Yorker* (April 4, 1994): 64–86.

Bierman, Kenneth J. "How Will Libraries Pay for Electronic Information?" *Journal of Library Administration* 15 (1991): 67–84.

Billings, Harold. *Magic & Hypersystems: Constructing the Information-Sharing Library*. Chicago: ALA, 2002.

Birdsall, William F. "Breaking the Myth of the Library as Place." In *The Myth of the Electronic Library: Librarianship and Social Change in America*. Westport, Conn.: Greenwood, 1994, 7–29.

Bishop, Ann P. "The National Research and Education Network (NREN): Promise of a New Information Environment." *ERIC Digest* (November 1990) EDO-IR–90–4.

Brod, Craig. "How to Deal with 'Technostress.'" *Office Administration and Automation* 45 (August 1984): 28–47.

Buckland, Michael K. "Documentation, Information Science, and Library Science in the U.S.A." *Information Processing & Management* 32 (1996): 63–76.

Buckland, Michael K., and Clifford A. Lynch. "The Linked Systems Protocol and the Future of Bibliographic Networks and Systems." *Information Technology and Libraries* 6 (June 1987): 83–88.

———. "National and International Implications of the Linked Systems Protocol for Online Bibliographic Systems." *Cataloging and Classifications Quarterly* 8 (1988): 15–31.

Bushman, John. "Asking the Right Questions about Information Technology." *American Libraries* 21 (December 1990): 1026–1030.

Coyle, Karen. "Access: Not Just Wires." Paper presented at the annual meeting of the Computer Professionals for Social Responsibility (CPSR). San Diego, October 1994.

December, John, and Neil Randall. *The World Wide Web Unleashed 1996.* Indianapolis: Sams, 1995.

Deegan, Marilyn, and Simon Tanner. *Digital Futures: Strategies for the Information Age.* New York: Neal-Schuman, 2002.

De Gennaro, Richard D. "Technology and Access in an Enterprise Society." *Library Journal* 114 (October 1, 1989): 40–43.

D'Elia, George, Corinne Jorgensen, and Joseph Woelfel. "The Impact of the Internet on Public Library Use: An Analysis of the Current Consumer Market for Library and Internet Services." *Journal of the American Society for Information Science and Technology* 53 (2002): 802–820.

De Rosa, Cathy, Lorcan Dempsey, and Alane Wilson. *The 2003 OCLC Environmental Scan: Pattern Recognition: A Report to the OCLC Membership.* Dublin, Ohio: OCLC, 2004.

Digital Libraries Initiative. [Online] Available at *http//dli.grainger.uiuc.edu/national.htm.* (Accessed July 8, 2003.)

Dugan, Robert E. "Information Technology Budgets and Costs: Do You Know What Your Information Technology Costs Each Year?" *Journal of Academic Librarianship* 28 (July 2002): 238–243.

Emerging Technologies Research Group. *The 1997 American Internet User Survey* [Online]. Available at *http://etrg.findsvp.com/internet/overview.html* (Accessed July 1, 1997.)

Fielden, Ned L., and Lucy Kuntz. *Search Engines Handbook.* Jefferson, N.C.: McFarland, 2002.

Fox, Edward A., and Shalini R. Urs. "Digital Libraries." In *Annual Review of Information Science and Technology.* Vol. 36. Medford, N.J.: Information Today, 2002, 503–590.

Gomery, Douglas. "In Search of the Cybermarket." *The Wilson Quarterly* (summer 1994): 9–17.

Greenstein, Daniel. "Digital Libraries and Their Challenges." *Library Trends* 49 (fall 2000): 290–303.

Grosch, Audrey N. *Library Information Technology and Networks.* New York: Marcel Dekker, 1995.

Hahn, Trudi Bellardo. "Pioneers of the Online Age." *Information Processing and Management* 32 (1996): 33–48.

Internet2. [Online] Available at *www.internet2.edu.* (Accessed July 8, 2003.)

Jackson, Mary E. "The Advent of Portals." *Library Journal* 127 (September 15, 2002): 36–39.

Kovacs, Diane. *Building Electronic Library Collections.* New York: Neal-Schuman, 2000.

Lankes, R. David. "The Foundations of Digital Reference." In *Digital Reference Service in the New Millennium: Planning, Management, and Evaluation,* edited by R. David Lankes, John W. Collins, III, and Abby S. Kasowitz. New York: Neal-Schuman, 2000.

Lankes, R. David, John W. Collins, III, and Abby S. Kasowitz, eds. *Digital Reference Service in the New Millennium: Planning, Management, and Evaluation.* New York: Neal-Schuman, 2000.

McClure, Charles R. "Foreword." In *Digital Reference Service in the New Millennium: Planning, Management, and Evaluation,* by David R. Lankes, John W. Collins III, and Abby S. Kasowitz, xiii–xiv. New York: Neal-Schuman, 2000.

McKenna, Mary. "Libraries and the Internet." *ERIC Digest* (December 1994) Syracuse, ERIC Clearinghouse on Information and Technology.

Media Metric. "comScore Media Metrix Search Engine Ratings." [Online] Available at *www.searchenginewatch.com/reports/article.php.* (Accessed November 4, 2003.)

Mediamark Research. "64.2 Million American Adults Regularly Use the Internet." [Online] Available at *www.mediamark.com/mri/docs/prcs_s99.htm* (Accessed March 21, 2000.)

Mutch, Andrew, and Karen Ventura. "The Promise of Internet2." *Library Journal* 128 (summer 2003): 14–16.

National Coordination Office for Computing, Information, and Communications. Next Generation Internet Initiative. [Online] Available at *www.ccic.gov/ngi/background.html* (Accessed December 28, 1997.)

National Information Standards Organization. "Information Retrieval: Application Service Definition and Protocol Specification." Bethesda, Md.: NISO, 1994.

NCES. *Public Libraries in the United States: Fiscal Year 2001.* Washington, D.C.: U.S. DOE, 2003.

NCSA (National Center for Supercomputing Alliance). *A Beginner's Guide to HTML.* [Online] Available at *www.ncsa.uiuc.e . . . /WWW/HRMLPrimerPl.html* (Accessed July 3, 1997.)

Olsen, Florence. "Internet2 at a Crossroads." *Chronicle of Higher Education* 49 (May 16, 2003).

Pinfield, Stephen, et al. "Realizing the Hybrid Library." D-Lib Magazine, October 1998. [Online] Available at www.dlib.org/dlib/october98/10pinfield.html.

Progressive Librarians Guild. "Progressive *Librarians Guild"* [Online]. Available at *http://home. earthlink.net /~rlitwin/PLG.html.* (Accessed January 6, 1998.)

Rider, Freemont. *The Scholar and the Future of the Research Library: A Problem and Its Solution.* New York: Hadham, 1944, 99. Cited in Buckland, 65.

Rutenbeck, Jeff. "The 5 Great Challenges of the Digital Age." *Netconnect* (fall 2000): 30–33.

Schottlaender, Brian E.C., and Mary E. Jackson. "The Current State and Future Promise of Portal Applications." In *The Bowker Annual: Library and Book Trade Almanac.* 48th Edition. Edited by Dave Bogart. Medford, N.J.: Information Today, 2003, 279–290.

"Sharp Increase in Internet Use at Public Libraries." *American Libraries* 29 (January 1998): 11.

Smith, Abby. *The Future of the Past: Preservation in American Research Libraries.* 1999. [Online] Available at *www.clir.org/pubs/reports/pub82/pub82text.html.* (Accessed August 28, 2003.)

————. *Why Digitize?* Washington, D.C.: Council on Library and Information Resources, 1999.

Tees, Miriam H. "Competencies for the Mid-Sized Special Library." In *Future Competencies of the Information Professional.* SLA Occasional Paper Series, Number One. Washington D.C.: SLA, 1991.

Tennant, Roy. "Internet Basics." *Eric Digest 18* (October 1992): EDO-IR–92–7.

Tenner, Edward. "Learning from the Net." *Wilson Quarterly* (summer 1994): 18–28.

University of South Carolina at Beaufort Library. "Bare Bones 101." [Online] Available at *www.sc.edu/beaufortlibrary/lesson1.html.* (Accessed November 3, 2003.)

Webster's Third New International Dictionary. Springfield, Mass.: G & C Merriam, 1970.

Whitney, Gretchen, and Stuart Glogoff. "Automation for the Nineties: A Review Article." *Library Quarterly* 64 (July 1994): 319–331.

World Almanac and Book of Facts, 1999. New York: World Almanac Books, 1999.

World Wide Web Consortium. [Online] Available at www.w3.org/Consortium. (Accessed October 31, 2003.)

Wright, Cheryl D. "Introduction." In *Digital Library Technology Trends.* [Online] Available at *www.sun.com/products-n-solutions/edu/whitepapers/pdf/digial_library_trends.pdf.* (Dated August 2002; Accessed July 22, 2003.)

4

Information Policy: Stakeholders and Agendas

INFORMATION POLICY STAKEHOLDERS

The importance of information in our society can hardly be overestimated. As we increasingly recognize the critical nature of information, policies that affect information creation, organization, use, and dissemination become equally critical. This chapter is devoted to a discussion of the major information policy issues with special attention to national policies that affect libraries. Institutions such as libraries, museums, and archives also create information policies that can affect the citizenry's access to information. The information policies specifically created by libraries have a significant effect on their collections and services, and Chapter 5 is devoted entirely to this subject.

Information policy is any law, regulation, rule, or practice (written or unwritten) that affects the creation, acquisition, organization, dissemination, or evaluation of information. Most often, information policy is discussed in terms of governmental legislation. This legislation usually focuses on areas such as information technologies for educational and industrial uses, telecommunications, privacy issues, computer regulations and crimes, copyright and intellectual property, and government information systems (Burger 1993).

In American society, discussion of information policy highlights a fundamental tension between entrepreneurship and democracy. Under capitalism, information can be viewed as a commodity, a form of property that can provide a competitive edge. Insofar as such information can be held privately, there is a strong incentive for individuals to discover new information and apply it to products and services that both advance society and increase personal wealth. On the other hand, the democratic values of society promote information and access to it as a right. Democratic traditions promote the free flow of ideas as essential if a free society is to prosper. This is not to say that capitalism and democracy are incompatible; it is to suggest that information policy in a democratic society requires a balancing of social, economic, and political interests.

Not surprisingly, there are a variety of stakeholders in the information policy process, stakeholders who are deeply concerned about information from a legal and political perspective. These stakeholders include business, government, information producers and disseminators, and the public.

Business and Industry

Because information is critical to competition, business and industry are very active in influencing policies that will affect the dissemination and restriction of information. Business and industry have special interests in both the discovery of new knowledge and the organization of current knowledge.

POLICIES AFFECTING THE DISCOVERY AND EXPLOITATION OF NEW KNOWLEDGE TO IMPROVE PRODUCTIVITY AND PROFITS

Business and industry have a strong need to control knowledge and to protect proprietary information, such as new inventions or discoveries. Patent and copyright laws are needed as well as laws that permit the restriction of an employee's use of protected knowledge even after separation from employment. For example, employers can use a "no competition" clause in contracts so that an employee cannot reveal secret information about an employer's processes or inventions. Similarly, organizational policy may prevent an employee from working for a competitor. Such restrictions are needed to maintain a competitive edge with domestic and foreign competitors and to ensure organizational survival.

THE ORGANIZATION OF CURRENT KNOWLEDGE FOR PURPOSES OF ACCESS

Organizations need access to information to prosper. The extent to which government policies permit easy and inexpensive access to information can have a substantial effect on an organization's ability to function effectively in competitive national and international environments.

Government

Political bodies are well aware that information is essential for decision making and action. Local, state, and federal governments are obligated to collect, organize, and evaluate information. The federal government does this through government hearings, the information-gathering activities of executive offices such as the Department of Labor or Department of State, the FBI law-enforcement investigations, or by the CIA's political-military assessments. Government is also in the business of disseminating and controlling information. To this end, the government promulgates regulations to restrict information, such as information affecting national security, and plays a role in selecting what information is published and made available to the public (or the press) and what information is not. Laws such as the Freedom of Information Act and the National Security Act form part of the process that defines the role of government in the dissemination and control of information.

Information Producers, Disseminators, Transmitters, or Telecommunicators

Although these stakeholders could be considered part of business and industry, they form a critical subgroup that takes a special interest in information policy because of the profound effect such policies might have on them. Information producers and disseminators include the telecommunications businesses such as telephone, television, cable, and radio industry; producers of videos, DVDs, and audio tapes; the print and publishing industry; the computer industry, including database producers and vendors; and, of course, libraries. A particular subgroup within these information producers and disseminators is known as the "digerati." According to West (2001) the digerati form "the broad group of individuals who invent, create, develop, manage, and sell a wide spectrum of information technologies. They have job titles like 'chief executive officer,' 'chief technology officer,' 'chief information officer,' 'manager of information systems,' 'software developer,' 'software engineer,' 'programmer,' 'vice president of sales,' and 'director of marketing'" (p. 12). Because these individuals have special knowledge and control of technology companies and research, they can be particularly influential in the policy making arena.

One can imagine any number of laws and regulations that can either promote or diminish the effectiveness of information producers and disseminators. Laws affecting competition, pricing of services, the right to tape programs, taxation, postal rates, and royalties and laws concerning libel or invasion of privacy could all have profound implications for these organizations. Libraries as information disseminators have a special role and exercise a special interest because they are among the few whose motivations are not profit-oriented.

The American Citizen and Those Organizations that Represent their Interest

In a democratic society, each citizen is a major stakeholder. The manner by which information flows in our society has a direct effect on our ability to make informed judgments and to take deliberative action. The subtlest shift in policy may affect the extent to which we receive accurate, up-to-date, and sufficient information, and who receives this information. For American citizens, defining rights to information is a critical function. Dowlin (1987) argues, for example, that citizens have rights to information that would help them deal with their environment, such as information related to their health, safety, careers, and their government, including information on political issues and candidates.

A fundamental value that underlies the transfer of information in a democratic society is the right of individuals to information, and with it comes the expectation that information policies will support that value. The extent to which information policies affect these rights is a critical consideration. Individual citizens, however, do not always have a significantly strong voice. Consequently, a variety of organizations try to represent the public's interests on information policy issues, including the American Library Association (ALA), the American Civil Liberties Union, and Computer Professionals for Social Responsibility. Clearly, there can be a vigorous clash of interests, and this produces a dynamic and sometimes unsettling tension in our society.

THE POLITICO-ECONOMIC CHARACTER OF INFORMATION

Fundamental to our understanding of information policy is the fact that, whether we like it or not, information is being reconceptualized from something merely useful for improving understanding to something that can be seen as a commodity in and of itself. This reconceptualization could potentially threaten the existence and well-being of libraries. This transformation has been fostered, in large part, by computers with dramatically increased capacity to store and process information and by the increasing sophistication of telecommunications, which permits computers to transmit data throughout the world almost instantaneously.

The value of having the right information at the right time, or the value of depriving others of information to gain an advantage, has become so obvious, that it was inevitable that individuals would see the economic and political value of information. Hence, information becomes a commodity—something to be bought, sold, or controlled in and of itself. The economic characterization of information can be seen in the use of the common metaphor, "information marketplace." This change has been likened in significance in at least one commentary (Vagianos and Lesser 1989) to the profound changes created with the invention of the printing press. To equate this change with the invention of printing might be hyperbole, but it is certainly a change with troubling implications. The view of information as a commodity could create for information providers like libraries an uneasy and potentially unethical accommodation with the economic "haves"—to the great disadvantage of the economic "have nots" (Blanke 1989).

Once the metaphor of the economics of information takes hold in the public consciousness, it is an easy assumption that all information should have economic value or price. The result may be that social, cultural, and creative knowledge, traditionally provided for free, may be curtailed or extinguished. The economic advantage of information may be becoming so powerful that those who are advantaged by its creation, dissemination, use, and control may not wish public institutions like libraries to have much of a role in the process. In the future, librarians may not serve as major players in defining how and at what price information will be used. The diminution of the library's role may be accelerated because the technology of information is blurring the traditional model of library work, a model that presupposes a depository to organize and disseminate information. Vagianos and Lesser (1989) argue, in fact, that the "standalone depository is at an end" (p. 10). The more others perceive that information has less and less to do with libraries and more and more to do with technology and telecommunications, the less libraries will be perceived as important in the information policy process. Similarly, as information technologies spawn an increasing variety of information channels such as electronic networks and the Internet, the temptation to think of information as a commodity, rather than a right, intensifies. What, then, are some of the major information policy issues facing librarians and citizens today?

Protecting the Privacy of Citizens

There is growing concern that unauthorized individuals can gain access too easily to records with information on our health, financial affairs, or buying habits. Consequently, there is an interest in protecting a citizen's privacy from third-party intrusions—from individuals or governments. Federal and state governments have promulgated legislation attempting to define a citizen's right of access to files maintained about them and the rights of others to access these same files. These are broadly referred to as Privacy Acts and Public Records Acts. Some acts are designed to protect privacy in specific areas, such as the Right to Financial Privacy Act of 1978, which deals with protection of financial records; the Electronic Communications Privacy Act of 1986, which deals with the privacy of cellular phones; and the Communications Assistance for Law Enforcement Act of 1994, which in part deals with the privacy of cordless phones and data communications (Science Applications International Corporation 1995).

Privacy has become a particularly important information policy issue for libraries because of governmental attempts to obtain borrowing information on individuals through their circulation records. This has led to the creation of many state "Confidentiality of Circulation Records" statutes that provide fairly complete protection against third-party access to borrowers' records, while still providing limited access by governmental agencies for specific reasons. Despite these acts, libraries have become increasingly concerned about patron privacy because of the special provisions of the USA Patriot Act which may compel libraries to provide information about their patrons and, at the same time, prevent them from informing patrons about such requests.

Promoting the Freedom of Information

Certainly, the need to protect the privacy of citizens is vital, but it is also vital that citizens have a right to information regarding governmental activities. This balance between privacy and public records is constantly being tested and redefined. Ironically, some of the same acts that serve to protect an individual's privacy are also ones that ensure rights of access when legitimate interests arise. For example, the protection of a citizen's right to government information is also defined in the family of public records acts, the most prominent being the first of these acts, the federal Freedom of Information Act of 1966. This act was meant to ensure that government records that were not specifically protected by national security or other valid reasons would be made available for inspection by members of the public. The intent was to prevent governments from withholding information merely because they thought that the information would be embarrassing or would be a political liability. The federal act was followed by many state acts, which define the records to which the public has access and usually exempts specific records from public access. These might, but do not necessarily, include law-enforcement investigation records, adoptions, and personnel or medical records. Interestingly, there is also concern that some information that traditionally has been public record is now being shielded from use by the Patriot Act. Of particular concern is infrastructure information such as data on water resources or electrical grids.

The Production and Control of the Flow of Government Information

In recent years, there has been a systematic attempt to reduce the amount of material being produced by the federal Government Printing Office (GPO) to make production more efficient and to reduce the budget for this agency. One major change is the shift from paper printing to the use of electronic formats, including microfiche and Web-based access. The decision to use other formats as a matter of government information policy may have significant implications for the use of such materials. Although production in electronic formats may increase flexibility for searching, it may also present a barrier to many citizens who want to access it. Knowing how to use computers and peripheral equipment is but one possible obstacle for some citizens. Increased costs for using electronic media may be another barrier because libraries may be unable to afford the computer equipment, peripherals, and cost of printing.

The emphasis on cost consciousness is highlighted by what appears to be increasing control of information dissemination by the Office of Management and Budget (OMB). Its "Circular A–130, Management of Federal Information Resources" requires cost-benefit analysis of government information activities, and requires reliance on the private sector to disseminate government information and recover costs by charging users (American Library Association [ALA] 1991). If the information decision making of the OMB is strictly centered on financial aspects, the philosophical, pedagogical, and social benefits, which are not easily measured, may be underestimated. The end result will be the publication of material that makes a profit, not necessarily the publication of material of most value.

The trend toward the privatization of information and removing the responsibility for producing documents from the GPO may be equally problematic. This trend was accelerated during the Reagan administration, but it has continued. Since 1982 one-fourth of the 16,000 publications produced by the government has been eliminated (ALA 1991). The privatization of public information has far-reaching effects, and there are arguments for this trend on both sides. These arguments have, in part, been summarized by a major federal governmental commission, the National Commission on Libraries and Information Science (NCLIS) (1981, pp. vii–ix). NCLIS is a "permanent federal agency charged with advising the President and the Congress on policy matters relating to library and information services" (White House Conference 1991).

Pro-Privatization

1. Our society is founded on the traditional view that individual freedom and initiative, expressed through competitive private enterprise, are the best means of supplying the products and services needed by society.
2. Government entry into the marketplace can have a chilling effect on private sector investment in the generation, collection, and distribution of information.
3. When the government enters the marketplace, it interferes with the ability of the market mechanism to allocate resources to the optimum production of goods and services.
4. The private sector, if not threatened by the anti-competitive effects of government in the marketplace, can widen the distribution of government information as well as information from other sources.

Anti-Privatization

On the other hand, NCLIS has also identified the reasons why privatization is not desirable:

1. There is a need to ensure equitable, open access by the general public to information that has been generated, collected, processed, or distributed with taxpayer funds.
2. To participate fully in our democratic society, citizens must be informed and aware, regardless of their ability to pay for needed information.

3. Information needs that are not served by the marketplace must be met by the government.
4. The government has a role to play in stimulating the development of information as a resource for dealing with societal problems.

The concern over private publication of public information might be expressed in another way: private publication relies on a profit motive. This means that information that does not have a sufficiently clear market for making a profit may not be published. If the basis for publication is projected sales, a considerable amount of information may be restricted. Even if an item with poor sales potential is published, the price is bound to be high, which also may make access or acquisition prohibitive. This fact is exemplified in the publication of the *Federal Statistical Directory*. When published privately, the price tripled in the first year and was more than five times more expensive in the second. At the same time, it was removed from the Depository Library Program, which prevented depository libraries from acquiring it at no cost (ALA 1988). Furthermore, private publishers are permitted to copyright their version of the material even though the GPO cannot. Information produced privately is also exempt from the Freedom of Information Act. Such conditions may seriously restrict the ability of individuals to consult these documents, or even after consultation, to easily and inexpensively disseminate the information to others.

National Security Issues

An important area in which the government wants to restrict information as a matter of policy is information that could threaten the security of the nation. A recent manifestation of this desire is the establishment of the Department of Homeland Security.

HOMELAND SECURITY

September 11, 2001, or "9–11" produced shockwaves throughout the United States and the world. Because it demonstrated that the United States was vulnerable to a major terrorist attack, it precipitated a reevaluation of our national security system. This reevaluation has substantial impact in many areas including information access. Only a month after the destruction of the Twin Towers, on October 8, 2001, President George W. Bush established the Office of Homeland Security (OHS) within the White House. This office developed the first *National Strategy for Homeland Security*. The strategy consists of three objectives: "prevent terrorist attacks within the United States; reduce America's vulnerability to terrorism; and minimize the damage and recover from attacks that do occur" (Office of Homeland Security [OHS] 2002, p. vii). The policies and actions recommended in the national strategy related to many aspects of American life including protection of the critical infrastructure of the United States This infrastructure was defined in the Patriot Act (see the next section below) as "systems and assets, whether physical or virtual, so vital to the United States that the incapacity or destruction of such systems, and assets would have a debilitating impact on security, national economic security, national public health or safety, or any combination of those matters." The information and telecommunications sector were identified as part of that vital infrastructure, because it connects other critical sectors and is essential for the economic growth and development of the country.

The Office of Homeland Security placed high priority on the creation of laws that might assist in protecting the United States from terrorist acts. Among the major information-related initiatives proposed are those related to the following: (1) quick and efficient sharing of information regarding the cyber-infrastructure (with concomitant limitations of the same information to the public); (2) improving information sharing among intelligence and law enforcement (OHS, p. 48); (3) integrating information sharing across the federal government; (4) integrating information sharing among federal, state, and local government and law enforcement; and (5) adopting common "metadata" standards for data related to homeland security (OHS, pp. 55–58). Subsequent to the report, in November 2002 the Department of Homeland Security (DHS) was created as a Cabinet-level agency uniting 22 federal entities under the leadership of a secretary. The Secretary of the DHS was given significant responsibilities for developing a national plan to secure cyberspace.

Protecting the "cyber-infrastructure" was and is a high priority for the DHS. As a consequence, in 2002 the President created the Critical Infrastructure Protection Board (CIPB). CIPB is composed of representatives from government and the private sector and was originally charged with creating a "National Strategy to Secure Cyberspace." This strategy is intended to make secure all levels of cyberspace from the home and office to global networks. Its report was issued in February 2003. CIPB views cyberspace as the "nervous system" of the critical infrastructure of the country (Critical Infrastructure Protection Board

[CIPB] 2003, p. vii.). Yet, CIPB observes that "Without a great deal of thought about security, the Nation shifted the control of essential processes in manufacturing, utilities, banking, and communication to networked computers" (CIPB 2003, p. 5). This shift has left the U.S. cyber-infrastructure vulnerable despite current and concerted efforts to install virus protections, firewalls, and intrusion detection devices. Consequently, the strategic objectives of the national strategy to secure cyberspace are to "prevent cyber attacks against America's critical infrastructures; reduce national vulnerability to cyber attacks; and, minimize damage and recovery time from cyber attacks that do occur" (CIPB 2003, p. viii). These objectives are to be accomplished through developing a comprehensive national plan for securing information technology and telecommunications systems, providing crisis management support when and where threats exist, providing technical assistance to the private sector, improving coordination of federal agencies to provide warning and advice about protective measures, and conducting and funding research and development to help secure the technological infrastructure (CIPB 2003).

Whenever the government becomes involved in regulating the flow of information, no matter how noble the reason, a variety of issues arise. The Office of Homeland Security has recognized that there are privacy considerations as well as open access ones. However, the OHS notes that a balance must be struck between the needs of national security and the privacy and information access rights of the citizenry.

Of particular concern to the OHS is protecting the "Critical Information Infrastructure" (CII). Generally much scientific, technical, and economic information, including government information, is readily available either directly from the federal government on its Web sites or through government documents in local libraries. There is concern by the OHS that much of this information could be used by terrorists to inflict damage on essential governmental facilities. For this reason, the federal government has either recalled or removed information from public access, including information from the U.S. Geological Survey on water supplies, Department of Energy reports, and risk management plans from the Environmental Protection Agency (ALA 2003). Recently, the Department of Homeland Security has proposed regulations that broadly attempt to control access to this information by creating a new "protected" status and security category, "Sensitive Homeland Security Information." The OHS observes that:

> In making decisions about this category of information–such as whether
> to make it available on agency web sites–agencies must weigh the ben-
> efits of certain information to their customers against the risks that freely-
> available sensitive homeland security information may pose to the
> interests of the Nation. (OHS, p. 56)

The American Library Association and other organizations are deeply concerned about the withdrawal or restriction of government information and the effects of broad and indiscriminate application of a "protected" status to a wide range of information that would otherwise be available to the public. Government publications and access to government information electronically play a critical role for librarians and the citizenry. Decisions related to its availability and control determine what information people do and do not get. A variety of issues have been raised, especially by the Government Documents Round Table (GODORT) of ALA, particularly since the events of September 11, 2001, terrorist attacks. These concerns resulted in the appointment of a special ALA Task Force on Restrictions on Access to Government Information (RAGI). The report, completed in June 2003, expressed serious reservations about current government policy related to access to government information. It said in part:

> While acknowledging the need on the part of government to consider
> potential security risks when making public information available for
> access, it is the conclusion of the Task Force that recent federal govern-
> ment actions limiting access promote a climate of secrecy tending to upset
> the delicate balance between the public's need to access government
> information and perceived national security concerns. (ALA 2003, p. 4)

Of particular concern was a memorandum by Attorney General Ashcroft instructing executive agencies to interpret narrowly the Freedom of Information Act. The result of such a recommendation could have the effect of significantly reducing access to important information by the public. The task force was also concerned about an additional memorandum (the Card Memorandum) which tightened classification standards and even permitted the classification of materials that had not been previously classified. The task force issued ten recommendations which, when taken as a whole exhorted ALA vigorously to oppose attempts to restrict access to government information on the basis of national security assertions, to monitor activities that lead to restrictions, and to stimulate advocacy on the part of librarians to protect the rights of patrons to government information (ALA 2003).

Additional concern has arisen because of apparent attempts by local OHS personnel to remove or otherwise restrict access to government materials in public libraries. For example, in March 2003, local Homeland Security agents came to the Bluffton (OH) Public Library and the Lima (OH) Public Library to remove Haz-Mat and emergency-plan documents. These actions were taken without prior consultation with the libraries (ALA 2003).

As a consequence of many of these concerns, the ALA adopted two resolutions in 2003 ("Resolution on Withdrawn Electronic Government Information" and the "Resolution on Security and Access to Government Information") at its annual conference on June 25, 2003.

The USA Patriot Act

One of the direct consequences of the terrorist attack on September 11, 2001, was the passing of the USA Patriot Act. The act, signed by President George W. Bush on October 26, 2001, less than two months after the attack, amended at least 15 different statutes and has a variety of provisions dealing with such areas as tracking and intercepting communications, conducting foreign intelligence investigations, money laundering, and dealing with alien terrorists and victims. The law created a broadly defined new crime of "domestic terrorism," expanded the authority of domestic investigative agencies (such as the FBI) and broadened powers related to wiretaps, search warrants, pen/trap orders, and subpoenas. There are several provisions that could be applied to libraries, and the American Library Association and other library organizations have expressed serious concern about potential violations of patron's First Amendment or privacy rights.

Of great concern are the provisions of the act that amend the Foreign Intelligence Surveillance Act (FISA). FISA permits surveillance in the United States by foreign intelligence agencies and creates a Foreign Intelligence Surveillance court composed of selected federal judges. This court has the power to authorize FBI agents involved in foreign intelligence investigations to wiretap, search, or use pen/trap devices that can secretly identify the addresses of telephone calls to and from a particular phone. It also authorizes "roving wiretaps" that can trace a single person's communication on a variety of devices regardless of place. Hence one could track an individual's communication from a public phone, or an e-mail to a friend's computer, or track that individual's activity on a public library computer. In other words, it focuses on the person, not the place. This has raised serious Fourth Amendment search-and-seizure concerns. Ironically, FISA was enacted in 1978 as a reaction to disclosures that the FBI had conducted extensive surveillance of U.S. citizens over the previous two decades. The act was intended to regulate and restrict FBI conduct in this area (Minow 2002).

The Patriot Act significantly expanded the power of FISA. This included the broadening of the definition of "business records" that can be searched. Originally, the records were clearly defined such as those coming from a common carrier (such as airline, bus company), vehicle rental agencies, or businesses that provided public accommodations (such as hotels). The Patriot Act (Section 215) expanded this definition to "any relevant tangible item" which could include books, circulation records, or electronic records of Internet searches in libraries. If a request for such a record is made under the Patriot Act, *the request must be kept secret*; because of this "gag," the subject of the inquiry may not be informed, and there can be no general discussion of the incident with other librarians. Similarly, there is concern that such requests for library records can be authorized under the Patriot Act without the traditional finding of *"probable cause."* Rather, the FBI merely has to assert to the Foreign Intelligence Surveillance court that the information is needed as part of an ongoing investigation into terrorism. Such an assertion is done in a secret proceeding.

Requests for data on the actual number of times such requests have been made to libraries from the Department of Justice were met with the response that the information is classified. However, in fall 2003, Attorney General Ashcroft reported that no requests under Section 215 had been made to libraries, although he did not rule out making such requests in the future. Although Section 215 had not been used, in May 2003 the House Judiciary Committee reported that the FBI had visited about 50 libraries under the Patriot Act (FBI Has Visited 2003). The ALA and other organizations have been active to try to exempt bookstores and libraries from FISA court orders. If successful, attempts to get library and bookstore records would have to be pursued through regular court-ordered warrants with the concomitant standards for probable cause.

The response from many quarters from the library community has been strong in challenging the provision. The intensity of their reaction to this provision of the act prompted a response from Attorney General Ashcroft, who asserted that librarians had been "duped" into thinking Section 215 is a threat, and accused the ALA of fueling "baseless hysteria." On the other hand, librarian's concerns have also prompted several pieces of proposed legislation that would exempt bookstores and libraries from this provision of the act and a suit by the American Civil Liberties Union (ACLU) challenging the constitutionality of the provision.

The overall fear concerning the Patriot Act is that the normal checks and balances to protect individual rights have been eliminated. Because libraries have had a mixed experience with the FBI, especially with its Library Awareness Program of the 1970s and 1980s (see the next section below), the ALA has developed a series of policies and procedures to deal with the Patriot Act. These include the "Resolution Reaffirming the Principles of Intellectual Freedom in the Aftermath of Terrorist Attacks," "Privacy: An Interpretation of the Library Bill of Rights," and "Resolution on the USA Patriot Act and Related Measures that Infringe on the Rights of Library Users." This last resolution, adopted in January 2003, condemns the use of governmental power to suppress the free and open exchange of information and free inquiry, and exhorts libraries and librarians to support open access and user privacy. It further encourages libraries to inform their staff and public regarding the impact of governmental surveillance on their library activities.

LIBRARY AWARENESS PROGRAM

The provisions of the USA Patriot Act are not the first to worry librarians and raise concern over the investigatory powers of government. Unbeknownst to the library community, in the 1970s the Federal Bureau of Investigation launched a program known as the Library Awareness Program. This program was initiated because U.S. intelligence agencies had become concerned about foreign agents gathering unclassified scientific and technical information that could give them a technological edge. They believed that libraries were a fertile source for such information (Schmidt 1987). They also believed that libraries could be a source of recruitment for foreign agents. Consequently, the FBI began making inquiries in libraries around the country regarding the use of libraries by foreigners. Librarians became aware of it in June 1987, when two FBI agents came to the Math and Science Library at Columbia University. According to Schmidt's account, these agents asked a clerk questions about the use of the library by foreigners. A librarian who heard the conversation referred the agent to the head of the library. The head librarian reported this contact to the New York Library Association Intellectual Freedom Committee, which in turn reported it to the ALA. This led to an ALA investigation and subsequent Congressional hearings. The FBI agreed to discontinue the program but did not guarantee that it would not be started again.

National security is an important issue in our society, but so is the concern that the rationale of national security not be employed simply to suppress embarrassing information or to impede the free flow of ideas unnecessarily. Balancing these important interests will remain a challenge for all.

Transmission and Control of Information Across National Boundaries

The ability to disseminate information globally has raised some important questions. In a world in which satellites can instantaneously transmit information, in which substantial electronic computer storage is both practical and economical, and in which this information can be transmitted and retrieved by microcomputers in homes around the world, the globalization of information raises deep issues about the impact of the spread and control of such information. Although there may be many reasons to control dissemination of information, the United Nations has asserted an underlying principle that is familiar to all Americans. In its Universal Declaration of Human Rights, Article 19, it states:

> Everyone has the right to freedom of expression and opinion. This right includes freedom to hold opinions without interference and to seek, receive, and impart information and ideas through any media regardless of frontiers.

The international exchange of information is sometimes referred to as transborder data flow (TDF) and concerns itself primarily with the flow of digital information across borders for storage or processing in foreign computers. There are a variety of personal, economic, national, and sociocultural issues to be dealt with, which can only be briefly identified here.

PERSONAL ISSUES

Because individual records throughout the world are stored on computer systems, it has become common to transmit this information to various organizations both private and governmental. Attempts have been made, especially in Europe, to control the unnecessary transmission of personal information across national borders so that individual rights are protected at the same time that necessary information can be transmitted (Bortnick 1985).

ECONOMIC ISSUES

The information industry is worth billions of dollars, and nations naturally compete to dominate this market. This leads to international issues such as tariff and trade regulations that restrict or encourage the flow of information and information technologies. Similarly, different countries may impose special standards on equipment or insist on a pricing structure inconsistent with the producer (Bortnick 1985). Of considerable interest is placing tariffs on the information itself, not just on the equipment or information products used to transmit it.

NATIONALISTIC ISSUES

The concerns over national issues related to TDF have grown over the years. Among those is the fear of a foreign national dominating the information resources of one's country, usually the United States, but it could also imply other countries and multinational corporations. There is always a temptation on the part of a country to jump ahead by importing technologies, software, and information from another country. This usually means adopting the hardware, software, language, and cultural assumptions of the country that provides these means. Similarly, the importing of information technologies may inhibit a country's ability to create its own infrastructure to produce its own technologies. As nations become increasingly dependent on the technologies of another nation, this may be perceived as a potential threat to its sovereignty. Similarly, countries may define public and private information differently. Information readily and legally available in one country may not be legally available in another (for example, information on drugs or sexuality). Given the ease by which electronic information can be transmitted, this can generate much national concern.

Another issue is the protection of national-security information from electronic intrusion by another country. Electronic storage of highly sensitive government information is now common in many countries, and the fear that the information may be accessed and transmitted across international borders is a common and important consideration.

SOCIOCULTURAL ISSUES

Technologies transform fundamental values, assumptions, and activities within society. The introduction of such technologies that are not consistent with these values and assumptions may create social and cultural dislocations that are unanticipated and undesired. Could the introduction of information technologies increase the capacity of government leaders to control their populations? Could such technologies change the economic basis of a society from rural to urban? Could devoting fiscal and human resources to building a technological infrastructure divert needed resources from other vital activities such as agriculture or education?

The importation of new technologies from one country to another can also raise serious concerns about undue cultural influence or dominance. There is a fear that such technologies can influence populations through the messages that are received. Thus a developing nation, for example, may fear the influence and effect of technologies imported from a Western nation, especially in terms of the developing nation's own culture and traditional values.

Attempts to Control Artistic and Other Individual Expression

The government has attempted in a variety of ways to control the flow of certain types of information and expression. It has restricted information that is harmful to national security, libelous, slanderous, or which could incite individuals to violence. Among the other categories it has tried to limit are artistic expression, expression in opposition to the U.S. government, and sexually explicit materials.

ARTISTIC EXPRESSION

There is a long history in the United States of attempts to censor books, plays, and works of art. The suppression of such material has been of great concern to libraries. Although some works that were suppressed have been of questionable artistic merit, there are many other items that have reached the status of literary classics such as James Joyce's *Ulysses* and J.D. Salinger's *Catcher in the Rye*. Usually, it is obscenity statutes and postal regulations that have been used to regulate this type of information. Other tactics have also been used to limit artistic expression. Most notably, pressure has been put on funding federal programs such as the National Endowment of the Arts (NEA) because of objection to the content of some of the projects funded. Funding for NEA has been held up periodically and provisions of NEA law have been changed in an attempt to prevent what some view as offensive content. It is doubtful that attempts to use information policies to suppress artistic expression will abate in the near future. Attempts to regulate the content on the Internet through legislation (such as the Children's Internet Protection Act) are another example of this continued scrutiny.

EXPRESSION IN OPPOSITION TO THE U.S. GOVERNMENT

A variety of State Department, postal, and import regulations have been used to bar either speakers or information from entering the United States when the information provided is considered contrary to the interests of the U.S. government. Foreign nationals, for example, have been prevented from speaking at conferences, for example, members of the Irish Republican Army (IRA). Similarly, films considered to be propaganda have been prohibited. Some years ago this happened to a Canadian film on acid rain that was in opposition to the Reagan administration's view that acid rain was not a serious problem.

SEXUALLY EXPLICIT MATERIAL

Federal, state, and local laws usually prohibit the production, importation, and mailing of obscene materials. These federal laws have shaped a complex, sometimes opaque, policy. It is clear, for example, that child pornography is not permitted in our society. On the other hand, explicit sex-education books showing nude children might also be construed as obscene under the laws. Information policy on sexual information remains a confused matter because of court interpretations on obscenity laws. Because determination of obscenity is based on community standards, it is hard to know what material can be restricted and what cannot. What is clear is that laws are used to try to define and restrict such material.

Copyright or Intellectual Property Rights

One of the most complex legal and ethical issues facing information creators, disseminators, organizers, and users is the issue of copyright and intellectual property. Intellectual property includes a variety of products, including patents, trademarks, and publications (print, electronic, and audiovisual). Of course, a major issue in the field of library and information science is the copyright of publications. Central to this concern is determining to what extent the creator or publisher of information can control the copying and use of that information by others. This has been further complicated with the development of the Internet, which is changing our notion of "publication." Does something become a publication once it is available on the Internet? Given the ease with which versions can be changed, which version is copyrighted and how can it be protected? ALA considers this such a serious issue that one provision of its Code of Ethics is specifically devoted to respect for intellectual property rights, and the Association of Research Libraries has its own statement on this issue as well.

It is important to realize that the purpose of the copyright law is based on the power granted to the federal government in the U.S. Constitution. It states that the Congress has the power to "promote the Progress of Science and useful Arts, by securing for limited Times to Authors and Inventors the exclusive Right to their respective Writings and Discoveries" (U.S. Constitution, Article I, Section 8, Clause 8). The basic idea is that by rewarding individuals for their creative efforts, the society benefits.

This benefit cannot be assumed in each and every case, and from a constitutional perspective, information policies must consider a balance between the interests of those who deserve to profit from their ideas and creations and the rights of individuals to have access to and use of information. This balance can be very difficult to obtain, especially given the political power of the for-profit sector. Sometimes, it seems as though the current attitude is that the copyright law is primarily to protect the economic interests of publishers and producers. This tension has created considerable controversy. Librarians find themselves in the center of this controversy because they depend on authors and producers of information to maintain the reservoir of knowledge so critical to library functions. On the other hand, librarians also have a strong conviction that information access, either physical or electronic, should be available at minimum or no cost to the user. Hence librarians favor very generous copying privileges, and producers favor restricted ones.

The constitutional objective of promoting developments in the useful arts and sciences and rewarding creators for their original ideas is codified in federal law through the U.S. Copyright Act, its most recent version being passed in 1976. The act does not deal with the ideas themselves, but with ideas once they are "fixed" in some form—they may be fixed in a variety of formats, including print, DVD, or a record in an electronic database. Generally, copyright ownership resides with the author of the work, unless it is turned over to another individual or organization, such as a publisher. The Copyright Act protects eight categories of works:

- Literary works
- Musical works, including any accompanying words
- Dramatic works, including any accompanying music
- Pantomimes and choreographic works
- Pictorial, graphic, and sculptural works
- Motion pictures and other audiovisual works
- Sound recordings
- Architectural works (17 U.S.C. Section 102[a] [1988 & Supp V 1993])

Copyright interpretation has been complicated because so many documents are now made available in an electronic environment. In fact, by the late 1970s it had become clear to information producers and disseminators that the development of new technologies had raised a variety of critical issues. The 1976 Copyright Act does not explicitly identify electronic works as works protected by copyright legislation. However, the act itself does state that

> Copyright protection subsists, in accordance with this title, in original works of authorship fixed in any tangible medium of expression, now known *or later developed* [italics mine], from which they can be perceived, reproduced, or otherwise communicated, either directly or with the aid of a machine or device. (17 U.S.C. 102)

The House Report (1976), however, describing the legislative intent of the Copyright Act, reveals that a broad meaning was to be given to the concept of a "literary work" that would be protected by the act. In fact, the concept includes "computer databases, and computer programs to the extent that they incorporate authorship in the programmer's expression of original ideas . . ." (p. 566). Thus, ideas fixed in media such as DVDs or on a Web site are all subject to the copyright law.

The exclusive rights of the copyright owner are considerable. They include the rights:

1. to reproduce the copyrighted work in copies or phonorecords
2. to prepare derivative works based upon the copyrighted work
3. to distribute copies or phonorecords of the copyrighted work to the public by sale or other transfer of ownership, or by rental, lease, or lending
4. in the case of literary, musical, dramatic, and choreographic works, pantomimes, and motion pictures and other audiovisual works, to perform the copyrighted work publicly
5. in the case of literary, musical, dramatic, and choreographic works, pantomimes, and pictorial, graphic, or sculptural works, including the individual images of a motion picture or other audiovisual work, to display the copyrighted work publicly (17 U.S.C. Section 106 [1988 & Supp. V 1993])

As might be expected, those who produce original works, or who purchase the rights to reproduce such works, wish to restrict copying privileges by others. Librarians, on the other hand, wish to disseminate information as freely as possible. This is usually accomplished by loaning the material or making copies (or permitting others to make copies) of materials. The right to perform these functions is currently defined under two doctrines in the copyright law, the Right of First Sale and the doctrine of fair use.

RIGHT OF FIRST SALE

The Right of First Sale is the fundamental right that permits libraries and others to loan copyrighted materials to others. Under this right, the owner of a lawfully made copy is authorized "without the authority of the copyright owner, to sell or otherwise dispose of the possession of that copy . . . " (17 U.S.C., Section 109 [a] [1988]). The model by which libraries operate today and have operated in the past, is that they purchase an item (for example, book, periodical, film) and, once they have purchased it, they can subsequently loan that item without remunerating the copyright owner. The Right of First Sale supports the fundamental notion of "subsidized browsing" so important to libraries. That is, library funds are expended to purchase the item, hence, subsidizing the use by the library patrons. It is critical to keep this in mind, because electronic dissemination of information is substantially altering this notion. The implications of this will be discussed below.

FAIR USE

The doctrine of fair use, which has been developed over many years, identifies uses of copyrighted material that fall outside the control of the copyright owner. When an individual makes a copy under the fair-use doctrine, he or she is not required to get permission from the copyright owner. The complexity and subtleties involved in interpreting when a use is "fair use" are tremendous, and there is little doubt that with the introduction of electronic access, the issue will become even more complicated. The key provision of the Copyright Act is Section 107, which identifies four specific criteria that must be considered when determining whether a use constitutes fair use. They are:

1. the purpose and character of the use, including whether such is of a commercial nature or is for nonprofit educational purposes

2. the nature of the copyrighted work
3. the amount and substantiality of the portion used in relation to the copyrighted work as a whole
4. the effect of the use upon the potential market for or value of the copyrighted work (17 U.S.C. Section 107)

As a rule, the fair-use doctrine is more likely to apply when the use is noncommercial (used for educational or research purposes) and would have little effect on the profits of the copyright owner. There are many restrictions, however. For example, copying of films, videocassettes, and sheet music have more severe restrictions.

Librarians depend heavily on the fair-use doctrine in making copies for users or permitting patrons to make copies for themselves. An area of particular concern, however, for publishers is librarians making copies for interlibrary loan purposes, especially copies of periodical articles. Librarians, of course, would like to make such copies freely, but it is natural that the publishers should be concerned with loss of subscription income. The copyright law addresses this issue by permitting libraries to make individual copies of most copyrighted works, but not "in such aggregate quantities as to substitute for a subscription to or purchase of" a copyrighted item (17 U.S.C. 108 [g][2]). The law, however, does not clearly identify how much copying is too much. Fortunately, the issue was subsequently addressed by the National Commission on New Technological Uses of Copyrighted Works (CONTU). This commission was created while the 1976 Copyright Act was being drafted primarily to deal with the effects of computers on copyrighted works. However, it also agreed to address the issue of photocopying as well (CONTU 1978).

CONTU consisted of members from the legal profession, librarians, journalists and writers, consumer organizations, publishers, business executives, and officials of the Library of Congress and Copyright Office (CONTU 1978). The end product of their deliberations is known as the "CONTU Guidelines on Photocopying under Interlibrary Loan Arrangements" (CONTU 1978, p. 54). In an attempt to balance the interest of periodical publishers with those of libraries, CONTU attempted to clarify what was meant by "aggregate quantities as to substitute for a subscription . . . " (17 U.S.C. 108 [g] [2]). In doing so, they established a guideline that permitted libraries to make as many as five copies from a given periodical in a given calendar year (CONTU 1978). The guideline applies only to requests for periodical articles published within the last five years. The CONTU guidelines were subsequently incorporated as part of the legislative history of the 1976 Copyright Act (CONTU 1978). As such, they play an important role in guiding library photocopying practices for interlibrary loans.

For copying activities that involve print materials and that might exceed fair use, a mechanism has been established to assist in the payment of royalties to publishers. This is the Copyright Clearance Center (CCC). This center licenses photocopying by corporations and other institutions by creating agreements with a wide variety of journal publishers. Royalty payments are made to the CCC, which then grants the right to make copies of the material. The doctrines of fair use and Right of First Sale have served as important foundations defining the rights of access to information for many years.

With the growth and development of electronic publication on the Web, the 1990s saw concern on the part of publishers and librarians on how to interpret fair use in the electronic environment. In 1994 the Working Group on Intellectual Property Rights, a committee of the Information Infrastructure Task Force originally created by President Clinton, published a report called the "Green Paper." This document suggested that the traditional interpretations of fair use were difficult to apply in the digital environment. Consequently, the working group convened a "Conference on Fair Use" (CONFU), whose purpose was to bring together the users of information and copyright owners to review and discuss how fair use is to be applied in the digital environment, and if possible, what new guidelines for fair use should be created. Many participants were involved in discussions lasting more than four years. Regrettably, the effort produced very mixed success. Guidelines for educational multimedia were developed, and proposals for fair use guidelines related to digital images and some aspects of distance learning were also produced. Several other issues were deferred and the proposal for guidelines dealing with electronic reserves was not widely supported. In addition, the group considered it premature to draft guidelines for digital transmission of digital documents especially for purposes of interlibrary loan and document delivery (U.S. Patent and Trademark Office 1998). Academic libraries, in particular, were concerned that the proposals regarding digital images and e-reserves lacked balance between copyright owners and users of digital images, narrowed inappropriately the concept of fair use, overly restricted access to e-materials, placed unreasonable restrictions on course materials that could be included in reserves, and limited electronic access to too short a term (Association of Research Libraries 1997).

As a response, fourteen organizations including the ALA, the American Association of Law Librarians, the Association of American Universities, the American Council on Education, the Medical Library Association, and the Association of Research Libraries developed a statement enunciating important precepts and goals related to protecting fair use and liberal access to ideas. Among the statements were the following:

> We will work to extend the application of fair use into digital networked environments in libraries and educational institutions by relying on it responsibly to lawfully make creative use of information. . . .

> We will encourage our members to reject any licensing agreement clause that implicitly or explicitly limits or abrogates fair use or any other legally conveyed user privilege. (Association of Research Libraries 1997)

In the absence of firm guidelines for e-reserves, in 2003 the Association of College and Research Libraries (ACRL) of the American Library Association issued a "Statement on Fair Use and Electronic Reserves," which specifically addresses the four criteria for fair use under the copyright act. The guidelines suggest that libraries must "assess overall whether a use is fair" by employing the four criteria of Section 107. In addressing these criteria, the ACRL statement takes a liberal view of the amount that can be copied in so far as it is to meet the relevant teaching objectives of an instructor, and minimizes the importance of the effect such a use may have on the market, if the use is for legitimate educational purposes.

Recent Copyright Legislation/Activities

As electronic publishing and distribution has increased, the producers and distributors of electronic information and developers of electronic devices and software have been increasingly concerned about protecting their copyright and other proprietary interests. Two recent legislative acts are particularly notable:

THE UNIFORM COMPUTER INFORMATION TRANSACTION ACT (UCITA)

Significant concern has been voiced concerning the impact of and protection for electronic commerce, especially copyright protections for software, databases, and Web sites. The Uniform Computer Information Transaction Act (UCITA) was originally introduced as an amendment to the federal Uniform Commercial Code (UCC), which is intended to make commercial state contract laws consistent regarding the licensing of software, databases, and Web sites throughout the United States. UCITA covers only electronic products, such as software or electronically distributed materials, not books or other written materials. Ostensibly, it was designed to promote electronic commerce and update laws and regulations related to software use. Recognizing that a significant and growing part of the economy deals with information technology, there was concern that the current laws were not sufficient to cover this unique and vital area of growth. Although the purpose of increasing uniformity in such laws is usually laudable, UCITA contains provisions which have become quite controversial, and attempts to pass it as a federal law have not been successful. As a result, an alternative strategy has been developed especially by large software developers and sellers to introduce UCITA on a state-by-state basis.

Many aspects of the controversy over UCITA have an impact on free expression and the use of computer software. Among the major concerns are the following:

1.   UCITA makes the conditions set forth in "shrink-wrap" licenses binding. Shrink-wrap licenses are usually included in software products. These licenses set forth conditions of use, but the buyer is not aware of the conditions when the product is purchased and has no opportunity to negotiate the terms. In effect, sellers can hide the terms of purchase until after the purchase has occurred. Similarly, UCITA also covers "click-through" licenses, which are similar agreements that are discovered only after the product is loaded and the purchaser is trying to use the product. In general, the concept of making a contract usually implies that the parties are able to negotiate the terms, but there is no possibility for negotiation with such licenses. Courts have been skeptical about the binding character of such contracts, and UCITA is an attempt by software producers to seek legal support for their proprietary interests.

2.   Because the terms in shrink-wrap or click-through licenses tend to be quite restrictive, the right of fair use normally provided under the Copyright Act is subverted. Similarly, the terms and conditions in the license may permit the monitoring of use, which may, in turn, violate traditional privacy rights afforded to patrons by libraries.

3.   The act, through licensing terms, may prevent "reverse engineering" which permits examination of a computer program or electronic product for such purposes as debugging or developing products that add value to the program or product. Reverse engineering may also be needed to evaluate a product critically.

4.   The act stifles protections for free expression by permitting software producers to create "non-disclosure terms" in their licenses and thus take

legal action against individuals who criticize their products. This provision could substantially limit the ability of individuals to prepare and publish critical reviews of a software product.

5. The act limits the rights of users to sell or transfer licensed software which subverts the "Right of First Sale"under the Copyright Act.

6. The act permits software distributors to avoid liability for damage caused by defects in their software even if those defects are known to the seller but unknown to the buyer.

7. The application of UCITA is unclear if the particular product is a combination of print and electronic, e.g., a book with an accompanying CD.

8. The act allows the software seller to determine the forum in which state legal actions will be considered. Obviously, sellers are likely to select states where the laws are most amenable to them, such as UCITA states. Overall, there is a general concern that the bill seriously disturbs the balance that protects both sellers and consumers.

The argument for passage of UCITA has generally been economic: the State will benefit economically if software developers and producers are able to control their products and benefit financially from their products. Proponents argue that the new electronic age requires the development of new laws to regulate their distribution and use. Opponents, however, point out that the evidence that such a law really would promote substantive economic growth is very weak. In addition, they argue that the Copyright Act is adaptable and applicable to electronic products, and, along with the Digital Millennium Copyright Act and the No Electronic Theft Act, there is no need for additional regulation in this area.

To date, UCITA has been passed in very few states, notably, Maryland and Virginia, and a coalition of libraries, industry, and businesses has formed to resist its passage. As the implications of the provisions of the proposed law have become known, the momentum for passage has receded substantially. Nonetheless, the library community remains vigilant.

DIGITAL MILLENIUM COPYRIGHT ACT (DMCA)

The Digital Millenium Copyright Act (DCMA), signed into law on October 28, 1998, is the federal government's response to two international treaties: the 1996 World Intellectual Property Organization (WIPO) Copyright Treaty and the WIPO Performance and Phonograms Treaty. These treaties were designed to make more consistent copyright protections around the world. The DMCA has significant implications for information dissemination. In general it has been supported by software developers and those in the entertainment industry, while librarians, scientific researchers, and other academics have expressed serious misgivings about some of the provisions.

Provisions of concern include those making it unlawful to circumvent technological protection measures (TPMs) designed to protect electronic copyrighted works, and provisions that prohibit tampering with copyright management information (CMI) systems. Effectively, these provisions attempt to prevent the piracy of copyrighted information and prohibit the dissemination of information that might help others violate copyright restrictions.

Among several DMCA provisions are two critical ones. Section 1201 provides for protections against circumventions of technological measures of copyright owners to protect their materials. It prevents both unauthorized access to a copyrighted work and also prevents unauthorized copying of such a work. The manufacture, sale, or distribution of devices or services that would circumvent such copyright protections is unlawful. Section 1202 is designed to protect copyright management information systems (CMIs). Such CMIs may contain information about the author, title, owner, names of performers, and terms and conditions of use. Removing or altering such systems is unlawful under this section. The act does provide some exemptions for law enforcement, and for libraries under very limited conditions (U.S. Copyright Office 1998).

Although the act on its face seems to have the noble purpose of protecting the rights of copyright owners, others have argued that there are also some substantial negative consequences. These include the following:

1. Making a single copy of an article is a common practice in a library or other educational agency and is not a violation of the Copyright Act. Rather it is protected under fair use provisions. Yet this type of copying may be effectively prohibited by the software "protections" installed on electronic products. Although one might under fair use be able to make a copy, if a library should attempt to disable the copyright protections to make a fair use copy, it would be in violation of the DMCA. Given the vast amount of information that is available now and in the future, these technological protections could present a serious barrier to the dissemination of important knowledge.

2. Although the law was designed to prevent piracy of copyrighted materials, some large corporations have used the law to hinder competitors who, by breaking computer protection code were able to engineer products that could be used with the corporation's product. This form of reverse engineering is generally a lawful practice, but the ability to bring

lawsuits under the DMCA creates a burdensome expense to smaller companies. The end result may be a diminution of marketplace innovations.

3. Concern about civil and criminal liability under the DMCA for disseminating information on copyright protection devices has led researchers and others to delimit their discussions of copyright protection systems and publications of research on current security protocols. The effect on lines of research related to such encryption technologies is undetermined, but there is substantive concern regarding the impact on important research in this area.

THE TECHNOLOGY, EDUCATION, AND COPYRIGHT HARMONIZATION ACT (TEACH)

With the rapidly increasing use of distance learning and Web-based technologies for classroom instruction, educational institutions have sought more flexible interpretations of the Copyright Act when the use is for instructional purposes. In general, copyright law provided special and expanded rights to faculty members and teachers as long as they used the materials in the classroom. Generally, however, this applied to "face-to-face" instruction; in the distance learning environment these rights were significantly delimited.

As a response, the TEACH Act was passed on November 2, 2002, as part of the larger Justice Reauthorization legislation. The act attempts to deal with the ability of teachers in nonprofit educational institutions to use copyrighted material in the digital environment of distance learning without permission from the copyright owner, especially in the area of in-class performances and displays. The act expands the rights for transmitting performance of all nondramatic literary or musical works, and the transmission of "reasonable and limited portions" of other performances. The act deals only with materials that would be provided as part of "mediated instructional activities"; that is, it is material that the instructor would be using or playing *in the classroom*. It does not cover digital dissemination of supplemental reading materials. Therefore the traditional concept of fair use remains an additional and pertinent consideration (Harper 2002). Overall, the act liberalizes the opportunities to use and distribute such material, but also sets substantive restrictions and requires the active participation of numerous parties. This is especially true of the educational institutions themselves which must be more active in controlling access, and in developing and enforcing the necessary copyright policies. As Crews (2004) has observed:

> Much of the law is built around permitting uses of copyright works in the context of "mediated instructional activities" that are akin in many

respects to the conduct of traditional classroom sessions. The law anticipates that students will access each "session" within a prescribed time period and will not necessarily be able to store the materials or review them later in the academic term; faculty will be able to include copyrighted materials, but usually only in portions or under conditions that are analogous to conventional teaching and lecture formats.

Among the requirements of the TEACH Act are that only accredited nonprofit institutions are included, the institution must develop and enforce appropriate copyright policies, the institution must provide information materials on copyright responsibilities to faculty students and staff, special notification must be provided to students regarding copyright protections, and transmission of copyrighted materials must be only to enrolled students. This latter point places special responsibilities on the technology officers of an educational institution to ensure that access is limited only to appropriate parties and that controls must therefore be placed on the storage and dissemination of digital materials so they are available only to authenticated individuals and only for the designated period of time. Educational institutions must also ensure that digital rights management systems created by the producers to prevent retention or further distribution of the copyrighted material are not interfered with. Faculty also must ensure that the materials that they select for dissemination are an integral part of the classroom instruction, and that they control or supervise the dissemination of the material.

Librarians are not specifically mentioned in the act, but the role of libraries in assisting faculty and students in distance learning is substantial. Certainly, such functions as digital reserves and services that deliver electronic information to students are closely related concerns. Crews (2004) observes that this involvement can create some substantial opportunities for librarians, including (1) active participation in copyright policies, (2) locating and preparing electronic materials for dissemination, (3) locating alternative materials when copyright restrictions may be too restrictive for some materials, (4) assisting others in the interpretations of "fair use" in the digital environment, and (5) monitoring enforcement and interpretation of the TEACH Act.

DIGITAL RIGHTS MANAGEMENT (DRM)

While copyright and the concepts of fair use and the Right of First Sale have often governed the use of print and audiovisual materials, the growth of digital information and its relative ease to copy and distribute have created new concerns among producers and distributers. The result has been the growth of digital rights management (DRM). DRM is defined by Agnew (2003), as "the documentation and administration of rights for the access to and use of digital works" (p. 267). A broad spectrum of activities related to a digital product are the subject of such management, including access, viewing, copying, printing, editing, or transferring the digital data. At its heart, digital rights management is involved in controlling access to digital information unless special permissions or fees are obtained.

The rise of DRM in some senses is at odds with the traditional obligations associated with fair use. Agnew notes that the responsibility of deciding whether a particular use is a "fair use" has traditionally resided with the user; that is, the copyright holder placed good faith in the individuals using the material to ask for copyright permission when it was required. In general, it was nearly impossible to monitor how most people used copyrighted material. Such a vulnerability, however, is especially problematic in the digital environment where copies can be quickly created, disseminated widely, and altered by anyone with access to the digital information. As the commercial possibilities for digitized information have been realized and information has become "commoditized," the producers and distributors of this information have increasingly attempted to control use of their digital products. Such control could limit improper uses and hence lost income.

The result has been a variety of technological efforts to render it difficult to access, manipulate, distribute, and copy digital information. Often these efforts center on two areas: authentification (making sure that the user is in fact a valid user of the system—for example, is the user actually a faculty member at a university?) and authorization (ensuring that the user has the right to and proper degree of access to the system—for example, has the user paid the required fee, or is use limited in terms of access or ability to manipulate or alter the digital data?). Similarly, a system for the identification of electronic objects is being developed that might also make substantial contributions to managing digital property. This is referred to as the Digital Object Identifier (DOI). According to the DOI Foundation (2003) "The Digital Object Identifier is a system for persistent identification and interoperable exchange of intellectual property on digital networks. It provides an extensible framework for managing intellectual content in any form, at any level of granularity, and in any digital environment." The DOI consists of two parts: a prefix, which identifies the name of the organization, and a suffix, which identifies the specific entity. The DOI is sufficiently flexible to accommodate current identification systems such as the International Standard Book Number (ISBN) commonly used for published books. The number of DOIs assigned is growing rapidly approaching 10 million internationally by 2003 (Paskin 2003). Although the DOI was developed as a digital rights system, it also has much broader potential to assist in organizing objects on the Web. The DOI identifies the digital object itself, not its address; in other words, it is independent and could be searched independently. It is sometimes compared to a bar code for physical objects. However, the extent to which DOIs will be used beyond rights management remains to be seen.

There is little doubt that those who produce digital information have rights and interests in protecting the fruits of their labors. The problem resides in the fact that such controls may also inhibit what would normally be considered fair use of such material. In other words, the digital technologies used to control access subvert the types of access that are otherwise considered beneficial, for example, consulting or copying material from a source for educational or research purposes. Similarly, such technologies may inhibit the sharing of digital information, thus controverting the underlying principle of Right of First Sale which has been the historical foundation for library lending. If there is a cost every time digital information is shared, the costs could easily become prohibitive for libraries.

Libraries have a stake in DRM, and it is not merely due to their concern for limited access to digital information. As they increasingly digitize their own information or provide access to digital information, they, too, become engaged in DRM activities. Academic libraries, for example, have restrictions on access to their databases, as do public libraries (must one be a card holder or resident?). In such circumstances special passwords or other controls may be implemented to ensure that the user is authenticated. In addition, as libraries digitize their own collections, they may need to consider whether they are violating copyright by making such material so easily available for distribution and copying. Similarly, libraries have a long history of protecting the privacy and confidentiality of users; yet the need to control access also means that users may be identifiable and the nature of their use may be recorded. Such record keeping undermines the expectations of library users that their transactions are private and confidential.

THE OPEN SOURCE INITIATIVE

A countervailing force to the proprietary interests protected by copyright is the open source movement. This movement, begun in the mid–1980s, relates to the development of software products, including the source code, which are made available at little or no cost through a license. The defining characteristic of open source software is that the license provided to others encourages people to modify and improve the software and make the resulting improvements available to others for further enhancement. Traditionally, when a software company creates a product, they closely scrutinize for copyright violations products produced by others who claim that they have enhanced the original product or created a product that can be used with the original product. Products produced as open source become public rather than private property. This is, in fact, in many ways how the Internet and Web developed so rapidly. As the Open Source Initiative (2003), a nonprofit corporation created to encourage open source activities, explains it:

> The basic idea behind open source is very simple: When programmers can read, redistribute, and modify the source code of a piece of software, the software evolves. People improve it, people adapt it, people fix bugs. And this can happen at a speed that, if one is used to the slow pace of conventional software development, seems astonishing.

Open source software has grown rapidly since the 1980s, and some major products are based on open source software, most notably Linux, a server operating system. Dorman (2002) surmises that open source software may well become a significant computing trend because it has strong ethical, economic, and technical foundations. Certainly, one of the underlying values of librarianship is easy access to information. Any movement that welcomes open access to critical technical information that, in turn, could lead to significant technological progress for all rather than serving proprietary interests, would seem consonant with librarianship's values.

The potential for libraries to employ open source online systems is significant, especially given the high costs of online systems when purchased from traditional vendors. Work on open systems software for library management, document delivery, circulation, cataloging, and e-mail systems has already begun (Mickey 2001). It will take some time, however, for the potential influence of open source software in the library world to be assessed and understood.

Telecommunications Legislation

TELECOMMUNICATIONS ACT OF 1996/COMMUNICATIONS DECENCY ACT

There is no doubt that our society is becoming increasingly reliant on telecommunication systems to create, organize, and disseminate information. The dynamic character of telecommunications has led legislators to recognize the need for new legislation to address the issues that have arisen as this infrastructure has increased in sophistication. One result was the Telecommunications Act of 1996, signed by President Clinton on February 8, 1996. Interestingly, it was signed at the Library of Congress. Two aspects of the act have direct effects on libraries. One deals with the cost to libraries and other educational institutions to use telecommunication lines for access to the Internet. Under what is known as the Snowe-Rockefeller-Kerry-Exon provision, the legislation authorizes reduced rates (e-rates) for libraries, schools, and health care providers for access to the Internet. The implementation of these rates is through the Federal Communications Commission, which on May 7, 1997, created new rules that mandate substantial discounts of 20–90 percent for schools and libraries ("FCC Approves Telecom Subsidies" 1997). More than 30,000 schools and libraries benefit from these universal service discounts.

Another provision of the act, known as the Communications Decency Act (CDA), subjected a person who knowingly transmitted or displayed materials that might be construed as "indecent" to minors to fines and criminal penalties. Indecency was construed very broadly to include words as well as images. This provision was challenged by the ACLU, the American Library Association, and other organizations. The Supreme Court declared this section of the law unconstitutional and a violation of the First Amendment. Justice John Paul Stevens, writing for the majority of the Court, noted that the

> CDA lacks the precision that the First Amendment requires when a statute regulates the content of speech. . . . As a matter of constitutional tradition, in the absence of evidence to the contrary, we presume that governmental regulation of the content of speech is more likely to interfere with the free exchange of ideas than to encourage it. The interest in encouraging freedom of expression in a democratic society outweighs any theoretical but unproven benefit of censorship. (*Janet Reno v. American Civil Liberties Union et al.*)

It is expected that attempts to limit access to "indecent" materials will continue. In fact, a new law, the Children's Internet Protection Act, was passed in 2000 and has already successfully passed its first constitutional test.

CHILD ONLINE PROTECTION ACT (COPA)

The Supreme Court ruling on the CDA delayed but did not deter Congress from attempting to control content on the Internet that it deemed inappropriate. In 1998, it passed the Child Online Privacy Protection Act. In part, the act states:

> Whoever knowingly and with knowledge of the character of the material, in interstate or foreign commerce by means of the World Wide Web, makes any communication for commercial purposes that is available to any minor and that includes any material that is harmful to minors shall be fined not more than $50,000, imprisoned not more than 6 months, or both. (Section 231)

The law required that commercial distributors require credit-card certifications and adult access codes or pin numbers that restricted viewing of adult materials to adults only. The law was again challenged on constitutional grounds and the federal district court determined that the law was unconstitutional and granted a permanent injunction against its enforcement. Ultimately, the Supreme Court heard the case, and sent the case back to a lower court. As of the beginning of 2004, no court had ruled that the law is constitutional and it is not currently being enforced.

CHILDREN'S INTERNET PROTECTION ACT (CIPA)

A third attempt to control access to adult materials by minors was passed by the Congress in December 2000 and called the Children's Internet Protection Act. Under this act, public and school libraries cannot receive federal monies to provide access to the Internet unless they have an Internet access policy, and employ filtering software that blocks child pornography, images that are obscene, or items deemed harmful to juveniles. It should be noted that a complementary piece of legislation, the Neighborhood Children's Internet Protection Act (NCIPA), was also passed at the same time. NCIPA details specific aspects of the Internet safety policy and how it should be adopted.

Currently, the federal government provides substantial fiscal assistance through the E-rate program, which was created by the Telecommunications Act of 1996. Nearly $60 million in discounts were provided in 2002 alone. Another way federal monies are provided is through

Library Service and Technology Act (LSTA) grants to state agencies from the Institute of Museum and Library Services (IMLS). These grants are meant to help link libraries electronically with other social or educational agencies, or promote linking with electronic information networks. Nearly $150 million was appropriated for libraries in 2002 for this purpose, and in 2004, more than 95 percent of public libraries have Internet access. Unfortunately, in encouraging Internet access, the Congress worried that its funds were also being used, albeit unintentionally, to promote access to pornographic sites. These sites were being accessed either by patrons, minors, or adults, who wished to view the materials, or who sometimes left pornographic images for others to come upon unknowingly.

In order to limit such access, the Congress enacted CIPA. The act prohibits a library from receiving E-rate or Internet-related LSTA funds unless it has an Internet safety policy for minors that includes filtering software that blocks visual depictions considered obscene or harmful to juveniles. Certainly, filtering did not begin with the Congressional mandate, and many libraries provide some kind of filtering on at least some of their computers.

In 2002, responding to First Amendment concerns, the ACLU, American Library Association, and other organizations launched a court challenge to CIPA on constitutional grounds. The concern focused on the fact that filters are very imperfect tools for at least two reasons. First, filters block constitutionally protected sites as well as those that might be considered obscene. Second, filters block sites that might be considered obscene for young people, but not adults, thus reducing Internet access to only materials available to children.

Although a federal district court agreed that the CIPA provisions for filtering were unconstitutional, on June 23, 2003, the Supreme Court reversed the federal district court decision in a 5–4 vote. The majority, recognizing a compelling state interest in protecting young people from inappropriate materials, held that CIPA does not impose an unconstitutional condition on libraries, and that the Congress has broad powers to define limits on how its funds may be used. In fact, the Court held that Congress, in making such limitations, was actually aiding the selection activities of libraries in their "traditional role of obtaining materials of requisite and appropriate quality for educational and informational purposes" (*United States et al. v. American Library Association* 2002, p. 3.). It is notable however that the Supreme Court did not deny that filters remove constitutionally protected speech as well as obscenity, but the majority argued that the filters could be easily removed at the request of an adult. The Court left open the possibility of a subsequent challenge if libraries were subsequently unable to disable filters easily or if Internet access to constitutionally protected speech was otherwise burdened in a substantial way.

This decision raises numerous intellectual freedom concerns for libraries. At the least they include the following:

1. The use of filters blocks access for adults to constitutionally protected speech. Although the intent of CIPA is to block materials that are harmful to minors, the current state of technology and the design of filters inevitably lead to the blocking of sites that contain material that is constitutionally protected when viewed by adults. This situation is referred to as "overblocking." The blocking of constitutionally protected speech is anathema to the ALA Library Bill of Rights.

2. The Supreme Court in its plurality opinion did not deny that filters overblock; rather, the justices argued that as long as the filter could be easily disabled, there was little or no constitutional problem. The requirement, however, that filters be easily disabled, does not dispose of the intellectual freedom problem, but diverts it to another equally important concern—that requiring that a patron request that a filter be disabled places a barrier between the patron and the information. Such barriers have been specifically proscribed in the ALA interpretation on "Restricting Access to Library Materials." Although a patron's request to disable a filter may be innocent, it is likely that many patrons would be reluctant to make such a request because it raises the possibility that they may wish to consult material that is sexual or otherwise sensitive. It is analogous to the time when individuals had to ask a librarian for sexual materials that were stored in "closed" stacks.

3. The use of filters blocks access to speech which is constitutionally protected even for minors. Because of the design of filters, there is substantial evidence that they block sites that are totally unrelated to sexual material or other material construed as harmful. The Supreme Court was silent on the rights of minors to materials in libraries, and instead, emphasized the compelling interest of the State to protect them from harmful materials. Despite this omission, the ALA avows through the ALA Library Bill of Rights that age is not to be considered when access to information is involved, and the blocking of sites that are constitutionally protected for minors is a violation of our profession's intellectual freedom principles.

4. The ruling of the Supreme Court on CIPA, although sometimes characterized as a "narrow" decision, may be seen as an encouragement for the passage of new state laws modelled on CIPA. These laws may be written more broadly and erode further the intellectual freedom rights of library users.

Education Legislation

Various library- and education-related legislation and policy statements have a considerable effect on the information infrastructure, including libraries. Among the most notable items are the "No Children Left Behind" intiatives through the Elementary and Secondary Education Act, and the Higher Education Act.

ELEMENTARY AND SECONDARY EDUCATION ACT 1965/1994 AND THE NO CHILD LEFT BEHIND ACT OF 2001

The Elementary and Secondary Education Act of 1965 (ESEA) was created to supplement state and local support to improve the quality of education for elementary and secondary schools, both public and private. Much of the act has been devoted to helping support programs for children with special needs or low income. Title II was the first provision designed to enhance the collections of school libraries and includes monographs, periodicals, and AV materials. At the time of the original passage of the act, nearly one-third of the students in school attended schools without libraries. ESEA helped resolve this problem by providing monies for textbooks, library resources, and other instructional materials. Since its enactment, funds have been used for development of curriculum and instruction, staff training and development, selection and purchase of instructional and library materials for pupils and teachers, setting of educational standards, demonstration of media programs, support of special-education programs, support for at-risk children, materials for bilingual studies, and support for the acquisition of materials in areas of social problems (Krettek 1975).

In 1994 the Improving America's School Act was passed as a reauthorization of the ESEA. This act contained a variety of provisions focusing on contemporary issues facing elementary and secondary education. Among the purposes identified for support were the following:

1. encouraging equal access to a quality education, especially for children in poverty;
2. encouraging parental participation in schooling;
3. upgrading the quality of instruction through professional development programs for teachers, administrators, and other school staff;
4. promoting the development and implementation of technology throughout school systems, using technology to enhance curricula and instruction and for administrative support;
5. providing funds to prevent violence and drug abuse in schools by sup-

porting local organizations and agencies and helping them to develop and improve their violence- and drug-abuse programs;

6. encouraging the use of magnet schools to improve equal access to a quality education and reduce the effects of discrimination on minorities;
7. promoting innovative education programs and practices;
8. developing effective bilingual education programs;
9. ensuring that Native Americans, Native Hawaiians, and Alaskan Natives receive a high quality education while respecting their native cultures;
10. encouraging the coordination of health and social service agencies with school systems;
11. providing funds for improving the physical facilities of schools; and
12. providing technical assistance to school systems and other agencies in developing, administering, and implementing their educational programs (U.S. Department of Education 1997).

On June 8, 2002, the Elementary and Secondary Education Act was again reauthorized, this time entitled the No Child Left Behind Act of 2001 (NCLB). This act is considered a sweeping revision of the ESEA, redefining the role of the federal government in K–12 education. According to the U.S. Department of Education (2003), the act is based on four principles: "stronger accountability for results, increased flexibility and local control, expanded options for parents, and an emphasis on teaching methods that have been proven to work." The act:

Requires States to set challenging State standards in reading and mathematics and to perform annual testing in grades 3–8. Progress must be reported based on race, gender, ethnicity, disability poverty level, and level of English proficiency in hopes of identifying particular groups that may not be progressing as rapidly as others. Data will be made available through annual report cards on school performance.

Provides the parents of students attending schools that are not meeting standards the opportunity to attend better schools and receive funds for transportation to those schools.

Provides students attending persistently poor performing schools with additional funds to obtain supplemental education services from the private or public sector.

Gives State and local education agencies greater flexibility in allocating expenditures to programs covered by ESEA.

Makes a strong commitment to ensuring that all children can read by the end of the third grade. This will be accomplished by supporting the Reading First Initiative increasing Federal funds in research-based reading instruction programs. Additional funds will be provided to local educational agencies for screening and diagnostic assessment of reading ability and for literacy and early language development programs.

Provides funding for demonstration projects that permit the consolidation and flexible use of Federal funds in return for commitment to higher academic performance. (U.S. Department of Education 2003)

Because the NCLB emphasizes reading, student achievement, and testing so strongly, it highlights not only the critical role of teachers, but also of school library media specialists. Whelan (2004) describes the act as a "golden opportunity" and recommends that librarians become experts on their state curriculum standards and then determine how they can form partnerships with classroom teachers to meet those standards. Given the strong emphasis on reading in the NCLB, Whelan argues that librarians can also find strategies to obtain federal funds under the act for library materials. To the extent that school library media specialists can demonstrate that they are essential to meet the curricular standards of their states, they can become substantial beneficiaries of the act.

HIGHER EDUCATION ACT OF 1965/1992/1998

The Higher Education Act of 1965 (HEA) was passed to support the educational programs of colleges and universities. HEA was designed to focus on four areas: improving student financial assistance; supporting services and activities that would help students, especially disadvantaged students, to graduate from high school, enter a postsecondary institution, and complete its program; providing aid to academic institutions; and improving K–12 teacher training at a postsecondary institution (Almanac of Policy Issues 2002).

HEA was reauthorized in 1986, 1992, and 1998. The current titles of the law deal with such areas as promoting teacher quality, improving institutional aid and student assistance, promoting international education programs, and improving graduate and postsecondary programs. Financial assistance to students is a key aspect of HEA, which funds such programs as the Pell Grant, the Federal Family Education Loans, and Federal Work Study.

Additional provisions of the HEA provide assistance to the institutions themselves to improve their academic programs. In this regard, institutions are authorized to support groups that have been historically underrepresented, including Native Americans and African Americans, and certain institutions such as historically black colleges and universities have been targeted for assistance. HEA also places emphasis on teacher training, with funds for teacher education and recruitment programs, and assisting teachers to use technology. The most recent amendments also require that teacher preparation programs report on rates of success of their students on licensing exams, and require the states to report on programs that are not performing well. Recent amendments have also encouraged the development of distance learning programs at the postsecondary level, and created new reporting requirements for academic institutions on the costs of higher education and tuition increases.

The HEA is now due for reauthorization and a variety of issues are currently stimulating debate. Among the concerns of the legislators are the following:

- Ensuring that the available financial aid packages actually provide the means and incentive for minorities and disadvantaged students to attend and complete postsecondary education. This aspect is particularly worrisome as total student debt rises with tuition increases.
- Combating the rising costs of a college education, especially college tuition, by increasing federal aid to students and concomitantly withholding or limiting federal funds from institutions that increase tuition too greatly.
- Developing a means of holding academic institutions that receive federal monies responsible for specific educational outcomes. This requirement might include attaching funding to rates of graduation, licensing, and certification.

Library Legislation

THE LIBRARY OF CONGRESS

Some of the most critical library legislation deals with the activities of the Library of Congress (LC). LC was established in 1800 and is the closest thing the United States has to a national library (especially in conjunction with the National Library of Medicine, the National Agricultural Library, and the National Archives). LC is one of the great repositories of the world, with more than 126 million items, an operating budget exceeding $525 million, and staff of more than 4,000 individuals. Its stated mission is "to make its resources available and useful to the Congress and the American people and to sustain and preserve a universal collection of knowledge and creativity for future generations" (Library of Congress 2003). The use and collection of LC for 2002 is summarized in Figure 4.1.

Figure 4.1
Summary of Selected Data Concerning the
Library of Congress for 2002

Number of on-site patrons and visitors	1,000,000
Number of items in collection	126,060,980
Cataloged books	18,993,274
Nonclassified items	97,371,821
Audio materials (disks, tapes, talking books)	2,614,253
Maps	4,863,681
Microforms	13,352,501
Visual materials	13,740,323
Electronic transactions per month	51,700,000
Number of staff	4,085
Total appropriations	525,837,000

Source: Library of Congress. "Year at a Glance—Fiscal Year 2002." [Online] Available at *www.loc.gov/about/reports/index.html*.

The programs funded by the Congress and implemented by the LC are many and varied. Historically, some of its programs have had a profound influence on librarianship. For example, as developers of MARC, LC transformed and made uniform the bibliographic record, which in turn greatly accelerated the development of bibliographic utilities.

Today, LC sponsors many exhibits, literary events, and symposia, and produces many publications. Similarly, the Copyright Office is part of the Library of Congress, and the considerable repository of materials at LC is primarily the result of the federal Copyright Law, which requires that publishers deposit at the Library of Congress two copies of each item published. Although LC is not required to retain material sent to it, this federal law provides a means of creating a central repository for much of the material printed in the United States. The historical and research implications are manifest.

The Library of Congress's highest priority is service to Congress through its Congressional Research Service (CRS). LC also provides reference services to the public in its reading rooms and through its Web site. In cooperation with the Online Computer Library Center (OCLC), it provides an online reference service called "Question-Point" which provides patrons with a collaborative network of reference librarians throughout the United States, 24 hours a day. A less immediate online reference service, the "Ask a Librarian Service," provides responses to queries submitted online within five business days. In addition, in 2002 alone, LC undertook more than 811,000 research assignments through its Congressional Research Service. It also provides limited services to the general citizenry; for example, it provides materials to the blind and physically handicapped. More than 232 million audiovisual and braille items were circulated in 2002 to more than 500,000 users.

LC has also placed considerable emphasis on the history of the United States through its American Memory Project. Originally begun as a CD-ROM project, the American Memory Project is now an online resource created by LC as part of the National Digital Library Program. The project consists of collections of primary source and archival materials relating to American culture and history. These collections represent a critical contribution to a national digital library. Photographs and documents can be searched full text by keyword. To date, using its American Memory Web site, LC has digitized more than 7.8 million historical items.

Another related program of considerable interest is the National Digital Information Infrastructure and Preservation Program (NDIIPP). For some time LC has recognized that digital technologies produce information that is often impermanent and fragile. Such material may be easily lost, and not easily recovered. Because such material may have significant historical value, LC has served as a pioneer in preserving it. Created in 2001 by Congress with approximately $100 million in funding, NDIIPP's stated mission is to "develop a national strategy to collect, archive and preserve the burgeoning amounts of digital content, especially materials that are created only in digital formats, for current and future generations" (National Digital Information Infrastructure and Preservation Program [NDIIPP] 2003). The vision of NDIIPP is "to ensure access over time to a rich body of digital content through the establishment of a national network of committed partners, collaborating in a digital preservation architecture with defined roles and responsibilities" (NDIIPP 2003, p. 5). Among the activities for the NDIIPP for the next three to five years are to develop cooperative agreements for the selection and preservation of digital materials, develop business models that provide incentives for institutions to preserve digital content, and develop standards and best practices for digital preservation technologies and techniques.

THE DEPOSITORY LIBRARY PROGRAM

The federal government not only seeks information in great quantities, it produces great quantities. As the nation's largest printer, the government produces publications in monumental number and variety. The Depository Library Program is intended to make a selected, albeit substantial, number of these documents available to the citizenry by providing approximately 1,300 libraries with copies of this material. These libraries are both public and academic, and some receive more complete sets of these documents than others. Nonetheless, such a program makes vast quantities of information available for public consumption. For example, in 2002 the Government Printing Office (GPO) distributed more than 30 million government publications in print, microform, and electronic format. In addition, another 31 million were downloaded electronically from GPO Access, which provides free public access to thousands of electronic information products from the government (Sherman 2003). Because of the importance of the depository program, recent attempts to reduce funding for this program have concerned many people. In addition, as mentioned above, with the movement toward privatization of government information, such materials may not find their way to depository libraries. This change would result in a reduction of available information to the citizenry.

THE LIBRARY SERVICES ACT, THE LIBRARY SERVICES AND CONSTRUCTION ACT, THE LIBRARY SERVICES AND TECHNOLOGY ACT, AND THE MUSEUM AND LIBRARY SERVICE ACT OF 1996/2003.

Since 1956 the federal government has passed legislation to foster improved library services in the United States. Originally this legislation was meant to redress the considerable inequalities evident in library services in cities compared to those in rural areas. Consequently, the Library Services Act addressed the needs of public libraries serving fewer than 10,000 people. Funds were funnelled through the state library agencies. The restriction on size of libraries to be served was removed in 1964, and the legislation's name was changed to the Library Services and Construction Act (LSCA). For years, LSCA has been the largest single provider of federal assistance to libraries (Molz 1990). As the title change reflects, the funding was expanded to include not only improving library services, but also library construction. Over the years, a variety of titles (sections) have been added to the bill for potential funding. Until fairly recently, the titles included funding for public library services (Title

I), construction (Title II), interlibrary cooperation (Title III), services for Indian tribes (Title IV), foreign-language materials acquisition (Title V), and library-literacy programs (Title VI). Programs under LSCA were administered by the Department of Education.

In the 1990s regular, politically partisan attempts were made to re-move or reduce funding from various titles, with varying success. In 1995 and 1996 concerted efforts were made to change the legislation to deemphasize construction in favor of developing information technolo-gies. The resulting legislation, however, did not clearly reflect these de-sires. On October 1, 1996, the Library Services and Technology Act (LSTA) was signed by President Clinton. Funds for construction remained the same, while there were decreases in funding for resource sharing and increases in funding for public services, especially for programming for children and literacy (*Slolist* 1996). LSTA reorganized the programs under the old LSCA, placing them under a newly formed Institute of Museum and Library Services rather than under the Department of Education.

The Institute of Museum and Library Services (IMLS) is an inde-pendent federal agency. It emphasizes life-long learning by providing grants to 15,000 museums and 122,000 libraries throughout the United States. IMLS was created through the Museum and Library Services Act of 1996 and reauthorized in 2003. IMLS tries to encourage leadership and innovation in libraries and museums by emphasizing their educa-tion role. The current grants under IMLS are provided to all types of libraries, with an aim toward improving access to information, espe-cially through technology, promoting equal access, and assisting the underserved. Approximately $180 million was allocated for library ser-vices in FY2003. IMLS also sponsors research and convenes forums and conferences that emphasize "best practices." The recent reauthorization places emphasis on a variety of issues, including (1) providing strong support for recruiting and educating the next generation of librarians; (2) updating LSTA to promote access to and sharing of resources, and to promote economic delivery of service to the citizenry; and (3) signifi-cantly increasing State Library Agency grants to promote statewide li-brary services through access to electronic databases (IMLS 2003).

NATIONAL COMMISSION ON LIBRARIES AND INFORMATION SCIENCE ACT

Created in 1970, the National Commission on Libraries and Information Science (NCLIS) is a nonpartisan, independent agency, charged by Con-gress to assess continuously the problems that face libraries and to find ways to harness the potential of libraries. The commission is comprised of 16 members, 14 appointed by the President with Senate confirmation. The two remaining members are the Librarian of Congress and the Director of the Institute for Museum and Library Services. According to NCLIS, the commission:

- reports directly to the White House and the Congress on the implementation of national policy
- conducts studies, surveys, and analyses of the nation's library and information needs
- promotes research and development activities
- conducts hearings and issues publications as appropriate
- develops overall plans for meeting national library and informational needs and for the coordination of activities at the federal, state, and local levels, and provides policy advice to IMLS Director regarding financial assistance for library services (National Commission on Library and Information Science 2003)

Areas of recent concerns for the commission have included the creation, dissemination, and availability of government information in electronic form, and the role of school library media centers in educational achievement and literacy. Following September 11, 2001, the commission also examined the potential role that libraries could play after a terrorist attack or natural disaster. Also, the Commission has developed a Library Statistics Program. This program is a cooperative effort with the National Center for Education Statistics (NCES), the Institute for Museum and Library Service, and the National Information Standards Organization (NISO). The program encourages national collection of library data and helps to develop models of data collection, particularly in the area of network statistics and performance measures for public libraries. Recently, however, questions have been raised concerning the need for NCLIS, and on several occasions the Office of Management and Budget (OMB) has proposed that no funds be allocated, arguing that other agencies could perform the work of NCLIS. So far, the OMB recommendations have been rejected by Congress and funding has continued, but some NCLIS programs have been curtailed (Willard 2003).

INFORMATION POLICY ISSUES IN THE ELECTRONIC ENVIRONMENT

First Amendment/Intellectual Freedom

Freedom of speech is one of the primary rights accorded to each citizen. This freedom protects not only the right to express oneself, but also to receive information. The Internet can certainly be perceived as a new and vital forum to express and hear the opinions of others. In addition, the Internet has been characterized by some as the last area where a "frontier" spirit reigns. It is a highly individualistic and attractive channel of communication; people have felt free to express themselves on any subject in any manner they see fit. Clearly, there is a strong interest in assuring the rights of free speech on the Internet. This implies not only that the content of what people say be protected, but also that the system permit free and open access to the network so people are able to express themselves, and that the system be designed so that effective two-way communication is available. In addition, the network should ensure that, despite its increasing privatization, there will be "public spaces" where people can express themselves freely on the issues of the day.

At the same time, some serious questions have been raised regarding uncontrolled speech on the Internet and the appropriateness of some of the subjects discussed, especially those that involve sexual topics, (for example, bestiality, sado-masochism). Explicit sexual images as well as language can also be found. Similarly, some individuals have expressed highly unflattering opinions about other individuals on the Internet. This type of vituperative expression is referred to as *flaming*. Such issues raise a whole range of questions:

1. Who should have access to the Internet?
2. Should children have access at the same level as adults?
3. Should certain types of expressions or subjects be restricted or excluded on the Internet?
4. What are the legal liabilities involved if individuals send or download questionable material on the Internet?
5. Do obscenity laws apply in the Internet environment? Currently, there are a variety of laws being proposed to regulate certain types of expression on the Internet. No doubt this will be a continually evolving aspect as First Amendment rights are applied to the electronic environment.

Privacy

Marc Rotenberg (1994), from Computer Professionals for Social Responsibility (CPSR), has stated that "protection of personal privacy may be the single greatest challenge in facing the developers of the National Information Infrastructure" (p. 50). Internet communication involves many different activities, including sending and receiving e-mail messages, transmitting and downloading files, participating in electronic discussion groups, and commercial activities involving the purchase and sale of goods and services. These activities take place in the privacy of one's own home or in the work setting. Many Internet users are under the impression that their identities are confidential; in reality, they can usually be discovered easily. To what extent are our communications protected and private? Who can read our electronic messages, and under what circumstances? CPSR has proposed a "Code of Fair Information Practices" (see Figure 4.2) that reflects important privacy and other related concerns (Rotenberg 1994).

INTELLECTUAL PROPERTY

As noted above, traditionally, intellectual property has been protected by copyright laws (as well as patent and trademark law). The properties being protected were physical representations. Today, with electronic access, the producers of information tend to retain control of the infor-

---

Figure 4.2
Code of Fair Information Practices

---

1. The confidentiality of electronic communications should be protected.
2. Privacy considerations must be recognized explicitly in the provision, use, and regulation of telecommunication service.
3. The collection of personal data for telecommunication services should be limited to the extent necessary to provide the service.
4. Service providers should not disclose information without the explicit consent of service users. Service providers should be required to make known their data collection practices to service users.
5. Users should not be required to pay for routine privacy protection. Additional charges for privacy should be imposed only for extraordinary protection.
6. Service providers should be encouraged to explore technical means to protect privacy.
7. Appropriate security policies should be developed to protect network communications.
8. A mechanism should be established to ensure the observance of these principles.

Reprinted with permission: Marc Rotenberg 1994. (Originally published in Rotenberg, Marc. "Code of Fair Information Practices." *Educom Review* March/April 1994, p. 51.)

mation (the intellectual property). Traditionally, the creator of the information sold a physical item (book, periodical), which under the doctrine of the Right of First Sale could then be loaned as many times as the item would sustain the uses. But online access is regulated as much, or more, by licensing and leasing agreements as by copyright. It is not uncommon for such agreements to be negotiated before these services are provided. The agreements set forth the conditions under which the library may disseminate the information and provide a very different context for the dissemination of information from the past. Because these agreements are mutually agreed upon, they are governed by contract laws, a fundamentally different set of laws. Most notably, where the intent of copyright law had the primary objective to advance developments in the arts and sciences, the basis of contract law has no such idealistic motive. Rather, contract law is written to benefit the parties who enter into the contract; benefits to the society at large are entirely incidental. For the producers and distributors of the information there is no need to consider the social issues at all—merely the economic ones. Because libraries often must sign a licensing agreement before they can gain access to the information in a particular product, they exercise far less control over their ability to disseminate this information than under the Right of First Sale. Indeed, if a library discontinues its lease on an information product, it can lose its access to the information, both current and retrospective. Control of the intellectual property thus remains and resides with the producer of the information, and although the fair use doctrine still applies, these rights can be limited by the contracts that libraries sign. The extent to which this control will be maintained in the future may well depend on the policies and practices to be established in the years to come regarding use of information on electronic networks. To address this problem, six library associations—the American Library Association, the Association of Research Libraries, the American Association of Law Libraries, the Association of Academic Health Sciences Libraries, the Medical Library Association, and the Special Libraries Association—developed a group of 15 principles when negotiating licenses for electronic resources (American Library Association, [ALA] 1998). Among the issues addressed are the need for clear statements in the agreement concerning the nature of the access rights obtained, liability or lack thereof for unauthorized use, protection of users' privacy and confidentiality, rights to make archival copies, and protection of rights under the current copyright law (ALA 1998).

The implications for network access, however, remain unclear. The development of digital technologies and the tremendous advances in the development of electronic networks have created an entirely new situation when it comes to copying information. Today, all types of information, visual, audio, and print, can be digitized and stored electronically. This information can then be uploaded, downloaded, and otherwise made available on electronic networks. This information can then be copied many times without loss of quality in copying and sent to literally hundreds or thousands of individuals. The problem of copying and sharing files has become especially notable as it relates to MP3 technology.

MP3, which stands for MPEG Audio Layer III, is a file format that permits the compression of audio files to less than one-tenth of their original size. This compression is accomplished by removing parts of the sound that are inaudible to normal hearing. MP3 technology permits audio files (speech or music) to be loaded and downloaded on the Internet with minimal compromise to the quality of the recording. It also permits the transfer of music on CD into computer files. MP3 players have a download interface and a variety of control features that permit the downloading, playback, and manipulation of the digitized audio file.

The digitization of music into easily transferable packages has raised many issues; most notably the ability to share files electronically permits millions of computer users to share music without purchasing a copy from the recording producers. Stevens (2000) has observed that "MP3 is more than an algorithm, a format, and software—MP3 is a culture, a movement, a religion, almost" (p. 115). Today, there are thousands of sites from which MP3 files can be downloaded, and there are many software and hardware products that support the MP3 format.

Of course, the recording industry has been very active in trying to prohibit the sharing of audio files, which, they argue, is a violation of copyright law. Some court decisions have supported their position, but the decisions are more likely to affect institutional attempts to make such files available, rather than individual users' attempts. Nonetheless, the recording industry has also attempted to reach individual file sharing by pursuing places where individuals may be sharing many files, such as universities. By warning universities that their networks may be supporting illegal activities, the industry is encouraging them to actively limit potential copyright violations by their students. The Recording Industry Association of America (RIAA) has also begun suing individuals who share files, especially those who share large collections of digital music.

Similarly, control over intellectual property in the electronic environment is an international issue. There have been previous international treaties on intellectual property, including the Berne Convention for the Protection of Literary and Artistic Works (1971) and the Rome Convention for the Protection of Performers, Producers of Phonograms and Broadcasting Organizations (1961). But more recent developments in networked communication technologies have made it clear that these treaties are inadequate for the dramatically changed information environment. To this end, the World Intellectual Property Organization (WIPO), an agency of the United Nations, has been active in developing the legal and administrative controls over intellectual property disseminated across international boundaries. In December 1996, at a WIPO conference held in Geneva, a new WIPO Copyright Treaty was adopted. This treaty deals with literary and artistic works, including works of an electronic nature. Among its central features is the extension of copyright protection to computer programs, including their copying, distribution, and rental (WIPO 1997). Interestingly a major issue for debate at the conference was whether accessing a Web page, which requires that the computer store the data in RAM on a temporary basis, constituted making a copy—and hence requiring permission from the copyright owner. After much debate and controversy, the treaty did not grant copyright to this type of temporary storage. In other words, the copy must be fixed or distributable in a tangible form (Blum 1997).

Universal and Equal Access

The Web is now a primary channel of communication in the United States, providing a wide range of information services to homes, offices, organizations, and governmental agencies. But does everyone have access to the Web? Services and products in this society are not equitably distributed. Geographic, social, and economic conditions often lead to inequitable access. Rural areas, for example, often have far inferior access to goods and services, including information services. Equality of access will require that diverse groups have access to the Web, and that access to basic services be available and affordable for all. In addition, opportunities to develop the skills to search the Web effectively must also be widely available or the inevitable digital divide will result regardless of the availability of the Web itself.

Given the ubiquity of Internet access, is universal access inevitable? Although the evidence for some years was that the number of Internet users was growing in the United States, the last few years have suggested that the number of users has leveled off. Will there be a permanent group of individuals who are unable to access the Web? Currently, the cost to connect to the Internet from home is considered modest by many, but for the poor it may be prohibitive. As noted in Chapter 1, there is strong evidence of a digital divide in the United States, a divide that maintains a society of information "haves" and "have nots." If one presumes that in a democratic and capitalistic society access to information is essential to govern and to succeed economically, then the Web should, to a large extent, be barrier free. This means that use of the system should incur minimum or no cost to the user, and should be conveniently available to all. But in order to ensure universal access, it is important to consider not only access to the Web, but access to particular information on it. Given the increasing commercialization of the Web, much of the information on it will increasingly be restricted to those who can pay to access it. This inequity raises vital questions for libraries who can serve as a great equalizer by subsidizing user access to this information.

Interoperability and Stability

The amount of information that is available on the Web is tremendous, but this does not mean that it is easy to access this information. The policies governing the design of the Web must ensure high levels of reliability, possess a wide array of functions, and permit easy access to information. The Web must be designed to be adaptable so that new functions can be added as they are developed. It must also be able to withstand heavy use, natural disasters, and attempts to sabotage the system. In addition, if the Web is to work to maximum advantage, the various computer networks should be able to function seamlessly and promote effective transmission of information between the various networks.

The ability of computer systems to communicate with each other is called *interoperability*. Among many requirements, a key to attaining interoperability is the acceptance of national standards. Many of these standards are currently under development by the American National Standards Institute (ANSI) and the National Information Standards Organization (NISO). One of the most important standards adopted by

ANSI is NISO standard Z39.50. The standard was developed with the cooperation of librarians and computer scientists and establishes rules for the search, location, and communication of certain types of information between computer networks. Its focus is on the search for and transmission of bibliographic and abstracting information and, therefore, has a critical impact on information retrieval functions. Without it, the sharing of electronic information so vital to librarians and researchers would be nearly impossible. The participation of librarians in the setting of these standards has given them the opportunity to have significant input into information transfer standards. Continued participation should provide an opportunity for leadership into future developments (Ward 1994).

SUMMARY

As the value of information increases, there will be more and more stakeholders, each trying to maneuver governmental information policies to serve their needs. Librarians, like all other participants, must actively monitor the information-policy climate and aggressively make their case for the values that they strive to preserve. Because librarians are generally oriented toward service rather than profit, their voice is democratic and represents a vital advocate for the tradition of an open marketplace for ideas. There has been a long tradition of library and education legislation that has supported the role of libraries in this process. But the growth of electronic technologies and the emphasis on the Web as an economic stimulus have created competitors more interested in gain than in universal access. This may be both just and natural in a capitalistic society, but it makes it doubly important that libraries have a place in the information policy debate.

REFERENCES

Agnew, Grace, and Mairead Martin. "Digital Rights Management: Why Libraries Should Be Major Players." In *The Bowker Annual: Library and Book Trade Almanac*. 48th edition. Edited by Dave Bogart. Medford, N.J.: Information Today, 2003, 267–278.

"ALA Lead Plaintiff in Lawsuit to Fight Communications Decency Act." ALAWON 5, no. 5 (February 26, 1996).

Almanac of Policy Issues. "Higher Education Act: Reauthorization Status and Issues." [Online] Available at *www.policyalmanac.org/education/archive/crs_higher_education.shtml*. (Accessed June 24, 2003.)

American Library Association. "Homeland Security Agents Pull Ohio Libraries' Haz-Mat Documents." *American Libraries*, [Online] Available at *www.ala.org/ ala/alonline/currentnews/newsarchive/2003/april2003/homelandsecurity.htm.* (Accessed July 22, 2003.)

———. "Less Access to Less Information by and about the U.S. Government: XVII: A 1991 Chronology: June–December." Washington, D.C.: ALA, 1991.

———. *Newsletter on Intellectual Freedom.* March 1988.

———. "Principles for Licensing Electronic Resources." [Online] Available at *www.ala.org/washoff/ip/license.html.* (Accessed January 7, 1998.)

———. *Restrictions on Access to Government Information (RAGI) Report.* Chicago: ALA, 2003.

American Library Association, Task Force on Restrictions on Access to Government Information. *Restrictions on Access to Government Information (RAGI) Report.* Chicago: ALA, 2003.

Association of Research Libraries. "CONFU Concludes: ARL Rejects Guidelines." [Online] Available at *www.arl.org/newsltr/192/confu.html.* (Dated 1997.)

———. "Lack of Consensus on Fair Use Guidelines: A Hot Topic for ALA and CONFU." [Online] Available at *www.id.ucsb.edu/detche/library/www/ confu2.htm.* 1997

Barlow, John Perry (Internet message): "The Life of Mind." Davos, Switzerland: The Cyberspace Society List. Electronic Frontier Foundation, February 8, 1996.

Blanke, Henry T. "Librarianship and Political Values: Neutrality or Commitment?" *Library Journal* 114 (July 1989): 39–43.

Blum, Oliver. "The New WIPO Treaties on Copyright and Performers' and Phonogram Producers' Rights." [Online] Available at *http://www.voncerlach.ch/ wipo.htm#2A.* (Accessed January 1997.)

Bortnick, Jane. "National and International Information Policy." *Journal of the American Society for Information Science* 36 (1985): 164–168.

Burger, Robert H. *Information Policy: A Framework for Evaluation and Policy Research.* Norwood, N.J.: Ablex, 1993.

Computer Professionals for Social Responsibility. *Serving the Community: A Public Interest Vision of the National Information Infrastructure.* Palo Alto, Calif.: CPSR, 1993.

"Congressional Oversight Committee Reviews Library of Congress." ALAWON 5, no. 28 (May 17, 1996).

CONTU (National Commission on New Technological Uses of Copyrighted Works). *Final Report. July 31, 1978.* Washington, D.C.: GPO, 1978.

Crews, Kenneth D. "New Copyright Law for Distance Education: The Meaning and Importance of the TEACH Act." [Online] Available at *www.ala.org/ washoff/teach.html.* (Accessed January 29, 2004.)

Critical Infrastructure Protection Board. *National Strategy to Secure Cyberspace.* Washington, D.C.: White House, 2003.

Dorman, David. "Open Source Software and the Intellectual Commons." *American Libraries* 33, no. 11 (December 2002): 51–54.

Dowlin, Kenneth E. "Access to Information: A Human Right?" In *Bowker Annual.* 32nd ed. New York: Bowker, 1987, 64–68.

"E-mail Message." ALAWON 5, no. 2 (February 1, 1996).

"FBI Has Visited About 50 Libraries." [Online] Available at *http:// libraryjournalreviewsnews.com*. (Accessed May 27, 2003.)

"FCC Approves Telecom Subsidies for Libraries, Schools." *American Libraries* 28 (June/July 1997): 12.

Government Printing Office. "What is the GPO?" [Online] Available at *www.access.gpo.gov/public-affairs/5–99facts.html*.

Harper, Georgia. "The TEACH Act Finally Becomes Law." [Online] Available at *http://utsystem.edu/ogc/ intellectualproperty/TeachActCheckList.pdf*. (Accessed January 29, 2002.)

House Report. *House Report No. 94–1476, Copyright Act*. In *United States Code: Congressional and Administrative News*. 94th Congress-Second Session 1976. St. Paul, Minn.: West, 1976, 5659–5823.

IMLS. "Institute of Museum and Library Services." [Online] Available at *www.imls.gov*. (Accessed November 17, 2003.)

Information Infrastructure Task Force. *Intellectual Property and the National Information Infrastructure*. Washington D.C.: IITF, 1995.

———. *The National Information Infrastructure: Agenda for Action*. Washington D.C.: IITF, 1993.

International Digital Identifier Foundation. "Introductory Overviews." [Online] Available at *www.doi.org/overview*. (Accessed May 4, 2004.)

Janet Reno v. American Civil Liberties Union et al. Cited in Citizen Internet Empowerment Coalition. "Supreme Court Opinion" [Online] Available at *www.ciec.org/ SC_appeal/opinion.shtml*. (Accessed June 26, 1997.)

Krettek, Germaine. "Library Legislation, Federal." In *Encyclopedia of Library and Information Science*. Vol. 15. New York: Marcel Dekker, 1975, 337–354.

Library of Congress. "Welcome from the Office of the Librarian." [Online] Available at *www.loc.gov/about*. (Accessed May 30, 2003.)

McKenna, Mary. "Libraries and the Internet." *ERIC Clearinghouse on Information Technology*, Syracuse University, 1994.

Mickey, Bill. "Open Source and Libraries: An Interview with Dan Chudnov." *Online* (January 2001). [Online] Available at *www.onlinemag.net/OL2001/ mickey1_01.html*. (Accessed June 23, 2003.)

Minow, Mary "The USA Patriot Act." *Library Journal* 127 (October 1, 2002): 52–55.

Molz, R. Kathleen. *The Federal Roles in Support of Public Library Services: An Overview*. Chicago: ALA, 1990.

National Commission on Libraries and Information Science. "Mission." [Online] Available at *www.clis.gov/about/mission.html*. (Accessed May 12, 2004).

National Commission on Libraries and Information Science. Public Sector/Private Sector Task Force. *Public Sector/Private Sector Interaction in Providing Information Services*. Washington, D.C.: NCLIS, 1981.

National Digital Information Infrastructure and Preservation Program. "Mission Statement." [Online] Available at *www.digitalpreservation.gov*. (Accessed November 24, 2003.)

———. *Preserving Our Digital Heritage: Plan for the National Digital Information Infrastructure and Preservation Program*. Washington D.C.: Library of Congress. [Online] Available at *www.digitalpreservation.gov/repor/ndipp_plan.pdf*.

Office of Homeland Security. *National Strategy for Homeland Security*. Washington., D.C.: White House, 2002

Office of Technology Assessment (OTA). *Informing the Nation: Federal Information Dissemination in an Electronic Age*. Washington, D.C.: OTA, 1988.

Open Source Initiative (OSI). "Welcome." [Online] Available at *www.opensource.org*. (Accessed June 23, 2003.)

Paskin, Norman. "DOI: A 2003 Progress Report." *D-Lib Magazine* 9 (June 2003). [Online] Available at *www.dlib.org/dlib/june03/paskin/06paskin.html*.

Rotenberg, Marc. "Privacy and the National Information Infrastructure." *Educom Review* 29 (March/April 1994): 50–51.

Schmidt, C. James. "Rights for Users of Information: Conflicts and Balances Among Privacy, Professional Ethics, Law, National Security." In *Bowker Annual*. 32nd ed. New York: Bowker, 1987, 83–90.

Science Applications International Corporation (SAIC). *Information Warfare: Legal, Regulatory, Policy and Organizational Considerations for Assurance*. Washington, D.C.: Pentagon, 1995.

Sherman, Andrew M. "United States Government Printing Office." In *The Bowker Annual: Library and Book Trade Almanac*. 48th edition. Medford, N.J.: Information Today, 2003, 66–78.

Slolist@winslo.state.oh.us (State Library of Ohio Listserv). (Accessed October 18, 1996.)

Stevens, Al. "Into the World of MP3." *Dr. Dobb's Journal* (September 2000): 115–120.

Tenner, Edward. "Learning from the Net." *The Wilson Quarterly 18* (summer 1994): 18–28.

United Nations. "Universal Declaration of Human Rights." [Online] Available at *www.un.org/Overview/rights.html*. (Accessed May 12, 2004.)

United States et al. v. American Library Association, Inc. et al. "Syllabus." Supreme Court of the United States. October Term, 2002.

U.S. Copyright Office. *The Digital Millennium Copyright Act of 1998: U.S. Copyright Office Summary*. December 1998

U.S. Department of Education. *Goals 2000: Educate America*. Washington, D.C.: DOE, 1994.

———. "H.R. 6: Improving America's Schools Act of 1994." [Online] Available at *www.ed.gov/legislation/ESEA/toc.html*. (Accessed June 22, 1997.)

_____. "No Children Left Behind Act of 2001." [Online] Available at *www.ed.gov/offices/OESE/esea*. (Accessed June 24, 2003.)

U.S. Patent and Trademark Office. *The Conference on Fair Use: Final Report to the Commissioner on the Conclusion of the Conference on Fair Use*. [Online] Available at *www.uspto.gov/web/offices/dcom/lia/confu/confurep.htm*. (Dated 1998.)

Vagianos, Louis, and Barry Lesser. "Information Policy Issues: Putting Library Policy in Context." In *Rethinking the Library in the Information Age*. Washington, D.C.: GPO, 1989, 9–42.

Ward, Maribeth. "Expanding Access to Information with Z39.50." *American Libraries* 25 (July/August 1994): 639–641.

West, Cynthia K. *Techno-Human Mesh: The Growing Power of Information Technologies*. Westport, Conn.: Quorum, 2001.

Whelan, Debra Lau. "A Golden Opportunity." *School Library Journal* (January 2004): 40–42.

White House Conference on Library and Information Science. *Information 2000: Library and Information Services for the 21st Century.* Washington, D.C.: GPO, 1991.

Willard, Robert S. "National Commission on Libraries and Information Science." In *The Bowker Annual: Library and Book Trade Almanac, 2003.* 48th edition. Medford, N.J.: Information Today, 2003, 103–109.

WIPO (World Intellectual Property Organization). "WIPO Copyright Treaty." [Online] Available at *www.wipo.int/eng/diplconf/distrib/94dc.htm.* (Accessed April 23, 1997.)

5

Information Policy
as Library Policy:
Intellectual Freedom

LIBRARY INFORMATION POLICIES

The general subject of information policy bears a specific relationship to
the field of library and information science. Although not usually discussed in this context, the fact is that the policies and practices that are
established and implemented by libraries regarding the creation, organization, use, and dissemination of the knowledge contained within libraries are themselves information policies, and they have tremendous
impact on the accessibility of information contained within those
libraries.

Organization of Materials and Collections

At the very center of library function is the ability to organize library
collections so that they can be easily accessed by patrons and librarians.
The policies affecting this organization are, therefore, some of the most
important information policies that a library establishes. Generally, as a
matter of policy, libraries use one of two basic types of information organization for their materials: the Dewey Decimal Classification (DDC)
or the Library of Congress Classification System (LCC). These systems
and related systems such as the Library of Congress Subject Headings
and the use of the Anglo-American Cataloguing Rules (AACR2) will be
discussed in Chapter 6.

Selection and Collection Development Policies

Although selection and collection development policies are not commonly thought of as information policies, they are, in fact, the guiding forces in determining the nature and type of information that is provided to library users. Libraries generally employ two basic information policies when building their library collections: collection development policies and selection criteria. These are very closely related but distinct.

A collection development policy takes a broad view of the collection. It answers such questions as: What is the fundamental mission(s) of the library? What subjects should be collected and in what depth should each of the subjects be collected? What types of formats should be included in the collection and what should be the balance among these formats? Who are the library users and what types of materials and services should be provided to meet their needs? What cooperative relationships should be established with other libraries and other information providers? Answers to these questions provide considerable direction to the library. A collection development policy serves many purposes: (1) as a planning tool to determine the use of monetary resources and staff; (2) as a guide to selectors in developing their collections; (3) as a means to ensure that collections are developed consistently over time and through changes of staff; (4) as a means to train new library staff; (5) as a statement of philosophy; and (6) as a defense in case of challenges to library materials (not an uncommon occurrence in many libraries).

Selection criteria, on the other hand, are used to select individual items or small groups of items. Obviously, the individual selections should be consistent with the wider objectives of the collection development policy, but there remains a need to assess each item to determine if it is of sufficient quality, even if it seems to fit within the parameters established by the collection development policy. Selection criteria may vary in complexity from library to library, but there are some conventional criteria.

Authority. Knowledge and reputation of the author or of the organization producing the item.

Appropriateness. Match of the item to the intended users. For example, is the age level appropriate?

Accuracy or timeliness. The accuracy of the content and its currency.

Physical characteristics: The quality of the binding, paper, or material on which the information is stored. The size and quality of the print.

Collection fit. The contribution the item makes to the collection, the appropriateness of the item in relation to the collection development plan, the balance it provides to other points of view.

Demand. The popularity of the item and likelihood of use by library patrons.

Content. The quality of the information or narrative and the clarity of its organization.

Special characteristics. The availability of such features as indexes, bibliography, notes, prefaces, introductions, teacher guides, and interpretive material.

There are many other criteria that might be applied depending on the nature of the work and the format. For example, as more and more information products become available on the Web, additional criteria for selection are required. Although some of the selection criteria above can be applied equally to Web sites, additional questions must also be asked. These include, but are not limited to, the following:

- What does the domain name indicate, i.e., is the Web site authored by one individual, or is it prepared by an educational institution, commercial enterprise, or organization?
- Are there additional links that are useful?
- Over time are the links updated?
- What Web sites "link to" this Web site?
- Can you get into the site easily?
- Does the site download information quickly?
- Can you navigate on the site easily?
- Is there an effective internal search engine to search the site?
- Is the Web site accessible to those with disabilities, such as visual or aural impairments?

In addition, the rise of new information technologies has forced libraries to consider information policies that address the balance of items that will be possessed physically by the library (for example, books, periodicals, videos) and information that will be accessed electronically (for example, by searching information resources on the Web). Further, the decision to access information electronically through sources such as the Web raises a variety of information-policy issues regarding the library's responsibility to control access to some types of information that would not otherwise be selected by the library (for example, certain sexually explicit electronic files) or to impose age restrictions on users of these networks.

Service Policies as Information Policy

The policies that a library establishes to encourage or discourage library use are also information policies. Even the simplest of policies can have significant implications for information access. For example, the establishment of library hours can be seen as an information policy because it affects when individuals can have access to the information. More obvious policies include

- *circulation policies*. Thèse policies include length of loan periods and renewal policies. They may also include the designation of some materials as noncirculating, requiring that the materials be used inside the library.
- *reference policies*. These policies include those affecting the types of services provided and the restrictions on such services. Examples are policies that set a time limit for the provision of reference service to an individual patron or a restriction based on the type of research (e.g., restricting service provided to students doing their homework or restricting the answering of contest questions). They may also include reference philosophy issues such as the belief that reference service should be primarily instructional, assisting the patron to learn how to get to information (quite common in academic and school libraries), in contrast to the belief that reference service means getting the patron the answer (more common in public library adult reference service or in special libraries). Such policies affect the nature of library service and the type of information provided.
- *personnel and staffing policies*. Library service remains a labor-intensive activity. Therefore, the type and size of the service staff have a direct effect on the quantity and quality of information services that can be provided. If a library decides to hire subject experts in a particular field (e.g., business or genealogy), this will affect the use and depth of service provided. The same may be said if knowledgeable children's librarians are hired to develop in-depth children's services.

Preservation as Information Policy

Libraries have many purposes and one of the oldest is the preservation of the human record. Unfortunately, for a number of reasons many library materials are deteriorating. These include poor environmental conditions, such as unstable temperatures or improper levels of humidity; improper handling of materials by patrons and library staff; natural disasters such as fire and flood; and the presence of insects that damage materials. Perhaps the most prominent reason, however, involves the nature of the materials themselves. Most print materials published since the 1850s are printed on paper that is highly acidic. This acidity was introduced by the process used to make the paper. As the years pass, the acid slowly breaks down the paper, making it dry and brittle. The result is that the paper literally crumbles, whether it is being used or not. Many libraries, especially research libraries that maintain materials for many years, are suffering severely from this deterioration, and there is far too little money available to restore or preserve most of these materials. As a consequence, a substantial part of the written record may eventually be lost.

The preservation policies that are established by libraries are critical information policies because in many ways they are decisions as to what ideas or materials will continue to exist especially in the digital environment. Libraries, for example, may have policies on what materials will be microfilmed or repaired. They may have a disaster plan in case of unpredictable natural events like fires, or intentional events such as arson or even terrorist acts. Recently, the federal government increased funding for the preservation of scholarly materials. With the available technologies such as microfilm and emerging technologies involving digitization, more materials might eventually be saved. As mentioned in Chapter 4, the Library of Congress has initiated two major projects to digitize a sizeable portion of its collection: the National Digital Library Program (NDLP) and the National Digital Information Infrastructure and Preservation Program (NDIIPP).

Intellectual Freedom as Information Policy

Most prominent among the information-policy issues for libraries are those related to intellectual freedom. Intellectual freedom issues are implicated in librarianship when a variety of activities are performed, such as selecting materials, not selecting or weeding materials, classifying materials, physically locating materials in the collection, establishing reference service policies, establishing administrative policies such as those requiring confidentiality, and creating policies that directly affect access to library materials or electronic access to information.

Concern for the protection of intellectual freedom is certainly as important now as it has ever been. Some have noted that attempts to censor library materials have been on the rise since the 1980s, and what has become most prominent has been the increased number of groups, in contrast to individuals, that are systematically attempting to influence the character of library collections (Abbott 1990). Such attempts come from groups across the political spectrums. Consequently, the array of materials that have been challenged over the years is quite varied. In 2002 among the most challenged books were J.K. Rowling's *Harry Potter* series, Phyllis Reynolds Naylor's *Alice* series, S.E. Hinton's *Taming the Star Runner*, David Pilkey's *Captain Underpants*, Mildred Taylor's *Roll of Thunder, Hear My Cry*, Katherine Peterson's *Bridge to Terabithia*, and Jean Craighead George's *Julie of the Wolves*. Many of these items are challenged yearly. Among the perennial favorites are Maya Angelou's *I Know Why the Caged Bird Sings*, Robert Cormier's *The Chocolate War*, and Mark Twain's *The Adventures of Huckleberry Finn*. The *Harry Potter* series topped the list of banned books for 2002. The most common reasons for challenges are "sexual explicitness," "offensive language," and "unsuited to the age group" (American Library Association 2003).

Movies have also been challenged. Sex and violence in movies are of major concern, but there have also been some surprises such as *Snow White, The Little Mermaid*, and *My Friend Flicka*. In addition, there have been broad-based attempts to create legislation that would limit the range of materials and services that could be provided through library collections and services.

Attacks on works such as those noted above highlight a fundamental value of most library and information work: the need to preserve intellectual freedom and the responsibility to resist censorship. Censorship is an act or set of acts by government, groups, or individuals (including librarians) to restrict the flow of information or ideas, usually because the content is considered offensive for political, religious, or moral reasons. The Code of Ethics and the ALA Library Bill of Rights (discussed below) place libraries securely within this context. However, intellectual freedom is a much larger concept than censorship. It deals with protecting the free flow of ideas or information. It is based on the fundamental belief that the health of a society is maintained and improved when ideas can be created and disseminated without governmental, political, or social impediment. Such an idea is hardly innocent; in some cases, it may lead to the propagation of heinous ideas with deleterious results. Such a view presumes, however, that the best way to combat a bad idea is not to suppress it, but to produce a better idea, and that the only alternative to censorship is free expression. It also presumes that the generation of good ideas is increased when there is unimpaired freedom to produce them. There are those who fear that some ideas may be so clearly harmful that they should be restricted. These individuals are prone to acts of censorship.

As an issue, censorship and the protection of intellectual freedom are of prime importance to many libraries and the profession as a whole. On its surface, it seems obvious that the former should be inhibited and the latter promoted. Regrettably, the situation quickly becomes opaque. The protection of intellectual freedom is, in fact, one of the most difficult aspects of library work and is the cause of much professional controversy. At the root of the problem are what librarians often perceive as conflicting moral, ethical, personal, social, and legal obligations. Some of these obligations form powerful motivators to restrict access to some library materials, while other obligations serve as countervailing forces, encouraging unrestricted access. By making these forces more explicit, a better understanding can be reached as to why librarians sometimes have a difficult time making decisions on this issue.

OBLIGATIONS THAT TEND TO *RESTRICT* ACCESS

The obligation to act in accordance with one's personal values. Each individual, through childhood training and experience, has developed certain moral precepts that form one of the bases for action. Information providers do not surrender these precepts just because they pass through the doors of the library. This is not to say that information providers should impose these precepts, but it is clear that certain circumstances that occur within libraries are more likely to evoke an interest in applying them than others. A common example would be the distribution of materials that promote bigotry. Librarians could believe that providing such material would be harmful, especially to children, and be inclined to restrict access.

The obligation to protect, preserve, and maintain the values of one's community and those of the society as a whole. As already noted, libraries and librarians do not exist outside the context of the society of which they are a part. Quite naturally, librarians and the libraries perceive themselves as part of the community. Many librarians not only work in the community but also live in it and participate in its many social, political, recreational, and cultural activities. Similarly, most libraries, public and school in particular, depend on local communities in terms of dollars and local friends and boosters. If a librarian values the community, then there is a general feeling that the collection and services provided should reflect its needs and desires. Indeed, the librarian may feel that the promotion of such values is both necessary and worthwhile. Under such circumstances, purchasing materials that represent values substantially different from the community's or that would offend a significant number of community members may seem inappropriate and a source of unnecessary conflict. This would tempt the librarian to restrict such materials.

The obligation to protect children from harm. Few obligations are as indisputable as the obligation of members of the society (no matter what their profession or job) to protect from exploitation those who are defenseless or vulnerable. What group would fall more clearly into this category than children? The society even recognizes that many groups dealing with children—teachers, health-care workers, social workers, university researchers—are obligated to monitor harm done to children and to report such harm to authorities. Although most librarians, as a rule, are not required by law to monitor such harm, it is unreasonable to presume that librarians have no stake in caring for and protecting children. Indeed, a central historical tradition of library work is nurturing children and developing their minds through exposure to books and other library materials. Can one reasonably say that if one believes that books and other library materials can improve children, that they cannot also harm them? This is a common argument by those who wish to restrict materials to young people, and it can be an attractive argument for librarians in some instances.

The obligation to protect the survival of the library. There are few obligations dearer to the librarian than the preservation of the library as an institution, and the survival of an institution is an important factor in ethical decisions. Generally, actions that would threaten the library's survival are anathema to librarians. They are therefore put in the position of making an economic and political calculation when making decisions about the selection, organization, and dissemination of library materials when they fear that the existence and use of certain materials would threaten the fiscal and political support of the community. Libraries are commonly threatened in this way by those who wish to restrict materials. Citizens, for example, may threaten to campaign against current or improved funding for library services.

OBLIGATIONS THAT TEND TO *INCREASE* ACCESS

The obligations that tend to restrict access are not trivial; in fact, they enlighten us regarding the realistic pressures that many librarians face in performing their work. But there are other obligations that are taken quite seriously by librarians and which often lead them to resist the temptation to restrict access to materials.

The obligation to protect the rights of patrons to free access to ideas and information in a democratic society. A value held dear by many librarians is the importance of providing information to those who seek it. This view may be held deeply on both a professional and personal level and often reflects a complementary belief in democracy as the most effective form of government. Holding such a belief requires that the citizenry be educated in order to make informed choices and that being informed means being able to read and view materials with different points of view. In order to make good citizens, the library must provide a variety of ideas. It is a premise of democratic societies that opposing points of view are aired, not suppressed, and that it is up to the people to make a decision. Such a viewpoint means that materials that are considered heinous and patently false may be part of the collection because they represent a point of view present in the society. Swan (1986) notes that we have a commitment to protect the flow of information, whether it is true or false, because a citizen's search for truth in a democratic society means exposure to all types of ideas, and freedom of expression requires that the untrue be heard as well as the true. Indeed, sometimes what is considered false in one generation becomes the truth of another. In this sense, the suppression of untruths can be dangerous to the flow of ideas. Indeed, falsehoods can often be quite useful in the learning process.

This obligation is also viewed by librarians as an obligation to preserve and support the First Amendment of the U.S. Constitution. It is well understood by most librarians that the First Amendment plays a central role in the establishment, maintenance, and protection of libraries and their patrons. The First Amendment forms the foundation of the right that publishers and creators of materials have to produce the products central to libraries. The First Amendment, however, not only provides people with the right to express themselves, it establishes a corollary right to receive expressions protected by that amendment. The library is a primary place for citizens to receive this information, hence the First Amendment protects patrons in the use of libraries and helps defend librarians in their selections. As such, librarians feel that restricting access to library materials contravenes the letter and spirit of this amendment, and restrictive actions taken by themselves and others diminish its authority and effect.

The obligation to educate children. As noted above, librarians feel strongly that a critical purpose of most libraries is to advance the education of the young. Although some feel that this process requires that some ideas be restricted, others would argue that children who are free to explore ideas become healthy adults and better educated citizens. In addition, many librarians feel that the obligation to restrict access rests with the parents alone and that librarians should not attempt to displace this obligation. The obligation to educate children is usually accomplished in libraries through careful collection development, responsive reference services, entertaining and educational programming, and cooperation with outside agencies such as schools and social-service agencies.

Of course, what is meant by education can be a complex concept. Those who wish to restrict access to ideas might argue that education means inculcating the values and behaviors of the majority of the society into the young. Others contend that education involves exposing the young to many different points of view and giving them the decision-making skills to make up their own minds. This argument was a fundamental issue in one of the most important Supreme Court cases on school censorship, *Island Trees v. Pico* (1982). For contemporary librarianship, the obligation to educate children generally has meant that access to information should be unrestricted, and this has been supported by a variety of formal statements from the American Library Association (ALA). For example, in the document "Kids Need Libraries," which was prepared by the ALA prior to its participation at the White House Conference on Library and Information Services in 1990, a set of needs for children was clearly identified (Mathews, Flum, and Whitney 1990). These needs include the following:

- The belief in a worthwhile future and their responsibility and desire to contribute to that future.
- A positive sense of self-worth.
- The ability to locate and use information and the awareness that this ability is an essential key to self-realization in the Information Age.
- Preparation to use present-day technology and to adapt to a changing technological world.

- Equal access to the marketplace of ideas and information.
- The ability to think critically in order to solve problems.
- The ability to communicate effectively—to listen, to speak, to read, and to write.
- Preparation to live in a multicultural world and to respect the rights and dignity of all people.
- The desire and ability to become lifelong learners.
- Creative ability to dream a better world. (pp. 33–37)

These needs strongly imply unimpeded access to materials and information available in libraries, but they also suggest that the librarian plays a critical role in guiding children so that they become thoughtful, well-informed citizens with abilities to discover the information they need for themselves.

The obligation to preserve the values of one's profession. Through formal library education and on-the-job-training, most librarians and library employees become acquainted with the accepted professional standards of library service. In terms of intellectual freedom, these are best expressed in the ALA's Library Bill of Rights and its interpretations. These obligations are also reiterated in the Code of Ethics of both the ALA and the American Society for Information Science and Technology (ASIST).

When such doctrines are properly taught, the library worker develops a strong obligation to provide a wide range of materials that are openly available to all, including children. The preservation of professional values can form a powerful source of resistance when attempts to restrict materials are made—so powerful that some librarians prefer to lose their positions rather than sacrifice these principles.

Central to the preservation of professional values in libraries is the conviction that the selection of materials is based on professional judgment rather than personal interest. Although personal preferences are hard to avoid, what distinguishes professional judgment from personal bias in the selection process are reasonably objective criteria on which selection judgments are based. These criteria usually include the factors listed in the Selection and Collection Development Policies section above. Lester Asheim (1954) has characterized the difference between selection and censorship in the following way:

> To the selector, the important thing is to find reasons to keep the book. Given such a guiding principle, the selector looks for values, for virtues, for strengths, which will overshadow minor objections. For the censor, on the other hand, the important thing is to find reasons to reject the book. His guiding principle leads him to seek out the objectionable

features, the weaknesses, the possibilities for misinterpretation. . . . The selector says, if there is anything good in this book let us try to keep it; the censor says, if there is anything bad in this book, let us reject it. And since there is seldom a flawless work in any form, the censor's approach can destroy much that is worth saving. (pp. 95–96)

Upholding professional values by selecting a wide array of materials for reasons unrelated to personal liking or taste is crucial. The breadth of library collections is a reflection of that belief.

Research on Censorship and Intellectual Freedom

Many librarians respect the principles of intellectual freedom, but find it much more difficult to practice it in the real world for a variety of reasons. Almost any debate on censorship, intellectual freedom, and libraries will provoke discussion over at least some of the obligations noted above. Although the basic value of intellectual freedom is strong in the library profession, individual librarians often feel ambivalent. This ambivalence may, in part, be based on the historical roots of the profession. In the nineteenth and well into the twentieth century, there was little doubt that librarians felt it was their duty to restrict access to library materials or to refuse to acquire materials that were deemed to have an unfortunate effect on patrons—adults and children. The library literature is replete with admonitions of librarians to obtain only the most wholesome materials. As Dewey (1876) noted, "only the best books on the best subjects" were to be collected (p. 5), and there was considerable debate as to whether patrons should be exposed to such works as romances. The women who were hired as librarians at the end of the nineteenth century were expected to represent the values of polite middle-class society and to steer individuals from good to better books (Garrison 1972).

Interestingly, the ambivalence of librarians toward intellectual freedom has been documented in research on librarians for many years. Serebnick (1979) in reviewing the research drew some informative conclusions: censorship in the schools and public libraries was reported in the research as early as the 1950s. The source of school censorship was not just principals and parents, but to a large extent the librarians themselves, often without prompting. In many cases, the librarians simply did not buy books if they thought they would be controversial, or at the least would restrict their access (Eakin 1948; Fiske 1959). In other words, much censorship was self-imposed, associated with the belief that books could actually harm the children.

Serebnick also found that there was considerable ambivalence on the part of librarians, and subsequent research has supported this. Studies of senior high school librarians and public librarians in the Midwest in the 1960s and 1970s revealed that a significant proportion of librarians had weak or wavering views about censorship and that there was little correlation between asserting a belief in intellectual freedom and actually censoring materials (Farley 1964; Busha 1971). Again, much of the censorship was self-imposed and occurred more often with materials that had pictures than with those that were unillustrated. The propensity to restrict materials was greatest among school librarians, followed by public, and then academic librarians; librarians with the stronger educational backgrounds were less likely to restrict materials (Pope 1973).

More recent research has focused on challenges in schools, and provides an enriched perspective on censorship issues. One study, titled *Limiting What Students Shall Read*, conducted by the Association of American Publishers in 1981, focused on a large sample survey of 1,891 public elementary- and secondary-school librarians, library supervisors, principals, and district superintendents using mail and telephone surveys. Many challenges to library materials were reported. Nearly one-third of the librarians reported at least one challenge in the previous year, and in 30 percent of the challenges the material was altered, restricted, or removed. Perhaps a bit different from previous research was that a large percentage of the challenges came from outside: more than 50 percent of the challenges came from parents. About 10 percent of the challenges came from teachers, and 6 percent from the school-board members (Association of American Publishers 1981). In a subsequent study, Hopkins (1993) sampled more than 6,500 U.S. school systems. She found that challenges came from both within and outside of libraries. Challenges from within, especially by principals, were the most problematic, because the item was least likely to be retained in this circumstance. In addition, the political aspect of protecting library materials was also highlighted as Hopkins noted that support from media and outside groups played a significant role in protecting materials from removal. Librarians were found to be most supportive of intellectual freedom when they had a high level of confidence in their own abilities.

Major Concerns of Those Who Wish to Censor Materials

The movement to censor library materials is unabated. What is it that bothers people so much that they believe that people, especially children, should not be able to obtain certain materials in libraries?

OFFENSIVE SUBJECTS

Probably the single most important factor that prompts a desire to censor is content. Content issues can be broken down into two categories: offensive subjects and offensive language. In terms of offensive subjects, two of the greatest concerns are sexual content and violence. This is not to suggest that these are the only themes that lead to censorship attempts. Other content areas are those that appear to undermine the "traditional family," are antireligious, are anathema to authority, are antidemocratic, or offend various groups such as African Americans, Asians, or Native Americans.

Sexual content. Many individuals are concerned that sexual subject matter is inappropriate in libraries, especially if that material is available to minors. Some may argue, for example, that sex-education materials should be provided by the parents, and children's access to them in the library should be restricted. Similarly, some argue that certain materials promote "perverse" sexual behaviors and adversely affect the attitudes of young people. This was the central focus of the debate over *Daddy's Roommate* and *Heather Has Two Mommies*, which were written for children and dealt with the family life of homosexual couples. But objections do not stop with minors alone; sexual materials that are too explicit may not be seen as acceptable for anyone, even adults. For this reason, it is common for censorship issues to arise over sex-education materials or any materials that have sexually explicit images, words, or lyrics.

Violent content. A second content issue is violence. Certainly, this is a subject of great concern to most people. Does exposure to violent behavior in books and films promote unacceptable behavior? There is some evidence that regular exposure to violence may, in fact, harden us (Huesmann 1986). Repeatedly watching people get shot and stabbed diminishes the shock of these disturbing actions. We are less shocked by such explicit violence than we were in the 1950s or 1960s. Are libraries promoting our insensitivity to violence by making available materials that harden us to violent acts? In addition, there is concern in the psychosocial literature that regular exposure to violent material might make us more likely to commit violent acts or, at least, increase our levels of aggressiveness. Libraries, as has been mentioned before, are imbedded in the society. As this society grows ever more concerned with the violence within it, people are searching for those aspects that might promote or foster this violence. Some find library materials to be one of those factors, and their contention may have greater power because the fear of violence is so prevalent in our world.

Offensive language. Another common area of concern is the language contained in materials. The language used in print and AV materials has become progressively colorful over the years. Today, explicit sexual slang and profanity are commonplace in many works. The use of such language, it is feared, serves as a role model for subsequent behavior, especially for young people, and like violence, there is concern that we become used to this type of language in everyday speech.

Concern with Formats

Although the censorship of print materials has been around for thousands of years and continues today, the focus of much concern is within the realm of audiovisual materials. Perhaps what underlies this concern is that the visual medium is especially effective; our visual senses are among the strongest. Therefore, we may be more deeply and immediately affected by what we see on the screen than by what we read in a book. Audio materials have also come under attack in recent years. Lyrics from rap music have been particularly vulnerable to requests for limitation and removal. One argument is that the combination of the words and music makes the message much more powerful than the use of the words alone. It is hard to deny that music can sometimes intensify an experience; that is why movies have musical accompaniments at strategic parts. Whether it actually produces deleterious effects, however, has yet to be demonstrated. Of course, of major concern today is easy access to the Web. Because the Web provides extremely broad access to visual, audio, and textual materials, great concern has been expressed about the potentially negative effects of Web exposure.

Concern for Children

The most heated censorship debates often center around those affecting children. This is reasonable, because it is presumed that young people are the most vulnerable to undesirable influences and need to be protected. As a historical footnote, the first obscenity case in English law occurred around 1860. The court was concerned with the effects of obscene materials on "vulnerable minds." Interestingly, this case did not deal with sexual materials but with anti-Catholic pamphlets. Our fear

of the harmful effects of ideas on youth goes back even further, to classical Greek times: the reason that Socrates was put to death was for corrupting the youth of Athens. Today, even those individuals who are
resistant to censorship in general may experience qualms when it comes
to permitting materials with adult themes to be circulated to the young.

Defending unrestricted access to such materials is probably the most
difficult intellectual freedom task that libraries perform, and the matter
is further complicated by legal concerns. Although obscenity statutes
are quite common in the United States, they are seldom useful as selection criteria. However, approximately 48 states now have what is referred
to as "harmful to juvenile" statutes. These statutes attempt to create an
obscenity standard for youth that is easier to meet than the standards
set for obscenity for adults. See Figure 5.1 for an excerpt from one such
law.

There are many vagaries associated with such a law, and one can
see how its application could be troublesome to a librarian. The librarian is not just confronted with the natural fears of people who believe
that some books might have the tendency to corrupt, but with the possibility that an irate citizen or public official might employ legal means to
restrict or eliminate library materials from the shelves.

The World Wide Web and the Debate Over Filtering

The ubiquity of the Web and its relative ease of use permit access to
millions of Web sites for millions of users. One of the problems, however, is that some Web sites, most notably those that are sexually explicit, are considered by some to be harmful, especially to minors. An
individual might deliberately access these sites, be exposed accidently
to them while searching for other sites, or be exposed to the sites by
third parties wishing to harass or otherwise disturb the user. In any case,
the desire to restrict all or most of these sites is a common interest of
parents and others, and this has created a market for techniques that
can selectively restrict or filter access to them.

Because exposure to the Web arises not only at home or in the workplace, but in public places such as schools and libraries, there has been
considerable interest by some in ensuring that access in these locations
be controlled through filters. In addition, federal legislation and judicial
decisions, especially the Children's Internet Protection Act (CIPA) and
the subsequent Supreme Court decision upholding its constitutionality,
have made some type of filtering mandatory in instances in which a

Figure 5.1
Sample of Harmful to Juvenile Statute
(Ohio Revised Code)

§ 2907.31. Disseminating matter harmful to juveniles.

(A)   No person, with knowledge of its character or content, shall recklessly do any of the following:

    (1)   Directly sell, deliver, furnish, disseminate, provide, exhibit, rent, or present to a juvenile, a group of juveniles, a law enforcement officer posing as a juvenile, or a group of law enforcement officers posing as juveniles any material or performance that is obscene or harmful to juveniles;

    (2)   Directly offer or agree to sell, deliver, furnish, disseminate, provide, exhibit, rent, or present to a juvenile, a group of juveniles, a law enforcement officer posing as a juvenile, or a group of law enforcement officers posing as juveniles any material or performance that is obscene or harmful to juveniles;

    (3)   While in the physical proximity of the juvenile or law enforcement officer posing as a juvenile, allow any juvenile or law enforcement officer posing as a juvenile to review or peruse any material or view any live performance that is harmful to juveniles.

(B)   The following are affirmative defenses to a charge under this section that involves material or a performance that is harmful to juveniles but not obscene:

    (1)   The defendant is the parent, guardian, or spouse of the juvenile involved.

    (2)   The juvenile involved, at the time of the conduct in question, was accompanied by the juvenile's parent or guardian who, with knowledge of its character, consented to the material or performance being furnished or presented to the juvenile.

    (3)   The juvenile exhibited to the defendant or to the defendant's agent or employee a draft card, driver's license, birth record, marriage license, or other official or apparently official document purporting to show that the juvenile was eighteen years of age or over or married, and the person to whom that document was exhibited did not otherwise have reasonable cause to believe that the juvenile was under the age of eighteen and unmarried.

(C)   (1)   It is an affirmative defense to a charge under this section, involving material or a performance that is obscene or harmful to juveniles, that the material or performance was furnished or presented for a bona fide medical, scientific, educational, governmental, judicial, or other proper purpose, by a physician, psychologist, sociologist, scientist, teacher, librarian, clergyman, prosecutor, judge, or other proper person.

Figure 5.1 (Continued)

---

(2) Except as provided in division (B)(3) of this section, mistake of age is not a defense to a charge under this section.

(D) (1) A person directly sells, delivers, furnishes, disseminates, provides, exhibits, rents, or presents or directly offers or agrees to sell, deliver, furnish, disseminate, provide, exhibit, rent, or present material or a performance to a juvenile, a group of juveniles, a law enforcement officer posing as a juvenile, or a group of law enforcement officers posing as juveniles in violation of this section by means of an electronic method of remotely transmitting information if the person knows or has reason to believe that the person receiving the information is a juvenile or the group of persons receiving the information are juveniles.

(2) A person remotely transmitting information by means of a method of mass distribution does not directly sell, deliver, furnish, disseminate, provide, exhibit, rent, or present or directly offer or agree to sell, deliver, furnish, disseminate, provide, exhibit, rent, or present the material or performance in question to a juvenile, a group of juveniles, a law enforcement officer posing as a juvenile, or a group of law enforcement officers posing as juveniles in violation of this section if either of the following applies:

(a) The person has inadequate information to know or have reason to believe that a particular recipient of the information or offer is a juvenile.

(b) The method of mass distribution does not provide the person the ability to prevent a particular recipient from receiving the information.

(E) If any provision of this section, or the application of any provision of this section to any person or circumstance, is held invalid, the invalidity does not affect other provisions or applications of this section or related sections that can be given effect without the invalid provision or application. To this end, the provisions are severable.

(F) Whoever violates this section is guilty of disseminating matter harmful to juveniles. If the material or performance involved is harmful to juveniles, except as otherwise provided in this division, a violation of this section is a misdemeanor of the first degree. If the material or performance involved is obscene, except as otherwise provided in this division, a violation of this section is a felony of the fifth degree. If the material or performance involved is obscene and the juvenile to whom it is sold, delivered, furnished, disseminated, provided, exhibited, rented, or presented, the juvenile to whom the offer is made or who is the subject of the agreement, or the juvenile who is allowed to review, peruse, or view it is under thirteen years of age, violation of this section is a felony of the fourth degree.

---

library receives federal e-rate or LSTA monies related to Internet access. Similarly, state "harmful to juvenile" laws have prompted some libraries to implement filtering to protect themselves from criminal liabilities.

Filters, otherwise referred to as "blocking software" or "content filters" perform the function of preventing access to certain Internet sites. Filters accomplish this access prevention primarily in two ways:

Keyword or word blocking. Compares Web page content with a list of disapproved words or phrases. This type of blocking is among the easiest to implement, but also the most inexact because it tends to block many sites inappropriately.

Site blocking. Compares Web pages to a list of disapproved sites. For the most part, the staff of the software company creates the list of sites to be blocked, although some filters allow for additional sites to be blocked and for some blocked sites to be unblocked. In general, companies do not permit the list of sites blocked to be known, arguing that it would put them at a competitive disadvantage. Because new Web sites are being created daily, filters that rely on site blocking must be constantly updated.

Blocking software, which is usually installed either on a local computer or on a server, relies on categories which are identified as either those to be blocked or permitted. The categories most commonly blocked reflect sexuality, nudity, profanity, and violence. Some organizations have tried to help both Web site developers and users "label" Web sites so that filtering can be performed more effectively. The Internet Content Rating Association (ICRA), for example, is an independent organization that permits Web authors to complete a questionnaire that describes their sites, especially regarding the presence or absence in the site of profanity, nudity and sexual content, violence, gambling, drugs, or alcohol. ICRA then generates content labels based on the responses of the Web site creators. These labels can then be used by parents when setting their browsers to accept or reject access to certain sites. Such organizations argue that commercial sites that lack these controversial features will find that such labeling may diminish the chance that their sites are filtered and increase the chance that their sites will be considered "child friendly." In addition, many adult-oriented sites may find it desirable to demonstrate their willingness to exclude minors (Internet Content Rating Association 2003).

Although few would dispute the desirability of reducing exposure to young people to violent, hateful, or pornographic sites, a variety of issues make the implementation of filters problematic. Among these issues are the following:

Overblocking. Filters tend to block sites that were not intended to be blocked. This fact raises important constitutional issues in that it deprives individuals access to information that is constitutionally protected. The irony of overblocking is sometimes manifest, as in the case of the Flesh Public Library in Ohio whose filter blocked access to its own Web site. More seriously, important information such as material on human sexuality or health can be blocked. The Kaiser Family Foundation reported, for example, that information on diabetes, sexually transmitted diseases, depression, and suicide have been blocked by these filters (Edward 2002). Among other sites that have been blocked by filtering software are sites dealing with Georgia O'Keeffe and Vincent Van Gogh, a U.N. report on HIV/AIDS, and the home pages of the Traditional Values Coalition, the Wisconsin Civil Liberties Union, and the National Coalition to Prevent Censorship. Filters have also blocked the Declaration of Independence, *Moby Dick*, and "The Owl and the Pussy Cat."

Underblocking. Kranich (2004) notes that filters often give parents a false sense of security, citing one study by the Kaiser Family Foundation which revealed that filters failed to block access to 10 percent of pornographic sites. Filters often fail to block a significant percentage of sites that they were intended to block. Another study in *Consumer Reports* found that even the "best" sites failed to block 20–30 percent of the objectionable sites. Some filters failed to block 50–90 percent of the objectionable sites (American Libraries 2001).

Subjective and discriminatory judgment. The criteria used for blocking sites is subjective, and may tend to screen out "controversial" subjects and sites that contain constitutionally protected speech. The line between what is legally obscene and what may be simply "offensive" can be a thin one, and it is not clear that software developers can create systems that can make such distinctions. The problem is exacerbated by the refusal of many filtering manufacturers to provide information on the subjects and sites that are specifically blocked. Even when it comes to filtering sites for young people, Kranich (2004) observes that filters do not discriminate sites that may be inappropriate for a six-year-old, but not for a sixteen-year-old.

Susceptibility to errors. Producers of filtering products often rely on automated systems for making content decisions. This type of "mindless mechanical blocking" inevitably leads to many mistakes (Heins and Cho 2001). Unfortunately, artificial intelligence programs are simply not yet sufficiently refined to make the subtle distinctions necessary to screen out only the sites that were intended to be screened. The impact of these errors in some cases could be small, in others it could deprive users of important information. Filters on local computers tend to be less reliable than filters installed on servers, and they have more problems involving conflicting software.

Vulnerability to dismantling. Filtering software can often be bypassed by knowledgeable users including young people. The belief that filters solve or substantially reduce children's access to sexuality, profanity, or violence is questionable.

Computer problems. Blocking software can produce computer problems that affect computer performance during installation, maintenance, upgrades, and removal.

Privacy. Filtering software can, in some cases, monitor Internet use, including time, date, which computer was used, and specific sites accessed. This capability jeopardizes the confidential use of library resources by patrons.

Despite some of the problems with filters, a variety of arguments support the need for some types of filtering. There is little doubt that the Internet contains access to sites that are extremely violent or hateful, and that contain explicit sexuality sometimes portraying criminal or violent acts (such as rape). Although some might argue that adults should be able to view such material freely, most would argue that such imagery is not appropriate for young people. The Supreme Court, in its ruling on CIPA, described the protection of children from such material as a "compelling interest" of the State.

Proponents argue that filters, although imperfect, are the most feasible way currently known to provide such protections. It is true that libraries have for years, through their selection criteria and collection development policies, explicitly or implicitly chosen not to collect pornographic materials, and it could be argued that filters are simply a logical extension of that process. Perhaps the most avid defense of filters has come from David Burt, a librarian, who also has been working in the filtering industry. Burt (1997) has expressed particular concern that the level of exposure to pornography in public libraries is much larger than public librarians admit. His arguments include the following: (1) Although keyword blocking has its problems, the better filters can have this feature disconnected, leaving the more accurate site-blocking feature to govern access. (2) Better filters are increasing in their refinement so that fewer nonpornographic sites related to sexuality are blocked. (3) Libraries have always restricted the choices of patrons to some extent to material deemed appropriate. Restricting sites that are pornographic is neither new nor undesirable. (4) Although filters do perform some type of "preselection" activity before librarians can review the material, this fearure is not new; publisher approval plans have been preselecting materials for years. (5) The claim that filters are unconstitutional misconstrues what filtering is; filters restrict access to materials that are not yet part of the library collection. This process is no different from deciding not to select some materials, and as such it is not ipso facto censorship or violation of constitutional rights. As Auld (2003) has observed, "Despite the onslaught of reports denying their effectiveness, filters, when managed properly, can and do achieve a virtually pornography-free online environment while only minimally affecting access to constitutionally protected speech" (p. 38).

These arguments, however, have not been viewed as compelling by the American Library Association and other organizations, which oppose the use of filters. Among the pertinent resolutions and policies passed by the ALA regarding filtering are "Resolution on Opposition to Federally Mandated Internet Filtering," "Guidelines and Considerations for Developing a Public Library Internet Use Policy," and "Resolution on the Use of Filtering Software in Libraries." Of great import to the ALA is that filters in fact deprive both young people and adults of constitutionally protected speech and that libraries have a special obligation to protect such access. The Internet is viewed as simply another important forum for speech which requires First Amendment protection. The introduction of filters reduces access to only those sites on the Internet that would be accessible by minors. The ALA suggests that there are other less restrictive means for ensuring that children do not use the Internet inappropriately in libraries, including supervision of their Internet use while in the library.

Libraries will continue to deal with the problem of filters for some time. For example, libraries that do not receive federal monies are not required to filter their computers unless additional state or local laws require it. Among the strategies used to deal with the problem are:

1. creating Internet use policies that clearly indicate appropriate and inappropriate use of library computers and establish penalties for violations of the policy.
2. installing filters on all computers.
3. installing filters on some terminals, for example, those in the children's area but not those in the adult area.
4. installing filters but setting them to the least restrictive levels.
5. asking librarians to supervise Internet use and informing patrons when their use is inappropriate.
6. controlling Internet access (especially on unfiltered machines) through the use of library cards or "smart cards."
7. installing privacy screens, so that material considered "offensive" by some cannot be easily viewed accidentally.
8. installing computers in locations not easily viewed by third parties, to prevent accidental exposure to offensive material.

The recent Supreme Court decision in CIPA has not settled the issue of filtering for libraries. Although it is clear that filtering is not currently considered an unconstitutional violation of patron rights, the Court indicated that filters must be easily disabled for adult patrons, and that if this is not accomplished, adult patrons who believe their First Amendment rights are being violated might find a sympathetic ear should a case be brought before them.

THE INFORMATION POLICIES OF THE AMERICAN LIBRARY ASSOCIATION

As can be seen by the previous discussion, librarians struggle with their perceived obligations—personal, professional, and organizational. In addition, the society itself is attempting to come to grips with its many problems and influences. In response to these pressures, ALA has established over the years a variety of policies meant to guide librarians in protecting the rights of their patrons. Most of these policies have been created by ALA's Intellectual Freedom Committee (IFC). The IFC was created in 1940, one year after the first version of the Library Bill of Rights was passed. The purpose of the IFC was to help promote and protect the values espoused by the Library Bill of Rights. It has accomplished this task primarily by developing policies and written interpretations of the Library Bill of Rights over the years (ALA 2002). These policies have provided national guidance to the library community on some of the most complicated issues that face librarians. Given the tremendous burden of this responsibility, in 1967 an administrative unit called the Office of

Intellectual Freedom (OIF) was created. The OIF was established to relieve the administrative burden on the IFC and to coordinate intellectual freedom activities. OIF is responsible for implementing the intellectual freedom policies that are adopted by ALA. It also presents conference programs, collects data, and generally promotes the concept of intellectual freedom. Policy making remains in the jurisdiction of the IFC (ALA 2002).

Copies of the policies promulgated by the IFC and passed by ALA Council, as well as background on them, can be found in OIF's *Intellectual Freedom Manual* (ALA 2002) and also at the ALA Web site (*www.ala.org*). Below is a brief discussion of some of the major ALA information policies. They have been broken down into four basic areas: philosophical foundations, access issues, modification of materials, and administrative aspects.

Philosophical Foundations

Library Bill of Rights. The fundamental obligations of libraries and library professionals are clearly defined by the central document of the American Library Association: the Library Bill of Rights (see Figure 5.2).

These provisions, first adopted in 1939 and revised on numerous occasions, create a positive obligation to select materials for the entire community and to reject censoring of materials based on the characteristics of the author (Section 1); to select materials with a wide array of viewpoints and to reject censoring materials due to doctrinal disapproval of content (Section 2); to reject censorship and to cooperate with others to fight the abridgement of free speech (Sections 3 and 4); to provide library materials and services to all individuals regardless of their characteristics (Section 5); and to permit equitable access to library facilities (Section 6).

Understanding how to apply the Library Bill of Rights is not always easy, especially when one is attempting to balance the entire range of obligations noted above. This challenge has been recognized by the ALA, which has consequently issued a variety of formal interpretations to assist librarians. Many of these will be noted below.

The Freedom to Read Statement and the Intellectual Freedom Statement. The Freedom to Read Statement was originally adopted in 1953 and revised in 1972. It was jointly prepared by ALA and the American Book Publishers Council. This philosophical statement is directed at both publishers and librarians. It concerns itself with how important reading is

---

Figure 5.2
The Library Bill of Rights

The American Library Association affirms that all libraries are forums for information and ideas, and that the following basic policies should guide their services.

1.   Books and other library resources should be provided for the interest, information, and enlightenment of all people of the community the library serves. Materials should not be excluded because of the origin, background, or views of those contributing to their creation.

2.   Libraries should provide materials and information presenting all points of view on current and historical issues. Materials should not be proscribed or removed because of partisan or doctrinal disapproval.

3.   Libraries should challenge censorship in the fulfillment of their responsibility to provide information and enlightenment.

4.   Libraries should cooperate with all persons and groups concerned with resisting abridgement of free expression and free access to ideas.

5.   A person's right to use a library should not be denied or abridged because of origin, age, background, or views.

6.   Libraries which make exhibit spaces and meeting rooms available to the public they serve should make such facilities available on an equitable basis, regardless of the beliefs or affiliations of individuals or groups requesting their use.

—Adopted June 18, 1948. Amended February 2, 1961, June 27, 1967, and January 23, 1980, by the ALA Council.

Reprinted with permission from the American Library Association.

to our democratic society and the inadvisability of permitting suppression of ideas due to perceived controversial or immoral material. Among the key points argued in this statement are that the greatest diversity of views, both unorthodox and orthodox, is in the public's interest; that the possession of materials does not constitute an endorsement of the ideas contained within them; that librarians should not permit the labelling of works as subversive or dangerous; and that it is the responsibility of publishers and librarians to protect people's freedom to read, to oppose censorship, and to provide access to a diversity of ideas. Perhaps the document's most notable assertion is the recognition of the importance of the freedom to read, its promise, and its dangers:

> We do not state these propositions in the comfortable belief that what people read is unimportant. We believe rather that what people read is deeply important; that ideas can be dangerous; but that the suppression of ideas is fatal to a democratic society. Freedom itself is a dangerous way of life, but it is ours.

The Intellectual Freedom Statement expresses the position of the ALA Council and the Freedom to Read Foundation, which is closely associated with ALA. The document closely parallels the *Freedom to Read Statement*, asserting the importance of our freedom of expression and, through seven propositions, asserting the need for diverse collections and the obligation to resist attempts at censorship by individuals or groups. In addition, there is a statement of professional concern regarding the fact that library professionals are often subjected to threats of legal, financial, or personal pressures to bow to censorious attempts. The statement reasserts our obligation to resist such attempts.

Freedom to View Statement. In response to the growing interest in AV materials, the Educational Film and Video Association adopted a statement in 1979 protecting the rights of viewers and creators of AV materials. Titled the Freedom to View Statement, this document (Figure 5.3) parallels in many ways the rights asserted in the Library Bill of Rights.

Privacy: An Interpretation of the Library Bill of Rights. The ALA has a long tradition of policies and statements affirming the right to privacy of library patrons. Underlying this advocacy is the belief that if patrons cannot use materials and make inquiries free from public exposure or governmental intrusion, they will not be free to explore controversial topics. Such exposure and criticism creates a "chilling effect" on the First Amendment rights of library users. Adopted in 2002 *Privacy: An Interpretation of the Library Bill of Rights* reaffirms that protecting the privacy rights of patrons is an ethical obligation of libraries and librarians, and patrons have a right to be free from unreasonable intrusion or surveillance of their library use. The interpretation also emphasizes that library users have a right to know about policies and procedures related to

---

Figure 5.3
Freedom to View

The FREEDOM TO VIEW, along with the freedom to speak, to hear, and to read, is protected by the First Amendment to the Constitution of the United States. In a free society, there is no place for censorship of any medium of expression. Therefore, we affirm these principles:

1. It is in the public interest to provide the broadest possible access to films and other audiovisual materials because they have proven to be among the most effective means for the communication of ideas. Liberty of circulation is essential to insure the constitutional guarantee of freedom of expression.

2. It is in the public interest to provide for our audiences, films and other audiovisual materials which represent a diversity of views and expression. Selection of a work does not constitute or imply agreement with or approval of the content.

3. It is our professional responsibility to resist the constraint of labeling or prejudging a film on the basis of the moral, religious, or political beliefs of the producer or film maker or on the basis of controversial content.

4. It is our professional responsibility to contest vigorously, by all lawful means, every encroachment upon the public's freedom to view.

—Drafted by the Educational Film Library Association's Freedom to View Committee, and adopted by the EFLA Board of Directors in February 1979.

Reprinted with permission from the American Library Association.

records that contain personal information about them, such as circulation records. Collection of personal information should be limited to only what is necessary to accomplish the mission of the library.

Intellectual Freedom Principles for Academic Libraries: An Interpretation of the Library Bill of Rights. Although the Library Bill of Rights was written with many types of libraries in mind, it has often been perceived as applicable primarily to public libraries. Intellectual Freedom Principles for Academic Libraries provides a specific application of the Library Bill of Rights to academic libraries. Among its provisions, the interpretation affirms the critical importance of intellectual freedom in the development of academic library collections and services, and emphasizes the necessity of (1) protecting patron privacy, (2) developing collections and services that meet the institutional mission, (3) preserving and replacing materials on controversial topics, and (4) providing open and unfiltered access to the collection and information.

Access Issues

Restricted Access to Library Materials. Although it is clear that preventing individuals from exposure to materials considered offensive by simply not selecting them is censorship, can the library simply restrict access to materials it believes are problematic? The interpretation Restricted Access to Library Materials indicates that such an action places a barrier between the patron and the collection. When libraries try to restrict access to various areas of the library using such techniques as closed shelving (shelves available only to staff), "adults only" sections, or restricted shelving areas, it is de facto suppression of ideas. But aren't there some legitimate reasons to restrict access to some materials? The association recognizes that it is acceptable to restrict access to materials for special reasons, such as to protect materials from mutilation or theft, but these should not be used as a pretense for censorious activity.

Free Access to Libraries for Minors. Although the temptation to restrict access is usually most powerful when young people are involved, and it is perfectly reasonable that librarians, as noted above, feel a special concern for children, ALA, through the promulgation of its policy Free Access to Libraries for Minors clearly states that library materials are not to be restricted on the basis of the patron's age. Hence reading areas restricted to adults, collections limited to adults or teachers, or restricted access to interlibrary loan all would constitute a violation of the ALA Library Bill of Rights because they restrict access to library materials. In this policy, ALA also asserts a key position in regard to access for young people:

> The American Library Association opposes libraries restricting access to library materials and services for minors and hold that it is the parents—and only parents—who may restrict their children—and only their children—from access to library materials and services. (ALA 2002, p. 92)

In other words, the library does not serve in loco parentis (in the place of the parent), and the focus of responsibility for controlling the reading, viewing, or listening habits of children is vested with the parent alone.

Access for Children and Young People to Videotapes and Other Nonprint Formats. Because of the growing prominence of nonprint formats, ALA established a second interpretative document, entitled Access for Children and Young People to Videotapes and Other Nonprint Formats, in 1989. This document reaffirms the association's stand that materials should not be restricted on the basis of the patron's age and specifically rejects policies that set minimum age limits or the costs of nonprint materials as a reason for restriction. Libraries are also cautioned about the inappropriateness of using Motion Picture Association of America (MPAA) ratings as a means of restricting access, but the document also protects the inclusion of such ratings when they appear on the film or video from the distributor. Removal of such ratings would constitute expurgation.

Economic Barriers to Information Access. Over the years, libraries have charged fees for a variety of reasons, but these fees have generally been minimal. With the increasing number of formats, expanding demands to purchase new technologies, and serious constraints on library budgets, libraries have experienced increasing temptations to charge substantial fees for library services. This policy affirms that free access to information is the fundamental mission of publicly-funded libraries, and that fees *ipso facto* create barriers to such access. The policy states unequivocally that access to information in whatever format should be provided equitably and that charging fees for materials, services, and programs is anathema to the concept of free and equal access. Ability to pay should not govern ability to know.

Access to Library Resources and Services Regardless of Gender or Sexual Orientation. In recent years, discussion of sexual orientation has become commonplace, and there have been continuing efforts by many groups to advocate for the rights of gays and lesbians, as well as other groups. Consistent with ALA's general philosophical stand on free and equal access to libraries, the association affirms the rights of individuals to use libraries regardless of sexual orientation. In addition, Access to Library Resources and Services Regardless of Gender or Sexual Orientation explicitly rejects the nonselection of materials because of the sexual orientation of the creator.

Access to Electronic Information, Services, and Networks. There is no doubt that the Internet has become a major source of information for librarians and library users. This has raised some very important issues for libraries, because the databases that can be accessed may contain controversial or "adult" material. The potential and real problems that have arisen prompted ALA to create a new interpretation of the ALA Library Bill of Rights in 1996 directly addressing this issue. It is clear that Access to Electronic Information, Services, and Networks reflects the consistent position of ALA regarding the right of access to information for all library users. This policy asserts that "users should not be restricted or denied access for expressing or receiving constitutionally protected speech." It also asserts that access should not be limited because some content may be controversial and that minors have equal rights of access to electronic information sources. Similar to earlier interpretations, this one places the burden of restricting access to information on the parents of minors rather than on the librarian. In addition, the policy asserts that users of electronic information services and networks in libraries should have their rights to privacy and confidentiality protected.

Access to Resources and Services in the School Library Media Program. Schools are especially common locations for attempts to restrict information. In part this is a reflection of the in loco parentis function of schools. Parents expect schools to protect their children from harm; indeed, schools are legally obligated to do so. Some parents believe that this harm extends to exposure to "unhealthy" materials. Access to the Web has exacerbated the problem because there is a general lack of control over the content of materials on it.

Because of the high probability that schools will experience attempts to restrict access, the ALA has recognized the importance of specifically addressing the problems of school library media centers. Access to Resources and Services in the School Library Media Program notes that the underlying value of intellectual freedom should be sustained by school libraries and that the ALA Library Bill of Rights applies in these settings. ALA recognizes the school library as a place where different sides of an issue should be available and where the collection should reflect the heterogeneous society in which schools exist. Access to the collection should be free and open, and attempts to restrict materials should be resisted. It places the burden of broad collections and reflecting diverse points of view directly in the hands of the school librarian.

Statement on Library Use of Filtering Software. Of primary importance to the ALA is the protection of library users from violations of their First Amendment rights. Because filters, due to overblocking, deprive both adults and young people of access to material that is constitutionally protected, the ALA opposes their use. Among the specific concerns of the ALA in addition to overblocking, is that filters can impose the point of view of the developer of the filtering software, that producers do not identify what sites are being blocked, that the criteria used to block sites is poorly defined, and that parents, not the library, should be responsible for regulating the Internet use of their children. ALA passed the Statement on Library Use of Filtering Software in July 1997, and revised it in November 2000.

Resolution Reaffirming the Principles of Intellectual Freedom in the Aftermath of Terrorist Attacks. The shocking events of September 11, 2001, produced legislation such as the Patriot Act. Although some of the provisions of this act may well have been very important and useful, the ALA, as well as other groups concerned about the civil liberties of individuals, grew concerned that some of the provisions of the act promote potentially oppressive behavior on the part of governmental officials. The fear that the legitimate exercise of free speech might be compromised led to the passing of the Resolution Reaffirming the Principles of Intellectual Freedom in January 2002. In it, ALA reaffirms its opposition to government censorship and suppression of news and government information, exhorts libraries to protect the privacy and confidentiality of their users, and affirms the importance of dissent and timely provision of information to the citizenry.

Resolution on the USA Patriot Act and Related Measures that Infringe on the Rights of Library Users. As with the above resolution, this resolution, passed in January 2003, expresses its concern that the Patriot Act in some of its provisions inappropriately expands the authority of the federal government to investigate its citizens and non-citizens. Such authority threatens the privacy rights of patrons using the library and impedes the dissemination of knowledge. As such, the ALA declares that the act is "a present danger to the constitutional rights and privacy rights of library users. . . . " Without unimpeded access to libraries and free inquiry within them, the purpose of libraries and their democratic mission cannot be fulfilled. The resolution exhorts libraries to educate patrons about the possible excesses of the Patriot Act, and to take action to ensure that the privacy rights and the rights of inquiry of library users are not adversely affected.

MODIFICATION OF MATERIALS

Expurgation of Library Materials. Sometimes a librarian may be tempted to alter library materials rather than restrict the item itself. This might mean obliterating text or altering or excising a photograph. Any attempt to alter material in this way is considered to be expurgation of library materials and, hence, is a type of restricted access. As such, it is considered a violation of the ALA Library Bill of Rights.

Statement on Labeling. It is normal to organize materials by classifying them. For example, we label some books "history," others as "science." This is not generally a concern to the ALA insofar as the labeling does not attempt to restrict access to such materials. ALA's concern is with affixing a prejudicial label to materials or separating materials through a prejudicial system. For example, labeling materials "adults only" or "teachers only" would have a tendency to restrict access. As noted above, placing MPAA ratings on videos and DVDs unless already provided by the distributor, is considered a violation of this policy.

ADMINISTRATIVE ASPECTS

Challenged Materials. From time to time, individuals challenge materials in the library, insisting that the materials be removed or restricted. Challenges can produce very difficult times for a library because of the potential of political pressure as well as the possibility of unpleasant media exposure. Nonetheless, such attempts can threaten the dissemination of ideas and as such challenge the basic principles of intellectual freedom. The policy on challenged materials asserts that libraries should have a clear materials-selection policy and that materials that conform to that policy should not be removed simply because individuals place legal or extra-legal pressures on the library. Rather, the library should protect such materials and insist, at the least, on an adversary hearing so that such requests can be closely scrutinized. This is not to say that a library should never remove materials that it has selected, but doing so under pressure should be avoided.

Policy on the Confidentiality of Library Circulation Records. When individuals take out a book from a library, it is normally assumed that no one else has access to the information regarding what was checked out (i.e., the circulation record). Underlying the privacy of circulation records is the belief that if individuals think that their reading habits can be scrutinized, they might feel pressure or embarrassment. This can create a chilling effect on an individual's use of the library, and essentially restricts the right to use the library and the ideas contained within.

From time to time such information is, in fact, requested. Usually this is done by an arm of law enforcement: a police officer or prosecutor. In some cases, FBI agents have requested circulation records. ALA policy asserts that any records that associate an individual with particular materials are confidential and should be released only after a subpoena has been issued and after the library is satisfied that the subpoena is properly issued. This means that libraries should usually insist on a court hearing to ensure that they are required to turn over the records.

Guidelines for the Development and Implementation of Policies, Regulations, and Procedures Affecting Access to Library Materials, Services, and Facilities. These guidelines, adopted in 1994, were prompted by a court case known as the "Kreimer case," which involved the rights of a homeless individual who was removed from a public library for inappropriate behavior. There was much debate over this issue because the library community felt that it was important to ensure the rights of each individual to use the library, even one who may behave differently. At the same time, the library community wanted to ensure that an individual's behavior could be controlled so that others could use the library effectively.

Because the case was so controversial, the library community looked to ALA for guidance on the development of rules and regulations regarding patron behavior. The guidelines presented make it clear that patron-behavior rules should be no more restrictive than absolutely necessary, should be consistent with constitutional protections of citizens, and should be consistent with the ALA Library Bill of Rights and the mission of the library. The guidelines further condemn focusing on specific groups of people, such as children or the homeless, and assert that local guidelines should be clearly written and that an appeal procedure be available.

These information policies are only some of the policies and statements made by the ALA addressing the dissemination of information by libraries. ALA also takes professional positions on national and interna-

---

Figure 5.4
The Glasgow Declaration on Libraries, Information
Services and Intellectual Freedom

Meeting in Glasgow on the occasion of the 75th anniversary of its formation, the International Federation of Library Associations and Institutions (IFLA) declares that:

IFLA proclaims the fundamental right of human beings both to access and to express information without restriction.

IFLA and its worldwide membership support, defend and promote intellectual freedom as expressed in the United Nations Universal Declaration of Human Rights. This intellectual freedom encompasses the wealth of human knowledge, opinion, creative thought and intellectual activity.

IFLA asserts that a commitment to intellectual freedom is a core responsibility of the library and information profession worldwide, expressed through codes of ethics and demonstrated through practice.

IFLA affirms that:

- Libraries and information services provide access to information, ideas and works of imagination in any medium and regardless of frontiers. They serve as gateways to knowledge, thought and culture, offering essential support for independent decision-making, cultural development, research and lifelong learning by both individuals and groups.
- Libraries and information services contribute to the development and maintenance of intellectual freedom and help to safeguard democratic values and universal civil rights. Consequently, they are committed to offering their clients access to relevant resources and services without restriction and to opposing any form of censorship.
- Libraries and information services shall acquire, preserve and make available the widest variety of materials, reflecting the plurality and diversity of society. The selection and availability of library materials and services shall be governed by professional considerations and not by political, moral and religious views.
- Libraries and information services shall make materials, facilities and services equally accessible to all users. There shall be no discrimination for any reason including race, national or ethnic origin, gender or sexual preference, age, disability, religion, or political beliefs.

Figure 5.4 (Continued)

- Libraries and information services shall protect each user's right to privacy and confidentiality with respect to information sought or received and resources consulted, borrowed, acquired or transmitted.

IFLA therefore calls upon libraries and information services and their staff to uphold and promote the principles of intellectual freedom and to provide uninhibited access to information.

Statement prepared by the International Federation of Library Associations and Institutions (IFLA), Free Access to Information and Freedom of Expression (FAIFE) Committee and approved by the Governing Board of IFLA 27 March 2002, The Hague, Netherlands. Proclaimed by the Council of IFLA 19 August 2002, Glasgow, Scotland. Reprinted with permission.

---

tional issues that affect the information rights of its citizenry and those of the world.

An International Declaration

Although the ALA Library Bill of Rights is the centerpiece that guides librarianship in the United States, it is instructive to remember that the battle for freedom of expression is a concern throughout the world. In 2002 the International Federation of Library Associations (IFLA) celebrated its 75th Anniversary. At this meeting, it passed the "Glasgow Declaration" (see Figure 5.4) It is a fitting expression of the universal concern for the free flow of ideas and the ability of all to express those ideas. The close kinship with the Library Bill of Rights is manifest.

SUMMARY

Libraries are critical information providers, and part of their function is to make information policies. The policies that they adopt on the selection, organization, and dissemination of the information they possess determine in large part their effectiveness. Few such policies are as important as those related to intellectual freedom and resistance to censorship. Libraries represent a special forum: a place where library users should be able to find a broad range of points of view on topics of interest. Some of these topics may be quite controversial, and there may be a tendency on the part of the public, and library staff as well, to consider restricting access or even removing some of these materials for fear of public response or the effects these materials may have, especially on the young. These concerns have been exacerbated as video and Web-based formats have become a larger part of library collections. Although some of the concerns may have merit and tempt librarians to restrict access to library materials, there are also countervailing professional obligations and policies that provide guidance. The intellectual freedom policies, adopted by the ALA, serve as both a philosophical and instrumental foundation for the practices of libraries and librarians.

The task of defending intellectual freedom is a very difficult one. Libraries and librarians have often been subjected to intense pressures as they defend items in their collection. There is little reason to believe that these problems will dissipate. On the contrary, with the increasing use of the Web, it is likely that the problems will increase. Only a firm understanding of the principles of the profession can provide the necessary rationale to protect patrons' rights to read and view the library materials of their choosing.

REFERENCES

Abbott, Randy L. "Pressure Groups and Intellectual Freedom." *Public Library Quarterly* 10 (1990): 43–61.

American Libraries, April 2001, p. 23.

American Library Association. "Banned Books Web Site." [Online] Available at *www.ala.org*. (Accessed June 27, 2003.)

————. *Intellectual Freedom Manual*. 6th ed. Chicago: ALA, 2002.

Asheim, Lester. "The Librarian's Responsibility: Not Censorship but Selection." In *Freedom of Book Selection*. Edited by Frederic Mosher. Chicago: ALA, 1954: 95–96.

Association of American Publishers, American Library Association, and Association for Supervision and Curriculum Development. *Limiting What Students Shall Read*. Washington, D.C.: Association of American Publishers, 1981.

Auld, Hampton. "Filters Work: Get Over It." *American Libraries* 34 (February 2003): 38–41.

Burt, David. "In Defense of Filtering." *American Libraries* 28 (August 1997): 46–48.

Busha, C.H. "The Attitudes of Midwestern Public Librarians toward Intellectual Freedom and Censorship." Unpublished dissertation. Indiana University, 1971. Cited in Serebnick (1979).

Dewey, Melvil. "The Profession." *Library Journal* (June 15, 1989): 5. Reprint of article in *American Library Journal* 1 (September 1876): 5.

Eakin, M. L. "Censorship in Public High School Libraries." Master's thesis. Columbia University, 1948. Cited in Serebnick (1979).

Edward, Ellen. "Web Filters Block Health Information." *Washington Post*, December 11, 2002, p. A02.

Farley, J.J. "Book Censorship in the Senior High Libraries of Nassau County, N.Y." Unpublished dissertation. New York University, 1964. Cited in Serebnick (1979).

Fiske, Marjerie. *Book Selection and Censorship: A Study of School and Public Libraries in California*. Berkeley: University of California Press, 1959. Cited in Serebnick (1979).

Garrison, Dee. "The Tender Technicians: The Feminization of Public Librarianship." *Journal of Social History* 6 (winter 1972–1973): 131–156.

Heins, Marjorie, and Christina Cho. *Internet Filters: A Public Policy Report*. Free Expression Policy Project, National Coalition Against Censorship, fall 2001.

Hopkins, Dianne McAfee. "A Conceptual Model of Factors Influencing the Outcome of Challenges to Library Materials in Secondary School Settings." *Library Quarterly* 63 (January 1993): 40–72.

Huesmann, L. Rowell. "Psychological Processes Promoting the Relation between Exposure to Media Violence and Aggressive Behavior by the Viewer." *Journal of Social Issues* 42 (1986): 125–139.

Internet Content Rating Association. [Online] Available at *www.icra.org?_en/about/*. (Accessed July 10, 2003.)

Island Trees Union Free School District v. Pico 102 S. Ct. 2799 (1982).

Kranich, Nancy. "Why Filters Won't Protect Children or Adults." *Library Administration and Management* 18 (winter 2004): 14–18.

Kreimer v. Bureau of Police for the Town of Morristown, et al. 765 F. Supp. 181 (D.N.J. 1991).

Lamolinara, Guy. "Metamorphosis of a National Treasure." *American Libraries* 27 (March 1996): 31–33.

Mathews, Virginia H., Judith G. Flum, and Karen A. Whitney. "Kids Need Libraries: School and Public Libraries Preparing the Youth of Today for the World of Tomorrow," *School Library Journal* 36 (April 1990): 33–37.

National Commission on Libraries and Information Science. "The Role of Fees in Supporting Library and Information Services in Public and Academic Libraries." Washington, D.C.: NCLIS, 1985. In *Fees for Library Service: Current Practice and Future Policy*. Vol. 8 of *Collection Building* (1986): 3–17.

Pope, M. J. "A Comparative Study of the Opinions of School, College, and Public Librarians Concerning Certain Categories of Sexually Oriented Literature." Unpublished dissertation. Rutgers University, 1973. Cited in Serebnick (1979).

Serebnick, Judith. "A Review of Research Related to Censorship in Libraries." *Library Research* 1 (1979): 95–118.

Swan, John. "Untruth or Consequences." *Library Journal* 111 (July 1, 1986): 44–52.

6

Information Organization: Issues and Techniques

Information has an entropic character: it does not organize itself, rather, it has a tendency toward randomness. Unless there are ways to organize it, it quickly becomes chaos. The primary purpose of organizing library collections is to meet the various information needs of library users. Given the amount of knowledge that is currently available and its projected growth, librarians and other information providers have logical, albeit sometimes complex, ways to arrange and to promote retrieval of information within their libraries as well as outside library walls.

Considering the vastness of today's information, and the inevitable and explosive growth of knowledge in the future, it is daunting to consider the task of organizing it so it is accessible. Existing in its unorganized state, it is, for all intents and purposes, impossible to access except by accident and serendipity. Libraries and other information organizations cannot operate in this manner, and although the issue of how knowledge is organized in society is an interesting one, the crucial concern for librarians is how information is organized within a library, within a database or on the Web. A library's fundamental purpose is to acquire, store, organize, preserve, disseminate, or otherwise provide access to the vast bodies of knowledge already produced. Organizing knowledge in libraries means organizing many types of information and media: information stored in physical items such as books, video recordings, or pictures. It means organizing virtual information, that is, information stored electronically in words, sounds, or images. It also means organizing the records that serve as representations of these items, such as catalog cards or the electronic bibliographic records in library computerized catalogs.

The notion of knowledge organization within a library can be very broad. For example, access to knowledge can be organized by the media used to record that knowledge (for example, print or audiovisual); by user (for example, children, adults, vision-impaired); by genre (for example, westerns, mysteries, fiction, nonfiction); or even by size (as with "oversize" shelving). Obviously, except in the smallest of collections such general forms of organization are usually not sufficient to locate most information effectively, but they do constitute useful forms of organization within a library.

The library itself can be viewed as one type of information retrieval system. Its content is a database, which is organized in such a way as to produce effective access to that content. Any information retrieval system has at least two parts: a database and a system for retrieval of the database. The database of the library would be its contents: the books, periodicals, audiovisual materials, and other items in the collection. The system would include the hardware, software, rules, policies, and management used to effect retrieval of the information in the database. The library catalog might also be considered an information retrieval system in itself. The database is the content or information (the electronic records or the cards in a manual system and the descriptions of the items in the catalog), the retrieval system would be the hardware, management, software, rules, policies, and procedures by which the catalog records are prepared (file preparation) and manipulated for access purposes. Classification schemes can also be seen as information retrieval systems. For example, the content is the classification scheme and the numbers that stand for the content; the retrieval system is the alphabetical and numerical rules that govern the system. Indeed, Bates (1986) has argued that a reference book itself is a retrieval system. As can be seen from these examples, a library is not only an information retrieval system, but it relies on many other information retrieval systems that function within it.

Although it is sometimes difficult to locate information or items in libraries, what is truly remarkable is that despite the incredible range and diversity of information they contain, the right information is frequently located. This is due in large part to the intricate systems and techniques that have been developed to organize the content of libraries. These systems and techniques have been developed and implemented by catalogers, archivists, information retrieval system designers, bibliographers, and indexers, all of whom assist information seekers by designing effective systems to retrieve information.

An important aspect of knowledge retrieval, and one that constitutes an important focus of this chapter is the concept of access points. Those designing information systems or those who make these systems available create the access points. The access points are employed by users of these systems, including librarians, to locate the desired material or information. There are many types of access points in a library. They can be access points in a bibliographic record, such as author, title, and subject headings, or they can be something as basic as a library sign naming a subject area or indicating the range of classification numbers located in a shelving range. Access points can also be human, such as access provided at the reference desk by a reference librarian. All of these provide points of access to the library collection. Knowledge retrieval involves much more than just these access points: other important aspects of knowledge organization and retrieval include shelf arrangement and indexes and bibliographies as systematic summaries and pointers to full texts.

Libraries, in order to accomplish their purposes, employ various intellectual tools, sometimes referred to as intellectual technologies. These tools help arrange knowledge in such a way as to promote retrieval of that knowledge. Effective organization of knowledge, however, is extremely difficult to accomplish: the organizing principles must be relatively easy to apply, and easy to understand by both information professionals and users, and they must reflect, to the greatest extent possible, the way that people ordinarily seek out information.

But even in the best of organizational systems, the individual information seeker is an essential variable. Individuals seek information with their own mental constructs, and no system can account for each of these constructs. In other words, no particular organization of information will satisfy each information seeker's needs perfectly (Mann 1993). Nonetheless, libraries, through their intellectual tools, provide an efficient means of retrieving a vast amount of information.

Svenonius (2000) has pointed out that the best systems for organizing information rely on certain intellectual foundations. These foundations include:

1. An ideology, formulated in terms of purposes (the objective to be achieved by a system for organizing information) and principles (the directives that guide their design).
2. Formalizations of processes involved in the organization of information, such as those provided by linguistic conceptualizations and entity-attribute relationship models.
3. The knowledge gained through research, particularly that expressed in the form of high-level generalizations about the design and use of organizations systems.
4. Insofar as a discipline is defined by its research foci, the key problems that need to be solved if information is to be organized intelligently and information science is to advance. (p. 1)

It is obvious that in this brief chapter a complete or sufficient discussion of knowledge organization is unattainable. The primary discussion, therefore, will center on the intellectual tools that promote retrieval of information. There are many such tools and those discussed in this chapter are ones that play a prominent role in the organization of the knowledge contained within libraries, although many of them play equally important roles in other types of information systems. The intellectual tools that will be discussed are (1) classification systems, (2) controlled vocabulary including thesauri and lists of subject headings including the Library of Congress Subject Headings, (3) the library catalog including the Anglo-American Cataloging Rules (AACR2), (4) indexes, abstracts, and bibliographies, and (5) electronic databases. These tools are not mutually exclusive; indeed, some rely heavily on others. For example, the library catalog and electronic databases rely heavily on controlled vocabulary. These have been selected as influential tools that affect how knowledge is organized in libraries. Following a discussion of these tools, the challenges facing the organization of the Web will be reviewed.

CLASSIFICATION SYSTEMS

A method fundamental to information access in libraries is through disciplinary and subject access. Although the concepts of discipline and subject are closely related, they are distinct. Put very simply, a subject is what an item is about; a discipline is a related body of knowledge that defines a particular approach. Take for example, the subject of the origin of humans. A book on the origin of humans that examines it from scriptural text is likely to be placed within the discipline of religion; a book on the same subject (the origin of humans) that focuses on physical processes and evolution is likely to be placed in the biosciences: same subject, different disciplines. Despite these differences, however, disciplines and subjects share many similarities when it comes to searching for information. Two basic systems that provide such access will be considered here: classification systems and controlled vocabularies.

One of the fundamental organizing principles libraries employ is called classification. Classification "is the act of organizing the universe of knowledge into some systematic order" (Chan 1994, p. 259). This organization provides "a descriptive and explanatory framework for ideas and a structure of the relationships among the ideas" (Kwasnik 1992, p. 63). Classification schemes attempt to identify knowledge and the interrelationships among knowledge. In this way, one is "connected" not only to a specific item, but also to other items on the same subject or items on related subjects. Good classification systems reflect the interconnectedness of ideas; they not only help searchers locate material but also help them to think about related aspects of their search and identify materials that embody those aspects.

Generally, libraries conceive of the universe of knowledge in terms of broad-based classification systems that are discipline oriented. Of course, items in a collection can be and are classified using many organizational principles that are not discipline based, for example, by author, as in a typical fiction collection. However, it is clear that classification by discipline is a fundamental and dominant intellectual technology for the arrangement and retrieval of items and information in libraries.

Among their many uses, classification schemes perform a direct and critical function: they provide a basis for the physical arrangement of library materials. There is a close relationship, of course, in how items are physically arranged on the shelf and the intellectual principles used to organize the knowledge contained within those items. Library classification schemes provide a means of organizing full texts—the items on the shelf (Mann 1993). Such classification systems function in at least two helpful ways: they help to locate specific items on the shelf and they serve as a means to place items treating the same or related subjects in the same area (this is referred to as *collocation*). Hence, as classification systems provide for the physical arrangement of library materials they also permit the grouping of like materials within the same area, thereby providing a means of discovering items of interest through browsing.

Two classification systems dominate in American libraries: the Dewey Decimal Classification (DDC) and the Library of Congress Classification (LCC). These schemes were devised originally to organize books—the traditional medium for information. In more recent times they have been adapted for use with other media. These classifications will be briefly discussed below because of their ubiquity and importance in American librarianship. Suffice it to say, these systems are quite complex, and the superficial discussion below is meant only to identify a few of their major characteristics.

Dewey Decimal Classification

The most common library classification system is the Dewey Decimal Classification (DDC), which has formed the foundation of library organization since 1876, when it was first proposed by Melvil Dewey. DDC was devised to arrange items and collections of items in a logical fashion using Arabic numerals. It is the most widely used classification system in the world; it is used in 135 countries and translated into more than 30 languages. It is certainly the classification system best known by most library users in the United States. Ninety-five percent of all U.S. public and school libraries, a quarter of all college and university libraries, and one-fifth of all special libraries use this system (OCLC 2004).

The DDC divides knowledge into *classes*; these classes represent traditional academic disciplines. There are ten main classes that are intended to encompass the universe of knowledge. Each of these main classes is assigned a specific numerical range. The main classes are shown in Figure 6.1.

Figure 6.1
Dewey Decimal Classification
Main Classes

000	Generalities
100	Philosophy, parapsychology and occultism, psychology
200	Religion
300	Social Sciences
400	Language
500	Natural sciences and mathematics
600	Technology (Applied Sciences)
700	The arts
800	Literature (Belles-lettres) and rhetoric
900	Geography, history, and auxiliary disciplines

Each item that falls within the scope of one of these classes is assigned a number within that range. The number assigned is called a *class number*. The internal logic within a main classification is hierarchical: that is, within a main discipline or class, there are various subclasses or subdivisions, and the subclasses are variously subdivided with greater and greater specificity. Each subclass is assigned a range of numbers within the range of the main class. For example, the items classed in the 640s deal with home economics and family living. Items in the 641s deal with food and drink, while those items dealing with household furnishings would be classed in the 645s (Dewey Decimal Classification 1996, p. 640). The class number becomes longer as the subclass of the discipline becomes more specific. To this end, decimals are used. Hence, the number 795 applies to games of chance, 795.4 applies to card games, 795.41 applies to "games in which skill is a major element," and 795.412 applies to poker, except in my own case in which skill is not involved (Dewey Decimal Classification 1996, p. 794). The length of the decimal notation can extend to many digits, reflecting highly detailed subdivisions of a discipline.

The DDC is a remarkable system of library organization and has served library users for more than a century. Obviously, both the physical and intellectual organization of library collections is directly affected by this system. Interestingly, although DDC affects the physical location of items in the collection, a key feature of this system is that it provides for "relative location" rather than a fixed one. Before DDC, books in libraries were numbered based on physical location in the library. Books had only one fixed location. In DDC, the numbers assigned to books are not related to a particular place, but in relation to other books (Chan 1994). Hence, the actual physical locations of materials could change as long as the books remained in appropriate relation to each other (any shelver shifting books will tell you this!).

This is not to say that DDC is without problems. Among the problems is that the system is a closed one. The range of numbers is limited between 000 and 999, and the disciplines they designate have already been assigned. As new disciplines arise, they must be accommodated within the existing ten classes, and in many cases this is not easy. Disciplines that were undeveloped or unknown at the time the DDC was created are today often crowded into narrow ranges. In the twentieth century a major problem arose with the growth of the social sciences. More recently, the rise of computer technologies, which, of course, were unanticipated in Dewey's time, have also necessitated considerable modifications. DDC has been revised many times to reflect needed changes, but the changes themselves can cause problems because altering classification practices may entail substantial work on the part of libraries. A second problem is that DDC places heavy emphasis on knowledge created and disseminated in European and North American culture. This reflects the nineteenth-century biases from which the system emerged. There has been a concerted effort in previous years to remove the Christian and Western biases from the system, and the newest edition (the 22nd) continues the effort to eliminate these biases. Of course, these problems are not solely those of DDC: most other classification systems also share these difficulties because they also reflect the times in which they are created.

Library of Congress Classification

The Library of Congress Classification (LC Classification or LCC) was developed at the turn of the century to deal with the ever-growing size of the Library of Congress's collection. Although DDC and other existing classification systems influenced the development of LC Classification, the system is unique and was developed for the practical purposes of organizing and accessing the Library of Congress collection. Other libraries that tend to adopt LC Classification are often academic libraries with large collections. LC Classification is an alpha-numeric system. Each class number begins with one to three letters followed by one to four integers. Decimals can be used to expand the class. The letters represent the main class and subclass divisions followed by the integers that further subordinate the discipline. Hence a notation that begins with the letter P deals with language and literature, while PT stands for German literature.

There are 20 main classes, as shown in Figure 6.2.

There are specific subclasses for a variety of the main classes. For example, under the class K (law), there are specific schedules for laws of the United States, Germany, United Kingdom and Ireland, Latin America, and Canada.

Some Challenges with Classification Systems

KEEPING CLASSIFICATION SYSTEMS UP-TO-DATE

Classifications such as DDC and LCC rely heavily on disciplinary approaches. Without a crystal ball, it is difficult to predict new disciplines or significant changes within disciplines such as the emergence of new

Figure 6.2
Library of Congress Main Classes

A	General Works
B	Philosophy; Psychology and Religion
C	Auxiliary Sciences of History
D	General and Old World History
E-F	American History
G	Geography; Maps; Anthropology; Recreation
H	Social Sciences; Economics and Sociology
J	Political Science
K	Law (General)
L	Education
M	Music
N	Fine Arts
P	Language and Literature Tables
Q	Science
R	Medicine
S	Agriculture
T	Technology
U	Military Science
V	Naval Science
Z	Bibliography; Library Science

subdisciplines. Similarly, some disciplines become obsolete. Attempts to respond to these changes can sometimes be quite cumbersome and present major problems to classification systems. For example, the introduction of new disciplines or subdisciplines may force the creation of new classification numbers and the alteration of old ones. Policy and economic implications can be considerations for libraries if they decide to adjust their collections and catalog to reflect these changes.

THE LIMITED APPLICATION OF CLASSIFICATION SYSTEMS FOR PERIODICALS AND OTHER FORMATS

Mann (1993) has observed that the current use of library classification schemes does not normally provide assistance in retrieving information from certain types of documents: most notably periodical articles and audiovisual materials. Library classification systems themselves have not been used to assign classification numbers to periodical articles (although theoretically this is possible). In addition, the systems themselves were designed for books, and the great advantage of the systems was to permit browsing of similar materials in the same location. Other formats can seldom be shelved with the book materials. As a result, the application of classification in libraries generally has not allowed classification schemes to accomplish one of their basic goals when other formats are considered (Mann 1993). It should be noted that this is not a failing of the conceptual scheme of the classification system. The system itself could be used to assign numbers to individual periodical articles or audiovisual materials. Perhaps with the growth of automated indexing of periodical articles, the assignment of classification numbers will become commonplace. But currently, such systems have not been employed for this purpose.

CONTROLLED VOCABULARY

A second crucial intellectual technology is controlled vocabulary. A controlled vocabulary is "a list of preferred and nonpreferred terms produced by the process of vocabulary control" (National Information Standards Institute [NISO], Z39.19-2003, p. 35). Vocabulary control is "the process of organizing a list of terms (a) to indicate which of two or more synonymous terms is authorized for use; (b) to distinguish between homographs; and (c) to indicate hierarchical and associate relationships among terms in the context of a thesaurus or subject heading list" (NISO, Z39.19-2003, p. 38). Decisions regarding which terms will be used to refer to authors, titles, or subjects are referred to as authority control. With authority control, one term is selected for use. The list of accepted terms used in a controlled vocabulary is referred to as an authority list. Such vocabularies, however, consist of more than just the words or vocabulary itself; they consist of rules for assigning terms, methods for describing relationships among terms, and a means for changing and updating terms (Meadows 1992).

Controlled vocabularies play crucial roles especially when seeking subject-related information, but they provide consistency in the assignment and use not only of subject terms or headings, but also of author and title terms. Controlled vocabularies are vital for effective use of indexes and thesauri and are essential for the collocating function of the library catalog. One is using a controlled vocabulary when consulting subject headings in a card catalog or online catalog; one is experiencing a controlled vocabulary when consulting the index terms in a periodicals index or when searching a computerized bibliographic database. Every time one encounters a well-prepared index at the back of a book, it is a controlled vocabulary at work.

Controlled vocabularies provide important information to the user. The following are some of the issues they deal with.

Synonymy. A variety of terms can mean the same thing. Organizers of information must select and consistently apply the same term so that searchers can retrieve information effectively. (Of course, those selecting such terms also can create references from synonymous terms to the one selected for use, e.g., *see* references in the library catalog.)

Hierarchical relationships. Controlled vocabularies can reveal when a concept identified by a term is contained within a larger concept also identified, e.g., references to *broader terms* or *narrower terms.*

Associative relationships. Controlled vocabularies help identify related terms (concepts) that could serve to broaden and enrich an information search.

Homographs. Sometimes, terms spelled the same way may represent different concepts. Controlled vocabularies reveal this ambiguity and refer information seekers to the appropriate terms, e.g., China (the country) versus china (the table setting).

Obviously, this type of information provides valuable information and it is easy to see why controlled vocabularies are important in databases and in libraries. Consider the problem of synonymy in the library catalog. Suppose there were no vocabulary control for the subject headings in a library catalog. Catalogers could choose any terms they wished to describe the contents of the items they catalog. Consider if, when creating catalog entries on aircraft, catalogers could choose any number of terms such as aircraft, airplanes, planes, or flying machines to describe the content of various items on this subject. A catalog user would then need to look in at least four places to find all the material, *if* the user could think of each of these terms and any others that might seem reasonable. Clearly, if different terms are assigned to describe the same content in different items, it becomes very difficult to retrieve those items.

Controlled vocabularies reduce error and ambiguity and guide the user to the proper place. This guidance is provided in part by showing relationships between terms in a controlled vocabulary. Hence, when a user consults a given term, the controlled vocabulary may suggest terms that are broader or narrower or give the proper equivalent term used by the controlled vocabulary. Examples of these relationships will be discussed further in the context of the Library of Congress Subject Headings.

Thesauri

A critical tool intended to promote retrieval of information through the use of a controlled vocabulary is the thesaurus. A thesaurus is "a controlled vocabulary of terms in natural language that are designed for postcoordination" (NISO 2003, p. 1). Indexers and catalogers use such a vocabulary to determine precisely what terms to assign as access points to a record or document. Users of indexes, catalogs, and databases can use thesauri to locate the proper terms for searching or to discover related terms and subjects. According to the National Information Standards Organization, thesauri accomplish four purposes:

> (1) Translation: To provide a means for translating the natural language of authors, indexers, and users into a controlled vocabulary used for indexing and retrieval; (2) Consistency: To promote consistency in the assignment of index terms; (3) Indication of Relationships: To indicate semantic relationships among terms; (4) Retrieval: To serve as a searching aid in retrieval of documents. (NISO 2003, p. 1)

As can be seen from these purposes, thesauri play critical roles in structuring access as well as in assisting in retrieval itself.

Thesauri usually consist of a core list of index terms, usually single words but sometimes combinations of words, phrases, or names. Terms in a thesaurus are sometimes referred to as descriptors. The terms comprising the core list are the ones determined to be acceptable for use to gain access to the information system (for example, catalog, database, index). Associated with these terms are additional terms that are not used for direct access to the information system, but which, if consulted first, will direct a user to the appropriate term for use. These are sometimes referred to as lead-in terms. Such an expansion is critical to a thesaurus because individuals trying to gain access to a particular information system are usually not aware of the terms that were selected. Rather they come with their own vocabulary and their own ideas as to which terms reflect the subject matter. As with controlled vocabularies, the terms selected are also enriched by notations about other associated terms and their relationships. Although thesauri have been in existence for many years, they have become especially important in the use of automated information retrieval systems. Such thesauri provide a wide variety of available terms for those assigning terms to documents for access and for searchers seeking information. Examples of such thesauri include the *ERIC Thesaurus* and *INSPEC Thesaurus*.

Subject Heading Lists

Lists of subject headings provide critical access points for finding information. The list of greatest importance for libraries is the Library of Congress Subject Headings (LCSH), which has worldwide influence. LCSH is best known for its applications to library catalogs and serves as an authoritative source of subject headings not only for library catalogs but for many indexes. Among its significant advantages is that it controls terms for the information organizer (for example, cataloger or indexer) and the information seeker (the user or librarian).

Subject headings have a special relationship to the classification system and provide an additional means of retrieving information. Classification puts subjects into the context of disciplines. For example, information on horses can appear in an animal (biology) class, in sports (horse racing), and in pets. Subject headings, in contrast, list subjects outside the disciplinary context, so a search on horses retrieves items about horses regardless of their disciplinary context. As a by-product, subject headings act as a kind of index to the classification scheme. That is, by identifying a subject through a subject heading, one also discovers the classification number or numbers assigned to that subject.

The LC subject headings are developed by the Library of Congress to provide subject access to the collections of the Library of Congress. They are widely used, in part, because they are one of the few *general* (nondisciplinary) controlled vocabularies in English. LC uses these headings in MARC records (discussed below), which in turn means that all other libraries and other organizations that use the MARC records also have the advantage of the LC subject headings. The dominance of these subject headings highlights their importance in providing effective and complete access to library collections.

The subject headings list contains many different types of headings, listed in an alphabetical arrangement. Among the types of headings used are (1) single nouns or terms (e.g., "Lifeguards"), (2) adjective with a noun (e.g., "Life-saving apparatus"), (3) prepositional phrases (e.g., "Life-saving at Fires"), (4) compound or conjunctive phrases (e.g., "Lifting and carrying"), (5) phrases or sentences (see Figure 6.3).

Figure 6.3
Sample Library of Congress Subject Headings

Survival swimming
Life-saving apparatus
VK1460-VK1481
  BT Survival and emergency
      equipment
  NT Emergency vehicles
      Immersion suits
      Life-boats
      Life-preservers
      Life rafts
      Life-saving nets
      Line-throwing guns
      Line-throwing rockets
      Submarine rescue vehicles
  —**Law and legislation** *(May Subd*
    Geog)
Life-saving at fires *(May Subd*
  Geog) TH9402-TH9418
  BT Fire-escapes
      Fires
      Rescue work
Life-saving nets
  TH9418
  BT Life-saving apparatus
Life-saving stations *(May Subd*
  Geog)
  VK1460-VK1471
  BT Life-saving
  NT Lifeboat service
Life science engineering
  USE Bioengineering
Life science publishing *(May Subd*
  Geog)
  BT Life sciences
      Publishers and publishing
      Science publishing
Life sciences *(May Subd Geog)*
  UF Biosciences
      Sciences, Life
  BT Science
  NT Agriculture

Biology
  Life science publishing
  Medical sciences
  Medicine
  —**Bibliography**
  RT Life sciences literature
  —Moral and ethical aspects
  USE Bioethics
Life sciences ethics
  USE Bioethics
Life sciences libraries *(May Subd*
  Geog)
  UF Libraries, Life sciences
  BT Scientific libraries
  NT Agricultural libraries
      Biological libraries
      Medical libraries
  —**Collection development**
  (May Subd Geog)
  BT Collection development (Li-
      braries)
Life sciences literature *(May Subd*
  Geog)
  QH303.6
  BT Scientific literature
  RT Life sciences—Bibliography
  NT Agriculture literature
      Biological literature
      Medical literature
Life skills *(May Subd Geog)*
  Here are entered works that dis-
cuss a combination of the skills
needed by an individual to exist in
modern society, including skills re-
lated to education, employment, fi-
nance, health, housing, psychology,
etc.
  UF Advice-for-living books
      Basic life skills
      Competencies, Functional
      Coping skills

Everyday living skills
  Functional competencies
  Fundamental life skills
  Living skills
  Personal life skills
  Problems of everyday liv-
  ing, Skills for solving
  Skills, Life
  BT Interpersonal relations
      Social learning
      Success
  NT Conduct of life
      Self-help techniques
      Social skills
      Study skills
      Survival skills
  —**Handbooks, manuals, etc.**
  UF Life skills guides
  SA *subdivision* Life skills guides
      under classes of persons and
      ethnic groups
  —**United States**
  NT Hispanic Americans—Life
      skills guides
      Vietnamese Americans—
      Life skills guides
Life skills guides
  USE Life skills—Handbooks,
      manuals, etc.
Life span, Productive *(May Subd*
  Geog)
  UF Productive life span
      Work life
      Working life
  BT Age and employment
      Aged
      Life cycle, Human
      Mortality
      Occupations
Life span prolongation
  USE Longevity

Figure 6.3 (*Continued*)

Life stages, Human
  USE Life cycle, Human
Life style *(May Subd Geog)*
  HQ2042-HQ2044
  Here are entered theoretical
works on an individual's distinc-
tive, recognizable way of living,
and the behavior that expresses it.
  UF Counter culture
      Lifestyle
      Social environment
      Style, Life
  BT Human behavior
      Life cycle, Human
      Manners and customs
      Quality of life
  NT Living alone
**Life support systems (Critical
care)**
(May Subd Geog)
  RC86.7
  BT Critical care medicine
**Life support systems (Space envi-
ronment)**
  UF Man in space
  BT Bioengineering
      Environmental engineering
      Human engineering
      Space flight—Physiological
      effect
     Space medicine
  NT Closed ecological systems
      (Space environment)
      Extraterrestrial bases
      Space cabin atmospheres
      Space ships
      Space suits
      Space vehicles—Oxygen
      equipment
      Space vehicles—Water-sup-
      ply
Life tables
  USE Mortality—Tables
Life testing, Accelerated
  USE Accelerated life testing
Life time light (Portrait sculpture)
  USE Strong, Brett-Livingstone,

  1953-
  Life time light
Life without death (Tale)
  USE Youth without age and life
      without death (Tale)
Life zones *(May Subd Geog)*
  QH84
  UF Biogeographic zones
      Zones, Life
  BT Biogeography
      Ecology
  NT Crop zones
      Hybrid zones
Lifeboat crew members *(May Subd
  Geog)*
  BT Life-saving
      Lifeboat service
Lifeboat service *(May Subd Geog)*
  BT Life-boats
      Life-saving stations
  NT Lifeboat crew members
Lifecare communities
  USE Life care communities
Lifecycle, Human
  USE Life cycle, Human
Lifeguards *(May Subd Geog)*
  GV838.72-GV838.74
  UF Life guards
  BT Life-saving
      Swimmers
Lifeline earthquake engineering
  (May Subd Geog)
  BT Earthquake engineering
Lifelong education
  USE Continuing education
Lifestyle
  USE Life style
Lifjell (Telemark fylke, Norway)
  BT Mountains—Norway
Lifoma (African people)
  USE Foma (African people)
Lifou language
  USE Dehu language
Lift (Aerodynamics)
  UF Aerodynamic forces
  BT Aerodynamic load
      Aerodynamics

  RT Drag (Aerodynamics)
  NT Flaps (Airplanes)
      Ground-cushion phenom-
      enon
      Stalling (Aerodynamics)
  —**Computer programs**
Lift fans
  UF Fans, Lift
      Lifting fans
  BT Air jets
      Fans (Machinery)
  RT Ground-effect machines
  NT Fan-in-wing aircraft
Lift irrigation *(May Subd Geog)*
  BT Irrigation
Lift net fishing
  SH344.6L5
  UF Dip net fishing
      Lift nets
  BT Fisheries
      Fishing nets
Lift nets
  USE Lift net fishing
Lift-off from the moon
  USE Artificial satellites—Lunar
      launching
Lift stations
  USE Pumping stations
Lifters, Vacuum
  USE Vacuum lifters
Lifthrop family
  USE Liptrap family
Lifting and carrying
  T55.3L5
  UF Carrying weights
  BT Materials handling
  NT Slings and hitches
      Vacuum lifters
      Weight lifting
Lifting and carrying (Jewish law)
  BT Jewish law
      Prohibited work (Jewish
      law)
Lifting fans
  USE Lift fans
Lifting-jacks
  TJ1430-TJ1435

The headings can also include a variety of subheadings under important terms. These subheadings can take many forms, such as division by time (e.g., nineteenth century), geography (e.g., France), or form of item (e.g., dictionary).

Decisions made by the Library of Congress regarding the terms used to denote a particular subject can dramatically affect the ability of a library user to locate the information or item desired. For this reason, there is a *syndetic* structure to the LC subject headings. A syndetic structure is one that links related terms, a structure that is common in such vocabularies generally. The use of related terms allows a searcher to identify those subjects that may relate to the one under investigation as well as identify the "correct" term used by the Library of Congress. To this end, major terms are linked to other subject terms or phrases. These links can be to broader terms (BT), to narrower terms (NT), or to the equivalent terms that are the accepted terms (USE). For example, for the subject heading "Life-saving apparatus" there is a reference to the broader term "Survival and emergency equipment" and to the narrower term "Emergency vehicles." For the term "Life science ethics," the LC subject headings indicate that the term used in the catalog is "Bioethics" (USE). Indexers and catalogers use this structure to provide the helpful *see* and *see also* references in catalogs and indexes.

The Library of Congress Subject Headings, although dominant, are not the only subject headings in common use. Smaller public libraries, for example, use the Sears List of Subject Headings. This is a simplified list, similar to LCSH, but the terms and structure are less complex. On the other end of the spectrum is the highly technical Medical Subject Headings (MeSH) created by the National Library of Medicine for searching *Index Medicus*, a database of medical materials.

Over the years, however, critics have expressed concern that some of the headings employed are inadequate. One criticism suggests that the subject headings reflect a cultural bias. Perhaps the most notable and outspoken professional advocating this view is Sanford Berman. Berman (1971) has argued for many years that the "LC list can only 'satisfy' parochial, jingoistic Europeans and North Americans, white-hued, at least nominally Christian (and preferably Protestant) in faith . . . and heavily imbued with the transcendent, incomparable glory of Western civilization" (p. ix). Berman has repeatedly exposed subject headings that suggest racial or religious prejudices and stereotypes. LC has also made modifications to headings considered discriminatory largely in response to Berman's criticisms (University of Illinois 1996). Berman

(1981) has also suggested that there aren't nearly enough "people help-ing descriptors," or popular terms, rather than the formal terms often devised by LC (p. 96). As a consequence, people may approach the cata-log with a popular term only to find that there is no such term, and they may be unable to locate the correct synonym. Among other concerns are that the subject terms have an academic bias that is unconducive to ap-plications in public libraries. Also, there is concern that the subject head-ing terms become outdated quickly. Newer items stored under outdated terms may not be located, because the user is using the more modern term in the search. The need to use the latest editions of the LCSH to obtain effective access to the information contained in the catalog and hence in the collection itself becomes obvious.

The development of electronic information access and the Web have also raised the possibility that LCSH might be applicable in this nontra-ditional environment. But as O'Neill and Chan (2003) have observed, "LCSH's complex syntax and rules for constructing headings restrict its application by requiring highly skilled personnel and limit the effec-tiveness of automated authority control" (p. 1). Nonetheless, its quality makes it an appropriate model to serve as a foundation for new systems that may be more flexible. To this end, led by OCLC, the Library of Con-gress and the Association for Library Collections and Technical Services of the American Library Association (ALCTS), the Faceted Application of Subject Terminology (FAST) has been developed as a simplified vo-cabulary based on LCSH. FAST is designed to apply in the Web envi-ronment and is intended to meet three goals: "it should be simple in structure (easy to assign and use) and easy to maintain; it should pro-vide optimal access points; [and] it should be flexible and interoperable across disciplines and in various knowledge discovery and access envi-ronments including the online public access catalog (OPAC)" (O'Neill and Chan 2003, p. 2). FAST will retain the LC subject headings in an authority file, but simplify the rules for syntax, so that it can be used by individuals with little training and experience. The original authority file for FAST will contain two million authority records. It is hoped that such a system will help provide effective access to a Web environment.

THE LIBRARY CATALOG

One of the fundamental limitations to collections of physical objects (such as books or periodicals) is that they can only be in one place at one time: only one physical arrangement of materials or group of materials can exist at a time. In order to overcome this limitation and to increase the modes of access, the library arranges representatives or surrogates of that knowledge in alternative arrangements. Historically, the surrogates were first organized only by author. With the development of card technology and the ability to produce duplicate cards, title and subject access were added to author access. Today, catalog records provide fundamental access to the library collection by author, title, and subject. Hence, if books are arranged alphabetically by author's last name on the shelf, the surrogates can be simultaneously arranged by subject, title, or discipline. A catalog that arranges records in one alphabetical file is called a *dictionary* catalog. Catalogs that have separate subject catalogs are called *divided* catalogs. Catalogs that arrange their records by classification number are called *classified* catalogs. While card catalogs may have separate physical files, one electronic catalog can provide the same search options, and more, and perform the search far more efficiently.

The library catalog, whether physical cards (the manual catalog) or electronic records, is an important intellectual technology that attempts to present much of the knowledge in the library in a systematic fashion. A catalog lists materials that comprise a collection, which in libraries usually focuses on the book collection. The records in a catalog are surrogates for the materials in that they represent items in the collection. Classification numbers on the cataloging record combined with the classification number on the material itself effect retrieval of materials in a library collection.

The library catalog is critical for libraries because it represents a substantial proportion of the total knowledge contained in the library collection or information system. In fact, the contemporary library catalog also provides access to electronic indexes and other information retrieval tools that expand the library resources far beyond its own collection.

Among the earliest and most influential attempts to define the purpose of the catalog was made by Charles Ami Cutter, who developed what he terms the "objects" of the catalog in his *Rules for a Dictionary Catalog* (1904).

As shown in Figure 6.4, Cutter's first two objects describe the two basic access functions of catalogs: the finding function and the collocation function. Hence, the catalog is designed to locate items and to bring items of similar characteristics (such as author or subject) together. As Tillett (1991) observes, "a library catalog should facilitate finding a desired item and should enlighten us about related items by displaying, in one place, all items that share a common characteristic, be it author, title,

---

Figure 6.4
Cutter's Objects of the Catalog

Objects

1. To enable a person to find a book of which either
   (a) the author
   (b) the title   } is known
   (c) the subject
2. To show what the library has
   (d) by a given author
   (e) on a given subject
   (f) in a given kind of literature
3. To assist in the choice of a book
   (g) as to its edition (bibliographically)
   (h) as to its character (literary or topical)

Source: Cutter, Charles Ami. *Rules for a Dictionary Catalog*. Washington, D.C.: GPO, 1904, p. 12.

or subject, and informing us of relationships to other materials" (p. 150). The objectives of the catalog were reaffirmed by the International Federation of Library Associations (IFLA) at the International Conference on Cataloguing Principles in 1961, which included 53 countries. At the conference the "Statement of Principles" (or "Paris Principles") were adopted, which established basic principles for access. The function of the catalog as described in the "Statement of Principles" is shown in Figure 6.5.

The goal of a catalog is not only to permit individuals to find items that they already know exist, but also to help them find items of which they were previously unaware (Layne 1989, p. 188).

The catalog as an intellectual technology provides more than an access function, however; it also provides systematic description of items in the collection. Some of the descriptive functions of the catalog include:

1. To state significant features of an item; to identify an item.
2. To distinguish one from other items by describing its scope, contents, and bibliographic relation to other items.
3. To present descriptive data that respond best to the interests of most catalog users.

Figure 6.5
Functions of the Catalogue

---

2.   Functions of the Catalogue

The catalogue should be an efficient instrument for ascertaining

2.1   whether the library contains a particular book specified by
(a) its author and title, *or*
(b) if the author is not named in the book, its title alone, *or*
(c) if the author and title are inappropriate or insufficient for identification, a suitable substitute for the title; and

2.2   (a) which works by a particular author and
(b) which editions of a particular work are in the library.

Source: International Federation of Library Associations. "Statement of Principles: Adopted at the International Conference on Cataloguing Principles, Paris, October, 1961." Annotated edition by Eva Verona. London: IFLA, Committee on Cataloguing, 1971, xiii.

---

4.   To provide justification for access points, that is, to make clear to users why they have retrieved an item, for example, to discover that a particular person authored or illustrated or adapted a particular work. (Carlyle 1996)

These descriptive functions provide valuable information by supplying needed information about the item and ensuring that the item is actually the one sought. This leads naturally to a discussion of a key element of catalogs and other information organizing tools—the bibliographic record itself.

Bibliographic Records (For Print or Machine-Readable Catalogs)

A fundamental aspect of designing information systems for retrieval is the creation of records that represent the items needed. These representations are sometimes referred to as surrogates. The content in these records is referred to as the bibliographic description. The entire record is referred to as the bibliographic record. Such information representations can be found in a variety of locating tools, including the library catalog, bibliographies, indexes, and abstracts. The records in these tools are intended to represent the actual item of knowledge in one way or another. A bibliographic record consists of a series of data elements (for example, author, title, place and date of publication, subject heading). Those elements that are created specifically for retrieval of bibliographic records are called access points or index terms. It should be noted that calling records surrogates implies that they always serve to guide the user to another item—the item referred to by the surrogate. But in reality, this is not always the case. There are times when a bibliographic record can, in and of itself, provide the information needed, and in this sense can be seen itself as part of the body of knowledge to be retrieved.

Some bibliographic records contain just a little information, while others may be quite detailed, but their purpose is always the same: to represent a unique item, for example, a particular version or edition, sometimes referred to as a manifestation of the same work. For example, there are many versions or manifestations of *Alice in Wonderland*. A bibliographic record has to provide sufficient information to distinguish one manifestation from another and relate the particular item being described to other items.

The challenge of being able to relate the various manifestations of a work has led to the concept of "bibliographic families." Smiraglia (2001) defines a bibliographic family as "that set that includes all texts of a work that are derived from a single progenitor" (p. 75). The texts that are derived have a "derivative bibliographic relationship" to the original. As an example, Smiraglia identifies some of the possible manifestations of a novel. They include but are not limited to:

1. the first edition of the published novel
2. subsequent editions with changes
3. translated editions of the first or subsequent editions of the novel
4. a screenplay of the novel
5. a motion picture

Other manifestations might include radio versions, abridgements, or adaptations including musical works or plays. Smiraglia observes that even the smallest bibliographic families are complex, but the largest families are commonly those works that would appear in academic research libraries. If one could effectively identify common bibliographic relationships among family members, the results could be used to collocate the family members and increase access to this complexly related group of materials. As Smiraglia and Leazer (1999) point out: "The development of direct and explicit control of bibliographic families would greatly enhance the user's ability to navigate the bibliographic universe" (p. 494).

The actual construction of bibliographic records is a complex task, and there is considerable discussion as to how much and what type of information is needed to represent an item. In fact, surrogates must reflect subtle intellectual distinctions. For example, there is a distinction between a particular book (the physical object) and the "work," which is embodied not only in a particular book but in many books. Hence, the work *Moby Dick* is embodied in many books of the same name, including many editions or translations. Creating a bibliographic record requires that the physical character of the book and the intellectual character of the work be properly described and differentiated. As Lubetzky (1985) has observed, "a *book* is not an independent entity but represents a particular *edition* of a particular *work* by a particular *author* . . . " (p. 190).

The creation of bibliographic records is guided by codes that provide standards or rules for the creation of such surrogates. The common process for providing bibliographic descriptions is called descriptive cataloging. Traditionally, these descriptions were found on catalog cards; today, they are more likely to appear on an online catalog screen, but the principles are the same.

There are two major factors that have dramatically affected descriptive cataloging over the last two decades. First is the economic advantage realized by shared cataloging efforts, and second is the use of computer technologies in the cataloging process (Delsey 1989). Cooperative efforts for standardized cataloging depend heavily on computerized bibliographic utilities such as OCLC, and this cooperation is promoted primarily through the efforts of the Library of Congress through its National Coordinated Cataloging Program. In this program, responsibility for descriptive cataloging is shared among the Library of Congress, designated libraries, and bibliographic utilities such as OCLC and the Research Library Group (RLG). Obviously, if one standard computer-generated record can be created for use by all or most libraries, significant fiscal and human resources are saved.

Bibliographic utilities and libraries rely on codes and standards to help make consistent their bibliographic descriptions. Codes that standardize bibliographic descriptions are important: standardization makes it easier for individuals to use a variety of information systems and databases and makes production of bibliographic records more economical since only one standard record need be generated. The movement for standardization has increased substantially in the last few decades, with major interest being generated on the international level. Primary activity for the international standardization for descriptive cataloging is currently being promulgated by the International Federation of Library Associations (IFLA). In 1971, for example, IFLA promulgated, through its program for international standardization, the International Standard Bibliographic Description for Monographs (ISBD(M)). In the years following, standards were subsequently developed for serials (ISBD(S)), printed music, maps, and other nonbook materials. These standards identify the key components for bibliographic description, the punctuation, and the preferred order for the components. Fortunately, these standards have been incorporated in individual cataloging codes, including AACR2. IFLA has continued these standardization activities through its Universal Bibliographic Control program.

Similarly, major constituencies involved in the creation of cataloging records are also working to improve bibliographic access. Most notably, in 1992 the Library of Congress, OCLC, and the RLG formed the Cooperative Cataloging Council to "facilitate an increase in the number of mutually acceptable bibliographic records available for use by the cooperative community" (Cromwell 1994, p. 415). This cooperative was succeeded by the Program for Cooperative Cataloging (PCC) in 1995. Of course, perfect standardization may not be possible, or even desirable, as variations in languages, cultural values, types of users, and purposes of institutions may be sufficiently great to create a need for variation in bibliographic description.

Today, there is considerable discussion regarding the need for various levels of cataloging. Given the economic stresses felt by libraries and the differences in library patrons' needs for detailed bibliographic description, some have argued that not all items have to be described with the same detail. They point particularly to research that suggests that patrons use only a few elements of the bibliographic description when searching for information, most notably, author, title, publisher, and place of publication (Svenonius 1990). These findings are somewhat controversial, but it is common for libraries to use more than one level of description, notably minimal-level cataloging and full-level cataloging. The minimal level was designed for materials considered to be less important than others and to help speed up the cataloging process, especially when backlogs were present (Cromwell 1994). The use of the minimal level remains controversial, although its use is commonplace, and there has also been an attempt to create a level of cataloging somewhere between minimal and full. This level is referred to as core-level standards, developed by the Cooperative Cataloging Council, which attempts to identify the essential elements of a bibliographic record requiring greater description than minimal level, but less than full (Cromwell 1994). These standards share a similar purpose in their creation: to accommodate the tremendous budget problems of libraries, to speed up the cataloging process for some materials, to reduce backlogs, and to make items available more quickly to users. But there is ongoing concern that less description is likely to mean a substantive decrease in the quality of information provided to the searcher. The importance of such a concern cannot be overestimated.

Anglo-American Cataloguing Rules

The primary code used to create bibliographic description for library catalogs is the Anglo-American Cataloguing Rules (AACR). It is not the first set of rules proposed for cataloging. Indeed, AACR is descended from a set of rules proposed by Antonio Panizzi for the British Museum library in 1841. The American Library Association promulgated rules for descriptive cataloging in 1908 and revised them several times. The Library of Congress used its own internal rules for description until the 1960s, when there was a strong interest in developing international standards for cataloging and in accommodating the use of computers. The first code designed specifically to accommodate these interests was the Anglo-American Cataloguing Rules (AACR1), promulgated in 1967. These rules recognized the importance of the "Paris Principles" written in 1961 and were developed with these principles in mind. AACR1 included rules for choosing access points for description (the method for describing the material) and for cataloging nonbook materials.

Although the intention was to create international standards, the practices of American, Canadian, and British libraries varied on many points (actually a separate edition was issued for British libraries), and as might be expected, the rules needed to undergo constant revision and enhancements. This ultimately led to a major revision of AACR1 in 1974 by international representatives from various national library associations and representatives from Canada, Great Britain, and the United States. The resulting revision is called the Anglo-American Cataloguing Rules Second Edition (AACR2) and incorporates International Standard Book Description (ISBD) standards. AACR2 represents an international standard for bibliographic description and continues to be revised. Amendments to the rules have occurred frequently in recent years with revisions published in 1999, 2001, and 2002. With the growth of the Internet and ever-increasing likelihood that electronic resources will play a greater role in information access, it is expected that the rules will continue to evolve.

BIBLIOGRAPHIES, INDEXES, AND ABSTRACTS

In addition to classified arrangements and library catalogs, there are other tools that represent common and important additions to the librarian's arsenal of organizing devices in the library. These tools not only play an important role in identifying and locating materials in the library; they also extend one's retrieval capabilities beyond those of the classified collection or library catalog. Among these are bibliographies, indexes, and abstracts, which can come in print, microform, and electronic formats. The effectiveness of these tools relies heavily on their ability to apply many of the intellectual technologies previously described, most notably the principles involved in controlled vocabulary, including the assignment of subject headings or descriptors.

A bibliography is a list of materials or items usually restricted in some way, such as by subject, form (for example, periodicals), or coverage (for example, items published before 1900). As a rule, bibliographies are intended to lead the user to the sources they identify. Bibliographies centralize bibliographic information: they are another form of collocation. Some include a brief note or summary of the contents and are referred to as annotated bibliographies. There are basically two types of bibliographies: systematic bibliography and analytical bibliography. Systematic bibliographies generally focus on a particular subject or are designed for a particular purpose. They are sometimes further subdivided into enumerative bibliographies and subject bibliographies. The latter is self-explanatory; it is a bibliography in a particular subject area. Enumerative bibliography is designed to provide an extensive list of items, but not necessarily on a specific subject. A catalog is an enumerative bibliography, as is a national bibliography. Analytical bibliography (also known as descriptive bibliography) is a list of items that carefully focuses on the physical aspects of the item so that historical and comparative analyses can be effected. In such bibliographies careful attention is paid to the physical characteristics of various editions, and they identify any characteristics of the item that would permit a scholar to place the item in its historical or aesthetic context (Bates 1976).

An index is "a systematic guide designed to indicate *topics* or *features* of *documents* in order to facilitate retrieval of documents or parts of documents" (NISO 1995, p. 8). This very broad characterization is especially appropriate for automated indexes. Such indexes consist of five components: terms, rules for combining terms, cross-references, a method for linking headings, and a particular order of headings, or search procedure (NISO 1995). More simply, an index can be viewed as an alphabetized list of items that direct the searcher to further information. It can point to content within a given work (for example, an index in the back of a book) or to items located outside the work (such as a periodical index). For example, when a searcher uses an index in the back of a book, the index term provides the appropriate section or page numbers within the work where information denoted by the term is provided. Indexes can provide retrieval information for most types of materials, including books, periodical articles, and dissertations. Other indexes have features much the same as bibliographies, for example, periodical indexes such as *Readers' Guide to Periodical Literature* or the *Social Sciences Citation Index*. These tools provide bibliographic citations arranged under various index terms. These terms might include, but are not limited to, subject terms, author names, article or book titles. Some indexes are devoted to a specific discipline, such as *Art Index*, while other indexes are considerably more general, such as *Magazine Index*; some are devoted to a single publication like the index for *National Geographic* or the *New York Times Index*. Given the proliferation of journals and the tremendous increase in the number of published articles over the years, the periodical index provides an essential pathway for the location of up-to-date material.

There are two major methods of indexing: precoordinate indexing and postcoordinate indexing. In precoordinate indexing, the indexer coordinates all the indexing terms at the time of the indexing. That is, the control over the combining of terms or indicating relationships between terms is done prior to the information seeker's use of the retrieval system. Postcoordinate indexing permits searchers to coordinate index terms of their own choosing (within the bounds of the controlled vocabulary) at the time of searching. This method is most common in (although not exclusively restricted to) electronic information retrieval systems in which the searcher selects combinations of search terms and connects them by logical operators, such as the Boolean terms *and*, *or* or *not*. Obviously, postcoordinate indexing permits great flexibility when using electronic indexes.

An abstract is "a brief and objective representation of the contents of a document or an oral presentation" (NISO 1997, p. 1). Whether prepared by the author or not, it is a form of surrogate that summarizes the contents of a document so that readers can determine if the document is appropriate for their purposes. Because of their abbreviated character abstracts can serve many useful purposes. For example, abstracts serve as a current awareness tool, a quick way to stay up to date; they also provide information seekers with access to a large body of literature that can be scanned quickly, including material in foreign languages (Pao 1989).

An abstract usually includes a bibliographic citation indicating where the entire text of an item can be located. It can be quite detailed or brief, but generally it attempts to describe key aspects of the document. There are two varieties of abstracts: *informative abstracts* and *indicative abstracts*. Informative abstracts represent and summarize the content of all major aspects of the material. Indicative abstracts briefly summarize what the document is about and include results when they are significant. Abstracts, however, are neither critical nor evaluative (Pao 1989); this differentiates an *abstract* from an *annotation*, which is a "brief explanation of a document or its contents, usually added as a note to clarify a title" (NISO 1997, p. 1) or a *review*, which is usually a more extensive summary of a document that includes evaluation and comment. Tools that arrange abstracts so that they can be accessed by index terms are especially useful knowledge location tools. Such tools often arrange the abstracts by broad classifications or subjects. The tools operate like periodical indexes except that they also contain abstracts, providing the searcher with even more information to help decide if consulting the full text would be helpful. Examples of such tools would be *Psychological Abstracts* or *Library and Information Science Abstracts*.

The intention of bibliographies, abstracts, and indexes is to centralize bibliographic information for materials that may exist in a variety of physical locations, to arrange it in a systematic way, and often to provide the information needed to locate the items for use. As such they represent important finding tools for both the librarian and the library user. But it also must be kept in mind that such tools have their limitations. They often reflect the cultural or theoretical biases of their authors or, due simply to economic limitations, are not complete. Some tools, notably those published as books, may quickly become outdated, especially in disciplines that change rapidly or in which new information is produced at a rapid pace. Few periodical indexes and abstracts are comprehensive; they seldom index *all* periodicals that might have an article in the pertinent subject area. Hence, some journals may not be indexed or may be only partially indexed. This is not to underestimate the importance of these tools. Rather, it highlights the complexity of trying to represent large bodies of knowledge. Information professionals must understand that all intellectual technologies and tools have their deficiencies; our confidence should not be placed entirely in any one item.

SHELF ARRANGEMENT

The manner in which a library physically arranges its items plays a critical role in the ability of the user to retrieve the desired information. The arrangements must take into account a wide variety of subjects, formats, and uses. Theoretically, a library could assign accurate and highly precise classification numbers to items, but arrange the materials on the shelf randomly, ignoring the benefits of the classification system. Such randomness might promote serendipity but is hardly efficient retrieval! Of course, shelf arrangement in libraries is not random and reflects a variety of organizational models. The models that predominate in libraries are alphabetical, numerical, and disciplinary. Clearly, most library collections begin with the premise that items of the same subject or from the same discipline are shelved together.

The proximity of subjects is effected through the use of the major classification systems (DDC and LC). Because the disciplines are designated by numerical notations (DDC) or alphanumeric notations (LC), subject proximity is created through the alphabetical/numerical sequences. Alphabetical arrangement predominates in fiction collections in public libraries, which are usually arranged in alphabetical order by author's last name and not generally classified by number. It should also be noted that discipline affects the arrangement even when the numbers for the disciplines are not sequential. For example, one might place language materials and literature close together (grouping 800s and 400s in Dewey), perhaps because users of one are also frequent users of the other. This suggests, as noted above, that other models of knowledge organization may also operate in libraries. These models are usually more general, but certainly are quite common. For example, collections may be organized by (1) type of materials (indexes, general reference materials, periodicals), (2) format (videocassettes, audiocassettes, computer software, microforms, print materials), or (3) user (children's, young adult, adult, vision-impaired).

THE ORGANIZATION OF KNOWLEDGE WITHIN ELECTRONIC INFORMATION RETRIEVAL SYSTEMS

Electronic information retrieval systems include a wide variety of tools. The online catalog is an example of such a system, as are periodical indexes, and other online databases. Understanding their basic structure is critical, because these systems are integral components of information access in libraries and other information centers and will continue to grow in importance as they are accessed both within the library and remotely through the Web.

Records and Fields

The foundation of electronic databases is in many ways similar to the card catalog: it is the record. A record is the information stored concerning a particular document. Each record refers to a document and consists of a series of fields. Fields are units of information within a record; that is, each field is a special area into which a specific category of information is added. Hence, in a bibliographic record there may be an author field, title field, an issue or volume field, a subject heading or descriptor field, and perhaps a field for special comments or notes. Database designers create these records and fields, but they do not necessarily select the access points to these records. Rather, it is common that the vendors who make these databases available determine which fields will actually be searchable and which ones will simply be displayed. The searchable fields may vary depending on the vendor, but the overall effect is to increase dramatically the number of access points that a searcher can use in locating information sources.

One of the most important developments for libraries regarding the creation of electronic records and fields was the development of MARC. MARC stands for Machine Readable Cataloging and was developed by the Library of Congress in the mid-1960s. The intention was to create a standard machine-readable format for bibliographic description. MARC is in reality a communications tool, designed for the creation and sharing of bibliographic information in a computerized or online environment. Today, MARC is the standard for the creation of bibliographic records.

MARC consists of various fields, also called identifiers or tags, each associated with specific information concerning a bibliographic entity (see Figures 6.6 and 6.7). There are many possible fields, including the basic ones such as author fields, title fields, subject fields, and publisher fields.

Additional fields include those for series, notes, related titles, and physical description. The effect of the MARC format can hardly be overestimated. MARC made possible the first substantive use of computer technologies for libraries—the centralized preparation of catalog cards

---

Figure 6.6
Selected MARC Fields

010	LC card number
020	International Standard Book Number
050	Library of Congress Classification Number
082	Dewey Decimal Classification Number
100	Personal author main entry
245	Title proper, subtitle, and statement of responsibility
246	Variant form of title
250	Edition statement
260	Publication information
300	Physical description
440	Series
500	General note
505	Contents note
650	Subject heading
700	Personal author added entry

---

for libraries—and its development also made possible the establishment of bibliographic utilities such as OCLC. The impact on collection development and resources sharing has been tremendous.

However, the MARC format was developed primarily as a cataloging format, and the organization of knowledge in other types of computer databases designed can be quite different. Abstracting and indexing databases, for example, use a variety of formats. The types of fields available and the type and number of searchable fields may also be different. The situation, however, is not totally chaotic. Some database producers in common subject areas have agreed to substantially the same formats. For example, Chemical Abstracts Services (CAS) and Biosciences Information Services (BIOSIS) use standardized record formats. Nonetheless, there is definitely a need for greater standardization.

MARC 21

MARC 21 is the latest version of the LC MARC format. MARC 21 is not a new format, but the harmonization of the format should greatly improve global access sharing of bibliographic records. In fact, MARC 21 is now being used not only in the United States and Canada, but also in Australia, New Zealand, many Latin American countries, the Middle East, and Asian countries including China. The United Kingdom is ex-

---

Figure 6.7
Sample MARC Record with Fields*

020	ISBN 1-56308-354-X
050	PS374.P63R67 1995
082	016.813009
100	Herald, Diana Tixier.
245	Genreflecting: a guide to reading interests in genre fiction / Diana Tixier Herald.
250	4th ed.
260	Englewood, Colo.: Libraries Unlimited, 1995.
300	xxvi, 367 p.; 25 cm.
500	Rev. ed. of: Genreflecting / Betty Rosenberg, 3rd ed. 1991.
504	Includes bibliographical references and indexes.
650	American fiction—Stories, plots, etc.
650	Popular literature—Stories, plots, etc.
650	English fiction—Stories, plots, etc.
650	Fiction genres—Bibliography.
650	Fiction—Bibliography.
650	Reading interests.
700	Rosenberg, Betty. Genreflecting.

*Record modified

Reprinted with permission from Online Computer Library Center.

pected to use MARC 21 in the near future (Radebaugh 2003).

MARC 21 brings together the U.S. and Canadian MARC formats and also updates MARC to include access to Web pages in library catalogs. There are now fields to permit the adding of URLs, FTP sites, and other computer addresses. In addition hypertext links can now be embedded into the bibliographic record so that a link to a Web site can be accomplished directly from that record. Although some have questioned the applicability of the MARC 21 format in the Web environment, others believe it can be used effectively in this way (Radebaugh 2003).

Standardization of Records

With the ever-expanding volume of documents, the need to standardize the format and organization of records has become critical. Considerable help in standardization of records as well as other information-related activities is provided by the National Information Standards Organization (NISO). NISO is accredited by the American National Standards Institute (ANSI) to create and maintain technical standards for information and for other organizations that exchange data. NISO develops standards only after a considerable process of consultation and participation by individuals and organizations that would be affected by the standard under development. When NISO believes a consensus has been reached, a standard is issued (although sometimes not all participants agree with a standard, even when it is issued in its final form). Compliance with the standard is voluntary, but the use of standardized formats can be of considerable value, both financial and instrumental. Among the many standards that are relevant to libraries are the following:

Z39.2	Information Interchange Format
Z39.4	Guidelines for Indexes and Related Information Retrieval Devices
Z39.9	International Standard Serial Numbering
Z39.14	Guidelines for Abstracts
Z39.18	Scientific and Technical Reports—Organization, Elements, and Design
Z39.19	Guidelines for the Construction, Format, and Management of Monolingual Thesauri
Z39.41	Printed Information on Spines
Z39.48	Permanence of Paper for Publications and Documents in Libraries and Archives
Z39.50	Information Retrieval: Application Service Definition and Protocol Specification
Z39.63	Interlibrary Loan Data Elements
Z39.84	Syntax for the Digital Object Identifier
Z39.85	Dublin Core Metadata Element Set

Files

A file is a group or collection of records that share common characteristics. A library catalog may be seen as a file of works with the shared characteristic that they are contained within the library. Of course, there are many other types of files. Electronic files are referred to as databases, and there are literally thousands of such databases. The way that files are arranged in a database is referred to as file organization. Just like in a physical file, the logical structure of organization within an electronic file determines how well information retrieval can be effected. Generally, storage of files is logically organized around a key field. That is, the collection of records in the file is organized around a single field, such as a field containing the record number or the author's name. For example, a common arrangement of files is alphabetical: hence, a database may be arranged alphabetically by author's name. This results in a linear or sequential file. The files arranged by key field make up the main file. Of course, database searching for anything but the simplest databases must be much more flexible than being searchable by the key field. This is certainly true of the online catalogs and databases that librarians use. The searching of most files is supplemented through the use of inverted files, which serve as indexes to the main file. An inverted file consists of particular fields that are associated with particular records within the database. Hence, if the key field is an author field, other inverted files may contain title words or subject heading terms or descriptors. Searching on any of these terms leads to the identification of documents associated with that term. Although there are other ways to organize computers, such as list chains and clustered files, the inverted file is the fundamental organization for searching electronic databases (Pao 1989).

THE INTERNET ERA AND THE SEMANTIC WEB: ORGANIZING KNOWLEDGE ON THE INTERNET/WORLD WIDE WEB

A current and growing problem facing all seekers of information is how to deal with the deluge of information available on the Internet or World Wide Web. Of course, a major problem is that the Internet was developed as a decentralized system in which there is minimal control of content and organization. Obviously, such a system has great advantages in that the freedom to produce and make information available is maximized. But a significant disadvantage is the lack of standardization. It is obvious from the discussion in this chapter that the standardization of information organization can make vast amounts of information accessible. This improved access has been especially true in libraries. Unfortunately, this standardization is not available on the Web.

With the growth of information retrieval through online computer systems and the Web, alternative techniques for describing, organizing, and retrieving documents are being developed. Most notable has been the development of the Standard Generalized Markup Language (SGML), which was originally developed in 1970 as the Generalized Markup Language (GML) (Gaynor 1996). SGML provides a standardized means to describe various classes of documents and to identify the elements that comprise each class. Classes are characterized by document-type definitions (DTD), which also identify the structure of the document by identifying the necessary and optional elements. Each element for a class is assigned a code number. Hence, one class of document might be poem, and among its elements might be lines, stanzas, couplets, and author (Gaynor 1996). SGML can describe content as well as structure in a document. For example, it can identify phone numbers, chemical structures, and citations within a document. It also permits the addition of nonbibliographical elements that can provide evaluative and analytical information for electronic documents. Overall, the use of SGML permits a hierarchical structure in which the bibliographical information, analytical information, and the full text itself can be "tagged" for retrieval. In this environment, retrieval can be very flexible and informative: each element or combination of elements, including whole documents, could be manipulated electronically and retrieved.

The consistent application of SGML in the creation or processing of documents residing in online systems has substantial implications for effective retrieval of not only individual documents, but of the individual elements. SGML is accepted as both a national and international standard (ISO 8879). In addition, items in MARC format can be "translated" into SGML, making the application even broader for library use. Perhaps the most far-reaching application of SGML is the development of Hypertext Markup Language (HTML). This markup language is the fundamental language used to create Web documents on the World Wide Web. It permits an individual to structure a Web page, display images, and create links to other pages or documents so that individuals can navigate the Web.

HTML has been described by Miller and Hillman (2002) as the "first layer or first tier" (p. 57) of a three-tiered Web. HTML assigns a simple set of tags to describe a Web document and permits the ability to share documents based on these tags. But the extent of sharing has been limited especially when the document was rich in information. The second tier was established through the creation of XML files, which permit a greater degree of document sharing. XML stands for Extensible Markup Language. Approved by the World Wide Web Consortium (W3C) in 1998, XML is a subset of SGML and is compatible with both SGML and HTML. Where HTML focuses on how information is displayed, XML describes the information content of an electronic document. It was first conceived for use on the World Wide Web, but it can be used for general electronic publication as well. As Desmarais (2000) notes, XML "is not a single, fixed format like HTML, nor is it a replacement for HTML. XML is a metalanguage that lets users design their own markup languages to meet specific applications or industry needs. It provides a standard way for describing and exchanging data regardless of its nature, how the sending system stored it, or how the receiving system will use it" (p. 10). A particular advantage of XML documents is that they can be created in one application, but used in others without conversion; as such, XML has encouraged open-source solutions and stimulated the development of products that cross operating systems. XML is expected to be widely used and advantageous to helping describe and organize Web contents. Indeed with the development of XML, a new version of HTML, called XHTML, has been developed. XHTML is written in XML and can be viewed on current browsers and also used for XML documents (Lemay and Colburn 2003).

Although HTML and XML through their linking features can reveal *that* two or more documents are related to one another, they are not able to describe *how* one document is related to another. The tags used in HTML and XML do not in and of themselves have much meaning. Understanding how objects on the Web are connected or related requires that the system actually understand the meaning within the tags, and by understanding the meaning within the tags, the system goes a long way to understanding the meaning of the Web pages themselves and how their meanings relate. The goal of a Web that would permit computers to relate Web sites on the basis of their meaning, referred to as the "Semantic Web," was a fundamental aim of the early Web creators. The Semantic Web "is not a separate Web but an extension of the current one, in which information is given well-defined meaning, better enabling computers and people to work in cooperation" (Berners-Lee, Hendler, and Lassila 2001, p. 40). The potential of a Semantic Web where Web sites are related as to their meaning would be truly remarkable. Although it is still a vision, we may be approaching a day when it may now be, at least in part, attainable.

Currently, meaning is absent except for the basic notion that one page is "linked to" another. The Semantic Web moves beyond the notion of relationships such as "Link to," to richer relationships such as "Works for," "is Author of," or "Depends on." The Semantic Web, according to Miller and Swick (2003) "is based on the idea of having data on the Web defined and linked such that it can be used for more effective discovery, automation, integration and reuse across various applications" (p. 11).

The tools used to create and develop this semantic relationship is the third layer of the Web, and much of the activity devoted to its creation comes from the World Wide Web Consortium. A key component in the development of the Semantic Web is the Resource Description Framework (RDF). RDF is an application of XML and provides a framework for creating metadata. As Berners-Lee, Hendler, and Lassila (2001) note, "In RDF, a document makes assertions that particular things (people, Web pages or whatever) have properties (such as 'is a sister of,' 'is the author of') with certain values (another person, another Web page)" (p. 40). As Semantic Web researchers develop the necessary rules and logic, and exploit the potential of RDF, one may soon see new and exciting opportunities to exploit the knowledge represented on the Web.

Metadata

Underpinning all aspects of organizing the Web is the concept of "metadata." As Web sites have proliferated and digital libraries have emerged as a major source of information in the electronic information environment, metadata has become the critical means of locating and using them. Librarians have been dealing with the concept of metadata for many years in the nonelectronic environment, except it has been known as the elements of cataloging: subject headings, classification numbers, indexing, and bibliographic description. Metadata performs the same function in the electronic environment in that it describes and creates access points for electronic resources. Clyde (2002), however, notes one significant difference between the work of catalogers and those who assign metadata:

> The major difference is that while cataloging, classification and indexing are usually carried out by disinterested library professionals who are creating finding tools for library users, metadata is usually (but not always) created by the creator of the digital resource, and often with the specific aim of promoting that resource by achieving high search engine rankings and bringing "traffic" to a web site. (p. 1)

Metadata is data about data. There are three basic types of metadata used in the context of digital libraries. *Descriptive metadata* describes objects or collections in a way that makes them searchable by search tools. Metadata descriptions often coincide with the traditional elements of bibliographic description including author, title, and subject. *Structural metadata* describes format or the relationship between individual information objects in the same way that individual chapters might be related to an entire book (Wright 2002). *Administrative metadata* assists in the management and preservation of the digital objects or collections. It assists in digital rights management and also indicates what player might be needed to use the data.

As with traditional rules for cataloging, standards for metadata are being developed. The Dublin Core Metadata Initiative (DCMI) is probably the most prominent and defines a set of elements for resource description in the online environment. A metadata system that possesses these standardized elements might make it possible for many individuals who lack the expertise of a professional cataloger to describe their Web sites and assign terms that could significantly aid others in accessing them. Conceived in 1995 at an OCLC-sponsored workshop, DCMI is an "open forum for the development of standards for interoperable online metadata in support of a broad range of purposes and business models" (OCLC 2003). Its emphasis is collaborative and international. The primary mission of DCMI is three-fold:

1. Developing metadata standards for discovery across domains.
2. Defining frameworks for the interoperation of metadata sets.
3. Facilitating the development of community- or disciplinary-specific metadata sets that are consistent with items 1 and 2. (OCLC 2003)

A wide variety of individuals and organizations are participating in this initiative on an international scale, including the Library of Congress, National Science Foundation, OCLC, the National Center for Supercomputing Applications, the national libraries of Australia and Canada, archives and museums, educational institutions, digital libraries, governmental agencies, networks, publishers, and knowledge managers.

DCMI strives to create metadata standards that possess four critical characteristics:

Simplicity: The Dublin Core is intended to be usable by non-catalogers as well as resource description specialists. Most of the elements have commonly understood semantics of roughly the complexity of a library catalog card.

Semantic
Interoperability: In the Internet Commons, disparate description models interfere with the ability to search across discipline boundaries. Promoting a commonly understood set of descriptors that helps to unify other data content standards increases the possibility of semantic interoperability across disciplines.

International
Consensus: Recognition of the international scope of resource dis-
                covery on the Web is critical to the development of ef-
                fective discovery infrastructure. The Dublin Core ben-
                efits from active participation and promotion in some
                20 countries in North America, Europe, Australia, and
                Asia.
Extensibility: The Dublin Core provides an economical alternative to
                more elaborate description models such as the full
                MARC cataloging of the library world. Additionally, it
                includes sufficient flexibility and extensibility to encode
                the structure and more elaborate semantics inherent in
                richer description standards (OCLC 2003).

The Dublin Core data element set includes the following:

Element Name   Definition

Title: A name given to the resource.
Creator: An entity primarily responsible for making the content
                of the resource.
Subject: A topic of the content of the resource.
Description: An account of the content of the resource.
Publisher: An entity responsible for making the resource available.
Contributor: An entity responsible for making contributions to the
                content of the resource.
Date: A date of an event in the life cycle of the resource.
Type: The nature of genre of the content of the resource.
Format: The physical or digital manifestation of the resource.
Identifier: An unambiguous reference to the resource within a
                given context.
Source: A reference to a resource from which the present re-
                source is derived.
Language: A language of the intellectual content of the resource.
Relation: A reference to a related resource.
Coverage: The extent or scope of the content of the resource.
Rights: Information about rights held in and over the resource.
                (OCLC 2003)

These elements have been formally endorsed as the NISO Standard
(Z39.85–2001) and are the basis for the proposed ISO international
standard.

It should be noted that the Dublin Core provides the important basic elements for resource description in an electronic environment. There are also specialized applications and standards for describing particular types of objects as well. These include, for example, the Content Standards for Digital Geospatial Metadata (CSDGM) for objects such as maps and gazetteers, Categories for the Description of Works of Art (CDWA) for describing art objects, and Learning Object Metadata (LOM) for learning objects such as syllabi, lecture notes, simulations, and educational kits.

SUMMARY

As the universe of knowledge expands, the demands placed on systems to organize this universe increase. The focus on libraries often falls on the information-giving function. But information cannot be effectively retrieved unless it is properly organized. New information channels, such as the Web, have produced great excitement, and it is a constant refrain that you can get "everything on the Web." This, of course, is the problem—too much, rather than too little information is there, and the information environment in which it resides is disorganized. The organization of knowledge will continue to be a central issue for those in library and information science who have been dealing with this problem for years. It is hoped that those who produce and make available the vast new sources of information will recognize the expertise of librarians and information scientists and the technologies that they have developed to gain some control over this ever-expanding universe.

REFERENCES

Bates, Marcia. "Rigorous Systematic Bibliography." *RQ* 16 (fall 1976): 2–26.
———. "What Is a Reference Book? A Theoretical and Empirical Analysis." *RQ* 26 (fall 1986): 37–57.
Berman, Sanford. *The Joy of Cataloging: Essays, Letters, Reviews, and Other Explosions.* Phoenix, Ariz.: Oryx, 1981.
———. *Prejudices and Antipathies: A Tract on the LC Subject Heads Concerning People.* Metuchen, N.J.: Scarecrow, 1971.
Berners-Lee, Tim, James Hendler, and Ora Lassila. "The Semantic Web." *Scientific American* 284 (2001): 34–43.
Carlyle, Allyson. "Descriptive Functions of the Catalog." (Unpublished class materials). Kent, Ohio: Kent State University, SLIS, 1996.

Chan, Lois Mai. "General Principles of Classification." In *Cataloging and Classification: An Introduction*. New York: McGraw-Hill, 1994. 259–284.

Clyde, Anne. "Metadata." *Teacher Librarian* 30 (December 2002): 45–47.

Cromwell, Willy. "The Core Record: A New Bibliographic Standard." *Library Resources and Technical Services* 38 (October 1994): 415–424.

Cutter, Charles Ami. *Rules for a Dictionary Catalog*. Washington, D.C.: GPO, 1904.

Delsey, Tom. "Standards for Descriptive Cataloguing: Two Perspectives on the Past Twenty Years," In *The Conceptual Foundations of Descriptive Cataloging*. Edited by Elaine Svenonius. San Diego: Academic Press, 1989, 51–60.

Desmarais, Norman. *The ABCs of XML: The Librarian's Guide to the eXtensible Markup Language*. Houston: New Technology, 2000.

Dewey Decimal Classification and Relative Index. 21st ed. Edited by Joan S. Mitchell et al. Albany: Forest Press, 1996.

Gaynor, Edward. "From MARC to Markup: SGML and Online Library Systems." *ALCTS Newsletter* (Supplement) 7 (1996): A–D.

Kwasnik, Barbara H. "The Role of Classification Structures in Reflecting and Building Theory." In *Advances in Classification Research: Proceedings of the 3rd ASIS SIG/CR Classification Research Workshop*. Vol. 3. Medford, N.J.: Learned Information, 1992, 63–81.

Layne, Sara Shatford. "Integration and the Objectives of the Catalog." In *The Conceptual Foundations of Descriptive Cataloguing*. Edited by Elaine Svenonius. San Diego: Academic Press, 1989, 185–195.

Lemay, Laura, and Rafe Colburn. *Web Publishing with HTML and XHTML in 21 Days*. 4th ed. Indianapolis, Ind.: Sams, 2003.

Levy, David M., and Catherine C. Marshall. "Going Digital: A Look at Assumptions Underlying Digital Libraries." *Communications of the ACM* 4 (April 1995): 77–84.

Lubetzky, Seymour. "The Objectives of the Catalog." In *Foundations of Cataloging: A Sourcebook*. Littleton, Colo.: Libraries Unlimited, 1985, 186–191.

Mann, Thomas. *Library Research Models: A Guide to Classification, Cataloging, and Computers*. New York: Oxford University Press, 1993.

Meadows, Charles T. *Text Information Retrieval Systems*. San Diego: Academic Press, 1992.

Miller, Eric, and Diane Hillmann. "Libraries and the Future of the Semantic Web: RDF, XML, and Alphabet Soup." In *Cataloging the Web: Metadata, AACR, and MARC21: ALCTS Papers on Library Technical Services and Collections*. Edited by Wayne Jones, Judith R. Ahronheim, and Josephine Crawford. Lanham, Md.: Scarecrow, 2002, 57–64.

Miller, Eric, and Ralph Swick. "An Overview of W3C Semantic Web Activity." *Bulletin of the American Society of Information Science and Technology* 29 (April/May 2003): 8–11.

National Information Standards Organization [NISO]. "Guidelines for Abstracts." [Z39.14–1997.] Bethesda, Md.: NISO, 1997, revised 2002.

———. "Guidelines for the Construction, Format, and Management of Monolingual Thesauri." [Z39.19-2003.] Bethesda, Md.: NISO, 2003.

———. "Guidelines for Indexes and Related Information Retrieval Devices." [TR-02-1997]. Bethesda, Md.: NISO, 1997.

OCLC. "An Overview of the Dublin Core Metadata Initiative." [Online] Available at *http://dublincore.org/about/overview*. (Accessed July 2, 2003.)

———. "Dewey Services." [Online] Available at *www.oclc.org//dewey*. (Accessed January 15, 2004.)

O'Neill, Edward T., and Lois Mai Chan. "FAST (Faceted Application of Subject Terminology): A Simplified LCSH-Based Vocabulary." World Library and Information Congress: 69th IFLA General Conference and Council. 1–9 August 2003. Berlin, Germany.

Pao, Miranda. *Concepts of Information Retrieval*. Englewood, Colo.: Libraries Unlimited, 1989.

Radebaugh, Jackie. "MARC Goes Global—and Lite." *American Libraries* 34 (February 2003): 43–44.

Smiraglia, Richard P. *The Nature of 'A Work': Implications for the Organization of Knowledge*. Lanham, Md.: Scarecrow, 2001.

Smiraglia, Richard P., and Gregory H. Leazer. "Derivative Bibliographic Relationships: The Work Relationship in a Global Bibliographic Database." *Journal of the American Society for Information Science* 50 (1999): 493–504.

Svenonius, Elaine. "Bibliographical Control." In *Academic Libraries: Research Perspectives*. Edited by Mary Jo Lynch and Arthur P. Young. Chicago: ALA, 1990, 38–68.

———. *The Intellectual Foundation of Information Organization*. Cambridge, Mass.: MIT, 2000.

Tillett, Barbara B. "A Taxonomy of Bibliographic Relationships." *Library Resources and Technical Services* 35 (April 1991): 150–158.

University of Illinois. "Sanford Berman Recipient of the 1996 Robert B. Downs Intellectual Freedom Award." [Online] Available at *http://alexia.lis uiuc . . . text/news/downs96.html*. (Accessed November 18, 1996.)

Vizine-Goetz, Diane and Joan S. Mitchell. "Dewey 2000." In *Annual Review of OCLC Research, 1995*. Dublin, Ohio: OCLC, 1996. 16–19.

Wright, Cheryl D. "Introduction." Sun Microsystems, Inc. *Digital Library Technology Trends*. August 2002. [Online] Available at *www. Sun.com/products-n-solutions/edu/ whitepapers/pdf/digital_library_trends.pdf*. (Accessed July 22, 2003.)

7

From Past to Present: The Library's Mission and Its Values

Libraries, in one form or another, have been around a very long time. Some have referred to them as "cultural agencies." They are, as Augst (2001) has observed, "a social enterprise, physical infrastructure, a symbolic site of collective memory. . . . Historically the library has borne the particular weight of defining culture and devising means for its practical administration" (p. 6).

Libraries satisfy a fundamental need of society: the need to have the society's records readily accessible to the citizenry. Now there are so many records a library cannot conceivably store them all, and although the place where records are stored may change in the future, the society continues to need access to organized information—perhaps more than ever before. Librarians must address the issues of which records should be stored, what types of records, who should have access to them, and for what purpose? Understanding the historical context in which libraries emerged provides a helpful context for answering these questions and offers a useful rudder to guide our course into the future. For this reason, we will make a brief excursion into the past to identify some of the major historical developments that defined the different missions that libraries have undertaken. This will provide a basic context for understanding the mission of present-day libraries and the libraries of the future.[1] Although the history of libraries in Asia, South America, Africa, and other parts of the world are important for study, this historical overview is confined to events primarily in Western Europe which form the foundation of libraries and librarianship in the United States. In addition, historical attention is limited to developments in the United States beginning with the settlement of the American colonies.

THE MISSIONS OF LIBRARIES IN HISTORY

Not all societies can have libraries; at least three prerequisite conditions are required for libraries to prosper (Harris and Johnson 1984). First, libraries require *centralization*. Libraries do not prosper in nomadic conditions; there must be a stable "place" for the materials. The centralization of population in cities and towns was a critical precondition for the development of libraries. Even a small stable population such as a university or monastery can serve as a sufficient concentration to produce a library. Second is *economic growth*. Libraries cannot prosper when the primary energies and resources of the community are devoted to subsistence; they require a certain commitment of wealth and time. Similarly, wealth makes individual philanthropy possible, and libraries, in particular American libraries, have relied on philanthropy for much of their development. Finally, libraries require *political stability*. They cannot flourish where the political climate is unstable. In times of revolt and political chaos libraries are bound to be destroyed, and history has seen the destruction of many great libraries when empires fell or in times of war or other armed conflicts.

The Earliest Mission: Maintaining a Records Archive

No one knows when the first library was established, but at least two factors provided a significant impetus for their creation: the invention of writing and the rise of a commercial culture. The earliest written records of a society were found in Sumerian temple libraries in Mesopotamia around 3000 BC. The Sumerian temple library was, for the most part, a commercial archive (Kramer 1961). Temples were the social and economic center of Sumerian communities. They conducted business, managed estates, and lent money. The records of these temples included "commercial accounts, grammatical exercises for young scribes, mathematical texts, treatises on medicine and astrology, and collections of hymns, prayers and incantations" (Dunlap 1972, p. 2). Some historical and literary works as well as early codifications of law have also been found (Harris and Johnson 1984). In addition to temple libraries, there have also been discoveries of municipal and government libraries that held business records as well as deeds, contracts, tax lists, and marriage records (Harris and Johnson 1984).

The form of writing used to record this information is known as cuneiform. It involved impressing a square-shaped or triangular-tipped stylus into clay tablets. There is evidence that some of the temples had schools that taught the art of writing and trained clerks to keep records of accounts (Dunlap 1972). Thus, it appears that the initial impetus for writing was primarily for administrative and practical business purposes, not for religious ones (Childe 1965).

Because of the complexity of some of these records and the number of clay tablets that must have been required, Harris and Johnson (1984) suggest that there must have been an organized arrangement for these materials. One wonders about the first librarians. The possibility of a "Marian, the Sumerian Librarian" wandering about some clay stacks gives us pause. We do know that the Sumerians had "Masters of the Books" or "Keepers of the Tablets" who were well-educated scribes or trained by scribes. Sometimes priests served in this capacity (Harris and Johnson 1984). Their specific duties, however, are unknown.

The Religious and Practical Mission of Egyptian Libraries

Parallel with the development of early libraries in Sumeria, the Egyptian culture was also producing written records. The form of writing used by the Egyptians is known as hieroglyphics and was pictorial in nature. The writing material was made from papyrus reeds that were flattened, rolled, and stored as scrolls (Jackson 1974).

The earliest Egyptian libraries probably emerged around 2400 B.C. As with Sumerian libraries, they were most often associated with Egyptian temples that were both religious and cultural centers. The libraries stored food, educated scribes, dispensed justice, and served both as historical archives and working libraries for learning the practical, spiritual, and medical arts. One early Egyptian library at Edfu, known as the "House of Papyrus," had a collection of practical and spiritual materials that included writings on administration, magic, astronomy, astrology, and medicine (Thompson 1962; Shera 1976). Egyptian libraries were particularly notable for their medical writings, which included pharmacological information as well as materials on diagnosis and treatment of diseases and surgery (Harris and Johnson 1984).

There were also extensive private collections among royalty and individual, wealthy Egyptians. Palace collections probably contained governmental records as well as philosophical or religious materials. Perhaps the most notable royal Egyptian library was that associated with Pharaoh Ramses II in Thebes between 1200 and 1300 B.C. This library may have had as many as 20,000 scrolls (Nichols 1964). Legend has it that, based on the work of the Greco-Roman historian Diodorus Siculus, the portal above the library was inscribed with the words "Healer of the Soul" (Jackson 1974). Such an inscription suggests the presence of both spiritual and medicinal materials, but evidence is lacking concerning the actual contents.

Egyptian "librarians" were also scribes, often highly placed officials or priests. The Egyptian priest or scribe was held in high esteem because the ability to read and write was so rare. Writing itself may well have been considered a sacred activity, thus giving the scribes considerably more power than today's librarian (Harris and Johnson 1984).

The Mission of Scholarship and Research

THE LIBRARY OF ASHURBANIPAL

The mission of libraries was broadened by the Assyrians in Mesopotamia around the eighth century B.C. The Assyrian King, Ashurbanipal, expanded a library begun by his great-grandfather, Sargon II, at his palace in Nineveh. Ashurbanipal believed that the library should not only maintain archival records, but also serve as a current source of reference materials and contribute to the education of future generations (Dunlap 1972). To this end, Ashurbanipal directed a group of scholars and assistants to collect clay tablets produced from other lands. The result was that thousands of tablets were collected on a wide variety of subjects. Many of these tablets were translated from their original language into Assyrian. The collection contained Sumerian and Babylonian materials, including literary texts, history, omens, astronomical calculations, mathematical tables, grammatical and linguistic tables, and dictionaries, as well as commercial records and laws. There is evidence that the collection was organized with the titles arranged by subject and listed in registers. Some of the clay tablets had markers to help in locating and shelving them. There is also evidence of a "keeper of the books," suggesting a librarian, but nothing else is known regarding the duties or character of this individual (Jackson 1974).

The library of Ashurbanipal was the greatest library of its time, providing a rich collection of materials and information on Mesopotamia and its culture. At its height, it was estimated to have as many as 30,000 clay tablets, two-thirds of which were collected during Ashurbanipal's reign (Dunlap 1972). Taken as a whole, the Royal Library at Nineveh was a remarkable achievement. The size of the library collection was a direct result of a concerted effort to collect a vast amount of material on a variety of subjects; the collection was developed, at least in part, for future generations; the materials were often translated; the materials were systematically organized, marked, and arranged; and a "librarian" played a significant role in the library's activities. No doubt, part of the reason for the library's existence was to glorify Ashurbanipal's greatness. But all of the characteristics noted above also suggest that the Royal Library can be seen as the first attempt to build a collection for reference and research.

THE ALEXANDRIAN LIBRARY

Advancing the scholarly mission of libraries was one of the notable contributions of the Greeks to the history of libraries. Two factors contributed to this influence. First, before the fifth century B.C., Greece had been an oral culture, and consequently there was little need for libraries. However, beginning with the teachings of Socrates, Plato, and especially Aristotle, along with the philosophical schools that they established, reading and written records became more commonplace (Dunlap 1972). Second, the values of reading and learning were spread through the conquests of Alexander the Great, although Alexander himself was not directly responsible for the building of libraries.

Following Alexander's death in 323 B.C., his conquered lands were divided among five Macedonian generals, one of whom, Ptolemy Soter (Ptolemy I), was given Egypt. Ptolemy had great respect for learning and he encouraged the emigration of many scholars to Egypt, especially Alexandria, which became a center of culture and learning. Ptolemy and his son Ptolemy Philadelphus (Ptolemy II), with the help and encouragement of Demetrios of Phaleron, founded the Alexandrian Museum and Library. The mission of the library was ambitious—to collect the entirety of Greek literature. To accomplish this, the founder went to great and sometimes questionable lengths. The Alexandrian, like the library of Ashurbanipal before it, aggressively collected materials throughout the known world (Harris and Johnson 1984). In addition, Ptolemy frequently confiscated cargoes of books in ships that came to Alexandria (Hessel 1955). Copies were made of the originals and then the copies were returned to the owners (Thompson 1962). The items were subsequently organized and edited, and many of them were translated into Greek by scholars from many countries.

The collection was stored in two buildings: a major structure called the Brucheion and a smaller library called the Serapeum. This latter structure may have provided some service to students and the public, but the primary purpose of the library was scholarship (Harris and Johnson 1984). The library was used by scholars for general as well as special research. It was divided into ten great Halls, each Hall representing a separate area of learning. There were also some smaller rooms for individuals involved in special studies (Parsons 1952).

The Alexandrian was also notable for its librarians, many of whom achieved great personal fame, such as the scholar Callimachus. Callimachus is especially known for his *Pinakes*, which was the subject catalog of the library holdings. The *Pinakes* contained 120 scrolls with entries for each document, including author and title. Because some entries included historical or critical remarks, some library historians regard the *Pinakes* as more than a library catalog, suggesting that it may have also served as a history of Greek literature (Jackson 1974). The scrolls were arranged into ten subject classes. Within each class, there were subdivisions. Authors were arranged alphabetically within each class as well. It is reported that under Callimachus's guidance the library exceeded more than a half-million items (Blackburn 2003).

The Alexandrian possessed the strength of any great research collection: a tremendous range of material and scholars to collect and maintain the collection. The comprehensiveness of the collection was beyond comparison for its time. As noted above, at its height it may have contained more than a half-million items, but the actual size of the collection relies on various accounts of questionable reliability (Parsons 1952; Jochum 1999). It is unclear when and how the Alexandrian was destroyed. Some have claimed that at least part of it was set afire when Caesar invaded Alexandria in 48 B.C., but there is at least some reason to doubt the veracity of this claim (Jochum 1999). Blackburn (2003) has argued that the scrolls which had supposedly been warehoused and destroyed by the fire, had actually been removed by the librarian to protect them and substituted with straw. According to Blackburn (2003) these scrolls still await discovery! Nevertheless, the Alexandrian deteriorated with the decline of the Greek Empire and by the third century A.D. suffered badly from pillaging and destruction.

The Mission of Personal Status and Public Use: The Roman Libraries

With the rise of the Roman Empire, the mission of libraries appeared to shift. The Romans possessed few, if any, libraries during the early years of their history. However, following the conquest of Greece, during which time the collections of Greek libraries were plundered, possessing a library became a symbol of status and rank, as well as personal pride, for many generals and the aristocracy. By the first century A.D. there were a large number of books and private libraries in Rome, and in Roman country houses private libraries abounded. Aristotle's library, for example, was brought to Rome in the first century B.C. by the Roman general Sulla (Thompson 1962). Cicero made his library "the heart of his home" (Hessel 1955, p. 6), and had a library in each of his villas (Dunlap 1972).

As with the Greeks, there also appeared to be some impetus among the Romans to serve the "public." Julius Caesar planned to build the first public library in Rome, but died before it was completed. His consul, Asinius Pollio, is given credit for this accomplishment. Two additional public libraries were created by the emperor Augustus, and by the fourth century A.D. there were as many as 29 public libraries in Rome (Boyd 1915). These libraries were usually associated with Roman temples, but included public records and general literature as well as religious items.

It appears that the materials contained in both the private and public libraries may have been available for borrowing under rare circumstances (Harris and Johnson 1984). One wonders what the penalty for returning materials late might have been? The existence of public libraries, however, should not conjure up the same image as that of the modern public library. It is likely that less than 10 percent of the Roman citizenry could read (W. Harris, 1989), and it is quite probable that access to public library collections was limited to the wealthy and educated classes of Rome. Some library historians have speculated that the public libraries may have served more often as a public forum for recitation of works by Roman authors than as a resource or lending library (Dix 1994; W. Harris, 1989).

For most of the years of the Roman Empire, the Romans recorded their history and accounts using papyrus scrolls, like the Greeks before them. There were some obvious disadvantages to the scrolls; they were bulky and it was more difficult to find one's place because there were no pages. During the first century A.D., due to persecution and the need to record religious text quickly and in readily transportable form, the early Christians abandoned the scroll and replaced it with the parchment codex (book). By the fourth century A.D., the codex was in widespread use and had replaced papyrus scrolls (Thompson 1962).

With the decline of the Roman Empire, the rise of Christianity, and the invasions from Northern Europe, the libraries of the empire were destroyed. Libraries did not entirely disappear from Western Europe, but their form and function changed substantially. As Western Europe plunged into political, economic, and social chaos, the archival and scholarly missions of libraries were sustained through the growth of Byzantine and Moslem libraries and the monastic libraries of Western Europe.

The Reemergence of the Scholarly Mission: The Byzantine and Moslem Libraries

Although the Western Empire was in serious decline by the fourth century A.D., the Eastern Empire under the leadership of the Christian emperor Constantine was flourishing. The center of the Byzantine Empire was the newly founded city of Constantinople. Constantine and the Byzantine culture valued education and writing, and it is in Constantinople that the Imperial Library was founded under the auspices of Constantine's son, Emperor Constantius, in 353 A.D. (Jackson 1974). Although the Eastern Empire was more influenced by Greek culture and traditions than Rome, the Imperial Library contained Christian and Latin works in addition to Greek materials (Harris and Johnson 1984).

By 450 A.D. the library had been expanded to an impressive 100,000 items. Constantinople contained not only the Imperial Library, but a large university library and the library of the leader of the Eastern Church, the Patriarch. The mission of these libraries was scholarly and religious, and this mission played an invaluable part in the sustenance of Western society. As Harris and Johnson (1984) have noted, "of the Greek classics known today, at least seventy-five percent are known through Byzantine copies" (p. 83). Without this preservation of materials, the Renaissance would not have been possible.

The same can be said concerning the achievements of the Moslem Empire, which flourished by the middle of the seventh century until 1000 A.D. Because of the respect afforded reading and learning in this culture, libraries became commonplace in private homes, royal palaces, and universities throughout the Moslem world. The caliphs in many of the major cities were scholars and literati (Thompson 1962). Spain had 70 libraries, Baghdad 36, and "every important city in Persia had its library" (Thompson 1962, p. 353).

The earliest major library was the Royal Library in Damascus, which contained materials from throughout the world on a wide variety of topics, including medicine, philosophy, history, and literature (Harris and Johnson 1984). Later, during the eighth and ninth centuries, Baghdad became the cultural center for the study of Greek medical, scientific, and philosophical works and "abounded with libraries" (Thompson 1962, p. 351).

In addition, research and learning were furthered by large libraries located in Moslem universities. There were, for example, major universities in Baghdad, Cairo, and Cordoba. The Cairo library may have held more than 200,000 volumes, and the library at Cordoba was reported to contain between 400,000 and 600,000 volumes—larger than the Alexandrian (Harris and Johnson 1984; Thompson 1962). Like the Byzantine libraries, Moslem libraries contained not only Arabic works, but Persian literature as well as Greek and Latin philosophy and science. As such, Moslem libraries made a substantial contribution to the preservation of Western culture by preserving the central works of Western thought. The Western world owes a particular debt to the Moslems for preserving the works of Aristotle, whose works were quite popular, and many of his writings were translated into Arabic for use by Arabic scholars (Harris and Johnson 1984). With the decline of the Moslem Empire, however, the fate of libraries was sealed.

The Religious Mission: Monastic Libraries of the Middle Ages

With the fall of the Roman Empire, social and political chaos led to economic instability throughout Western Europe. Inevitably, a decline of libraries followed. Only one major Western institution was able to sustain the critical preconditions for library development, the Christian monastery. Monasteries provided a means of geographically, as well as spiritually, isolating Christian adherents from the disorder that had spread throughout society. These monasteries were well established by 500–550 A.D. The mission of the monastic library was threefold: to provide a place for spiritual reflection, to archive religious texts, and to reproduce religious and sometimes secular texts.

Perhaps the best exemplar of the religious mission of the monastic library comes from the Benedictine Order established in 529 A.D. in Monte Casino, Italy. The monastic life in this monastery and the Benedictine monasteries founded thereafter were guided by the Rules of St. Benedict. One of the rules was that each monk was to be given one book for study each year (Clanchy 1979). Other rules included copying books as a fundamental aspect of monastic life. Copying was done in a special room called the scriptorium. Sometimes copying was used as a punishment for a recalcitrant monk, and the quality of the copy often left much to be desired (Shera 1976).

It should be kept in mind, however, that according to St. Benedict, the purpose of monastic life was to concentrate on spiritual matters and to avoid secular thoughts. Reading and copying books were seen as a means to maintain an ascetic life, not to become educated per se. For example, books were often read to monks when they were dining, but it was not to enlighten them, but to keep their minds from straying to frivolous or worldly matters. The purpose of copying was not to create more useful and instructive texts, but to keep the monks busy (Thompson 1962).

Other monasteries founded in Ireland, Switzerland, Scotland, France, and Great Britain emphasized books and copying in a different vein. For example, if one were copying religious texts, one would be expected to derive inspiration from them. Many of these monasteries produced fine, illuminated manuscripts intended to reveal the spiritual beauty of God. These works of art reflected the copyist's realization that he was representing sacred words from the scripture. Their physical beauty, however, might also have been fascinating to the laity and may even have served as an early incentive to literacy (Clanchy 1979).

Regardless of whether the purpose of reading and copying books was to learn, to inspire, or to achieve an ascetic life, the fact is that many books were saved and copied during this time, thus preserving the writings of antiquity. One should not, however, give too much credit to the monks. As Thompson has observed, "it is equally true their preservation was as often due to neglect and mere chance as it was to conscious intent . . . the medieval scriptorium was more often a treadmill for meaningless labor than it was a shrine where the expiring flame of literary culture was sedulously preserved" (Thompson 1962, pp. 30–31).

One other aspect of medieval monastic life deserves mention. One could argue that modern library and information science began with another monastic tradition: the Dominicans. Among the rules of the

Dominican friars are those related to finding a good location for the library, providing adequate shelving, organizing the library by subjects, marking the spines of books with their titles, replenishing and weeding the collection, establishing hours of operation, and selling duplicate titles (Clanchy 1979). Certainly these are reflective of some of the duties of the modern librarian.

The Educational Mission of Libraries: Cathedral and University Libraries of the Late Middle Ages

The mission of Western libraries to educate reemerged in the late Middle Ages (800–1200 A.D.). With the growth of cities and towns and the improvement in trade and other economic and social conditions, there was a concomitant improvement in the intellectual climate. The increasing respect for learning made fertile conditions for libraries once again.

By 1100 large cathedrals in major cities were the administrative centers for bishops and archbishops and training centers for priests and other religious functionaries (Harris and Johnson 1984). The mission of the cathedral libraries, unlike the monastic libraries, was to support the educational program of the cathedral and encourage study. The cathedral libraries were larger than most monastic ones and were less dominated by religious works (Shera 1976). Although some of the cathedral libraries were substantial, such as those in Verona and Monte Casino, Italy, or at the cathedrals at Rheims and Chartres in France, none were anything resembling the size of the larger libraries of the Moslem Empire (Dunlap 1972).

Although the church continued to be a vital part of the life of the late Middle Ages, it was also in a period of transition. The cities were producing a middle class, and there were those among the laity and intellectual aristocracy who did not rely on church teaching to guide their intellectual pursuits (Hessel 1955). These developments, coupled with the dominance of less contemplative and more secularly involved religious sects such as the Dominicans and Franciscans, spawned the establishment of academic centers in Bologna, Paris, and Oxford. These institutions supported not only theological studies, but also classical and professional instruction in law, medicine, and philosophy. Initially, the first universities did not have libraries; rather, students bought their books from booksellers. The first university library appeared at the University of Paris in the mid-thirteenth century, and subsequently at Oxford and Cambridge among others (Shera 1976). These libraries were often small, well under 1,000 items, but their mission to support and expand the educational mission of the university served as a bridge from the domination of the medieval church to the birth of the Renaissance (Harris and Johnson 1984; Shera 1976).

The Humanistic Mission and the Reemergence of the Library for Personal Status

The period following the Middle Ages was a time of considerable economic, social, and political ferment, with much of it centered in Italy, most notably Venice and Florence. Contributing factors included the rise of secular monarchies, an increased sense of nationalism, a decline in the power of the church, an increase in literacy, an emerging interest in natural sciences, an expanding interest in secular politics, and a reawakening of the philosophical traditions of ancient civilization, most notably the Greek and Roman thinkers. This fervor for the knowledge of the ancients and for new secular knowledge rather than spiritual enlightenment characterizes much of what is referred to as Renaissance Humanism.

The Renaissance was primarily an aristocratic enthusiasm, and great private libraries were developed by leading literary figures such as Petrarch and Boccaccio, who themselves were sponsored by popes or the Renaissance princes, for example, the dukes of Urbino and the Medici. These sponsors were passionate book collectors as both a matter of personal vanity and a genuine interest in secular learning. They sent agents throughout Western Europe to locate and retrieve the manuscripts stored in the deteriorating monastic libraries. Sometimes the manuscripts were copied but, at other times, enthusiastic agents confiscated (saved?) these items for posterity by bringing them to their sponsors. As a result, Renaissance libraries were richly appointed and filled with beautifully illuminated texts. They served as places for scholarship, but also as places where aristocrats could "display their sensitivity to classical Latin" (Jackson 1974, p. 107).

Although the Renaissance princes may have taken the notion of the private library as personal aggrandizement to its highest form of ostentatious display, it was hardly a new concept or new mission (remember Ashurbanipal and the wealthy Romans?). One might reasonably contend as Dunlap (1972) does, "Had it not been for the enthusiasm of a few collectors of that age . . . we should certainly possess only a small part of the literature, especially that of the Greeks, which is now in our hands" (pp. 106–107).

Promoting National Pride: The Mission of the National Libraries

The growth of secular monarchies and nationalism is consistent with the emergence of a new type of library with a special mission—the national library. Early examples of such libraries arose in the seventeenth century in England, France, Germany, Denmark, and Scotland. The eighteenth and nineteenth centuries saw national libraries in Austria, Italy, Sweden, Norway, Greece, Spain, and Ireland among others (Gates 1976). What distinguishes these libraries is not simply their large collections; rather their special mission was to preserve the cultural heritage of the countries in which they were situated. This meant developing a comprehensive collection of materials by and about the country, including books, manuscripts, documents, and other records.

In order to meet this mission, a unique collection development technique was employed: the creation of a "depository" right. That is, some nations passed laws requiring that at least one copy of each item published within the country be sent to the national library. This was accomplished, for example, in England in 1610, when an agreement was made between the Stationers' Company (which licensed publications in England) and the Bodleian Library of Oxford University. This agreement stipulated that one copy of each book published would be given to the Bodleian in return for limited borrowing privileges (Jackson 1974). In essence, this meant that all items, or nearly all items, published would become part of the national collection. In the United States, this depository right is held by the Library of Congress and, although it is not officially our national library, it is a very close approximation.

Making Modern Missions Possible: The Printing Press

If one can identify a single historical development that affected all library collections in a profound way, it would be the invention of the printing press in 1454 in Mainz, Germany. The invention of the printing press had broader effects than those on libraries, but there is no doubt that libraries would never be the same following its genesis, and it is impossible to consider the modern mission of libraries without considering some of the changes that the printing press wrought. Eisenstein (1979) identified many effects of the printing press. Some of these are summarized below.

The ability to produce an authoritative version. Before the time of printing, copies were made by hand. This laborious process sometimes produced extraordinary works of art, but more often less-than-perfect versions: copiers made mistakes or even intentionally omitted or amended text. The printing press could produce identical copies.

The ability to produce more titles and copies. The sheer volume of printed materials increased dramatically as use of the printing press increased. Obviously hand copying was slow and arduous and, although multiple copies were made, overall they were small in number. In the sixteenth century, after the printing press had had some time to develop, more than 100,000 different books were printed in Europe alone (Harris and Johnson 1984). The implication for libraries is obvious: the size of library collections could increase substantially. In addition, by making more copies available, more collections could develop.

The ability to cover more subjects. With an efficient means to produce materials, there was an opportunity to spread many more ideas. For example, in the first decade of printing, ending in 1460, the publications consisted of four typically medieval categories: sacred literacy (Bibles and prayer books), learned literacy (works of grammar and scholastic works such as those of Thomas Aquinas), bureaucratic literacy (official documents such as papal bulls and indulgence certificates), and vernacular literacy (works in the language of the people, notably German readers) (Clanchy 1983). During the second decade of the press, the breadth of subjects increased and spread beyond medieval thinking. Obviously, the communication of different ideas can have a profound effect on society. In fact, one of the earliest effective uses of the printing press was to spread the ideas of Martin Luther, who disseminated his religious tracts throughout Europe using this method. The effect of the subsequent Protestant Reformation can hardly be overestimated.

The creation of new techniques for the organization of published materials. Given the growth in size and subject diversity of library collections, new techniques for organizing and classifying materials became necessary. This eventually led to the complex systems we have today in the Dewey Decimal or Library of Congress classification systems.

The stimulation of literacy and education for the general population. When books are scarce, only a few can have access to them. As more books became available, it was inevitable that more people would learn to read. This, in turn, would eventually generate the market for library users.

In sum, the invention of the printing press, coupled with the reawakening of secular and scientific interests during the Renaissance ultimately formed the foundation for the growth in number and size of libraries and consequently for a broader and wider mission for libraries.

LIBRARIES IN THE UNITED STATES: NEW MISSIONS

As we move to the next period in the development of library missions, it is time to leave the European continent. The seventeenth and eighteenth centuries were formative periods in American life, and as the focus of this book is on the United States, the balance of this discussion will concentrate on American libraries. It is notable that Americans and libraries have had a healthy and active relationship for more than 200 years. McMullen (2000) has observed that there were more than 10,000 libraries of 80–85 different types in the United States before 1876, many of them concentrated in the Northeast, Mid-Atlantic, and East North Central portion of the country. Their variety was impressive: agricultural libraries, antiquarian society libraries, art society libraries, church libraries, county libraries, government libraries, historical society libraries, hotel reading rooms, ladies' libraries, law libraries, mechanics' libraries, medical libraries, prison libraries, public libraries, railroad libraries, saloon reading rooms, scientific and engineering libraries, sewing circle libraries, state libraries, university libraries, and YMCA libraries. Obviously, a discussion of all the different types of libraries lies outside the scope of this book, but it is important to reflect on the character and purposes of some of the major types that formed the foundation of libraries today.

There were few libraries in America during the early part of the seventeenth century, and those few libraries were in New England. The social preconditions were not yet in place: people were struggling for subsistence, there were few urban settings, and there was limited economic development or individual wealth. America was an agrarian society that depended on manual labor, and the literacy rate in the general population was low. Near the end of the seventeenth century, libraries began to grow significantly in the South Atlantic region, primarily through the growth of religious libraries and the work of Reverend Thomas Bray (McMullen 2000). In England in the late seventeenth century, Bray, an Anglican clergyman, advocated for libraries devoted solely to religious purposes. To this end, he created the Society for the Propagation of the Gospel, which established parish libraries throughout England. His interest soon spread to America, and by the 1700s 70 parish libraries were established in the United States (Harris and Johnson 1984).

A few private libraries were found in the colonial homes of ministers, doctors, and other prominent citizens. In general, these libraries were less a form of status or recognition, however, and more a resource for practical or spiritual materials to deal with the problems confronting settlers in the New World. Most of these collections were quite small. In addition, there were also a few modest college libraries. Harvard University, founded in 1636, possessed a small library of approximately 5,000 volumes by the mid-eighteenth century; Yale University, founded in 1700, held around 2,500 volumes by 1750 (Harris and Johnson 1984). The sparsity of college libraries is a reflection of the sparsity of the college educated. By 1775 fewer than one in a thousand citizens had attended any college (Hanson 1989). By 1792 only nine colonial colleges were established that had libraries. The libraries themselves were not located in separate buildings, but in rooms within buildings in which other functions were performed.

The size of the typical collection was small for several reasons: the low number of book titles produced in the United States at the time, lack of fiscal resources, and lack of recognition for the library's role in academic life. The growth of the collection depended primarily on donations. If a college had a library, it was usually open infrequently and usually had no librarian to provide assistance. For example, Harvard did not have a librarian until 1667. When assistance was available, it was usually a faculty member who served only secondarily as a part-time librarian (Harwell 1968). Book selection was accomplished usually by a committee of trustees or faculty members (Hamlin 1981; Shiflett 1994). Professional librarians were generally not part of college staff until the end of the nineteenth century (Hamlin 1981).

The Mission of Self-Improvement: The Social Libraries of the Eighteenth Century

As in Europe, the seventeenth and eighteenth centuries in America were a time of considerable political stability and growth in scientific and technical knowledge. With these advances and the development of mechanical technologies, the industrial revolution soon led to the growth of the economy with concomitant growth in individual and community wealth. This in turn meant that some of the more fortunate citizens had more leisure time, time which could be spent pursuing self-development. These were fertile conditions for the emergence of new libraries and missions.

During the first half of the eighteenth century two such library models emerged: the social library and the circulating library. According to Shera (1965) "the social library was nothing more than a voluntary association of individuals who had contributed money toward a common fund to be used for the purchase of books" (p. 57). Two types of social libraries eventually emerged: proprietary libraries and subscription (association) libraries. Proprietary libraries operated on the principle that those who contributed money for the library actually owned the material purchased; in essence, they were stockholders. In subscription libraries, the fees contributed permitted the participants to use and circulate the collection, but they did not have ownership of the items themselves (Shera 1965). The collections of social libraries were often quite small, as was their membership, many having less than 300 books, and most fewer than 50 members.

The mission of the social library was to assist self-improvement and the search for truth. Many of its members had a genuine love of literature and believed that the common use of such materials led to character improvement and, through discussion with others, increased knowledge, as well. One of those who believed in the value of self-improvement was Benjamin Franklin. Franklin is given credit for establishing in 1728 the first, although short-lived, library in Philadelphia, called the Junto. He founded a second library, also in Philadelphia, which he referred to as a "subscription library" in 1731. It survives today as the Philadelphia Library Company.

The social library became quite popular throughout New England in the latter half of the eighteenth century and well into the nineteenth. The mission of self-improvement was not restricted to scientific, technical, or professional pursuits but served whatever group decided to create the collection. Hence, although there were social libraries that had relatively aristocratic and well-educated clients, there were also YMCA libraries, agricultural libraries, "ladies clubs," and mechanics libraries, all developed to meet the special interests of less affluent, and often less educated, members of the community. There were also many general-interest social libraries that did not focus on one particular subject but nonetheless met the educational needs of its members. Their collections often contained religious materials, history, travel, and literature (not to be confused with popular fiction, of which there was little in these collections). Although social libraries may have had materials of a more diverting nature, their purpose was not to appeal to mass tastes, but to one's "better angels."

Given the voluntary nature of social libraries, their ability to accomplish their missions was deeply affected by the ability of their members to sustain the library. Often these libraries relied on one or a few benefactors, and shifting economic times, depressions, wars, and social unrest led to the relatively quick demise of many. Nonetheless, the legacy of the social library is significant. Not only did the development of library collections for self-improvement become ingrained in America and form the basis of an important aspect of public library service, but the core of many future library collections once were the remnants of abandoned social libraries. To those defunct libraries, the American public library owes much for its early inventory.

The Mission of Mass Appeal: The Circulating Library

While the social library was attempting to meet the need for self-improvement and edification with informative materials, there was contemporaneously a second mission pursued by a different type of library: the circulating library (sometimes referred to as the rental library). Although England had circulating libraries many years before America, the first circulating libraries in America arose in the 1760s. Their mission was to satisfy public demand and popular tastes, especially the demand for fiction. The popular novels of this time consisted mostly of romances (much like today!) and the appearance of these novels was fairly well established in America by 1790. Although there were few romances by American authors, there was ample supply of popular foreign novels published by American presses. There may have been as many as 350 foreign titles published in America from 1789 to 1800, compared to 35 titles by American authors (Shera 1965). Serving mass tastes appears to have been as profitable in colonial times as it is today; many of these libraries prospered and spread throughout New England.

The distinguishing feature of circulating libraries was their profit-making character. Usually they were associated with another commercial enterprise such as a printer or bookstore. From this perspective, the circulating library's purpose, first and foremost, was to make money. The majority of the collection was fiction although there were some holdings of literature, history, and theology. Overall, the materials were intended for entertainment rather than education. Either the books were rented or individuals were charged a membership fee that allowed them to borrow a designated number of materials over a specified period of time.

It is worth noting that circulating libraries often incurred the wrath of certain segments of society who were concerned with the immoral effects of popular reading. As sometimes happens today in public libraries, circulating libraries were suspected of corrupting youth, usually because of the corrupting effects of the popular novels—especially the French ones (Shera 1965).

Just as the social library formed the basis for many early public library collections and provided some of the philosophical underpinnings as well, the circulating library also made several contributions to public library philosophy and service. For example, despite its profit motive, its mission to appeal to popular taste echoes in contemporary public library service. In addition, Kaser (1980) notes that circulating libraries were the first to provide (1) service to women, (2) newspapers and magazines, (3) extended hours of service, (4) reading areas in the library itself, and (5) outreach services, including the home delivery of books. These are substantive contributions. The circulating library's survival, however, was ultimately threatened by its low status and competition from tax-supported public libraries (Kaser 1980).

The Library in Support of Commercial Profit: The Rise of Special Libraries for Business and Industry

Although the circulating library as a money-making venture failed to catch on, its spirit of free enterprise was certainly consistent with a capitalistic economy, one of the central elements of American society. Shortly after the start of the industrial revolution, public libraries started collections for factory workers, technical workers, craftsmen, and managers (Kruzas 1965). Not long thereafter, American business and industry discovered the instrumentality of the library. The roots of the business library go back to the mechanics, mercantile, and factory libraries established at the beginning of the nineteenth century. Generally, however, with the exception of a few law or insurance firm libraries, most libraries associated with private enterprise in the past were used for education, consultation with professional literature, or diversion. Their purpose was not to provide direct assistance in conducting business itself.

At the beginning of the twentieth century, however, there emerged a new library whose purpose was the "direct application of recorded information to the practical goals of profit-seeking business enterprises"

(Kruzas 1965, p. 109). The purpose of the commercial library was to promote the profitability of the company. Hence, these libraries collected
only materials that focused on the direct needs of the enterprise. Interestingly, this led to the collection of materials unfamiliar to many libraries: records, documents, papers, announcements, reports, and, by the 1920s,
microfilm. Emphasis was on providing reference service to the organization rather than on collection development itself: providing the information to the individual who needed it was much more important than
revealing to the requester where to find the information. This remains a
fundamental characteristic of special libraries to this day. The concerns
of these types of libraries helped promote the creation of the Special
Libraries Association in 1909, and these libraries also served as a primary impetus for fostering new technologies that would access information rather than documents. As noted in the previous chapter on information science, this shift in emphasis was also an important foundation for the rise of information science and the exploitation of information technologies in libraries.

*The Mission of Supporting Teaching and Research: The American Academic
Library*

Although the educational mission of libraries emerged as early as the
Alexandrian library, the mission of the library in the modern American
academic institution did not evolve until the latter part of the nineteenth
century when most universities were established (Hamlin 1981). There
are historical reasons for this late development. From the colonial period to the Civil War, the curriculum of academic institutions followed a
classical model. Areas emphasized were theology, philosophy, history,
and the trivium of the liberal arts—grammar, rhetoric, and logic (Hanson
1989). The faculty taught from a single text or, at best, a few books. Classroom recitation was strongly emphasized (Hamlin 1981). Such methods
produced little need for libraries, and academic collections remained
small throughout this period.

Several developments in the mid-nineteenth century substantially
changed academic institutions and produced the foundation of modern
academic libraries' missions. In particular, the library was recognized as
a critical factor necessary to support the curriculum and research for
students and faculty. Three important changes led to this recognition;
changes in the curriculum, the rise of the research model, and the Morrill
Land Grant Act of 1862.

Changes in the Nature of the Curriculum

Fundamental to the advancement of the academic library was the evolution of teaching methods and subject matter in academia as a whole. With the rise of the sciences and the industrial revolution, the need to change the classical nature of the college curriculum arose. Industry and manufacturing were demanding graduates with practical education rather than an understanding of the classics (Hanson 1989). Realization of the need for change started slowly, but by the 1840s the curriculum often included courses in the natural sciences. In 1850 Brown University began the first elective system, including courses in the sciences and languages (Shiflett 1994). Although the elective system did not spread rapidly, it served as the model for the modernization of the academic curriculum. As the breadth of the curriculum expanded, access to materials became an increasingly important issue, concomitantly increasing the importance of the library. Teaching methods also changed. Seminars, laboratories, and independent study emerged as an alternative to the recitation techniques of the past (Hanson 1989).

The evolution of the academic curriculum and its implication for librarianship were recognized early by Melvil Dewey (1888):

> The colleges are waking to the fact that the work of every professor and every department is necessarily based on the library; text books constantly yield their exalted places to wiser and broader methods; professor after professor sends his classes, or goes with them, to the library and teaches them to investigate for themselves, and to *use* books, getting beyond the method of the primary school with its parrot-like recitations from a single text. (p. 136)

The Rise of the Research Model

As the classical model of the curriculum changed, there was also a change in the perception of the role of research, which had not traditionally been a part of academia. At the turn of the eighteenth century at the University of Berlin in Germany, however, a model of the modern university emerged. This model saw the faculty member as an independent researcher. The notion of objective scholarship was promoted and an expansive faculty research agenda was encouraged (Shiflett 1994). Given the obvious need for published resources for research, the library increasingly played a critical role. The reforms in German higher education did not go unnoticed at some of the more prestigious academic institutions in the United States, and many American students were sent to Germany to study. These individuals, in turn, brought the new concept of research coupled with teaching back with them (Shiflett 1994).

Although these ideas had some effect on American higher education throughout the nineteenth century, it was not until 1876 that this model was explicitly adopted with the founding of Johns Hopkins University. Emphasis was placed on research as a key function of the university. The seminar model of teaching was emphasized and students were encouraged to consult a wide variety of published sources. Soon thereafter, Harvard, Cornell, and Columbia Universities adopted this teaching approach (Jones 1989). The need for a library with current and deep collections was essential to fulfill this function and the result was to increase substantially the importance and centrality of the academic library.

THE PASSAGE OF THE MORRILL LAND GRANT ACT OF 1862

Although most colleges founded before the Civil War were private and sectarian, by the nineteenth century it became clear that the higher education of the citizenry was also a matter for the state. Beginning in the East and South, universities were founded in many states including Vermont, Maine, North Carolina, Georgia, New York, Pennsylvania, Massachusetts, and Kentucky. By midcentury, the federal government recognized that it could play an important role by providing grants of land to states for educational purposes. This led to the passage of the Morrill Land Grant Act in 1862, which allocated 30,000 acres of public land per senator or house member for educational use. The act was specifically designed to promote agriculture and the mechanical arts, and the universities founded as a result of the act emphasized applied sciences and technology (Hamlin 1981). The act resulted in the establishment of many major state universities including the Ohio State University and the University of Illinois.

Fortunately, the growth of the academic library coincided with the systematic development of professional education for librarians, with the founding of the American Library Association (ALA) in 1876, and the establishment of the first library school in 1887 (Jones 1989). As the demands for collection development, selection, and library service grew, there were increasing numbers of trained librarians who could nurture the fertile environment for scholarship and teaching. Although the mission of academic libraries continues to evolve, the need to support the academic curriculum and provide research support for faculty remain the academic library's primary functions.

Supporting the School Curriculum: The Mission of the American School Library

There were a few publicly supported schools in Massachusetts and New York during the colonial period, but in general publicly supported schools were a rarity. In the middle Atlantic states and the South, parochial and private schools were more common (Hanson 1989). In general, schools in the colonial period focused on elementary-level education— a level considered sufficient to create an efficient force of manual laborers. There were a few secondary schools in the colonial period, but they were available to only a small number of students preparing for a limited number of colleges (Hanson 1989). It was not until the second half of the nineteenth century that the modern school system began to emerge. In 1852 Massachusetts passed the first compulsory school attendance laws. Other states followed and by 1890, half of the states had compulsory attendance laws. At the same time, more and more schools, including secondary schools, many of which had libraries, were being built.

The earliest attempt to support public school libraries occurred in 1835 when the New York state legislature under the leadership of Governor DeWitt Clinton passed a law that permitted school districts to apply some of their tax receipts to create and maintain school libraries. By 1875, 20 states had passed similar legislation (Knight and Nourse 1969). Unfortunately, many of these efforts to assist school libraries proved unsuccessful. The laws often allocated money for books, but not for administration and maintenance. In addition, sometimes money allocated for books went to teachers' salaries. The result was poorly developed, poorly maintained libraries that were seldom used (Knight and Nourse 1969; Cecil and Heaps 1940). Although these libraries had great potential, they did not perform their central mission. Gillespie and Spirt (1983) suggest, however, that these legislative endeavors to create and maintain public school libraries established the idea that public funds were an appropriate means to support school libraries, and that school libraries could play a useful role in public school education.

By the last decade of the nineteenth century, the number of school libraries, especially in high schools, began to increase substantially, and by 1895 it was estimated that there were from 2,500 to 4,000 school libraries in the country (Knight and Nourse 1969). The earliest example of funding for school libraries with a material effect on curriculum support occurred in 1892 when the state of New York passed legislation providing matching funds to purchase library books for school districts. The books purchased from these funds first had to be approved by the Department of Public Instruction. These approved books consisted of "reference books, supplementary reading books, books related to the curriculum, and pedagogical books for use by teachers" (Gillespie and Spirit 1983, p. 3). Some of them could even be taken out of the library!

New York notwithstanding, public school education in America continued to emphasize rote memorization and teaching from a single text. Consequently, there was little need for, or emphasis on, school libraries. Fortunately, there were several groups that were concerned, among them the National Council of Teachers of English (NCTE), the National Education Association (NEA), and ALA. In 1914 the NCTE formed a standing committee on school libraries and ALA formed a School Library Section (Cecil and Heaps 1940). In 1915 the NCTE conducted a national survey, and the findings expressed serious concern about the adequacy of school libraries. This prompted the NEA and ALA to appoint a joint committee headed by Charles Certain to study the condition of school libraries and develop standards for them. Certain's first report focused on high schools and was published in 1920. The second report focused on elementary schools and was published in 1925. Both reports concluded that school libraries were seriously deficient. The standards prepared by Certain's committee described the library as "an integral part of the daily life of the school" and included several significant recommendations (Certain 1925, p. 5). First they emphasized the centrality of "materials of instruction," that is, curricular support. Second, they emphasized a centralized collection. The centralization of materials in the school had been an issue for some years with some arguing for small library collections in each classroom, and others arguing for centralized location and control of library materials. Third, they emphasized library instruction as a duty of school libraries. Fourth, they emphasized the integral character of the school library within the total setting of school life. Certain's reports were significant in that they proposed the first national standards for school libraries and these standards were endorsed by both ALA and NEA (Gillespie and Spirit 1983).

One should not assume, however, that Certain's report led to the quick development of centralized and modern school libraries, though it certainly made a major contribution. Fortunately, in addition to the report, there were other significant factors that contributed to progress in that direction. Among them were the changes looming on the horizon as a result of the educational reform movement, which Certain (1925) anticipated:

> Modern demands upon the public school presuppose adequate library service. Significant changes in methods of teaching require that the school library supplement the single textbook course of instruction and provide for the enrichment of the school curriculum. (p. 1)

The decade of the 1920s was indeed an era of reform in public education. John Dewey and the progressive education movement introduced a variety of new educational theories that contributed to the emergence of the modern school library and its mission (Gillespie and Spirt 1983). Among the new principles of learning advanced by Dewey and the reformers were the following: (1) a child's growth and development, rather than subject matter, should be the central focus of the school; (2) education should involve children learning through a variety of experiences and exploring a variety of subjects; (3) children learn best when they are exploring subjects of interest to them; and (4) schools should be a social experience that teaches the children how to be self-directed (Fargo 1930). These "radical" ideas resulted in a more varied school curriculum requiring access to a much wider range of materials. Responding to children's interests, encouraging exploration, and providing a broad range of experiences could only highlight the importance of a school library. As Fargo (1930) observed:

> With such a program, it is obvious that the library stands in a far more vital relationship to the school than before. Under the older tradition, books other than texts were desirable; in the new school they are indispensable. They are not the accompaniment of the school's activities; they are its warp and woof. (pp. 31–32)

Other influences that contributed to the emergence of the modern school library included the encouragement and studies of the U.S. Office of Education, NEA, ALA, the Carnegie Corporation, and the North Central Association of Colleges and Secondary Schools (Cecil and Heaps 1940; Gillespie and Spirt 1983). The combination of changing teaching philosophies and the evaluations and standards developed by NEA and ALA had a substantial impact on establishing the foundations of the school library and its mission—to support the curriculum by providing current and appropriate materials for students and teachers.

The Mission of Serving the Public: The American Public Library

The social library and the circulating library each performed a unique mission: the former to educate and enlighten, and the latter to satisfy popular taste. Both of these libraries contributed to the development of the modern public library and its very special mission—the mission of serving the public. The term "public library" refers generically to public support of a library. Using this broad definition, there were approximately 3,600 public libraries in the United States by 1876. Most of these, however, were associated with academic institutions, public schools, or social libraries. As we apply the term today, there were very few public libraries. By 1880 only seven of the sixteen largest cities in the United States had municipally supported public libraries. What we mean when we speak of "public" libraries, today, is very specific to certain fundamental characteristics shared by all American public libraries.

Supported by Taxes. They are usually supported by local taxes, although over the years there have been exceptions. The notion of public support through taxation is rare before the nineteenth century. As noted in earlier discussions, prior to this time, libraries were most often sponsored or subsidized by private citizens, religious orders, or royal families.

Governed by a Board. This board is specifically appointed to serve the public interest. Boards have usually consisted of prominent citizens charged with ensuring that the library provides materials that serve the community.

Open to All. A fundamental tenet is that the library is accessible to everyone in the community. This is not to say that all want to come or all have been made to feel welcome; various groups have not found public libraries friendly or accommodating to their needs. But in principle, the libraries are open to all.

Voluntary. People are not forced to come; the use of the library is entirely up to them. This distinguishes it from other educational institutions, such as public schools. Its voluntary nature is also part of the underlying social philosophy of the nineteenth century in which self-improvement was considered an important value.

Established by State Law. This point is not generally well understood. During the early development of libraries, serious questions arose concerning whether a town could create a public institution and tax its citizens for its maintenance without the state's approval. As a consequence, a key aspect of the creation of public libraries was the passage of "enabling legislation" on the part of the states that permitted the creation of public libraries on the local level. In rare instances, public libraries are not only "enabled" by state legislation, they are financed by state monies. Such is the case in Ohio today, where 5.7 percent of the state's income tax is earmarked for the funding of public libraries.

Provides Services Without Charge to the User. Although some public libraries charge a small fee for copying and interlibrary loans, the overwhelming number of services are provided without fees. This issue may become more problematic in the electronic marketplace, but there is considerable professional resistance to fees for library services.

There is and will continue to be a debate as to when and where the first "public" library in the United States was established. Some have suggested that the honor belongs to Peterborough, New Hampshire, because in 1834 "there for the first time an institution was founded by a town with the deliberate purpose of creating a free library that would be open without restriction to all classes of the community—a library supported from the beginning by public funds" (Shera 1965, p. 169). One thing is certain; there is no dispute as to where and when the first *major* public library was established. In March of 1848 the Massachusetts legislature authorized the city of Boston to provide municipal support for a public library. The Boston Public Library, founded 20 years after Peterborough, in 1854, receives credit for being the first major public library. There is no question that the establishment of the Boston Public Library was a landmark in library development. Interestingly, however, there has arisen an informative debate regarding the reason for its founding that touches at the heart of the mission of public libraries. For this reason, some discussion of this debate is worthwhile.

The creation of the Boston Public library can be seen in at least two lights: first, as a natural outgrowth of prevailing social attitudes and developments at work by the mid-nineteenth century; and second, as the result of efforts by a group of specific individuals who, for whatever reason, concluded that a public library was an appropriate institution for the citizens of Boston.

Not only the emergence of the Boston Public library, but that of public libraries in general, can be seen as a natural outgrowth of other institutional developments of the period. For example, urbanization in America had reached a point at which there was considerable centralization of municipal services. As cities matured and prospered economically, their political and bureaucratic structure also matured. Boston was typical of a prospering and stable urban environment, where wealth had accumulated both generally and among specific individuals. In such sophisticated urban settings, it was not uncommon to have a highly developed urban infrastructure provide basic services, such as water, sanitation, public health, fire, water, and education. As a result, when the issue of a public library was first raised in Boston, it was perceived from an administrative point of view as a logical extension of city services.

Similarly, by the mid-nineteenth century, there was growing interest in literature in general and in American literature in particular as well as in book production, which served to promote a climate conducive to public libraries. The concept of a public library for Boston was first advanced more than a decade before its establishment by a noted French actor and ventriloquist of the time, Nicholas Marie Alexandre Vattemare. Vattemare was especially energetic in trying to promote an exchange of international materials. In the 1840s he proposed that several of the major private libraries in Boston agree to combine into one public institution to facilitate this exchange. This proposal met with some favor from local officials, but the libraries resisted, and Vattemare's proposal did not succeed. Nonetheless, the public discussion on this issue continued for some time and helped maintain the necessary political and social momentum that would ultimately produce the desired result more than a decade later.

There were also other more general social forces at work that promoted public library development. For example, it was a time when people believed that individuals could be improved morally and socially by the good efforts of others, as well as by their own efforts. An associated belief was that social institutions could also uplift and improve individuals. Examples of such institutions included the church, but in New England at this time there was, in fact, a declining power of the conventional churches and a strong emphasis on the power of reason. More consistent with the temper of the times, and still evident today, was the belief that public schools were a vital force in the socialization of the population. The concept of the public library was closely allied with this belief, and this relationship was made explicit by Melvil Dewey, who stated in 1876 that popular education was actually divided into two parts: "the free school and the free public library" (1989, p. 5). He thought of the library as a school and of the librarian as a teacher, and indeed, the librarians of the latter half of the nineteenth century saw themselves as agents of social improvement. Wiegand (1989) characterized this attitude as the "ideology of reading" (p. 100). This ideology held that there was good reading and bad reading; the former led to good conduct, the latter to unacceptable conduct. The implication, of course, was that librarians were to buy only the good reading.

The responsibility to improve people lay not only with social institutions. Members of the upper classes still believed in noblesse oblige and assumed that they too bore responsibility to provide the means by which others could improve themselves. This implied a duty on the part of the wealthy and better educated to improve the poor and uneducated in so far as these individuals wanted to be improved. Thus American philanthropy became one of the critical foundations for the growth of the public library for years to come. Libraries were seen as an ideal institution to help those less fortunate. This was, ostensibly, an underlying reason for the philanthropy of Andrew Carnegie, who asserted in his 1889 *Gospel of Wealth*:

> This, then, is held to be the duty of the man of wealth: To set an example of modest, unostentatious living, shunning display or extravagance; to provide moderately for the legitimate wants of those dependent upon him; and, after doing so, to consider all surplus revenues which come to him simply as trust funds, which he is called upon to administer, and strictly bound as a matter of duty to administer in the manner which, in his judgment, is best calculated to produce the most beneficial results for the community—the man of wealth thus becoming the mere trustee and agent for his poorer brethren, bringing to their service his superior wisdom, experience, and ability to administer, doing for them better than they would or could do for themselves. (1962, p. 25)

The growth of libraries and librarianship during the nineteenth century was deeply rooted in these beliefs (Nielson 1989). In the 1840s Boston found itself with numerous individuals who had both the wealth and power to generate a civic interest in libraries. Most notable were the efforts of Charles Ticknor and Edward Everett. Ticknor was the educated son of a wealthy Boston merchant. He assumed that social change was possible if accomplished gradually, and he believed that public schools and libraries could improve social and political stability by promoting the education of the general population (Ditzion 1947). Everett was a Unitarian clergyman, teacher, scholar, and at one point, governor of Massachusetts. A strong advocate of the public schools, Everett's beliefs were less populist and more academic than Ticknor's. He saw in the public library the opportunity for those no longer attending schools to continue their studies. He believed the public library could extend one's education by providing educational materials, not just for scholars, but for professionals and merchants. The efforts of Ticknor, Everett, and others finally convinced the Boston city fathers to appoint a Joint Standing Committee on the Library, which in turn recommended the appointment of a board of trustees. The Boston Public Library opened in the spring of 1854. Its mission was to meet the educational convictions of Everett and the popular needs espoused by Ticknor.

What then can we deduce about the historic mission of the public library? Clearly, it shared the educational mission of American public schools. But in what way was the mission of the public library distinct from the public schools? First, the public library could satisfy the interest in reading and learning for all ages, not just for those who were in school; second, it was a means to self-improvement in an age when self-education was still a vital means for improving one's chances in the society. Third, it was intended to produce more thoughtful people, individuals capable of making balanced and well-reasoned judgments in a democratic society that depended on their judgments at the voting booth. Such citizens would serve as a strong and stabilizing force to the democratic society. The nobility of these objectives is rewarding to those who reflect on the foundations of public librarianship from today's vantage point. Much of this same rationale is used to defend libraries today from attacks of various kinds, both fiscal and philosophical.

More recently, however, this historical account of the motivations of the founders of the Boston Public Library has met with skepticism, most notably from Michael Harris (1973), whose "revisionist" interpretation provides a considerably different perspective. Although few of the facts are disputed, Harris has challenged the notion that it was humanitarian, idealistic, or democratic impulses that prompted the leaders of Boston society to create the public library. Rather, Harris reminds us that the founders were among the Boston "Brahmins," a highly privileged, politically conservative, and aristocratic class that dominated the social, economic, and political life of the city. Harris argues that the founders were far less concerned with making educated democrats than with socializing the wave of immigrants who were flowing into Boston in great numbers. He suggests that the immigrants were perceived as unruly and subject to undue influence by political demagogues and other unscrupulous politicians who could foment political and social instability within the genteel confines of Boston. In other words, the creation of the Boston Public Library was another strategy of elitist aristocrats to maintain class stratification and ensure the social order that had benefited them. If the aristocrats controlled what was taught about the social and political institutions of American society, the immigrants would accept those institutions, institutions that were controlled and shaped by the elites. In this conceptualization of the public library, libraries and librarians are seen as agents of authority and social control, implementing restrictive rules, and generally unfriendly to hoi polloi. How could they be otherwise, run by board members appointed by elites, who were themselves elites? Further, Harris has suggested that the public library collection was not designed for the common person, but catered to the educated and upper classes. He argues that this pattern has been repeated time and again as evidenced by the fact that public libraries then and today are run by elites and attended by a disproportionately large number of upper- and middle-class patrons.

Harris's position has been challenged by other library historians. Dain (1975), for example, noted that there is insufficient historical evidence for some of Harris's strongest assertions. Further, she points out that just because elites created the first public libraries does not mean ipso facto that other classes were not well served by them. She notes that the authoritarian nature of early public libraries was a reflection of all public institutions of the time. She argues that public libraries make earnest efforts to attract a variety of users, and offers as evidence the extended hours of operation on Sundays and evenings, information services, open stacks, classification systems, branches, children's rooms and services, meeting rooms for community groups, cooperative activities with schools, interlibrary loan, and special services for immigrants.

Although Harris's position is controversial, it reminds us that comfortable views of history are not without their problems and that the mission of public libraries had multiple philosophical underpinnings, some of them countervailing and incompatible. Are public libraries the cauldrons of democracy or the tools of social control? Perhaps these missions coexist in a dynamic tension that remains unresolved.

ANDREW CARNEGIE AND THE PUBLIC LIBRARY

The events of the latter half of the nineteenth century probably exacerbated this tension. In many ways Andrew Carnegie personified it. Carnegie was a Scottish immigrant who, through hard work and ingenuity, prospered in the iron and steel industry. He amassed a huge fortune exceeding $330 million, 90 percent of which went into charitable trusts. Carnegie's philosophy of stewardship certainly marked him as a prominent exponent of noblesse oblige, but his philanthropy served many. From 1886 to 1919 Carnegie donated $56 million to construct more than 2,000 library buildings, many of them public libraries, in more than 1,400 communities, large and small, in the United States. The communities that requested Carnegie's money often did so as a source of civic pride. The libraries built with Carnegie's largesse were their libraries, not Carnegie's, and their shelves were stocked with materials of local interest, not Carnegie's. In fact, the specifically local character of today's public library collections and services may be a direct result of the special conditions and restrictions that Carnegie required with every donation. First, the money that Carnegie provided was for building construction only, not for the purchase and maintenance of library materials or for staff. This, in essence, guaranteed the local character of library collections. Second, Carnegie required that all recipients of his money must contribute an annual sum equal to 10 percent of the money donated to build collections and hire staff. This created a tradition of shared government support of public libraries and defined local governance. The town, through its appointed board, was in control, not Carnegie. The inevitable result was that the mission of the Carnegie public library was shaped by local interest: library collections did not necessarily reflect the views of Carnegie but of the local community and popular taste. Thus one of the fundamental missions of public libraries, to meet the needs of the local community, may be derived from the Carnegie model of local taxation and local governmental control. Indeed, Carnegie may well have done more to establish this model than the Boston Public Library. After all, Carnegie contributed mightily to making the public library commonplace throughout the United States.

WOMEN'S CLUBS AND THE PUBLIC LIBRARY

One cannot leave the discussion of the forces that shaped public libraries without noting the significant contributions of women's voluntary organizations, most notably women's clubs. Paula Watson has conducted considerable research in this area and much of the information that follows relies on her findings.

Women's clubs became commonplace following the Civil War as it became more acceptable for women to seek an education, especially self-education. Some of these clubs were local, while others were affiliated nationally with the General Federation of Women's Clubs. Like similar organizations devoted to education, "the members were imbued with the idea of the importance of books in improving the quality of life" (Watson 1994, p. 235). Their support for improving women's education extended to developing libraries for use by members of their local community. Watson suggests that women's clubs contributed in significant ways to the development of more than 470 public libraries between 1870 and 1930. Although the exact percentage of public libraries established through the efforts of women's clubs in the early part of the twentieth century is unclear, Watson estimates that it may have ranged between 50 and 75 percent of the total. In some instances the clubs provided support for additional materials and club members volunteered as librarians. Some women's clubs were influential at the state level, lobbying for library legislation and the need for state library commissions (Watson 1994). Although many of the members of the women's clubs were aristocrats, or at least middle class, and therefore potentially subject to Harris's criticisms, their contributions to advancing the public library are substantial. Their stated mission of self-education and improvement is firmly in line with the history and values of their era, and the results were salutary.

Meeting Popular Tastes: Quality Versus Demand

It is also worth noting that from the beginning, the public library has been challenged by the mission of satisfying popular tastes. As public libraries proliferated, much discussion arose concerning the popular novel. Charles Ticknor advocated that a collection of popular materials should be part of the library's collection for the entertainment of readers. But serious concerns were raised by others that popular novels would lower morals. It was even suggested by some that too much fiction reading might cause insanity! Should the collection of the library include such diversions? What would be the effect on young people? Some librarians felt that popular fiction might serve to bring less-educated readers into the library where they would then be exposed to a better quality of literature. Even among librarians with serious misgivings, most had at least some popular novels on their shelves. They realized that if they wanted library users, they would need popular fiction. Generally, these collections were not overly stocked with "cheap" novels, but offered works by Flaubert, Zola, Fielding, and Balzac. This did not protect libraries, however, from censorship attacks. The works of these masters were perceived as scandalous at the time.

SERVING ETHNIC GROUPS AND MINORITIES: A MISSION OF INCLUSIVENESS

During the nineteenth century, America experienced major immigrations from many countries, and in many areas, especially cities, America was a multicultural and polyglot nation. Amidst this influx of new peoples, the concerns regarding the education and socialization of the immigrants was a natural outgrowth of the progressivist philosophy of the times. This philosophy viewed the function of educational institutions as improving society and advancing the democratic tradition (Du Mont, Buttlar, and Caynon 1994). For many, this meant that immigrant groups needed to be assimilated into the American mainstream. Because of their numbers, Europeans were considered to be a particularly difficult challenge (Stern 1991). Libraries were "to furnish fuel for the fires beneath the great melting pot" (Roberts 1912, p. 169). What better group to select and provide the necessary material than librarians? Many librarians took this responsibility quite seriously and numerous articles in professional periodicals offered advice on providing services and understanding the needs of immigrants. Some librarians exhibited an almost missionary zeal in their efforts to bring the benefits of reading to the general public.

Nonetheless, it is true that the public library of the nineteenth century was used primarily by white, middle and upper classes. Ethnic minorities were largely excluded from the benefits of library service (Trujillo and Cuesta 1989). There is relatively limited evidence, however, to determine whether public libraries intentionally excluded ethnic groups, or whether librarians and trustees were simply uninformed as to how to serve them effectively.

It was not until the turn of the century that the library's mission began a systematic effort to provide service to ethnic groups. This was also a time of considerable immigration with more than 20 million arriving in the first quarter of the century (Stern 1991). Although some librarians recognized that each ethnic group had a literature and culture worth preserving and transmitting, the primary emphasis was on integration of immigrants into the American way of life. Library collections and services included books and newspapers written in native languages; programs on U.S. citizenship; classes in English; story hours in native languages; programs on American history and culture; supplementary materials to support school curricula; and help for immigrants in reading letters, sending messages to social service agencies, writing checks, and completing citizenship forms (Stern 1991; Du Mont, Buttlar, and

Caynon 1994). In 1917 ALA created a Committee on Work with the Foreign Born whose job it was to collect and disseminate information on how to help educate immigrants on American values and the English language (Stern 1991). The committee produced numerous guides to assist in this process.

Perhaps the most notable organizational response to serving ethnic groups and minorities was the creation of branch libraries in urban areas. Branches provided extension services that could reach special populations, especially industrial workers and those who did not speak English (Ditzion 1947). Branches also offered special services to children. By 1900 many public libraries had a separate room for children's books and services. What better place to educate the first generation of immigrant children in the ways of American life (Du Mont, Buttlar, and Caynon 1994)?

Sadly, there were some minorities and ethnic groups that did not receive much attention from librarians, most notably, African Americans and Hispanics. Prior to the Civil War, the majority of African Americans lived in the South and were forbidden to read. After the Civil War there were a few public libraries in the South, but library services for African Americans were severely restricted or nonexistent (Trujillo and Cuesta 1989). Even into the 1930s there was considerable evidence that funding for library services to African Americans in the South was not commensurate to the proportion of African Americans in the community (Gleason 1941). There were few services and what was available was often offered only in segregated circumstances: separate branches, poorly funded school libraries, restricted privileges at main libraries, and a few independent African-American libraries (Du Mont, Buttlar, and Caynon 1994). Sometimes the same library served both blacks and whites but had separate entrances, collections, and reading areas. The establishment of black branches was usually funded by the philanthropy of whites or the activities of both black and white churches or civic organizations (Cresswell 1996).

There were a few notable exceptions to this picture, in particular, the work of Thomas Fountion Blue, who pioneered library service to African Americans in Louisville, Kentucky. Blue was a graduate of the prestigious Hampton Institute and Richmond Theological Seminary. He was placed in charge of a segregated branch of the Louisville Free Public Library in 1905. This was the first branch for African Americans in any American city (Josey 1994). His services and library training programs for African Americans were considered a national model (Josey

1970). Similarly, the Negro Public Library in Nashville, Tennessee, which opened in 1916 as a branch of Nashville's Carnegie Library, focused on service to children. Under the leadership of the African American branch librarian, Marian Hadley, who studied under Thomas Fountion Blue, and the librarian of the Carnegie Library, Margaret Kercheval, a solid children's collection was developed and services such as story hours were also offered (Malone 2000). Nonetheless, in general, public library service to people of color was poor or nonexistent, and it was not until the 1960s activist movements that sponsored demonstrations, sit-ins, and "read-ins" that library services became widely available to African Americans, especially in the South (Graham 2001).

Regrettably, ALA was not outspoken on the issue of library service to African Americans until the 1960s when the Civil Rights movement made it impossible to ignore (Du Mont, Buttlar, and Caynon 1994). Generally, until the 1960s the association viewed itself as representing a national constituency of librarians, including those in the South, who favored segregation. ALA did not want to be perceived as judging the political or social beliefs of its members and viewed segregationist policies as a local matter. There was also concern that too much agitation on the issue would create more resistance in the South and bring unfavorable publicity to those public libraries who were desegregating quietly (Cresswell 1996; Josey 1994).

The problems, of course, were not only in the South. Evidence that northern libraries also engaged in discriminatory practices was available, but generally overlooked. For example, communities that received Carnegie dollars often spent the money on the provision of service to whites in the community but not to African Americans; or far less money was spent, resulting in inferior service. As the historian John Hope Franklin (1977) observed, "one searches in vain for an indignant outcry on the part of the professional librarians against this profanation of their sacred profession and this subversion of their cherished institutions" (p. 13).

It was not until 1961 that the ALA took a firm stand regarding service to African Americans as well as all other citizens, advocating equal library service to all. At its midwinter meeting, the association passed an amendment to the Library Bill of Rights that made clear that an individual's library use "should not be denied or abridged because of his race, religion, national origins or political views." Regrettably, the response of many communities toward opening their libraries to ethnic minorities, especially African Americans, was met with disappointingly strong opposition. In Virginia, for example, the citizens of Danville and Petersburg voted to close their public libraries rather than to desegregate them (Cresswell 1996).

Hispanics experienced a similar lack of quality and quantity in public library services. Among the earliest documented services were those provided by Pura Belpre at the New York Public Library beginning in 1921 (Guerena and Erazo 2000). But this was clearly the exception. In his study of library services to Hispanics, Haro (1981) found that libraries are often perceived as one of many Anglo institutions that are designed and controlled by Anglos to serve Anglos:

> While most Mexican Americans, even the poor and illiterate, aspire to better education, the public library is not seen as a vehicle to attain it. The public library is viewed by far too many Mexican Americans, particularly within the lower classes, as an Anglo institution which has never cared about their needs, which does not hire their people, and which engages in the disproportionate distribution of resources to satisfy first the demands of an Anglo society. (p. 86)

The Civil Rights Movement of the 1960s was a critical turning point in ensuring that African Americans and Hispanics were equally included in the mission of public libraries. The earlier public library movement focused primarily on assimilating ethnic cultures into the American mainstream. The Civil Rights Movement of the 1960s was also a struggle for ethnic self-determination (Stern 1991). Groups such as African Americans and Hispanics did not necessarily desire to be assimilated; rather they argued for equal opportunity and rights to the advantages that American society had to offer. The concept of the melting pot was replaced by a concept of a multicultural society.

The focus on minorities and disadvantaged groups in the United States produced several pieces of progressive legislation affecting libraries. Most notable was the passage of the Library Services and Construction Act (LSCA) in 1964, which served as the major force in developing library services. LSCA specifically provided funding for libraries to develop services and collections for ethnic, disadvantaged, and underserved groups. Similar funding was provided with the passage of the Higher Education Act for colleges and universities (Trujillo and Cuesta 1989).

Libraries responded to these initiatives by hiring individuals from ethnic groups, collecting reference resources on ethnic cultures and experiences, creating criteria to make library collections inclusive of all members of the community, developing outreach programs to attract minorities, offering information and referral programs for minorities, and building collections that were more responsive to the needs of various ethnic groups.

There was also a significant professional response through library associations and organizations. In the late 1960s a considerable number of ALA members expressed concern that the association had done little to secure open access for all citizens and to address issues of equality and social justice within the profession and in society at large. The ALA response was to create the Social Responsibilities Round Table (SRRT) in 1970. Among SRRT's purposes is "to act as a stimulus to the association and its various units in making libraries more responsive to current social needs"(American Library Association [ALA] 1997, p. 135). SRRT has been very active over the years addressing a variety of issues, including advocating for international human rights and rights for racial minorities and gays, securing rights for the poor and homeless, and promoting equal rights for women. Their focus has been both on the library profession and on policies and practices of the society as a whole (West 1997).

Additional organizations were established as a result of the turmoil and activities of the 1960s. One such ALA-affiliated advocacy group is REFORMA (The National Association to Promote Library Service to the Spanish Speaking), which was established in 1971. This organization's stated purpose is to foster the development of library collections that include materials written in Spanish as well as materials that are oriented to Hispanics, to encourage the recruitment of bilingual librarians and staff, to develop services and programs for Hispanics, to educate Hispanics regarding the services and materials available in libraries, and to lobby to maintain library services for Hispanics (REFORMA 1997). Similar to REFORMA, the Black Caucus of ALA has worked since 1970 on behalf of African-American librarians and the African-American community. Among its purposes are to encourage ALA to focus on the information needs of the African-American community, to promote services to that community, and to encourage the creation of information resources about African Americans for dissemination to the wider community (Black Caucus 1997).

Stern (1991) has observed that in the last decade there have been changes in emphasis in developing library services to ethnic groups and minorities. He notes that the traditional focus regarding services to ethnic groups has been based on the perception of this community as "disadvantaged." However, since the 1980s the approach has shifted some-what to serving the "ethnically enfranchised." In this sense, members of ethnic communities are seen "as equal partners with nonethnic residents in the fight to improve the quality of their lives and the communities in which they reside" (Stern 1991, p. 96). Some of the resulting library col-lections are developed less for self-improvement than to empower.

The public library mission to serve the various ethnic communities in the United States continues to grow and evolve. The White House Conference on Library and Information Services held in 1991 reaffirmed the need to respond to the needs of an increasingly multicultural soci-ety. Its recommendations included providing financial and technical assistance to promote service to multicultural populations and popula-tions with disabilities, promoting outreach services to traditionally underserved populations, and encouraging support for training library and information science professionals to serve multicultural needs (White House Conference 1991). Today, ALA has a variety of committees and round tables that monitor minority issues in addition to the ones noted above. These include the Minority Concerns and Cultural Diversity Committee, the ALA Office for Literacy and Outreach Services (OLOS), the LITA (Library and Information Technology Association)/LSSI (Li-brary Systems & Services) Minority Scholarship in Library and Infor-mation Technology Subcommittee; LITA/OCLC Minority Scholarship Subcommittee, and the Minorities Recruitment Committee of the New Members Round Table (ALA 1997).

Although there have been concerted efforts to provide library ser-vices to ethnic minorities, few would argue that the problems of un-equal service have vanished. Prominent issues remain including the need for recruitment and retention of a diverse library workforce, concern for the reduction in federal funding for library services to ethnic communi-ties, and the need for good research on the impact of the programs and services that have been developed to serve these communities (Trujillo and Cuesta 1989).

SUMMARY: SERVING THE PUBLIC

Today's public libraries serve as archives of commercial and historical records; they contain religious and liturgical works and interpretations; they offer a place for students, scholars, academics, and the general citi-zenry to study; and they provide a source for edifying reading. These services reflect the historic missions of libraries in the past to: (1) support the education and socialization needs of society, (2) meet the informational needs of a broad spectrum of citizens, (3) promote self-education, and (4) satisfy the popular tastes of the public. Whether these missions were undertaken to control the masses or to make them more effective citizens will be a subject of continuing debate. Nonetheless, as the missions of the public library have been revealed, they suggest that the modern public library's purposes and practices rest on a rich historical foundation.

THE MISSION AND FUTURE OF THE MODERN AMERICAN LIBRARY

Today's libraries and librarians confront a host of destabilizing factors: the flood of information, constant innovations in technology, economic and political demands and stresses, as well as numerous social problems. De Rosa, Dempsey, and Wilson (2004) observe that the purpose of libraries is evolving:

> It has become increasingly difficult to characterize and describe the purpose of and the experience of using libraries and other allied organizations. The traditional notions of "library," "collection," "patron" and "archive" have changed and continue to change. The relationships among the information professional, the user and the content have changed and continue to change. (p. ix)

What will be the mission and values of the library in the future? It is clear from history that the mission of libraries is shaped by the societies in which they exist. The values and attitudes that evolve within a given society are the self-same forces and attitudes that mold and shape its institutions. Thus, it is to our advantage to examine some of the influential values and attitudes in today's environment that are likely to shape our future.

Forces that Shape the Future: Attitudes

ATTITUDE TOWARD GOVERNMENT AGENCIES

The society's confidence, or lack thereof, in government agencies to perform their tasks will have a direct effect on the society's willingness to continue providing fiscal resources to operate them. Lack of confidence will produce diminished funding, which in turn will result in shrinking services, a situation that has been demonstrated in several states from

the 1990s to early 2000s, for example, California. As government funding has declined, so has funding for libraries. Of course, other factors
play a role, including the general health of the economy and individuals' personal financial condition. Nonetheless, as the public demands
greater and greater accountability from its public institutions, libraries
will be forced to demonstrate their contribution to the community. Failing to do so may well affect both the quality of services provided and
the means by which they are delivered. For example, library services
and materials may be offered on a cost-recovery basis with fees being
charged directly for services rendered.

ATTITUDE TOWARD EDUCATION

Because libraries are so closely linked with education, the society's attitude toward education is a critical factor in the library's survival. In a
society where learning is highly valued and libraries are perceived as
positive contributions to education, libraries are likely to receive considerable support. It is safe to say, however, that among the general public there
has been a considerable decline in confidence in public school education.
This is a substantial change from the 1950s, when Americans were much
more confident in the ability of their public schools to educate the young.

Two alternative scenarios for libraries are possible. A loss of confidence in the public schools could lead to decline in confidence and support for all agencies perceived as primarily educational. In this case,
public library funding and support may suffer. A second alternative may
have the opposite effect: if the public schools are perceived as failing,
citizens may expect the library to strengthen its role in the education of
its citizenry as a substitute for the deficiencies of schools. In this case
libraries may assume greater status and responsibility for encouraging
young people to read, developing their collections to support curricula,
and providing increased educational programming.

ATTITUDE TOWARD SERVING ALL SEGMENTS OF SOCIETY

There is considerable contemporary debate over the role of government
agencies in helping various groups in our society. Libraries have mir-
rored this ambivalence, going through periods of activism to recruit new
groups of people who were not traditional users, and at other times focusing on the library's traditional clientele. Bernard Berelson (1949), in a
major study of library use in 1949, concluded that the library should

focus on its natural constituency—the better educated, middle-class in-dividual who represented the typical user of public libraries at that time. This constituted 10 percent of the adult population. Certainly, there are librarians today who feel that the energies and resources of libraries should be devoted to those individuals who are its most likely users. Underlying this belief is the essentially voluntary and passive nature of libraries; if people want to use a library, they do so. Others have argued that the library should be reaching out to those groups, who, for what-ever reason, have not taken advantage of this tax-supported resource. These individuals may have not received adequate education to develop literacy skills or may have been victims of discrimination. The extent to which the society sends a clear message as to how public institutions function in meeting the needs of various groups will help shape the library's direction. Surely, if the library directs its attention to frequent users, it is likely to devote resources to materials and services quite dif-ferent from those it would use if it attempts to meet the needs of those for whom the library has not been a regular contact.

ATTITUDE TOWARD THE IMPORTANCE OF READING

If the society believes that reading, and by inference, literacy, is impor-tant, then it is likely that libraries will have great support. In addition, if reading is considered critical, then the materials and services of libraries are likely to reflect this value. This might include strong print collec-tions and considerable emphasis on children's reading programs, adult literacy programs, and support for school reading programs. If reading is undervalued, or other values are placed above it (for example, the value of visual entertainment), then emphasis might be placed on differ-ent services such as audiovisual services, materials, and programming. Of course, this is not to say that audiovisual materials in and of themselves are incompatible with reading, only that what is emphasized in terms of how resources will be allocated will differ depending on the value placed on reading itself. If, in fact, we are moving to a more visual society, and we presume that libraries are extensions of the values of our society, then we would expect changes in our library collections and services.

ATTITUDE TOWARD LITERATURE

Throughout history, libraries have been seen as archives of the great literature of the world. Yet, today, many libraries appear to offer more popular materials and less literature. One might well argue that this is because most people neither value fine literature nor desire to read it. The argument is well taken. One study of American reading habits found that less than 1 percent of reading materials read by the public were what one would call "literature" (Zill and Winglee 1989). No matter what one thinks of this situation, a society that does not value literature is not likely to expect its libraries to devote many resources to its collection and preservation, especially, if other types of materials or services are valued more highly.

ATTITUDE TOWARD TECHNOLOGY

There is no doubt that new information technologies are influencing almost every aspect of our lives and specifically altering the way we create, organize, store, and disseminate information. The enthusiasm with which a society accepts these new technologies and the reservations it may have concerning them will undoubtedly affect those institutions involved in information transfer in profound ways. That libraries now possess a wide array of these information technologies and are experiencing many pressures regarding their access and control is testimony to the impact that the technological culture has already had on library services.

   These attitudes, as well as others, influence the mission of today's library and will, no doubt, significantly affect the future of library services and materials. The dramatic nature of some of these changes has led some to speculate that the new technologies have totally revolutionized our society, so much so that the traditional missions of libraries may be obsolete. Enthusiasts of this view see books and print-on-paper being replaced by the virtual electronic library where information seekers will simply go online from their homes or offices to find what they need. The library without walls will become a reality without libraries (Harris and Hannah 1992). Although such predictions may be hyperbole, it is clearly true that the introduction of new technologies has exacerbated and magnified many of the problems and challenges that libraries face.

Forces that Shape the Future: Values

As we began this chapter, the library was identified as fundamentally serving a social purpose and reflecting social values. Values are strongly held beliefs that serve to guide our actions. When we think of values we associate them with words such as "convictions" or "principles" more than with words like "opinions." Values structure our experience and provide insight when we make important decisions affecting our future and that of others. Institutions and professions have values just as individuals have them. These values provide for institutional and professional stability and consistency when important issues arise. It has been suggested that the American society and the American library may be entering a new era. Whether that is true or not, it may be instructive to check our compasses before embarking.

Trying to identify what the values of librarianship are is a source of controversy, especially in the public library world. Gorman (2000, 2001) has identified eight values for consideration which are very briefly characterized below:

1. *Stewardship:* Preserving and making available the human record and ensuring that librarians maintain and update their skills as needed.
2. *Service:* Serving the best interests of the society as a whole and treating each individual with equal respect.
3. *Intellectual Freedom:* Promoting the freedom of inquiry and expression.
4. *Rationalism:* Acting reasonably and in an orderly, systematic manner.
5. *Literacy and Learning:* Promoting both the ability to read and the capacity to understand more complex text.
6. *Equity of Access:* Ensuring that access is available to all and recognizing that some groups such as the poor, rural populations, the aged, and members of minorities have been placed at a disadvantage which librarians should act to overcome.
7. *Privacy:* Ensuring that the activities of library patrons including circulation records and reference inquiries are treated as private.
8. *Democracy:* Supporting democratic institutions by ensuring a broad range of materials and open access to information.

While these are certainly worthy values, others have taken different approaches to identify the values of the field. Koehler (2003), for example, surveyed 1,900 librarians and other information workers from around the world and from different types of libraries. Although differences were found, certain basic values seemed to emerge. "Service to the patron" appeared to be the most commonly identified value, but others were consistently noted as well, including the values of intellectual freedom, information literacy, and equal access.

Fairly recently the American Library Association undertook the task of identifying what it refers to as the "core values" of librarianship. Although the ALA had promulgated a variety of policies on values such as intellectual freedom and ethical conduct, there was no one document that clearly enunciated all the critical values of the field. The need for such values was noted at the ALA's first Congress on Professional Education (COPE) in May 1999. This resulted in the appointment of a Core Values Task Force. By April 2000, the task force had prepared a "Statement on Core Values." It identified the following as the core values of the field:

- Connection of people to ideas
- Assurance of free and open access to recorded knowledge, information, and creative works
- Commitment to literacy and learning
- Respect for the individuality and the diversity of all people
- Freedom for all people to form, to hold, and to express their own beliefs
- Preservation of the human record
- Excellence in professional service to our communities
- Formation of partnerships to advance these values (ALA 2000)

No doubt, the statement expresses some of the deeply held convictions of the field. Some however were unimpressed: one editorial writer described the statement as "a bland homogenization of euphemisms" (Buschman 2000). Among ALA members the statement received a mixed response, and these values have not been formally adopted by the association. Sager (2001), reflecting on the many reasons proffered for the failure to get consensus on core values, identified a variety of reasons given for the tepid response of ALA members: (1) the core values dilute other existing policies of the association, most notable those of the Intellectual Freedom Committee and the Social Responsibilities Roundtable; (2) existing policies of ALA already express the core values of the field; (3) the core values statement is too brief to give an adequate account of the field's values; (4) there was insufficient input into the core values from various segments of the library community; (5) more time was needed to analyze the various revisions to the draft statements; and (6) it was unrealistic to believe that a consensus was possible. Whether these criticisms are fair and accurate depends on one's point of view; what is clear is that the profession appears to be unprepared at this time to adopt a sweeping statement on its values. No doubt, the ALA will continue to explore this issue in the years to come.

Interestingly, the Association of College and Research Libraries (2000), a division of ALA, has been able to identify its core values as they apply to academic libraries. They are the following:

- Equitable and open access to information
- Service

- Intellectual freedom
- Cooperation, collaboration, and sharing of resources
- Commitment to the profession of librarianship
- Fair use
- Education and learning
- Commitment to the use of appropriate technology
- Knowledge as an end in itself
- Conservation and preservation of knowledge
- Diversity
- Scholarly communication and research
- Global perspective

The machinations of library associations notwithstanding, it would be useful to discuss in more detail some values that seem to be pervasive as they apply to libraries in the United States. The following is a more detailed discussion of some of them.

VALUE 1: THE VALUE OF SERVICE

Perhaps the most distinctive feature of library and information science, in contrast, for example, to computer science, is that the purpose of the field is to communicate knowledge to people. This is more than just "meeting an information need," which is the common parlance for the activities of the contemporary library. Underlying this notion of service is not just the betterment of the individual, but the betterment of the community as a whole. This activity, of bringing knowledge to people and the society, is the sine qua non of the profession. It also distinguishes it from business and industry in that, for most libraries, and certainly for publicly funded ones, the generation of profit is not the fundamental purpose; rather it is helping others. Pierce Butler (1951) characterized this notion succinctly over 50 years ago:

> The cultural motivation of librarianship is the promotion of wisdom in the individual and the community . . . to communicate, so far as possible, the whole of scholarship to the whole community. The librarian undertakes to supply literature on any and every subject to any and every citizen, for any and every purpose. . . . [These actions], in the long run, will sharpen the understanding, judgment, and prudence of the readers and thus sustain and advance civilization. (pp. 246–247)

Libraries and librarianship are about serving people and the society as a whole. Service to others has been the foundation of American librarianship for more than one hundred years, and this notion of service seems to apply to librarianship no matter what type of library or information service is involved. As Finks (1989) has recently observed:

> Our natural reaction to the approach of a patron is not irritation at being interrupted, but delight at another chance to help someone pick his or her way through our beloved maze. It is, we should admit, a noble urge, this altruism of ours, one that seems both morally and psychologically good. (p. 353)

Winter (1988) has pointed out that librarianship emerged as one of the service-oriented professions of the nineteenth century, in contradistinction to the profit-centered, capitalistic enterprises emerging at the same time. Librarianship grew out of the same American well-spring as nursing, social work, teaching, medicine, law, and the clergy. In addition, part of this service orientation may well be related to the fact that American libraries, at least since the latter half of the nineteenth century, have been numerically, as distinguished from bureaucratically, dominated by women. When women entered the workforce of the nineteenth century, their activities were expected to conform to the stereotypes of appropriate behavior for their gender (Garrison 1972). Women occupied professions that distinguished themselves by their nurturing characteristics: teaching, nursing, social work, and librarianship among them. Garrison (1972) refers to nineteenth-century librarians as "tender technicians" (p. 131). Serving others, usually at a sacrificial wage one might add, was part and parcel of librarianship as with other such occupations.

Interestingly, some have suggested more recently that an emerging business model for library service is seriously distorting this service orientation. As fiscal resources dwindle, more and more pressure is exerted on libraries to act as businesses, emphasizing concepts such as increased productivity, pricing information as a commodity, and "repackaging" information services to market as products for sale. This business approach has led to the use of management techniques, technologies, and marketing strategies often borrowed directly, and with mixed success, from the private sector. Estabrook (1982) argues that this rationalization of library practice using a business model could change the very nature of library service, with unhappy results. For example, it could lead to libraries only serving their most successful clients, those who are easiest to serve and satisfy and hence most cost-efficient, and ignoring those difficult to serve or reluctant to use library services.

Despite these misgivings, the preoccupation of many libraries and librarians with quality service is testimony to the persistence of this value in most libraries—whether in the private or public sector. Part of the reason for service's tenaciousness may be that it has played such an explicit role in the stated philosophical values of librarianship for so long. This can be observed directly in the thinking of one of the most notable philosophical figures in the history of librarianship, S.R. Ranganathan. Ranganathan (1892–1972) was a major figure in the development of a variety of theoretical issues in library and information science, most notably in classification theory and in developing basic principles for the field. He conducted much of his work and study in India, beginning the first school of library science there. His contribution is international in scope, and his work has influenced American librarianship as well as librarianship in other countries. Ranganathan examined the most fundamental underpinnings of libraries and librarianship. In 1931, he observed:

> The vital principle of the library—which has struggled through all the stages of its evolution, is common to all its different forms and will persist to be its distinguishing feature for all time to come—is that it is an instrument of universal education, and assembles together and freely distributes all the tools of education and disseminates knowledge with their aid. (Ranganathan 1931, p. 354)

Ranganathan (1931) proposed five laws of library science that have remained a centerpiece of professional values and that reflect his deeply held conviction that the library is dedicated to the service of people. A brief review of these laws provides a surprisingly contemporary perspective on the central value of library service.

Books Are for Use. Looking back to earlier historical uses of libraries, Ranganathan observed that books were often chained to prevent their removal and that the emphasis was on storage and preservation rather than use. He did not reject the notion that preservation and storage were important, but he asserted that the purpose of such activities was to promote the use of the item. Without the use of materials, there is little use to libraries. Certainly, this is even more obvious today. In the past, one needed to protect most materials because, before the invention of the printing press, they were rare and difficult to produce. Today, for most library materials there are many copies, often obtainable at reasonable cost. By emphasizing use, Ranganathan refocused the attention of the field to access-related issues, such as the library's location, loan policies, hours and days of operation, such mundanities as library furniture, and the quality of staffing. Ranganathan's law is certainly a contemporary one. Much emphasis is now being placed on quality of "customer" service and developing a "customer" orientation. Given the attitude of society that public institutions need greater accountability, this orientation is both healthy and essential for survival.

Books Are for All. This law suggests that every member of the community should be able to obtain materials needed. It is an important egalitarian principle that certainly forms the foundation of much public library ideology. Ranganathan felt that all individuals from all social environments were entitled to library service, and that the basis of library use was education, to which all were entitled. These "entitlements," however, were not without some important obligations for both libraries/librarians and library patrons. Among these were that librarians should have excellent first-hand knowledge of the people to be served, that collections should meet the special interests of the community, and that libraries should promote and advertise their services extensively to attract a wide range of users. In addition, Ranganathan felt that library selectors should emphasize materials that were strong, well written, and well illustrated. On the other hand, library users should be advocates for library service, follow the rules and regulations of the library, keep the library in good order, and take out only materials that are needed.

Ranganathan understood that to accomplish this purpose, society would have to contribute. For example, he argued that the state is obligated to provide the financial resources through taxation and legislation so that all people could be served by libraries. In addition, the state should create a state-library authority, with a state librarian, whose duty it would be to ensure library service by creating institutions for that purpose. Similarly, the local library authority is obligated to provide service to all individuals in their local areas.

Every Book Its Reader. This principle is closely related to the second law but it focuses on the item itself, suggesting that each item in a library has an individual or individuals who would find that item useful. Ranganathan argued that the library could devise many methods to ensure that each item finds its appropriate reader. One method involved the basic rules for access to the collection, most notably the need for open shelving (direct access by patrons to the book collection). Ranganathan saw the system of open shelving as critical because it gave users the chance to examine the collection freely, much the same way they could examine their own collections at home. As Ranganathan noted, "In an open access library, the reader is permitted to wander among the books and lay his hands on any of them at his will and pleasure" (p. 259). Another aspect of the library that improved the chances for a match of reader with book involved collection arrangement. Ranganathan suggested that the collection arrangement should be by subject if the most effective access was to result. He was not dogmatic, however, about the uniformity of this arrangement, and he possessed a very modern sense of the need for marketing library materials. Evidence of this is his suggestion that the library set up displays of selected materials that singled out collections of books, such as a section for newly acquired materials. He also suggested special reading areas for popular materials. Another aspect of library service that would improve matching books with readers is the use of trained professional staff who could evaluate library collections through surveys, provide reader's advisory services, conduct programs such as story hours, provide extension services, and select good books. Finally, the library could promote and market its services to readers through publicity, library displays, library publications, and public activities such as festivals.

Save the Time of the Reader. This law is a recognition that part of the excellence of library service is its ability to meet the needs of the library user efficiently. To this end, Ranganathan recommended the use of appropriate business methods to improve library management. He observed that centralizing the library collection in one location provided distinct advantages. He also noted that excellent staff would not only include those who possess strong reference skills, but also strong technical skills in cataloging, cross-referencing, ordering, accessioning, and the circulation of materials. All of these functions would contribute to timely service to the user. In a way he anticipated, although not necessarily predicted, the more competitive information marketplace of today in which the information seeker has more than one option available for finding material and information traditionally provided by libraries.

The Library Is a Growing Organism. Perhaps one of the most sagacious observations made by Ranganathan is this principle. Ranganathan described this as the "fundamental principle" that governs library organization (p. 326). Remarkably, it anticipates the management theorists of the 1960s, who argued that organizations are not self-sufficient; they do not exist autonomously. Rather, they exist, like living organisms do, within an environment in which the primary challenge is to survive.

Ranganathan said it this way: "It is an accepted biological fact that a growing organism alone will survive. An organism which ceases to grow will petrify and perish" (p. 326). Clearly, the notion expressed by Ranganathan is kindred to the later theorists who perceived the library as a dynamic institution constantly subject to changes. Ranganathan's perspective however focused more on the need for internal change than on changes in the environment itself. He argued that library organizations must accommodate growth in staff, the physical collection, and patron use. This involved growth in the physical building, reading areas, shelving, and in space for the catalog. Because of the inevitable growth in the collections, he anticipated increased need for security against theft (book lifts forecast increased demand) and a need to design traffic flow to permit easy movement around the floors. Ranganathan also recognized that personnel structure and decision making would also be affected by this growth. He anticipated the increased division of labor among administrative, technical, and reference staff and recommended that an administrative staff council be created to assist in the operations and organization of the library. This clearly anticipated the participatory decision-making movements of the 1960s and beyond.

These laws represent the quintessential principles of library service and reflect the continuing and persistent value of service to those the profession serves. These laws are also an explicit recognition that the principles that we accept for our discipline are not merely theoretical niceties; on the contrary, they are the driving forces, or should be the driving forces, for structuring library collections, services, and staff.

These values are clearly important both in terms of historical and contemporary library service. Interestingly, they have been recently revisited by Gorman (1995), who advanced five "new laws" as updates to Ranganathan's. Gorman asserts the following five laws:

Libraries Serve Humanity. This is a restatement of the service ethic that permeates librarianship, recognizing that the "dominant ethic of librarianship is service to the individual, community, and society as a whole" (p. 784).

Respect All Forms by Which Knowledge Is Communicated. In Ranganathan's time, print materials dominated library materials. For this reason, his principles talk of books and readers. But today, there are many more ways in which knowledge is packaged in libraries. According to Gorman, "each new means of communication enhances and supplements the strengths of all previous means" (p. 784). It is certainly true that most of the time new means of communication merely add to the repertoire of communication techniques provided by the society. This new principle suggests that library workers should not fear that new forms of communication will replace print; rather, librarians should exploit all media to advance library service.

Use Technology Intelligently to Enhance Service. The obligation of librarians is neither to resist new technologies nor to use technology uncritically. Rather, it is to recognize the potential of some technologies in accomplishing the missions of libraries. To the extent that new technologies can offer tremendous advantages to library service, they should be applied in a constructive and intelligent manner.

Protect Free Access to Knowledge. The historical concept of the library as one of the foundations of democratic institutions remains as important today as ever. The controls and centralization that new technologies can produce have exacerbated many of the problems involved in protecting the intellectual freedom of patrons. The legacy of our culture and other cultures must be freely transmitted to all; otherwise freedom is threatened and tyranny promoted.

Honor the Past and Create the Future. A central value of librarianship is the recognition that the past serves as a guide for the future. The library has been a central institution for archiving our cultural record and the cultural records of other societies. To this end the library must not only focus on the new information that is constantly being produced but protect the historical record as well.

Value 2: Reading and the Book Are Important

A central value of libraries and library workers has been and continues to be a deep and abiding respect for both reading and the book. Consider some of the advantages that books possess:
Books . . .

- are generally lightweight and very portable; they're easy to take to the beach or to bed
- require no electricity (except when it's dark)
- require no additional equipment such as video display terminals, printers, etc.
- require little maintenance and repair, and when repair is needed it is

usually quite inexpensive and can be accomplished by an individual with minimal training; no service contract is needed

- require no diagrams or documentation to use
- can get pretty damp and dusty and still function
- can be dropped on the floor with little damage
- are comparatively cheap
- can be browsed easily and contain finding aids, such as an index, that are relatively easy to use (compared with using Boolean logic)
- provide a large number of thoughtful and interconnected ideas in one place that can be read from start to finish or scanned in sections;
- are an excellent source for stimulating the imagination;
- store easily
- can be written in and text can be easily underlined for emphasis during later reading and study
- require little knowledge to operate
- can last a very long time, especially when printed on acid-free paper

This is not to say that each of these features is unique to books, but in combination they represent a very impressive technology. It is highly unlikely that any electronic technology, although each has its own distinct advantages, will possess the combination of advantages available in the book in the near future.

But the book has many advantages quite aside from its technical character. Neill (1992) argues, for example, that books stimulate more active involvement and diminish the passivity common when viewing television or movies; they are able to convey more complex concepts and psychological conditions than television and movies and more closely approximate real life; they stimulate intellectual activity; and exposure to books often leads to improved understanding, discovery, and growth in our personal lives.

The fact that librarianship values reading greatly is also seen in the library's concern for those who cannot read. The sad truth is that in this ever more complex information environment, there are many who are unable to read. It is especially regrettable to know that the United States is far from immune from this problem. According to UNESCO, the United States ranks 70th in the percentage of literate adults among 211 nations (Kurian 2001). This is a significant decline since 1950. Millions of U.S. adults are unable to read an eighth-grade level book, and many of these individuals are unable to read simple but essential items such as bus schedules, newspapers, and maps. For such individuals, the world of information is dramatically inaccessible.

It is no surprise then, that libraries, with their strong history of the book as their primary material, would continue to emphasize books and reading, even while images continue to dominate the popular media. It is no doubt a reason why many library professionals feel a sense of ambivalence when they see more and more library collection expenditures for audiovisual materials and electronic technologies.

VALUE 3: RESPECT FOR TRUTH AND THE SEARCH FOR TRUTH

When individuals seek answers to questions, they expect the library to provide timely and accurate information, and library professionals would consider themselves remiss if they provided inaccurate information. Certainly, the provision of accurate information is a duty of the information provider. This respect for truth should, however, be separated from the search for truth that must also be promoted. Often library users are in the process of investigating issues for themselves that are much more complex than simply asking for an answer to a single question. Libraries are intended to assist individuals in this investigatory process. The consequence of assisting in this process may require the library to collect materials that contain information which is false as well as true. Swan (1986) has noted that librarians must have the untrue on their library shelves as well as the true, because sometimes these sources prove quite revealing to those exploring complex issues. One may, for example, know that the ideas in Hitler's *Mein Kampf* are outrageous and false, but the historical analysis of such ideas may prove quite useful in teaching individuals about the truth of our past and the dangers that may still lie in the future. Making such material unavailable may impede one's understanding of the truth. Similarly, respecting the search for truth requires that the librarian reduce barriers in this search. This may mean protecting the privacy rights of patrons by refusing to supply information concerning circulation records to others; it may mean not restricting library materials by practices that place a barrier between the patron and the information. Protecting the search for truth means collecting and defending the many points of view of authors and creators and respecting each individual's search for knowledge.

VALUE 4: TOLERANCE

A complementary value to the search for truth is that of tolerance. Tolerance has played a critical role in the finer moments of American history, as has intolerance in some of our most ignominious times. Tolerance has a special relationship to truth; tolerance admits of the possibility that our ability to judge the truth is flawed, and that there may be many "truths," or that the truth in some cases may not be known. It presumes that more than one perspective on a subject may be reasonable and that exposure to many ideas may help us understand and approach the truth. The value of tolerance thus suggests that library collections possess a variety of perspectives on a wide array of topics. It suggests that information professionals try to be nonjudgmental in terms of the value or direction of a library user's inquiry. Without such a value, library collections would be little more than the dogmatic assertions of the majority.

VALUE 5: THE PUBLIC GOOD

The notion of the public good is fundamental to library service and has at least three implications for the library. First, it implies that people and society as a whole are changed, and, in the long run, improved by ideas, no matter what format of these ideas. It implies that ideas improve the quality of a person's life and the life of the community. There is little reason for libraries to exist if one does not believe that people can be improved by using them. Improvement may not be the only reason for libraries, but it is an essential function. Examples include stimulating an interest in reading among young children, helping children in their school work, providing training information to adults, providing programming for mothers or the elderly, and providing information to clients to advance their knowledge and careers.

Second, the notion of the public good implies that the citizen has a right to good entertainment, that people have a right to enjoy life, and that the library has a role in promoting pleasure. Certainly the presence of copious fiction, romance, travel, and popularized science and history attests to the strong feelings that librarians have about this dimension of library service. The notion of "healthy entertainment" has been carried over into modern library service from the nineteenth-century concern that the provision of healthy entertainment would deter citizens from embarking on unhealthy ones.

It is interesting that the value of the public good is sufficiently ambiguous to accommodate both the "improvement" function and the "entertainment" one. As noted earlier regarding the historical mission of the public library, the attempt to accommodate this dual mission has accounted for considerable debate in librarianship, especially when it comes to allocation of resources for the library collection. This debate, sometimes characterized as the "quality versus demand" debate, centers on defining the library's primary purpose: Is it to educate or to entertain? Nelson (1978) in a classic statement on the issue suggested that the public library has become too laden with trivialities and entertainment to truly respond to the needs of its citizenry, that its emphasis on meeting immediate entertainment needs has led it to forget its more important social responsibilities. She argued that the library should serve as a community information center rather than an entertainment center.

Perhaps part of the tension can be elucidated by examining the third implication of seeking the "public good." The public good implies that librarians perform their tasks in a selfless manner, placing service to the community above personal interest. An especially thorny problem relates to identifying who or what is the community that the librarian serves. This struggle is perhaps best seen when discussing the public library and the extent to which public libraries should serve the middle-class, better-educated, and wealthier members of the public who historically have used it, and the extent to which seeking the public good requires that the librarian actively seek out those who could benefit from library services but for whom the library has been an unwelcome and unresponsive institution, that is, the poor, members of minorities, and the undereducated.

Blanke (1989) has suggested that the librarian's quest for political neutrality has led it to serve the more powerful by default—that librarianship's lack of activism or advocacy for the information "have-nots" has led libraries to "uncritically accommodate . . . society's dominant political and economic powers" (p. 39). This has led libraries to adopt a business ethic with marketing attitudes that promote the charging of fees and the privatization of information sources. Accepting an active political role in defense of the information-needy in contrast to focusing on the interests of the wealthy and powerful places in relief the question of our valuing the public good and the ethical duty implied by that value.

VALUE 6: JUSTICE

This value pertains both to the public and to staff. It implies that each individual has equal access to library and information services. It also implies that every person should be respected as an individual, and the delivery of inadequate service is a violation of such a value. Related to this, McCook (2001) has argued that the underlying goal of our profession is *information equity*. She observes that "inherent in this goal is so-cial justice–working for universal literacy; defending intellectual free-dom; preserving and making accessible the human record to all" (p. 81). The concept of justice is very complex and a distinction, noted by the philosopher John Rawls (1958), is especially appropriate in the library context. Rawls has noted that justice cannot be understood merely as equality; it must include fairness. Equality implies an equal amount; fairness implies the amount that is needed or deserved. This is an im-portant distinction for librarianship, because in some circumstances it implies that ethical action requires fair rather than equal service or treat-ment. Unequal service might be an ethical obligation if the needs of in-dividuals differ. This recognizes, for example, that children may receive unequal service, because their needs are different from that of adults. The value of justice implies that we do not provide equal service, but that we provide service that recognizes extenuating or special circum-stances. This does not imply that equality is absent in the concept of justice or library ethics; equality of access to library services is basic to the concept of library and information service. Part of the challenge to the librarian is knowing when to apply principles of fairness and when ensuring equality is the appropriate response.

VALUE 7: AESTHETICS

Among all the informational and entertainment materials that are part of library collections there exists a core of materials that are collected because they possess the elements of extraordinary creativity—they are the works of genius that live on. Although librarians value great diver-sity in materials, there is a special respect for humankind's greatest cre-ations, those that make a special contribution to the society and civiliza-tion. The great music, art, literature, and philosophy of the past, as well as those modern works that appear to have like potential are often prized by libraries, even when their circulation levels are low. These works oc-cupy a special place for librarians and often receive special consider-ation for preservation.

SUMMARY

One could quarrel with one value or another or argue that among some libraries some of these values are less important, or not important at all.

Figure 7.1
Libraries: An American Value

Libraries in America are cornerstones of the communities they serve. Free access to the books, ideas, resources, and information in America's libraries is imperative for education, employment, enjoyment, and self-government.

Libraries are a legacy to each generation, offering the heritage of the past and the promise of the future. To ensure that libraries flourish and have the freedom to promote and protect the public good in the 21st century, we believe certain principles must be guaranteed.

To that end, we affirm this contract with the people we serve:

> We defend the constitutional rights of all individuals, including children and teenagers, to use the library's resources and services;

> We value our nation's diversity and strive to reflect that diversity by providing a full spectrum of resources and services to the communities we serve;

> We affirm the responsibility and the right of all parents and guardians to guide their own children's use of the library and its resources and services;

> We connect people and ideas by helping each person select from and effectively use the library's resources;

> We protect each individual's privacy and confidentiality in the use of library resources and services;

> We protect the rights of individuals to express their opinions about library resources and services;

> We celebrate and preserve our democratic society by making available the widest possible range of viewpoints, opinions and ideas, so that all individuals have the opportunity to become lifelong learners—informed, literate, educated, and culturally enriched.

Change is constant, but these principles transcend change and endure in a dynamic technological, social, and political environment.

By embracing these principles, libraries in the United States can contribute to a future that values and protects freedom of speech in a world that celebrates both our similarities and our differences, respects individuals and their beliefs, and holds all persons truly equal and free.

Adopted by the Council of the American Library Association February 3, 1999

Surely, the diversity of libraries makes attempts to generalize extremely difficult. Nonetheless, the values discussed above account for much of the direction libraries take and for their misgivings and resistance when these values are threatened. Libraries have occupied important places, if not central roles, in many societies throughout history. Shera (1965) characterized libraries as "social agencies," rather than social institutions, because he saw them as instrumentalities designed to support a social institution. That is, he argued that social institutions were essential foundations of a society, while social agencies provided important support for those institutions. In this sense, Shera saw American libraries as important supports for institutions such as education. This would fit the picture of libraries throughout history; their mission has primarily supported other more fundamental institutions: religion, government and education. This support function is a particularly important aspect of the library's mission, which is a mission with a special relationship to the people it serves. Shera (1984) described it in this manner:

> That purpose is to make accessible the graphic records of human culture, so that people may understand the totality of the environment in which they find themselves and their own place in it. (p. 387)

There are many environments in which we find ourselves; and there are many cultures that must be understood. The library helps orient us economically, educationally, religiously, politically, and aesthetically to those cultures and environments. Perhaps the best summary of the value of libraries is expressed in the 1999 statement by the American Library Association (see Figure 7.1).

ENDNOTE

1. I am indebted to Professor Donald Krummel, whose example in teaching library history at the University of Illinois first suggested to me addressing issues in library history from the perspective of the missions of libraries.

REFERENCES

American Libraries. "REFORMA's Rite of Passage: Coming of Age in Austin." *American Libraries* 27 (October 1996): 20–23.

American Library Association. *ALA Handbook of Organization, 1997–98*. Chicago: ALA, 1997.

──────. "Librarianship and Information Service: A Statement on Core Values." (5th Draft), (28 April 2000). [Online] Available at *www.ala.org*. (Accessed July 18, 2003.)

──────. *Congress on Professional Educaton: Focus on Education for the First Professional Degree: Librarianship and Information Service: A Statement on Core Values, Fifth Draft*. [Online] Available at *www.ala.org*. (Accessed September 18, 2003.)

Association of College and Research Libraires. "ACRL Strategic Plan 2005." [Online] Available at *www.ala.org/ACRLPrinterTemplate.cfm?Section= Strategic_Plan1 &Template=*.

Association of College and Research Libraries. "ACRL Strategic Plan 2005." [Online] Available at *www.ala.org*. (Accessed July 18, 2003.)

Augst, Thomas. "American Libraries and Agencies of Culture." *American Studies* 42 (fall 2001): 5–22.

Berelson, Bernard. *The Library's Public: A Report of the Public Library Inquiry*. New York: Columbia University, 1949.

Black Caucus of the American Library Association. Mission and Purposes of the Black Caucus of the American Library Association. [Online] Available at *www.bcala.org/mission.htm* . (Accessed December 26, 1997.)

Blackburn, Robert H. "The Ancient Alexandrian Library: Part of It May Survive!" *Library History* 19 (March 2003): 23–34.

Blanke, Henry T. "Librarianship and Political Values: Neutrality or Commitment?" *Library Journal* 114 (July 1989): 39–43.

"Book Buying Habits of Americans Revealed in Study." *Library Hotline* 21 (February 3, 1992): 2.

Boyd, Charence Eugene. *Public Libraries and Literary Culture in Ancient Rome*. Chicago: University of Chicago Press, 1915.

Buschman, John. "Editorial: Core Wars." *Progressive Librarian* 17 (summer 2000). [Online] Available at *www.libr.org/PL/17_Editorial.html*. (Accessed September 18, 2003.)

Butler, Pierce. "Librarianship as a Profession." *Library Quarterly* 21 (October 1951): 235–247.

Carnegie, Andrew. "The Gospel of Wealth." In *The Gospel of Wealth and Other Timely Essays*. Edited by Edward C. Kirkland. Cambridge, Mass.: Harvard University Press, 1962. Originally published in the *North American Review* 148 (June 1889): 653–664.

Cecil, Henry L., and Willard A. Heaps. *School Library Service in the United States: An Interpretive Survey*. New York: H.W. Wilson, 1940.

Certain, Charles C. *Elementary School Library Standards*. n.p.: National Education Association, 1925.

──────. *Standard Library Organization and Equipment for Secondary Schools of Different Sizes*. Chicago: ALA, 1920.

Childe, V. Gordon. *Man Makes Himself*. London: Watts, 1965.

Clanchy, Michael. *From Memory to Written Record*. Cambridge, Mass.: Harvard University Press, 1979.

————. "Looking Back from the Invention of Printing." In *Literacy in Historical Perspective*. Edited by D. P. Resnick. Washington D.C.: Library of Congress, 1983.

Cresswell, Stephen. "The Last Days of Jim Crow in Southern Libraries." *Libraries and Culture* 31 (summer/fall 1996): 557–573.

Dain, Phyllis. "Ambivalence and Paradox: The Social Bonds of the Public Library." *Library Journal* 100 (February 1, 1975): 261–266.

De Rosa, Cathy, Lorcan Dempsey, and Alane Wilson. *The 2003 OCLC Environmental Scan: Pattern Recognition: A Report to the OCLC Membership*. Dublin, Ohio: OCLC, 2004.

Dewey, Melvil. "Libraries as Related to the Educational Work of the State." (1888) In *Melvil Dewey: His Enduring Presence in Librarianship*. Edited by Sarah K. Vann. Littleton, Colo.: Libraries Unlimited, 1978, 136.

————. "The Profession." *Library Journal* 114 (June 15, 1989): 5. Reprinted from *American Library Journal* 1 (1876).

Ditzion, Sydney H. *Arsenals of a Democratic Culture*. Chicago: ALA, 1947.

Dix, T. Keith. "'Public Libraries' in Ancient Rome: Ideology and Reality." *Libraries & Culture* 29 (summer 1994): 282–296.

Du Mont, Rosemary Ruhig, Lois Buttlar, and William Caynon. *Multiculturalism in Libraries*. Westport, Conn.: Greenwood, 1994.

Dunlap, Leslie W. *Readings in Library History*. New York: R.R. Bowker, 1972.

Eisenstein, Elizabeth L. *The Printing Press as an Agent of Change: Communications and Cultural Transformations in Early Modern Europe*. Cambridge: Cambridge University Press, 1979.

Estabrook, Leigh. "The Library as a Socialist Institution in a Capitalist Environment." In *The Economics of Information*. Edited by Jana Varlys. Jefferson, N.C.: McFarland, 1982, 3–16.

Fargo, Lucile F. *The Program for Elementary Library Service*. Chicago: ALA, 1930.

Finks, Lee W. "Values Without Shame." *American Libraries* 20 (April 1989): 352–356.

Franklin, John Hope. "Libraries in a Pluralistic Society." In *Libraries and the Life of the Mind in America*. Chicago: ALA, 1977.

Garrison, Dee. "The Tender Technicians: The Feminization of Public Librarianship." *Journal of Social History* 6 (winter 1972–1973): 131–156.

Gates, Jean Key. *Introduction to Librarianship*. New York: McGraw-Hill, 1976.

Gillespie, John T., and Diana L. Spirt. "School Library to Media Center." In *Administering the School Library Media Center*. New York: Bowker, 1983.

Gleason, Eliza Atkins. *The Southern Negro and the Public Library*. Chicago: University of Chicago Press, 1941.

Gorman, Michael. "Five New Laws of Librarianship." *American Libraries* 26 (September 1995): 784–785.

————. *Our Enduring Values*. Chicago: ALA, 2000.

————. "Values for Human-To-Human Reference." *Library Trends* 50 (fall 2001): 168–182.

Graham, Patterson Toby. "Public Librarians and the Civil Rights Movement: Alabama, 1955–1965." *Library Quarterly* 71 (January 2001): 1–27.

Guerena, Salvador, and Edward Erazo. "Latinos and Librarianship." *Library Trends* 49 (summer 2000): 138–181,

Hamlin, Arthur T. *The University Library in the United States: Its Origins and Development*. Philadelphia: University of Pennsylvania Press, 1981.

Hanson, Eugene R. "College Libraries: The Colonial Period to the Twentieth Century." In *Advances in Library Administration and Organization*. Vol. 8. Greenwich, Conn.: JAI, 1989, 171–199.

Haro, Roberto P. *Developing Library and Information Services for Americans of Hispanic Origin*. Metuchen, N.J.: Scarecrow, 1981.

Harris, Michael. "The Purpose of the American Public Library." *Library Journal* 98 (September 15, 1973): 2509–2514.

Harris, Michael H., and Stanley Hannah. "Why Do We Study the History of Libraries? A Meditation on the Perils of Ahistoricism in the Information Era." *LISR* 14 (1992): 123–130.

Harris, Michael, and Elmer D. Johnson. *History of Libraries in the Western World*. Metuchen, N.J.: Scarecrow, 1984.

Harris, William V. *Ancient Literacy*. Cambridge, Mass.: Harvard University Press, 1989.

Harwell, Richard. "College Libraries." In *Encyclopedia of Library and Information Science*. Edited by Allen Kent, Harold Lancour, and William Z. Nasri. New York: Marcel Dekker, 1968, 269–281.

Hessel, Alfred. *A History of Libraries*. New Brunswick, N.J.: Scarecrow, 1955.

Jackson, Sydney L. *Libraries and Librarianship in the West: A Brief History*. New York: McGraw-Hill, 1974.

Jochum, Uwe. "The Alexandrian Library and Its Aftermath." *Library History* 15 (May 1999): 5–12.

Jones, Plummer Alston Jr. "The History and Development of Libraries in American Higher Education." *College and Research Libraries News 50* (July/August 1989): 561–565.

Josey, E.J. *The Black Librarian in America*. Metuchen, N.J.: Scarecrow, 1970.

———. "Race Issues in Library History." *Encyclopedia of Library History*. Edited by Wayne A. Wiegand and Donald G. Davis Jr. New York: Garland, 1994, 533–537.

Kaser, David. *A Book for a Sixpence: The Circulating Library in America*. Pittsburgh: Beta Phi Mu, 1980.

Knight, Douglas M., and E. Shepley Nourse. *Libraries at Large: Tradition, Innovation, and the National Interest*. New York: R.R. Bowker, 1969.

Koehler, Wallace. "Professional Values and Ethics as Defined by 'The LIS Discipline.'" *Journal of Education for Library and Information Science* 44 (spring 2003): 99–119.

Kramer, Samual Noah. *Sumerian Mythology, A Study of Spiritual and Literary Achievement in the Third Millennium B.C.* New York: Harper, 1961.

Kruzas, Anthony Thomas. *Business and Industrial Libraries in the United States, 1820–1940*. New York: SLA, 1965.

Kurian, George Thomas. *The Illustrated Book of World Rankings*. 5th ed. Armonk, N.Y.: Sharpe, 2001.

From Past to Present 321

Malone, Cheryl Knott. "Books for Black Children: Public Library Collections in Louisville and Nashville, 1915–1925." *Library Quarterly* 70 (April 2000): 179–200.

McCook, Kathleen de la Peña. "Social Justice, Personalism, and the Practice of Librarianship." *Catholic Library World* 72 (December 2001): 80–84.

McMullen, Haynes. *American Libraries Before 1876*. Westport, Colo.: Greenwood, 2000.

Neill, Sam D. "Why Books?" *Public Library Quarterly* 12 (1992): 19–28.

Nelson, Anne. "How My Hometown Library Failed Me." *Library Journal* 103 (February 1, 1978): 317–319.

Nichols, Charles L. *The Library of Ramses the Great*. Berkeley, Calif.: Peacock, 1964.

Nielson, Brian. "The Role of the Public Services Librarian: The New Revolution." In *Rethinking the Library in the Information Age*. Washington, D.C.: GPO, 1989, 179–200.

Parsons, Edward A. *The Alexandrian Library*. Amsterdam, N.Y.: Elsevier, 1952.

Ranganathan, S.R. *The Five Laws of Library Science*. New York: Asia, 1963. First published 1931.

Rawls, John. "Justice as Fairness." *Philosophical Review* 67 (1958): 164–194.

REFORMA. The National Association to Promote Library Services to the Spanish Speaking. [Online] Available at *www.reforma.org* (Accessed December 26, 1997.)

Roberts, F.B. "The Library and the Foreign Citizen." *Public Libraries* 17 (1912): 166–169.

Sager, Don. "The Search for Librarianship's Core Values." *Public Libraries* 40 (May/June 2001): 149–153.

Shera, Jesse. *Foundations of the Public Library*. Chicago: Shoestring, 1965.

———. *Introduction to Library Science: Basic Elements of Library Service*. Littleton, Colo.: Libraries Unlimited, 1976.

———. "Librarianship and Information Science." In *The Study of Information: Interdisciplinary Messages*. Edited by Fritz Machlup and Una Mansfield. New York, Wiley, 1984.

Shiflett, O. Lee. "Academic Libraries." In *Encyclopedia of Library History*. Edited by Wayne A. Wiegand and Donald G. Davis Jr. New York: Garland, 1994, 5–15.

Stern, Stephen. "Ethnic Libraries and Librarianship in the United States: Models and Prospects." In *Advances in Librarianship*. Vol. 15. Edited by Irene P. Godden. San Diego: Academic Press, 1991, 77–102.

Swan, John. "Untruth or Consequences." *Library Journal* 111 (July 1, 1986): 44–52.

Thompson, James Westfall. *Ancient Libraries*. Hamden, Conn.: Archon, 1962.

Trujillo, Roberto G., and Yolanda J. Cuesta. "Service to Diverse Populations." In *ALA Yearbook of Library and Information Science*. Vol. 14. Chicago: ALA, 1989, 7–11.

Watson, Paula. "Founding Mothers: The Contribution of Women's Organizations to Public Library Development in the United States." *Library Quarterly* 64 (July 1994): 233–269.

West, Jessamyn. "Social Responsibilities Round Table." [Online] Available at *www.jessamyn.com/srrt* (Accessed November 20, 1997.)

White House Conference on Library and Information Services. *Information 2000: Library and Information Services for the 21st Century.* Washington, D.C.: Superintendent of Documents, 1991.

Wiegand, Wayne A. "The Development of Librarianship in the United States." *Libraries and Culture* 24 (winter 1989): 99–109.

Winter, Michael F. *The Culture and Control of Expertise: Toward a Sociological Understanding of Librarianship.* Westport, Conn: Greenwood, 1988.

Zill, Nicholas, and Winglee, Marianne. "Literature Reading in the United States: Data from National Surveys and Their Policy Implications." *Book Research Quarterly* 5 (fall 1989): 24–58.

8

Ethics and Standards: Professional Practices in Library and Information Science

But if indeed we have no philosophy, then we are depriving ourselves of the guiding light of reason, and we live only a day-to-day existence, lurching from crisis to crisis, and lacking the driving force of an inner conviction of the value of our work.

—D. J. Foskett, 1962

The essence of the librarian's obligation can best be expressed in terms of function and purpose, and these should be explicitly stated. Librarians are behaving properly (or ethically) when they act in such a way that they fulfill their function, thereby fulfilling the function of the library.

—Lee W. Finks, 1991

As professionals, we are responsible to those we serve and to each other. As citizens, we are committed to using our special knowledge for the good of society. And as members of the worldwide human family, we take responsibility to preserve and protect human dignity.

—Martha M. Smith, Editorial, 1993

In previous chapters, we looked at the mission and values of libraries. Although it may not constitute a "philosophy of librarianship," as Foskett refers to it above, it is clear that libraries play important roles and that the values that underlie them are basic to democratic processes. There are many ways that libraries accomplish their missions and thus support their values; one of these ways is through ethical conduct. Through such conduct we recognize that librarians and information professionals are moral agents, responsible to themselves, others, and the society as a whole. The ethical conduct of information professionals is an affirmation of the critical values of service, respect for others, and the need to improve society. Ethics provide a framework for conducting essential information functions, instituting policies, and developing strategies for service. Without them, we are, as Foskett observes above, merely "lurching" about—stumbling in the dark.

Ethical deliberations are extremely complex for at their base they deal with the fundamental questions of "right" and "wrong." Ethics is mostly about how people should be treated and how one should act, if one wishes to act rightly. The discussion of ethics has deep philosophical, religious, and legal roots, and the divergent points of view of many disciplines make much fodder for debate and disagreement. These debates will not be explicated here; this chapter is not intended to determine once and for all what is "right" or "wrong" in a given instance. Rather, it will identify some of the major principles, codes, obligations, and situations that are part of our professional environment. In this way, a clearer picture of the many ethical issues that information professionals face may emerge.

Historically, what the field has identified as the focus of ethical concern has varied. Du Mont (1991) has suggested three periods, each with different ethical orientations. The earliest period includes the years prior to 1930. During this time, American librarianship focused attention on its responsibility to the library collections themselves. It was a formative time for libraries, and much attention was directed to collection creation and maintenance. The issues included explicitly moral concerns with the potentially corrupting influence of library materials. The second period occurred between 1930 and 1950. During this time, ethical attention focused on the human aspects of library service, on staff and patrons. This focus was a recognition that staff members, for example, were not simply cogs in the library's wheel, but individuals with human needs. Issues such as job security, working conditions, education, and training arose. The focus on human needs was a recognition that patrons were people whose treatment and needs should be understood. Emphasis was directed toward the obligation to deliver quality service and maintain good relations with the public. This period also focused on the issue of the ethical obligation to provide free access to information. This attention may, in part, have been produced by the rise of fascism in Nazi Germany (Harris 1973) and resulted in the adoption of major intellectual freedom documents such as the ALA Library Bill of Rights and the ALA Code of Ethics. In the final period, since 1960, the ethical attention has been drawn to the broader needs of society as a whole. Emphasis has been on improving the public good, promoting social justice, and taking socially progressive political positions. The more general concept of social responsibility extends beyond the current employees of the library or the individuals who were current users of the library, to the society beyond. Issues such as affirmative action and the needs of the underserved have become important ethical issues. In addition, the ethical responsibilities of the reference librarian in answering questions have been questioned. For example, Hauptman (1976) queried whether reference librarians would provide information on building a car bomb, and Dowd (1989) questioned whether reference librarians would or should provide information on freebasing cocaine. The underlying question was whether reference librarians can be totally neutral in the performance of their duties, or whether social consequences of the information should be considered.

There is still continuing and growing interest in professional ethics. Several conferences have focused on this issue, and a publication, the *Journal of Information Ethics* is now well established. Nonetheless, despite this increasing attention, today's work world allows very little time for reflection. Realistically, practitioners seldom have time to consider the broader ethical implications of their work. It is not that these are considered unimportant considerations, but often they can only be properly considered and evaluated when there is time to deliberate. One study of Management Information System (MIS) professionals found that there was a strong perception among a significant number of them that there were many opportunities for MIS professionals to act unethically. This perception was further substantiated when the respondents were asked about their knowledge of unethical conduct. In fact, a fifth of the respondents indicated that they were aware of incidents in which MIS managers had acted improperly. This does not mean, however, that the information professionals condoned the unethical conduct. To the contrary, 70 percent stated that the interests of the employer do not always come first; that the interests of the society may rise above the interest of the employer. In fact, nearly all the respondents made it clear that there are broader social responsibilities that MIS professionals must uphold over and above the professional responsibility to the employer and that one's general ethical obligations do not end when one enters the work-place (Vitell and Davis 1990).

The issue of ethics in a professional context is about our dealings with and treatment of people and involves a complex relationship between information producers, intermediaries, and consumers. Froehlich (1992) has identified at least seven stakeholders in the information dissemination process who are affected by our actions. These stakeholders include authors, publishers, database producers, database vendors or networks, information professionals, the organization and managers, and the end-users or consumers. The actions of information professionals affect and are affected by these various stakeholders, and the ethical ramifications are complex.

Froehlich (1992) proposes an ethical model that reveals three basic elements in professional ethics: self, organization, and environment. The self is the moral agent, the person who must act or suffer the consequences of the actions of others; the organization is the institution that is also a moral agent that acts in an autonomous manner and directs the actions of others; the environment includes the standards of the community or professional societies that create an ethical context in which the self and organization operate. Ethical stresses can often be characterized by the interactions and imperatives that arise for each of these elements. These interactions and imperatives may not be easily or consistently balanced, and as a result, ethical frictions and dilemmas arise. Hence, there may be a conflict between the self as a person and the self as an employee or a member of an organization. For example, the librarian may have a personal belief that certain material contains morally offensive content. As an individual moral agent, the librarian may believe that such material is inappropriate for dissemination; at the same time, as a librarian, there are organizational and professional standards of conduct that may dictate that the material be freely disseminated. Such conflicts may be infrequent for some and commonplace for others, but they are inevitable for most.

The need for discussion of ethical concerns is highlighted by the fact that librarianship is a service-oriented profession; our most important stakeholder is our user. As Finks (1991) has observed, "the basic function of the library is to optimize the value of recorded information for humankind" (p. 86). The decisions made by librarians and other information workers may determine who receives information and who does not. Failure to perform this function is a violation of professional ethics. Accomplishing this function, however, requires a careful balancing of interests, realizing that often, even when the interests are balanced, both benefits and harms may arise.

FACTORS IN ETHICAL DELIBERATIONS

Most of the time, librarians do not think consciously about the ethical ramifications of what they do. As with ethical conduct generally, our behavior follows from habit. It is only when a special situation arises that ethical dissonance arises. In these situations we may feel qualms about what to do, and there is general agreement that there should be standards of conduct to limit unethical actions. In addition, ethical constraints apply not only to individuals but to organizations. Libraries and other information organizations are not value-neutral; they act, make choices, affect human beings, and receive, allocate, and disseminate resources in ways analogous to individuals. They too have ethical obligations.

When one considers ethics for a given discipline or for the practitioners in that discipline, it is not necessarily to suggest that ethics are different for that discipline than for others. On the contrary, there are very few disciplines in which normal ethical practices do not apply. Rather, it is to say that there may be special situations that arise within a particular professional context to which ethics must be applied. Understanding these situations, being familiar with the ethical prescriptions of the field, and reflecting on the factors that must be considered when making ethical deliberations is important if informed and appropriate actions are to be taken. Certainly such issues arise in library and information science, and practitioners must become aware and sensitive to these issues.

Part of the complexity of dealing with ethics in library and information science is that it has at least two focuses. One focus might be called *information ethics*. Information ethics among other things is an area of applied ethics concerned with the use and misuse of information. This would include such areas as the ownership of information, intellectual property rights, free or restricted access to information, use of government information, assuring privacy and confidentiality, data integrity, and the international flow of information. A second focus deals with professional behavior specifically. This is referred to as *professional ethics*. Professional ethics deals with how we apply ethical principles to our decisions and actions as information professionals (Smith 1993a). Fortunately, for discussion purposes, information ethics and professional ethics are closely related and often overlap. It is more a matter of emphasis rather than unique content, and often discussion of one cannot proceed satisfactorily without discussion of the other.

Regardless of focus, when attempting to make ethical judgments, those who make decisions often find themselves with a residue of dissatisfaction, even when they think they have made the best decision. Part of this ambivalence may be the result of the organizations and practitioners being subject to competing demands from a variety of sources, including the public, clients, board members, administrators, and staff. Attempts to satisfy so many parties require a very careful balancing of interests and frequently produce ethical tensions. When ethical decisions are being considered, there are at least four factors that affect the deliberative process: social utility, survival, social responsibility, and respect for the individual. These factors may not be explicitly considered by the individuals making the decision; often they are obscured. But they are often implicit and underlie the decision-making process. These factors are not in themselves ethical principles, but they are critical considerations. In fact, it is the constant attempt to balance these factors that often makes decisions so difficult from an ethical perspective.[1]

Factor 1: Social Utility

Organizations, especially public ones, are intended to serve important social ends. Libraries are certainly among those institutions that have a socially desirable purpose. For example, academic libraries are intended to advance society by educating students and producing research that will improve society; public libraries are created to meet the educational, informational, and recreational needs of the general public; and school libraries are expected to prepare students to enter the job market and to provide them with the general life skills to function effectively in society. The extent to which the purpose of an organization can accomplish its social purpose is its social utility. Because this is a desired end, decisions and actions taken that would aid an organization in accomplishing its social purpose can be seen as ethically desirable.

However, sometimes ethical conflicts can arise when attempting to meet the goals of the organization, and sometimes, albeit unintentionally, helping the library may have a negative effect on other institutions. For example, the library may compete with other worthy public institutions for a limited amount of public monies. Hence city parks, law enforcement, or schools, all of which need funds, might suffer from the political successes of the library. Similarly, ethical qualms may arise when the library develops collections that might have a detrimental effect on local businesses. For example, the development of entertainment DVD and videocassette collections might pose a threat to some video stores. From a staffing perspective, ethical concerns may arise if a library director or supervisor needs to release an employee who is unable to perform his or her library-service duties effectively. The employee may be a likeable individual who is making an earnest effort. The decision to terminate may, therefore, produce considerable ethical discomfort despite the fact that keeping the employee will impair the library's function.

Factor 2: Survival

A key requirement for an organization is that it survive. This is no different from individuals. It is generally presumed that individuals are acting correctly when they act to preserve their own lives. Without survival, organizations would not exist to perform the functions for which they were created. As such, it is reasonable to assume that, insofar as an organization performs a worthy purpose, it would have an ethical obligation to maintain itself.

Libraries confront issues related to their survival regularly. Perhaps the most obvious example is when some members of the community object to a particular item or items held in the library collection. When censorship attempts arise, the protests are often linked to threats to the library's funding sources. Unhappy citizens may threaten to campaign against a levy or lobby political bodies to reduce funding. Under these circumstances, the library's leadership may consider bowing to pressure because the continued existence of the library is considered more important than the retention of a few items in the library collection. Such an example highlights how the various factors can come into conflict. For example, in a censorship case, the factor of survival may conflict with the factor of social utility: by protecting the library's fiscal survival, one may be sacrificing the purpose for which the library was established—free access to all types of ideas, even objectionable ones.

Factor 3: Social Responsibility

Not only do organizations have an ethical obligation to fulfill the specific purposes for which they were created. They also function in the society-at-large, and it is generally recognized that organizations have an obligation to serve the larger society. It seems reasonable that public organizations have a particular obligation to act on behalf of the society because they receive their fiscal support from that society. Librarians and administrators recognize that they have social responsibilities as well as responsibilities to survive and perform their particular functions. There are a variety of actions and decisions that are taken in libraries that indicate that social responsibilities are important to them. For example, there may be a policy to order as many items as possible on acid-free paper to minimize pollution and the need for replacement copies. Alternatively, library policy may actively promote equal-employment opportunity to ensure that all members of the society have an equal opportunity for library positions. Of course, in attempting to meet social responsibilities, there may be conflicts with other factors. For example, purchasing materials on acid-free paper may be more costly to the organization, which in turn may have a negative impact on the survival of the organization.

Factor 4: Respect for the Individual

A fundamental factor in ethical deliberations concerns how individuals are treated. This factor implies that individuals must be treated with dignity and respect, and that employees and patrons have a right to act as they see fit, insofar as they do not violate the dignity and respect of others.

Libraries and other information organizations strive to accommodate this factor in many ways. For example, libraries are open to all persons. In the area of collection development, librarians develop the collections tailored to individual interests as well as for "the masses." Librarians pay special attention to building collections that represent a wide range of materials, reflecting diverse perspectives and in a variety of formats. Respect for the individual is also recognized when libraries protect the privacy of patrons, for example, when protecting the privacy of their circulation records. Respect for the individual is also reflected in the managerial and administrative practices of the organizations. This is a factor when the rules and policies are developed so that individuals are treated fairly and employee privacy is respected.

Of course, as with the other factors, conflicts can occur. For example, in terms of collection development, a library director may feel that appealing to the broader mass tastes, rather than to individual tastes, improves the prospects of the library's survival because then the public will be more inclined to support the library, and there is less possibility of public dissatisfaction with controversial selections. By appealing to popular taste, the director puts greater emphasis on the factor of survival and less on respect for the individual. Conflicts with the factors may also occur when dealing with respecting an individual's privacy. For example, the staff may comply with law-enforcement authorities who request the circulation record of a patron who may have committed a serious crime. In this circumstance, one may feel that the factor of social responsibility, i.e., aiding society in the apprehension of criminals, outweighs the factor of respect for the individual.

All of the factors mentioned above are important to librarians. Balancing them is a complex and challenging task. Although experience and professional codes and guidelines may provide some assistance, each situation has its own unique circumstances. There is no simple formula for determining which factor weighs more heavily in a given situation. Rubin and Froehlich (1996) suggest that the concerns of libraries involved in ethical deliberations are reflected in four questions:

1. To what extent is the survival of the organization threatened?
2. To what extent will the purpose of the organization be benefitted or harmed?
3. To what extent is the organization or employee socially responsible or irresponsible when acting in a particular manner?
4. To what extent are the actions of the organization or individuals acting in its behalf harming or benefitting other individuals, organizations, or the profession? (p. 41)

CATEGORIES OF ETHICAL CONCERN

Consider some of the many categories of ethical concern within the library and information context:

Free Access to Information/Effects of Information

The ethical ramifications of information dissemination are considerable and touch virtually all activities and policies of libraries. In general, however, much of the energy and ethical attention in this area have focused on the responsibility to maintain intellectual freedom. The ALA Code of Ethics explicitly refers to intellectual freedom as a central ethical doctrine (Section 2), and the American Society for Information Science's ASIS Professional Guidelines refer to "free and equal access" (American Library Association [ALA] 1995; American Society for Information Science [ASIS] 1994). This is no doubt a correct emphasis, and the profession has created numerous additional information policies to protect this freedom (see detailed discussion in Chapter 5). Nevertheless, one must be careful not to exclude other potentially pertinent considerations that fall into the ethical domain. Most notable has been an ongoing debate in our profession about our social responsibilities. That is, to what extent do libraries serve to improve and protect society? In this regard, what is a library's obligation to limit access to materials that might be socially unhealthy or promote materials that are considered beneficial to the health of the society? This duality between protecting individual rights and the imperatives of acting in a socially responsible manner creates a critical tension for ethical decision making. Smith (1993b) characterized this tension as a dynamic relationship between three components: (1) freedom, meaning intellectual freedom; (2) information democracy, that is, promoting the need for social equity in information; and (3) responsibility, or the obligation to promote the social good.

Such considerations can complicate discussion of ethical issues in information dissemination and may account for the ambivalence librarians feel about providing all types of information to anyone. Baker (1992) articulated this consideration as "Do no harm" (p.8). Baker was referring specifically to the activities of library administrators, not to intellectual freedom issues, but the underlying notion applies to library users as well. It suggests that library activities should minimize harm to others and reminds us that ethics deal not only with protecting the rights of others, but also their welfare. For example, there is debate over whether librarians should freely disseminate materials about suicide to minors. Similarly, there is some evidence that exposure to violent materials may lead to levels of increased aggressive behavior; as a consequence, some librarians are concerned about the dissemination of violent materials to minors (Green and Thomas 1986). It is not being suggested here that librarians should act as censors, but it is to say that considering the effects of information on the patron lies well within the domain of ethical deliberations, and that intellectual freedom issues, although clearly intimately related, do not exhaust the important considerations when making ethical decisions.

Selection Decisions

Selection decisions are extremely important for libraries because they determine the nature of the library collection. At the most basic level, there is an ethical obligation to use appropriate selection criteria, to hire qualified selectors, and to develop an efficient system for the procurement of selected items. The mission of libraries is to meet the needs of users, thus decisions should generally be made for the benefit of users. This seems obvious, but ethical issues may arise. For example, selectors may select items that are of particular interest to them, rather than their patrons. Selectors might acquire items simply because they are popular and increase the chance for improved funding. They may select items that fail to meet their selection criteria because of pressure from administrators or powerful members of the community. Perhaps even more common, sometimes selectors fear that a particular selection will be both popular and controversial and fail to select it. It could be a well-known and heavily promoted, sexually explicit or violent book, video, or DVD. In each of these cases, ethics are a factor.

Privacy

Respect for privacy is a fundamental concept in a democratic society, and with the increasing computerization and networking of information, the problems are magnified further. Not only library records, but medical, financial, and credit records, and consumer information are now part of national and international networks. Information professionals are rapidly developing the skills to access this type of information, and the potential to invade the privacy of these records is considerable. In terms of libraries, one can conceive that without privacy protections individuals may decide not to seek out information because they feel that subsequent public exposure may subject them to censure or intimidation. Librarians, therefore, try to protect user privacy as much as possible. The issue becomes especially sensitive in the area of circulation records. In the broader information environment, there are privacy issues regarding proprietary information. For example, competitors may attempt to access information that is the property of another organization through deception or other inappropriate means, violating the privacy rights of these organizations.

Copyright

Although copyright is fundamentally defined and treated as a legal concept subsumed under the broader notion of intellectual property, it is also an ethical issue. At its heart is the question of whether individuals should copy the intellectual work of others without asking the originator's permission. Librarians often make copies of materials or encourage others to do so without seeking copyright permission. This encouragement is not done with the intention of depriving copyright owners of their rights, but in fulfillment of the library's mission to provide information to their citizenry. This situation highlights the fundamental question: To what extent does the creator of a work have the right to control its dissemination following publication? Interestingly, there are competing ethical considerations here. If the library's mission is to promote the dissemination of information to all users to fulfill its democratic mission, then is it not ethically bound to disseminate as much information as possible? Essentially, are not librarians ethically obligated to test the bounds of others' control over the dissemination of information? Librarians feel an ethical tension to respect and protect the rights of both authors and patrons. They want authors to profit, but they do not want to permit authors and publishers to unnecessarily restrict and control the flow of information. As more and more information becomes available electronically, the ethical debate will no doubt flourish.

Information Organization

The challenge of organizing information (for example, through classification, controlled vocabulary, and bibliography) has been central to American librarianship since its early development. Usually, this task is considered strictly a conceptual and procedural one. It is largely a question of techniques: which ones are best, which ones are the easiest to understand and use? From time to time, however, there are ethical issues that confront us, because how information is organized directly affects the effectiveness of our services. Some types of information organization may reflect prejudices and biases of the organizer. For example, a cataloger may classify some materials as adult that are really aimed at young people, because the cataloger believes the material is inappropriate for children. These biases, whether intentionally applied or not, may deprive or inhibit access to information, inappropriately silencing the voices of authors or producers who have a right to be heard. Such actions violate a fundamental value of librarianship: excellence in service.

How knowledge is organized may also be a broader reflection of the society's attitudes. The Dewey Decimal Classification System has been criticized for diminishing the importance of writings from non-

Western cultures. The library's primary mission is to organize materials for access—as we organize them we must consider what values, prejudices, or preconceptions affect this access.

The ethical ramifications of organizing knowledge suggest that there is a substantial ethical contribution that is made by an often overlooked department in this regard—technical services. Perhaps this oversight results from the fact that technical services is perceived as having only an oblique relationship to the patron. But the purpose of technical services is the same as all other library functions: to provide the highest quality of service to the user. In fact, the relationship between the patron and technical services is direct, because it is technical services that often determines how access will be provided and the ease with which information and materials can be obtained. As Bierbaum (1994) notes, "The mission of technical services is to provide bibliographical and physical access to collections and information" (p. 13). Among other things, this implies that the technical services professionals have the ethical obligation to maintain high bibliographic standards, to process materials efficiently and effectively, to reduce barriers to information, to keep up with technical and professional issues in technical services, and to resist censorship.

Information Policy

The information policies of nations, communities, libraries, and other information organizations may have a profound effect on access to information in society. Information policies of ethical import include the economic, social, and cultural impact of laws and regulations governing information technologies, national and international policies affecting the ability of citizens to access information, and the effects of organizational policies and practices on information access.

In the latter case, there is no doubt that libraries are replete with policies that affect the organization and dissemination of information. Among them are reference service policies, intellectual freedom policies, circulation and registration policies, and policies on access to meeting rooms. Obviously, these policies could have profound effects on how patrons are treated and hence have serious ethical ramifications. Consider just a few such examples: restricting materials to those over eighteen; failing to develop policies or practices that attract users who are poor, disabled, or members of minority groups; revealing circulation records to others. All these raise important ethical questions.

Information Quality

The ethical obligations inherent in the value of service also extend to practices that affect the quality of information. To the extent that a library can, within the scope of its activities, ensure that the information it provides is timely and accurate, it preserves its service values. When libraries cannot ensure quality, they may well have the obligation to indicate to a user that there may be deficiencies, limitations, or biases to the information system being used. This has become especially problematic in any information environment in which the searcher is using automated databases and the Web. There may be a temptation to let consumers believe that these information systems are perfect systems that access all relevant information. We know that all databases have their limitations, biases, and deficiencies, and we know that the Web is filled with unreliable information. Information professionals have ethical duties, if not legal ones, to ensure that such systems are not misrepresented.

The notion of information quality suggests also its opposite—information malpractice. If one assumes that information professionals are just that—professionals—then they have an ethical obligation to maintain high professional standards in their work. One assumes that a doctor's recommendations are based on the most current thinking; the same can be said for the work of attorneys. When they fail to meet the standards of practice in their fields, then they are subject to charges of malpractice. Librarians and other information professionals may not have the same legal obligations, but the field recognizes that the ethical obligations to maintain the highest standards of service are similar to that of any profession. Hence, information professionals who produce inferior products, or misrepresent their capabilities to produce a quality product, may well be guilty, at least ethically, of malpractice.

Administration

Libraries and other information organizations inevitably have administrative and managerial components. The subject of business ethics is now commonplace in the management literature, and the concerns raised in this literature are no strangers to the library environment. Among the ethical issues facing both the employer and the employee are (1) the ethical use of consultants, (2) the ethical obligations that arise when dealing with vendors or others engaged in business with the library, and (3) ethical aspects regarding the treatment of personnel. The last category is a common and critical area of ethical concern and debate. Consider the following areas of potential ethical breaches when dealing with library personnel (Rubin 1990, pp. 34–35).

Violations of Privacy

- Revealing information about employees to individuals who do not need to know such information, or revealing information that may unnecessarily damage the individual's personal or professional reputation.
- Misusing personnel records or files, including inappropriate access to computer files.
- Collecting any personal information about employees that is not related to the necessary functions of the organization.
- Conducting inappropriate investigations of an individual's personal history or using irrelevant personal information to make a personnel decision.
- Conducting drug, alcohol, HIV, or other testing unless it is essential to the safe operation of the job or is directly related to the safety of others.
- Monitoring employees with video cameras or tape recorders without their knowledge or consent, unless significant and specific job-related reasons make such monitoring necessary.
- Using a polygraph unless there is clear and substantial reason for its use (e.g., in cases of suspected theft).
- Attempting to censor the writing or speech of employees unless such speech or writing would significantly damage the institution's ability to perform its essential function.

Misuses of Authority

- Showing favoritism to friends or relatives.
- Making personnel decisions out of anger or spite.
- Writing inaccurate job references for employees to prevent them from gaining other employment or to encourage their departure.
- Collecting job-related information from employees, without informing them of the potential consequences (e.g., for disciplinary action).
- Retaliating against employees who are outspoken or who have merely exercised their legal rights.
- Withholding information from an individual to ensure or promote job failure.

Organizational Inadequacies

- Designing a system of rewards that fosters cheating, sabotaging the work of others, or withholding important information, or that places emphasis only on quantity rather than quality (e.g., providing substantial financial rewards for higher library circulation).

- Paying wages and benefits that do not give minimal protection and security to employees.
- Creating a personnel system that discriminates or is unfair in administering essential personnel functions.
- Permitting the hiring and placement of individuals with a Master of Library Science degree in support-staff positions.
- Misusing behavior modification techniques to manipulate employees.
- Knowingly allowing employees to work in unsafe or unhealthy working conditions, especially without their knowledge or consent.

Archival Issues

An area often unrecognized as raising ethical issues involves materials
stored in archives. Such records play a critical role in the preservation of
materials through which history is written. Although some of the issues
confronted by archivists overlap with issues noted above, the special function of archives—the storage and dissemination of usually unique records
of long-term value—places special ethical burdens on the archivist.

The members of the Society of American Archivists (SAA) recognized this in their promulgation of their own Code of Ethics, most recently revised in 1992 and reprinted in Figure 8.1. This code deals with
many issues, including ethical issues, in the acquisition of and access to
archival collections, as well as defining business and research conduct.
Overall, there is a critical tension concerning the function of archival
services that can generate considerable ethical friction. One aspect of
this tension arises from the need first and foremost to preserve the archival records. This is recognized in the code as the critical purpose of
the archivist—to provide for the safety and protection of records of long-
term value. Obviously this means that adequate safeguards and preservation techniques are applied to preserve the integrity of the collections.
The second aspect that generates the tension concerns itself with the
concomitant responsibility to promote access to these records by ensuring that only reasonable restrictions be placed on their use. It is a natural
temptation for an archivist to do everything possible to preserve records,
but records are of little value if they cannot be consulted relatively easily. Hence, the archivist is ethically bound to minimize such restrictions
and to create the necessary finding aids so that the collection can be
used. This tension is certainly a part of much library and information
science work, but it is especially prevalent in archival records where the
works are likely to be rare and fragile.

Of special ethical interest is the issue of privacy. One can imagine
many instances in which a collection of letters and correspondence is

Figure 8.1
A Code of Ethics for Archivists, with Commentary*

The code is a summary of guidelines in the principal areas of profes-sional conduct. A longer commentary explains the reasons for some of the statements and provides a basis for discussion of the points raised. The Code of Ethics is in italic bold face; the commentary is in Roman type.

I. The Purpose of a Code of Ethics

The Society of American Archivists (SAA) recognizes that ethical decisions are made by individuals, professionals, institutions, and soci-eties. Some of the greatest ethical problems in modern life arise from conflicts between personal codes based on moral teachings, professional practices, regulations based on employment status, institutional poli-cies and state and federal laws. In adopting a formal code of profes-sional ethics for SAA, we are dealing with only one aspect of the archivist's ethical involvement.

Codes of ethics in all professions have several purposes in common, including a statement of concern with the most serious problems of pro-fessional conduct, the resolution of problems arising from conflicts of interest, and the guarantee that the special expertise of the members of a profession will be used in the public interest.

The archival profession needs a code of ethics for several reasons: (1) to inform new members of the profession of the high standards of conduct in the most sensitive areas of archival work; (2) to remind expe-rienced archivists of their responsibilities, challenging them to maintain high standards of conduct in their own work and to promulgate those standards to others; and (3) to educate people who have some contact with archives, such as donors of material, dealers, researchers, and ad-ministrators, about the work of archivists and to encourage them to ex-pect high standards.

A code of ethics implies moral and legal responsibilities. It presumes that archivists obey the laws and are especially familiar with the laws that affect their special areas of knowledge; it also presumes that they act in accord with sound moral principles. In addition to the moral and legal responsibilities of archivists, there are special professional concerns, and it is the purpose of a code of ethics to state those concerns and give some guidelines for archivists. The code identifies areas where there are or may be conflicts of interest, and indicates ways in which these con-flicting interests may be balanced; the code urges the highest standards of professional conduct and excellence of work in every area of archives administration.

This code is compiled for archivists, individually and collectively. Institutional policies should assist archivists in their efforts to conduct

---

Figure 8.1 (*Continued*)

---

themselves according to this code; indeed, institutions, with the assistance of their archivists, should deliberately adopt policies that comply with the principles of the code.

II. Introduction to the Code

Archivists select, preserve, and make available documentary materials of long-term value that have lasting value to the organization or public that the archivist serves. Archivists perform their responsibilities in accordance with statutory authorization or institutional policy. They subscribe to a code of ethics based on sound archival principles and promote institutional and professional observance of these ethical and archival standards.

Commentary: The introduction states the principal functions of archivists. Because the code speaks to people in a variety of fields—archivists, curators of manuscripts, records managers—the reader should be aware that not every statement in the code will be pertinent to every worker. Because the code intends to inform and protect non-archivists, an explanation of the basic role of archivists is necessary. The term "documentary materials of long-term value" is intended to cover archival records and papers without regard to the physical format in which they are recorded.

III. Collecting Policies

Archivists arrange transfers of records and acquire documentary materials of long-term value in accordance with their institutions' purposes, stated policies, and resources. They do not compete for acquisitions when competition would endanger the integrity or safety of documentary materials of long-term value, or solicit the records of an institution that has an established archives. They cooperate to ensure the preservation of materials in repositories where they will be adequately processed and effectively utilized.

Commentary: Among archivists generally there seems to be agreement that one of the most difficult areas is that of policies of collection and the resultant practices. Transfers and acquisitions should be made in accordance with a written policy statement, supported by adequate resources and consistent with the mission of the archives. Because personal papers document the whole career of a person, archivists encourage donors to deposit the entire body of materials in a single archival institution. This section of the code calls for cooperation rather than wasteful competition, as an important element in the solution of this kind of problem.

Institutions are independent and there will always be room for legitimate competition. However, if a donor offers materials that are not

Figure 8.1 (*Continued*)

within the scope of the collecting policies of an institution, the archivist should tell the donor of a more appropriate institution. When two or more institutions are competing for materials that are appropriate for any one of their collections, the archivists must not unjustly disparage the facilities or intentions of others. As stated later, legitimate complaints about an institution or an archivist may be made through proper channels, but giving false information to potential donors or in any way casting aspersions on other institutions or other archivists is unprofessional conduct.

It is sometimes hard to determine whether competition is wasteful. Because owners are free to offer collections to several institutions, there will be duplication of effort. This kind of competition is unavoidable. Archivists cannot always avoid the increased labor and expense of such transactions.

IV. Relations with Donors and Restrictions

Archivists negotiating with transferring officials or owners of documentary materials of long-term value seek fair decisions based on full consideration of authority to transfer, donate, or sell; financial arrangements and benefits; copyright; plans for processing; and conditions of access. Archivists discourage unreasonable restrictions on access or use, but may accept as a condition of acquisition clearly stated restrictions of limited duration and may occasionally suggest such restrictions to protect privacy. Archivists observe faithfully all agreements made at the time of transfer or acquisition.

Commentary: Many potential donors are not familiar with archival practices and do not have even a general knowledge of copyright, provision of access, tax laws, and other factors that affect the donation and use of archival materials. Archivists have the responsibility for being informed on these matters and passing all pertinent and helpful information to potential donors. Archivists usually discourage donors from imposing conditions on gifts or restricting access to collections, but they are aware of sensitive material and do, when necessary, recommend that donors make provision for protecting the privacy and other rights of the donors themselves, their families, their correspondents, and associates.

In accordance with regulation of the Internal Revenue Service and the guidelines accepted by the Association of College and Research Libraries, archivists should not appraise, for tax purposes, donations to their own institutions. Some archivists are qualified appraisers and may appraise records given to other institutions.

It is especially important that archivists be aware of the provisions of the copyright act and that they inform potential donors of any provision pertinent to the anticipated gift.

Figure 8.1 (*Continued*)

Archivists should be aware of problems of ownership and should not accept gifts without being certain that the donors have the right to make the transfer of ownership.

Archivists realize that there are many projects, especially for editing and publication, that seem to require reservation for exclusive use. Archivists should discourage this practice. When it is not possible to avoid it entirely, archivists should try to limit such restrictions; there should be a definite expiration date, and other users should be given access to the materials as they are prepared for publication. This can be done without encouraging other publication project that might not conform to the standards for historical editing.

V. Description

Archivists establish intellectual control over their holdings by describing them in finding aids and guides to facilitate internal controls and access by users of the archives.

Commentary: Description is a primary responsibility and the appropriate level of intellectual control should be established over all archival holdings. A general descriptive inventory should be prepared when the records are accessioned. Detailed processing can be time-consuming and should be completed according to a priority based on the significance of the material, user demand and the availability of staff time. It is not sufficient for archivists to hold and preserve materials: they also facilitate the use of their collections and make them known. Finding aids, repository guides, and reports in the appropriate publications permit and encourage users in the institution and outside researchers.

VI. Appraisal, Protection and Arrangement

Archivists appraise documentary materials of long-term value with impartial judgment based on thorough knowledge of their institutions' administrative requirements or acquisitions policies. They maintain and protect the arrangement of documents and information transferred to their custody to protect its authenticity. Archivists protect the integrity of documentary materials of long-term value in their custody, guarding them against defacement, alteration, theft, and physical damage, and ensure that their evidentiary value is not impaired in the archival work of arrangement, description, preservation, and use. They cooperate with other archivists and law enforcement agencies in the apprehension and prosecution of thieves.

Commentary: Archivists obtain material for use and must insure that their collections are carefully preserved and therefore available. They are concerned not only with the physical preservation of materials but even more with the retention of the information in the collections. Excessive delay in processing materials and making them available for use would cast doubt on the wisdom of the decision of a certain institution

---

Figure 8.1 (*Continued*)

---

to acquire materials, though it sometimes happens that materials are acquired with the expectation that there soon will be resources for processing them.

Some archival institutions are required by law to accept materials even when they do not have the resources to process those materials or store them properly. In such cases archivists must exercise their judgment as to the best use of scarce resources, while seeking changes in acquisitions policies or increases in support that will enable them to perform their professional duties according to accepted standards.

VII. Privacy and Restricted Information

Archivists respect the privacy of individuals who created, or are the subjects of, documentary materials of long-term value, especially those who had no voice in the disposition of the materials. They neither reveal nor profit from information gained through work with restricted holdings.

Commentary: In the ordinary course of work, archivists encounter sensitive materials and have access to restricted information. In accordance with their institutions' policies, they should not reveal this restricted information, they should not use specifically restricted information in their own research. Subject to applicable laws and regulations, they weigh the need for openness and the need to respect privacy rights to determine whether the release of records or information from records would constitute an invasion of privacy.

VIII. Use and Restrictions

Archivists answer courteously and with a spirit of helpfulness all reasonable inquiries about their holdings, and encourage use of them to the greatest extent compatible with institutional policies, preservation of holdings, legal considerations, individual rights, donor agreements, and judicious use of archival resources. They explain pertinent restrictions to potential users, and apply them equitably.

Commentary: Archival materials should be made available for use (whether administrative or research) as soon as possible. To facilitate such use, archivists should discourage the imposition of restrictions by donors.

Once conditions of use have been established, archivists should see that all researchers are informed of the materials that are available, and are treated fairly. If some materials are reserved temporarily for use in a special project, other researchers should be informed of these special conditions.

IX. Information about Researchers

Archivists endeavor to inform users of parallel research by others using the same materials, and, if the individuals concerned agree, supply each name to the other party.

Figure 8.1 (*Continued*)

Commentary: Archivists make materials available for research because they want the information on their holdings to be known as much as possible. Information about parallel research interests may enable researchers to conduct their investigations more effectively. Such information should consist of the previous researcher's name and address and general research topic and be provided in accordance with institutional policy and applicable laws. Where there is any question, the consent of the previous researcher should be obtained. Archivists do not reveal the details of one researcher's work to others or prevent a researcher from using the same materials that others have used. Archivists are also sensitive to the needs of confidential research, such as research in support of litigation, and in such cases do not approach the user regarding parallel research.

X. Research by Archivists

As members of a community of scholars, archivists may engage in research, publication, and review of the writing of other scholars. If archivists use their institutions' holdings for personal research and publication, such practices should be approved by their employers and made known to others using the same holdings. Archivists who buy and sell manuscripts personally should not compete for acquisitions with their own repositories, should inform their employers of their collecting activities, and should preserve complete records of personal acquisitions and sales.

Commentary: If archivists do research in their own institutions, there are possibilities of serious conflicts of interest—an archivist might be reluctant to show to other researchers material from which he or she hopes to write something for publication. On the other hand, the archivist might be the person best qualified to research in area represented in institutional holdings. The best way to resolve these conflicts is to clarify and publicize the role of the archivist as researcher.

At the time of their employment, or before undertaking research, archivists should have a clear understanding with their supervisors about the right to research and to publish. The fact that archivists are doing research in their institutional archives should be made known to patrons, and archivists should not reserve materials for their own use. Because it increases their familiarity with their own collections, this kind of research should make it possible for archivists to be more helpful to other researchers. Archivists are not obliged, any more than other researchers are, to reveal the details of their work or the fruits of their research. The agreement reached with the employers should include in each instance a statement as to whether the archivists may or may not receive payment for research done as part of the duties of their positions.

Figure 8.1 *(Continued)*

XI. Complaints About Other Institutions

Archivists avoid irresponsible criticism of other archivists or institutions and address complaints about professional or ethical conduct to the individual or institution concerned, or to a professional archival organization.

Commentary: Disparagement of other institutions or of other archivists seems to be a problem particularly when two or more institutions are seeking the same materials, but it can also occur in other areas of archival work. Distinctions must be made between defects due to lack of funds, and improper handling of materials resulting from unprofessional conduct.

XII. Professional Activities

Archivists share knowledge and experience with other archivists through professional associations and cooperative activities and assist the professional growth of others with less training or experience. They are obligated by professional ethics to keep informed about standards of good practice and to follow the highest level possible in the administration of their institutions and collections. They have a professional responsibility to recognize the need for cooperative efforts and support the development and dissemination of professional standards and practices.

Commentary: Archivists may choose to join or not to join local, state, regional, and national professional organizations, but they must be well-informed about changes in archival functions and they must have some contact with their colleagues. They should share their expertise by participation in professional meetings and by publishing. By such activities, in the field of archives, in related fields, and in their own special interests, they continue to grow professionally.

XIII. Conclusion

Archivists work for the best interests of their institutions and their profession and endeavor to reconcile any conflicts by encouraging adherence to archival standards and ethics.

Commentary: The code has stated the "best interest" of the archival profession—such as proper use of archives, exchange of information, and careful use of scarce resources, The final statement urges archivists to pursue these goals. When there are apparent conflicts between such goals and either the policies of some institutions or the practices of some archivists, all interested parties should refer to this code of ethics and the judgment of experienced archivists.

Adopted by the Council of the Society of American Archivists, 1992.
* *As of Spring 2004 the code was under revision and a new version may now be available.*

given to an archive by an individual, but those who wrote the correspondence, or who are the subject of the correspondence may not know that this material has been donated. Archivists are exhorted to protect the privacy of such individuals, especially if they had no control over the provision of such records to the archives. This highlights the careful balancing of interests required of archivists who must consider both the rights of access to information and the protection of the privacy of others.

Finally, archives may often find themselves in competition with other archives to obtain certain materials from donors. Archivists are expected to act ethically in the procurement of such materials, accurately representing the capacity of the archive to store and maintain such materials. Similarly, archivists must avoid competition that would work to the detriment of the preservation of such records, and they should not attempt to appropriate records already archived in other organizations.

PROFESSIONAL CONSIDERATIONS IN ETHICAL DELIBERATIONS

When considering professional ethics, the focus is on the ethical obligations and principles that arise when an individual is acting as an information provider. As noted earlier, most of our ethical actions are the result of our ethical education and training that we received as children. Consequently, as situations arise, we act almost automatically in most instances without taking much time to reflect on the ethical implications or bases of our acts. The fact that we often act out of habit highlights the power of our early ethical socialization. It also suggests that this same type of socialization is needed if the ethics of the profession are to be followed. Once the ethics of one's profession are inculcated, acting in accordance with them should also follow normally as part of our everyday behavior. This is not to say that one's personal ethics are necessarily in conflict or wholly distinct from one's professional ethics. In most cases, in fact, professional ethics can be seen as a specialized example of our normal ethical practices. From time to time, however, they may conflict.

Regrettably, it is not clear how the socialization process of inculcating professional ethics in information professionals takes place. The basic ethical principles are often reviewed in schools of library and information science, but such training is usually superficial and seldom systematic. The primary means of communicating ethical principles in the professions are through the codes of ethics mentioned earlier: ALA's Code of

Ethics (Figure 8.2), the ASIS Professional Guidelines (Figure 8.3), and SAA's Code of Ethics for Archivists (Figure 8.1). Other information-based disciplines also have codes of ethics, such as the ACM (Association for Computing Machinery) Code of Ethics and Professional Conduct and the Society of Competitive Intelligence Professionals, SCIP Code of Ethics for CI Professionals (see Appendix E).

Professional codes are important for at least four reasons: (1) they represent a statement of the fundamental values of the profession; (2) they are useful in teaching new librarians about the fundamental values of the profession; (3) reading (and rereading) them and listening to other professionals discuss and apply provisions of a code promotes the assimilation of important professional values; and (4) when particularly knotty ethical issues arise and important ethical concerns may be ignored, the professional code can serve as a decision-making guide and as a jog for one's conscience.

Codes, however, are not magic formulas. Unfortunately, because most of the individuals in a profession did not participate in the discussions that created the code, the rationale for each provision of the code is generally obscured. As a result, the code may appear to be unnecessarily arbitrary. This is especially problematic when a professional must justify acting in a manner consistent with the code. Unless there is a solid understanding of the code's rationale, the explanation is likely to sound dogmatic rather than like a thoughtful justification of professional conduct.

ALA Code of Ethics

Discussion of a need for an ethical code for librarians was sparse or nonexistent before the twentieth century. An early version, although not official, was discussed between 1903 and 1909. Two individuals contributed most to these early discussions: Mary Wright Plummer, director of the Pratt Institute Library School, and Charles Knowles Bolton, librarian of the Boston Athenaeum. The ALA actively considered adopting a code by 1928, but it was not formally adopted until 1938 (Lindsey and Prentice 1985). Interestingly, the ALA Library Bill of Rights was adopted just a year later. Together, these two documents form an important ethical foundation for librarianship. Revisions of the ethics code have been adopted over the years, in 1975 and 1981, and most recently in 1995.

The current ALA Code of Ethics explicitly recognizes the potential conflicts in values that are inherent in library work and establishes one

---

Figure 8.2
American Library Association Code of Ethics

As members of the American Library Association, we recognize the importance of codifying and making known to the profession and to the general public the ethical principles that guide the work of librarians, other professionals providing information services, library trustees, and library staff.

Ethical dilemmas occur when values are in conflict. The American Library Association Code of Ethics states the values to which we are committed, and embodies the ethical responsibilities of the profession in this changing information environment.

We significantly influence or control the selection, organization, preservation, and dissemination of information. In a political system grounded in an informed citizenry, we are members of a profession explicitly committed to intellectual freedom and the freedom of access to information. We have a special obligation to ensure the free flow of information and ideas to present and future generations.

The principles of this Code are expressed in broad statements to guide ethical decision making. These statements provide a framework; they cannot and do not dictate conduct to cover particular situations.

  I. We provide the highest level of service to all library users through appropriate and usefully organized resources; equitable service policies; equitable access; and accurate, unbiased, and courteous responses to all requests.
 II. We uphold the principles of intellectual freedom and resist all efforts to censor library resources.
III. We protect each library user's right to privacy and confidentiality with respect to information sought or received and resources consulted, borrowed, acquired, or transmitted.
 IV. We recognize and respect intellectual property rights.
  V. We treat co-workers and other colleagues with respect, fairness, and good faith, and advocate conditions of employment that safeguard the rights and welfare of all employees of our institutions.
 VI. We do not advance private interests at the expense of library users, colleagues, or our employing institutions.
VII. We distinguish between our personal convictions and professional duties and do not allow our personal beliefs to interfere with fair representation of the aims of our institutions or the provision of access to their information resources.
VIII. We strive for excellence in the profession by maintaining and enhancing our own knowledge and skills, by encouraging the professional development of co-workers, and by fostering the aspirations of potential members of the profession.

—Adopted by *ALA Council*, July 28, 1995
Reprinted with permission from theAmerican Library Association.

Figure 8.3
ASIS Professional Guidelines

Dedicated to the Memory of Diana Woodward

ASIS recognizes the plurality of uses and users of information technologies, services, systems and products as well as the diversity of goals or objectives, sometimes conflicting, among producers, vendors, mediators, and users of information systems.

ASIS urges its members to be ever aware of the social, economic, cultural, and political impacts of their actions or inaction.

ASIS members have obligations to employers, clients, and system users, to the profession, and to society, to use judgement and discretion in making choices, providing equitable service, and in defending the rights of open inquiry.

Responsibility to Employers/Clients/System Users

To act faithfully for their employers or clients in professional matters.

To uphold each user's, provider's or employer's right to privacy and confidentiality and to respect whatever proprietary rights belong to them, by

- limiting access to, providing proper security for and ensuring proper disposal of data about clients, patrons or users.

To treat all persons fairly.

Responsibility to the Profession

To truthfully represent themselves and the information systems which they utilize or which they represent, by

- not knowingly making false statements or providing erroneous or misleading information
- informing their employers, clients or sponsors of any circumstances that create a conflict of interest
- not using their position beyond their authorized limits or by not using their credential to misrepresent themselves
- following and promoting standards of conduct in accord with the best current practices
- undertaking their research conscientiously, in gathering, tabulating or interpreting data; in following proper approval procedures

---

Figure 8.3 (*Continued*)

---

for subjects; and in producing or disseminating their research results
- pursuing ongoing professional development and encouraging and assisting colleagues and others to do the same
- adhering to principles of due process and equality of opportunity.

Responsibility to Society

To improve the information systems with which they work or which they represent, to the best of their means and abilities by

- providing the most reliable and accurate information and acknowledging the credibility of the sources as known or unknown
- resisting all forms of censorship, inappropriate selection and acquisitions policies, and biases in information selection, provision and dissemination
- making known any biases, errors and inaccuracies found to exist and striving to correct those which can be remedied.

To promote open and equal access to information, within the scope permitted by their organizations or work, and to resist procedures that promote unlawful discriminatory practices in access to and provision of information, by

- seeking to extend public awareness and appreciation of information availability and provision as well as the role of information professionals in providing such information
- freely reporting, publishing or disseminating information, subject to legal and proprietary restraints of producers, vendors and employers and the best interests of their employers or clients.

Information professionals shall engage in principled conduct whether on their own behalf or at the request of employers, colleagues, clients, agencies or the profession.

(Adopted May 1992)

Reprinted with permission from the American Society of Information Science, Silver Spring, MD.

over-riding value: "commitment to intellectual freedom and freedom of access to information" (ALA 1995). Although not formally subdivided, the eight provisions of the code focus on three general areas: access issues, rights of authors and creators, and employment issues.

ACCESS ISSUES

Consistent with the overriding value cited in the preamble, three of the eight principles of the code deal directly with the issue of access to the library by patrons. The first section emphasizes the obligation to treat all equally, emphasizing the principle of equal treatment and access. The second section suggests that there is a positive obligation to promote intellectual freedom and to resist attempts to censor library materials. The third section is a recognition of the individual and the special nature of librarian-patron interactions. It highlights the "privileged" character, albeit not necessarily in the legal sense, of library use. To this end, the librarian is exhorted to protect the privacy of all patrons and to ensure that their interactions remain confidential.

RIGHTS OF AUTHORS AND CREATORS

Although the code of ethics places great emphasis on service to patrons, one section recognizes that the producers or creators of information are critical participants in this service process; they also deserve ethical treatment. Obviously, failure to recognize this aspect of information transfer and dissemination could seriously restrict the distribution of information products to libraries, with unhappy consequences for library service. To this end, Section IV of the code recognizes that authors and creators of works have the right to benefit from their creativity through their intellectual property rights. This is a clear reference to librarians' need to respect copyright protections.

EMPLOYMENT ISSUES

Employment issues actually comprise more provisions of the code than any other issue. One section deals with the interrelationships between employees and the need to create a sense of mutuality and community. These sections explore the treatment of fellow employees, the promotion of self-interest, the clash between personal and professional values, and the obligation to pursue and promote continuing education. Section V suggests that treating fellow employees in an ethical manner is itself an ethical obligation and part of the obligation to respect the rights and welfare of all employees. Section VI recognizes the essentially altruistic nature of the professional obligation. It admits to the fact that in some circumstances librarians could personally benefit from their employment relationship and reminds professionals that one's personal or private interests are not to be served above the interests of patrons, the employer, or other employees. Section VII focuses on a very delicate aspect of professional work. Each of us brings to the workplace a set of values, beliefs, and moral perspectives that govern our everyday behavior, but sometimes, acting in our professional capacity, we should act in the best interests of our clients. For example, what if a patron asks for a book that supports the concept of abortion, but we personally abhor it? Section VII suggests that we act to serve the patron, even if the material provided may violate our own values. Finally, Section VIII emphasizes the professional obligation to improve one's skills continually. In an increasingly complex information and technological environment, this is certainly a vital obligation. Interestingly, the obligation as set forth in this provision is broader than just self-improvement; it suggests that the obligation extends to the development of others. As such, it is especially pertinent to library decision makers and managers who have the capacity to create opportunities for training and development for their staffs.

ASIS Guidelines for Professional Conduct

The ethical guidelines from ASIS, as might be expected, are more broadly written, because they are aimed at information workers in all types of occupations, not just librarianship. These guidelines also recognize that some information services are part of private organizations and that the proprietary interests of such employers must be taken into account when making decisions concerning the dissemination of information.

Nonetheless, many of the underlying principles are similar to the ALA Code of Ethics. ASIS's code identifies three basic areas of ethical responsibility: (1) responsibilities to employers, clients, and systems users; (2) responsibilities to the profession; and (3) responsibilities to society. Like the ALA code, these guidelines consider the right to privacy, confidentiality, and fair treatment rights of clients, users, and employers. The ASIS Professional Guidelines, under the more general notion of protecting privacy and confidentiality, also highlight a critical obligation of those who design and administer information systems— to provide security for these systems. In addition, as in the ALA code, the responsibility to the profession includes the promotion of continuing education. The guidelines add, however, the responsibility not to misrepresent one's qualifications or the information system that is being used. The responsibility to the society also echoes that of the ALA code in the emphasis on free and equal access to information.

A cautionary note: professional ethical codes can be useful in setting an ethical context for employees who work within a given profession, but they are seldom sufficiently elaborate to be of great help. Such codes tend to be wooden documents that prescribe and proscribe general conduct, but because of their dogmatic character, seldom do they provide a deep understanding of the ethical issues that need to be addressed and resolved. This has not deterred the creation of codes, and additional codes have been suggested in librarianship. For example, Bierbaum (1994) has suggested a code of ethics for technical services, and Baker (1992) has suggested an ethical code for library administrators.

SPECIAL ETHICAL PROBLEMS WITH INFORMATION TECHNOLOGIES

Do Technologies Invite Ethical Lapses?

The deficiencies of ethical codes become more apparent when they are applied in today's technological environment. There is some reason to believe that these technologies may encourage or even promote unethical conduct. If so, then depending on formal ethical codes may be even less desirable and the need for careful ethical reflection more important. This is not to renounce traditional ethical concerns, but new information technologies can create new ethical dilemmas. It is worthwhile to consider some qualities of these new technologies that might promote unethical actions.

THE SPEED OF COMPUTERS

The speed of computers is one of their greatest attractions. Indeed, they are often promoted and advertised based on how fast the latest versions can perform their functions. However, the speed of computers also increases the temptation to act unethically because it suggests that one might be able to escape detection more easily. Stealing a file, for example, was much more difficult in the past. One had to enter a building or an office unobserved, locate a file drawer, locate a file, and either hide the file on one's person or make copies of the material. At each step, there was always the possibility of being detected. In contrast, the appropriation of a computer file by another computer is nearly instantaneous and chances of being caught severely limited.

COMPUTER USE IS OFTEN PRIVATE AND ANONYMOUS

Although some computer use is performed in public areas, most personal computer use is performed either in an office or at home. Generally, if one wants to work unobserved, the opportunities are available. Even if people are in the same room, it is relatively difficult for them to observe computer use without being noticed. Such privacy is very attractive to an individual who wishes to commit unethical acts. Similarly, the fact that the computer user is free from detection provides a sense of anonymity. The feeling that one cannot be "found out" tends to increase one's propensity to commit unethical acts.

COMPUTER ACCESS CAN BE ACCOMPLISHED FROM GREAT DISTANCES

In general, committing acts such as theft require that the thief be present when the item is stolen. Computers, on the other hand, permit accessing the item through telephone or cable lines. The result is that a computer file may be stolen by an individual in another city, state, or country. It is likely that such a thief is unlikely to feel vulnerable to detection, nor does the act require the same effort and stealth as the act of a "traditional" thief.

COPYING IS ACCOMPLISHED WITH GREAT EASE

The electronic medium is highly flexible. It is usually quite simple to download or make a physical copy of an electronic file while leaving the original unchanged. Under these circumstances, it is tempting to rationalize that nothing has actually been taken. Electronic theft is essentially an intellectual rather than artifactual act; electronic impulses are not nearly as tangible as paper or objects. Perhaps this is why individuals seem to have fewer misgivings about copying software than about copying a print edition of a work.

POTENTIAL AUDIENCE IS LARGE AND EASILY REACHED

Because of the nature of the Internet and Web, messages can now be sent quite easily to millions of individuals simultaneously—without the traditionally burdensome costs of postage, supplies, or long-distance tolls. Although this is a wonderful opportunity for communication, it also presents an opportunity for the unscrupulous to exploit large numbers of unwitting victims. In fact, a term has been coined to describe sending uninvited electronic messages, usually for business or commercial purposes: "spam" or "spamming." Because the available audience is so large, and the ease of communicating with them so great, the temptation to act unethically increases.

A Code of Ethics for Computer Use

It is interesting that there has been an explicit recognition of the ethical issues raised by computers. The "Ten Commandments of Computer Ethics," developed by the Computer Ethics Institute, is shown in Figure 8.4.

Figure 8.4
Ten Commandments of Computer Ethics

---

1. Thou shalt not use a computer to harm other people.
2. Thou shalt not interfere with other people's computer work.
3. Thou shalt not snoop around in other people's computer files.
4. Thou shalt not use a computer to steal.
5. Thou shalt not use a computer to bear false witness.
6. Thou shalt not copy or use proprietary software for which you have not paid.
7. Thou shalt not use other people's computer resources without authorization or proper compensation.
8. Thou shalt not appropriate other people's intellectual output.
9. Thou shalt think about the social consequences of the program you are writing or the system you are designing.
10. Thou shalt always use a computer in ways that insure consideration and respect for your fellow humans.

Reprinted with permission from the Computer Ethics Institute, P.O. Box 42672, Washington, DC 20015 (301) 469–0615. psullivan@brook.edu (*www.brook.edu/sscc/cei/cei_hp.htm*)

These commandments direct those who use computers to resist harming others or interfering with their work and to refrain from stealing or deceiving others with computers, violating copyright, or plagiarizing. They also recognize the need to respect others. As librarians increase their use of computers, it would be well for them to heed this code as well as their own profession's.

ETHICAL APPROACHES

When one sees how complex the ethical situation is for an information professional, it is tempting to try to create basic principles for ethical action. In large part, these principles are embodied in the ethical codes of the profession, and generally, they do a pretty good job, although sometimes they do fail us with their inevitable generality. Others have tried to restate or supplement these codes with additional principles, although none argue that their particular suggestions represent absolutes or a definitive list (Baker 1992; Rubin and Froehlich 1996). Froehlich (1992) summarized five of these principles as the obligations to minimize harm, to respect the autonomy of others, to act justly and fairly, to seek social harmony, and to comport with organizational, professional, and public trust.

Another approach to examining the desired ethical behaviors has been to subdivide the discipline, identifying three venues for ethical actions: the organizational, the professional, and the individual (Rubin and Froehlich 1996).

On the organizational level, there is little evidence that information organizations or agencies attempt to address ethical issues systematically. It is likely that concern for ethics most often arises, not because the actions themselves may be unethical, but because of an undesired result or diminished productivity. Nonetheless, among the approaches that have been taken to promote ethical conduct are: (1) establishing rules and regulations that clearly identify the ethical obligations of employee and management and clearly stating the penalties for ethical violations; (2) developing training and education programs that sensitize information professionals to ethical issues; (3) punishing individuals for ethical violations; (4) establishing an ethics code within the organization; (5) hiring and promoting individuals who demonstrate ethical behavior and understanding; and (6) developing a system of rewards that provides an incentive for ethical actions and a disincentive for unethical ones.

On the professional level, librarians and related information professionals have promulgated ethics guidelines and codes, as noted above. Professional associations also attempt to reinforce these codes through programs and speeches at association meetings and articles in professional publications. Some associations actually have the power of sanctions for unethical conduct. For example, the American Medical Association can withdraw a physician's power to practice, and the American Bar Association can prevent an attorney from practicing law. Such a sanctioning power, however, is not part of the arsenal of ALA or ASIS. It is through professional discussion and persuasion that the information professions attempt to promote ethical conduct.

Preventing unethical acts rests first and foremost on the individual level. Each of us is an individual moral agent and we do not give up our ethical obligations merely because we become employees. It seems clear that certain duties form a foundation for ethical conduct in the information profession. Some of the more obvious ones are that individuals should: (1) promote open, unbiased access to information; (2) maintain professional skills and knowledge; (3) act honestly with colleagues and consumers of information; (4) respect the privacy and confidentiality of others; and (5) provide the best service possible.

SUMMARY

No matter which principles or codes are used, it is clear that these statements reflect a consensus that the duties of information professionals are far greater than simply "doing their job." Their obligations follow from the more fundamental notions of respect for the individual and the desire to benefit the organization and the society. These are not new notions; on the contrary, they are quite old and seek expression in professional contexts. Ethical situations arise in many contexts for the information provider, and the ethical deliberations that ensue are complex. These deliberations often require a balancing of many interests and considerations: individual, organizational, and societal. If librarians and information specialists abide by fundamental ethical notions expressed in a professional context, the mission and values that underlie institutions like libraries can be preserved and sustained.

ENDNOTE

1. I am indebted to Dr. Thomas Froehlich, Kent State University, for many discussions on the ethical factors that affect deliberations in library and information science. The factors presented are a product of these discussions.

REFERENCES

American Library Association [ALA]. "Code of Ethics." *American Libraries* 26 (July/August 1995): 673.

American Society for Information Science [ASIS]. "ASIS Professional Guidelines." *Bulletin of the American Society for Information Science* 20 (1994): 4.

Baker, Sharon L. "Needed: An Ethical Code for Library Administrators." *Journal of Library Administration* 16 (1992): 1–17.

Bierbaum, Esther Green. "Searching for the Human Good: Some Suggestions for a Code of Ethics for Technical Services." *Technical Services Quarterly* 11 (1994): 1–18.

Dowd, Robert. "I Want to Find Out How to Freebase Cocaine; or Yet Another Unobtrusive Test of Reference Performance." *The Reference Librarian* 25–26 (1989): 483–493.

DuMont, Rosemary. "Ethics in Librarianship: A Management Model." *Library Trends* 40 (fall 1991): 201–215.

Finks, Lee W. "Librarianship Needs a New Code of Professional Ethics." *American Libraries* 22 (January 1991): 84–92.

Foskett, D. J. "The Creed of a Librarian: No Politics, No Religion, No Morals." Paper given at North Western Group, Reference, Special, and Information Section, Manchester Literary and Philosophical Society House, Manchester, England (March 27, 1962).

Froehlich, Thomas J. "Ethical Considerations of Information Professionals." *Annual Review of Information Science and Technology (ARIST)* 27 (1992): 292.

Green, Russell G., and Susan L. Thomas. "The Immediate Effects of Media Violence on Behavior." 42 (1986): 7–27.

Harris, Michael. "The Purpose of the American Public Library." *Library Journal* 98 (September 15, 1973): 2509–2514.

Hauptman, Robert. "Professionalism or Culpability? An Experiment in Ethics." *Wilson Library Bulletin* 50 (1976): 626–627

Lindsey, Jonathan A., and Ann E. Prentice. *Professional Ethics and Librarians*. Phoenix, Ariz.: Oryx, 1985.

Rubin, Richard. *Human Resources Management in Libraries: Theory and Practice*. New York: Neal-Schuman, 1990.

Rubin, Richard E., and Thomas J. Froehlich. "Ethical Aspects of Library and Information Science." *Encyclopedia of Library and Information Science*. Vol. 58 (Supplement). New York: Marcel Dekker, 1996, 33–52.

Smith, Martha M. "Editorial," *North Carolina Libraries* 51 (spring 1993a): 4.

————. "Information Ethics: Freedom, Democracy, Responsibility." *North Carolina Libraries* 51 (spring 1993b): 6–8.

Society of American Archivists. "Code of Ethics for Archivists." 1992.

Vitell, Scott, and Donald L. Davis. "Ethical Beliefs of MIS Professionals: The Frequency and Opportunity for Unethical Behavior." *Journal of Business Ethics* 9 (1990): 63–70.

9

The Library as Institution: An Organizational View

Institutions, including libraries, cannot be conceived as independent and self-sufficient entities whose survival relies solely on the efficient internal operation of the organization. Libraries must be thought of as organisms whose purpose is to adapt, as all organisms do, to a constantly changing environment. As organizational theorists have noted, simply surviving is an essential purpose and focus of an organization, and in this complex social, political, and economic climate, this task is no less an issue for libraries. Among the many environmental factors threatening the library's survival are the rapidly increasing costs of library materials and human resources, the reluctance of the public to provide continued and increased support for libraries, the increase in the diversity and quantity of published materials, the pressure to acquire computerized systems and resources, and the increasing power of publishers to control access to the information they produce and hence to control the costs of such information (Young 1994).

Libraries, as Wilson (1984) has noted, are part of the *bibliographic sector* in our society. This sector is "the assemblage of institutions and organizations that collectively take the output of the publishing industry and try to make it accessible for public use" (p. 389). Members of this assemblage include not only libraries, but publishers, materials retailers and wholesalers, networks, and indexing and abstracting services. The purposes of this sector are to provide both intellectual and physical access to information (Wilson 1984). Libraries, of course, provide both services, but there are other organizations that compete with them, and the competition is becoming keener all the time. Libraries are under threat from many quarters. Lack of money, lack of political support, social controversy arising from the materials and services that libraries provide, information competitors, changes in how information is produced and supplied, legal threats and constraints, personnel issues, demanding publics insisting on traditional and nontraditional materials and services, and technological changes are altering the very function and structure of libraries themselves. It is crucial, then, to understand the many ways in which libraries are organized and to identify some of the major issues confronting them as organizations.

There are many ways in which contemporary libraries are organized, but no matter what form the organization takes, libraries are designed to perform certain basic functions. These include (1) selecting materials and developing collections; (2) ordering and acquiring materials; (3) making information available through document delivery, electronic delivery of information, and the provision of information access mechanisms; (4) conserving and preserving materials; and (5) programming, including bibliographic and other forms of instruction in information access. Some libraries will place greater emphasis on some of these functions, and their organization may reflect these differences in emphasis.

In order to provide a general overview, the following discussion will emphasize a functional view of libraries as organizations. That is, it will attempt to identify the major functions that libraries perform and the units that are traditionally responsible for those functions. Suffice it to say that other forms of organization, such as matrix organizations, have evolved. Their influence may increase in years to come.

THE FUNCTIONAL ORGANIZATION OF LIBRARIES

For libraries to perform their essential functions, they are commonly divided into various units, with the number and types of units varying depending on the size and type of library. The units noted below are generally associated with those of a larger public library, although many other types of libraries also have them. Smaller libraries or libraries of different types may combine many functions within one unit. School library media centers, for example, tend to be very simple organizationally with few separate units; large university or public libraries are quite complex organizations and have many individual units.

Typically, the units in a library consist of boards of trustees, library administration, public service units, and support service units.

Boards (of Trustees)

In one fashion or another, most libraries are ultimately controlled by a board. Most board control is exercised directly in a public library where the chief administrator reports to an elected or appointed board of trustees. Boards generally possess the statutory authority to operate the library, as well as perform other organizational functions, as in the case of schools, academic institutions, and special libraries. The primary purpose of boards is to establish policies, strategic plans, goals, and directions for the library. In academic libraries, school library media centers, and special libraries, the control by the board is less direct in that the directors of these libraries generally report to other administrators, such as an academic dean, principal, or department head.

Library Administration

The administration includes the director and other individuals such as the treasurer, assistant or associate directors, and heads of administrative departments such as personnel, planning, and information systems. These individuals are responsible for the overall operation of the library. They contribute to policy creation, enforce those policies, administer personnel practices, conduct fiscal operations, and carry out planning functions.

Public Service Units

Many of the library departments are responsible for providing services and materials directly to the users. In addition, these departments often have direct responsibility for the selection of materials in their units. Each unit usually has at least one individual at the management level. The purpose of management levels in libraries is usually to oversee directly or indirectly units that perform specific service functions. Supervision of staff, participation in budgeting, and planning are often involved, as well as providing direct public service in many instances. Examples of management levels include heads of individual branches, departments, or divisions. There are several public service units.

Reference Department: This department's primary purpose is to meet the information needs of users. As a rule, the reference staff deals with user-initiated inquiries. Today, the department might be referred to variously by such terms as "Information Division," or "Information Center." Depending on the size of the library and its service philosophy, a library may have a single department responsible for giving information service to patrons or there may be many such departments. Larger reference departments are usually subdivided by subject (history, science, business), although they also may be organized by age or other characteristics of the user (children, adults, young adult, blind or visually impaired), or by geography (branches or decentralized libraries). Smaller libraries may have a single undivided department and its librarians may need to have a considerable breadth of knowledge to answer the questions of the various patrons who come to the reference desk.

The services provided by reference departments include, but are not limited to, answering information questions from print and nonprint materials and the Web, reader's advisory, assistance in locating materials, interpreting materials, preparing guides, instruction on how to use materials and services in the library (bibliographic/mediagraphic/Web instruction), maintenance of reference files, creation of reference Web sites, and conducting tours and programs. Reference staff may also select materials and electronic resources for the department and the library. In addition to these functions, reference librarians in school library media centers may offer story times and other programs for children, either in the library or in classrooms.

Circulation Department (Access Services): The term circulation implies the activity of dispensing or receiving library materials. The term coming into more popular use is "Access Services." No matter what it is called, its concern is the flow of materials and control over the conditions under which materials are used. The most common activities are checking materials out, receiving returned materials, and administering fines and procedures for late or lost materials. Circulation staff may also have control over periodicals, interlibrary loans, and materials held for restricted use (for example, reserve files in an academic library).

Audiovisual (AV) Department: With the growth in the popularity and variety of audiovisual materials, many libraries have separate AV departments. These departments include both materials and AV equipment and sometimes advice on AV programming. Organizationally, not all AV materials are necessarily included in this division. For example, music compact disks might still be found in a music or fine arts department, while videocassettes and DVDs might be found in an AV department.

Archives and Special Collections: This department deals with records that are of local or general historical importance. In addition, it often deals with materials that are considered rare or especially fragile. The size and scope of special collections departments vary tremendously. Research libraries (special, public, or academic) with special collections in specific areas are more likely to have actual departments that house, manage, and preserve the collection.

Special Services: Some libraries have departments that are designed to serve special clientele. For example, there may be departments for the blind or visually impaired. Other departments may be designed for those who are physically unable to come to the library; such departments might provide services to prisons or jails, service to nursing homes, or home visits. Bookmobile service could also be considered in this category.

Technical Services

Technical services are services that concern themselves with the preparation of library materials, including electronic information, in order to make such materials or information accessible to library users. Typically, the department consists of subdivisions including Acquisitions, Serials, and Cataloging and Classification. In addition, depending on the sophistication of the department, areas such as Preservation, Government Publications and Integrated Library Systems could also be part of Technical Services.

The challenges facing technical services are great and due in large part to the transformation of library collections into items that are physically retained and those items that are only "accessible" through electronic means. Gorman (1998) in discussing the issues facing technical services today notes that the term "collection" now includes four categories of items: (1) tangible materials (for example, books); (2) intangible materials owned by the library (for example, electronic resources on CD-ROM); (3) tangible materials not owned by the library (for example, materials available on interlibrary loan); and (4) intangible materials not owned by the library. Those charged with making all such knowledge available not only *in* the library but also *through* the intermediation of the library, are facing exciting and difficult challenges.

In addition, with the introduction and integration of automated systems, the workflow and coordination processes in Technical Services are changing. Traditional functions of specific units are now interrelated with the functions of other units. As noted by Younger, Gapen, and Johns (1998) this change, in turn, has led in some cases to the combining of traditional units, such as Acquisitions and Cataloging. They argue that the future of Technical Services will be shaped by many forces, and that there will be a

> focus on cost and product effectiveness, a client-centered mission, and managing an accelerating rate of change. Shrinking staff size, time-saving computing applications, less complicated cataloguing rules, streamlined workflows, and *outsourcing* . . . will be among the challenges in, and proposed solution to, managing technical services in the twenty-first century. (p. 174)

It is informative to summarize briefly some of the major functions of the units that comprise technical services.

ACQUISITIONS

The Acquisitions department deals with ordering and receiving materials. In addition, when materials are ordered but not received, Acquisitions is responsible for obtaining the delayed materials or determining why the materials are unavailable. This process is referred to as "claiming." Although in the past the concept of "acquisitions" also included both selection and collection development, these activities have now been separated and are usually performed by bibliographers, subject specialists, or other librarians. (They may also be performed in an automated fashion with protocols created by professionals.) Today, Acquisitions concerns itself more with the mechanics of the ordering process.

Schmidt and Ray (1998) identify the major processes of Acquisitions as ordering, claiming, and receiving materials. The procedures involved include bibliographic searching, order preparation and placement, online record maintenance, vendor assignment, correspondence, claiming, receiving materials, invoicing, and monitoring budgets and funds. The prospects for improving the efficiency of acquisition processes are good as the automated acquisition systems implemented by libraries become increasingly integrated with the systems of vendors and publishers.

SERIALS

The magazines, journals, newsletters and other serials that are a common part of library collections require a complex and coordinated process to ensure that they are available for user access. This process is referred to as *serials control*. Kao (2001) defines serials control as "Library tasks involved in managing serials titles and keeping them in good order and accessible to library users. Included are functions such as check-in, claiming, binding, replacement of back issues, and shelf maintenance" (p. 73). Among the challenges facing serials departments are assisting in the selection and evaluation of serials vendors, monitoring the costs of periodical subscriptions, and dealing with the growth of e-serials.

CATALOGING AND CLASSIFICATION

The Cataloging and Classification unit is responsible for bibliographic control. As such, its work focuses on descriptive and subject cataloging, copy cataloging, classification, and authority control. This work often involves use of bibliographic networks. The cataloging process generally consists of two types: copy cataloging and original cataloging. *Copy cataloging* usually involves creating a bibliographic record based on the preexisting record provided by another organization. Typically, the record is in the MARC format created by the Library of Congress and provided through a bibliographic utility such as OCLC. A suggested classification number is also provided, but may be modified by the local copy cataloger depending on the needs of the local collection. *Original cataloging* is work performed by a local cataloger and usually based directly on the item itself. Obviously, the expertise of an original cataloger is substantially greater than that required of a copy cataloger, hence the critical need for librarians who specialize in this area.

PRESERVATION

When thinking about the concept of "preservation" one usually considers activities associated with older, deteriorating materials. It is certainly worrisome and well-documented that substantial portions of many library collections, especially research and academic library collections, are embrittled due to the acidification of the paper used in their publication. Although dealing with deteriorating materials is certainly an essential aspect of any library's preservation program, concern for preservation begins with the proper handling of newly acquired materials as well as aging ones. The better the preservation techniques that are used from the start, the longer the material is likely to survive.

Preservation units deal with a variety of activities and techniques as part of their duties. Their functions include the following: preparing and administering the library's preservation program, assisting in the development and implementation of disaster plans, repairing and rebinding materials, deacidifying and/or encapsulating materials, and reformatting or digitizing and migrating materials. In many libraries, some of these functions are performed by units that are not specifically identified as "preservation" units. They may be situated in Collection Development or Technical Services departments; some are situated in Public Services while others may be independent units reporting directly to the director.

In an age in which there is great emphasis on new knowledge in electronic form, Preservation units remain critical if both important artifacts and the intellectual content of items of the past are to survive. In addition, as new knowledge is produced in digital form, such units will have to concern themselves more and more with how to preserve information stored in electronic formats: formats that are manifestly impermanent and easily altered or destroyed.

Support Units

There are also units in libraries that perform essential functions that are not, in themselves, providing direct service to the users. These support services, however, are needed if the library is to perform its service function. These units include the following:

Maintenance: Probably the least-visible and least-appreciated unit of a library is that of maintenance. This department ensures that the physical facilities operate smoothly and are appealing. The functions may vary considerably but generally include cleaning and housekeeping, maintaining and landscaping of grounds, heating, plumbing and electrical repair, and constructing displays. In small libraries, the maintenance department may perform some security functions as well.

Public Relations: Public relations units are intended to provide an important conduit for communication to the public and to listen to the public about the library. Among its functions are preparing promotional materials for library programs and agencies; designing systemwide programming activities; writing grants; managing communication with the public, the media, and political, civic, and religious leaders; and taking on crisis management when controversies arise.

Security: The need for a specific unit on security varies with the environment and nature of the community. Security problems can arise on a continuum from minor nuisances to major felonies. Security maintains a reasonably safe environment for users and staff. Its functions extend to patrolling the premises, protecting library property by monitoring users on the premises and when they exit, dealing with difficult or problem users, and contacting additional safety forces as needed.

Integrated Systems: A relatively new unit has emerged in some libraries with the increasing integration of technologies into all aspects of library service. Given the fiscal and human resources now devoted to information technologies, it has become clear that the need to coordinate the acquisition and use of such technologies is vital. For this reason, some libraries have created a separate department or appointed a specific individual to be responsible for these technologies. Generally, this unit deals with such activities as participating in the evaluation and selection of information technologies, training staff, trouble-shooting technological problems, and providing network security to prevent inappropriate or unauthorized use of the system, as well as viruses.

THE ORGANIZATION OF AUTHORITY IN LIBRARIES

The structure of organizations can also be understood in terms of sources of authority. Authority is the power to command or influence others. In most organizations, including libraries, there are usually three types of authority: bureaucratic, professional, and informal.

Bureaucratic Authority

The primary organizational structure of most libraries is bureaucratic. In a bureaucracy, one conceives of an organization as a group of formal positions that exist independently from the individuals who fill them. Different people may occupy these positions, but the positions themselves exist to fulfill basic organizational functions. Each bureaucratic position has at least three elements: (1) a set of clearly defined responsibilities, (2) an appropriate level of authority to meet these responsibilities, and (3) a set of clearly defined qualifications required for the individual to properly fill the position. In a bureaucracy, it is the responsibility of organizational leaders to rationally and objectively locate individuals who can satisfy the needs of the specific position. Personal considerations or any considerations unrelated to the required skills are to be ignored.

Within the bureaucratic structure, positions are arranged so their relationship to each other is clear. The most common arrangement is pyramidal and hierarchical. In such arrangements, a set of positions of similar character and authority report to a smaller number of positions of higher authority. For example, a group of reference librarians may report to the "head" of the reference department, the heads of various departments report to a "director." This hierarchical relationship is sometimes referred to as a "scalar chain of command." As the positions occupy a higher level in the hierarchy, the number of positions diminishes until there is a single position at the top (the director). In smaller organizations, the pyramid has far fewer levels and is therefore "flatter."

Bureaucratic authority rests on position rather than on the technical skills of the individual, and a bureaucracy relies on the authority to impose sanctions to get subordinates to obey (B. Lynch 1978). Individuals who leave a particular position no longer have the authority that is derived from it.

Professional Authority

Examining authority purely from a bureaucratic perspective provides an incomplete picture. Within the library bureaucracy is a professional activity—librarianship. Librarians derive professional authority by virtue of their expertise. Professional authority has evolved, in part, as a counterbalance to the profit-oriented traditions spawned in the factory system of the nineteenth century (Winter 1988). As Winter has observed,

> Professionalization is a way of dealing with the more immediate challenges of bureaucratic authority, in the everyday sense of fighting off the attempts of business to invade spheres of professional practice. (p. 13)

Similarly, Beverly Lynch (1978) characterizes this to some extent as a clash of ends: the purpose of bureaucracies is to increase organizational efficiency; the purpose of professionals is the provision of superior service, that is, effectiveness. This inevitably leads to internal frictions as librarians clamor for more services and materials, and bureaucrats resist on the basis of lack of resources. Bureaucratic authority clashes with professional authority when administrators make decisions that actually require professional, as well as administrative, expertise. Staff may, in fact, reject, sabotage, or otherwise make the work situation difficult if they believe that formal authority is being used by individuals to make decisions that lie outside their intellectual and professional ken. This is not, however, to suggest that all bureaucrats lack professional knowledge or care less about service. It does suggest that the bureaucratic character of managerial or administrative positions themselves involve different perspectives and concerns that lead to inevitable frictions with professional positions designed to deliver services.

Informal Authority

The third type of authority arises from the informal, social relationships among staff. It is defined by the persuasiveness of the individual or group or the personal relationship of that individual or group to those who are more powerful. These informal relationships are referred to as the "informal organization." Sometimes individuals or groups can be more powerful than the formal authority structures or than their expertise would warrant. Because libraries are labor intensive there is a relatively complex set of social relationships that define which individuals or groups are influential and which are less so. There is no reason to presume, however, that informal authority always works against the interests of those with formal authority.

Is Bureaucracy the Best Way to Organize Libraries?

One of the most common issues for discussion regarding the organization of libraries is whether a bureaucratic structure is best for library service. Hierarchical structures persist primarily for three reasons: (1) administrators believe that changes in the traditional decision-making structure can lead to chaos, (2) they believe that participatory decision making produces mediocre choices, and (3) they see participation as an abdication of their responsibility (Euster 1990). Although these reasons are not entirely without sense, do they represent convincing reasons for preserving a structure that may be unresponsive to the organizational needs of the future?

Some theorists suggest that bureaucratic structures are only best in organizations that exist in stable and predictable environments. In such an environment, where the dangers of and demands on the organization are predictable, features such as written rules and standardized procedures and practices are appropriate. In these settings, a methodical, deliberate, and centralized decision-making process is also appropriate. However, if the environment is unstable and the threats less predictable, it is necessary to be much more sensitive to environmental changes and to react to these changes quickly and effectively. To do this, more power has to be invested in those parts of the organization that are in close contact with the environment itself; this would generally be units that deal directly with "customers" (users) and that are constantly on the watch for new developments, such as new technologies or competitors. In such environments, decentralized authority seems more appropriate.

Euster (1990) argues that the increasing complexity of librarianship makes the traditional hierarchical structure obsolete, that "leadership and expertise must reside at all levels of the organization not just among designated leaders" (p. 41). No longer can one individual be expected to be sufficiently knowledgeable to make the necessary decisions. There is a need for the effective exchange of information among all individuals. The system must be designed to coordinate and share information so that decision making can be a joint process. Euster refers to the sharing of information for decision making, usually via automated systems, as "informating" the organization. Such systems convey critical information to the relevant parts of the organization so that decisions are made by whoever has the most information (p. 43).

Alternative organizational structures have been proposed that tend to decentralize decision making. Most notably, Martell (1983) has proposed a "client-centered" organization for academic libraries that tailors the structure directly to the needs of the users rather than to the needs of the bureaucracy. It is important to think anew about how libraries are organized. How well a library functions should be assessed by its ability to adapt to the changing and increasing demands of the environment in which it operates. Given the remarkable technological transformation occurring, it is likely that only structures that can respond rapidly and sensitively will survive and prosper in the years to come.

ORGANIZATION OF LIBRARIES BY TYPE

Another approach to library organization is to examine the various types: public, academic, school, and special. Although it is a convenient way of looking at libraries, it must be noted that within a given type there may be tremendous variation. The *American Library Directory 2002–2003* breaks down the number of U.S. libraries as seen in Figure 9.1.

PUBLIC LIBRARIES

The public library in the United States represents a unique contribution to the dissemination of knowledge to citizens. There are few countries that can boast of a tradition comparable to the historical contribution that this institution has made to create an informed citizenry. Public libraries have been part of American life for nearly 150 years, with the first large public library established in Boston in the 1850s (see Chapter 7). There are approximately 9,000 public libraries in the United States, and nearly 17,000 outlets when branch libraries are included. Total library collections exceed more than 760 million books and serial volumes, and more than 54 million audio and visual materials. Total operating income exceeds $7.7 billion, 77 percent of which comes from local funding, and less than 1 percent from federal sources (*Digest of Education Statistics 2002*).

Figure 9.1
Number of Libraries in the United States

Public libraries	16,598
Public libraries excluding branches	9,445
Public library branches	7,153
Academic libraries	3,480
Junior college libraries	1,082
University and college libraries	2,398
Special libraries including law, medical, and religious libraries	10,452
School and media center libraries	94,342

Sources: National Center for Education Statistics, *Digest of Education Statistics, 2002; American Library Directory 2002-2003.*

The broad-based public support that public libraries receive is not surprising. Americans are heavy users of their libraries. Despite the fact that public libraries are not used by all Americans in equal proportion, there are millions of library users. In 2001 more than 1.7 billion items were circulated (6.5 per capita); there were more than 296 million reference transactions. In addition, there were more than 1.1 billion visits, amounting to 4.3 visits per capita (National Center for Education Statistics [NCES] 2003). A Louis Harris national survey of 2,254 adults conducted in 1990 showed just how heavy public library use is in the United States. Two out of three of those interviewed (66 percent) indicated that they had used the services of a public library in the past year, and 42 percent of these had used the service twelve or more times a year (Westin and Finger 1991). A Gallup Poll in 1998 produced very similar results with 74 percent of the respondents indicating that they had visited the library at least once in the last 12 months. Individuals who had visited the library had used it primarily to take out books (81 percent), consult a reference librarian (65 percent), or use reference materials (61 percent). Interestingly, when individuals were asked if libraries will exist and be needed in the future despite all the advancements of computers, 90 percent believed that they will (Gallup 1998).

Some studies have demonstrated somewhat less use. In 1996 the National Center for Education Statistics (1997) reported on the 1996 National Household Education Survey, which is an annual survey on educational issues. The survey included specific questions on public library use. The study revealed that 44 percent of U.S. households had at least one individual who had used the public library in the previous month. It also reported that 65 percent of the households had used the public library in the last year.

Although the results of studies of use differ, it is clear that annual library use is well above use in the past, which was closer to 10 percent. As a rule, the more frequent users are under 50 years of age, with at least a high school education and some college education. Generally, as income levels increase, so does library use; and whites are more likely to use libraries than African Americans or Hispanics. Nonetheless, the Harris data suggest that library use is considerable among minorities, with 58 percent of African Americans and 62 percent of the Hispanics indicating library use in the previous year (Westin and Finger 1991). Public library use also tends to increase in families with children (NCES 1997).

The National Household Education Survey also revealed that the most common use of the library was for enjoyment or hobbies (32 percent); followed by getting information for personal use, such as health or consumer material (20 percent); or using the library for school assignments (19 percent) (NCES 1997).

The organizational goal of the public library is broad—perhaps overly broad. This goal can be stated simply: to meet the informational, recreational, educational, and cultural needs of the community it serves. Although the goal can be stated simply, it is another matter to try to satisfy it. Its comprehensiveness taxes library resources and can lead to an unfocused use of these resources. The Public Library Association (PLA) has made attempts to help public libraries focus their goals through its public-library planning process. PLA has recommended that libraries select only a few basic roles from eight possibilities, and in this way they have a means of focusing their resources and energies (Palmour 1980). These roles include the following:

Community-Activities Center: The library is a central focus point for community activities, meetings, and services.

Community-Information Center: The library is a clearinghouse for current information on community organizations, issues, and services.

Formal Education-Support Center: The library assists students of all ages in meeting educational objectives established during their formal courses of study.

Independent-Learning Center: The library supports individuals of all ages who are pursuing a sustained program of learning on an independent basis.

Popular-Materials Library: The library features current, high-demand, high-interest materials in a variety of formats for persons of all ages.

Preschoolers' Door to Learning: The library encourages young children to develop an interest in reading and learning through services for children and for children with their parents or caregivers.

Reference Library: The library actively provides timely, accurate, and useful information for community residents.

Research Center: The library assists scholars and researchers who conduct in-depth studies, investigate specific areas of knowledge, and create new knowledge. (Palmour 1980, p. 28)

Obviously, the missions or groups of missions a library chooses may reflect the type of community that it serves. For this reason, one is likely to find a research mission selected by only the largest of public libraries where there is a business, technological, academic, or scientific infrastructure that would use these types of resources regularly. Suburban libraries or libraries located in small cities and towns are more likely to emphasize popular materials for the community and materials that support the education of the young. However, these generalities are not hard and fast, and certainly libraries can and do maintain multiple missions. With the ongoing competition from other information competitors, especially those in the electronic information environment, it is instructive to remember that the public library is an important *place*, and part of its essential mission is integrally related to its physical reality. Simon (2002) reminds us that as a place the public library has the ability to perform a variety of functions, including a community and social center, a play space for children, a study hall for students, a lifelong learning center for the community, a museum for community history, and a cultural center, to name just a few.

MAJOR ISSUES CONFRONTING PUBLIC LIBRARIES

The political climate. The inherently political nature of public librarianship is often overlooked and greatly underestimated, but it is a vital part of a public library's survival. The political considerations are not necessarily partisan—often they are quite the opposite as public library administrators attempt to preserve a nonpartisan and effective working relationship with the various political groups. The political character of public librarianship is further reinforced, in that public libraries rely almost entirely on public monies to finance their operations, and library board members are often appointed by local political powers. Balancing the various political interests is a complex and challenging task. Consider the various interests that are concerned with public library resources: the business community, governmental agencies and legislative bodies, schools and other educational institutions, religious groups, clubs and civic organizations, and parents. The expectations of each of these groups vary. These factors, coupled with increasing financial strains and a social climate that is often antagonistic to public institutions in general make the political complexities of running the public library considerable.

Financial stresses. There are a variety of factors combining to make life difficult for the public library. Most notable has been the economic slowdown in the first years of the twenty-first century and increasing public debt. De Rosa, Dempsey, and Wilson (2004) have observed that the fiscal debt for 2003 approached nearly $80 billion and the projected debt for 2004 is little better. Reliance on public funding is considerable: 87 percent of funding for libraries is through public dollars in the United States. Under the current circumstances, decreasing public support and reductions in programs are likely. Projections by the federal government suggest that public funding on the local and state level is expected to remain static or even decline in the near future. Many states, including major ones like California, New York, and Ohio, have suffered serious drops in public support for libraries, leading to reduction in hours and staffing and declining book budgets. Other sources of financial stress include the increasing prices of traditional library materials, especially periodicals, and additional costs incurred by use of the new information technologies. The additional costs of computer hardware and software, along with connection costs for electronic access, can also be considerable. These costs, coupled with static budgets, make the burden on public library service tremendous. Attempts to save money and improve operational efficiency have included outsourcing public library services to private vendors, with mixed results. Hennen (2003) recommends additional tactics to improve fiscal conditions, including pooling resources by combining individual libraries into library districts, raising additional funds by creating library foundations, developing e-commerce initiatives, assessing "impact fees" on new homes, and being more politically active by introducing legislation that would set aside a percentage of current property taxes to finance public libraries. The effectiveness of such recommendations will no doubt vary by locality, but public libraries must take a more aggressive, entrepreneurial approach if they are to survive and prosper in the years to come.

The introduction of new information technologies. New information technologies create more than financial challenges. Public library services, physical structures, and organizational charts are all being redesigned as information technologies permit an entirely new way of accessing information on a local, regional, national, and global scale. There is little doubt, for example, that the ubiquity of Web access has transformed many aspects of the information services provided by libraries. More than 96 percent of all public libraries now have access to electronic services and the Internet (NCES 2003). The new electronic information environment requires new types of staff and patron training, the development of new types of information resources, and knowledge of electronic publishing techniques. As Web access continues to grow, there will be changes to the way libraries view resource sharing, collection development, and access issues, including the prospect of filtering. There is mounting evidence that the citizenry expect their public libraries to integrate electronic technologies into their services. A survey by the Benton Foundation (1996) found that 60 percent of the respondents considered it very important for the public library to provide computers and online services, especially to those who do not have their own computers. Nearly the same percentage (58 percent) felt the librarians should have access to such services so that they can assist library patrons.

There is little doubt that the costs of both equipment and technical expertise will be considerable for public libraries. To this end the Microsoft Corporation, in cooperation with the ALA, has taken steps to assist public libraries in providing access to the Internet. As early as 1995 Microsoft began a pilot program known as Libraries Online, which was intended to help public libraries gain access to digital information. This was accomplished by donating the funds to obtain the necessary information technologies, as well as providing technical training. This program reached more than 200 libraries throughout the United States. In 1997 this concept was expanded by Bill Gates, the founder of Microsoft, and his wife, Melinda French Gates. They established the Gates Library Foundation, which was intended to promote the public library as a key access point for all citizens of the United States and Canada. Recognizing that computers have become a common aspect of public library service, since 1997 the foundation has emphasized working particularly with public libraries in low-income areas to provide the hardware and software required for community access to digital information. In addition, the foundation has supported computer training for library staff so that they can effectively obtain access to and manage digital information for their patrons and their communities. Millions of dollars have been allocated to accomplish these goals. Recent focus of the foundation on library activities are related to three areas: the U.S. Library Program, which continues to work with public libraries to provide access to computers and computer training; the International Library Initiatives, which support libraries around the world to expand electronic access; and the Native American Access to Technology program, which focuses on the unique information and training needs of Native Americans. According to the Bill and Melinda Gates Foundation (2003), the goal of this program is "to empower Native communities through increased access to digital information resources." Funds for preserving local culture through digital techniques, and training in digital skills are among the activities funded.

The new technologies may also create new libraries that serve as public libraries but are not physical structures in the traditional sense. For example, based originally on a classroom project at the University of Michigan School of Information, the Internet Public Library (IPL) was created. The IPL subsequently received funding from the W.K. Kellogg Foundation and the Andrew W. Mellon Foundation ("Internet Public Library" 1997). The mission of IPL is to provide free services to the Internet community including both adults and children, and to teach librarians how the digital environment can be exploited (Internet Public Library 1997). It explores best practices for providing library service by the Internet, and conducts research aimed at increasing our knowledge about digital libraries and librarianship. It is a 24-hour online service, with subject collections including Art & Humanities, Business, Computers, Education, Health, Science & Technology, and Social Science as well as a ready-reference service. It also provides special services to teens and children. The objective of IPL is not to replace local libraries, but to serve as a traditional library model enhanced by the capacities of the Internet (Internet Public Library 2001).

Measurement, evaluation, and planning of library services. Although there is almost universal agreement that public libraries provide an invaluable service, it is more difficult to quantify the contributions that public libraries make. For this reason, some years ago the Public Library Association (ALA) created the Public Library Development Program (PLDP) to help public libraries develop the techniques and skills to plan, measure, and evaluate their organizations. The result in part was to produce a variety of publications that could serve as important "how-to" guides to these important activities.

To some extent, a public library must be evaluated against the expectations of its local community. The best-known measurements for individual libraries or for comparison between individual libraries are those created by the PLA in its development of specific "output measures." First promulgated in 1982 in the work *Output Measures for Public Libraries* (Zweizig 1982) and subsequently revised in a second edition in 1987 (Van House et al. 1987), these works were intended to assist public libraries in the planning, measurement, and evaluation process, and to focus the libraries' attention on their local communities rather than on national standards. Among the measures suggested in these publications are a variety of *per capita* measures related to annual library visits, circulation, in-library materials use, reference transactions, and program attendance. In addition, a variety of rates was proposed, including the title fill rate, subject and author fill rate, and browsers' fill rate.

Many of the above measures, however, presume the delivery of traditional library services. Special challenges for measurement and evaluation have arisen as electronic networks have played central roles in the delivery of library services. To assist libraries in measuring these more elusive activities, Bertot, McClure, and Ryan (2001) have proposed additional measures so that public libraries can be recognized for the electronic resources and services that they provide. Among the measures proposed are the following: number of public access Internet workstations, number of virtual reference transactions, number of full-text titles available by subscription, number of database sessions, number of virtual visits to library networked resources, and number of users instructed.

Holt and Elliott (2003) have suggested that the increasing pressures of accountability from the public dictate more rigorous methods of analysis, most notably, the use of cost-benefit analysis (CBA) for public library performance. Certainly the cost of library services is a matter for interest; it is certainly not *free*. De Rosa, Dempsey, and Wilson (2004) have estimated that the cost to visit a public library, when such factors as travel time, time in the library (return travel time, and per capita library expenditures are taken into account) is $26.43 for someone with an annual income of $50,000, and $40.43 for someone with an income of $85,000. Holt and Elliott (2003) have suggested that CBA requires a shift in emphasis from outputs to *outcomes*. That is, there needs to be a change of focus from what libraries do, to what tangible benefits public libraries provide to their communities. The proposed cost-benefit measures include (1) consumer surplus, which is "the value that library users place on separately valued library services" (p. 429), and (2) contingent valuation, which involves how much an individual would be willing to pay rather than lose library service, or how much an individual would be willing to pay in taxes to have the current library services. Although the efficacy of such measures for public libraries remains unclear (very little research has yet been conducted using these measures), it is very likely that they will be important contributions to the arsenal of measures that could be useful as public libraries struggle to demonstrate their critical role in the community.

Other attempts have been made to provide comparative public-library service measurements using a ranking system. Most notable are the yearly rankings using Hennen's American Public Library Ratings (HAPLR). This system ranks public libraries nationally by five categories of population size. The rankings are based on weighted scores assigned to 15 measures dealing with such variables as circulation, expenditures, staff size, collection size, and number of visits. Some have criticized the measures, and even Hennen (2002) has noted the need to introduce additional measures related to electronic and Web use. Nevertheless, to date, Hennen's rankings are the only examples of national rankings available.

Of course, measurement and evaluation processes go hand in hand with planning processes. Over the years, the ALA, especially PLA, has been focused on developing strategic planning expertise within public libraries. The approach is primarily goal- and objectives-based. The first major planning document, *A Planning Process for Public Libraries*, was published in 1980 and established the need to identify primary and secondary roles for each library based on community needs, and to conduct community analyses to determine the appropriateness of the needs and if the needs are being met (Palmour 1980). This work was followed by enhancements and improvements in planning approaches leading to the publication of *Planning and Role-Setting for Public Libraries* (McClure et al. 1987), *Planning for Results* (Himmel and Wilson 1998), and, most recently, *The New Planning for Results* (Nelson 2001). In this latest version, topics such as designing and preparing for the planning process, identifying community needs, selecting service responses and activities, writing and communicating the plan, allocating resources and monitoring plan implementation are methodically discussed. As public accountability continues to grow, there is little doubt that planning, measurement, and evaluation techniques will be critical tools for public library survival.

Censorship issues. Attempts to restrict access to materials or remove them are hardly new to public libraries. But the current social climate suggests that citizens are becoming even more active in monitoring access to materials and services in public libraries. Interestingly, challenges are not only being made to individual items, but to the policies of libraries that permit controversial items to be selected and retained. In particular, there have been specific attacks on ALA, especially the ALA Library Bill of Rights, because it is perceived by some as an organization that is influential in developing individual public library policy. Censorship attacks on individual libraries are now including concomitant challenges to the authority of ALA. The result is that public librarians are forced not only to defend their own libraries, but also their professional association. Attempts to accommodate those who are unhappy with libraries' intellectual freedom policies have led some librarians to compromise by restricting access or eliminating materials. As use of the Web has become commonplace, public libraries are also facing requests by patrons to filter access at library terminals, especially those used by minors. With the passage of the Children's Internet Protection Act, these requests are even more likely to occur.

The quality versus demand problem. The breadth of a public library's mission makes it difficult to determine exactly how the mission should be implemented. An important area for decision making is selection and collection development, and one issue in particular prompts frequent and sometimes intense discussion. This involves the extent to which libraries purchase high-circulation materials of limited and ephemeral value versus their purchase of materials of lasting, educational value, even if these items are only rarely consulted. The most typical example of popular materials is the purchase of popular fiction and romances. This controversy is commonly referred to as the *quality versus demand* debate. It is not simply a black-and-white issue; public libraries order both highly popular materials and those that may be less popular but of more long-term value. Nonetheless, a great deal of money can be spent on popular or ephemeral materials, and the degree to which libraries emphasize one aspect over the other can substantially affect the allocation of resources.

Some of the fundamental arguments in support of acquiring a large number of highly popular materials are (1) these materials are heavily used, indicating that the library is meeting the demand of its community's needs; (2) these materials provide important diversion and entertainment, which is a valid and valuable purpose of public libraries; (3) high circulation is an important indicator of a library's success; and (4) high circulation assists the library in obtaining popular political support.

Arguments that emphasize the purchase of educational and less ephemeral materials include (1) the library is primarily an educational institution, not an entertainment one, hence collections should emphasize materials of lasting educational value; (2) high demand is artificially created by mass-market publishers, and libraries should not cater to what is basically a marketing campaign of popular publishers; (3) libraries have a duty to serve individual tastes and not cater to mass-market appetites; (4) there is already too much emphasis on circulation statistics (which promote the purchase of ephemeral popular materials) while such important statistics as in-house use of educational or reference materials (which support the selection of educational materials) are often ignored; and (5) mass-market materials have a degrading effect on the public's intellect (Bob 1982; Rawlinson 1981). As public library budgets remain tight, the allocation of scarce resources requires that libraries answer important questions about their primary functions so that they may make these allocations wisely.

Service to rural communities. Although Americans who reside in rural areas comprise about 17 percent of the total U.S. population, they live in four-fifths of the land area. Large urban libraries tend to get the greatest attention, but the fact is that more than 50 million people reside in nonmetropolitan areas in the United States. In the decade of the 1990s rural population grew more than 10 percent, and this growth was accounted for almost entirely by migration of metropolitan populations to nonmetropolitan ones (Economic Research Service 2004).

Given the large areas to be served and number of individuals involved, it is not surprising that rural public libraries number in the thousands. Yet despite their prevalence, rural libraries face many challenges. Vavrek (2003) notes that a rural library serving fewer than 25,000 people averages 3.5 paid, full-time equivalents in staff, a book collection of 26,000 volumes, and a total operating income of $155,000. The smallest of libraries possess even fewer resources. The challenges facing rural libraries are many and include (1) finding sufficient fiscal resources to maintain and improve rural library service; (2) providing network access to electronic resources and the Web, and supplying the technical expertise to support these networks and resources; (3) locating, hiring, and retaining professionally trained staff; (4) providing continuing education and training to staff who have not been professionally trained; (5) dealing with the impressive geographic barriers that inhibit rural library use (including the use of mobile services, Books by Mail programs, deposit collections, and institutional services to nursing homes and retirement facilities); (6) collaborating with local schools and homeschoolers; (7) providing reading, information, and computer literacy instruction for individuals and families; and (8) maintaining the library as a community center for use by clubs and organizations, and for continuing education and additional services for the rural population (Vavrek 2003; Johnson 2000).

Service to multicultural populations. As the United States population becomes increasingly heterogeneous ethnically and racially, the public library continues to diversify its library services. It is clear that various ethnic and racial groups have unique information needs and may require special services or approaches tailored to these needs. The history of the public library has been uneven in the service of these groups. Some public libraries have not been welcoming; they have been, as Harris (1973) has described, cold, authoritarian institutions. On the other hand, by the turn of the century, public libraries had developed specific programs for various immigrant, racial, and ethnic groups. The adaptation of public libraries to the needs of minority and ethnic populations faces many barriers. Du Mont, Buttlar, and Caynon (1994) have identified a variety of these barriers to multicultural services: shortages of resources, lack of multicultural staff, tensions between staff and members of ethnic and racial groups, lack of understanding of other cultures, competing demands among ethnic and racial groups, staff resentment toward the creation of new programs, lack of patron knowledge of libraries, and lack of time. Resolutions to these barriers require increased attempts to recruit minority librarians, greater staff development and training in services to various racial and ethnic groups, improved needs assessments, promotion and target marketing of library services, more support for research on service to ethnic and racial groups, and consideration of minority and ethnic populations in the design and implementation of library services. In addition, the library is becoming an important place to redress the problems created by the digital divide. Because there is substantial evidence that minorities have less access to the Internet in their homes, public libraries play a substantive and important role in providing access to this critical information source for such individuals.

Service to individuals with disabilities. It is estimated that 20 percent of the population have a disability, constituting the largest minority in the United States (Klauber 1998). Native Americans have the highest rates of disability followed by African Americans. In general, increasing disability rates are associated with lower incomes and formal levels of education. Similarly, because the rate of disabilities also increases with age, the maturing of the baby-boom populations will increase the number of individuals with disabilities in the future. These factors, combined with the fact that individuals with disabilities often have increased information needs, place a special burden on libraries to be responsive (Rubin 2001). The problem is exacerbated by the fact, as noted in previous discussions (see Chapter 1), that individuals with disabilities are part of the digital divide; they generally have less access to the Internet in their homes, and thus less access to information.

The earliest of library services specifically directed to individuals with disabilities was provided to the visually impaired, hospitalized, or otherwise institutionalized beginning in the nineteenth century. The first book delivery to the homebound (by horse and buggy) occurred in 1901. Library services for individuals with other disabilities did not begin until World War I. The signing of the Library Services and Construction Act in 1966, however, was a significant turning point authorizing Title IV-A and B funding to help state agencies and institutions improve their services (G. Casey 1971; Lovejoy 1983). Today, with public libraries' commitment to diversity and to service to all, it is expected that they would serve individuals with disabilities, just as they serve others.

Of course public libraries must deal with a variety of issues in providing such services. Most notably, they must ensure physical access to the building and services. Ramps, curb cuts, parking availability, elevators, signage, telephones, drinking fountains, alarm systems, and wider aisles are among the considerations that help ensure physical access. Access to library services requires consideration of a variety of other issues as well, including access to computers through assistive technologies (such as page-turning devices, modified keyboards, and speech input capability), machines that read print aloud, adjustable work stations, and computer hardware and software that enlarge print, speak, and produce braille. Accessible collections (including large print books, audio books and tapes, braille books, and closed-captioned DVDs and videos), are important considerations as well. Services such as extended loans and reserve periods, remote access to the catalog, library cards for caregivers, and programs that include signers may also be effective in meeting the needs of those with disabilities. Access to services beyond the library might include programs for the homebound, books by mail, and fax and e-mail services. Staff training to assist individuals with disabilities is also an important aid to such service (Klauber 1998; Rubin 2001).

Children's and young adult (YA) services. One of the great challenges of public library service is providing services to the young. Although the phrase "YA services" has been commonplace to designate service to teenagers, more recently the term "Teen services" has become quite popular and may well supplant "YA" in the future.

No matter what you call these programs, the public is a great supporter of public library services to the young. A recent survey of adults found that 83 percent believed it was very important for the library to provide storyhours and other children's programming (Benton Foundation 1996). Generally, services to youth are broken down into those serving children and those for young adults (YA), although the boundary line between them is often hard to distinguish and arbitrarily drawn. Nonetheless, it is clear that at their extremes they represent very different groups.

The magnitude of children's and YA services is often underestimated. Approximately 60 percent of all public library users are under the age of 18; 23 percent are between the ages of 12 and 18; 37 percent are younger than 12. Approximately 30 percent of all librarians specialize in services to young people (NCES 1995). A substantial portion, more than one-third, of all public library circulation is that of children's materials (Wright 1996), and children tend to borrow more materials than the general population. In addition, more than three-fourths of all attendees at public library programs are children (Zweizig 1993). Despite this considerable participation, only about one in five public libraries have a children's specialist and only 11 percent have a designated YA specialist (NCES 1995). In addition, despite the clear benefits of reading and library use for children, youngsters between the ages of 9 and 14 spend a little more than 1 percent of their waking hours reading, while they spend nearly 21 percent of their time watching television (Carnegie Corporation 1993).

What then are some of the major trends and challenges facing children's and YA librarians?

Demographic changes. Public libraries serve their communities, and over the years the demographics of these communities have changed. Most notably, they have become more racially and ethnically diverse. In addition, the social and family structure of the American family has changed. Many more children are living in single-parent and intergenerational families. Among adolescents between ages 10 and 17, 20 percent of the whites, 30 percent of Hispanics, and 50 percent of African Americans live in single-parent families. More than a fifth of these youngsters live in poverty or near poverty. Even in two-parent families, 60 percent of the mothers have jobs in the labor force (U.S. Bureau of the Census 1991). The children from these families sometimes have different experiences from those of children in the "traditional" family, in which the father went to work and the mother stayed home with the children. As a consequence, children's and YA services, collections, and programs are expected to respond sensitively to these changes. In terms of children's and YA services this means that collections and services reflect the racial and ethnic realities or alternative family structures with which these children deal. The effect has not only been in the collections, but in programming as well. Providing programs for latch-key children or "children at risk" and performing outreach functions at local daycare facilities have become more common.

Proliferation in the variety of quality of children's and YA materials. Providing an up-to-date children's and YA book collection has become a central challenge for public libraries. There is little question that children's and YA book publishing is one of the healthier segments of the publishing marketplace, and the result has been a marked proliferation in the number and variety of children's and YA materials. There are about 3,000–5,000 books published each year for children and young adults in the United States, many of increasingly high production quality. The number of children's authors and illustrators has also climbed correspondingly. Today, market segmentation has become so great that there are retail stores that specialize only in children's and YA materials. Similarly, the breadth and depth of various subject areas has substantially increased. These include works in a variety of formats including "pop-up" books. Many of these works, especially those for young children, are brilliantly illustrated using printing technologies that make the illustrated page a feast for youngsters' eyes. Fiction has grown in subject depth as well, confronting difficult situations including drug abuse, suicide, and divorce. Surprisingly, these subjects have been prepared not only for older children, but for young ones as well, for example, *Let's Talk About It: Divorce*, by Fred Rogers (1996).

Nonfiction has also seen growth in size and quality. Many of the new nonfiction works are well-researched, well-written works, prepared by knowledgeable authors reflecting a multicultural perspective. There are now, for example, far more biographies of minority individuals and women. Science books for children have also proliferated and include new or newly adapted illustration techniques (pop-up science books!) and even incorporate computer chips that emulate sounds. Picture books for very young children have been written on a wide range of subjects with exceptional artistic and literary merit. All this is good news, but the growth of these materials has placed significant burdens on collection development budgets. Children's and YA librarians must decide if they are going to purchase multiple copies of materials or try to purchase just one of many titles. Similarly, they must ensure not only that newly published materials are ordered, but that a high-quality core collection is maintained. Needless to say, as the cost of children's and YA materials rises so does the cost of maintaining a current collection.

Growth of services to special groups, preschoolers, and homeschoolers. Libraries are developing special programs for infants (lap-sit programs), toddlers, preschoolers, primary schoolers, and young adults. These programs also extend to alternative educational programs such as programs for homeschoolers who depend heavily on public libraries to act as their "school" library. Homeschooling groups can be quite demanding on public libraries and a careful balance must be struck to ensure that children's collections represent all of the needs of the community. Children's librarians are also providing training and resources to caregivers or parents who then can better employ library resources to the benefit of their children. Ultimately, libraries must devote considerable energy to developing a wide array of programs throughout the year and throughout the day and evening to accommodate the heterogeneous nature of our society.

Underlying the public library's attention to the youngest of children is the concept of "emergent literacy." Traditionally, studies of the ability to read focused on children in the early years of schooling. It is now understood that a child's development of reading skills is affected by experiences from birth onward. The ability to read has its origins in the child's early nonverbal and verbal interactions with others and the environment. Early experiences with language and books build a foundation on which literacy skills are built (Stratton 1996). Early engagement with informal literacy activities, even simple observation of such activities, can have substantial effects on the development of reading skills. Justice and Kaderavek (2002) note that emergent literacy skills are acquired by some at a different rate than others, and some patterns of acquisition and nonacquisition are disturbing. As might be expected, individuals with disabilities related to autism or other mental impairments are delayed in acquiring emergent literacy skills. Other individuals at risk of delayed emergent literacy skills are children in poverty, those with limited English proficiency, or those who have limited early access to literacy materials. The implications for public (and school) libraries are obvious. Byrne, Deerr, and Kropp (2003) recommend four critical services for public libraries to develop emergent literacy skills. These are "age-appropriate spaces, materials, programming, and the opportunity for parents to gain skills through modelling" (p. 42). Obviously, the programming for those at such an early age requires the cooperation and often the presence of a parent or caregiver and includes collection of materials that reflect the interests of children from 1 to 3 years of age. It is also critical that the librarian model behavior that promotes the interaction of the children with the activity. The librarian must encourage parents to read to their children at home and incorporate play in learning activities, including reciting and singing nursery rhymes. The focus of public libraries on emergent literacy is simply another example of how libraries' programming has followed important research to serve its current and potential users of any age.

The growth of electronic materials for children. In addition to the proliferation of materials, there is a marked increase in the variety of formats being developed for children and young adults. Most notable are developments in electronic information technologies including DVDs. Of course, computers have become an everyday part of children's experience, and the Web now provides a vast array of information for young people, including electronic encyclopedias and other reference materials. Web access, of course, creates completely new challenges of identifying the best Web sites and making them known and available to children, parents, and teachers.

Outreach. The changing family structure has challenged libraries to consider moving outside the four walls of their buildings to provide alternative library services. For example, with the increasing number of families in which both parents work, there has been a proliferation of daycare and preschool programs. This is an opportunity for children's and YA librarians to network with outside agencies: schools, Head Start programs, daycare centers, and other agencies that work with young people. Some public libraries are sending their library professionals into these establishments to provide programs that were traditionally provided only at the library. Similarly, some libraries are preparing predesigned kits of print and AV materials that can be borrowed by various agencies serving children at remote sites, and they are preparing lists of appropriate Web sites for their use. No doubt, this type of outreach is vitally important, but it is also costly in terms of personnel and time. Nonetheless, children's need for library materials is critical. If children cannot come to the library, then librarians have made a commitment to take materials and services to them.

Intellectual freedom. The issues of censorship and intellectual freedom are always at the forefront of library services to children and young adults, and the problem has been exacerbated by the increasing use of electronic networks, especially the Web. Indeed, with the passage of the Children's Internet Protection Act (see Chapter 4), children's and YA librarians face new challenges to abide by the law and protect the information access rights of the young. This challenge will also be discussed further below in the section on School Library Media Centers. It should be kept in mind, however, that in terms of intellectual freedom, the public library differs fundamentally from the school library media center in at least two important ways:

(1) Public libraries do not serve in loco parentis, that is, in the place of the parent. As a consequence, they have more freedom in the dissemination of materials to young people. By the same token, parents and some political groups are putting considerable pressure on public libraries to act as monitors and censors.

(2) Public libraries contain materials primarily published or produced for adults. School library media centers seldom have adult materials, except those for teachers, on their shelves. Given ALA policy on open access to public library materials, there is considerable concern about children's reading, viewing, or hearing material that has been prepared for adults. The intensity of this issue is likely to increase, not only because of the increasingly graphic nature of violence and sexual activity in visual and audio materials, but also because access has been expanded even more through the availability of the Internet in public libraries. The political and legal tensions that are sure to arise will require ever more vigilance on the part of librarians to protect the rights of minors to library materials. To some extent, ALA has tried to accommodate the concerns of parents and other adults by establishing a Web site that links to over 700 educational and recreational sites for parents and their children ("ALA Launches Web Site" 1998).

Public library–school library media center cooperation. As the challenges of providing library service to diverse communities and family structures continue, cooperation between public libraries and schools becomes even more important. Cooperative programs can include class visits by school librarians, extended loans to teachers, provision of information on Web resources for teachers, coordination of curricular units with available public library materials, provision of library instruction and library tours to students by public librarians, and participation of public and school librarians on joint education-related committees. Despite the obvious advantages of school–public library cooperation, there are also factors that tend to inhibit cooperation:

1. Because schools and public libraries are often separate political subdivisions, a concerted effort must be made to promote cooperation.
2. There is little or no administrative or board support for cooperation.
3. Schools (classrooms and libraries) and public libraries tend to be understaffed; teachers and librarians focus their time and attention primarily on the duties within their own institutions.
4. Limited fiscal resources reduce the time and staffing available for cooperation.
5. Public librarians are sometimes wary that their cooperation is really being used as an inappropriate subsidy of the school budget. That is, the public library budget is being used to support services that should be provided by the school budget.
6. There is insufficient expertise to develop effective cooperation.

Perhaps the ultimate in public library–school library media center cooperation is the "combined school-public library facility." In an age when citizens want their public institutions to cooperate and to maximize fiscal efficiencies, combining libraries is, at least on the surface, attractive. Certainly there are examples of successful combinations, and there are significant advantages to students who, in one place, have librarians trained to assist them, and a collection that is usually much larger than the traditional school library collection. On the other hand, a variety of issues are matters of concern. These issues include:

- Who will manage the library?
- How will use of the facility be determined?
- How are complaints handled?
- How can parking be assured to public library patrons?
- Who determines policies related to materials access?
- How are costs allocated?
- Who is expected to perform cataloging and processing functions?
- What are the legal liabilities of a joint use facility?
- Do students and teacher retain priority access at certain times of day?
- Are there two separate staffs?
- Do school regulations for behavior apply?
- How will staff problems be handled if the school district is unionized but the library staff is not?
- Will fines and fees be different for students and teachers from those for regular patrons?
- How will conflicts between school library and public library staff members be handled? (Owens 2002; J. Casey 2002; Blount 2002)

Despite these problems, the advantages of shared resources, expanded hours, increased economies, shared technologies, shared expertise, and potential community approbation make this a tempting alternative.

School Library Media Centers

The American Association of School Librarians (AASL) and the Association of Educational and Communication Technology (AECT) define school library media centers in the following way:

> A school library media center is defined as an organized collection of printed and/or audiovisual and/or computer resources which (a) is administered as a unit, (b) is located in a designed place or places, (c) makes resources and services accessible and available to students, teachers, and administrators. (Ingersoll and Han 1994, p. 8)

In a general sense, the school library media center has one central function—to support the curriculum of the school. The fiscal and human resources are directed to this end. There are many secondary, albeit important, functions that the school library media center performs as well. It stimulates the imagination of young people, it promotes critical thinking, it exposes young people to diverse points of view on important topics, it provides exposure to the cultural differences that exist in the world, and it provides some entertaining diversions as well.

School library media centers are imbedded in much larger organizations. On one level, although there may be a school librarian who exercises immediate control, ultimate control and supervision of the library is the concern of the school's principal. Alternatively, school library media centers may be governed by a special administrator in charge of curriculum for the entire school system, who may be responsible for selection or approval of materials for all of the schools' library media centers. Finally, because school library media centers exist as part of the entire school system, they are governed by a school board, whose administrative powers are delegated to a school administration. This administration often consists of a superintendent and assistants. Although these individuals seldom get involved in direct supervision or control, they often become involved when there are complaints about materials.

The school library media centers in the United States have nineteenth-century origins, but there were actually very few of them until the twentieth century. Their development was accelerated in the twentieth century by many factors. In the 1920s impetus for school library media centers grew because of the development of regional accrediting agencies, which promoted the need for trained librarians (Woolls 1994). At this time, the National Education Association's (NEA's) Committee on Library Organization and Equipment published the first standards for junior and senior high schools. In 1925 the NEA created standards for elementary schools. The K–12 standards were published in 1945 (American Library Association [ALA] 1998). In the 1950s another push was given when the Soviet Union launched Sputnik. The successful placing of a satellite in space by the United States's rival created considerable social and political upheaval as Americans feared they would soon be militarily inferior to their adversary. The space race thus gave a strategic significance to efforts to improve the American educational system. One of the results was substantial increases in federal funding for elementary and secondary education, especially to improve curricula and the training of teachers. It was a logical extension to provide money to expand the library collections of these schools.

Expansion of school library media center collections began in the 1960s, and additional standards were promulgated in 1960 and 1969 to reflect the library's increasing sophistication. This decade saw the development of strong political support. The political support was expressed primarily through the passage of the Elementary and Secondary Education Act (ESEA) in 1965, which provided federal support to purchase materials for schools and libraries (see Chapter 4) and resulted in a tremendous expansion of school library media center collections. The growth of school library collections and the variety of formats collected, including AV materials, led to the creation of new standards in 1975, emphasizing the importance of a strong media collection (Brodie 1998).

Today, the mission of the school library media center reflects a dynamic and broad perspective of the role of the librarian and the library. These roles have been expressed by AASL, a division of ALA, in its work *Information Power* (ALA 1998). First published in 1988, and revised in 1998, *Information Power* shifts the focus of traditional school library practice from building and managing collections to developing students as lifelong learners. It also creates the first nationally published information literacy standards (Brodie 1998). The philosophy underlying *Information Power* is that the primary mission of the school library media center is "to ensure that students and staff are effective users of ideas and information" (ALA 1998, p. 6). This mission is accomplished in three ways: "by providing intellectual and physical access to materials in all formats; by providing instruction to foster competence and stimulate interest in reading, viewing, and using information and ideas; [and] by working with other educators to design learning strategies to meet the needs of individual students" (ALA 1998, p. 6). In turn, the role of the library media specialist is four-fold: (1) to serve as a teacher, collaborating with students and teachers to evaluate the learning and information needs of all; to instruct students and assist in curriculum development; (2) to serve as an instructional partner, developing policies and curricula that improve the information literacy skills of students and collaborating with teachers to design meaningful learning activities that involve the development of information skills; (3) to serve as an information specialist by evaluating, acquiring, and making available information resources and by modeling strategies for effective information seeking; and (4) to serve as a program administrator, helping to create and implement policies for the library media center, manage library staff, and serve as an advocate for the program (ALA 1998). Eisenberg (2002) has concisely summarized the school library media specialist's role in the following way:

> School librarians *teach* meaningful information and technology skills that can be fully integrated with the regular classroom curriculum. They *advocate* reading through guiding and promoting it. And they *manage* information services, technologies, resources and facilities. (p. 47)

In 2002 it was estimated that there were more than 94,000 school library media centers located in 95 percent of the public schools and 86 percent of the private schools. The size of the workforce in these libraries is considerable. More than 66,000 librarians and 99,000 support staff work in school library media centers alone (ALA 2002). But the picture is not entirely bright. For example, a quarter of all schools have no school librarian. In addition, the average age of a librarian is 45, with 50 percent planning to retire in the next 12 years. In schools, there is only one school librarian for every 953 students (Minkel 2003). The potential shortage of school library media specialists could have significant and unfortunate consequences.

In addition, the contemporary school library media center faces many challenges. *School Library Journal* identifies annually some of these issues in their "Biggest Challenges" column. It is revealing simply to identify the challenges for 2002 and 2003 (Ishizuka, Minkel, and St. Lifer 2002; Whelan 2003). These include the following: gaining the respect of school administrators, making information literacy matter, satisfying the growing demand for librarians, riding out fiscal uncertainty, managing the filtering challenge, partnering with the principal, staying on top of technology, managing time effectively, recruiting qualified librarians, getting behind literacy efforts, and taking an advocacy stance. Reviewing these topics reveals important themes: communication and advocacy to administrators, meeting the need for new librarians, dealing with technology (including the Web), coping with budget problems, promoting information literacy, and managing time. Below is a more detailed discussion of some of the critical issues facing school library media centers:

ENSURING THAT THE LIBRARY PLAYS AN INTEGRAL ROLE IN THE FUNCTION OF THE SCHOOL

Central to the philosophy of *Information Power* is the idea that the librarian and library be perceived as a central feature of the school and that the librarian be seen as a collaborator in developing effective learning strategies. If school library media centers are to thrive in the future, they must be recognized for their importance to the function of the school. Too often, the library is considered an expensive appendage to the educational process rather than an integral part. This viewpoint is especially ironic, given the evidence of the relationship of school library media centers to academic achievement. Lance, Welborn, and Hamilton-Pennell (1993) found that students who score higher on norm-referenced tests tend to come from schools with larger library staff and larger school library media collections. In addition, high academic performance of students was also correlated with school library media centers in which librarians served in an instructional and collaborative role. The size of the library staff and the collection were the best predictors of academic performance, with the exception of the presence of at-risk conditions, such as poverty. These findings have been consistently supported in additional studies (Lance, Rodney, Hamilton-Pennell 2000). This research highlights the fact that school librarians need to communicate clearly and cooperate closely with teachers, principals, and administrators. By demonstrating the importance of the library and its ability to contribute to the school's mission, greater political and fiscal support is more likely to follow. Fortunately, there is some evidence that library media specialists are having an impact. Lau (2002) reports that in a survey conducted by *School Library Journal*, 66 percent of the school librarians responded that their principals are very supportive of library collaborations with teachers, 46 percent of the librarians teach classes, 95 percent instruct students on how to use print and online resources, and 30 percent recommend and evaluate vendors for potential classroom textbook purchases. Ninety percent reported that they are satisfied with their jobs and the amount of respect they receive.

DEALING WITH THE INCREASES IN TECHNOLOGY

Schools have devoted considerable resources to educational technologies. In many ways they are leaders in this area. They have incorporated television as a part of classroom teaching for years. To this they have added laser discs, videocassettes, CD-ROMs, DVDs, and computers. Of course, the impact of access to the Internet has been dramatic and rapid. The number of public school classrooms with access to the Internet increased from 77,853 in 1995 to 81,066 in 2001. In addition, the proportion of elementary and secondary school students using computers at school rose from 70 percent in 1997 to 84 percent in 2001 (*Digest of Education Statistics 2002*). As technologies and technological use increase, the school library media center will have to respond in kind, meeting increasing demands in terms of costs, staffing, training, equipment, and physical facilities. In addition, as students increasingly view the Web as the most common channel to get information, librarians play a special role in identifying the many resources that are available in the Web environment, and in training and educating both students and teachers on how to locate and evaluate Web sites. Similarly, librarians must be able to organize Web sites for local access.

THE IMPORTANCE OF INFORMATION LITERACY

With the increasing use of technologies in the classroom and the media center, it is clear that students need to be well educated on how to locate and evaluate information. The underlying rationale for this education, however, has been broadened in recent years. The purpose is not only to develop these skills so that students can be more proficient academically, but also as lifelong learners. As the American Association of School Librarians has noted in its latest version of *Information Power* (ALA 1998):

> Central to this new context is the idea of the "learning community."
> This phrase suggests that all of us—students, teachers, administrators,
> and parents as well as our local, regional, state, national, and international communities—are interconnected in a lifelong quest to understand and meet our constantly changing information needs. (p. 2)

Such a perspective places information acquisition, dissemination, and use in the broader context of social responsibility. It is not enough to be a good locater and evaluator of information; it is the responsibility of all to continue to learn and to contribute what we have learned to our society in a beneficial manner. As a consequence, ALA (1998) has created nine information literacy standards which all students should meet. These standards not only involve how to access, evaluate, and use information, but also define what it means to be an independent, lifelong learner, and what responsibilities we have to contribute to the learning community in a responsible manner. The standards are as follows:

Standard 1: The student who is information literate accesses information efficiently and effectively.

Standard 2: The student who is information literate evaluates information critically and competently.

Standard 3: The student who is information literate uses information accurately and creatively.

Standard 4: The student who is an independent learner is information literate and pursues information related to personal interests.

Standard 5: The student who is an independent learner is information literate and appreciates literature and other creative expressions of information.

Standard 6: The student who is an independent learner is information literate and strives for excellence in information seeking and knowledge generation.

Standard 7: The student who contributes positively to the learning community and to society is information literate and recognizes the importance of information to a democratic society.

Standard 8: The student who contributes positively to the learning community and to society is information literate and practices ethical behavior in regard to information and information technology.

Standard 9: The student who contributes positively to the learning community and to society is information literate and participates effectively in groups to pursue and generate information. (pp. 8–9)

DEALING WITH DECLINING FUNDS IN SCHOOLS

There is little doubt that some citizens have limited confidence in their school systems. This, coupled with a general feeling among taxpayers that they have been taxed enough, has led to a resistance to increasing their tax burden for the public schools. The damage to schools from this trend is magnified by the need for additional monies to accommodate the rapid changes in learning technologies and the proliferation of excellent print materials published today for young people. Some urban school districts have been hit particularly hard. Because schools are undergoing financial strains, there is an understandable temptation to place existing resources directly into teaching along with classroom materials and activities. Such a reallocation merely increases the drain on dwindling school library media center financial resources and diminishes the opportunity for the libraries to assist teachers effectively in the learning process.

ADDRESSING THE SHORTAGE OF CERTIFIED LIBRARY MEDIA SPECIALISTS

For some years, it has become clear that the labor force of librarians, including those working in schools, is aging. Everhart (2002) reports that in the next 12 years, approximately 68 percent of school librarians will leave their profession. Already, this trend has resulted in a severe shortage of certified media specialists nationwide. A recent survey has suggested that the number of states experiencing severe shortages has risen from 12 states in 2000 to 30 in 2002. Previously these shortages appeared to concentrate in inner cities and rural areas, but now the problem has spread to suburban areas as well (Everhart 2002). The American Library Association is now actively developing strategies to assist in the recruitment of certified media specialists, and schools of library and information science are beginning to respond by offering more school library media programs, some using online and interactive video delivery systems. In addition, the Institute for Museum and Library Services is developing initiatives to help alleviate the shortage. If professional programs are unable to respond quickly to this pressing need, more and more individuals without the necessary training will be hired—and school systems are already tempted to replace certified media specialists with paraprofessionals to meet fiscal demands. The resulting loss in quality and vitality of the media center would be a disturbing result.

DEALING WITH CENSORSHIP OF LIBRARY MATERIALS

There are few issues in librarianship that generate so much heat and so little light as censorship. Schools have traditionally been vulnerable to censorship attempts, especially because they are supposed to serve *in loco parentis*. The general issue of censorship is dealt with in Chapter 5, but schools represent, in some sense, a unique situation. Among the crucial issues that define school censorship problems are (1) the differing views of the function of schools and school library media centers and (2) the rights and powers of school boards versus the rights of students and parents. These issues have been battled out in years of court cases, many of which have resulted in unclear or contradictory conclusions. This judicial ambivalence was highlighted in one of the most important school library media center cases, which reached the United States Supreme Court. This case is now referred to as the "Island Trees" case, or "Pico," named after Stephen Pico, the student who filed the complaint (Board of Education 1982). The purpose here is not to review in detail this particular case, or the legal issues per se, but to discuss briefly some of the fundamental issues raised by the legal and philosophical arguments found in the various cases.

The functions of schools and school library media centers. Defining the functions of schools can have profound consequences on how one perceives the functions of school library media centers. There are at least two fundamentally differing accounts. One can view the schools as a place to inculcate the values of the local community—the majority values. Such a view perceives the school as an instrument of particular values. Children, in this sense, are perceived as highly vulnerable to outside influences and need protection until they are old enough to know that these influences are problematic. Such a view is, in itself, not wholly unreasonable. It seems obvious that children do need protection from physical abuse, and some might argue that this is easily extended to intellectual harm as well. The purpose of schools is to inculcate the students with specific orthodox attitudes as well as basic knowledge. Exposure to unorthodox points of view would be undertaken only under conditions in which substantial control is exercised to ensure that the views are not mistakenly understood as acceptable or reasonable alternatives. From this perspective, the school library media center represents a potential problem. Most obvious is that the school library media center has traditionally been a place of voluntary attendance, where the materials are voluntarily selected by the student. Some guidance may be involved, but as a rule, there is considerably less guidance and control over exposure and interpretation of materials in the library than in the classroom. If the inculcation of values is to be effected, one function of the librarian or library worker would be to monitor each student's selections. In many cases, this is a practical impossibility. The alternative is that the library exercises very careful and restrictive selection of materials and, most likely, restrictive access to materials for some, usually younger, children.

The second perspective is to view the school as a place where students are exposed to a wide variety of points of view. The function of the school is to familiarize students with many perspectives, emphasize critical thinking skills and judgment-making skills. It is not the school's place, however, to assert a particular perspective or attempt to inculcate the specific values of the local or majority community. It attempts to prepare students to discriminate among ideas so they can make future judgments on important issues in which there are many differing opinions. The school library media center in this setting would likely function quite differently. The library collection would likely contain many perspectives, some unorthodox as well as orthodox, and the librarian's function would be less supervisory and controlling. Access would tend to be unrestricted.

These two perspectives have been painted here as polar opposites, although there are certainly many gradations that reflect the realities of school library media centers. All schools educate about values, and all try to get students to think, more or less. But how one perceives a school's primary purpose is likely to affect one's attitude seriously when one hears that a book on suicide, one by a revolutionary, or books that contain explicit language about sex are part of the library collection. Those who subscribe to the former view are much more likely to restrict or control materials.

Similarly, even in schools in which the indoctrination of local or majority values is paramount, a more subtle distinction might be made regarding its school library media center. One can perceive, for example, that the function of the classroom is different from the function of the school library media center. One can argue that the classroom is the place where values are communicated and still believe that the school library media center's purpose is different, a place for exposure to a wide array of ideas, even those that are unorthodox. In this sense, the concept of the library carries with it the supposition that it is a special forum—a place where many different, even controversial and subversive, ideas may coexist. In this way, a distinction between classroom purposes and library purposes is possible. Obviously, if one perceives the library as a special forum for ideas, the library collection would predictably be more catholic in perspective, no matter what the defined purpose of the classroom.

The rights of school boards and students (and parents?). Censorship problems in schools also arise from the friction created by the conflicting authority of the school board and the rights of young people. Traditionally, school boards have exercised considerable legal authority and power in the United States. Generally, education falls primarily within the province of the states. States have delegated the authority to local school boards which have been given broad authority to run their school systems, including the selection of teachers, curricular materials, and materials for the school library media center. There is little doubt that school boards are responsible for school library media centers, but it is seldom their central focus. From time to time, school boards are surprised to discover that some of the materials on the school library media center shelf are not to their liking or the liking of parents. Problems usually arise when parents file objections to materials their children have selected from the school library media center. But objections also arise from principals, teachers, students, and school board members themselves. When challenges occur there is a tendency in many cases to restrict or withdraw the material, especially when there are no formal policies for selection and reconsideration of these materials.

The actions of school boards to remove or restrict materials may often go unchallenged. Although the rights of young people may be limited, the courts have recognized that students do not give up First Amendment rights and due-process rights just because they are in school. This highlights the delicate balance that must be struck in schools concerning the rights of school boards to run their schools as they see fit and the individual rights of citizens, including young people, to First Amendment and due-process protection. The balance is dynamic. As one court decision noted:

> A library is a storehouse of knowledge. When created for a public school it is an important privilege created by the state for the benefit of the students in the school. That privilege is not subject to being withdrawn by succeeding school boards whose members might desire to "winnow" the library for books the content of which occasioned their displeasure or disapproval. (*Minarcini v Strongsville City School District* 1977)

Similarly, in the *Island Trees* case, the Supreme Court noted that the school board members "possess significant discretion to determine the content of their school libraries" (Board of Education 1982, p. B3922). But the court also noted that the school board cannot exercise its discretion in a "narrowly partisan or political manner" (Board of Education, p. B3922). If the school board intended to deprive students of access to ideas just because the board didn't like those ideas, then the board was violating the constitutional rights of the students. Interestingly, the Supreme Court left open the possibility that the school board could remove materials that were "pervasively vulgar" or were educationally unsuitable, especially if the board followed a well-structured procedure to review and evaluate those materials.

The lack of clarity regarding the legal rights of boards, the place of the school library media center, and the rights of students literally ensures that more problems await on the horizon. The problem will be magnified as the library media center collections expand to include resources on the Internet. There is certainly plenty of dissent in our society regarding what is suitable material for young people, and the school library media center will remain a lightning rod of political controversy in this arena.

Academic Libraries

The academic library has been extant in the United States since the seventeenth century, beginning with the library at Harvard. There were nine colonial colleges with libraries by 1792, though the collections were quite small (Jones 1989). The model of classical learning in vogue at that time emphasized theology and required little "library" study. Well into the nineteenth century, the collections were too small to have a separate structure for the library, and the library collection was not emphasized in academic instruction. Often, professors, academic departments, and college debating societies maintained their own collections, which were superior to that of the academic library (Jones 1989). It wasn't until the latter half of the nineteenth century that academic libraries as we know them began to prosper. Their emergence was a result of a change in academic orientation, away from the classical model of education that emphasized religion, rhetoric, and the classics, and toward professional, technical and scientific, and social scientific education. This change was heavily influenced by European trends of industrialization and the promotion of the German model of the university, which identified research as a central role of the university. In the United States, its premier exponent was Johns Hopkins University, which set a model for other universities. As American higher education adapted to this model, the role of the library grew in status. It was a logical place to centralize research collections and provide a place for consultation of these materials. Over the years, support for developing academic libraries has come from outside as well as from within academic institutions, including the American Library Association and its division the Association of College and Research Libraries, the Association of Research Libraries, and the federal government. The result has been the significant growth of academic library collections, the creation of separate library buildings, and increased staffing of these facilities. Today, the academic library plays a vital role in curricular support, teaching, research, publication, and self-education.

The term "academic" library is a generic one applying to many different varieties of institutions. Overall, a library is an academic one if it serves an educational institution providing a curriculum beyond the primary or secondary level. This would include universities, four-year colleges, and community and junior colleges. As with school library media centers, the academic library is embedded in a larger bureaucracy. Usually, the library is headed by a director or dean who reports directly to a higher level academic administrator. The academic library does not have an independent purpose; its functions are directly related to the function of the larger academic institution. In a general sense, its purpose is to serve the students and faculty of the academic community, and to a lesser extent the administration and staff of the institution and the greater academic community that exists nationally and internationally. In addition, the academic library may provide some service to the local community by way of making materials available to local citizens.

The type and sophistication of materials in the library collection will reflect the mission of the academic institution. Areas of emphasis usually revolve around two aspects: teaching (curriculum support) and research (publication). Various types of academic libraries tend to emphasize different aspects of academic life. Major university libraries, for example, tend to emphasize research and graduate programs. The collections include many current research journals, special collections, rare materials, dissertations, and theses as well as general monographs. The general curricula are still supported, but much of the library's financial resources will be devoted to research materials for faculty and graduate work. This may also be true for some four-year liberal arts colleges, but less so. For the most part, the liberal arts college tends to deemphasize graduate programs and emphasizes a well-rounded education to undergraduates. Hence the collection is primarily for curricular support. Insofar as the college expects research and publication from its faculty, the library will be expected to provide a supporting collection, but focus is likely to fall in the teaching area. Community and junior colleges devote almost all of their energies to teaching and continuing education in the community, and their collections and services reflect this emphasis.

Outsell (2003a) has observed a variety of trends that are shaping academic libraries today. Among them are that academic libraries are reporting to higher levels of administrative authority, suggesting increasing influence at the administrative level; the mission of academic libraries is broadening and becoming more global; academic libraries are fostering more "self-service" models and personalized services; budgets are flat and staffing on the decline; and there is a slow transition to the digital library environment somewhat impaired by lack of good archiving techniques for digital data.

Academic libraries, like school libraries, face a variety of challenges and issues. Albanese (2003) identified seven: (1) recruitment, education, and retention of librarians; (2) the role of the library in academic enterprise; (3) impact of information technology on library services; (4) creation, control, and preservation of digital resources; (5) chaos in scholarly communications; (6) support of new users; and (7) higher education funding. A more detailed discussion of some of these and other issues facing academic libraries is below.

PRESERVATION/CONSERVATION

A far-reaching problem that academic libraries face is the serious deterioration of their library collections and inadequate resources to preserve them. Academic libraries are particularly vulnerable because they retain their collections for long periods of time so that they may be consulted when needed. Preservation and conservation are two closely related but distinct concepts. Although definitions differ, Cloonan (2001) notes that today conservation usually refers to the "physical treatment of individual library materials, while preservation refers to the care of library materials in the aggregate (for example, by monitoring environmental conditions)" (p. 232).

There are many sources of the preservation problem facing academic libraries, but the primary one is acid paper. The acidity introduced in the paper-making process is self-destructive. The result is that over a period of years, the acidity in the paper dries the paper until it is brittle. Once brittle, simply touching or turning the pages can lead to the paper's crumbling. Because most books and other print materials have been printed on acid paper since the 1860s, the magnitude of the brittle book problem in research libraries is immense. The Council of Library Resources has estimated that there are more than 75 million brittle books in American research libraries alone, and to preserve just 3 million of them would cost over $200 million (Byrnes 1992). The simple fact is that there are few dollars to expend in this area when money must be diverted to collect the ever-expanding amounts of new knowledge available in new formats. The problem is exacerbated by a variety of other factors as well. These include improper use of materials by patrons and staff, improper heating and air conditioning, improper lighting, poor plumbing, fire hazards, insects, poor security to prevent theft and mutilation, and the lack of a disaster plan when and if flood or fire arise. In response, libraries develop preservation programs that include using proper storage facilities, devising collection development plans that recognize the need to purchase and treat materials from a preservation perspective, implementing effective environmental controls, using reformatting and migrating techniques for materials that are physically deteriorating, creating disaster recovery plans, physically treating materials in need of repair and restoration, and providing staff and user education (Cloonan 2001).

Despite these efforts, Smith (1999) has warned that "two things can be said definitively about future library collections: not all recorded information will survive, and we will never be able to predict accurately which information will be in demand by scholars in the future" (p. 4). On the national level, Smith identifies four basic questions that must be addressed:

1. How do we document the information to be saved, on what medium, and using what standards?

2. How do we record the fact that a title has been preserved?
3. What should be preserved?
4. Who should be responsible for accomplishing the preservation? (p. 9)

Information stored in the new electronic formats brings additional changes in the area of preservation that were totally unanticipated in the early 1990s. Digital data have tremendous flexibility; they can be easily manipulated, updated, and altered. This flexibility, however, is a double-edged sword: what can be easily altered may be difficult to preserve in its original form. The impermanence of digital data presents a variety of challenges for preservationists. Among them are the following:

1. There is lack of durability of some electronic formats. Hard drives and disks are vulnerable to many problems. Compared to some new media, the print form has been a highly stable format overall. Acid-free paper can last for hundreds of years; even many acid papers can last for decades.
2. The digital world presents different challenges from the analog (physical items) world. It is very difficult to determine which is the *original* item and which is the copy. Also, it is difficult to determine authenticity (i.e., has the item been altered or manipulated electronically?).
3. Electronic data have a tendency to deteriorate over time. Information stored in electronic formats must, therefore, be monitored and periodically refreshed or transferred onto new storage devices lest the integrity of the data be lost.
4. Electronic formats quickly can become obsolete. Continuous innovations in information technologies will likely produce new storage formats. As the hardware changes, how do we deal with the previous formats?
5. Similarly, when preserving digital data, it is critical that the mechanisms to read the data are also preserved. (Cloonan 1993, 2001)

As a result of these serious problems, major universities and the federal government have increased their efforts to preserve materials. The strategies that have been developed include digitizing significant collections at the Library of Congress. Emphasis has been on preserving important research collections, but there have also been cooperative preservation efforts among smaller academic libraries. It must be noted, however, that digitization projects are at this time more *access* initiatives than they are preservation initiatives. Because digital data are neither fixed nor permanent, they will have to be constantly refreshed to be preserved. In fact, Smith (1999) has noted ironically that providing greater access to collections through digitization often increases demand for the original items, thus increasing the chance of deterioration of the original through greater use. Similarly, Cloonan (2001) has expressed concern that attention to digitization projects may, in fact, divert attention from important preservation initiatives.

THE GROWTH OF AGGREGATED FULL-TEXT DATABASES

As more and more information, periodicals, and books are digitized, academic libraries have struggled to choose those databases that are most productive for their libraries. The last few years have seen a significant growth in the popularity of full-text aggregated databases, such as EBSCO, Proquest, and LexisNexis. Librarians find these aggregated databases serve them well both academically and economically, and in general, they are popular with students. The amount of information contained in these databases is great and a cost advantage often arises because the purchases are made collectively; in many cases prices are negotiated by state consortia. Such databases also are particularly amenable to the current trend in distributed education. As more and more students take their courses online, the library needs to supply these resources electronically, especially to students who do not have access to research libraries in their location (Albanese 2001). Of course, such databases generally do not contain historical periodicals or documents. As a consequence, they provide only part of what is needed in the scholarly environment. Nonetheless, the introduction of electronic information access is creating a revolution in the academic library environment. In some cases, remote access may well have resulted in a drop in in-house library use. For example, among ARL libraries, the number of reference transactions has dropped an average of 2.7 percent per year since 1991 and in-house use of library materials has dropped an average of 3.8 percent per year over the same period. The decline, however, has actually been sharper as the higher number of reference transactions actually occurred in 1997, and the highest in-house use in 1995 (Association of Research Libraries [ARL] 2003a). Despite concerns about the impact of the electronic information environment, it also provides many opportunities for librarians to emphasize their information-seeking skills in the chaotic world of the Web and to make the academic library a portal for all types of information. There is certainly no doubt that the growth of electronic resources and access is substantially changing the academic library environment. As noted by the Association of Research Libraries (2003a):

The World Wide Web has revolutionized the way libraries are delivering services, enabling them to offer more value ranging from remote access to online catalogs, indexing and abstracting tools, and full-text resources delivered at the user's desktop. The delivery of new and innovative services through digitization projects and distance learning technologies is transforming the brick-and-mortar library model to a virtual model. We are still in the early stages of a long transition period where a hybrid model will reign. (p. 19)

What will happen at the end of that "long transition period" remains to be seen.

INCREASING COSTS OF PERIODICALS AND OTHER MATERIALS

Academic libraries rely heavily on periodicals to support their research and teaching. Journals often provide some of the most current information on a topic, especially when compared to books. Researchers rely heavily on periodicals in their field to maintain their currency in their areas of expertise. The Association of Research Libraries estimates that research libraries now serve 10 percent more students and 16 percent more faculty than they did in 1986. Yet print serials budgets are shrinking. One survey suggests that the percentage spent on print serials is expected to drop from 43 percent to 35 percent in a three-year period; monographs from 38 percent to 31 percent. Although part of the problem is the ever-increasing costs of periodicals, there is also expected to be increased expenditures for e-serials (Albanese 2001).

Although the full-text aggregated databases have been of help in controlling costs, substantial numbers of periodicals are still purchased as separate items. Unfortunately, the cost of such periodicals has risen significantly in the last decade, and, generally much faster than the cost of books. For example, the cost increase for periodicals and serials averaged 8.6 percent and 5.8 percent in 2001, respectively, while academic books rose only 0.4 percent in the same year. The situation is exacerbated because academic institutions often have substantial science and technology programs, and it is in this area that inflation has been the worst. Medical periodicals, for example, have increased 19 percent in cost since 2000 (*Bowker Annual* 2003). Foreign publications are also a special problem. Unlike most public and school library media centers, academic libraries often require a substantial collection of materials published from foreign countries. Foreign currency fluctuations alone can create substantial fluctuations in the costs of materials, and the conversion of many European countries to the euro has introduced additional complications in tracking real costs. Constant vigilance concerning foreign publishers is required.

The effects of these financial pressures are troubling. The Association of Research Libraries reports that declines in the purchases of serials and monographs have been occurring since 1986, and, coupled with increasing prices for these works, the overall purchasing power of research libraries has declined substantially. In fact, the price of serials has risen an annual average of 7.7 percent since 1986. This trend, combined with annual average increases of 6.7 percent for library materials in general, 3.1 percent for monographs, and 4.7 percent for salaries, places research libraries in considerable fiscal jeopardy (ARL 2003a). In 2004 even the most prestigious of universities, such as Harvard University, Cornell University, and the University of California have announced large cuts in their serials budgets to deal with diminishing budgets ("Harvard, Cornell Slash Journal Subscriptions" 2004). Although some of these fiscal challenges are mitigated by online access, especially to periodicals, it is clear that considerable pressures on academic libraries remain.

DECLINING BUDGETS

Most academic institutions are constantly struggling for fiscal security. These struggles are acute in public institutions where the political climate for taxation is generally negative. Given the inflationary pressures and increasing costs of operation of academic institutions, the decline in fiscal support often leads to cuts in expenditures. In this climate, academic institutions compete with other public agencies, such as schools and social service organizations, for these dwindling resources. The problem is similarly acute in private institutions that rely on tuition, donations, and investments to stay financially stable. Regardless of whether the institution is private or public, the academic library must compete with other academic departments and agencies for the few dollars that remain. This comes at an especially unfortunate time because academic libraries are experiencing a need for increased dollars for traditional library resources and for developing information technologies, including the accompanying peripherals for effective operation, for example, ergonomically designed furniture. These many and varied costs place considerable responsibility on the academic library to make the most of its resources.

Information Literacy

As in school library media centers, the role of the academic library and librarian is evolving. The increasing complexity of the information environment, especially in the academic domain, presents both challenges and opportunities to enrich that role. Although the collection management and information access functions of academic libraries remain critical roles, growing emphasis is being placed on the librarian as teacher and guide, whose function is, in part, to develop information skills in students not only for academic purposes, but for lifelong learning. As Owusu-Ansah (2001) has observed, the changing environment calls "for an extended role for academic libraries in the formation of the intellectual aptitude of the student. These libraries must no longer just acquire, organize, disseminate, and preserve information, but they must also instruct in the strategies for retrieving, evaluating, and using information" (p. 285).

Academic librarians have been performing an instructional role for many years, but as the role of the library is increasingly challenged by external access to information from the Web, librarians are recognizing the need to capitalize on the added value they can provide by helping students navigate and effectively exploit the Web.

Consequently, in January 2000 the Association of College and Research Libraries (ACRL) approved five information literacy competency standards for higher education. Each standard is accompanied by specific performance indicators. The five standards are the following:

Standard 1: The information literate student determines the nature and extent of the information needed.

Standard 2: The information literate student accesses needed information effectively and efficiently.

Standard 3: The information literate student evaluates information and its sources critically and incorporates selected information into his or her knowledge base and value system.

Standard 4: The information literate student, individually or as a member of a group, uses information effectively to accomplish a specific purpose.

Standard 5: The information literate student understands many of the economic, legal, and social issues surrounding the use of information and accesses and uses information ethically and legally.

THE CRISIS IN SCHOLARLY PUBLISHING

Academic libraries are facing an unprecedented crisis in their attempt to collect and provide access to scholarly materials at reasonable cost to their academic institutions and users. Although such materials may come in many forms (books, letters, reports, memoranda), the major problems revolve around journals, which often play a central role in scholarly endeavors. A variety of important issues related to scholarly publishing are confronting academic and research libraries. These issues include:

1. Affordable access to scholarly materials is being threatened especially due to the continuing increases in the price of academic journals. This crisis has been developing since the 1980s as the costs of journals, especially scientific ones have far outpaced inflation and library budgets. The price of periodicals has increased 38.5 percent from 1997 to 2001 (*Bowker Annual* 2003), and libraries are spending more and more funds to purchase fewer and fewer titles. Not only are fewer journals being purchased, but the fiscal burden to purchase journals has required that academic libraries shift their resources away from the purchase of books and monographs. The Association of Research Libraries reports that "the typical research library has foregone purchasing 90,000 monographs over the past 15 years" (ARL 2003b).

2. The growth of electronic journals at first may have been seen as a panacea for the high cost of paper and publication, but it has created its own set of problems. As more and more materials become available only electronically, the publisher and vendor of the electronic database maintains control over its content. The result has been a shift from purchasing a physical object owned by the library, to being permitted access usually only through a negotiated license. Consequently, use of material in the database is no longer governed by copyright or fair use, which has permitted generous sharing of scholarly information, but through the license or negotiated contract, which can provide far fewer rights to users than the Copyright Act affords. The growth of e-journals also increases the complexity of archiving and preserving journal information. New methods of storage must be maintained, and decisions regarding who should preserve such materials and for how long may affect the ability of scholars to use such materials in the future.

3. Large journal publishers, especially in the sciences, have been able to dominate the marketplace and make large profits at the expense of aca-

demic and research libraries. Subscription prices of science journals are often in the thousands of dollars, and without significant competition, these price increases are likely to continue. Since these journals are essential for the educational and research function of academic libraries, these libraries have little choice but to transfer their already declining monographic budgets to their serials budgets, with the attendant narrowing of their monographic collections.

4. Major journal publishers are undergoing numerous mergers that reduce competition and result in significant increases in prices. ARL reports that of the "13 major STM [science, technology, and medicine] publishers in 1998, only 7 remained by the end of 2002" (ARL 2003b).

The academic and research community has responded to these problems. One approach is the creation of the Scholarly Publishing and Academic Resources Coalition (SPARC) in June 1998. SPARC is a worldwide alliance of academic institutions, research libraries, and other organizations. Originally an initiative of the Association of Research Libraries, SPARC's intention is to correct the perceived imbalance of power between journal publishers and the scholarly community. This goal would be accomplished by increasing access to scholarly publications through the creation of a more competitive marketplace with lower cost journals publishing high-quality research. In part, this model implies creating noncommercial publishing operations, which could serve as alternative authoritative channels for scientists and technicians to publish their materials, most notably in electronic format. The underlying rationale is that scientists will choose alternatives that could disseminate their findings widely (R. Johnson 2003). In order to encourage new competitors, SPARC maintains an alternative publisher partnership program that works with scientific societies, university publishers, and other organizations to establish alternative journals that attract authors of high reputation. The major focus is on STM (science, technology, and medicine) titles, because these are among the most expensive journals to access, although the organization is also moving into the field of economics. SPARC members assist by subscribing to these new journals to provide fiscal support. SPARC also is engaged in educating the academic community and others about the issues facing academic publishing today.

In addition, in March 2000 many concerned parties, including the Association for Research Libraries, Johns Hopkins University, Indiana University, Pennsylvania State University, and numerous other research and academic institutions, met to discuss the scholarly communication crisis. Concluding that the current system was simply too costly, they produced "Principles for Emerging Systems of Scholarly Publishing." These principles are as follows:

1. The costs to the academy of published research should be contained so that access to relevant research publications for faculty and students can be maintained and even expanded. Members of the university community should collaborate to develop strategies that further this end. Faculty participation is essential to the success of this process.
2. Electronic capabilities should be used, among other things, to provide wide access to scholarship, encourage interdisciplinary research, and enhance interoperability and searchability. Development of common standards will be particularly important in the electronic environment.
3. Scholarly publications must be archived in a secure manner so as to remain permanently available, and, in the case of electronic works, a permanent identifier for citation and linking should be provided.
4. The system of scholarly publication must continue to include processes for evaluating the quality of scholarly work, and every publication should provide the reader with information about evaluation the work has undergone.
5. The academic community embraces the concepts of copyright and fair use and seeks a balance in the interest of owners and users in the digital environment. Universities, colleges, and especially their faculties should manage copyright and its limitations and exceptions in a manner that assures the faculty access to and use of their own published works in their research and teaching.
6. In negotiating publishing agreements, faculty should assign the rights to their work in a manner that promotes the ready use of their work and choose journals that support the goal of making scholarly publications available at reasonable cost.
7. The time from submission to publication should be reduced in a manner consistent with the requirements for quality control.
8. To assure quality and reduce proliferation of publications, the evaluation of faculty should place a greater emphasis on quality of publications and a reduced emphasis on quantity.
9. In electronic as well as print environments, scholars and students should be assured privacy with regard to their use of materials. (Principles for Emerging Systems 2003).

As can be observed from these principles, it is not simply the fiscal issues that are involved; rather, the entire process of evaluating and refereeing works, the preservation of materials, the assignment of publishing rights, and privacy rights in the digital environment are all of concern to scholars and academic institutions. Only through constant vigilance regarding these issues can the rights of scholars and students be balanced against the economic interests of academic publishers.

RECRUITMENT OF ACADEMIC LIBRARIANS

As with many types of libraries, there is considerable concern that there will be an insufficient supply of librarians in the near future. A variety of factors have been identified by the ACRL (2002) to explain this shortage. These include the aging of the librarian workforce, a poor image of the profession, flat or declining numbers of master's graduates in library and information science, relatively low salaries, and competition from other sectors of the economy. ACRL recommends new marketing and media campaign efforts, more promotion of the professional degree by programs in library and information science, as well as more effort to identify and support students who may be interested in academic librarianship, and greater activity related to promotion and partnerships among individual academic institutions. In addition, ACRL is concerned with retention of academic librarians once they have entered the labor force. To this end, the association recommends creating a more stimulating and flexible work environment through job rotation and job sharing, flexible work schedules, and the assignment of more interesting and challenging duties. Needless to say, increases in salary would also be a stimulant for retention. The challenge for academic libraries is considerable. There is little reason for optimism regarding substantial increases in salaries, but in the last several years academic librarians have recognized the seriousness of the projected dearth of professionals and are taking new and concerted efforts to reverse the trend.

THE INFORMATION COMMONS

University teaching strategies continue to evolve, especially as technology has transformed the learning environment. Among the notable changes have been a greater emphasis on active learning, cooperative or collaborative learning among students, and group study. Some academic libraries have attempted to reassess how they deliver their service in light of these changes in pedagogy. One adaptation is the creation of the "information commons" (IC). In general, an information commons is a single physical space which has been configured to offer a variety of library services, usually emphasizing digital resources. Within such a space are computer workstations (including multimedia workstations) for students, with access to the Internet and local databases, the online catalog, and software to prepare assignments. In addition, reference materials, reference staff, and computing staff are available for consultation and support. Additional academic support for tutoring and writing may be available, and spaces for group work are provided.

Obviously, the creation of an IC requires careful planning, significant resources, and adequate staffing, training, and funding. It also requires a productive liaison with faculty whose assignments and attitude toward the commons must encourage its use (MacWhinnie 2003). Will the IC improve the ability of academic libraries to adapt and integrate the new strategies for teaching and learning? Beagle (2002) suggests that the IC must evolve into a "testbed for instructional support and knowledge discovery" (p. 287). He argues that given the growing use of learning technologies that lie outside the library, we must find ways for librarians, faculty, and students to "shape" and integrate the information space: librarians must be able to organize and make digital content available, teachers must be able to locate and bring online resources together, and students need to be able to locate and use the digital content. In addition, Beagle argues that the IC has the potential to go beyond instructional support and become a discovery system that transcends individual disciplines and permits the student to exploit more effectively the expansive digital environment. Whether an evolving IC will help secure the survival of the academic library as a vital component of the academic enterprise remains to be seen. But it is clear that the IC is an increasingly common adaption in the academic environment.

Special Libraries and Information Centers

School and academic libraries are relatively easy to identify and define. Special libraries and information centers are somewhat more difficult, because of their immense variety. There is no one definition that can aptly accommodate the variety of special libraries and information centers, and usually a distinction is made between the two. Mount (1995) defines special libraries as "information organizations sponsored by private companies, government agencies, not-for-profit organizations or professional associations" (p. 2). The definition would also include special subject units in public and academic departments. Information centers are seen as "special libraries with a very narrow scope" (Mount 1995, p. 3). One example might be a library devoted to a special metal, for example, an aluminum library. Under this view, then, an information center is subsumed under the broader notion of special library.

The "roots" of special libraries and information centers can be traced to the ancient and medieval periods since libraries in those times tended to focus on a particular mission (Wiegand and Davis 1994). The archival functions of Sumerian libraries might fit the special library pattern, or the monastic libraries might be considered special religious libraries. Nonetheless, the special library, as we know it, is probably better located in the eighteenth and nineteenth century. Mount (1995) places the date at 1777 with the founding of the army library at the Military Academy. White (1984) suggests that the earliest special libraries were associated with scientific and historical societies. Early legal and medical collections provided training in law and medicine. The development of social libraries that focused on the specific and often professional or technical interests of their clientele also serve as early models of special libraries and information centers—mercantile and mechanics libraries represent examples. Libraries associated with commercial firms were found as early as the 1880s. Reflecting the growth of science, technology, and industrial development, there was considerable growth in the special library entering the twentieth century. This development was sufficient to generate an interest in an association specifically designed to serve special libraries and information centers, hence the creation of the Special Library Association (SLA) in 1909. By 1910 there were probably about a hundred special libraries and information centers. This number grew rapidly to about one thousand by 1920. The major growth occurred after World War II, exceeding ten thousand in the 1960s. Information centers, as defined above, arose in this latter period and started primarily in scientific and technical laboratories (Mount 1995).

As society recognized that quick access to up-to-date information is the cornerstone of a competitive intellectual and economic climate, the role of special libraries and information centers became obvious. Recognition of the importance of quick access accounts for White's projection that special libraries and information centers will grow in number about 5 percent per year—a significant contrast to traditional public and academic libraries (White 1984). The continuing growth in the number of special libraries and information centers is attributable to at least three forces: the rapid increase in the amount of information, continuing development in information technologies, and the recognition of how important information has become as an essential resource for organizational survival (Christianson, King, and Ahrensfeld 1991). From an organizational perspective, the importance of special libraries and information centers is likely to increase. As more and more information is stored in electronic formats and the importance of the written document or monograph declines, especially in the areas of science, technology, and business, the function of special libraries and information centers appears more and more relevant and vital.

Although it may be difficult to define today's special library or information center, it may be useful to highlight some of their most important characteristics. White (1984) has attempted to identify these characteristics. They can be summarized as follows:

Special libraries and information centers:
- tend to emphasize the provision of information for practical purposes rather than instruction on how to find the information or a physical document
- generally involve the librarian researching and finding the answer for the client, rather than the client expecting to locate the answer with the librarian's assistance
- tend to give librarians a great deal of autonomy because those requesting the information are unfamiliar with the function of information centers
- tend to have a relatively small number of users, and restricted access to relatively small, but highly specialized collections
- are directly and narrowly related to the mission of the organization in which they are located, and must regularly demonstrate their usefulness in order to survive
- tend to work for organizations with managements that are not library oriented; rather management is oriented to the goals of the larger organization, and the library staff itself represents only a small fraction of the total organizational workforce

The list above suggests that special libraries and information centers tend to operate in a more entrepreneurial environment, often within private, profit-oriented organizations—quite different from most other types of libraries. Generally, special libraries and information centers serve their special clients or sponsors, in contrast to public libraries and institutions that tend to serve anyone. Also, special libraries and information centers are in many instances expanding their functions and image well beyond the concept of the traditional library, promoting the idea that they provide "knowledge services" or "content management services." As St. Clair, Harriston, and Pellizzi (2003) explain:

> Knowledge Services is about establishing social communities; about creating the social infrastructure, a foundation of trust, and a collaborative environment in which all stakeholders contribute to the successful achievement of the parent organization's mission. (p. 11)

There are probably between 14,000 and 21,000 special libraries and information centers in the United States, depending on how they are defined. There are approximately 35,000 special libraries and information centers worldwide.) The heterogeneous character of special libraries and information centers is highlighted by noting the various divisions (see Figure 9.2) of the Special Libraries Association (SLA), an association specifically created to serve these libraries (SLA 2003).

Today, special libraries and information centers are confronting many important issues: scarce resources, defining and promoting their roles and consequent low customer awareness, lack of recognition of the value of special libraries, keeping up with how information is stored and located, copyright issues, the demands of individualized service, and poor cooperation from management. Below is a brief discussion of some of these issues.

THE BURDEN OF SCARCE RESOURCES

Few special libraries and information centers are publicly funded. Their existence depends on keeping their labor costs low and their productiv-

---

Figure 9.2
Types of Special Libraries Based
on Special Libraries Association Divisions

Advertising and Marketing	Military Librarians
Biomedical and Life Sciences	Museums, Arts, and Humanities
Business and Finance	News
Chemistry	Petroleum and Energy Resources
Education	Pharmaceutical and Health
Engineering	Technology
Environment and Resource	Physics, Astronomy and
Management	Mathematics
Food, Agriulture and Nutrition	Science-Technology
Information Technology	Social Science
Legal	Solo Librarian
Leadership and Management	
Materials Research and Manufacturing	Transportation

ity high. As might be expected, especially in our highly competitive times, stresses on the budget are considerable. Outsell (2003b) reports, for example, that the budgets of corporate information centers declined 7 percent from 2002 to 2003. In addition, operating costs are rising; vendor prices, for example, are increasing and putting considerable strain on the ability of special libraries to use their databases (Outsell 2003b). This creates a considerable burden for information managers because the organizations expect high performance with minimum expenditures. As a consequence, library staffs tend to be quite small. Mount (1995) reports, for example, that nearly one-third of special libraries and information centers have three or fewer people, and only 1 percent have more than 20 people. The profitability of the organization may well depend on the timeliness and accuracy of information provided by the library staff—the challenge is tremendous.

NEED TO DEFINE, PROMOTE, AND MEASURE THE VALUE OF THE LIBRARY'S ROLE WITHIN THE ORGANIZATION

Even if a library is functioning well, within the corporate environment especially, each department is often in competition for scarce resources. Because a library seldom produces a product of its own for sale, it is often viewed as a "cost center" rather than a "profit center." This means that the library and librarians must justify their existence in other ways or be trimmed from the budget. Attempts to tighten budgets or changes in administration can seriously jeopardize a special library or information center's survival. Therefore special libraries must actively promote their product—information—as something that improves the performance of others and the organization as a whole, and be able to demonstrate how performance improvements arise. Librarians and information managers must be able to measure and evaluate their effectiveness and be able to communicate and market the value of their libraries in a measurable, clear, and businesslike manner. In the final analysis they must be able to demonstrate that they save time, increase productivity, improve the organization's response to competitive threats, and provide a return to shareholders (if they are for-profit) (Kassel 2002).

One technique currently promoted for the evaluation of special libraries is *benchmarking*. Benchmarking involves comparing a library's performance with the performance of others, in order to identify the best practices and improve the efficiency and effectiveness of the operation. The benchmark becomes a standard against which the performance of the library can be assessed. The Special Libraries Association considers benchmarking sufficiently important that it is incorporated as a skill among its competencies (Henczel 2002). Another technique being employed is called the "balanced scorecard." This approach attempts to evaluate the library from four perspectives: customer, internal, innovation and learning, and financial. The organization develops targets for each area and then measures success in obtaining the targets (Mathews 2003).

Overall, in evaluating special libraries, particular attention is paid to demonstrating that the library has a positive return on investment (ROI), which usually involves focusing on outcome measures. As Matthews (2003) has noted:

> For the special library, there is compelling evidence that libraries provide information services that have real value to the larger organization. This value may be in the form of accomplishments, time savings, and financial impacts—both financial savings and increased revenues. (p. 28)

Need to Keep Up with How Information Is Being Stored and Located Within the Field

Because there is less emphasis on the package in which information comes and more on the information itself, it is necessary that the information be provided, in whatever form, quickly and accurately. Given that a large proportion of special libraries and information centers deal with technical, scientific, and economic information, it is crucial that the most timely information be procured. Meeting this responsibility entails increased reliance on information technologies. Special librarians must, therefore, be on the cutting edge of innovation, constantly updating their knowledge. Kassel (2002) has identified a variety of new skills that the special librarian must possess. These include Web searching skills, Internet teaching skills, knowledge of competitive intelligence, ability to conduct market research, analysis and writing skills, and intranet development skills.

Dealing with Copyright Issues

The ability to make copies is an extremely important method of disseminating current information. This is especially important in research-related contexts. The application of copyright restrictions to special libraries and information centers has raised considerable concern. The issue was highlighted in a 1992 case called *American Geophysical Union v Texaco*. A research scientist at Texaco, a for-profit company, made copies of eight articles from various journals from the company library for future research purposes. Although the copying of materials for research purposes generally meets the "fair use" criteria, the court found that the purpose was commercial rather than research, that the researcher copied the entire article rather than just small parts, and that Texaco's action had a deleterious effect on the market of journal publishers. That is, the company could have taken alternative actions that would have accomplished the same research purpose while respecting the copyright privilege of the journal, for example, ordering more journal subscriptions, ordering copies from a document delivery service, or paying additional royalties to the Copyright Clearance Center (designed to reimburse publishers). These arguments led the court to find in favor of the publisher. This is a very disturbing ruling for special libraries and information centers. The activity of copying articles is an extremely common and important method of keeping current in a researcher's area of interest. This case was upheld on appeal to the Second Circuit court and Texaco ultimately settled the suit at considerable expense ("Court Upholds Ruling" 1994; "Texaco Settles" 1995). This decision is likely to have a substantial impact on academic libraries as well as special libraries and information centers, and it might require librarians to inquire of patrons the purpose of making the copies. Such an action would be unparalleled and raise serious privacy and intellectual freedom issues.

Of course, all the issues related to copyright in the digital environment for other libraries (see Chapter 5), also apply to special libraries. The issue may be even more problematic because of the "for-profit" character of many of these libraries.

THE DEMANDS OF INDIVIDUALIZED SERVICE

A major challenge of special library service is to deliver the information on request as quickly as possible. The services are specifically tailored to the needs of the organization and the people making the query. This requires highly flexible library service and the ability of the special librarian to work under considerable time pressure as the information may be vitally important but lose its utility after a short period of time.

HUMAN RESOURCES IN THE LIBRARY AND INFORMATION WORKFORCE

A good overview of the labor force can be determined from U.S. Bureau of Labor Statistics (2002) data. Estimates of the librarian workforce vary, but usually range from about 135,000 to 150,000 (see Figure 9.3). Compared to the workforce of computer scientists and systems analysts, computer software engineers, and computer and information systems managers, librarians are but a small fraction of information professionals. A similar disparity is found when comparing the number of librarians to primary, secondary, and elementary teachers, who now exceed 4 million.

Support staff in libraries (library assistants, library technicians) comprise approximately 200,000 workers. This number also represents a small percentage when compared to 5 million information and record clerks. This number is not to say that the size of the total library work force is trivial, as it approaches more than 350,000.

The racial and gender characteristics of the labor force are also revealing when compared to other occupations (see Figure 9.4). It comes as no surprise that librarianship is comprised primarily of women: 82 percent of all librarians are female. The profession is primarily white: less than 8 percent of librarians are African Americans and just over 5 percent are Hispanic. The representation of African Americans and Hispanics is even lower in academic libraries. The *ARL Annual Salary Survey 1996–97* (1996) reports that in research libraries blacks comprise 3.7 percent of the professional workforce, and Hispanics 2.2 percent. Comparisons to other information professions suggest that librarianship may be quite different, especially in regard to gender distributions. For example, the proportion of women to men is reversed when dealing with computer systems analysts and scientists. Only 28 percent of this workforce is female, while the percentage of African Americans and Hispanics is similar to that of librarianship.

It is also revealing to examine the projected growth of the workforce to the year 2010 (see Figure 9.3). According to the Bureau of Labor Statistics (2003), the growth of the library workforce is expected to be slow. A 7 percent gain among librarians is expected over the 2000–2010 period, with more rapid, but still very modest, growth for library assistants (19.7 percent) and library technicians (19.5 percent).

As might be expected, labor force growth will be much greater in information technology occupations than among librarians (see Figure

9.3). For example, positions for computer scientists and systems analysts are expected to grow 59 percent, database administrators 66 percent, and network and computer systems administrators 82 percent from 2000 to 2010. Although labor force growth among librarians is expected to be slow, it is important to note that librarianship as a profession is aging and that many of the opportunities for librarian positions will come from replacement rather than growth in new positions. In fact, according to the Bureau of Labor Statistics, 60 percent of employed librarians were 45 years old or older (Figure 9.5); and it is expected that more than 46 percent of all librarians over 45 will be leaving the workforce by 2008 (Dohm 2000). From 2000 to 2010, approximately 76 percent of total job openings for librarians will be due to replacement. By contrast only 29 percent of computer scientists or computer analysts are 45 and older, and only 13 percent of their positions will be available due to replacement. For network and computer systems administrators, only 5 percent of their positions will be available due to replacement (Figure 9.3).

It is difficult to predict the shape of the library workforce in the future. But some significant labor force issues have arisen that have a significant effect on library organizations.

The Persistently Low Numbers of Minority Librarians

The potentially large number of openings in the labor force for librarians places in relief the importance of being able to recruit new librarians. Michael Rogers (2003) has noted that recruiting prospective librarians has been difficult over the years for many reasons, including low salaries, an image of stodginess, and the perception that librarians are primarily bureaucrats who shuffle books from place to place. The inability to recruit is especially notable when it comes to recruiting a diverse workforce.

The lack of diversity in the librarian labor force has been a major concern to the profession for many years. Of course, the concept of diversity can be defined in many ways: by age, level of education, income, religion, nationality, ethnicity, race, and types of life experiences. But a central focus of diversity in the library profession has been on race and ethnicity. As a profession, librarianship has not attracted a large number of individuals from various ethnic and racial groups. Consequently, recruitment of these underrepresented groups has been among the major objectives of a variety of professional associations, including the ALA,

Figure 9.3
Employment by Occupation, 2000 and Projected 2010
Library and Information Science and Related Occupations

Occupation	Employment Number (in 000's) 2000	Employment Number (in 000's) 2010	Projected Change 2002-2010 (Laborforce Growth) Number (in 000's)	Projected Change 2002-2010 (Laborforce Growth) Percent	Total job openings 2000-2010 Number (in 000's)	Percent Replacement Percent
Computer and information systems managers	453	513	150	47.9	203	26
Computer specialists	2,903	4,894	1,991	68.6	2,259	12
Computer programmers	585	680	95	16.2	217	57
Computer scientists and systems analysts	459	729	269	58.6	309	13
Computer systems analysis	431	689	258	59.7	296	13
Computer software engineers	697	1,361	664	95.4	711	7
Database administrators	106	176	70	65.9	74	5
Network and computer systems administrators	229	416	187	81.9	197	5

Primary, secondary, and special education teachers	4,284	4,995	711	16.6	1,663	57
Archivists, curators, and museum technicians	21	24	3	11.9	7	57
Librarians	149	160	10	7.0	41	76
Library technicians	109	130	21	19.5	70	70
Audio-visual collection specialists	11	13	2	13.6	3	33
Licensed practical and licensed vocational nurses	700	842	142	20.3	322	56
Information and record clerks	5,099	6,105	1,006	19.7	2,047	51
Library assistants, clerical	98	118	19	19.7	63	70
Printing occupations	534	543	8	1.6	20	60
Bookbinders and bindery workers	105	113	8	7.3	36	67

Source: Based on data provided by U.S. Department of Labor, Bureau of Labor Statistics, Employment Projections. "Employment by occupation, 2000 and projected 2010."

Figure 9.4
Racial and Gender Characteristics
of Selected Occupations, 2002

Occupation	Percent Female	Percent African American	Percent Hispanic
Librarians	82.0	7.8	5.1
Social workers	74.0	22.7	8.6
Library clerks	79.2	10.6	6.2
Teachers, except college	75.0	10.1	6.1
Computer systems analysts	27.8	6.9	5.2

Source: U.S. Department of Labor, Bureau of Labor Statistics. "Table 11: Employed Persons By Detailed Occupation, Sex, Race, and Hispanic Origin." (Online) Available at ftp.bls.gov. Accessed December 23, 2003.

the Black Caucus of the American Library Association, REFORMA, and the Asian/Pacific American Librarians Association.

The fact that there remains significant underrepresentation among ethnic and racial groups suggests strongly that there may be structural aspects of the educational and employing institutions that tend to discourage minorities from applying and being retained. For example, it may be that schools of library and information studies and employers are not devoting enough energy to recruitment. Effective recruitment strategies might increase the number of candidates from minority groups. Similarly, library schools may need to assess whether their schools are providing the necessary academic and financial support for minority students so that once admitted they can remain in the academic programs. There may, of course, be other external factors as well. The master's degree requirement may disproportionately screen out minorities, who, for a variety of reasons including discrimination, have been unable to obtain higher academic degrees at the same rate as others. Additionally, members of some ethnic and racial groups may not consider librarianship as a career because they have not been introduced to it as a career option. In addition their experiences with libraries may have been negative, and hence, working in a library may appear less desirable, or they may have access to more highly paid career options. Demographically, the United States is increasing in its heterogeneity and the field must constantly evaluate its practices so that the library workforce reflects this heterogeneity.

Figure 9.5
Employed Persons by Occupation and Age (Annual Average 2001)
Age Categories Expressed as Percent of Total

n in 000's

Occupation	Total 16+	16-19 n / %	20-24 n / %	25-34 n / %	35-44 n / %	45-54 n / %	55-64 n / %	65+ n / %
Archivists and curators	28	0 / 0	2 / 07	9 / 32	7 / 25	8 / 29	2 / 07	0 / 0
Computer systems analysts and scientists	1,810	11 /01	123 / 07	649 / 36	583 / 32	334 / 18	99 / 05	10 / 06
Information clerks	2,029	190 /09	368 / 18	434 / 21	408 / 20	363 / 19	187 / 09	79 / 01
Librarians	203	2 / 01	0 / 04	17 / 08	51 / 25	80 / 39	39 / 19	5 / 02
Library clerks	150	23 / 15	25 / 17	14 / 09	22 / 15	36 / 24	18 / 12	12 / 08
Social workers	782	3 / 00	56 / 07	244 / 31	175 / 22	210 / 27	81 / 10	14 / 02
Teachers (excluding post secondary)	5,473	89 / 02	408 / 07	1,305 / 24	1,300 / 24	1,645 / 30	611 / 11	115 / 02

Source: Based on U.S. Bureau of Labor Statistics, Division of Labor Force Statistics. "Employed Persons by Detailed Occupation, Sex and Age. Annual Average 2001."

Sex Discrimination

Analysis of gender-based data in the library labor force suggests differences in the wages and placement of women. A survey of recent library school graduates in 2002 revealed that men were paid 7.1 percent more on average than women, with an average wage gap of $2,836. Although the percentage of difference may vary by region, the average salary of women entering the profession is less than men in all regions of the country and in all types of libraries (Maata 2003). Similarly, women occupy a disproportionately low number of management and administrative positions compared to their general representation in the librarian workforce. For example, although women occupy approximately 80 percent of all public librarian positions, they serve in only 65 percent of the public library directorships. The average salary for male public library directors is nearly 17 percent greater than for females. In academic libraries, although females occupy about 65 percent of academic librarian positions, they hold only 43 percent of the directorships. The average salary of male academic library directors is 8 percent higher than that of their female counterparts (M.J. Lynch 2000; American Library Association 1986). Among ARL university libraries, women comprise approximately 64 percent of the professional staff, but only 48 percent of the directorships. The salary gap, however, is narrow, with only a 1 percent difference in favor of males in ARL directorships. On the other hand, the gap is closer to 6 percent when all ARL professional positions are taken into account (Kyrillidou and Young 2002).

Explanations have ranged widely regarding this disparity, including the assertion that men have a higher motivation to manage, which would incline them to apply for managerial or administrative positions. However, when research has been conducted on the difference in the motivation to manage between male and female librarians, no differences in motivation have been detected (Swisher, DuMont, and Boyer 1985). Men, on average, may have more years of managerial or library experience or more formal education, but research suggests that even when these factors are taken into consideration, there is a disparity in the representation of women in higher-level positions (Heim and Estabrook 1983). Certainly, the appearance of discrimination against women in management positions is hardly unique to librarianship, but its presence in a field numerically dominated by women makes it doubly regrettable and ironic. The abolition of discrimination is essential for a healthy labor force.

The Creation of New Technology-Oriented Positions

With the proliferation of new information technologies, special competencies have entered our field that were not there several decades ago. Knowledge of computer systems, including their evaluation, operation, maintenance, and replacement, has become essential for at least some library staff. In addition, with the Web emerging as a dominant information-seeking technology, the development of new competencies is being required of those performing reference positions. In some instances, positions requiring these skills have led to the creation of new job categories. Some of these categories may require levels of skill equivalent to or exceeding those of librarians, and their place in the organizational hierarchy in terms of pay, responsibility, and authority may be problematic.

Support/Professional Strains

Support staff play a vital role inside libraries and these roles are quite various. A support staff worker can be a clerical employee, paraprofessional, bookkeeper or accountant, public relations officer, business manager, computer programmer, or systems analyst. The organizational, political, and pay relationships within libraries are becoming more and more complex. These complexities become especially problematic with the new information technologies. New information technologies have given impetus for some support staff to increase their authority and responsibilities. Traditional clerical workers are becoming "desk-top publishers" or "database managers." How library administrators deal with this issue could have serious implications for the morale and productivity of their staffs.

SUMMARY

The complex and various functions of libraries are reflected in their organization. It is not surprising that libraries are often organized in conventional bureaucratic and hierarchical fashion: they have prospered quite nicely over the years employing these organizational patterns. However, today's environment is constantly presenting challenges that require rapid and effective responses. Many of the difficult issues that librarians face are caused by situations and events that lie outside their direct control. Common environmental influences in libraries are decreasing budgets and increasing inflation, the rapid expansion of knowledge, the obsolescence of knowledge, and the growth of new technologies. Other challenges are unique to various types of libraries. No matter what the source of these challenges, libraries, as organizations, will need to maintain clarity of mission, design their functions, and harness their human resources to ensure that the library users' needs are effectively satisfied.

REFERENCES

"ALA Launches Web Site with Links for Kids." *American Libraries* 29 (January 1998): 11.

Albanese, Andrew Richard. "Moving from Books to Bytes." *Library Journal* 126 (September 1, 2001): 52–54.

———. "The Top Seven Academic Library Issues." *Library Journal* 128 (March 15, 2003): 43.

American Library Association (ALA). *Academic and Public Librarians: Data by Race, Ethnicity and Sex.* Chicago: ALA, 1986.

———. *Information Power: Building Partnerships for Learning.* Chicago: ALA, 1998.

———. *Information Power: Guidelines for School Library Media Programs.* Chicago: ALA, 1988.

———. *Library Advocacy Now! Kids Can't Wait.* Chicago: ALA, 1996.

———. *Number Employed in Libraries: ALA Library Fact Sheet 2.* [Online] Available at *www.ala.org.* (Accessed 2002.)

American Library Directory 2002–2003. 56th ed. Medford, N.J.: Information Today, 2002.

ARL Annual Salary Survey 1996–97. Edited by Martha Kyrillidou and Kimberly A. Maxwell. Washington, D.C.: ARL, 1996.

ARL Annual Salary Survey 2001–02. Edited by Martha Kyrillidou and Mark Young. Washington, D.C.: ARL, 2002.

Association of American Publishers, American Library Association, and Association for Supervision and Curriculum Development. *Limiting What Students Shall Read.* Washington, D.C.: Association of American Publishers, 1981.

Association of College and Research Libraries (ACRL/ALA). "Information Literacy Competency Standards." [Online] Available at *www.ala.org.* (Accessed December 11, 2003. Document dated 2000.)

Association of College and Research Libraries (ACRL/ALA). *Recruitment, Retention & Restructuring: Human Resources in Academic Libraries.* ACRL, Ad Hoc Task Force on Recruitment and Retention. Final Draft. May 20, 2002.

Association of Research Libraries (ARL). *ARL Statistics 2001–2002.* Edited by Martha Kyrrillidou and Mark Young. Washington, D.C.: ARL, 2003a.

———. "Framing the Issues: Open Access." [Online] Available at *www.arl.org/scomm/open_access/framing.html.* (Accessed July 25, 2003b.)

Beagle, Donald. "Extending the Information Commons: From Instructonal Testbed to Internet2." *Journal of Academic Librarianship* 28 (September 2002): 287–296.

Benton Foundation. *Buildings, Books, and Bytes.* Washington, D.C.: Benton Foundation, 1996.

Bertot, John Carlo, Charles R. McClure, and Joe Ryan. *Statistics and Performance Measures for Public Library Networked Services.* Chicago: ALA, 2001.

Bill and Melinda Gates Foundation "About Us." [Online] Available at *www.gatesfoundation. com/AboutUs.* (Accessed November 30, 2003.)

Blount, Patti. "Double Your Fun with a Combination Public-High School Library." *Public Libraries* 41 (September/October 2002): 254–255.

Board of Education, Island Trees Union Free School District v. Pico [42 CCH S. Ct. Bull.] (1982).

Bob, Murray C. "The Case for Quality Book Selection." *Library Journal* 107 (September 15, 1982): 1707–1710.

The Bowker Annual: Library and Book Trade Almanac. New Providence, N.J.: Bowker, 1996, 1999, 2003.

Brodie, Carolyn. "A History of School Library Media Center Collection Development." In *The Emerging School Library Media Center: Historical Issues and Perspectives.* Edited by Kathy Howard Latrobe. Englewood, Colo.: Libraries Unlimited, 1998, 57–73,

Bureau of Labor Statistics. "The Job Outlook in Brief." *Occupational Outlook Quarterly* 40 (spring 1996): 3–43.

Byrnes, Margaret M. "Preservation and Collection Management: Some Common Concerns." In *The Collection Building Reader.* Edited by Betty-Carol Sellen and Arthur Curley. New York: Neal-Schuman, 1992, 57–63.

Byrnes, Marci, Kathleen Deerr, and Lisa G. Kropp. "Book a Play Date: The Game of Promoting Emergent Literacy." *American Libraries* 34 (September 2003): 42–44.

Carnegie Corporation of New York. *A Matter of Time: Risk and Opportunity in the Nonschool Hours: Executive Summary.* New York: Carnegie, 1993.

Carson, C. Herbert. "Beginner's Luck: A Growing Job Market." *Library Journal* 121 (October 15, 1996): 29–35.

Casey, Genevieve. "Library Service to the Handicapped and Institutionalized." In *Library Trends* 20 (October 1971): 350–366.

Casey, James. "The Devil Is in the Details." *Public Libraries* 41 (September/October 2002): 252.

Christianson, Elin B., David E. King, and Janet L. Ahrensfeld. *Special Libraries: A Guide for Management.* 3rd ed. Washington, D.C.: SLA, 1991.

Cloonan, Michele Valerie. "The Preservation of Knowledge." *Library Trends* 41 (spring 1993): 594–605.

———. "W(h)ither Preservation?" *Library Quarterly* 71 (2001): 231–242.

Coleman, Jim. "The RLG Conspectus: A History of Its Development and Influence and a Prognosis for Its Future." In *Collection Assessment: A Look at the RLG Conspectus.* Edited by Richard J. Wood and Katina Strauch. Binghamton, N.Y.: Haworth, 1992, 25–43.

"Court Upholds Ruling that Texaco Violated Copyright." *American Libraries* 25 (December 1994): 974.

Debons, Anthony, Esther Horne, and Scott Croneweth. *Information Science: An Integrated View.* Boston: G.H. Hall, 1988.

De Rosa, Cathy, Lorcan Dempsey, and Alane Wilson. *The 2003 OCLC Environmental Scan: Pattern Recognition*. Dublin, Ohio: OCLC, 2004.

Digest of Education Statistics 2002. Washington, D.C.: National Center for Educational Statistics, 2002.

Directory of Special Libraries and Information Centers. 17th ed. Edited by Joanna M. Zakalik. Detroit: Gale, 1994.

Dohm, Arlene. "Gauging the Labor Force Effects of Retiring Baby-Boomers." *Monthly Labor Review* 123 (July 2000): 17–25.

Du Mont, Rosemary Ruhig, Lois Buttlar, and William Caynon. "Multiculturalism in Public Libraries." In *Multiculturalism in Libraries*. Westport, Conn.: Greenwood, 1994, 37–51.

Economic Research Service, Department of Agriculture. "Briefing Room: Rural Population and Migration." [Online] Available at *www.ers.usda.gov/briefing/Population*. (Accessed January 27, 2004.)

Eisenberg, Mike. "This Man Wants to Change Your Job." *School Library Journal* 48 (September 2002): 47–49.

Euster, Joanne R. "The New Hierarchy: Where's the Boss?" *Library Journal* 115 (May 1, 1990): 41–44.

Everhart, Nancy. "Filling the Void." *School Library Journal* 48 (June 2002): 44–49.

Ferguson, A.W. "The Conspectus and Cooperative Collection Development: What It Can and Cannot Do." In *Collection Assessment: A Look at the RLG Conspectus*. Edited by Richard J. Wood and Katina Strauch. Binghamton, N.Y.: Haworth, 1992, 105–114.

Gallup Organization. *Usage and Perception Study*. Lincoln, Neb.: Gallup, June 1998.

"Gates Foundation to Invest $400 Million in Libraries." *American Libraries* 28 (August 1997): 14.

Gates Library Foundation. Gates Library Foundation Background. [Online] Available at *www.glf.org/background.html*. (Accessed December 17, 1997.)

Gorman, Michael. "Technical Services Today." In *Technical Services Today and Tomorrow*. 2nd edition. Edited by Michael Gorman. Englewood, Colo: Libraries Unlimited, 1998, 1–7

Harris, Michael. "The Purpose of the American Public Library." *Library Journal* 98 (September 15, 1973): 2509–2514.

"Harvard, Cornell Slash Journal Subscriptions." *American Libraries* 35 (January 2004): 23–24.

Heim, Kathleen, and Leigh S. Estabrook. *Career Profiles and Sex Discrimination in the Library Profession*. Chicago: ALA, 1983.

Henczel, Sue. "Benchmarking Measuring and Comparing." *Information Outlook* 7 (July 2002): 12–20.

Hennen, Thomas J. Jr. "Great American Public Libraries: The 2002 HAPLR Rankings." *American Libraries* 33 (October 2002): 64–68.

———. "Performing Triage on the Budgets in the Red." *American Libraries* 34 (March 2003): 36–39.

Himmel, Ethel E., and William James Wilson. *Planning for Results: A Public Library Transformation Process*. Chicago: ALA, 1998.

Holt, Glen E., and Donald Elliott. "Measuring Outcomes: Applying Cost-Benefit Analysis to Middle-Sized and Smaller Public Libraries." *Library Trends* 51 (winter 2003): 424–440.

Ingersoll, Richard M., and Mei Han. *School Library Media Centers in the United States: 1990–91. Survey Report.* Washington, D.C.: GPO, 1994.

Internet Public Library. The Internet Public Library Mission Statement. [Online]. Available at *http://ipl.org* (Accessed December 11, 2003.)

"Internet Public Library." *American Libraries* 28 (February 1997): 56–57.

Ishizuka, Kathy, Walter Minkel, and Evan St. Lifer. "Biggest Challenges 2002." *School Library Journal* 48 (January 2002): 50–53.

Johnson, Linda. "The Rural Library: Programs, Services, and Community Coalitions and Networks." *Rural Libraries* 20 (2000): 38–62.

Johnson, Richard K. "Competition: A Unifying Ideology for Change in Scholarly Communications." [Online] Available at *www.arl.org/sparc/core/index.asp?page=a2*. (Accessed July 28, 2003.)

Jones, Plummer Alston Jr. "The History and Development of Libraries in American Higher Education." *College and Research Libraries News* 50 (July/August 1989): 561–564.

Justice, Laura M., and Joan Kaderavek. "Using Shared Storybook Reading to Promote Emergent Literacy." *Teaching Exceptional Children* 34 (March/April 2002): 8–13.

Kao, Mary Liu. *Introduction to Technical Services for Library Technicians.* New York: Haworth, 2001.

Kassell, Amelia. "Practical Tips to Help You Prove Your Value." *MLS: Marketing Library Services* 16 (May/June 2002): 1–3.

Klauber, Julie. "Living Well with a Disability: How Libraries Can Help." *American Libraries* 29 (November 1998): 52.

Kyrillidou, Martha. "Librarians' Salaries Continued to Increase." *ARL News Release.* March 29, 1996.

Lance, Keith Curry, Marcia J. Rodney, and Christine Hamilton-Pennell. *How School Librarians Help Kids Achieve Standards: The Second Colorado Study.* Castle Rock, Colo.: Hi Willo Research and Publishing, 2000.

Lance, Keith Curry, Lynda Welborn, and Christine Hamilton-Pennell. *The Impact of School Library Media Centers on Academic Achievement.* Castle Rock, Colo.: Hi Willo Research and Publishing, 1993.

Lau, Debra. "Got Clout?" *School Library Journal* 48 (May 2002): 40–45.

Lovejoy, Eunice. "History and Standards." In *That All May Read: Library Service for Blind and Physically Handicapped People.* Washington, D.C.: National Library Service for the Blind and Physically Handicapped, Library of Congress, 1983, 1–24.

Lynch, Beverly P. "Libraries as Bureaucracies." *Library Trends* 26 (winter 1978): 259–267.

Lynch, Mary Jo. "Know About Librarians." *American Libraries* 31 (February 2000): 8–9.

Maata, Stephanie. "Salaries Stalled, Jobs Tight." *Library Journal* 128 (October 15, 2003): 28–34.

MacWhinnie, Laurie A. "The Information Commons: The Academic Library of the Future." In *Portal: Libraries and the Academy.* Volume 3. Baltimore: Johns Hopkins, 2003, 241–257.

Martell, Charles R. *The Client-Centered Academic Library: An Organizational Model.* Westport, Conn.: Greenwood, 1983.

Mathews, Joseph R. "Determining and Communicating the Value of the Special Library." *Information Outlook* 7 (March 2003): 27–31.

McClure, Charles R., et al. *Planning and Role-Setting for Public Libraries: A Manual of Options and Procedures.* Chicago: ALA, 1987.

McKimmie, T. "Budgeting for CD-ROM in Academic Libraries: Sources and Impacts." *Library Acquisitions: Practice and Theory* 16 (1992): 221–227.

Minarcini v Strongsville City School District. 541 F 2d 577 (1977).

Minkel, Walter. "The Year in K–12 Libraries: School Librarians Redefine Themselves." In *The Bowker Annual: Library and Book Trade Almanac.* Medford, N.J.: Information Today, 2003, 10–14.

Mount, Ellis. *Special Libraries and Information Centers: An Introductory Text.* 3rd ed. Washington, D.C.: SLA, 1995.

National Center for Education Statistics [NCES]. *CES Schools and Staff Survey, 1991, and Statistics of Public and Private School Library Media Centers. 1985–86.* Washington D.C.: U.S. DOE, 1991.

———. *Public Libraries in the United States: Fiscal Year 2001.* Washington, D.C.: U.S. DOE, 2003.

———. *Report on Public Libraries, 1992.* Washington D.C.: U.S. DOE, 1994.

———. *School and Staffing Survey 1990–91.* Washington, D.C.: U.S. DOE, 1991. In *School Library Media Centers in the United States: 1990–91. Survey Report* by Richard M. Ingersoll and Mei Han. Washington, D.C.: American Institutes for Research in the Behavioral Sciences, 1994.

———. *Services and Resources for Young Adults in Public Libraries.* Washington, D.C.: GPO, August 1995.

———. *Use of Public Library Services by Households in the United States: 1996.* Washington D.C.: U.S. DOE, March 1997.

Nelson, Sandra. *The New Planning for Results: A Streamlined Approach.* Chicago: ALA, 2001.

Outsell. *The Changing Roles of Content Deployment Functions: Academic Information Professionals.* Burlingame, Calif.: Outsell, 2003a.

———. *The Changing Roles of Content Deployment Functions: Corporate Information Professionals.* Burlingame, Calif.: Outsell, 2003b.

Owens, Margaret. "Get It in Writing!" *Public Libraries* 41 (September/October 2002): 248– 250.

Owusu-Ansah, Edward K. "The Academic Library in the Enterprise of Colleges and Universities: Toward a New Paradigm." *Journal of Academic Librarianship* 27 (July 2001): 282–294.

Palmour, Vernon E., Marcia C. Bellassai, and Nancy V. DeWath. *A Planning Process for Public Libraries.* Chicago: ALA, 1980.

Principles for Emerging Systems of Scholarly Publishing. [Online] Available at *www.arl.org/scomm/tempe.html.* (Accessed July 28, 2003.)

Rawlinson, Nora. "Give 'Em What They Want!" *Library Journal* (November 15, 1981): 77–79.

"Riverside County Outsources Library—Again." *American Libraries* 28 (August 1997): 19.

Rogers, Fred. *Let's Talk About It: Divorce*. New York: Putnam, 1996.

Rogers, Michael. "Tackling Recruitment." *Library Journal* 128 (February 1, 2003) 43.

Rubin, Joyce Rhea. *Planning for Library Services to People with Disabilities*. Chicago: ALA, 2001.

Schmidt, Karen A., and Ron L. Ray. "The Ordering, Claiming, and Receipt of Materials." In *Technical Services Today and Tomorrow*. 2nd ed. Edited by Michael Gorman. Englewood, Colo.: Libraries Unlimited, 1998, 9–20.

Simon, Matthew. "Will the Library Survive the Internet? What Patrons Value in Public Libraries." *Public Libraries* 41 (March/April 2002): 104–106.

Smith, Abby. *The Future of the Past: Preservation in American Research Libraries*. Washington, D.C.: Council on Library and Information Resources, 1999.

Special Libraries Association [SLA]. [Online] Available at *www.sla.org*. (Accessed December 17, 2003.)

St. Clair, Guy, Victoria Harriston, and Thomas A. Pellizzi. "Toward World-Class Knowledge Services: Emerging Trends in Specialized Research Libraries." *Information Outlook* 7 (July 2003): 10–16.

Stratton, J.M. "Emergent Literacy: A New Perspective." *Journal of Visual Impairment & Blindness* 90 (May/June 1996): 177–183.

Swisher, Robert, Rosemary Ruhig DuMont, and Calvin J. Boyer. "The Motivation to Manage: A Study of Academic Librarians and Library Science Students." *Library Trends* 34 (fall 1985): 219–234.

Tenopir, Carol. "Electronic Reference in Academic Libraries in the 1990s." In *Annual Review of OCLC Research*. Dublin, Ohio: OCLC, 1995, 66–68.

"Texaco Settles Copyright Case." *American Libraries* 26 (July/August 1995): 632–634.

U.S. Bureau of the Census. *Current Population Reports, Series P-20, No. 450: Marital Status and Living Arrangements: March 1990*. Washington, D.C.: GPO, 1991.

U.S. Department of Labor, Bureau of Labor Statistics, Employment Projections. "Employment by Occupation, 2000 and Projected 2010."

Van House, Nancy A., et al. *Output Measures for Public Libraries*. 2nd ed. Chicago: ALA, 1987.

Vavrek, Bernard. "Rural Public Library Services." In *Encyclopedia of Library and Information Science*, 2nd ed. Edited by Miriam Drake. New York: Marcel Dekker, 2003, 2550–2555.

Westin, Alan F., and Anne L. Finger. *Using the Public Library in the Computer Age*. Chicago: ALA, 1991.

Whelan, Debra Lau, ed. "Greatest Challenges for 2003." *School Library Journal* 49 (January 2003): 48–50.

White, Herbert S. *Managing the Special Library*. White Plains, N.Y.: Knowledge Industry, 1984.

White House Conference on Library and Information Science. *Information 2000: Library and Information Services for the 21st Century*. Washington, D.C.: GPO 1991.

Wiegand, Wayne, and Donald G. Davis, eds. "Special Libraries." In *Encyclopedia of Library History*. New York: Garland, 1994, 597–599.

Wilson, Patrick. "Bibliographical R&D." In *The Study of Information: Interdisciplinary Messages*. Edited by Fritz Machlup and Una Mansfield. New York: Wiley, 1984, 389–397.

Winter, Michael F. *The Culture and Control of Expertise: Toward a Sociological Understanding of Librarianship*. Westport, Conn: Greenwood, 1988.

Woolls, Blanche. *The School Library Media Manager*. Englewood, Colo.: Libraries Unlimited, 1994.

Wright, Lisa A. "Public Library Circulation Rises Along with Spending." *American Libraries* 27 (October 1996): 57–58.

Young, Peter R. "Changing Information Access Economics: New Roles for Libraries and Librarians." *Information Technology and Libraries* 13 (June 1994): 103–114.

Younger, Jennifer A., D. Kaye Gapen, and Cecily Johns. "Technical Services Organization." In *Technical Services Today and Tomorrow*. 2nd ed. Edited by Michael Gorman. Englewood, Colo.: Libraries Unlimited, 1998, 165–181.

Zweizig, Douglas L. "The Children's Services Story." *Public Libraries* 32 (January/February 1993): 26–28.

———. *Output Measures for Public Libraries*. Chicago: ALA, 1982.

10

Librarianship: An Evolving Profession

Librarianship is in the midst of a great change. It is a traumatic one for many, in part because rapid change has not been an aspect that librarianship has generally had to deal with; the field has remained stable for many years. Since the late nineteenth century, whatever changes have occurred have been incremental and evolutionary, not revolutionary, and the role of the librarian has remained relatively constant for more than a hundred years. In many ways, the slowness of change in librarianship has been good. It has created a solid historical identity and important precedents for its actions and goals. From these traditions emerged the central values and duties of librarianship on which the changes in contemporary librarianship may be squarely built.

Historically, the librarian has been closely tied with the physical institution of the library. One does not usually think of librarians without also thinking of the library in which they ply their trade. Is the entire identity of the librarian inextricably linked to this physical entity? If the new world of information transfer can be accomplished without such a physical institution, will the librarian also disappear? Are librarians capable of thinking of performing their tasks without a physical library, and is the rest of the world capable of thinking of them in this way as well? Will there be librarians without libraries? Will we be calling them something different, as some are being called today—"information consultant," "information specialist," "information manager" or "knowl-edge manager"?

Such a concern may be more an exercise in hysteria than reality. There is no evidence that libraries are or will be vanishing in the near future. However, it is quite possible that a substantial number of librarians (or whatever we will call them in the future) will be working outside the traditional library building. The librarian of tomorrow may be quite different. The library may have its quiet places for contemplation and study, but it is not a sedate place, it is dynamic, and those who choose librarianship will need to be adaptable, patient, able to withstand uncertainty, and amenable to learning new things. The stable environment of the past is being replaced by a dynamic environment in which the content and function of the institution is constantly being revised and modified by technological, political, and economic change. How the profession comes to be defined will be the result of a dynamic interaction between the qualities of the profession, its capacity to adapt, and the demands placed upon it by society at large.

Libraries and the profession of librarianship are closely linked; what happens to one is likely also to affect the other. This chapter will focus on three aspects of the profession: the forces that shaped education for librarianship, the current struggle for professional identity, and the forces and challenges facing librarianship in the future.

AN HISTORICAL OVERVIEW OF PROFESSIONAL EDUCATION

The education and training of American librarians have been closely related to developments in professional education and to economic developments as well. As noted in the chapter on the mission and values of libraries (Chapter 7), early American libraries were small and relatively unsophisticated. In most libraries, if staff existed they were very small in number and often functioned in a custodial capacity. Scholarly librarians did exist in the mid-nineteenth century. They were usually found in more sophisticated academic institutions and were invariably male. These individuals were described as "Bookmen" by Pierce Butler (1951) in his history of the profession, because they were scholars, not technicians. Their numbers, nonetheless, were generally small.

Until 1850 there was no training to speak of for those who worked in the library except trial and error. One simply learned on one's own and followed the example of others. Sometimes a novice librarian would contact other experienced librarians for advice and counsel. The earliest type of training, apprenticeship, probably emerged between 1850 and 1875. Apprenticeship involved learning a trade through practical experience under the tutelage of another more experienced individual. A librarian would find an individual who was interested in librarianship and have that person work in the library under close observation.

Another route of professional development consisted of informative publications from private publishers, the United States government, or the American Library Association. *Publishers Weekly*, for example, began during this time, 1872. Although it focused on the publishing industry, there were small sections devoted to librarians. The major publication that provided tremendous support for library training was the *American Library Journal*. Created in 1876 as the official organ of the newly created ALA, this journal (which was soon renamed *Library Journal*) was the first to devote itself to the interests of librarians. It published articles, summaries of ALA conference proceedings, and a section titled "Notes and Queries," which printed responses to questions and comments from librarians. Many of these questions were queries about cataloging and classification, circulation, library buildings, library equipment, and funds. *Library Journal* (*LJ*) was filled with advice to novitiates. In the very first issue, Justin Windsor (1876), associate editor and director of the Boston Public Library, wrote an article in which he advised new librarians on learning about the management of libraries. To this end he recommended that the notiviate (1) locate whatever printed materials on librarianship are available; (2) locate similar libraries and ask for their rules and reports; (3) study the materials received; (4) evaluate the extent to which other libraries are good comparisons to the library in question; (5) contact an experienced librarian; and (6) do what seems to come naturally. He also warned the novitiate that if he did not have time to do this research and analysis, then he should "resign your trust to some one who has" (p. 2).

Another significant source of publications for the librarian was the U.S. Office of Education, which produced publications for educators. The most significant publication affecting library education was the bureau's landmark study issued in 1876, *Public Libraries in the United States of America: Their History, Condition, and Management*. A substantial body of statistical data was presented on more than 3,600 public libraries, and data on other types of libraries were included as well. As part of this work, the bureau issued a manual including articles written by noted authorities on librarianship. The topics included such areas as management, administration, history, cataloging, popular reading, and library buildings. In essence, it was the first authoritative library reader (*Public Libraries* 1876). These early beginnings produced a sparse literature and little formal training for librarianship. The dearth of training reflected both the relatively small number of libraries and little recognition of the potential of libraries and librarians to the society as a whole.

The period from about 1876 to 1923 marks a critical and complex time in the development of library education, and there were a variety of forces at work that created the foundations for the professionalization of librarianship. Among these were the following:

The Decline of the Classical English and Apprenticeship Models of Education and the Rise of the Model of Technical Education

American education during the nineteenth century was generally shaped by the dominant immigrant population: the British. This model emphasized study of the classical languages, religion, literature, and grammar. With the rise of the industrial revolution, training models needed to change. This change was also needed because it was becoming apparent that training for the factory environment required a more efficient type of training than traditional apprenticeship. In the traditional apprenticeship system, which was designed for training an individual for a craft, only a few individuals could be trained at a time for a specialized, narrowly defined job. With industrialization, many people had to be trained for positions in factories that might be quite similar from factory to factory. Education had to accommodate many people and provide a more generalized approach, employing the general principles and practices the job required. A classical education was inappropriate, and apprenticeship was too inefficient. The rise of technical schools and the vocational emphasis of these educational institutions fit well into the needs of libraries. Exposure to the European technical education model was provided at various International Fairs and Expositions in Europe and the United States, and some library leaders, among others, attended them and found the model attractive (C. White 1976).

The Influence of Andrew Carnegie and the Growth of Libraries

The latter half of the nineteenth century saw a tremendous expansion in the number of libraries. For example, 551 public libraries were established between 1825 and 1850, but more than 2,200 were established in the ensuing 25 years (*Public Libraries* 1876, p. xvi). There were many reasons for this rapid increase, especially at the end of the nineteenth century, including an increased recognition of the important role of libraries in research and teaching. Andrew Carnegie's focus on libraries led to his financing the construction of 3,000 libraries throughout the world, a large proportion of which were public libraries built in the United States. The proliferation of libraries had the inevitable effect of increasing the demand for library workers. Although professionally trained librarians were not required for many of these libraries, especially in the nineteenth century, it was clear that library workers were still needed.

The Influence of Melvil Dewey and the Professionalization of Librarianship

There is little dispute that Melvil Dewey was the prime force in the professionalization of librarianship during the latter part of the nineteenth century. Dewey was not alone in promoting the field of librarianship and library education, but he was a central figure whose energy and devotion advanced the profession. It is not possible to discuss all of Dewey's accomplishments, but three will be noted here that were clearly important in establishing the professional foundations for the field.

First, Dewey provided a fundamental context through which materials and disciplines could be understood and organized through his development of a decimal classification system. His earliest experience with libraries came while he was a student working in the library at Amherst College. After graduation, Dewey remained at Amherst and served as the librarian. It became clear to Dewey that the existing classification system simply did not provide the flexibility and clarity that was desired. The development of a new and more efficient way to organize materials was just the type of project that would have been of interest to Dewey. He was fascinated with labor-saving routines and devices. His fascination was, no doubt, part and parcel of the excitement generated by the possibilities of industrialization. Dewey, for example, was a member of organizations promoting the use of metrics and simplified spelling (hence, *Melvil* rather than *Melville*). The classification system was heavily promoted by Dewey and grew in popularity over the years. In terms of the profession, its use clearly represented a stabilizing force as it provided a fundamental and important theoretical principle by which basic activities of the profession could be organized.

Second, Dewey was an early promoter of professional identity on a national level. Although the need for a professional association had been discussed in the 1850s, the time was not right for its creation. In 1876 Dewey was a guiding force in organizing a national meeting of librarians in Philadelphia. On the final day of the meeting, the American Library Association was founded with Melvil Dewey as its secretary. From the perspective of the sociology of professions, the creation of a national professional association is an important guidepost. It substantially increases professional identity, helps to identify important issues, and establishes standards of service and conduct. The founding of ALA did that for librarianship and, perhaps just as important, it provided librarianship with an identity to those outside the profession. It also provided a common forum for the discussion of ideas and problems. The first conferences, for example, discussed such issues as classification, indexing, and protecting materials from abuse.

Third, Dewey was instrumental in the creation of the first major professional library journal, also in 1876. Dewey's orientation, both in the creation of the association and the journal, was pragmatic. The establishment of the *American Library Journal* was intended to assist librarians in the daily performance of their duties. The emphasis was practical, not theoretical, concentrating on the problems a librarian in the United States would face. Dewey served as one of its editors. The attractiveness of such a journal was not lost on the newly created American Library Association. In 1877 it was adopted as the official organ of ALA, and the name was shortened to *Library Journal*.

Although Dewey's work tended to focus on the technical aspects of the profession, he also believed that librarianship was a serious profession with a serious, moralistic, and prescriptive purpose to make people better. The idea of improving people by providing healthy reading would not have been considered a curious notion in those times. Dewey (1876) had some clear notions on this subject, which he directly conveyed in his brief article "The Profession" in *Library Journal*. He argued that individuals are influenced by print materials and that librarians could be quite influential by buying the right materials for their library. Dewey was the consummate social engineer:

> He must see that his library contains, as far as possible, the best books on the best subjects, regarding carefully the wants of his special community. Then, having the best books, he must create among his people, his pupils, a desire to read those books. He must put every facility in the way of readers, so that they shall be led on from good to better. . . .

Such a librarian will find enough who are ready to put themselves under his influence and direction, and, if competent and enthusiastic, he may soon largely shape the reading, and through it the thought, of his whole community. (p. 5)

The idea that it is the librarian's duty to shape a community's thinking is strong stuff. At the very least, it implies that books have considerable power. This power could be used for good or evil. The librarian's duty was moral and pedagogical, to provide the "better" books and to improve people so that they could be exposed to even better works in the future.

The Beginning of Library School Training

At the same time that there was a proliferation of libraries in the latter half of the nineteenth century, and with it an increased need for library workers and trained librarians, there occurred a transition from library work performed by scholars in relatively academic settings to library work focused on routines and practices (Butler 1951). It seems reasonable that if librarianship involved technical manipulations and routines, training needed to be provided.

Up to this time apprenticeship was generally an informal process. Then in 1879 Dewey tried to promote a system of organized apprenticeship that would provide systematic training under the auspices of various librarians and libraries. The librarians would advise the apprentices on library matters and suggest readings and areas of study. Dewey suggested that the teachers be knowledgeable librarians and that the apprenticeship be associated with a substantial library (Vann 1961). Little interest, however, was generated from this proposal, and it received a cool reception at ALA. Traditional apprenticeship remained one of the typical ways by which a librarian learned his or her trade and was being provided at such notable institutions as the Boston Public Library, Boston Athenaeum, and Harvard University. There were also summer schools at Amherst College and library training classes at major public libraries such as those in Los Angeles, Denver, and Cleveland. There were also special classes in library techniques at academic or technical institutes. All of these, however, were usually brief and unsystematic in terms of curricula.

A fortuitous event occurred in 1883. Dewey's reputation for his work at Amherst had grown considerably and quickly, and consequently he was recruited to apply for the head librarian's position at Columbia

University. His discussion with the president of Columbia, F.A.P. Barnard, and the board of trustees before his hire included the discussion of the need for formal training of librarians. This was met with enthusiastic support on the part of President Barnard and sufficient support from the board, although it is not clear that the board actually understood the full import of Dewey's suggestions. Dewey accepted the appointment in 1884, and the first library school, called the School of Library Economy, opened on January 1, 1887, with a class of 20 students: 3 men and 17 women (Vann 1961). As might be expected, the program of instruction at the school was pragmatic, including selection, reader's aids, bibliography, repair of materials, administration, and issues related to the catalog. The program also included practice work so that the students could actually perform the work of their intended profession. This was not to say that Dewey felt that anyone with some technical training could be a librarian. Rather, as Wiegand (1999) has observed, Dewey believed that only people with the appropriate "character" should be accepted into the profession; character in this nineteenth century sense meant "moral potential," a potential for self-refinement and improvement. The proposed length for the original instructional program was three months, although it was also proposed that students follow their instruction by a substantial period of work experience and then return to the school for several months of further instruction (Vann 1961). The total period was about two years, and some of the students actually followed this course. Unfortunately, Dewey's relations with university officials were tense, and there was a feeling that he had not correctly represented the school to the board, especially in relation to the problematic presence of women as students in the school. Indeed, when the trustees discovered that women would be attending, they voted to deny Dewey the use of Columbia's classrooms. The students met across the street from the Columbia campus in a converted storeroom. Wiegand (1999) describes the inauspicious beginning of the school as a "bootleg operation" (p. 18). By 1888 it was clear that Columbia would close the school.

Dewey, anticipating these events, accepted a position as head of the New York State Library in Albany. The state library agreed to have the school transferred there, thus preserving the only formal education program for librarians in the country. Dewey remained the director of the library school, but he was preoccupied with other professional responsibilities at the time. Consequently, the daily operations became the responsibility of Mary Salome Cutler Fairchild, who taught at Albany for 16 years and served as its vice-director (Maack 1986). Fairchild had worked both as a cataloger and a cataloging instructor under Dewey at Columbia. Fairchild's view of library education differed somewhat from Dewey's: hers emphasized more theoretical and cultural aspects of the field while Dewey emphasized the practical aspects, viewing libraries as businesses. For example, Dewey emphasized book selection through the use of standard reviews, while Fairchild emphasized that the librarian should have a broad knowledge of books and an understanding of people's tastes in order to select books (Wiegand 1996). Nonetheless, as Gambee (1978) observes, Fairchild gave "form and substance to the Dewey dream" (p. 168) through her able administration and inspiring pedagogy. Gambee notes that she commanded much loyalty from her students and alumnae, and she is credited with establishing and maintaining the high standards of admission and high quality of education that made Albany the standard of library education.

The success of the program at Albany led to its imitation in other locations. By 1900 there were four major library schools: University at Albany, SUNY, Pratt Institute (1890), Drexel University (1892), and the Armour Institute (1893), which became the State Library School at the University of Illinois in 1897 (Vann 1961). Among the directors of these schools were found some of the future women leaders of the library profession—individuals who helped to shape library education and librarianship for years to come.

Pratt was originally established in 1890 to train staff of the Pratt Institute library, and the school experienced a considerable period of growth and development under the leadership of Mary Wright Plummer. Plummer was a member of the first library school class at Columbia and one of its best students. She was an ardent advocate for library school training and became director of Pratt Institute's library and library school in 1895. Under her leadership, the school broadened its purpose to train librarians for other public library positions (Brand 1996). This involved extending the training program from six months to two years, making it equivalent to the best training provided (Vann 1961). The curriculum underwent considerable enrichment during this period, developing specialized courses in children's work and historical courses in cataloging and bibliography (Brand 1996). In 1896, Plummer experimented with a second year of specialization designed to train librarians to work in more scholarly libraries. Special courses in bibliography, advanced cataloging, and courses on the histories of books, bindings, and engravings were offered. Three years later, Plummer started a second-year specialization in children's librarianship (Karlowich and Sharify 1978; Maack

1986). Despite the difficulties of women acting as leaders and administrators in an era when women were not expected to play such roles, Plummer would eventually become the second female president of ALA and director of the library school of the New York Public Library (Weibel and Heim 1979).

Drexel's library training program, as well as the library itself, was directed by Alice Kroeger, also a graduate of Dewey's library school after it had moved to Albany. Kroeger's program was deliberately like the one created by Dewey, including course work in cataloging, literature, bibliography, history of books, and library management. The similarities to Dewey's program helped establish this type of curriculum as the model for library education (Vann 1961; Grotzinger 1978a). In addition to serving as the major instructor at the library school, Kroeger had many contributions. She was a prolific author and presenter at ALA conferences. At a time when there were few texts for the library school student, she published the first major text on reference materials as well as a work on book selection.

The Armour Institute, established in 1893 in Chicago, Illinois, was the first library school in the Midwest. It began under the leadership of Katharine Lucinda Sharp, another graduate of Dewey's library school. Sharp's view of library education was heavily influenced by Dewey, especially the idea that librarians could have power because they could influence people's access to print materials (Grotzinger 1966). Sharp's program took one year with the possibility of a second year of advanced work. The advanced training included work in bibliography courses in specialized areas and the history of printing and libraries; a specialized children's program was also available (Vann 1961). Sharp was not satisfied with the existing admission requirements at Armour and wanted to develop a program comparable to that of Dewey's (Grotzinger 1966). She was especially interested in being able to award a degree, rather than a certificate, for library training. She established such a notable program that two universities became interested in it: the University of Wisconsin and the University of Illinois. As a consequence, she successfully and amicably negotiated a transfer of the program to the University of Illinois, where she would serve as head of the school and head of the university library as well. She also held the title of full professor. This enabled her to use the library as a laboratory for practice work for her students (Grotzinger 1978b; Maack 1986). The program that she developed in terms of academic requirements was comparable to that at Dewey's school in Albany (Vann 1961). Sharp did much to establish the academic respectability of library education and, although she was only able to establish a four-year program leading to a bachelor's degree, she was an early proponent of placing library education on the graduate level. During her tenure, the school was "constantly the center of experimentation and innovation" (Grotzinger 1966, p. 304). She was an innovative curriculum designer, adding courses on documents, extension work, and research methods to the library school curriculum (Grotzinger 1978b). She also involved students in the life of the community. These students created travelling collections, conducted storyhours, and organized collections (Grotzinger 1966). As a consequence, Sharp was highly respected as a library educator and librarian and was twice elected ALA vice-president.

The number of library schools continued to grow in the ensuing decades. There were 15 such programs by 1919, 10 of them founded by women (Maack 1986). They varied in many ways including length of program, type of degree or certificate awarded, and requirements for admission. The M.L.S. was not awarded except at Albany until the 1920s. The master's at Albany was given only after two years of education beyond the baccalaureate (sometimes referred to as the "sixth-year degree"). The bachelor's of library science (B.L.S.) was awarded by most schools, and this was given after one year of library education following the regular baccalaureate degree, sometimes referred to as the "fifth-year degree" (Robbins-Carter and Seavey 1986).

As the number of library schools grew, ALA took a greater interest in their development. The other traditional methods of library training remained and coexisted uneasily with the developing library schools. The library schools wanted ALA to recognize and endorse them as the appropriate forum for library training. Instead, the association created the ALA Committee on Library Training at the end of the nineteenth century. This committee had many transformations, but an important development occurred in 1902 when the committee was asked to make a review of library training programs. This review resulted in the issuance of standards for library education in 1903. These standards reflected no commitment to any particular type of library education strategy. ALA chose to promulgate standards for the various types of library education rather than identify which type was most desirable. Subsequent standards were issued in 1905 and 1906, again with the same equivocations: a politic choice in an association badly divided over this issue.

The tensions regarding standards for library education became acute in the period between 1910 and 1920. ALA continued to have an interest in library education, including the establishment of a Section on Professional Training. This section conducted some superficial examination of the programs being offered by various organizations, but as far as making a commitment to the library schools was concerned the association continued to keep them at arm's length. The reluctance to endorse the library schools as the only appropriate form of library education led the library schools to create their own organization, the Association of American Library Schools, in 1916. Although it had little influence over ALA activities, it did establish an identity for the library schools that had been lacking. Library school educators were not simply thinking about the political value of ALA endorsement. Their concerns were both administrative and curricular. Among their issues were establishing consistent standards for admission to library school programs, establishing standards for instructors, determining the length of programs, determining the types of degrees to be awarded, establishing the proper balance between practical and theoretical approaches, and developing a system for transferring credits from one school to another (Vann 1961).

It was neither ALA nor the American Association of Library Schools that had the most effect on the future direction of library education. Rather, it was the Carnegie Corporation, established by Andrew Carnegie to administer his philanthropic activities after his death. The corporation continued to provide funds for public libraries, but had begun to suspect that the libraries, after being built, were often inadequately supported. This, despite the fact that generally Carnegie agreed to provide money for buildings only if the recipient of his largesse would agree to commit 10 percent of the amount donated each year to maintain the library. This led the corporation to appoint Alvin Saunders Johnson in 1915 to determine the condition of the libraries built with Carnegie funds and to explore the adequacy of library schools. Johnson's report in 1916 suggested that there were serious problems. He observed that those working in libraries were often poorly trained. He criticized the quality of many of the programs and suggested that the corporation assist in the recruitment of better-qualified individuals through scholarships, provide financial assistance to library schools and summer-school programs, and shift the emphasis in the corporation's philanthropy by providing money to improve library service rather than for buildings (Vann 1961).

Johnson's report was met with concern by the Carnegie Corporation. The corporation then subsidized a major study directed solely toward library education, and the library schools in particular. The corporation appointed C.C. Williamson to undertake this study. Williamson had the ideal combination of credentials. He was a political economist, a graduate of Columbia, and a professor of economics at Bryn Mawr. He had served as head of the Economics and Sociology Library at the New York Public Library, and at the time of his appointment was head of the Municipal Reference Library in New York. Williamson conducted a close examination of 15 library schools and a final report was issued in 1923. Referred to as the "Williamson Report," its historic importance to library education is unquestioned. A summary of some of his major findings and recommendations are noted below.

1. There is a difference between clerical and professional work. Professional work deals with theory and the application of principles and requires a broad education, including four years of college. Clerical work involves the following of rules and as such requires far less education. Professional, rather than clerical, instruction should be provided by library schools.
2. Library schools do not agree on the subjects that should be taught or the emphasis of subjects. Different schools devote much more time to one subject than to others.
3. The schools' curricula must reflect constant reexamination so that the most current practices can be taught rather than relying on traditional practices.
4. The breadth of content required for adequate library school instruction cannot be realized in only one year of education.
5. There is considerable inconsistency in entrance requirements. Library schools should require a college education (or its equivalent) for entrance.
6. Many current library school instructors are not trained to teach college graduates. Many lack college degrees themselves, few have had training or experience in teaching, and nearly one-third have had no library experience. There is too much reliance on lectures and few good textbooks. Low salaries of teachers need to be corrected, and library schools need to find ways to recruit teachers of better quality. Schools must also provide financial incentives for teachers to produce texts.
7. To recruit students, library schools should maintain high educational standards and provide fellowships and scholarships to make library training more attractive.
8. The library school should be part of an academic department in a university. This conforms with the model that other professional schools have used. Universities are better able to maintain academic standards and increase the status of these programs, and public libraries are unable to devote the resources necessary to maintain these standards.
9. Library programs should consist of two years of schooling. The first year should consist of a general program of study; the second year should be highly specialized. This will involve cooperative efforts with other local educational institutions.

10.   There is little incentive for librarians who are currently employed to seek continuing education. Continuing education at this point is centered on subprofessional workers; this needs to be remedied by schools that direct their attention to the enrichment of professional education. Correspondence schools should be considered.
11.   There are no fixed standards of training for librarians. The setting of standards should begin with the profession, and once established should eventually be made part of the law. The American Library Association should create a system of voluntary certification of librarians regulated by a national certification board.
12.   The national certification board should also serve as an agency for accreditation of library schools. (Williamson 1923)

The Williamson Report represents a breakthrough for library education. Although many of the issues raised were not original with Williamson, his report represented a culmination of the historical forces that were working to define library education for this century. Because of the imprimatur of the Carnegie Corporation, the report could not be ignored. It established the essentially theoretical and professional nature of the discipline and appropriately located the focus of the education of librarians at the university. In addition, because Williamson sets forth a college degree as an entrance requirement, it is clear that he considered library education to be on the graduate level (Williamson 1923). Thus the master's degree became the appropriate degree. In a broader sense, the Williamson Report affirmed that a substantial part of librarianship was, or should be, a form of education, rather than simply training. Further, it forced the profession to consider the importance of consistency and high quality in the curricula, administration, and teaching in library schools. Interestingly, some of Williamson's recommendations were not heeded, most notably the certification of librarians. Likewise, only a few library schools have adopted a two-year program of study.

After the issuance of the Williamson Report all other forms of library education did not simply vanish nor did the profession at large uncritically accept its recommendations. But its impact was considerable and marked the eventual death knell for all other forms of professional education. ALA responded by creating the Temporary Library Training Board in 1924, which soon became the Board of Education for Librarianship (BEL). The BEL prepared standards for library education in 1925 and 1933, which helped establish master's-level education for one year of education beyond graduate school (Robbins-Carter and Seavey 1986). By the early 1950s most library schools had adopted the "fifth-year" master's degree for their model.

The Carnegie Corporation's response to the report was even more concrete. Williamson had revealed many weaknesses and inconsistencies in library schools, and there was obviously a considerable need to improve them. In the ensuing 15 years, the Carnegie Corporation gave nearly $2 million to 17 library schools to accomplish this. Perhaps the corporation's most notable achievement during this time was the special attention it paid to the lack of research and quality texts for instruction. It was determined that the best way to resolve this problem was to support the creation of a graduate program for librarians—a program that would lead to the Ph.D. The school, called the Graduate Library School, was established at the University of Chicago in 1926, and the doctoral program began in 1928. Rayward (1983) argues that "library science" as opposed to librarianship emerged with the creation of the Graduate Library School because it emphasized theoretical approaches that involved applying the scientific and research tools of other disciplines to library work.

The Graduate Library School at the University of Chicago made special contributions to librarianship. First, its faculty was quite diverse, drawing faculty members with expertise from a variety of fields, including sociology and history. These individuals applied the established methodologies from other academic disciplines to the problems of librarianship. Second, the faculty focused on research. Because the faculty were primarily scholars rather than practitioners, they produced a considerable body of research, which formed the foundation for further research. Finally, the school sponsored many conferences and programs on major issues in the profession. These conferences drew practitioners and other library school faculty together and resulted in numerous publications, which also served as texts.

The Carnegie Corporation during this time also provided funding for the first school specifically designed to train African American librarians. The Hampton Institute Library School was created by a Carnegie grant in 1925. Given the concentration of African Americans in the South at that time, it is notable that before 1925 there was only one accredited library school in the South, Emory in Atlanta, but it did not admit African Americans until 1962 (L. Campbell 1977; McPheeters 1988). What library training was available was primarily through training programs in libraries or, in very rare instances, attendance at a predominantly white library school. By 1925 there was only one African American graduate of a library school—Edward Williams, librarian of Howard University (L. Campbell 1977). Obviously, with the growth of colleges for African Americans and the presence of primary and secondary schools that served them, there was a growing need for librarians. The fact that such a school was not founded until 1925 is related to the lack of library services for African Americans up to this time. It was only because philanthropic organizations such as the Carnegie Corporation and the Julius Rosenwald Fund focused on library services in the South that the issue of library service to African Americans was highlighted (L. Campbell 1977). To this end, the founder and first director of the Hampton Institute Library School, Florence Rising Curtis, played a significant role. Rising Curtis was a graduate of Dewey's school in Albany. Before coming to Hampton, she had had a distinguished career in the profession. She taught for 12 years at the University of Illinois's library school and had also been vice-director at the Drexel Institute school. She played a major role in the establishment and operation of the Association of American Library Schools, serving as its first secretary (Davis 1978). At Hampton, she was not only largely responsible for the quality of instruction to library school students, but she was devoted to improving library service throughout the South for African Americans. The Hampton Institute produced some notable library graduates during its existence, including Virginia Lacy Jones, who was to become the dean of the Atlanta University School of Library Service, and Wallace Van Jackson, library director at Virginia State College and a teacher at Hampton Institute, who made substantial contributions to academic library service for African Americans (L. Campbell 1977). Unfortunately, with the decline in the philanthropic resources on which the school depended, the school was closed in 1939. Although the loss of the Hampton Institute Library School was significant, it was just two years later, fortunately, that its role was continued by a school established at Atlanta University under the urging of its president, John Hope (Davis 1978).

The Great Depression and World War II placed severe burdens both on the development of libraries and on librarianship. Following the war, library educators continued to analyze and reanalyze their methods of education. Many of their concerns echoed those of Williamson. Educators were especially concerned that the curricula of many schools still emphasized routines rather than theory, and there was considerable variation in quality among the schools. In 1951 the Board of Education for Librarianship issued a new set of standards for library education that finally required five years of post–high school education (in other words, a master's degree) as the standard for professional education. This ended once and for all the alternative forms of library education. In

1956 the ALA Committee on Accreditation (COA) was formed and given the responsibilities of reviewing and accrediting library school programs, a task that it holds to this day.

The decades of the 1950s and 1960s were a fruitful period for libraries and librarians. In particular, the expanding economy, the Baby Boom, the passage of the Library Services Act, and federal legislation supporting the development of elementary, secondary, and higher education institutions and their libraries all led to a significant expansion of libraries and library collections. This concomitantly resulted in an increased need for librarians and provided a fertile market for spawning library schools. By the 1970s there were more than 70 accredited library schools with accredited master's programs in the United States and Canada. This might be considered the "heyday" of library schools, at least judging by the numbers, for the following two decades produced a considerable ebb. This decline included the elimination of library schools with considerable reputations, including those at the University of Chicago and Columbia. By 1999 there were 56 ALA-accredited library school programs in the United States and Canada (see Appendix C). There may be many reasons for this decline, including economic and social conditions. With the recession of the 1980s, there were deliberate, self-conscious attempts at universities to reduce costs. Taxpayers became ever more reluctant to finance higher education, and politicians and board members found the budgets for higher education a tempting arena in which to cut costs. Internally, schools of library and information science (LIS) are not, as a rule, high-profile departments. They are rarely mentioned when speaking of the reputation of an academic institution, nor do they produce many major donors in comparison with law or medical schools. In addition, LIS programs have traditionally not built strong links with other academic departments and have low visibility and prestige within the academic community. Many of these schools failed to develop an energetic alumni network. The result is that higher education administrations have found library schools fairly easy targets for closing, and because of their lack of connections with other academic departments, they find few defenders when closing decisions are made (Paris 1988). Boyce (1994), dean of a school of library and information science, has suggested that such closings may not be all bad. He suggests that library schools try to improve the quality of their academic programs and the profession set higher academic standards. Boyce suspected that an additional one-third to one-half of the remaining library schools might close. It appears, however, that the precipitous decline has ended, and it is hoped that the remaining library schools have learned from the experiences of those less fortunate.

Contemporary LIS Education and Training: Background and Challenges

LIS STUDENTS

Although concern has been expressed that the overall number of library school graduates has declined (enrollment peaked in 1992), the decline has been minimal. In 2002, 4,923 master's degrees in library and information science were conferred, in comparison to 4,877 in 2000. As might be expected, a high percentage is female (80 percent). In 2002 there were more than 15,000 master's students enrolled in accredited master's programs in the United States and Canada (Association for Library and Information Science Educators [ALISE] 2003). The largest group of male and female students are between the ages of 25 and 34 (45 percent and 38 percent respectively). The maturity of the students may be a reflection of many factors. Librarianship is considered a career of "late deciders," because it is not usually considered a first career choice. It is unlikely, for example, that recent college graduates are counseled that librarianship is a good career. It does not have high visibility or status, nor does it appear to offer competitive salaries compared to many other occupations. Similarly, given the numerical dominance of women in its labor force, it is often a career that for many is delayed during their early child-bearing years. It is notable that in 2002 approximately 17 percent of the male enrollees and 24 percent of the women enrollees were forty-five or older: overall more than one in five enrollees were 45 years or older (ALISE 2002).

LIS PROGRAMS

Programs in library and information science (LIS) have undergone a substantial evolution at the turn of the twenty-first century. This, in turn, has led educators to rethink a substantial part of their curricula. The evolution has in large part been precipitated by the expansion of information technologies and the resulting changes in the way that information is being created, organized, accessed, and disseminated. This can be seen in the name of the schools that were traditionally known as schools of library science. Today, with minor variations, most are known as one of the following:

School of Information Science and Policy
School of Library and Information Studies
School of Library and Information Science
School of Information Studies
School of Information

The introduction of "information studies" is a recognition of at least three factors: (1) information rather than books has become a central focus of many programs, (2) information technologies are significantly influencing the basic functions of libraries, and (3) there is a considerable market for information specialists, who may or may not be associated with libraries, whom schools of library and information science can educate and train. This recognition has been formalized by the American Library Association, which has determined that programs of education for librarianship will be referred to officially as programs in "Library and Information Studies."

INTEGRATION OF INFORMATION TECHNOLOGIES INTO THE CURRICULUM

Because information technologies play such an important role, LIS curricula have had to make substantial changes. They have had to integrate new information into current courses and add a wide variety of courses, including information storage and retrieval, networking, and programming, to an already full course of study. In addition, because the Web plays such a central role in the information access, core competencies now must actively involve Web-related skills, including access and search skills, evaluation and training skills, and electronic publishing competencies.

COMPETITION FROM OTHER ACADEMIC DISCIPLINES

As the function of libraries and library education has become more generically related to the broader concept of information access, the content in a variety of disciplines tends to overlap with LIS programs. For this reason, academic disciplines such as computer science, communications studies, and business have developed programs that mirror many aspects of LIS. In some cases, this has led to a combining or integration of library science programs with other departments. LIS programs must walk a fine line between broadening their curricula and retaining their unique identities. Failure to do so results in loss of fiscal and human resources, and sometimes even more troubling, the loss of departmental identity within the institution.

FINANCIAL STRESSES

The integration of information technologies into LIS programs has substantially increased the costs of operation. The costs are rather impressive: computer hardware and software, support materials such as books and periodicals, peripherals, maintenance and replacement of computers, network and telecommunication costs, and hiring individuals to support the computer systems. This is in addition to the costs of hiring faculty to instruct in these new and developing areas and the costs of supporting faculty training to use the new technologies. The pressure on academic programs, including schools of library and information studies, to produce new revenue streams has been substantial. Response to such pressure has included the development of new programs (for example, bachelor's programs in information studies) and increased fund-raising and marketing activities. Allard (2000), for example, has recommended a variety of marketing strategies, including creating a logo, adopting a slogan for the program, and publicizing program successes. In addition, she has suggested targeting particular groups, such as alumni and businesses, and preparing special messages for each.

CONTINUING EDUCATION

Continuing education involves the improvement of the knowledge, skills, and abilities of individuals in their professional performance. With the rapid changes occurring in the information environment, much of the knowledge conveyed in library and information science programs quickly becomes obsolete. Consequently, many LIS programs have recognized that there is a significant need to continue the education of graduates, as well as to provide training for other library employees. Adding to the pedagogical burdens of LIS faculty can be problematic. Therefore, these programs must develop techniques to identify the specific course content needed by returning students.

DISTANCE EDUCATION

The economic pressures in higher education have led administrators to search for techniques to increase enrollments while delivering education at minimum costs. With developments in telecommunications, it has now become possible to deliver education to remote sites using interactive video and Web-based instruction. These techniques are being employed by many LIS programs today. As of 2003 there were 38 LIS programs offering accredited master's program by distance learning (ALA 2003).

This form of education brings its own set of issues. Among these are (1) how to ensure that the quality of education provided in distance learning is equal to that provided in the traditional classroom; (2) how to provide the variety of courses and specialities offered at the "main" campus; (3) how to create a sense of educational community for students who may have little face-to-face contact with faculty members and other students; (4) how to train faculty to employ new distance learning technologies effectively; (5) how to administer distance-learning programs; and (6) how best to assess academic performance in the distance-learning environment. Many of these issues are not unique to distance education, but they must be addressed yet again with the development of these new techniques for delivery of library education.

TRAINING LIBRARIANS TO SERVE ETHNIC AND MINORITY POPULATIONS

The American population is becoming increasingly heterogeneous. Today, the four major minority populations—Native Americans, African Americans, Hispanics, and Asians—comprise approximately one-third of the U.S. population; in the next century, whites are likely to become a minority population. In many large cities, minorities comprise the majority, or, at least, a very substantial proportion of the urban population. In order to serve these populations it has become increasingly necessary for LIS programs to recruit more minority M.L.S. students and to provide some focus on how to serve ethnic and minority populations.

The challenge of minority recruitment, especially of African Americans, has been recognized for decades. The relatively few African-American librarians and their lack of ALA involvement at the higher levels were among the main reasons for the creation of the Black Caucus of ALA in 1970 under the chairmanship of E.J. Josey. Minority recruitment is also a focus of other library associations supporting diverse ethnic backgrounds, such as the Asian/Pacific American Library Association (APALA). Current minority enrollments in M.L.S. programs remain well below 10 percent. In 1997 the ALA undertook a special program, the "Spectrum Initiative," in an attempt to confront directly the ethnically

homogeneous character of the library profession. This initiative originally undertook the goal of educating as many as 50 library school students annually for a three-year period with the objective of doubling
the number of librarians of color. Subsequent support from ALA presi-
dents has led to creating a fund that would extend the initiative indefi-
nitely. As of 2002 the total number of Spectrum Scholars was 227 ("Four
Years of Progress" 2002).

McCook and Geist (1993) have suggested additional ways to improve the situation, including development of cooperative partnerships
between LIS schools and employers, greater monetary support for minority students, more active recruitment activities in undergraduate and
secondary education programs, recruitment in nontraditional settings
such as military and community colleges, and creation of an educational
environment more conducive to minority students. In addition to recruitment, LIS schools need to develop education programs that provide training sensitive to cultural and language differences and to the
special information needs of these populations.

IDENTIFICATION OF COMPETENCIES FOR LIBRARY AND INFORMATION PROFESSIONALS

What knowledge and skills are essential for the education of librarians?
What constitutes the core of information needed for education and training of LIS professionals? Beverly Lynch (1989), for example, in her examination of courses in LIS programs, found only a small number of
core courses on which there was agreement, and little agreement as to
what constituted courses for specialization in the field.

As the field of library and information science expands, the potential areas for training and education will expand further. Given the variety of competencies that are possible, LIS programs need to identify those
that are essential, so that graduating students will have a basic level of
knowledge and skill to perform their jobs. This will require a careful
understanding of the dynamic library and information job market and
tailoring of the curricula to meet the needs of this market. Will this mean
a reduction of theoretical material and a significant increase in practical
"how-to" material on information technologies? Main (1990) has suggested that this is the desirable course:

> There is no longer a need to be concerned with theoretical and philo-
> sophical issues. What we must be concerned with is what enables us to

survive in a competitive world, namely information technology. And information technology is a practical discipline. (p. 228)

Such a view is quite different from that advanced by Williamson in 1923, and other academics would no doubt argue that the challenges and issues raised by these same information technologies make understanding the philosophical issues even more important today. Similarly, it is argued that there is a need to increase librarians' theoretical understanding so that they can perform the planning, evaluation, and decision-making functions that will be so vital in the rapidly evolving information environment. As Beverly Lynch (1989) has noted:

> The shaping of the future of librarianship rests not on the vocational skills necessary to the time, but on the principles common to all specialization in the field. The professional expects library education to be built on a solid intellectual foundation. (p. 81)

No doubt, these different perspectives will generate tensions within LIS programs for years to come.

An underlying aspect of this debate centers on the centrality of the M.L.S. for professional education. As the professional model of education has developed in the latter part of the twentieth century, formal education has become increasingly important. This is based on the notion that within a profession is a substantive body of theoretical knowledge and principles upon which professional practice is based. Obviously, this is a critical point for LIS education. Even today there are some who assert that there is not a sufficient body of theoretical education to require graduate academic training. As Hauptman (1987) has asserted:

> There is not even any mandatory *a priori* knowledge necessary to function effectively as a librarian of any persuasion. Any intelligent college graduate can begin working in a special, public, or academic library and quickly learn the skills necessary to catalog, do reference work, manipulate overrated computer systems, or even administer. (pp. 252–253)

Hauptman describes the work of the librarian as "90% clerical" and asserts that librarians create a mystique regarding their work. The patron can often learn to perform some library functions in only a short time. Jerry Campbell (1993) takes a different view but raises the same issue. He argues that the computer revolution has created the need for greater and greater technical proficiencies and that the failure to alter library education significantly may lead to its obsolescence. As he notes, "the MLS may no longer be a viable credential given the nature of the technological and practical challenges we face in everyday library work" (p. 560).

On the other hand, there are many who would disagree with the diminution of LIS education and the master's degree. Librarianship, like many professions, is a combination of work that appears routine and work that requires theoretical and conceptual knowledge and judgment. Such a view does not see librarianship so much as a set of individual tasks, as it does a field that performs an essential social and political function demanding a broad understanding of the nature of knowledge, information, people, and society. It requires an understanding that permits us to evaluate, make judgments, and set future courses of action. For example, knowing the name of a particular source may be useful for answering a specific query, but understanding people's information needs and how to identify and evaluate them requires a different type of understanding. This latter type of understanding helps librarians design their information systems, choose areas of emphasis, and design methods for encouraging the use of such systems. The same may be said for understanding the principles of selection, the effects of information policy, the uses of technology, the manner by which knowledge is organized, and the principles that guide the operation of information-giving institutions. As Herbert White (1986) has noted, the master's degree is not so much a qualification for a particular position, as it is a qualification for entry into the profession.

The American Library Association (1996) has recognized the importance of graduate education among its own policy statements. In part, it states:

> The American Library Association supports the provision of library services by professionally qualified personnel who have been educated in graduate programs within institutions of higher education. . . . The American Library Association supports the development and continuance of high quality graduate library/information science educational programs of the quality, scope and availability necessary to prepare individuals in the broad profession of information dissemination.
>
> The American Library Association supports education for the preparation of professionals in the field of library and information studies (LIS) as a university program at the master's level. (p. 137)

This supporting statement is strong but not unequivocal. It does not, for example, insist that all professional librarians possess a master's degree from an accredited LIS program. The importance of the master's degree in library science became quite public when a legal challenge was lodged against its use as a criterion for hiring a librarian at Mississippi State University in the 1980s. Title VII of the Civil Rights Act protects various classes from discrimination by age, race, color, religion, or disability. The act extends to protecting individuals from being discriminated against in the hiring process, especially when an irrelevant characteristic or qualification is considered in that process. In other words, employers are obligated to employ only those criteria that directly relate to the individual's ability to perform the job. Glenda Merwine sued Mississippi State University when she was not hired for a librarian's position at the Veterinary Medicine Library. Although the case, *Glenda Merwine v. Board of Trustees for State Institutions of Higher Education* (Holley 1984) had many complications, one of her arguments was that she was denied employment because she did not possess a master's degree from a program accredited by ALA. Interestingly, ALA did not take a stand on the issue, but several prominent library educators did testify. The court found that no reasonable alternative to the master's degree had been provided and that the master's degree was both relevant and broadly accepted as the professional degree. This case did not permanently resolve the possibility of subsequent challenges, but an adverse decision would have seriously damaged the professional degree's standing. In addition, it put the profession on notice that it must be able to clearly articulate why the professional degree is essential. Nor has it inoculated the profession from attacks from other sources, most notably the Office of Management and Budget of the federal government, which has challenged the need for a master's from an accredited LIS program for some positions that previously required it.

EVALUATION OF LIBRARY EDUCATION

Since the 1950s the ALA Committee on Accreditation has served as the formal professional means of quality control for LIS education. Only LIS programs on the master's level are accredited. The purpose of such accreditation is to assure that LIS programs are of sufficient quality to provide library service. There are no formal bodies assessing LIS education at the doctoral level.

The accreditation standards have changed as the field has evolved and as schools have expressed their dissatisfactions with the evaluation process. In 1992 a new set of standards replaced those created in 1972

(ALA 1992). Each standard is considered to be an essential component of a master's degree LIS program. The standards address six basic areas: Mission, Goals, and Objectives; Curriculum; Faculty; Students; Administration and Financial Support; and Physical Resources and Facilities. Contemporary accreditation places strong emphasis on the school's ability to articulate its own mission, to develop planning mechanisms to implement its mission, and to provide effective methods for evaluating the outcomes of its educational program. In addition, reflecting the development of alternative teaching approaches, the standards explicitly recognize that LIS education can be provided through nontraditional mechanisms such as by interactive video or online instruction. The standards, however, remain the same regardless of the delivery technique.

Although the need for accreditation is strong, not all library educators are satisfied with the current standards and approach. Saracevic (1994) has suggested that allowing schools to set their own missions is illogical and focuses too much attention on setting their own objectives rather than developing a basic curriculum centered on the content and theoretical foundations of the field. Saracevic is concerned that universities in which LIS programs are located perceive them as vocational institutions rather than academic departments. Without the necessary theoretical underpinnings, library schools are in jeopardy of closure.

BALANCING THE INTERESTS OF LIBRARY PRACTITIONERS AND LIBRARY EDUCATORS

For some time, practitioners in libraries have expressed increasing concern about the diminution of emphasis on librarianship as opposed to aspects of information science. Practitioners have grown increasingly uneasy about the curriculum of LIS schools, especially regarding the lack of required courses that some believe are "core" to the discipline, including reference and cataloging. This concern is coupled with the projected labor force shortages for librarians in the near future, most notably in the areas of cataloging, and services to children. These concerns have been taken very seriously by the American Library Association, which convened a Congress on Professional Education; the congress has met three times since 1999. At the first congress the participants focused on library education that led to the master's degree and attempted to reach a consensus on the values and core competencies of the profession. Although a consensus was not reached, the discussions led to the formation of task forces on competencies and core values of the profession. The second congress focused on continuing professional education for librarians and library staff, and the third conference focused on education for library support staff.

Library educators, on the other hand, have noted that, although they respect the needs of librarianship, they must also pay attention to the lessons learned only recently when schools of library and information science education were being eliminated. The universities in which they reside demand new strategies. Indeed, Koenig and Hildreth (2002) have observed that, due to the relatively small size of individual schools of library and information studies, the "standalone library school" may be rapidly coming to an end as LIS programs are compelled to combine with schools of communication, journalism, education, and management. They perceive that LIS programs must either grow significantly in size or be merged with other programs.

It appears certain that in order for LIS schools to survive they must increase enrollments and be responsive to attracting a wider range of information professionals. Educators note that the fiscal realities and strains on universities require that LIS programs demonstrate their capacity to increase revenues. Universities expect LIS schools to broaden their market, and seek students who can be trained and educated for the information marketplace as well as the library marketplace. This expectation has resulted in the provision of new programs and degrees in addition to the master's in library and information studies. If LIS schools fail to make these changes, it is difficult to see how universities can accept the ever-increasing costs of graduate education in library and information studies. Undoubtedly, there will be a continuous need for library educators and library practitioners to communicate their concerns to their institutions. Regrettably, Moran (2001) has observed that so far these communications have often only increased the friction between them. It is hoped that the future will bring greater consensus and mutual understanding.

DETERMINING FUTURE DIRECTIONS: THE KALIPER PROJECT

The future and direction of education in library and information studies is unclear. Conrad and Rapp-Hanretta (2002) have identified a variety of internal and external forces that are shaping LIS education overall. Among the external forces are advances in technology, changing employer expectations of employee skills, need for ongoing training, changing patterns of educational financing (including reduced governmental funding), and increasing corporate funding. Internal factors include changing modes of information access and dissemination (for example, the Web), the increasing entrepreneurial culture of universities, shortages of faculty, and trends toward reorganization. Van House and Sutton (2000) suggest that two broad forces are shaping the future of LIS: the rapidly changing information environment and the changing university environment in which LIS programs are housed. Most notably, they argue that as the value of information becomes increasingly clear, new information competitors, such as computer science and business administration, are becoming powerful information competitors threatening the traditional jurisdiction of library and information science. This competition in turn produces an internal university environment that is unstable, with various disciplines competing for students and university resources. Van House and Sutton warn that LIS must make substantial adaptations to survive. The authors suggest that, while not abandoning the institutional focus LIS has on libraries, a concerted effort must be made for LIS to broaden its "niche," making LIS education less library-centered and more information-centered.

Given the many dynamic forces shaping library education, there has been an attempt to assess the state and direction of library education as a whole. With the support of the W.K. Kellogg Foundation and the active partnership of the Association for Library and Information Science Education, the KALIPER Project was initiated. Conducted between 1998 and 2000, the purpose of the project was "to analyze the nature and extent of major curricular change in LIS education" (ALISE 2000, p. 3). Led by a KALIPER advisory committee, five "scholar teams" were created, comprised primarily of faculty and doctoral students from schools of library and information science. Using a variety of techniques including data collection, interviews, surveys and case studies of 26 schools, the KALIPER Advisory Committee concluded that library and information science is a "vibrant, dynamic, changing field that is undertaking an array of initiatives" (ALISE 2000, p. 1). The report also identified six trends that aptly reflect the current and continuing issues that LIS education faces:

Trend 1:   In addition to libraries as institutions and library-specific operations, Library and Information Science (LIS) curricula are addressing broad-based information environments.

Trend 2:   While LIS curricula continue to incorporate perspectives from other disciplines, a distinct core has taken shape that is predominantly user-centered.

Trend 3:   LIS schools and programs are increasing the investment and infusion of information technology into their curricula.

Trend 4:   LIS schools and programs are experimenting with the structure of specialization within the curriculum.

Trend 5:   LIS schools and programs are offering instruction in different formats to provide students with more flexibility.

Trend 6:   LIS schools and programs are expanding their curricula by offering related degrees at the undergraduate, master's, and doctoral levels. (ALISE 2000)

There is little doubt that these trends will continue to affect schools of library and information science for many years to come.

THE LIBRARY PROFESSION: THE STRUGGLE FOR PROFESSIONAL IDENTITY AND PURPOSE

Librarianship, for some time, has been occupied, some might say preoccupied, with the question: "Are we a profession?" This self-reflection has created a substantial literature, but leaves the question unresolved. As early as 1876 Melvil Dewey thought he had resolved the issue in his editorial in the first issue of *Library Journal* when he pronounced, "The time has come when a librarian may, without assumption, speak of his occupation as a profession" (p. 5). Few, however, have accepted this pronouncement as final. Underlying the concern over the professional question are some substantial issues, and the stakes are high: recognition as a profession could lead to increases in status and concomitant increases in wages and authority.

Do Librarians Have a Distinctive Function?

To a substantial degree, the professional status of librarianship rests on the belief that librarians do special things and possess special expertise. This is sometime referred to as the "asymmetry of expertise," implying that the client or patron places special trust in the knowledge of the professional (Abbott 1988, p. 5). The historical image of the library and librarian and their source of authority was based in part on the fact that the library performed an essentially unique function in a unique way. It was, after all, often the only place in town with a substantial collection of materials that was well-organized and readily available to its users, and it had librarians who had at least some idea how to locate the right materials. This gave the librarian, if not a monopoly, a limited amount of control over some types of knowledge. It was a clearly identified institution where such knowledge could be obtained. Abbott (1988) identifies the type of knowledge over which librarians had control as "qualitative information" (p. 216), in contrast to quantitative information, which would be provided by professionals such as cost accountants, statisticians, and engineers. Librarians "had physical custody of cultural capital" (p. 217) which they organized and disseminated for either education or entertainment.

But now librarianship is in competition with many other information agencies that may also provide information. In turn, this competition leads to a struggle for professional jurisdiction (Abbott 1988). The effect of this competition may change the internal functions of library work. For example, Nielsen (1989) argues that the traditional and classical library model of a reference librarian able to answer any reference question put to him or her is changing significantly. There are several factors involved in this transformation:

> (1) increasing availability of remote and local end-user search systems both in and outside libraries, and artificial intelligence systems with icon-based interfaces for responding to both routine and non-routine questions; (2) a user population increasingly sophisticated in a variety of computing application areas; (3) availability of improved software products that encourage library users to integrate computing applications in their day-to-day work; and (4) pervasive availability of computing power and textual, numeric and graphic data commonly accessible in machine-readable form. (p. 190)

The points raised by Nielsen in the late 1980s are even more poignant today as the Web has become a ubiquitous technology for millions of Americans. It is no accident that the term digital or virtual "library" is prominent among the traditional library's information competitors. Certainly, to whatever extent the librarian was perceived as having control over access to knowledge, this perceived control will continue to be challenged and will likely deteriorate further.

Mason (1990) echoes deterioration in the distinctiveness of the library profession, placing it within the broader confines of the information profession. He has identified seven major information professions: accountant, archivist, librarian, records manager, information systems analyst, management scientist, and museum curator. The duty of the information professional according to Mason is "to get the right *information* from the right *source* to the right *client* at the right *time* in the form most suitable for the use to which it is to be put and at a *cost* that is justified by its use" (p. 125). The information professional's purpose is to improve a client's knowledge. Today, one could add several other categories, including information entrepreneurs, information architect, content manager, or knowledge manager. All this suggests that the librarian cannot claim sole jurisdiction to this area as a lawyer might claim such jurisdiction for the law.

On the other hand, Winter (1988) sees a distinctive characteristic to the field. He has identified three basic functions of librarians: classification of knowledge to organize it, indexing recorded knowledge so that that knowledge can be accessed, and understanding the formal and informal organization of various bodies of knowledge. Librarianship is engaged in a metascience that attempts to understand not one body of knowledge, but the organization of many bodies of knowledge and their interrelationship. On the face of it, this seems to provide some convincing substance to the argument that librarianship is indeed a profession, for these functions cannot be accomplished without considerable knowledge, both theoretical and practical. Yet it does not follow that librarianship is the only occupation concerned with these functions; other occupations also perform similar functions.

Winter (1988) argues that "mediating between the user and the public record of knowledge is the special province of the librarian" (p. 6). This special province harkens back to a fundamental value of the field, that of service. Librarianship is quintessentially serving a special *social* function, rather than just a specific activity. It is engaged in a social service, emphasizing the welfare of people over profit. Its model historically reaches back to an age in which professions were meant to improve the society: clergy, lawyers, doctors, teachers, nurses, social workers. These professions were dedicated to the betterment of people, not increases in profit, which were characteristics of positions in business and industry. As Abbott (1988) has observed, the professions "stood outside the new commercial and industrial heart of society" (p. 3). Librarians serve the public good by providing library service, by bringing people in contact with the vast body of public knowledge. In doing so, librarians support fundamental democratic values by emphasizing equality of access to knowledge. This cannot be assumed of other information professionals such as accountants, management scientists, computer scientists, or systems analysts. Underlying the special character of librarianship is not its techniques, but its fundamental values. The significance of librarianship lies not in mastery of sources, organizational skills, or technological competence, but in *why* librarians perform the functions they do. The fact that librarianship tends to encompass the vast body of print, audiovisual, and electronic information increases the importance of these underlying values further and differentiates it from other, even kindred, professions such as museum curators or historical society professionals.

Is Librarianship a Profession?

The debate over the distinctiveness of librarianship will continue, and this lack of clarity spills over into the question of whether it can rightfully be called a profession at all. Traditionally, the debate has been placed in the broader sociological context of defining professions more generally. The most popular approach, although not necessarily the most intellectually satisfying, is called trait theory. In this theory, professions are accepted or rejected based on whether they possess certain traits. Among these traits are that a profession:

1. *Possesses a substantial body of theoretical knowledge that forms the intellectual foundation of the profession.* Practitioners hence possess considerable expertise and knowledge of principles that are based on a systematically organized body of knowledge and usually acquired through a significant amount of formal education.
2. *Permits a substantial amount of autonomy.* Individuals practicing in the profession generally exercise their own professional judgment and, within the bounds of the canons of their profession, are free to act in accordance with these judgments.
3. *Exercises control over the conduct of its practitioners through licensure and a code of ethics.* Professions are often recognized by established codes that give the profession the authority to control entrance into the profession and to sanction practitioners if their conduct falls outside professional bounds. This is sometimes referred to as *structural powers* (Reeves 1980, pp. xix–xx). The power to license practitioners, to regulate their conduct and to withdraw the power to practice the profession is usually vested in the appropriate professional association, such as the American Bar Association or the American Medical Association. The enforcement of conduct within a profession is not only established by law; it is also defined by codes of ethics promulgated by the respective professional association. Violations of this code can lead to sanctions including suspension or revocation of the license. In many professions, however, the professional association does not have the power to sanction or legally control the activities of its professionals. Nonetheless, these bodies can still influ-

ence the nature of the professional work and the standards of work and conduct through education and standard setting. Such bodies exercise normative rather than structural power over their professionals (Reeves 1980).

4. *Possesses a dominant altruistic rather than self-interested purpose.* That is, professions place as their primary purpose the betterment of others and society at large. Professions provide an important service to the society, and their values emphasize the provision of such service over the personal and pecuniary interests of its practitioners. Professions are, in this sense a "calling" rather than an occupation. This is reflected in the origin of professions which arose from the clergy and served as a profession of faith. Professions in their modern sense emerged in considerable numbers in the latter part of the nineteenth century and the early part of the twentieth (law, medicine, nursing, teaching, librarianship), and it is notable that they arose in contrast to the many other factory-oriented occupations of the period. Professions had as their central value service to others rather than production and profit.

5. *Possesses a monopoly over the practice of the profession.* This can be seen prominently in the areas of law and medicine. These professions, in large measure, possess singular control over their fields. It is, in fact, unlawful for others not certified by their respective associations to practice law or medicine, and usually those who attempt to do so are barred from the basic institutions of the profession, such as the courts or practice in hospitals. Even in these fields the monopoly is not complete, but it is substantial.

6. *Possesses professional associations.* These associations serve many vital functions, including providing a professional identity to members; defining and enforcing the standards for the education needed, and accrediting the institutions that provide that education; enforcing standards of conduct; providing continuing education; providing a centralized forum, e.g., conferences and institutes, for the discussion of issues and research; and producing publications for dissemination of research and professional information.

Librarianship shares some of these traits. It is service-oriented and altruistic rather than profit-making in its orientation. It has professional associations that hold conferences, produce publications, promulgate codes of ethics and, in the case of ALA, provide an accrediting function. Yet, upon reviewing these traits, one could argue that librarianship does not meet these qualifications in some very important areas. Most notably, the power of the professional associations is very limited. They do not control the licensing of practitioners and they possess no power to sanction practitioners whose conduct violates its professional codes. In other words, there is no monopoly exercised by librarianship, although the field does possess normative authority, including the standards of conduct and work of librarians. One reason for the lack of strong structural control in the profession may be because many of its functions, such as finding and disseminating information, can be generalized and performed outside the library context. Similarly, arguments are frequently made that the discipline lacks a theoretical basis and that the formal education is primarily training rather than theoretical knowledge or principles. It is further argued that any necessary knowledge probably could be acquired just as well on the job as in the classroom. In addition, the formal graduate training, one year in most cases, is not equal to the extensive training required in other professions.

The trait view of professions, however, has been seriously criticized. For example, the extent to which a profession possesses particular traits is difficult to measure, and setting a criterion for how much of a particular trait is required for an occupation to be considered a profession is problematic. An alternative, and perhaps more appropriate, view of librarianship as a profession has been discussed by Winter (1988), who uses a "control model" based on the work of various sociologists. In this view, the nature of a profession is based on the power of that profession and the nature of the control that it exercises over practitioners. Underlying this view is the notion that an occupation and a profession are actually two related but distinct phenomena: a profession is a set of practices that control an occupation. In many ways, professions are more like unions than they are a particular occupation. Hence where one can speak of "unionized" occupations (for example, auto workers), one can also speak of "professionalized" occupations, which identifies a certain type of control that is exercised (p. 44). The professional control model emphasizes higher educational degrees and intellectual and theoretical knowledge in contrast to unionized control, which relies on work background and manual skills.

The control model, however, does not assume that all control is centered among the practitioners of the profession. There are, in fact, three types of control that dominate the intellectual activities of the profession. These are "collegial control," "client control," and "mediated control." In collegial control, the occupation is controlled by those who provide the service. For example, doctors and lawyers tend to control their practices in regard to their patients. In a client-controlled profession, the clients who use the services determine their wants, their needs, and the means by which they are satisfied. In the mediated type of control, there is a balance between collegial control and client control. Winter (1988) suggests that almost all professions are moving toward mediated control. Even in medicine, for example, patients are exercising a great deal more control over their medical treatment than in the past. Librarianship seems to fall in the mediated control category. Some clients will seek information and the librarian may have a great deal of autonomy in resolving that need; in other cases, the client may ask for a specific item or set of items. The librarian merely locates the information demanded by the user.

The proliferation of information technologies may also be an important factor that affects professional control or the lack thereof. Birdsall (1982) suggests that these technologies have stimulated a trend toward deprofessionalization or the creation of new professional models. Computerization, it is asserted, tends to make expert knowledge and technique much more widely available than in the past. In Winter's (1988) terms, it tends to promote a more client-controlled model. According to Birdsall (1982), the newer professions will not be characterized by a monopoly over special knowledge, but a recognition that the society is moving toward a self-help or self-reliant model of service. The purpose of the new professional is not to control knowledge or prescribe what the client must do, but to teach the client to become more and more self-sufficient. Birdsall suggests that the helping professions such as librarianship, social work, and education fall into this category of professional.

What becomes clear is that the amount and type of control exercised by librarianship may have great impact on how others perceive the profession. This in turn affects status and influence. The increasing awareness that information is a vital resource in our society, and the many economic, technological, and political forces used to control the creation and dissemination of this information, could have tremendous impact on who can have access to information, what type, and how much. Librarians have recognized the importance of influencing policies and practices in this arena, and their role and contribution could have a significant influence on whether librarians will be considered professionals. If librarians are perceived as having unique and expert knowledge of the organization and dissemination of information, and if they are seen as integral to the information dissemination process, then it is likely that they will be heard in the information-access debate. The stakes are high.

What Is the Image and Personality of Librarians?

How are librarians perceived, and do the perceptions match the reality? It is commonly believed by librarians that their image is negative: they are aging spinsters, have their hair in a bun, and wear sensible shoes and glasses. In addition, librarians believe that they are perceived as authoritarian and controlling, stern in appearance, ready to say "Shhsh" at the slightest disturbance. Male librarians experience additional concerns. They believe that they are seen as anomalous, part of a "woman's" profession, and therefore as ineffectual or effeminate. This fear is great enough that men are less likely than their female counterparts to admit that they are librarians. They tend to refer to themselves more in terms that sound less feminine, for example, they are more likely to identify themselves as information scientists rather than librarians (Morrisey and Case 1988). Such stereotypes about men and women in librarianship can have pernicious effects. Not only can they affect the influence of librarians in the information environment, but they also impede recruitment of librarians and affect the status and growth of the profession as a whole.

But how much of librarians' fears are real? It is true that some professions are perceived as feminine and others masculine. For example, in 1988 Beggs and Doolittle (1993) found that among 129 occupation titles, "Head Librarian" was considered the sixth most feminine. The only occupations considered more feminine were manicurist, registered nurse, receptionist, private secretary, and prima ballerina. Interestingly, this study replicated a 1975 study that placed "Head Librarian" as the ninth most feminine, suggesting that the stereotyping has increased. This study also suggested that gender stereotyping of professions is greater among males than females. This does not necessarily mean that the traits portrayed in a "feminine" profession are problematic. Morrisey and Case (1988) specifically studied perceptions of male librarians by college students and found that the perception was often quite positive. They found that the most common terms to describe male librarians were "organized," "approachable," "logical," "friendly," "patient," and "serious" (p. 457). Their conclusion was that male librarians perceived themselves in a much more negative light than others did. Schuman (1990) observed that although there are negative images in the media about librarians, the supposition that all such images are negative is unfounded. She points out that such notable writers as Sinclair Lewis, Sherwood Anderson, Henry James, and Edith Wharton depicted librarians in nonstereotypical manners, and that these nonstereotypical depictions were not uncommon in fiction. Furthermore, the media's occasional portrayal of librarians in a negative light may well be in line with how the media portray most other professions. What occupation does not receive a negative portrayal in the media? Lawyers and politicians receive their share of media ignominy. Even if current images of librarians are somewhat negative, perhaps the future is brighter. One study of 117 children between the ages of 4 and 15 by Duffy (1990) examined whether children had a positive attitude toward librarians. Duffy found that 50 percent responded positively when asked if they would like to become librarians. Many of the young people had little idea of what librarianship involves, and saw the profession in terms of many of the stereotypes—the quiet of libraries, the apparent ease of the job, and the disciplinary atmosphere. In addition, the power of societal attitudes and socialization still played a role, girls were more likely to respond positively than boys, and the older children were less likely to endorse librarianship as a career. It appears that gender-role stereotyping is still in operation, and as children grow older they seem to receive societal messages that librarianship is a less desirable career than others.

More recent interpretations of the librarian's image using a "cultural studies" approach suggest that librarians would be best to accept the popular culture stereotype of the librarian as a "loveless frump" or "old maid," and use the stereotype to their advantage. Such theorists point out that popular images are tenacious, and it is easier to alter the meaning of them than to try to actively resist them. Adams (2002) and Radford and Radford (2003) argue that rather than vehemently objecting to the persistent image of the old-maid librarian, librarians should accept and transform it using such techniques as parody, mimicry, and humor to change the significance of the stereotype in the same way that gays and lesbians have transformed the term "queer." The 1995 film *Party Girl*, in which a young woman is transformed from a self-centered, fun-obsessed individual into a serious-minded librarian, and Web sites such as "Lipstick Librarian" (www.lipsticklibrarian.com) are seen by cultural studies theorists as good examples of ways in which the stereotype can be used to librarians' advantage.

Studies of the personalities of librarians have been conducted for many years and generally have focused on either public or academic librarians. The first major study was conducted by Alice Bryan in 1948. The study was part of a much larger study of public libraries in general, called the *Public Library Inquiry*. Bryan (1952) found that librarians were submissive and lacked qualities of leadership. Since then, a variety of studies have provided additional data that have been summarized by Agada (1984, 1987); these data suggest that, in general, both male and female librarians exhibit personality traits of deference, passivity, nonassertiveness, and self-abasement. Studies using the Myers-Briggs

Type Indicator (MBTI) suggest that librarians tend to be introverted. In terms of the MBTI typologies, the majority of librarians fall into one of two typologies: Introversion, Sensing, Thinking, Judging (ISTJ) or Introversion, Intuitive, Thinking, Judging (INTJ). Among the characteristics of individuals who fall into these two types are determination and perseverance, independence, a drive to work hard, the desire to innovate, and placing of a high value on competence (Scherdin 1994). Other studies have found librarians to be resistant to change, lacking initiative, and disinterested in decision making. These traits persist regardless of whether the studies were of academic or public librarians. Interestingly, there is little evidence that, despite the stereotype, librarians are authoritarian in character. One should also hasten to add that these traits were not considered to be pathological in character and, generally, librarians' personalities fell well within normal ranges. One should, of course, be very careful about trying to apply these findings to individuals. Fisher (1988), in reviewing many personality studies of librarians, concluded that many of the personality tests applied were flawed, and overall, there was no one distinct personality type for a librarian.

Nonetheless, from a historical perspective, the findings of passivity among librarians might, in part, be attributable to the numerical predominance of women in the library profession. Dee Garrison (1979) suggests in her work *The Apostles of Culture* that this legacy has brought low status to the profession. The numerical predominance of women has been a part of American librarianship, especially American public librarianship, since the latter half of the nineteenth century. The first woman clerk was hired by the Boston Public Library in 1852; by 1878 two-thirds of the library workforce was female, and by 1910 more than 75 percent of library workers were women (Garrison 1972). In these years, women were expected to be passive and deferent. Professions that women were permitted to enter were "service" oriented and would thus reflect these traits. Since that time, the proportion of women in the workforce has varied little.

The entrance of women into the library labor force was an outgrowth of several factors. The rapid growth of public libraries produced a substantial need for library workers. However, these libraries were poorly funded, so there was a need to locate individuals who were willing to work for low pay. Women represented just such a group. Male library leaders and managers openly acknowledged the desirability of hiring women because they would be willing to work for half the pay. Librarianship fit the values of work for women at the time. It was not considered fitting for women to enter the labor force except under special circumstances; women were expected to marry and remain in the home. If this proved unfeasible, there was a narrow range of jobs that would be considered acceptable, mostly related to nurturing or educational activities, such as teaching and nursing. For all intents and purposes, these positions permitted women to bring their home-making and child-raising skills into the workplace. They were, therefore, considered dispositionally suited to librarianship, because the library was seen as a civilizing and nurturing environment (Garrison 1972). This all fit very well into the nineteenth-century value of the possibility of individual moral improvement and the capacity of books and reading to effect moral development. Indeed, librarianship was sometimes described as missionary activity. The fact that the profession still draws at least some individuals to its ranks who share these convictions is, in part, a legacy of these historical forces and confirmation that the service aspect of librarianship is still deeply ingrained.

Garrison (1972) has suggested that the feminization of public librarianship created an inferior image for the profession, an image it may not have had, had it remained the domain of male scholars as in previous decades. In other words, an occupation that once had considerable potential had been depressed in terms of status because it had been appropriated into the sphere of women. This sphere generally did not include leadership: women were not perceived as potential heads of libraries, especially of the larger libraries, but rather as support workers—leadership, after all, was not a characteristic generally located within a woman's character. Further, it was assumed, albeit incorrectly, that her physical nature was more delicate and could not tolerate the rigors of administration. Indeed, administrative responsibilities might even lead to mental illness!

The legacy of this attitude still persists: women librarians comprise a disproportionately low percentage of administrative positions in both public and academic libraries. There are several possible explanations for this trend. Women tend to have more career breaks due to family and marital responsibilities, and they begin their library careers later than men. They also tend to remain within the same organization longer than men, which reduces the number of promotional opportunities. When they do move to other libraries, they are more likely than their male counterparts to relocate because of spouses' job changes. This often entails accepting the only positions available to them, rather than positions involving promotion. The underrepresentation of women in administrative positions, however, is not fully accounted for by the reasons noted above—*sex discrimination still appears to play a role* (Heim and Estabrook 1983).

Internally, the distribution of positions by gender may also reflect sensitivity to problems with image and status. Women are more likely to serve as children's librarians or in cataloging positions; men are more likely to seek technology-oriented and managerial positions, despite the fact that males have no greater motivation to manage than female librarians (Swisher, Du Mont, and Boyer 1985). The former categories reflect values of nurturance or attention to detail, the latter categories reflect technical competence, leadership, or managerial skills. Male children's librarians are a rarity and no doubt raise eyebrows, no matter how undeservedly, when encountered. The predominance of men in the technical and managerial categories further supports the theory that men are uneasy working in a field whose traditions are perceived as "feminine." In the general labor force, technological and managerial positions are still dominated by males; male librarians may find that occupying such positions within libraries mitigates their occupational ambivalence. In turn, it may further serve to depress the status and pay of women. As Hildenbrand (1989) observes, librarians in children's services and cataloging generally receive lower pay than librarians in other positions despite the fact that these are basic functions in libraries. These inequalities in specialties are another example of the messages sent to women that their work is of less value and status.

The apparent passive nature of the profession has led Garrison (1972) to lament that librarianship has not encouraged or drawn to it those with the necessary leadership or aggressiveness to establish librarianship in the pantheon of professions—precisely because of its passivity. As Garrison observes:

> Specifically lacking in the librarian's professional service code are a sense of commitment, a drive to lead rather than to serve and a clear-cut conception of professional rights and responsibilities. The feminization of library work is a major cause of these deficiencies. (pp. 144–145)

Although the facts seem clear—that librarianship appears to have relatively low status, that women predominate numerically, that the profession shows segregation in job by gender, and that there is a disproportionately large number of males in administrative and managerial positions—Garrison's explanations for these conditions have been sharply criticized by some social historians, especially those who focus on gender as a critical aspect of historical analysis (Hildenbrand 1992, 1996). Sometimes described as a "feminist" approach or "gendered history," this approach contends that understanding the status and place of women in librarianship necessitates an understanding of the historical, political, and social relationships between men and women, especially in terms of how power is distributed (Hildenbrand 1996). Hildenbrand (1992) argues that the traditional historical analysis applied to library history is biased. For example, important women in the history of librarianship are largely ignored while the achievements of prominent males are studied in detail. Garrison is criticized for attributing to women the responsibility for their poor status in the profession, rather than attributing it to the pernicious attitudes of the times and for failing to recognize the importance of the historical achievement of women librarians. Hildenbrand (1992) argues that a reanalysis of the history of the role of women in librarianship would reveal that they were responsible for its rapid growth, the increase in the quality of library workers, and the growth of a national purpose to public libraries.

Consistent with Hildenbrand's concerns, Roma Harris (1992) has suggested that librarians' self-consciousness with their image is counterproductive, especially when it leads to a self-deprecation of their profession. Such self-criticism leads to blaming the victim and denigrating worthy "feminine" traits rather than focusing on why society places such low status on nurturing activities. For Harris, the disparaging of caring attitudes and the lionizing of management, research, and technical expertise (considered male traits) is tantamount to endorsing and perpetuating the suppression of women. That the deprecation of these traits occurs by both men and women in the profession is equally disturbing.

Maack (1997) suggests that striving for the status traditionally associated with male-dominated professions such as law and medicine is misdirected. Rather, she argues that there is a need for a reconceptualization of professions to replace the understanding of professions that focuses only on the traditionally male-oriented factors of control and authority. The new concept would admit of three different types of professions: high-authority professions, such as law and medicine; indirect or product-oriented professions, such as engineering and architecture; and empowering professions, such as education, social work, and library and information science. In empowering professions, "the professional shares expertise with the goal of enabling clients to use knowledge in order to take control of their own lives or their own learning" (p. 284). It is a collaborative, client-centered activity in which sharing and facilitation are fundamental activities of the professional. Such a profession contrasts clearly with high-authority professions in which "the professional offers prescriptions, directives, or strategies that the client must follow" (p. 284). In the client-centered model, it is not power and authority that dominate, but the desire to develop abilities and promote confidence in clients so that they can deal with their own problems and challenges. Accepting the concept of empowering professions eliminates the need to strive to be like law or medicine and recognizes the vitality of a profession that increases the independence and abilities of others.

What Is the Future Role of Librarians?

Will librarians be performing the fundamental role of locating information in a chaotic information world? Few groups have as much familiarity with meeting information needs as librarians. In conjunction with information scientists, who explore the information needs not only of library users, but of information seekers more generally, librarians should play a vital role in designing and using information systems in a manner that helps people solve their own information problems.

It is likely that a good part of the librarian's functions will be shaped by the rapidly changing information technologies, especially the tremendous increase in information found outside the library itself. Will librarians of the future perform more direct evaluation of information for library users in the future? The issue has been raised by Rice (1989), who observed that librarians have never had difficulty in making judgments about what should be included in library collections, but find it very difficult to make judgments advising patrons about the quality and accuracy of information they provide. There are many difficulties in deciding for the patron which information is more valuable but, as Rice points out: "There is seldom a problem in finding information nowadays. The problem is usually in sorting through all of it and deciding which is best" (p. 59). Rice suggests that future librarians will exert much greater effort in consulting, teaching, and advising individuals in their search for information, and such activities will become an essential part of the librarians' function. This role will be advanced as the library "collection" consists increasingly of information available through networks. Many patrons will feel adrift in this sea of information and expect the librarian to provide advice and counsel on the reliability and value of various information sources. Certainly, the ubiquity of the Web increases this feeling of being "at sea" with all this information. Nonetheless, it is also unlikely that librarians will be perceived as having sufficient expertise to determine which information is of value for a particular patron and which is not. As Wiegand (1998) has noted, many other professionals in various disciplines believe they have greater expertise and authority to evaluate information in their own fields, and they are unlikely to relinquish authority over their professional terrain to librarians.

It is also possible that librarians will be playing roles similar to those of the past, but that some roles will expand while others will diminish. For example, *Library Journal* briefly reported on a survey of 1,000 librarians conducted by Jones e-global library in fall 2001. The results suggested that librarians perceived their most significant roles as instructing patrons in navigating the Web, directing patrons to appropriate information resources, evaluating collections, organizing resources, creating programs, creating e-resources, and establishing digital archiving. Interestingly, although many of these functions were seen as still being quite important five years from now, creating e-resources and establishing digital archiving were the only two seen as increasing in importance ("Projecting Librarians' Roles" 2002). Baruchson-Arbib and Bronstein (2002) conducted a survey of experts in the field of library and information science that seemed to confirm the idea that change will occur in an evolutionary, rather than revolutionary, fashion. The experts perceived that the traditional library model would not be replaced by a virtual one, but that the traditional model would undergo significant changes, especially in regard to accessing information outside the library. Similarly, they saw the role of professionals as increasingly user-centered rather than organization-centered and that there was greater need for LIS professionals to understand how individuals seek and use information. In addition, they saw the need for librarians to be more aggressive in marketing and promoting their services to the community, and to develop the skills needed to accomplish these activities.

It is possible, nonetheless, that the changes occurring in the information environment may require reconceptualizing the role of the librarian. The librarian of the twenty-first century, according to Debons (1985), will be seen as an "information intermediary," performing at least three basic functions:

- *Diagnosis*: Estimating the information need. The librarian as diagnostician employs analytical interviewing techniques to assess the patron's personal abilities, the level of information required, the appropriate type of information package, appropriate cost, and method of delivery.

- *Prescription*: Organizing the information and processing to meet the patron's needs.
- *Evaluation*: Determining if the diagnosis and prescription was effective. (p. 27)

Although the model appears rather "medical" in nature and may be an incomplete picture of all the functions of the future librarian, it provides an important context for the information-giving function that librarians often perform. The focus of the model is to adapt to the users' special needs and problems and to see the library as an information system. Adopting such a model is likely to require a restructuring of library policies and practices to reflect individual constituencies. Information systems are only effective if they meet client needs rather than the needs of the bureaucracy. This means that librarians will need to conduct a regular analysis of the information needs of their constituencies and an analysis of organizational barriers to access. Similarly, they must constantly improve access to information through increased networking and exploitation of information technologies.

SUMMARY

Information does not organize itself, the order must be imposed, and librarians and information scientists perform a valuable service in imposing this order. Although part of this function is accomplished through classification systems and controlled vocabularies, a major part of the task goes to the librarian, who applies organizing systems so that the information needs of patrons will be met. The role of the future librarian will be to anticipate and satisfy the information needs of patrons and to collect or provide access to the information that will be needed. The librarian will meet not only individual needs, but ensure that systems and services are effectively designed so that future needs can be met. The librarian of the future will be an information needs assessor, information evaluator, information planner, information services manager, and information instructor. One may well argue that this has been the role of librarians throughout their history, but it is clear that the challenge and breadth of their responsibilities have grown substantially. If they are able to adapt to the new information environment, they may well remain important contributors to controlling an ever-expanding information universe.

This is an exciting prospect, but there are pitfalls as well. The shift in emphasis toward accessing information through electronic technologies may have unintended negative consequences to the profession. Information technologies have focused librarians' activities on techniques for information access—emphasis being on locating specific information or citations. It is a role that fits comfortably in a society that sees information as a commodity, a role that can be comfortably exploited by those who know the value of information and can use it profitably. As such, the technical character of the knowledge needed to access information and the value of the knowledge that can be accessed tends to raise the status of the librarian (at least temporarily) insofar as he or she is perceived as possessing the special skills to find the knowledge needed. Yet librarians in a rush to exploit this trend may not be considering all the consequences. Estabrook (1981) has warned that this enthusiasm may be short-lived, as those with greater capital recognize the potential of information control and appropriate the information marketplace for themselves.

Perhaps even more important, will the emphasis on electronic information access lead librarians to neglect other obligations? Finding pieces of information has always been part of the librarian's role, but this role has traditionally been subsumed under larger purposes: the humanistic and democratic values of traditional librarianship, a tradition with the goal of helping people or providing education. Information provision is only one part of this function. The humanistic values in librarianship were referred to as the "cultural motivation" of librarianship by Butler (1951). This motivation was "the promotion of wisdom in the individual and in the community" (p. 246). The librarian was to foster understanding and judgment within the citizenry and society. From this perspective, librarians are educators, individuals who enrich the lives of library users through their advice and guidance. They foster the love of reading, provide intellectual stimulation, bring those not familiar with libraries into their confines, provide instruction so that library users can continue to grow and develop intellectually throughout their lives, and provide entertainment and diversion from an often weary world. It is not technological competence that forms the basis of such a model; it is service to people. What makes the role attractive is not merely satisfying an information need but caring about people, solving human problems, and improving lives.

The librarian is thus battered on the rocks of Scylla and Charybdis: needing to respond to rapidly changing modes of information access and the demands of those who require the most technologically intensive services and equipment and, at the same time, trying to satisfy traditional readers and promote library services among those with poor or nonexistent reading skills. These are not entirely incompatible obligations. Rather, the key question is whether the traditional social values of librarianship should form the context for the exploitation of information technologies by librarians, or whether the new information technologies create a new social context that changes the meaning and significance of libraries and librarians.

REFERENCES

Abbott, Andrew. *The System of Professions*. Chicago: University of Chicago, 1988.

Adams, Katherine C. "Loveless Frump as Hip and Sexy Party Girl: A Reevaluation of the Old-Maid Stereotype." *Library Quarterly* 70 (July 2000): 287–301.

Agada, John. "Studies of the Personality of Librarians." *Drexel Library Quarterly* 20 (spring 1984): 24–45.

———. "Assertion and the Librarian Personality." In *Encyclopedia of Library and Information Science*. New York: Marcel Dekker, 1987, 128–144.

Allard, Suzie. "LIS Education Development: Strategies for Improving Awareness, Part II." *Journal of Education for Library and Information Science* 41(summer 2000): 244–249.

American Library Association. "ALA Policy Manual: Policy 56.1." *ALA Handbook of Organization*, 1995–96. Chicago: ALA, 1996.

———. *Directory of Institutions Offering Accredited Master's Programs in Library and Information Science*. [Online] Available at *www.ala.org*. (Accessed January 13, 2004.)

———. *Standards for Accreditation of Master's Programs in Library and Information Studies*. Chicago: ALA, 1992.

———. Office of Library Personnel Resources. *Academic and Public Librarians: Data by Race, Ethnicity and Sex*. Chicago: ALA, 1986, 7, 13.

Association for Library and Information Science Educators [ALISE]. *Library and Information Science Education Statistical Report 2002*. Edited by Evelyn H. Daniel and Jerry D. Saye. Reston, Va.: ALISE, 2003.

———. *Educating Library and Information Science Professionals for a New Century: The KALIPER Report: Executive Summary*. Reston, Va.: ALISE, 2000.

Baruchson-Arbib, Shifra, and Jenny Bronstein. "A View to the Future of the Library and Information Science Profession: A Delphi Study." *Journal of the American Society for Information Science and Technology* 53 (March 2002): 397–408.

Beggs, Joyce M., and Dorothy C. Doolittle. "Perceptions Now and Then of Occupational Sex Typing: A Replication of Shinar's 1975 Study." *Journal of Applied Social Psychology* 23 (1993): 1435–1453.

Birdsall, William F. "Librarianship, Professionalism and Social Change." *Library Journal* 107 (February 1, 1982): 223–226.

Boyce, Bert R. "The Death of Library Education." *American Libraries* (March 1994): 257–259.

Brand, Barbara B. "Pratt Institute Library School: The Perils of Professionalization." In *Reclaiming the American Library Past: Writing the Women In*. Edited by Suzanne Hildenbrand. Norwood, N.J.: Ablex, 1996, 251–278.

Bryan, Alice. *The Public Librarian*. New York: Columbia University, 1952.

Bushman, John. "Asking the Right Questions about Information Technology." *American Libraries* (December 1990): 1026–1030.

Butler, Pierce. "Librarianship as a Profession." *The Library Quarterly* 21 (October 1951): 235–247.

Campbell, Jerry D. "Choosing to Have a Future." *American Libraries* 24 (June 1993): 560–566.

Campbell, Lucy B. "The Hampton Institute Library School." In *Handbook of Black Librarianship*. Edited by E.J. Josey and Ann Shockley Allen. Littleton, Colo.: Libraries Unlimited, 1977, 35–46.

Conrad, Clifton F., and Kim Rapp-Hanretta. "Positioning Master's Programs in Library and Information Science: A Template for Avoiding Pitfalls and Seizing Opportunities in Light of Key External and Internal Forces." *Journal of Education in Library and Information Science* 43 (spring 2002): 92–104.

Davis, Donald G. Jr. "Curtis, Florence Rising." In *Dictionary of American Library Biography*. Edited by Bohdan S. Wynar. Littleton, Colo.: Libraries Unlimited, 1978, 108–109.

Debons, A. "The Information Professional: A Survey." In *The Information Profession*. Proceedings of a Conference Held in Melbourne, Australia (November 26–28, 1984). Edited by James Henri and Roy Sanders. Melbourne, Australia: Centre for Library Studies, 1985.

Dewey, Melvil. "The Profession." *Library Journal* 114 (June 15, 1989): 5. Reprinted from *American Library Journal* 1 (1876).

Dictionary of American Library Biography. Edited by Bohdan S. Wynar. Littleton, Colo.: Libraries Unlimited, 1978.

Duffy, Joan R. "Images of Librarians and Librarianship: A Study." *Journal of Youth Services in Libraries* 3 (summer 1990): 303–308.

Estabrook, Leigh. "Productivity, Profit, and Libraries." *Library Journal* 106 (July 1981): 1377–1380.

Fisher, David P. "Is the Librarian a Distinct Personality Type?" *Journal of Librarianship* 20 (January 1988): 36–47.

"Four Years of Progress: The Spectrum Initiative Leads On." *American Libraries* 33 (August 2002): 16–17.

Gambee, Budd L. "Fairchild, Mary Salome Cutler." In *Dictionary of American Library Biography*. Edited by Bohdan S. Wynar. Littleton, Colo.: Libraries Unlimited, 1978, 167–170.

Garrison, Dee. *The Apostles of Culture: The Public Librarian and American Society, 1876–1920*. New York: Free Press, 1979.

———. "The Tender Technicians: The Feminization of Public Librarianship." *Journal of Social History* 6 (winter 1972–1973): 131–156.

Grotzinger, Laurel A. "Kroeger, Alice Bertha." In *Dictionary of American Library Biography*. Edited by Bohdan S. Wynar. Littleton, Colo.: Libraries Unlimited, 1978a, 295–298.

———. *The Power and the Dignity: Librarianship and Katharine Sharp*. New York: Scarecrow, 1966.

———. "Sharp, Katharine Lucinda." In *Dictionary of American Library Biography*. Edited by Bohdan S. Wynar. Littleton, Colo.: Libraries Unlimited, 1978b, 470–473.

Harris, Roma M. *Librarianship: The Erosion of a Woman's Profession*. Norwood, N.J.: Ablex, 1992.

Hauptman, Robert, "Iconoclastic Education: The Library Science Degree." *Catholic Library World* 58 (May–June 1987): 252–253.

Heim, Kathleen, and Leigh Estabrook. *Career Profiles and Sex Discrimination in the Library Profession*. Chicago: ALA, 1983.

Hildenbrand, Suzanne. "A Historical Perspective on Gender Issues in American Librarianship." *The Canadian Journal of Information Science* 17 (September 1992): 18–28.

———. "Women in Library History: From the Politics of Library History to the History of Library Politics." In *Reclaiming the American Library Past: Writing the Women In*. Edited by Suzanne Hildenbrand. Norwood, N.J.: Ablex, 1996, 1–23.

———. "'Women's Work' within Librarianship." *Library Journal* 114 (September 1, 1989): 153–155.

Holley, Edward G. "The Merwine Case and the MLS: Where Was ALA?" *American Libraries* 15 (May 1984): 327–330.

Irvine, Betty Jo. *Sex Segregation in Librarianship: Demographic and Career Patterns of Academic Library Administrators*. Westport, Conn: Greenwood, 1985.

Josey, E.J. "Minority Representation in Library and Information Science Programs." *The Bookmark* 48 (fall 1989): 54–57.

Karlowich, Robert A., and Nasser Sharify. "Plummer, Mary Wright." In *Dictionary of American Library Biography*. Edited by Bohdan S. Wynar. Littleton, Colo.: Libraries Unlimited, 1978, 399–402.

Koenig, Michael E.D., and Charles Hildreth. "The End of the Standalone 'Library School.'" *Library Journal* 127 (June 15, 2002): 40–42.

Lynch, Beverly P. "Education and Training of Librarians." In *Rethinking the Library In the Information Age*. Washington, D.C: U.S. GPO, 1989, 75–92.

Maack, Mary Niles. "Toward a New Model of the Information Professions: Embracing Empowerment." *Journal of Education for Library and Information Science* 38 (fall 1997): 283–302.

———. "Women in Library Education: Down the Up Staircase." *Library Trends* 34 (winter 1986): 401–431.

Main, Linda. "Research versus Practice: A 'No' Contest." *RQ* 30 (winter 1990): 226–228.

Mason, Richard O. "What Is an Information Professional?" *Journal of Education for Library and Information Science* 31 (fall 1990): 122–138

McCook, Kathleen de la Peña, and Paula Geist. "Diversity Deferred: Where Are the Minority Librarians?" *Library Journal* 118 (November 1, 1993): 35–38.

McPheeters, Annie L. *Library Service in Black and White: Some Personal Recollections, 1921–1980*. Metuchen, N.J.: Scarecrow, 1988.

Moran, Barbara B. "Practitioners vs. LIS Educators: Time to Reconnect." *Library Journal* 126 (November 1, 2001): 52–55.

Morrisey, Locke J., and Donald O. Case. "There Goes My Image." The Perception of Male Librarians by Colleague, Student, and Self." *College and Research Libraries* 49 (September 1988): 453–464.

Nielsen, Brian. "The Role of the Public Services Librarian: The New Revolution." In *Rethinking the Library in the Information Age*. Washington, D.C.: GPO, 1989, 179–200.

Paris, Marion. *Library School Closings: Four Case Studies*. Metuchen, N.J.: Scarecrow, 1988.

"Projecting Librarians' Roles." *Library Journal* 127(February 1, 2002): 48.

Radford, Marie L., and Gary P. Radford. "Librarians and Party Girls: Cultural Studies and the Meaning of the Librarian." *Library Quarterly* 73 (2003): 54–69.

Rayward, W. Boyd. "Library and Information Sciences: Disciplinary Differentiation, Competition, Convergence." In *The Study of Information: Disciplinary Messages*. Edited by Fritz Machlup and Una Mansfield. New York: Wiley, 1983, 343–363.

Reeves, William Joseph. *Librarians as Professionals*. Lexington, Mass.: Lexington Books, 1980.

Rice, James. "The Hidden Role of Librarians." *Library Journal* 114 (January 1989): 57–59.

Robbins-Carter, Jane, and Charles A. Seavey. "The Master's Degree: Basic Preparation for Professional Practice." *Library Trends* 34 (spring 1986): 561–580.

Saracevic, Tefko. "Closing of Library Schools in North America: What Role Accreditation?" *Libri* 44 (November 1994): 190–200.

Scherdin, Mary Jane. "Vive la Difference: Exploring Librarian Personality Types Using the MBTI." In *Discovering Librarians*. Edited by Mary Jane Scherdin. Chicago: ACRL, 1994, 125–156.

Schuman, Patricia Glass. "The Image of Librarians: Substance or Shadow?" *Journal of Academic Librarianship* 16 (1990): 86–89.

Swisher, Robert, Rosemary Ruhig DuMont, and Calvin J. Boyer. "The Motivation to Manage: A Study of Academic Librarians and Library Science Students." *Library Trends* 34 (fall 1985): 219–234.

U.S. Office of Education. *Public Libraries in the United States of America: Their History, Condition, and Management: Special Report*. Washington D.C.: GPO, 1876.

Van House, Nancy, and Stuart A. Sutton. "The Panda Syndrome." *Journal of Education for Library and Information Science* 41 (winter 2000): 52–68.

Vann, Sarah K. *Training for Librarianship before 1923*. Chicago: ALA, 1961.

Weibel, Kathleen, and Kathleen M. Heim. *The Role of Women in Librarianship 1876–1976: The Entry, Advancement, and Struggle for Equalization in One Profession*. Phoenix: Oryx, 1979.

White, Carl M. *A Historical Introduction to Library Education: Problems and Progress to 1951*. New York: Scarecrow, 1976.

White, Herbert S. "The Future of Library and Information Science Education."

Journal of Education for Library and Information Science 26 (winter 1986): 174–181.

Wiegand, Wayne A. *Irrepressible Reformer: A Biography of Melvil Dewey*. Chicago: ALA, 1996.

———. "The Politics of Cultural Authority." *American Libraries* 29 (January 1998): 80–82.

———. "The Structure of Librarianship: Essay on an Information Profession." *Canadian Journal of Information and Library Science* 24 (April 1999): 17–37.

Williamson, Charles C. *Training for Library Service: A Report Prepared for the Carnegie Corporation of New York*. Boston: Updike, 1923.

Wilson, Patrick. "Bibliographical R&D." In *The Study of Information*. Edited by Fritz Machlup and Una Mansfield. New York: Wiley, 1983, 389–397.

Windsor, Justin. "A Word to Starters of Libraries." *American Library Journal* 1 (September 1876): 1–3.

Winter, Michael F. *The Culture and Control of Expertise: Toward a Sociological Understanding of Librarianship*. Westport, Conn.: Greenwood, 1988.

Selected Readings

The literature of library and information science is vast. The following list of readings is intended as a starting place for exploring this literature. The headings reflect the major subject matter in the book.

Ethical issues
Impact of technology
Information policy
Information policy and libraries
Information science
Intellectual organization of libraries
Librarianship
Libraries as organizations
Mission and values of libraries

Additional assistance is provided by the list of selected periodicals, indexes, and encyclopedias in Appendix A.

ETHICAL ISSUES

Books

Biegel, Stuart. *Beyond Our Control? Confronting the Limits of Our Legal System in the Age of Cyberspace.* Cambridge, Mass.: MIT, 2003.

Gorman, Michael. *Our Enduring Values: Librarianship in the 21st Century.* Chicago: ALA, 2000.

Hauptman, Robert. *Ethical Challenges in Librarianship.* Phoenix: Oryx, 1988.

———. *Ethics and Librarianship.* Jefferson, N.C.: McFarland, 2002.

Lancaster, F.W., ed. *Ethics and the Librarian: Proceedings of the Allerton Park Institute: Volume 31.* Urbana-Champaign, Ill.: Graduate School of Library and Information Science, University of Illinois, 1991.

Lindsey, Jonathan A., and Ann E. Prentice. *Professional Ethics and Librarians.* Phoenix: Oryx, 1985.

Lipinski, Tomas A. *Libraries, Museums, and Archives.* Lanham, Md.: Scarecrow, 2002.

Mason, Richard O., Florence M. Mason, and Mary J. Culnan. *Ethics of Information Management.* Thousand Oaks, Calif.: Sage, 1995.

Mintz, Anne P., ed. *Information Ethics: Concerns for Librarianship and the Information Industry.* Jefferson, N.C.: McFarland, 1990.

Severson, Richard J. *The Principles of Information Ethics.* Armonk, N.Y.: M.E. Sharpe, 1997.

Articles

Alfino, Mark, and Linda Pierce. "The Social Nature of Information." *Library Trends* 49 (winter 2001): 471–485.

American Library Association. "ALA Code of Ethics." *American Libraries* 26 (July/August 1995): 673.

"ASIS Professional Guidelines." *Bulletin of the American Society for Information Science* 20 (December/January 1994): 4.

Baker, Sharon L. "Needed: An Ethical Code for Library Administrators." *Journal of Library Administration* 16 (1992): 1–17.

Barnes, Robert F. "Some Thoughts on Professional Ethics Codes." *Bulletin of the American Society for Information Science* 12 (April/May 1986): 19–20.

Bierbaum, Esther Green. "Searching for the Human Good: Some Suggestions for a Code of Ethics for Technical Services." *Technical Services Quarterly* 11 (1994): 1–18.

Capurro, Rafael. "Moral Issues in Information Science." *Journal of Information Science* 11 (1985): 113–123.

Dowd, Robert. "I Want to Find Out How to Freebase Cocaine; or Yet Another Unobtrusive Test of Reference Performance." *The Reference Librarian* 25–26 (1989): 483–493.

Du Mont, Rosemary Ruhig. "Ethics in Librarianship: A Management Model." *Library Trends* 40 (fall 1991): 201–215.

Estabrook, Leigh. "The Library as a Socialist Institution in a Capitalist Environment." In *The Economics of Information*. Edited by Jana Varlys. Jefferson, N.C.: McFarland, 1982.

Finks, Lee W. "Librarianship Needs a New Code of Professional Ethics." *American Libraries* 22 (January 1991): 84–92.

———. "What Do We Stand For? Values without Shame." *American Libraries* 20 (April 1989): 352–356.

Ford, Nigel, David Miller, and Nicola Moss. "The Role of Individual Differences in Internet Searching: An Empirical Study." *Journal of the American Society for Information Science and Technology* 52 (2001): 1049–1066.

Fricke, Martin, Kay Mathiesen, and Don Fallis. "The Ethical Presuppositions Behind the Library Bill of Rights." *Library Quarterly* 70 (2000): 468–491.

Froehlich, Thomas J. "Ethical Considerations of Information Professionals." *Annual Review of Information Science and Technology (ARIST)* 27 (1992): 291–324.

———. "Ethical Considerations in Technology Transfer." *Library Trends* 40 (fall 1991): 275–302.

Goehner, Donna M. "Vendor-Library Relations: The Ethics of Working with Vendors." In *Understanding the Business of Library Acquisitions*. Edited by Karen Schmidt. Chicago: ALA, 1990, 137–151.

Gorman, Michael. "Values for Human-to-Human Reference." *Library Trends* 50 (fall 2001): 168–182.

Hauptman, Robert. "Professionalism or Culpability? An Experiment in Ethics." *Wilson Library Bulletin* 50 (April 1976): 626–627.

———, ed. *Ethics and the Dissemination of Information*. Special issue of *Library Trends* 40 (fall 1991): 199–375.

———, ed. *Journal of Information Ethics*. Jefferson, N.C.: McFarland, 1991–.

Hendrickson, Kent. "Library Vendors: How Do They Use Us?" *Library Acquisitions: Practice and Theory* 13 (1989): 121–123.

Koehler, Wallace. "Professional Values and Ethics as Defined by 'The LIS Discipline'" *Journal of Education for Library and Information Science* 44 (spring 2003): 99–119.

Lennon, Donald R. "Ethical Issues in Archival Management." *North Carolina Libraries* 51 (spring 1993): 18–22.

Mintz, Anne P. *Information Ethics: Concerns for Librarianship and the Information Industry: Proceedings of the 27th Annual Symposium of the Graduate Alumni and Faculty of the Rutgers School of Communication, Information, and Library Studies*. April 14, 1989. Jefferson, N.C.: McFarland, 1989.

Rathbun, Susan R. "Ethics Issues in Reference Service: Overview and Analysis." *North Carolina Libraries* 51 (spring 1993): 11–14.

Rodger, Joey. "Core Values: Our Common Ground." *American Libraries* 29 (October 1998): 68–71.

Rubin, Richard. "Ethical Issues in Library Personnel Management." *Journal of Library Administration* 14 (1991): 1–16.

———. "Moral Distancing and the Use of Information Technologies: The Seven Temptations." In *Ethics in the Computer Age: Conference Proceedings*. Gatlinburg, Tenn., November 11–13, 1994. New York: ACM, 1994, 151–155.

Rubin, Richard E., and Thomas J. Froehlich. "Ethical Aspects of Library and Information Science." *Encyclopedia of Library and Information Science*, 58 supp. New York: Marcel Dekker, 1996, 33–52.

Smith, Martha M., ed. *Information Ethics* Special issue of *North Carolina Libraries* 51 (spring 1993).

Vitell, Scott, and Donald L. Davis. "Ethical Beliefs of MIS Professionals: The Frequency and Opportunity for Unethical Behavior." *Journal of Business Ethics* 9 (1990): 63–70.

Weissinger, Thomas. "Competing Models of Librarianship: Do Core Values Make a Difference?" *Journal of Academic Librarianship* 29 (January 2003): 32–39.

Wengwert, Robert G. "Some Ethical Aspects of Being an Information Professional." *Library Trends* 49 (winter 2001): 486–509.

IMPACT OF TECHNOLOGY

Books

Arms, William Y. *Digital Libraries*. Cambridge, Mass.: MIT, 2000.

Billings, Harold. *Magic and Hypersystems: Constructing the Information-Sharing Library*. Chicago: ALA, 2002.

Birdsall, William F. *The Myth of the Electronic Library: Librarianship and Social Change in America*. Westport, Conn: Greenwood, 1994.

Cassell, Kay Ann. *Developing Reference Collections and Services in an Electronic Age*. New York: Neal-Schuman, 1999.

Deegan, Marilyn, and Simon Tanner. *Digital Futures: Strategies for the Information Age*. New York: Neal-Schuman, 2002.

De Rosa, Cathy, Lorcan Dempsey, and Alane Wilson. *The 2003 OCLC Environmental Scan: Pattern Recognition: A Report to the OCLC Membership*. Dublin, Ohio: OCLC, 2004.

Dreyfus, Hubert L. *On the Internet*. New York: Routledge, 2001.

Fielden, Ned L., and Lucy Kuntz. *Search Engines Handbook*. Jefferson, N.C.: McFarland, 2002.

Hacker, Scot. *MP3: The Definitive Guide*. Sebastopol, Calif.: O'Reilly, 2000.

Janes, Joseph, David Carter, Annette Lagace, Michael McLennen, Sara Ryan, and Schelle Simcox. *The Internet Public Library Handbook*. New York: Neal-Schuman, 1999.

Jones, Wayne, ed. *E-Serials: Publishers, Libraries, Users, and Standards*. 2nd ed. New York: Haworth, 2003.

Kovacs, Diane. *Building Electronic Library Collections*. New York: Neal-Schuman, 2000.

Lancaster, F.W. *Toward Paperless Information Systems*. New York: Academic, 1978.

Lancaster, F.W., and Amy Warner. *Intelligent Technologies in Library and Information Service Applications*. Medford, N.J.: Information Today, 2001.

Lankes, R. David, John W. Collins III, and Abby S. Kasowitz. *Digital Reference Service in the New Millennium: Planning, Management, and Evaluation*. New York: Neal-Schuman, 2000.

Laughlin, Sara, ed. *Library Networks in the New Millennium: Top Ten Trends.* Chicago: ALA, 2000.

Lazinger, Susan S. *Digital Preservation and Metadata.* Englewood, Colo.: Greenwood, 2001.

Lui, Lewis-Guodo, ed. *The Role and Impact of the Internet on Library and Information Services.* Westport, Conn.: Greenwood, 2001.

Pew Internet and American Life Project. *The Ever-Shifting Internet Population: A New Look at Internet Access and the Digital Divide.* Washington, D.C.: Pew, 2003.

Shuman, Bruce A. *Issues for Libraries and Information Science in the INTERNET Age.* Englewood, Colo.: Libraries Unlimited, 2001.

Smith, Abby. *Why Digitize?* Washington, D.C.: Council on Library and Information Resources, February 1999.

Smith, Mark, ed. *Managing the Internet Controversy.* New York: Neal-Schuman, 2001.

Sun Microsystems. *Digital Library Technology Trends.* [Online] Available at *www.sun.com/products-n-solutions/edu/whitepapers/pdf/digital_library_trends.pdf.* (Accessed July 25, 2003.)

Tennant, Roy, ed. *XML in Libraries.* New York: Neal-Schuman, 2002.

U.S. Department of Commerce. *A Nation Online: How Americans Are Expanding Their Use of the Internet.* Washington, D.C.: National Telecommunications and Information Administration, February 2002.

Weizenbaum, Joseph. *Computer Power and Human Reason*: From Judgment to Calculation. San Francisco: W.H. Freeman, 1976.

Articles

Bartlett, Virginia. "Technostress and Librarians." *Library Administration and Management* 9 (fall 1995): 226–230.

Bell, Steven J. "Is More Always Better?" *American Libraries* 34 (January 2003): 44–46.

Bennett, Scott. "The Golden Age of Libraries." *Journal of Academic Librarianship* 27 (July 2001): 256–259.

Birdsall, William F. "Breaking the Myth of the Library as Place." In *The Myth of the Electronic Library: Librarianship and Social Change in America.* Westport, Conn: Greenwood, 1994, 7–29.

Booth, Doris. "Searching for the Elusive eBook Market." [Online] Available at *www.authorlink.com/in010501_booth_ebook%20mkt.htm.* (Accessed September 2, 2003.)

Brod, Craig. "How to Deal with 'Technostress.'" *Office Administration and Automation* 45 (August 1984): 28–47.

Burbules, Nicholas C. "Paradoxes of the Web: The Ethical Dimensions of Credibility." *Library Trends* 49 (winter 2001): 441–453.

Bushman, John. "Asking the Right Questions About Information Technology." *American Libraries* 21 (December 1990): 1026–1030.

De Gennaro, Richard D. "Technology and Access in an Enterprise Society." *Library Journal* 114 (October 1, 1989): 40–43.

D'Elia, George, Corinne Jorgensen, and Joseph Woelfel. "The Impact of the Internet on Public Library Use: An Analysis of the Current Consumer Market for Library and Internet Services." *Journal of the American Society for Information Science and Technology* 53 (2002): 802–820.

Dorman, David. "Open Source Software and the Intellectual Commons." *American Libraries* 33 (December 2002): 51–54.

Dowlin, Kenneth E. "Distribution in an Electronic Environment, or Will There Be Libraries as We Know Them in the Internet World?" *Library Trends* 43 (winter 1995): 409–417.

Dugan, Robert E. "Information Technology Budgets and Costs: Do You Know What Your Information Technology Costs Each Year?" *Journal of Academic Librarianship* 28 (July 2002): 235–243.

Epstein, Jason. "Reading: The Digital Future." *New York Review of Books* 48 (July 5, 2001). [Online] Available at *www.nybooks.com/articles/14318*. (Accessed September 2, 2003.)

Fine, Sara F. "Terminal Paralysis or Showdown at the Interface." In *Human Aspects of Library Automation: Helping Staff and Patrons Cope*. Edited by Debora Shaw. Urbana-Champaign, Ill.: Graduate School of Library and Information Science, 1985, 3–15.

Fritch, John W., and Robert L. Cromwell. "Evaluating Internet Resources: Identity, Affiliation, and Cognitive Authority in a Networked World." *Journal of the American Society for Information Science and Technology* 52 (2001): 499–507.

Fritch, John W., and Scott B. Mandernack. "The Emerging Reference Paradigm: A Vision of Reference Services in a Complex Information Environment." *Library Trends* 50 (fall 2001): 286–305.

Gomery, Douglas. "In Search of the Cybermarket." *The Wilson Quarterly* 18 (summer 1994): 9–17.

Hahn, Trudi Bellardo. "Pioneers of the Online Age." *Information Processing and Management* 32 (January 1996): 33–48.

Janes, Joseph. "How to Think About Technology." *Library Journal* 127 (February 1, 2002): 30–32.

Janes, Joseph, Chrystie Hill, and Alex Rolfe. "Ask-an-Expert Services Analysis." *Journal of the American Society for Information Science and Technology* 52 (2001): 1106–1121.

Jerabek, J. Ann, Linda S. Meyer, and S. Thomas Kordinak. "'Library Anxiety' and 'Computer Anxiety': Measures, Validity, and Research Implications." *Library and Information Science Research* 23 (2001): 277–289.

Kirkpatrick, Cheryl H. "Getting Two for the Price of One: Accessibility and Usability." *Computers in Libraries* 23 (January 2003): 26–29.

Kling, Rob, and Ewa Callahan. "Electronic Journals, the Internet, and Scholarly Communication." *Annual Review of Information Science and Technology* 37 (2003), 127–177.

Lenhart, Amanda. *The Ever-Shifting Internet Population*. Washington, D.C.: Pew Internet and American Life Project, 2003.

Lewis, Marilyn P. "The Effects of Technology on Midcareer Librarians." *Library Trends* 50 (spring 2002): 717–724.

Lynch, Clifford. "The Battle to Define the Future of the Book in the Digital World."

[Online] Available at *http://firstmonday.dk/isssues/issue6_6/lynch/index.html*. (Accessed on September 2, 2003.)

Martinez, Michael E. "Access to Information Technologies Among School-Age Children: Implications for a Democratic Society." *Journal of the American Society for Information Science* 45 (July 1994): 395–400.

Max, D.T. "The Last Book." *Utne Reader* 104 (March–April 2001): 74–80.

Mickey, Bill. "Open Source and Libraries: An Interview with Dan Chudnov." *Online* (January 2001). [Online] Available at *www.onlinemag.net/OL2001/mickey1_01.html*. (Accessed June 23, 2003.)

Molyneux, Robert E., and Robert V. Williams. "Measuring the Internet." *Annual Review of Information Science and Technology* 34 (1999): 287–339.

Mutch, Andrew, and Karen Ventura. "The Promise of Internet2." *Library Journal* 128 (summer 2003): 14–16.

Noam, Eli M. "Will Books Become the Dumb Medium?" *Educom Review* 33 (March–April 1998): 18–24.

Ormes, Sarah. "An E-Book Primer." [Online] Available at *www.ukoln.ac.uk/public/earl/issuepapers/ebook.htm*. (Accessed October 1998.)

Pinfield, Stephen, Jonathan Eaton, Catherine Edwards, Rosemary Russell, Astrid Wissenburg, and Peter Wynne. "Realizing the Hybrid Library." [Online] Available at *www.dlib.org/dlib/october98/10pinfield.html*. (Accessed on July 8, 2003.)

Richey, Rodger, and Kris Klink. "The Embedded Hardware for the MP3 Revolution." *Electronic Engineering* 71 (September 1999): 55–60.

Rusbridge, Chris. "Towards the Hybrid Library." [Online] Available at *www.dlib.org/dlib/july98/rusbridge/07rusbridge.html*.

Smith, Abby. *The Future of the Past: Preservation in American Research Libraries.* [Online] Available at *www.clir.org/pubs/reports/pub82/pub82text.html*. (Accessed August 28, 2003.)

Whitlatch, Jo Bell. "Evaluating Reference Services in the Electronic Age." *Library Trends* 50 (fall 2001): 207–217.

DIGITAL LIBRARIES/WEB PORTALS

Fox, Edward A., and Shalini R. Urs. "Digital Libraries." *Annual Review of Information Science and Technology* 36. (2002): 503–589.

Greenstein, Daniel. "Digital Libraries and Their Challenges." *Library Trends* 49 (fall 2000): 290–303.

Jackson, Mary E. "The Advent of Portals." *Library Journal* 127 (September 15, 2002): 36–41.

Jasco, Peter. "XML and Digital Libraries." *Computers in Libraries* 22 (September 2002): 46–49.

Miller, Rush G. "Shaping Digital Library Content." *Journal of Academic Libarianship* 28 (May 2002): 97–103.

Schottlaender, Brian E.C., and Mary E. Jackson. "The Current State and Future Promise of Portal Applications." In *The Bowker Annual Library and Book Trade Almanac.* 48th ed. Medford, N.J.: Information Today, 2003, 279–291.

Schwartz, Candy. "Digital Libraries: An Overview." *Journal of Academic Libraries* 36 (November 2000): 385–393.

Wiederhold, Gio. "Digital Libraries, Value, and Productivity." *Communications of the ACM* 38 (April 1995): 85–96.

DIGITAL REFERENCE

Coffman, Steve. "So You Want to Do Virtual Reference?" *Public Libraries* Supplement 40 (2001): 14–29.

Janes, Joseph. "Digital Reference: Reference Librarians' Experiences and Attitudes." *Journal of the American Society for Information Science and Technology* 53 (2002): 549–566.

Lankes, R. David. "The Foundations of Digital Reference." In Lankes, R. David, John W. Collins III, and Abby S. Kasowitz. *Digital Reference Service in the New Millennium: Planning, Management, and Evaluation.* New York: Neal-Schuman, 2000: 1–100.

White, Marilyn Domas. "Digital Reference Services: Framework for Analysis and Evaluation." *Library and Information Science Research* 23 (2001): 211–231.

INFORMATION POLICY

Books

GENERAL

American Library Association, Task Force on Restrictions on Access to Government Information. *Restrictions on Access to Government Information (RAGI) Report.* Chicago: ALA, June 9, 2003.

Burger, Robert H. *Information Policy: A Framework for Evaluation and Policy Research.* Norwood, N.J.: Ablex, 1993.

Compaine, Benjamin, ed. *The Digital Divide: Facing a Crisis or Creating a Myth?* Cambridge, Mass.: MIT, 2001.

Computer Professionals for Social Responsibility. *Serving the Community: A Public Interest Vision of the National Information Infrastructure.* Washington, D.C.: CPSR, 1993.

Critical Infrastructure Protection Board. *National Strategy to Secure Cyberspace.* Washington, D.C.: White House, February 2003.

Harris, Lesley Ellen. *Licensing Digital Content: A Practical Guide for Librarians.* Chicago: ALA, 2002.

Hoffmann, Gretchen McCord. *Copyright in Cyberspace: Questions and Answers for Librarians.* New York: Neal-Schuman, 2001.

Horrigan, John B. *Consumption of Information Goods and Services in the United States.* Washington, D.C.: Pew Internet and American Life Project, 2003.

Information Infrastructure Task Force,Working Group on Intellectual Property Rights. *Intellectual Property and the National Information Infrastructure.* Washington, D.C.: Department of Commerce, September 1995.

Library of Congress. *To Preserve and Protect: The Strategic Stewardship of Cultural Resources.* Washington, D.C.: GPO, 2002.

Lynch, Clifford A. *Accessibility and Integrity of Networked Information Collections.* Washington D.C.: Office of Technology Assessment, 1993.

McClure, Charles R., Joe Ryan, and John Carlo Bertot. *Public Library Internet Services and the Digital Divide: The Role and Impacts from Selected External Funding Sources.* Tallahassee, Fla.: Information Use Management Policy Institute, School of Information Studies, 2002.

Mossberger, Karen, Caroline Tolbert, and Mary Stansbury. *Virtual Inequality: Beyond the Digital Divide.* Washington D.C.: Georgetown University Press, 2003.

National Digital Information Infrastructure and Preservation Program. *Preserving Our Digital Heritage: Plan for the National Digital Information Infrastructure and Preservation Program.* Washington D.C.: Library of Congress. [Online] Available at *www.digitalpreservation.gov/repor/ndipp_plan.pdf.*

Office of Homeland Security. *National Strategy for Homeland Security.* Washington., D.C.: White House, July 2002.

Office of Library Programs, Office of Educational Research and Improvement U.S. Dept. of Education. *Rethinking the Library in the Information Age.* Washington, D.C.: GPO, 1989.

Science Applications International Corporation. *Information Warfare: Legal, Regulatory, Policy and Organizational Considerations for Assurance.* Washington D.C.: Joint Staff, The Pentagon, 1995.

U.S. Department of Commerce. *Falling Through the Net: A Report on the Telecommunications and Information Technology Gap in America.* Washington D.C.: National Telecommunications and Information Administration, July 1999.

U.S. Department of Commerce. *Falling Through the Net II: New Data on the Digital Divide.* [Online] Available at *www.ntia.doc.gov/ntiahome/net2.* (Accessed on August 11, 1998.)

U.S. National Commission on Libraries and Information Science. *Libraries and the National Information Infrastructure: Proceedings of the 1994 Forum on Library and Information Services Policy.* Washington, D.C.: NCLIS, May 1994.

West, Cynthia K. *Techno-Human Mesh: The Growing Power of Information Technologies.* Westport, Conn.: Quorum, 2001.

Articles

Agnew, Grace. "Digital Rights Management: Why Libraries Should Be Major Players." In *The Bowker Annual Library and Book Trade Almanac.* 48th ed. Medford, N.J.: Information Today, 2003, 267–278.

Braman, Sandra. "Defining Information: An Approach for Policymakers." *Telecommunications Policy* 13 (September 1989): 242.

Horrigan, John B. *Consumption of Information Goods and Services in the United States.* Washington, D.C.: Pew Internet and American Life Project, 2003.

Lievrouw, Leah A., and Sharon E. Farb. "Information and Equity." *Annual Review of Information Science and Technology* 37 (2003): 499–540.

McCain, Roger A. "Information as Property and as a Public Good: Perspectives from the Economic Theory of Property Rights." *Library Quarterly* 58 (1988): 265–282.

McClure, Charles R., John Carlo Bertot, and John C. Beachboard. "Enhancing the Role of Public Libraries in the National Information Infrastructure." *Public Libraries* 35 (July-August 1996): 232–238.

McClure, Charles R., Mary McKenna, William E. Moen, and Joe Ryan. "Toward a Virtual Library: Internet and the National Research and Education Network." In *Bowker Annual*. 38th ed. New York: Bowker, 1993, 25–45.

Minow, Mary "The USA Patriot Act." *Library Journal* 127 (October 1, 2002): 52–55.

Reyles, Harold C. "Homeland Security and Information Management." In *The Bowker Annual Library and Book Trade Almanac*. 48th ed. Medford, N.J.: Information Today, 2003, 231–250.

Rothberg, Marc. "Privacy and the National Information Infrastructure." *Educom Review* 29 (March/April 1994): 50–51.

Shill, Harold B. "Privatization of Public Information: Its Impact on Libraries." *Library Administration and Management* 5 (spring 1991): 99–109.

Weingarten, Fred W. "The Next Generation Internet: Government Policy and the Future of the Net." *American Libraries* 28 (September 1997): 13–15.

———. "Technological Change and the Evolution of Information Policy." *American Libraries* 27 (December 1996): 45–47.

Copyright

Agha, Syed Salim. "Ethics and Copyright: A Developing Country Perspective." *IFLA Journal* 23 (1997): 251–257.

Anestopoulou, Maria. "Challenging Intellectual Property Law in the Internet: An Overview of the Legal Implications of the MP3 Technology." *Information and Communications Technology Law* 10 (2001): 319–337.

Bronmo, Ole. "Copyright Legislation, Fair Use and the Efficient Dissemination of Scientific Knowledge." *IFLA Journal* 23 (1997): 290–294.

Cornish, Graham P. "Electronic Copyright Management Systems: Dream, Nightmare or Reality?" *IFLA Journal* 23 (1997): 284–287.

Crews, Kenneth. *Copyright Essentials for Librarians and Educators*. Chicago: ALA, 2000.

English, Jane, and Kirti Jacobs. "Royalties and Payments: Why Pay for Copyright? What Are Words Worth?" *IFLA Journal* 23 (1997): 270–274.

Gasaway, Laura N. "Balancing Copyright Concerns: The TEACH Act of 2001." *Educause* Review 36 (November/December 2001): 82–83.

———. "The Teach Act." *Outlook* 6 (April 2002): 44–45.

Giavarra, Emanualla. "European Copyright User Platform." *IFLA Journal* 23 (1997): 288–289.

Greene, Lisa H., and Steven J. Rizzi. "Database Protection Legislation: Views from the United States and WIPO." *Copyright World* 37 (January 1997): 36–42.

Harris, Lesley Ellen. *Licensing Digital Content: A Practical Guide for Librarians*. Chicago: ALA, 2002.

Heller, James S. "The Impact of Recent Litigation on Interlibrary Loan and Document Delivery." *Law Library Journal* 88 (spring 1996): 158–177.

————. "The Public Performance Right in Libraries: Is There Anything Fair About It?" *Law Library Journal* 84 (spring 1992): 315–340.

Hoffmann, Gretchen McCord. *Copyrights in Cyberspace: Questions and Answers for Librarians.* New York: Neal-Schuman, 2001.

Jackson, Mary E. "Copyright: The Worrisome Element in Electronic Document Delivery." *Wilson Library Bulletin* 67 (December 1992): 81–82, 119–120.

Kahn, Brian, and Hal R. Varian, eds. *Internet Publishing and Beyond: The Economics of Digital Information and Intellectual Property.* Cambridge, Mass: MIT, 2000.

Kasaras, Kostas. "Music in the Age of Free Distribution: MP 3 and Society." *First Monday* [Online] Available at *www. firstmonday.dk/issues/issue7_1/kasaras/ index.html.* (Accessed on September 9, 2003.)

Neal, James G. "Copyright Is Dead…Long Live Copyright." *American Libraries* 33 (December 2002): 48–51.

Norman, Sandy. "Copyright and Fair Use in the Electronic Information Age." *IFLA Journal* 23 (1997): 295–298.

Parker, James. "PLR in a Copyright Context." *IFLA Journal* 23 (1997): 299–304.

Paskin, Norman. "DOI: A 2003 Progress Report." *D-Lib Magazine* 9 (June 2003). [Online] Available at *www.dlib.org/dlib/june03/paskin/06paskin.html.*

Pearse, Richard. "Library Open-Distribution Systems and Copyright Infringement in Canada and the United States." *Law Library Journal* 86 (summer 1994): 399–443.

Peck, Robert S. *The First Amendment and Cyberspace.* Chicago: ALA, 2000.

Sato, Seiji. "Libraries and Publishers in the Digital Environment." *IFLA Journal* 23 (1997): 263–265.

Stevens, Al. "Into the World of MP3." *Dr. Dobb's Journal* 25 (September 2000): 115–120

Tepper, Laurie C. "Copyright Law and Library Photocopying: An Historical Survey." *Law Library Journal* 84 (spring 1992): 341–363.

Vaidhyanathan, Siva. *Copyrights and Copywrongs.* New York: New York University, 2001.

Valauskas, Edward J. "Copyright: Know Your Electronic Rights!" *Library Journal* 117 (August 1, 1992): 40–43.

Webster, Duane E. "Copyright, Libraries, and the Electronic Information Environment: Discussions and Developments in the United States." *IFLA Journal* 23 (1997): 280–283.

NATIONAL SECURITY

American Libraries [Online]. "Homeland Security Agents Pull Ohio Libraries' Haz-Mat Documents." (April 7, 2003.) [Online] Available at *www.ala.org/ ala/alaonline/currentnews/newsarchive/* (Accessed on July 22, 2003.)

American Library Association. *Restrictions on Access to Government Information (RAGI) Report.* Chicago: ALA, 2003.

Computer Scientists for Social Responsibility. "The Clipper Chip: Frequently Asked Questions (FAQ)." (August 1995) [Online] Available at *www.cpsr.org/ program/clipper-faq.html.* (Accessed on September 7, 1997).

Doyle, Charles. *The USA PATRIOT Act: Legal Analysis.* Washington D.C.: Congressional Research Service, Library of Congress, 2002.

Electronic Frontier Foundation (EFF). *EFF Analysis of the Provisions of the USA PATRIOT Act*. (October 31, 2001.) [Online] Available at *www.eff.org/Privacy/ Surveillance/Terrorism/20011031 _eff_usa_patriot_analysis.html*. (Accessed on May 27, 2003.)

"FBI Has Visited About 50 Libraries." (June 15, 2003) *Library Journal*. [Online] Available at *http://libraryjournal.com/index.asp?layout=articleArchive &articleid=CA302414*. (Accessed on May 27, 2003.)

Minow, Mary. "The USA Patriot Act." *Library Journal* 127 (October 1, 2002): 52–55.

Molander, Robert C., Andrew S. Riddile, and Peter A. Wilson. *Strategic Information Warfare: A New Face of War*. (1996) [Online] Available at *www.rand.org* (Accessed on September 7, 1997).

Office of Homeland Security. *National Strategy for Homeland Security*. Washington D.C.: OHS, July 2002.

———. *The National Strategy to Secure Cyberspace*. Washington D.C.: OHS, February 2003.

Relyea, Harold C. "Information Policy." *Journal of Academic Librarianship* 27 (January 2001): 36–51.

Relyea, Harold C., and L. Elaine Halchin. "Homeland Security and Information Management." In *The Bowker Annual: Library and Book Trade Almanac*. 48th ed. Medford, N.J.: Information Today, 2003.

Science Applications International Corporation (SAIC). *Information Warfare: Legal, Regulatory, Policy and Organizational Considerations for Assurance*. Washington, D.C: Joint Staff, The Pentagon, 1995.

U.S. Congress. Office of Technology Assessment. *Information Security and Privacy in Network Environments*. OTA-TCT–606. Washington, D.C.: GPO, September 1994.

INFORMATION POLICY AND LIBRARIES

Books

Banks, Paul N., and Roberta Pilette. *Preservation: Issues and Planning*. Chicago: ALA, 2000.

Heins, Marjorie, and Christina Cho. *Internet Filters: A Public Policy Report*. New York: Free Expression Policy Project, National Coalition Against Censorship, 2001.

Reichman, Henry. *Censorship and Selection: Issues and Answers for Schools*. Chicago: ALA, 2001.

Swan, John C., and Noel Peattie. *The Freedom to Lie: A Debate About Democracy*. Jefferson, N.C.: McFarland, 1989.

White House Conference on Library and Information Science. *Information 2000: Library and Information Services for the 21st Century*. Washington, D.C.: GPO, 1991.

Articles

ACCESS TO FEDERAL INFORMATION

Cornwall, Gary T. "The Dissemination of Federal Government Information: Prospects for the Immediate Future." *Journal of Government Information* 23 (1996): 299–306.

Jobe, Margaret M. "Another Casualty." *Library Journal* 9 (May 15, 2003): 54–55.

———. "What a Difference a Year Makes." *Library Journal* 9 (May 15, 2002): 60–64.

Kadec, Sarah. "Public Access to Government Electronic Information." *Bulletin of the American Society for Information Science* 19–20 (October/November 1992): 22–24.

McConnell, Bruce W. "New Wine in Old Wineskins: U.S. Government Information in a Networked World." *Journal of Government Information* 23 (1996): 217–225.

Sherman, Andres M. "Statutory Reform of the U.S. GPO: A View from the GPO." *Journal of Government Information* 23 (1996): 265–279.

Sherman, Chris. "Vanishing Act: The U.S. Government's Disappearing Data." *Searchday* [Online] Available at *http://searchenginewatch.com/searchday/02/sd1219.vanish.html.* (Accessed on December 20, 2002.)

Shill, Harold B. "Privatization of Public Information: Its Impact on Libraries." *Library Administration and Management* 5 (spring 1991): 99–109.

Williams, Jane. "Recent Changes for Three Federal Library and Information Agencies: Lessons to the Field, Lessons from the Field, or Neither?" *The Bowker Annual 1997.* 42nd ed. New Providence, N.J.: R.R. Bowker, 1997.

INTELLECTUAL FREEDOM

Abbott, Randy L. "Pressure Groups and Intellectual Freedom." *Public Library Quarterly* 10 (1990): 43–61.

Adams, Helen R. "Privacy and Confidentiality." *American Libraries* 33 (November 2002): 44– 47.

American Library Association. *Intellectual Freedom Manual,* 6th ed. Chicago: ALA, 2002.

———. "Plain Facts About Internet Filtering Software." [Online] Available *www.ala.org/ala/pla/plapubs/org/technotes/internetfiltering.htm.* (Accessed on July 10, 2003.)

Asheim, Lester. "Not Censorship but Selection." *Wilson Library Bulletin* 28 (September 1953): 63–67.

———. "Selection and Censorship: A Reappraisal." *Wilson Library Bulletin* 58 (November 1983): 180–184.

Ayre, Lori Bowen. *Internet Filtering Options Analysis: An Interim Report.* InfoPeople Project, May 2001. [Online] Available at *www.infopeople.org/howto/ filtering/ Internetfilter_rev1.pdf.*

Becker, Beverley C., and Susan M. Stan. *Hit List for Children 2: Frequently Challenged Books.* Chicago: ALA, 2002.

Broderick, Dorothy. "Censorship: A Family Affair?" *Top of the News* 35 (spring 1979): 223–232.

Burt, David. "In Defense of Filtering." *American Libraries* 28 (August 1997): 46–48.

Consumer Reports. "Digital Chaperones for Kids." *Consumer Reports* 66 (March 2001): 20–23.

Doyle, Tony. "A Critical Discussion of 'The Ethical Presuppositions Behind the Library Bill of Rights." *Library Quarterly* 72 (2002): 275–293.

———. "A Utilitarian Case for Intellectual Freedom in Libraries." *Library Quarterly* 71 (2001): 44–71.

Edwards, Ellen. "Study: Web Filters Block Health Information." *Washington Post*, December 11, 2002, p. A02.

Elsner, Edward J. "Legal Aspects of Internet Filtering in Public Libraries." *Public Libraries* 40 (July/August 2001): 218–222.

Hopkins, Dianne McAfee. "A Conceptual Model of Factors Influencing the Outcome of Challenges to Library Materials in Secondary School Settings." *Library Quarterly* 63 (January 1993): 40–72.

International Federation of Library Associations and Institutions. "The Glasgow Declaration on Libraries, Information Services and Intellectual Freedom." [Online] Available at *www.ifla.org/faife/policy/iflastat/gldeclar-e.html*. (Accessed on June 25, 2003.)

Kranich, Nancy. "Why Filters Won't Protect Children or Adults." *Library Administration and Management* 18 (winter 2004): 14–18.

Minow, Mary. "Who Pays for Free Speech?" *American Libraries* 34 (February 2003): 34–38.

National Coalition Against Censorship. *Internet Filters: A Public Policy Report.* [Online] Available at *www.ncac.org/issues/internetfilters.html*. (Accessed on May 23, 2003.)

Schladweiler, Chris. "The Library Bill of Rights and Intellectual Freedom: A Selective Bibliography." *Library Trends* 45 (summer 1996): 97–125.

Serebnick, Judith. "A Review of Research Related to Censorship in Libraries." *Library Research* 1 (summer 1979): 95–118.

———. "Self-Censorship by Librarians: An Analysis of Checklist-Based Research." *Drexel Library Quarterly* 18 (winter 1982): 35–56.

Swan, John. "Untruth or Consequences." *Library Journal* 111 (July 1986): 44–52.

FEES

Bierman, Kenneth J. "Costs of Electronic Information." In *Encyclopedia of Library and Information Science*, vol. 54. New York: Marcel Dekker, 1994, 122–143.

———. "How Will Libraries Pay for Electronic Information?" *Journal of Library Administration* 15 (1991): 67–84.

Coffman, Stephen. "Fee-Based Services and the Future of Libraries." *Journal of Library Administration* 20 (1995): 167–186.

Coffman, Steve, and Helen Josephine. "Doing It for Money." *Library Journal* 116 (October 15, 1991): 32–36.

Halliday, Jane. "Fee or Free: A New Perspective on the Economics of Information." *CLJ* 48 (October 1991): 327–333.

Young, Peter R. "Changing Information Access Economics: New Roles for Libraries and Librarians." *Information Technology and Libraries* 13 (June 1994): 103–114.

PRESERVATION

Cloonan, Michele Valerie. "The Preservation of Knowledge." *Library Trends* 41 (spring 1993): 594–605.
———. "W(h)ither Preservation?" *Library Quarterly* 71 (April 2001): 231–242.
Cox, Richard J., and Lynn W. Cox. "Selecting Information of Enduring Value for Preservation." In *Rethinking the Library in the Information Age* 2 (April 1989). Washington, D.C.: GPO, 9–42.
Lamolinara, Guy. "Metamorphosis of a National Treasure." *American Libraries* 27 (March 1996): 31–33.
Rothenberg, Jeff. "Ensuring the Longevity of Digital Documents." *Scientific American* 272, no. 1 (January 1995): 42–47.

INFORMATION SCIENCE

Books

Allen, Bryce L. *Information Tasks: Toward a User-Centered Approach to Information Systems*. San Diego: Academic Press, 1996.
Baker, Sharon L., and F. Wilfred Lancaster. *The Measurement and Evaluation of Library Services*. 2nd ed. Arlington, Va.: Information Resources, 1991.
Brown, John Seely, and Paul Duguid. *The Social Life of Information*. Boston: Harvard Business School, 2000.
Buckland, Michael K. *Information and Information Systems*. New York: Praeger, 1991.
Campbell, Nicole. *Usability Assessment of Library-Related Web Sites: Methods and Case Studies: Guide #7*. Chicago: ALA, 2001.
Case, Donald O. *Looking for Information: A Survey of Research on Information Seeking, Needs, and Behavior*. San Diego: Academic Press, 2002.
Chandler, Alfred D., Jr., and James W. Cortada. *A Nation Transformed by Information: How Information Has Shaped the United States from Colonial Times to the Present*. New York: Oxford University Press, 2000.
Chen, Ching-Chih, and Peter Hernon. *Information Seeking: Assessing and Anticipating User Needs*. New York: Neal-Schuman, 1982.
Feather, John. *The Information Society: A Study of Continuity and Change*. London: Library Association, 1998.
Large, Andrew, Lucy A. Tedd, and R.J. Hartley. *Information Seeking in the Online Age: Principles and Practice*. New Providence, N.J.: Bowker-Saur, 1999.
Lester, June, and Wallace C. Koehler Jr. *Fundamentals of Information Studies*. New York: Neal-Schuman, 2003.
Machlup, Fritz, and Una Mansfield, eds. *The Study of Information: Interdisciplinary Messages*. New York: Wiley, 1983.

Maze, Susan, David Moxley, and Donna J. Smith. *Authoritative Guide to Web Search Engines*. New York: Neal-Schuman, 1997.

Morrogh, Earl. *Information Architecture: An Emerging 21st Century Profession*. Upper Saddle River, N.J.: Prentice Hall, 2003.

Neill, S.D. *Dilemmas in the Study of Information: Exploring the Boundaries of Information Science*. Westport, Conn.: Greenwood, 1992.

Norlin, Elaina, and CM! Winters. *Usability Testing for Library Web Sites: A Hands-On Guide*. Chicago: ALA, 2002.

Rosenfeld, Louis, and Peter Morville. *Information Architecture for the World Wide Web*. 2nd ed. Sebastopol, Calif.: O'Reilly, 2002.

Spool, Jared M., Tara Scanlon, Will Schroeder, Carolyn Snyder, and Terry DeAngelo. *Web Site Usability: A Designer's Guide*. San Francisco: Morgan Kaufmann, 1999.

Srikantaiah, T. Kanti, and Michael E.D. Koenig. *Knowledge Management for the Information Professional*. Medford, N.J.: Information Today, 2000.

Taylor, Robert S. *Value-Added Processes in Information Systems*. Norwood, N.J.: Ablex, 1986.

Westbrook, Lynn. *Identifying and Analyzing User Needs*. New York: Neal-Schuman, 2001.

Articles

Alfino, Mark, and Linda Pierce. "The Social Nature of Information." *Library Trends* 49 (winter 2001): 471–485.

Allen, Bryce L. "Cognitive Research in Information Science: Implications for Design." *Annual Review of Information Science and Technology (ARIST)* 26 (1991): 3–37.

Benoit, Gerald. "Data Mining." *Annual Review of Information Science and Technology* 36 (2002): 265–310.

Bergeron, Pierrette, and Christine A. Hiller. "*Competitive Intelligence*." *Annual Review of Information Science and Technology (ARIST)* 36 (2002): 353–390.

Bush, Vannevar. "As We May Think." *Atlantic Monthly* 176 (July 1945): 101–108.

Cappel, James J., and Jeffrey P. Boone. "A Look at the Link Between Competitive Intelligence and Performance." *Competitive Intelligence Review* 6 (summer 1995): 15–23.

Chatman, Elfreda A. "The Impoverished Life-World of Outsiders." *Journal of the American Society for Information Science* 47 (1996): 193–206.

Cronin, Blaise. "Information Warfare: Peering Inside Pandora's Postmodern Box." *Library Review* 50 (2001): 279–294.

Dervin, Brenda. "On Studying Information Seeking Methodologically: The Implications of Connecting Metatheory to Method." *Information Processing and Management* 35 (1999): 727–750.

———. "Useful Theory for Librarianship: Communication, Not Information." *Drexel Library Quarterly* 13 (July 1977): 16–32.

Dervin, Brenda, and M. Nilan. "Information Needs and Uses." *Annual Review of Information Science and Technology (ARIST)* 21 (1986): 3–33.

Durrance, Joan C. "Information Needs: Old Song, New Tune." In *Rethinking the Library* (1986). Washington, D.C.: GPO, 159–178.

Ellis, David. "The Dilemma of Measurement in Information Retrieval Research." *Journal of the American Society for Information Science* 47 (1996): 23–36.

———. "Paradigms in Information Retrieval Research." In *Encyclopedia of Library and Information Science*, vol. 54. New York: Marcel Dekker, 1994, 275–291.

Ellis, David, T.D. Wilson, Nigel Ford, Allen Foster, H.M. Lam, R. Burton, and Amanda Spink. "Information Seeking and Mediated Searching. Part 5: User-Intermediary Interaction." *Journal of the American Society for Information Science* 53 (2002): 883–893.

Harter, Stephen P. "Variations in Relevance Assessments and the Measurement of Retrieval Effectiveness." *Journal of the American Society for Information Science* 47 (1996): 37–49.

Hewins, Elizabeth T. "Information Need and Use Studies." *Annual Review of Information Science and Technology (ARIST)* 25 (1990): 145–172.

Jacoby, Jacob. "Perspectives on Information Overload." *Journal of Consumer Research* 10 (March 1984): 432–435.

Koenig, Michael E. "Information Services and Downstream Productivity." *Annual Review of Information Science and Technology (ARIST)* 25 (1990): 55–86.

Mann, Thomas. "The Principle of Least Effort." In *Library Research Models: A Guide to Classification, Cataloging, and Computers*. New York: Oxford University, 1993, 91–101.

Meola, Marc, and Sam Stormont. *Starting and Operating Live Virtual Reference Services*. New York: Neal-Schuman, 2002.

Miller, Stephen H. "Competitive Intelligence—An Overview." [Online] Available at *www.scip.org/Library/overview.pdf*. (Accessed on July 22, 2003.)

Nardi, Bonnie A., and Vicki O'Day. "Intelligent Agents: What We Learned at the Library." *Libri* 46 (June 1996): 59–88.

Palmquist, Ruth A. "An Overview of Usability for the Study of Users' Web-Based Information Retrieval Behavior." *Journal of Education in Library and Information Science* 42 (spring 2001): 123–135.

Savolainen, Reijo. "The Sense-Making Theory: Reviewing the Interests of User-Centered Approach to Information Seeking and Use." *Information Processing and Management* 29 (1993): 13–28.

Shaw, Debora. "The Human-Computer Interface for Information Retrieval." *Annual Review of Information Science and Technology (ARIST)* 26 (1991): 155–195.

Smith, Linda C. "Artificial Intelligence and Information Retrieval." *Annual Review of Information Science and Technology (ARIST)* 22 (1987): 41–77.

———. "Citation Analysis." *Library Trends* 30 (summer 1981): 83–106.

Society of Competitive Intelligence Professionals (SCIP). "Overview." [Online] Available at *www.scip.org/about/index.asp*. (Accessed on July 21, 2003.)

Taylor, Robert S. "Value-Added Processes in Libraries." In *Value-Added Processes in Information Systems*. Norwood, N.J.: Ablex, 1986, 71–95.

Wallace, Danny P. "Bibliometrics and Citation Analysis." In *Principles and Appli-*

cations of Information Science for Library Professionals. Edited by John N. Olsgaard. Chicago: American Library Association, 1989, 10–26.

Zhang, Ping. "Satisfiers and Dissatisfiers: A Two-Factor Model for Website Design and Evaluation." *Journal of the American Society for Information Science* 51 (2000): 1253–1268.

INFORMATION SEEKING

Bilal, Dania. "Children's Use of the Yahooligans! Web Search Engine. II. Cognitive and Physical Behaviors on Research Tasks." *Journal of the American Society for Information Science and Technology* 52 (2001): 118–136.

———. "Children's Use of the Yahooligans! Web Search Engine. III. Cognitive and Physical Behaviors on Fully Self-Generated Search Tasks." *Journal of the American Society for Information Science and Technology* 53 (2002): 1170–1183.

Chatman, Elfreda A. "The Impoverished Life-World of Outsiders." *Journal of the American Society for Information Science* 47 (1996): 193–206.

Ford, Nigel, David Miller, and Nicola Moss. "The Role of Individual Differences in Internet Searching: An Empirical Study." *Journal for the American Society for Information Science and Technology* 52 (2001): 1049–1066.

———. "Web Search Strategies and Approaches to Studying." *Journal for the American Society for Information Science and Technology* 54 (2003): 473–489.

Hsieh-Yee, Ingrid. "Children's Use of the Yahooligans! Web Search Engine: III. Cognitive and Physical Behaviors on Fully Self-Generated Search Tasks.." *Library and Information Science Research* 53 (2002): 1170–1183

———. "Research on Web Search Behavior." *Library and Information Science Research* 23 (2001): 167–185.

Krikelas, James. "Information-Seeking Behavior: Patterns and Concepts," *Drexel Library Quarterly* 19 (spring 1983): 5–20.

Kuhlthau, Carol C. "Inside the Search Process: Information Seeking from the User's Perspective." *Journal of the American Society for Information Science* 42 (June 1991) 361–371.

Lazonder, Ard W., Harm J.A. Biemans, and Iwans G.J.H. Wopereis. "Differences Between Novice and Experienced Users in Searching Information on the World Wide Web." *Journal of the American Society for Information Science* 51 (2000): 576–581.

Slone, Debra J. "The Influence of Mental Models and Goals on Search Patterns During Web Interaction." *Journal of the American Society for Information Science and Technology* 53 (2002): 1152–1169

Spink, Amanda, and Charles Cole. "Introduction to the Special Issue: Everyday Life Information-Seeking Research." *Library and Information Science Research* 23 (2001): 301–304.

Spink, Amanda, T.D. Wilson, Nigel Ford, Allen Foster, and David Ellis. "Information-Seeking and Mediated Searching. Part 1: Theoretical Framework and Research Design." *Journal of the American Society for Information Science and Technology* 53 (2002): 695–703.

Wilson, T.D., Nigel Ford, David Ellis, Allen Foster, and Amanda Spink. "Information Seeking and Mediated Searching. Part 2: Uncertainty and Its Correlates." *Journal of the American Society for Information Science and Technology* 53 (2002): 704–715.

Yu, Byeong-Min, and Seak-Zoon Roh. "The Effects of Menu Design on Information-Seeking Performance and User's Attitude on the World Wide Web." *Journal of the American Society for Information Science and Technology* 53 (2002): 923–933.

DEFINITION AND HISTORY OF INFORMATION SCIENCE

Borko, H. "Information Science: What Is It?" *American Documentation* 19 (January 1968): 3–5.

Brittain, J.M. "What Are the Distinctive Characteristics of Information Science?" In *Theory and Application of Information Research: Proceedings of the Second International Research Forum on Information Science.* August 3–6, 1977. London: Mansell, 1980, 34–47.

Buckland, Michael. "Documentation, Information Science, and Library Science in the U.S.A." *Information Processing & Management* 32 (January 1996): 63–76.

Herner, Saul. "Brief History of Information Science." *Journal of the American Society for Information Science* 35 (May 1984): 157–163.

Ingwersen, Peter. "Information and Information Science." In *Encyclopedia of Library and Information Science,* vol. 56. New York: Marcel Dekker, 1995, 137–174.

Miksa, Francis L. "Machlup's Categories of Knowledge as a Framework for Viewing Library and Information Science History." *Journal of Library History* 20 (spring 1985): 157–172.

Neill, S.D. "The Dilemma of Method for Information Research: Is Information Science a Science, Social Science, or Humanity?" In *Dilemmas in the Study of Information: Exploring the Boundaries of Information Science.* Westport, Conn.: Greenwood, 1992, 139–158.

Oppenheim, Charles. "The Institute's New Criteria for Information Science." *Journal of Information Science* 4 (1982): 229–234.

Rayward, Boyd. "Library and Information Sciences." In *The Study of Information: Interdisciplinary Messages.* Edited by Fritz Machlup and Una Mansfield. New York: Wiley, 1983, 343–363.

Saracevic, T. "Relevance: A Review of and a Framework for the Thinking on the Notion in Information Science." *Journal of the American Society for Information Science* 26 (November/December 1975): 321–343.

Schrader, Alvin M. "In Search of a Definition of Library and Information Science." *Canadian Journal of Information Science* 9 (June 1984): 59–77.

Shapiro, Fred R. "Coinage of the Term *Information Science.*" *Journal of the American Society for Information Science* 46 (1995): 384–385.

Shera, Jesse H., and Donald B. Cleveland. "History and Foundations of Information Science." *Annual Review of Information Science and Technology* 12 (1977): 249–275.

Warner, Julian. "W(h)ither Information Science?" *Library Quarterly* 71 (2001): 243–255.

Wellisch, Hans. "From Information Science to Informatics: A Terminological Investigation." *Journal of Librarianship* 4 (July 1972): 157–187.

Yuexiao, Zhang. "Definitions and Sciences of Information." *Information Processing and Management* 24 (1988): 479–491.

INFORMATION ARCHITECTURE / KNOWLEDGE MANAGEMENT

Blair, David C. "Knowledge Management: Hype, Hope or Help?" *Journal of the American Society for Information Science and Technology* 53 (2002): 1019–1028.

Davenport, Thomas H. "Some Principles of Knowledge Management." [Online] Available at *www.mccombs.utexas.edu/kman/kmprin.htm*. (Accessed on July 23, 2003.)

Farnum, Chris. "Information Architecture: Five Things Information Managers Need to Know." *The Information Management Journal* 36 (September / October 2002): 33–40.

Gotcha!. "What is Knowledge Management (KM)?" [Online] Available at *www.sims.berkeley.edu/courses/is213/s99/Projects/P9/web_site/about_km.html*. (Accessed on July 22, 2003.)

Gullikson, Shelley, Ruth Blades, Marc Bragdon, Shelley McKibbon, Mainie Sparling, and Elaine G. Toms. "The Impact of Information Architecture on Academic Web Site Usability." *The Electronic Library* 17 (October 1999): 293–304.

McInerney, Claire. "Knowledge Management and the Dynamic Nature of Knowledge." *Journal of the American Society for Information Science and Technology* 53 (2002): 1009–1018.

Rosenfeld, Louis. "Information Architecture: Looking Ahead." *Journal of the American Society for Information Science and Technology* 53 (2002): 874–876.

INTELLECTUAL ORGANIZATION OF LIBRARIES

Books

Berman, Sanford. *The Joy of Cataloging: Essays, Letters, Reviews, and Other Explosions*. Phoenix: Oryx, 1981.

———. *Prejudices and Antipathies: A Tract on the LC Subject Heads Concerning People*. Metuchen, N.J.: Scarecrow, 1971.

Carpenter, Michael, and Elaine Svenonius, eds. *Foundations of Cataloging: A Sourcebook*. Littleton, Colo.: Libraries Unlimited, 1985.

Chan, Lois Mai. *Cataloging and Classification: An Introduction*. New York: McGraw-Hill, 1994.

———. *A Guide to the Library of Congress Classification*. Englewood, Colo.: Libraries Unlimited, 2000.

Chan, Lois Mai, Phyllis A. Richmond, and Elaine Svenonius, eds. *Theory of Subject Analysis: A Sourcebook*. Littleton, Colo.: Libraries Unlimited, 1985.

Connell, Tschera Harkness, and Robert L. Maxwell, eds. *The Future of Cataloging: Insights from the Lubetzsky Symposium*. Chicago: ALA, 2000.
Desmarais, Norman. *The ABC's of XML: The Librarian's Guide to the eXtensible Markup Language*. Houston: New Technology, 2000.
Fensel, Dieter, James Hendler, Henry Lieberman, and Wolfgang Wahlster. *Spinning the Semantic Web: Bringing the World Wide Web to Its Full Potential*. Cambridge, Mass.: MIT, 2003.
Foskett, A.C. *The Subject Approach to Information*. 5th ed. Hamden, Conn: Linnet, 1996.
Gorman, Michael, ed. *Technical Services Today and Tomorrow*. 2nd ed. Englewood, Colo.: Libraries Unlimited, 1998.
Greenberg, Jane, ed. *Metadata and Organizing Educational Resources on the Internet*. New York: Haworth, 2000.
Jones, Wayne, Judith R. Ahronheim, and Josephine Crawford. *Cataloging the Web: Metadata, AACR, and MARC 21*. Lanham, Md.: Scarecrow, 2002.
Lancaster, F.W. *Indexing and Abstracting in Theory and Practice*. 3rd ed. Champaign, Ill.: University of Illinois, 2003.
———. *Vocabulary Control for Information Retrieval*. 2nd ed. Arlington, Va.: Information Resources, 1986.
Lubetzky, Seymour. *Principles of Cataloging: Final Report, Phase I: Descriptive Cataloging*. Los Angeles: Institute of Library Research, 1969.
Mann, Thomas. *Library Research Models*. New York: Oxford University Press, 1993.
Marcella, Rita, and Arthur Maltby. *The Future of Classification*. Brookfield, Vt.: Gower, 2000.
Pao, Miranda Lee. *Concepts of Information Retrieval*. Englewood, Colo.: Libraries Unlimited, 1989.
Ranganathan, S.R. *Elements of Library Classification*. 3rd ed. Bombay: Asia Publishing, 1962.
Rowley, Jennifer E. *Organising Knowledge: An Introduction to Information Retrieval*. 2nd ed. Aldershot, England: Gower, 1992.
Smiraglia, Richard P. *The Nature of 'A Work': Implications for the Organization of Knowledge*. Lanham, Md.: Scarecrow, 2001.
Soergel, Dagobert. *Organizing Information: Principles of Data Base and Retrieval Systems*. Orlando, Fla.: Academic Press, 1985.
Svenonius, Elaine, ed. *The Conceptual Foundations of Descriptive Cataloging*. San Diego: Academic Press, 1989.
———. *The Intellectual Foundation of Information Organization*. Cambridge, Mass.: MIT, 2000.
Taylor, Arlene. *The Organization of Information*. 2nd ed. Westport, Conn.: Libraries Unlimited, 2004.
Wilson, Patrick. *Two Kinds of Power: An Essay on Bibliographical Control*. Berkeley: University of California, 1968.

Articles

Baker, Nicholson. "Discards." *New Yorker* 70 (April 4, 1994): 64–86.
Bates, Marcia. "Rigorous Systematic Bibliography." *RQ* 16 (fall 1976): 7–26.

Berners-Lee, Tim, James Hendler, and Ora Lassila. "The Semantic Web." *Scientific American* 284 (2001): 34–43.

Clyde, Anne. "Metadata." *Teacher Librarian* 30 (December 2002): 45–47.

Cromwell, Willy. "The Core Record: A New Bibliographic Standard." *LRTS* 38 (October 1994): 415–424.

Dillon, Martin, and Erik Jul. "Cataloging Internet Resources: The Convergence of Libraries and Internet Resources." In *Electronic Resources: Selection and Bibliographic Control,* vol. 22. Edited by Ling-yuh W. Pattie and Bonnie Jean Cox. New York: Haworth, 1996, 197–238.

Franklin, Rosemary Aud. "Re-Inventing Subject Access for the Semantic Web." *Online Information Review* 27 (2003): 94–101.

Greenberg, Jane. "Metadata Generation: Processes, People and Tools." *Bulletin of the American Society for Information Science and Technology* 29 (December/January 2003): 16–18.

Henderson, Kathryn Luther. "'Treated with a Degree of Uniformity and Common Sense': Descriptive Cataloging in the United States—1876–1976." *Library Trends* 25 (July 1976): 227–271.

Jeng, Ling Hwey. "A Converging Vision of Cataloging in the Electronic World." *Information Technology and Libraries* 15 (December 1996): 222–230.

Mann, Thomas. "The Principle of Least Effort." In *Library Research Models: A Guide to Classification, Cataloging, and Computers.* New York: Oxford University, 1993, 91–101.

Miller, Eric, and Ralph Swick. "An Overview of W3C Semantic Web Activity." *Bulletin of the American Society for Information Science and Technology* 29 (April/May 2003): 8–11.

OCLC. "Dublin Core Metadata Initiative." [Online] Available at *www.dublincore.org.* (Accessed on July 2, 2003.)

Parsia, Bijan. "Semantic Web Services." *Bulletin of the American Society for Information Science and Technology* 29 (April/May 2003): 12–15.

Smiraglia, Richard P., and Gregory H. Leazer. "Derivative Bibliographic Relationships: The Work Relationship in a Global Bibliographic Database." *Journal of the American Society for Information Science and Technology* 50 (1999): 493–504.

Tennant, Roy. "MARC Must Die." *Library Journal* 127 (October 15, 2002): 26–28.

Thibodeau, Patrick. "The Web's Next Leap." *Computerworld* 37 (April 2003): 34.

Tillett Barbara B. "A Taxonomy of Bibliographic Relationships." *Library Resources and Technical Services* 35 (April 1991): 150–158.

Uschold, Michael. "Where Are the Semantics in the Semantic Web?" *AI Magazine* 24 (fall 2003): 25–36.

Vellucci, Sherry L. "Herding Cats: Options for Organizing Electronic Resources." *Internet Reference Services Quarterly* 1 (1996): 9–30.

———. "Metadata." *Annual Review of Information Science and Technology* 33 (1998): 187–222.

Ward, Maribeth. "Expanding Access to Information with Z39.50." *American Libraries* 25 (July/August 1994): 639–641.

Younger, Jennifer A. "Resources Description in the Digital Age." *Library Trends* 45 (winter 1997): 462–481.

Zeng, Marcia Lei. "Developing Control Mechanisms for Intellectual Access for

Discipline-Based Virtual Libraries: A Study of Process." In *Annual Review of OCLC Research 1995*. Dublin, Ohio: OCLC, 1996, 61–64.

LIBRARIANSHIP

Books

Abbott, Andrew. *The System of Professions*. Chicago: University of Chicago, 1988.

ALISE. *Educating Library and Information Science Professionals for a New Century: The KALIPER Report: Executive Summary*. Reston, Va: ALISE, July 2000.

American Library Association. *Congress on Professional Education: Focus on Education for the First Professional Degree: Librarianship and Information Service: A Statement on Core Values, Fifth Draft*. [Online] Available at *www. ala.org*. (Accessed September on 18, 2003.)

Baum, Christina D. *Feminist Thought in American Librarianship*. Jefferson, N.C.: McFarland, 1992.

Bruce, Harry, Raya Fidel, Peter Ingwersen, and Pertti Vakkari, eds. *Emerging Frameworks and Methods: Proceedings of the Fourth International Conference on Conceptions of Library and Information Science*. Greenwood Village, Colo.: Libraries Unlimited, 2002.

Eberhart, George M. Comp. *The Whole Library Handbook 3*. Chicago: ALA, 2003.

Gorman, G.E. *The Education and Training of Information Professionals: Comparative and International Perspectives*. Metuchen, N.J.: Scarecrow, 1990.

———. *Our Enduring Values*. Chicago: ALA, 2000.

Harris, Michael H., Stan A. Hannah, and Pamela C. Harris. *Into the Future: The Foundations of Library and Information Services in the Post-Industrial Era*. 2nd ed. Greenwich, Conn.: Ablex, 1998.

Harris, Roma M. *Librarianship: The Erosion of a Woman's Profession*. Norwood, N.J.: Ablex, 1992.

Hildenbrand, Suzanne, ed. *Reclaiming the American Library Past: Writing the Women In*. Norwood, N.J.: Ablex, 1996.

Josey, E.J., and Marva L. DeLoarch. *Handbook of Black Librarianship*. 2nd ed. Lanham, Md: Scarecrow, 2000.

Office of Library Programs, Office of Educational Research and Improvement U.S. Dept. of Education. *Rethinking the Library in the Information Age*. Washington, D.C.: GPO, 1989.

Scherdin, Mary Jane, ed. *Discovering Librarians*. Chicago: ALA, Association of College and Research Libraries, 1994.

Shera, J.H. *Sociological Foundations of Librarianship*. New York: Asia, 1970.

Vann, Sarah K. *Training for Librarianship before 1923*. Chicago: ALA, 1961.

White, Herbert S. *Librarianship—Quo Vadis?* Englewood, Colo.: Libraries Unlimited, 2000.

Wiegand, Wayne A. *Irrepressible Reformer: A Biography of Melvil Dewey*. Chicago: ALA, 1996.

Winter, Michael F. *The Culture and Control of Expertise: Toward a Sociological Understanding of Librarianship*. Westport, Conn: Greenwood, 1988.

Articles

THE PROFESSION

Abbott, Andrew. "The Order of Professionalization." *Work and Occupations* 18 (November 1991): 355–384.

Bak, Greg. "The Greatest Librarians of the World...Were Not Graduates of Library School." *Libraries and Culture* 37 (fall 2002): 362–378.

Balderrama, Sandra Rios. "This Trend Called Diversity." *Library Trends* 49 (summer 2000): 194–214.

Baruchson-Arbib, Shifra, and Jenny Bronstein. "A View to the Future of the Library and Information Science Profession: A Delphi Study." *Journal of the American Society for Information Science and Technology* 53 (2002): 397–408.

Berry, John N., III. "LIS Recruiting: Does It Make the Grade?" *Library Journal* 128 (May 1, 2003): 38–41.

Birdsall, William F. "Librarianship, Professionalism and Social Change." *Library Journal* 107 (February 1, 1982): 223–226.

Blackburn, Robert H. "The Ancient Alexandrian Library: Part of It May Survive!" *Library History* 19 (March 2003): 23–34.

Bobinski, George S. "Is the Library Profession Over-Organized?" *American Libraries* 31 (October 2000): 58–61.

Braun, Linda W. "New Roles: A Librarian by Any Name." *Library Journal* 127 (February 1, 2002): 46–47.

Budd, John. "Instances of Ideology in Discursive Practice: Implications for Library and Information Science." *Library Quarterly* 71 (2001): 498–517.

Budd, John M. "Jesse Shera, Sociologist of Knowledge?" *Library Quarterly* 72 (October 2002): 423–440.

———. "The Library, Praxis, and Symbolic Power." *Library Quarterly* 73 (2003): 19–32.

Buschman, John. "Editorial: Core Wars." *Progressive Librarian* 17 (summer 2000). [Online] Available at *www.libr.org/PL/17_Editorial.html*. (Accessed on September 18, 2003.)

Butler, Pierce. "Librarianship as a Profession." *The Library Quarterly* 21 (October 1951): 235–247.

Campbell, Jerry D. "Choosing to Have a Future." *American Libraries* 24 (June 1993): 560–566.

Davis, Donald G., Jr. "Education for Librarianship." *Library Trends* 25 (July 1976): 113–134.

Dawson, Alma. "Celebrating African-American Librarians and Librarianship." *Library Trends* 49 (summer 2000): 40–87.

Dewey, Melvil. "The Profession." *Library Journal* 114 (June 15, 1989): 5. Reprinted from *American Library Journal* 1 (1876).

Diamond, Randy, and Martha Dragich. "Professionalism in Librarianship: Shifting the Focus from Malpractice to Good Practice." *Library Trends* 49 (winter 2001): 395–414.

Drake, David. "The 'A' Factor: Altruism and Career Satisfaction." *American Libraries* 24 (November 1993): 922–924.

DuMont, Rosemary Ruhig, Lois Buttlar, and William Caynon. "The Case for Multiculturalism." In *Multiculturalism in Libraries.* Westport Conn.: Greenwood, 1994, 1–21.

———. "The History of Multiculturalism in Libraries." In *Multiculturalism in Libraries.* Westport Conn.: Greenwood, 1994, 23–35.

Eddy, Jacalyn. "'We Have Become Too Tender-Hearted': The Language of Gender in the Public Library, 1880–1920." *American Studies* 42 (fall 2001): 155–172.

Edwards, Ralph M. "The Management of Libraries and the Professional Functions of Librarians." *Library Quarterly* 45 (April 1975): 150–160.

Estabrook, Leigh. "The Growth of the Profession." *College and Research Libraries* 50 (May 1989): 287–296.

———. "Productivity, Profit and Libraries." *Library Journal* 106 (July 1981): 1377–1380.

Gorman, Michael. "Five New Laws of Librarianship." *American Libraries* 26 (September 1995): 784–785.

———. "Values for Human-to-Human Reference." *Library Trends* 50 (fall 2001): 168–182.

Graham, Patterson Toby. "Public Librarians and the Civil Rights Movement: Alabama, 1955–1965." *Library Quarterly* 71 (January 2001): 1–27.

Guerena, Salvador, and Edward Erazo. "Latinos and Librarianship." *Library Trends* 49 (summer 2000): 138–181.

Harris, Roma M. "Information Technology and the Deskilling of the Librarians." *Computers in Libraries* 12 (January 1992): 8–16.

Hildenbrand, Suzanne. "'Women's Work' Within Librarianship." *Library Journal* 114 (September 1, 1989): 153–155.

Holley, Edward G. "Librarians, 1876–1976." *Library Trends* 25 (July 1976): 177–207.

Huber, Jeffrey T. "Library and Information Studies Education for the 21st Century Practitioner." *Journal of Library Administration* 20 (1995): 119–130.

Koehler, Wallace. "Professional Values and Ethics as Defined by 'The LIS Discipline.'" *Journal of Education for Library and Information Science* 44 (spring 2003): 99–119.

Lancaster, F. Wilfred. "Whither Libraries? or, Wither Libraries." *College and Research Libraries* 50 (July 1989): 406–419.

Leber, Michele. "Putting Pay First." *Library Journal* 128 (April 1, 2003): 43–44.

Liu, Mengziong. "The History and Status of Chinese Americans in Librarianship." *Library Trends* 49 (summer 2000): 109–137.

Maack, Mary Niles. "Toward a New Model of the Information Professions: Embracing Empowerment." *Journal of Education for Library and Information Science* 38 (fall 1997): 283–302.

Mason, Richard O. "What Is an Information Professional?" *Journal of Education for Library and Information Science* 31 (fall 1990): 122–138.

McCook, Kathleen de la Peña. "Social Justice, Personalism, and the Practice of Librarianship." *Catholic Library World* 72 (December 2001): 80–84.

McCook, Kathleen de la Peña, and Paula Geist. "Diversity Deferred: Where Are the Minority Librarians?" *Library Journal* 118 (November 1, 1993): 35–38.

Miksa, Francis L. "Melvil Dewey: The Professional Educator and His Heirs." *Library Trends* 34 (winter 1986): 359–381.

Nelson, Anne. "How My Hometown Library Failed Me." *Library Journal* 115 (June 15, 1990): 82–85.

Office of Library Programs, Office of Educational Research and Improvement U.S. Dept. of Education. *Rethinking the Library in the Information Age.* Washington, D.C.: GPO, 1989.

Passet, Joanne E. "Men in a Feminized Profession: The Male Librarian, 1887–1921." *Libraries and Culture* 28 (fall 1993): 385–402.

———. "'You Do Not Have to Pay Librarians': Women, Salaries, and Status in the Early 20th Century." In *Reclaiming the American Library Past: Writing the Women In.* Edited by Suzanne Hildenbrand. Norwood, N.J.: Ablex, 1996, 207–219.

Patterson, Lotsee. "History and Status of Native Americans in Librarianship." *Library Trends* 49 (summer 2000): 182–193.

Piper, Paul S., and Barbara E. Collamer. "Male Librarians." *Journal of Academic Librarianship* 27 (September 2001): 406–411.

Quattrocchi, Ed. "An Outsider's Thoughts on the Education of Librarians." *American Libraries* 30 (April 1999): 82–85.

Radford, Gary P. "Trapped in Our Own Discursive Formations: Toward An Archaeology of Library and Information Science." *Library Quarterly* 73 (2003): 1–18.

Radford, Gary P., and Marie L. Radford. "Libraries, Librarians, and the Discourse of Fear." *Library Quarterly* 71 (2001): 299–329.

Rice, James. "The Hidden Role of Librarians." *Library Journal* 114 (January 1989): 57–59.

Sager, Don. "The Search for Librarianship's Core Values." *Public Libraries* 40 (May/June 2001): 149–153.

Trosow, Samuel E. "Standpoint Epistemology as an Alternative Methodology for Library and Information Science." *Library Quarterly* 71 (2001): 360–382.

Warner, Alice Sizer. "Librarians as Money Makers: The Bottom Line." *American Libraries* 21 (November 1990): 946–948.

Wiegand, Wayne A. "The Politics of Cultural Authority." *American Libraries* 29 (January 1998): 80–82.

———. "The Structure of Librarianship: Essay on an Information Profession." *Canadian Journal of Information and Library Science* 24 (April 1999): 17–37.

Yamashita, Kenneth A. "Asian/Pacific American Librarians Association—A History of APALA and Its Founders." *Library Trends* 49 (summer 2000): 88–108.

LIBRARY EDUCATION

Allard, Suzie. "LIS Education Development: Strategies for Improving Awareness, Part II." *Journal of Education for Library and Information Science* 41(summer 2000): 244–249.

Boyce, Bert. "The Death of Library Education." *American Libraries* 25 (March 1994): 257–259.

Buckland, Michael. "Education for Librarianship in the Next Century." *Library Trends* 34 (spring 1986): 777–787.

Buttlar, Lois, and William Caynon. "Recruitment of Librarians into the Profession: The Minority Perspective." *Library and Information Science Research* 14 (1992): 259–280.

Buttlar, Lois, and Rosemary Du Mont. "Library and Information Science Competencies Revisited." *Journal of Education for Library and Information Science* 37 (winter 1996): 44–62.

Carbo, Toni, and Stephen Almagno. "Information Ethics: The Duty, Privilege and Challenge of Educating Information Professionals." *Library Trends* 49 (winter 2001): 510–518.

Conrad, Clifton F., and Kim Rapp-Hanretta. "Positioning Master's Programs in Library and Information Science: A Template for Avoiding Pitfalls and Seizing Opportunities in Light of Key External and Internal Forces." *Journal of Education in Library and Information Science* 43 (spring 2002): 92–104.

Crowley, Bill, and Bill Brace. "A Choice of Futures: Is It Libraries Versus Information?" *American Libraries* 30 (April 1999): 76–79.

Curry, Ann. "Canadian LIS Education: Trends and Issues." *Education for Information* 18 (2000): 325–337.

Dalrymple, Prudence W. "The State of the Schools." *American Libraries* 27 (January 1997): 31–34.

Davis, Donald G., Jr. "Education for Librarianship." *Library Trends* 25 (July 1976): 113–134.

Hamilton-Pennell, Christine. "Getting Ahead by Getting Online." *Library Journal* 127 (November 15, 2002): 32–35.

Hauptman, Robert. "Iconoclastic Education: The Library Science Degree." *Catholic Library World* 58 (May/June 1987): 252–253.

Holley, Robert P. "The Ivory Tower as Preparation for the Trenches: The Relationship Between Library Education and Library Practice" *C&RL News* 64 (March 2003): 172–175.

Irwin, Ray. "Characterizing the Core: What Catalog Descriptions of Mandatory Courses Reveal About LIS Schools and Librarianship." *Journal of Education for Library and Information Science* 43 (spring 2002): 175–184.

Johnson, Carol P. "Domain Competencies and Minnesota's Voluntary Certification Program." *Public Libraries* 40 (July/August 2001): 228–234.

Koenig, Michael E.D., and Charles Hildreth. "The End of the Standalone 'Library School.'" *Library Journal* 127 (June 15, 2002): 40–42.

Maack, Mary Niles. "Women in Library Education: Down the Up Staircase." *Library Trends* 34 (winter 1986): 401–432.

Main, Linda, "Research Versus Practice: A 'No' Contest." *Journal of Education for Library and Information Science* 30 (winter 1990): 226–228.

Marcum, Deanna B. "Transforming the Curriculum: Transforming the Profession." *American Libraries* 27 (January 1997): 35–38.

McCook, Kathleen de la Peña. "Keeping the Library in Library Education." *American Libraries* 29 (March 1998): 59–63.

———. "Social Justice, Personalism, and the Practice of Librarianship." *Catholic Library World* 72 (December 2001): 80–84.

McGrath,William. "Explanation and Prediction: Building a Unified Theory of Librarianship." *Library Trends* 50 (winter 2002): 350–370.

Moran, Barbara. "Practitioners vs. LIS Educators: Time to Reconnect." *Library Journal* 126 (November 1, 2001): 52–55.

Nardini, Robert F. "A Search for Meaning: American Library Metaphors: 1876–1926." *Library Quarterly* 71 (April 2001): 111–149.

Naylor, Richard J. "Core Competencies: What They Are and How to Use Them." *Public Libraries* 39 (March/April 2000): 108–114.

Nichols, C. Allen. "Leaders: Born or Bred." *Library Journal* 127 (August 2002): 38–40.

Paris, Marion. "Why Library Schools Fail." *Library Journal* 115 (October 1, 1990): 38–42.

Pemberton, J. Michael, and Christine R. Nugent. "Emergent Field, Convergent Curriculum." *Journal of Education for Library and Information Science* 36 (spring 1995): 126–138.

Raphael, Laura B. "Far and Away: The Pros and Cons of a 'Long Distance' MIS." *American Libraries* 33 (October 2002): 50–52.

Rayward, W. Boyd. "Library and Information Sciences: Disciplinary Differentiation, Competition, Convergence." In *The Study of Information: Disciplinary Messages*. Edited by Fritz Machlup and Una Mansfield. New York: Wiley, 1983, 343–363.

Robbins, Jane. "Yes, Virginia, You Can Require an Accredited Master's Degree for That Job." *Library Journal* 115 (February 1, 1990): 40–44.

Robbins-Carter, Jane, and Charles A. Seavey. "The Master's Degree: Basic Preparation for Professional Practice." *Library Trends* 34 (spring 1986): 561–580.

Saracevic, Tefko. "Closing of Library Schools in North America: What Role Accreditation?" *Libri* 44 (November 1994): 190–200.

Schement, Jorge Reina. "A 21st-Century Strategy for Librarians." *Library Journal* 121 (May 1, 1996): 34–36.

Stoker, David. "Persistence and Change: Issues for LIS Educators in the First Decade of the Twenty First Century." *Education for Information* 18 (2000): 115–122.

Sutton, Stuart A. "KALIPER Project: Final Report-Trends, Trend Projections, and Crystal Ball Gazing." *Journal of Education for Library and Information Science* 42 (2001): 241–247.

Tenopir, Carol. "Educating Tomorrow's Information Professionals Today." *Searcher* 10 (July/August 2002): 12–15.

Terbille, Charles I. "Competing Models of Library Science: Waples-Berelson and Butler." *Libraries and Culture* 27 (summer 1992): 296–319.

Van House, Nancy, and Stuart A. Sutton. "The Panda Syndrome." *Journal of Education for Library and Information Science* 41 (winter 2000): 52–68.

White, Herbert S., "The Future of Library and Information Science Education." *Journal of Education for Library and Information Science* 26 (winter 1986): 174–181.

White, Herbert S., and Sarah L. Mort. "The Accredited Library Education Program as Preparation for Professional Library Work." *Library Quarterly* 60 (July 1990): 187–215.

Wiegand, Wayne A. "The Development of Librarianship in the United States." *Libraries and Culture* 24 (winter 1989): 99–109.

Wright, H. Curtis. "The Symbol and Its Referent: An Issue for Library Education." *Library Trends* 34 (spring 1986): 729–775.

Yontz, Elaine. "How You Can Help Save Library Education." *American Libraries* 34 (January 2003): 42.

Yontz, Elaine, and Kathleen de la Peña McCook. "Service-Learning and LIS Education." *Journal of Education for Library and Information Science* 44 (winter 2003): 58–68.

THE IMAGE OF LIBRARIANS

Adams, Katherine C. "Loveless Frump as Hip and Sexy Party Girl: A Reevalution of the Old-Maid Stereotype." *Library Quarterly* 70 (July 2000): 287–301.

Agada, John. "Assertion and the Librarian Personality." In *Encyclopedia of Library and Information Science,* vol. 42. New York: Marcel Dekker, 1987, 128–143.

———. "Studies of the Personality of Librarians." *Drexel Library Quarterly* 20 (spring 1984): 24–45.

Carmichael, James V., Jr. "The Male Librarian and the Feminine Image: A Survey of Stereotype, Status, and Gender Perceptions." *Library and Information Science Research* 14 (October–December 1992): 411–446.

Duffy, Joan R. "Images of Librarians and Librarianship: A Study." *Journal of Youth Services in Librarianship* 3 (summer 1990): 303–308.

Durrance, Joan C. "Librarians: The Invisible Professionals." In *Bowker Annual.* 35th ed. New Providence, N.J.: R.R. Bowker, 1990–1991, 92–99.

Fisher, David P. "Is the Librarian a Distinct Personality Type?" *Journal of Librarianship* 20 (January 1988): 36–47.

Lemkau, Jeanne Parr. "Men in Female-Dominated Professions: Distinguishing Personality and Background Features." *Journal of Vocational Behavior* 24 (February 1984): 110–122.

Morrisey, Locke J., and Donald O. Case. "'There Goes My Image.' The Perception of Male Librarians by Colleague, Student, and Self." *College and Research Libraries* 49 (September 1988): 453–464.

Radford, Marie L., and Gary P. Radford. "Librarians and Party Girls: Cultural Studies and the Meaning of the Librarian." *Library Quarterly* 73 (2003): 54–69.

Schuman, Patricia Glass. "The Image of Librarians: Substance or Shadow?" *The Journal of Academic Librarianship* 16 (May 1990): 86–89.

LIBRARIES AS ORGANIZATIONS

Books

American Association of School Librarians and Association for Educational Communications and Technology. *Information Power: Guidelines for School Library Media Programs.* Chicago: ALA, 1988.

American Library Association. *Information Power: Building Partnerships for Learning.* Chicago: ALA, 1998.

Association of College and Research Libraries. *Recruitment, Retention & Restructuring: Human Resources in Academic Libraries.* Chicago: ALA, 2002

Bertot, John Carlo, Charles R. McClure, and Joe Ryan. *Statistics and Performance Measures for Public Library Networked Services.* Chicago: ALA, 2001.

Bloch, R. Howard, and Carla Hesse. *Future Libraries.* Berkeley, Calif.: University of California, 1993.

Christianson, Elin B., David E. King, and Janet L. Ahrensfeld. *Special Libraries: A Guide for Management*, 3rd ed. Washington, D.C.: Special Libraries Association, 1991.

Clyde, Laurel A. *Managing InfoTech in School Library Media Centers.* Englewood, Colo.: Libraries Unlimited, 1999.

Council on Library and Information Resources. *Scholarship, Instruction, and Libraries at the Turn of the Century.* Washington, D.C.: CLIR, January 1999.

Cox, Richard J. *Vandals in the Stacks? A Response to Nicholson Baker's Assault on Libraries.* Westport, Conn.: Greenwood, 2002.

Erikson, Rolf. *Designing a School Library Media Center for the Future.* Chicago: ALA, 2001.

Grimes, Deborah J. *Academic Library Centrality: User Success Through Service, Access and Tradition.* Chicago: ACRL, 1998.

Hamlin, Arthur T. *The University Library in the United States: Its Origins and Development.* Philadelphia: University of Pennsylvania, 1981.

Hardesty, Larry, ed. *Books, Bytes and Bridges: Libraries and Computer Centers in Academic Institutions.* Chicago: ALA, 2000.

Hayes, Robert M. *Models for Library Management, Decision-Making, and Planning.* San Diego: Academic Press, 2001.

Heaviside, Sheila, Christina Dunn, Ray Fry, and Judi Carpenter. *Services and Resources for Children and Young Adults in Public Libraries.* Washington, D.C.: U.S. DOE, 1995.

John, Patricia LaCaille. *Rural Libraries and Information Services.* Champaign, Ill.: University of Illinois, Graduate School of Library and Information Science, 1995.

Jones, Patrick. *Connecting Young Adults and Libraries.* 2nd ed. New York: Neal-Schuman, 1998.

———. *New Directions for Library Service to Young Adults.* Chicago: ALA , 2002.

Kahn, Miriam B. *Disaster Response and Planning for Libraries.* 2nd ed. Chicago: ALA, 2003.

Kearney, Carol A. *Curriculum Partner: Redefining the Role of the Library Media Specialist.* Westport, Conn.: Greenwood, 2000.

Lance, Keith Curry, Lynda Welborn, and Christine Hamilton-Pennell. *The Impact of School Library Media Centers on Academic Achievement.* Castle Rock, Colo.: Hi Willow Research and Publishing, 1993.

Lance, Keith Curry, Marcia J. Rodney, and Christine Hamilton-Pennell. *How School Librarians Help Kids Achieve Standards: The Second Colorado Study.* San Jose, Calif.: Hi Willow Research and Publishing, 2000.

Lee, Stuart D. *Electronic Collection Development: A Practical Guide*. New York: Neal–Schuman, 2002.

Loertscher, David V. *Measures of Excellence for School Library Media Centers*. Englewood, Colo.: Libraries Unlimited, 1988.

Lougee, Wendy Pradt. *Diffuse Libraries: Emergent Roles for the Research Library in the Digital Age*. Washington D.C.: Council on Library and Information Resources, August 2002.

McClure, Charles R., Amy Owen, Douglass L. Zweizig, Mary Jo Lynch, and Nancy A. Van House. *Planning and Role-Setting for Public Libraries: A Manual of Options and Procedures*. Chicago: ALA, 1987.

McCook, Kathleen de la Peña. *A Place at the Table: Participating in Community Building*. Chicago: ALA, 2000.

McCook, Kathleen de la Peña, Barbara J. Ford, and Kate Lippincott, eds. *Libraries: Global Reach–Local Touch*. Chicago: ALA, 1998.

McNulty, Tom, ed. *Accessible Libraries on Campus: A Practical Guide for the Creation of Disability-Friendly Libraries*. Chicago: ACRL, 1999.

Molz, Redmond Kathleen, and Phyllis Dain. *Civic Space/Cyberspace: The American Public Library in the Information Age*. Cambridge, Mass.: MIT, 1999.

Mount, Ellis. *Special Libraries and Information Centers: An Introductory Text*. 3rd ed. Washington, D.C.: Special Libraries Association, 1995.

Nelson, Sandra. *The New Planning for Results: A Streamlined Approach*. Chicago: ALA, 2001.

Nelson, Sandra, Ellen Altman, and Diane Mayo. *Managing for Results: Effective Resource Allocation for Public Libraries*. Chicago: ALA, 2000.

Rubin, Rhea. *Planning for Library Services to People with Disabilities*. Chicago: ALA, 2001.

Rubin, Richard E. *Human Resource Management in Libraries: Theory and Practice*. New York: Neal-Schuman, 1991.

Van House, Nancy A., Mary Jo Lynch, Charles R. McClure, Douglas L. Zweizig, and Eleanor Jo Rodger. *Output Measures for Public Libraries*. 2nd ed. Chicago: ALA, 1987.

Vavrek, Bernard. *Assessing the Information Needs of Rural Americans*. Clarion, Pa.: Department of Library Science, Clarion University, 1990.

———. *Assessing the Role of the Rural Public Library*. Clarion, Pa: Department of Library Science, Clarion University, 1993..

Wallace, Danny P., and Connie Van Fleet. *Library Evaluation: A Casebook and Can-Do Guide*. Englewood, Colo.: Libraries Unlimited, 2001.

Walters, Virginia A. *Children & Libraries: Getting It Right*. Chicago: ALA, 2001.

Wellheiser, Johanna, and Jude Scott. *An Ounce of Prevention*. 2nd ed. Lanham, Md.: Scarecrow, 2002.

Westin, Alan, and Anne L. Finger, *Using the Public Library in the Computer Age: Present Patterns, Future Possibilities*. Chicago: ALA, 1991.

White, Herbert S. *Managing the Special Library*. White Plains, N.Y.: Knowledge Industry, 1984.

Whitesides, William L., Sr., ed. *Reinvention of the Public Library for the 21st Century*. Englewood, Colo.: Libraries Unlimited, 1998.

Wright, Kieth C., and Judith F. Davis. *Forecasting the Future: School Media Programs in an Age of Change.* Lanham, Md.: Scarecrow, 1999.

Articles

Ad Hoc Task Force on Recruitment and Retention Issues. "Recruitment and Retention: A Professional Concern." In *The Bowker Annual Library and Book Trade Almanac.* 48th ed. Medford, N.J.: Information Today, 2003, 291–302.

Albanese, Andrew Richard. "Moving from Books to Bytes." *Library Journal* 126 (September 1, 2001): 52–54.

Arp, Lori, and Beth S. Woodard. "Recent Trends in Information Literacy." *Reference and User Services Quarterly* 42 (winter 2002): 124–128.

Blosh, Marie. "Changing the Way We Do Business." *American Libraries* 34 (January 2003): 48.

Dohm, Arlene. "Gauging the Labor Force Effects of Retiring Baby-Boomers." *Monthly Labor Review* 123 (July 2000): 17–25.

Eason, Sue, ed. "The Roles of Professionals, Paraprofessionals, and Nonprofessionals: A View from the Academy." *Library Trends* 46 (winter 1998): 427–596.

Euster, Joanne R. "The New Hierarchy: Where's the Boss?" *Library Journal* 115 (May 1, 1990): 41–44.

Hernon, Peter, and Danuta A. Nitecki. "Service Quality: A Concept Not Fully Explored." *Library Trends* 49 (spring 2001): 687–708.

Klauber, Julie. "Living Well with a Disability: How Libraries Can Help." *American Libraries* 29 (November 1998): 52–55.

Lynch, Beverly P. "Libraries as Bureaucracies." *Library Trends* 27 (winter 1978): 259–267.

Mathews, Virginia H., Judith G. Flum, and Karen A. Whitney. "Kids Need Libraries: School and Public Libraries Preparing the Youth of Today for the World of Tomorrow." *School Library Journal* 36 (April 1990): 33–37.

Rader, Hannelore B. "Introduction." *Library Trends* 51 (fall 2002): 141–143.

Stahl, D. Gail. "The Virtual Library: Prospect and Promise, or Plus Ça Change, Plus C'Est la Même Chose." *Special Libraries* 84 (fall 1993): 202–205.

Tyckoson, David A. "What Is the Best Model of Reference Service?" *Library Trends* 50 (fall 2001): 183–196.

SPECIAL LIBRARIES

Arnold, Stephen. "Relationships of the Future: Vendors and Partners." *Special Libraries* 84 (fall 1993): 235–240.

Henczel, Sue. "Benchmarking Measuring and Comparing." *Information Outlook* 7 (July 2002): 12–20.

Kassell, Amelia. "Practical Tips to Help You Prove Your Value." *MLS: Marketing Library Services* 16 (May/June 2002): 1–3.

Matthews, Joseph R. "Determining and Communicating the Value of the Special Library." *Information Outlook* 7 (March 2003): 27–31.

Ojala, Marydee. "Core Competencies for Special Library Managers of the Future." *Special Libraries* 84 (fall 1993): 230–233.

Outsell. *The Changing Roles of Content Deployment Functions: Corporate Information Professionals*. Burlingame, Calif.: Outsell, 2003.

Piggott, Sylvia E.A. "Why Corporate Librarians Must Reengineer the Library for the New Information Age." *Special Libraries* 86 (winter 1995): 11–20.

St. Clair, Guy, Victoria Harriston and Thomas A. Pellizzi. "Toward World-Class Knowledge Services: Emerging Trends in Specialized Research Libraries." *Information Outlook* 7 (July 2003): 10–16.

Sykes, Jan. "Value as Calculation." *Information Outlook* 7 (March 2003).

SCHOOLS

Brodie, Carolyn S. "A History of School Library Media Center Collection Development." In *The Emerging School Library Media Center: Historical Issues and Perspectives*. Edited by Kathy Howard Latrobe. Englewood, Colo.: Libraries Unlimited, 1998, 57–73.

Eisenberg, Mike. "This Man Wants to Change Your Job." *School Library Journal* 48 (September 2002): 47–49.

Everhart, Nancy. "Filling the Void." *School Library Journal* 48 (June 2002): 44–49.

Garland, Kathleen. "An Analysis of School Library Media Center Statistics Collected by State Agencies and Individual Library Media Specialists." *School Library Media Quarterly* 21 (winter 1993): 106–110.

Ishizuka, Kathy, Walter Minkel, and Evan St. Lifer. "Biggest Challenges 2002." *School Library Journal* 48 (January 2002): 50–53.

Justice, Laura M., and Joan Kaderavek. "Using Shared Storybook Reading to Promote Emergent Literacy." *Teaching Exceptional Children* 34 (March/April 2002): 8–13.

Kuhlthau, Carol Collier, ed. *The Virtual School Library*. Englewood, Colo.: Libraries Unlimited, 1996.

Lance, Keith Curry, Lynda Welborn, and Christine Hamilton-Pennell. *How School Librarians Help Kids Achieve Standards: The Second Colorado Study*. Castle Rock, Colo.: Hi Willo Research and Publishing, 2000.

———. *The Impact of School Library Media Centers on Academic Achievement*. Castle Rock, Colo.: Hi Willow Research and Publishing, 1993.

Lau, Debra. "Got Clout?" *School Library Journal* 48 (May 2002): 40–45.

Mathews, Virginia H., Judith G. Flum, and Karen A. Whitney. "Kids Need Libraries: School and Public Libraries Preparing the Youth of Today for the World of Tomorrow." *School Library Media Quarterly* 18 (spring 1990): 167–172.

Minkel, Walter. "The Year in K–12 Libraries: School Librarians Redefine Themselves." In *The Bowker Annual Library and Book Trade Almanac*. 48th ed. Medford, N.J.: Information Today, 2003, 10–15.

Stratton, J.M. "Emergent Literacy: A New Perspective." *Journal of Visual Impairment & Blindness* 90 (May/June 1996): 177–183.

Whelan, Debra Lau. "Greatest Challenges for 2003." *School Library Journal* 49 (January 2003): 48–50.

Zweizig, Douglas, L. "The Children's Services Story." *Public Libraries* 32 (January/February 1993): 26–28.

ACADEMIC LIBRARIES

Albanese, Andrew Richard. "Deserted No More." *Library Journal* 128 (April 15, 2003): 34–36.
———. "Moving from Books to Bytes." *Library Journal* 126 (September 1, 2001): 52–54.
———. "The Top Seven Academic Library Issues." *Library Journal* 128 (March 15, 2003): 43.
Association of College and Research Libraries (ACRL/ALA). "Information Literacy Competency Standards." [Online] Available at *www. ala.org*. (Accessed on December 11, 2003.)
———. *Recruitment, Retention & Restructuring: Human Resources in Academic Libraries.* ACRL, Ad Hoc Task Force on Recruitment and Retention. Final Draft. May 20, 2002.
Association of Research Libraries. "Principles for Emerging Systems of Scholarly Publishing." [Online] Available at *www.arl.org/scomm/tempe.html*. (Accessed on July 25, 2003.)
Association of Research Libraries, Association of American Universities, and Pew Higher Education Roundtable. "To Publish and Perish." [Online] Available at *www.arl.org/scomm/pew/pewrept.html*. (Accessed on July 25, 2003.)
Bailey, Russell, and Barbara Tierney. "Information Commons Redux: Concept, Evolution, and Transcending the Tragedy of the Commons." *Journal of Academic Librarianship* 28 (September 2002): 277–286.
Beagle, Donald. "Extending the Information Commons: From Instructional Testbed to Internet2." *Journal of Academic Librarianship* 28 (September 2002): 287–296.
Bostick, Sharon L. "The History and Development of Academic Library Consortia in the United States: An Overview." *Journal of Academic Librarianship* 27 (March 2001): 128–130.
Clayton, Howard. "The American College Library, 1800–1860." *Journal of Library History* 3 (April 1968): 120–137.
Cook, Colleen, and Bruce Thompson. "Reliability and Validity of SERVQUAL Scores Used to Evaluate Perceptions of Library Service Quality." *Journal of Academic Librarianship* 26 (July 2000): 248–258.
Hurt, Charlene S. "A Vision of the Library of the 21st Century." *Journal of Library Administration* 15 (1991): 7–19.
Johnson, Richard. "Scholarly Publishing and Academic Resources Coalition (SPARC)." In *The Bowker Annual Library and Book Trade Almanac.* 48th ed. Medford, N.J.: Information Today, 2003, 185–192.
Jones, Plummer Alston, Jr. "The History and Development of Libraries in American Higher Education." *College and Research Library News* 7 (July/August 1989): 561–564.
MacWhinnie, Laurie A. "The Information Commons: The Academic Library of the Future." In *portal: Libraries and the Academy,* vol. 3. Baltimore: Johns Hopkins, 2003, 241–257.

Magner, Denise K. "Seeking a Radical Change in the Role of Publishing." *Chronicle of Higher Education* 46 (June 16, 2000). [Online] Available at *http:chronicle.com/ free/v46/41/41a01601.htm*. (Accessed on June 6, 2003.)

Marcum, James W. "Rethinking Information Literacy." *Library Quarterly* 72 (2002): 1–26.

Neal, James G. "Academic Libraries: 2000 and Beyond." *Library Journal* 121 (July 1996): 74–76.

Outsell. *The Changing Roles of Content Deployment Functions: Academic Information Professionals.* Burlingame, Calif.: Outsell, 2003.

Owusu-Ansa, Edward K. "The Academic Library in the Enterprise of Colleges and Universities: Toward a New Paradigm." *Journal of Academic Librarianship* 27 (July 2001): 282–294.

Primary Research Group. *The Survey of Academic and Special Libraries.* 2001 ed. New York: Primary Research Group, 2001.

Shuler, John A. "Freedom of Public Information Versus the Right to Public Information: The Future Possibilities of Library Advocacy." *Journal of Academic Librarianship* 28 (May 2002): 157–159.

Smith, Eldred, and Peggy Johnson. "How to Survive the Present While Preparing for the Future: A Research Library Strategy." *College and Research Libraries* 54 (September 1993): 389–396.

Stallings, Dees. "The Virtual University: Legitimized at Century's End: Future Uncertain for the New Millennium." *Journal of Academic Librarianship* 26 (January 2000): 3–14.

PUBLIC LIBRARIES

Auld, Hampton. "Combined School-Public Library Facilities: Opinions, Case Studies, and Questions to Consider, Part I." *Public Libraries* 41 (September/ October 2002): 248–255.

Birdsall, William F. "Community, Individualism, and the American Public Library." *Library Journal* 110 (November 1, 1985): 21–24.

Blount, Patti. "Double Your Fun with a Combination Public-High School Library." *Public Libraries* 41 (September/October 2002): 254–255.

Byrne, Marci, Kathleen Deerr, and Lisa G. Kropp. "Book a Play Date: The Game of Promoting Emergent Literacy." *American Libraries* 34 (September 2003): 42–44.

Casey, James. "The Devil Is in the Details." *Public Libraries* 41 (September/October 2002): 252.

Coffman, Steve. "What If You Ran Your Library Like a Bookstore." *American Libraries* 29 (March 1998): 40–46.

Connaway, Lynn Silipigni. "E-Book Trends in Public Libraries." *Public Libraries* Supp. 39 (2001) 27–29.

D'Elia, George, and Eleanor Jo Rodger. "Public Opinion About the Roles of the Public Library in the Community: The Results of a Recent Gallup Poll." *Public Libraries* (January/February 1994): 23–28.

Elsner, Edward J. "The Evolution of the PLA's Planning Model." *Public Libraries* 41 (July/August 2002): 209–215.

Guscott, John. "These Emerging Technologies Will Change Public Libraries." *Library Futures Quarterly*. [Online] Available at *www.library futures.com/ freereports/technology.htm*. (Accessed on January 29, 2003.)

Hennen, Thomas J., Jr. "Great American Public Libraries: The 2002 HAPLR Rankings." *American Libraries* 33 (October 2002): 64–68.

———. "Performing Triage on the Budgets in the Red." *American Libraries* 34 (March 2003): 36–39.

Hilyard, Nann Blaine. "Disabilities in the Library." *Public Libraries* 42 (January/ February 2003): 14–19.

Hoffert, Barbara. "Serving More with Less." *Library Journal* 128 (February 15, 2003): 42–44.

Holt, Glen E., and Donald Elliott. "Cost Benefit Analysis: A Summary of the Methodology." *The Bottom Line* 15 (2002): 154–158.

———. "Measuring Outcomes: Applying Cost-Benefit Analysis to Middle-Sized and Smaller Public Libraries." *Library Trends* 51 (winter 2003): 424–440.

———. "Proving Your Library's Worth: A Test Case." *Library Journal* 123 (November 1, 1998): 42–44.

Johnson, Linda. "The Rural Library: Programs, Services, and Community Coalitions and Networks." *Rural Libraries* 20 (2000): 38–62.

Klauber, Julie. "Living Well with a Disability: How Libraries Can Help." *American Libraries* 29 (November 1998): 52.

Leckie, Gloria J., and Jeffrey Hopkins. "The Public Place of Central Libraries: Findings from Toronto and Vancouver." *Library Quarterly* 72 (2002): 326–372.

Lynch, Mary Jo. "Economic Hard Times and Public Library Use Revisited." *American Libraries* 33 (August 2002): 62–63.

McCain, Mimi. "What's So Special About Special Needs?" *Public Libraries* 42 (January/February 2003): 51–54.

Nichols, LeeAnn. "Joint School-Public Libraries: Challenges and Opportunities." *Public Libraries* (November/December 2002): 312–314.

Oder, Norman. "A Precarious Holding Pattern." *Library Journal* 128 (January 2003): 55–57.

Owens, Margaret. "Get It in Writing!" *Public Libraries* 41 (September/October 2002): 248–250.

Quezada, Shelley. "Nothing About Me Without Me: Planning for Library Services for People with Disabilities." *Public Libraries* 42 (January/February 2003): 42–46.

Ring, Daniel F. "Has the American Public Library Lost Its Purpose?" *Public Libraries* 33 (July/August 1994): 191–196.

Rogers, Michael. "Tackling Recruitment." *Library Journal* 128 (February 1, 2003): 40–43.

Shearer, Kenneth. "Confusing What Is Most Wanted and What Is Most Used: A Crisis in Public Library Priorities Today." *Public Libraries* 32 (July/August 1993): 193–197.

Simon, Matthew. "Will the Library Survive the Internet?: What Patrons Value in Public Libraries." *Public Libraries* 41 (March/April 2002): 104–106.

Summers, William F. "The Concept of the Indispensable Public Library." *Public Libraries* 32 (July/August 1993): 212–215.

Vavrek, Bernard. "Rural Information Needs and the Role of the Public Library." *Library Trends* 44 (summer 1995): 21–48.

———. "Rural Public Library Services." In *Encyclopedia of Library and Information Science*. 2nd ed. Edited by Miriam A. Drake. New York: Marcel Dekker, 2003, 2550–2555.

William, Patrick. "How Should the Public Library Respond to Public Demand?" *Library Journal* 115 (October 15, 1990): 54–56.

MISSION AND VALUES OF LIBRARIES

Books

Benton Foundation. *Buildings, Books and Bytes: Libraries and Communities in the Digital Age*. Washington D.C.: Benton Foundation, 1996.

———. *Local Places, Global Connections: Libraries in the Digital Age*. Washington, D.C.: Benton Foundation, 1999.

Casson, Lionel. *Libraries in the Ancient World*. New Haven, Conn.: Yale, 2001.

Ditzion, Sidney H. *Arsenals of a Democratic Culture*. Chicago: ALA, 1947.

Dunlap, Leslie W. *Readings in Library History*. New York: R.R. Bowker, 1972.

Eisenstein, Elizabeth L. *The Printing Press as an Agent of Change: Communications and Cultural Transformations in Early-Modern Europe*. Cambridge, England: Cambridge University, 1979.

Hamlin, Arthur T. *The University Library in the United States: Its Origins and Development*. Philadelphia: University of Pennsylvania, 1981.

Haro, Roberto P. *Developing Library and Information Services for Americans of Hispanic Origin*. Metuchen, N.J.: Scarecrow, 1981.

Hessel, Alfred. *A History of Libraries*. New Brunswick, N.J.: Scarecrow, 1955.

Jackson, Sidney, L. *Libraries and Librarianship in the West*. New York: McGraw-Hill, 1974.

Josey, E.J., ed. *The Black Librarian in America*. Metuchen, N.J.: Scarecrow, 1970.

———. *The Black Librarian in America Revisited*. Metuchen, N.J.: Scarecrow, 1994.

Kruzas, Anthony Thomas. *Business and Industrial Libraries in the United States, 1820–1940*. New York: Special Libraries Association, 1965

Lerner, Fred. *The Story of Libraries: From the Invention of Writing to the Computer Age*. New York: Continuum, 1998.

Martin, Robert Sidney. *Carnegie Denied: Communities Rejecting Carnegie Library Construction Grants 1898–1925*. Westport, Conn.: Greenwood, 1993.

McCabe, Ronald B. *Civic Librarianship: Renewing the Social Mission of the Public Library*. Lanham, Md.: Scarecrow, 2001.

McMullen, Haynes. *American Libraries Before 1876*. Westport, Conn.: Greenwood, 2000.

Molz, Redmond Kathleen, and Phyllis Dain. *Civic Space/Cyberspace: The American Public Library in the Information Age*. Cambridge, Mass.: MIT, 1999.

Ranganathan, S.R. *The Five Laws of Library Science*. New York: Asia, 1963. First published 1931.

Sapp, Gregg. *A Brief History of the Future of Libraries: An Annotated Bibliography*. Lanham, Md: Scarecrow, 2002.

Shera, Jesse. *Foundations of the Public Library*. Chicago: Shoe String, 1965.

Thompson, James Westfall. *Ancient Libraries*. Hamden, Conn.: Archon, 1962.

Winger, Howard W., ed. *American Library History 1876–1976*. Urbana-Champaign: University of Illinois, Graduate School of Library Science, 1975. Published as *Library Trends* 25 (July 1976).

Wisner, William H. *Whither the Postmodern Library: Libraries, Technology, and Education in the Information Age*. Jefferson, N.C.: McFarland, 2000.

Articles

Augst, Thomas. "American Libraries and Agencies of Culture." *American Studies* 42 (fall 2001): 5–22.

Augst, Thomas, and Wayne Wiegand, ed. "Libraries as Agencies of Culture." *American Studies* 42 (fall 2001).

Baker, Nicholson. "The Author vs. the Library." *New Yorker* (October 14, 1996): 50–61.

Blackburn, Robert H. "The Ancient Alexandrian Library: Part of It May Survive!" *Library History* 19 (March 2003): 23–34.

Blanke, Henry T. "Librarianship and Political Values: Neutrality or Commitment?" *Library Journal* 114 (July 1989): 39–43.

Brabazon, Tara. "Double Fold or Double Take? Book Memory and the Administration of Knoweldge." *Libri* 52 (2002): 28–35.

Broderick, Dorothy. "Net or Not, People Need Libraries." *American Libraries* 29 (January 1998): 62–64.

Clayton, Howard. "The American College Library." *Journal of Library History* 3 (April 1968): 120–137.

Cox, Richard J. "Taking Sides on the Future of the Book." *American Libraries* 28 (February 1997): 52–55.

Cresswell, Stephen."The Last Days of Jim Crow in Southern Libraries." *Libraries and Culture* 31 (summer/fall 1996): 557–573.

Dain, Phyllis. "Ambivalence and Paradox: The Social Bonds of the Public Library." *Library Journal* 100 (February 1, 1975): 261–266.

Dowlin, Kenneth E. "Access to Information: A Human Right?" In *Bowker Annual*, 32nd ed. New York: R.R. Bowker, 1987, 64–68.

Dix, T. Keith. "'Public Libraries' in Ancient Rome: Ideology and Reality." *Libraries and Culture* 29 (summer 1994): 282–296.

Estabrook, Leigh, and Chris Horak. "Public vs. Professional Opinion on Libraries: The Great Divide?" *Library Journal* 117 (April 1, 1992): 52–55.

Garrison, Dee. "The Tender Technicians: The Feminization of Public Librarianship." *Journal of Social History* 6 (winter 1972–1973): 131–159.

Gorman, Michael. "Technostress and Library Values." *Library Journal* 126 (April 15, 2001): 48–50.

Hanson, Eugene R. "College Libraries: The Colonial Period to the Twentieth

Century." In *Advances in Library Administration and Organization*. Greenwich, Conn.: JAI, 1989, 171–199.

Harris, Michael. "The Purpose of the American Public Library." *Library Journal* 98 (September 15, 1973): 2509–2514.

Harris, Michael H., and Stanley Hannah. "Why Do We Study the History of Libraries?: A Meditation on the Perils of Ahistoricism in the Information Era." *LISR* 14 (April/June 1992): 123–130.

Harwell, Richard, and Roger Michener. "As Public as the Town Pump." *Library Journal* 99 (April 1, 1974): 959–963.

Jochum, Uwe. "The Alexandrian Library and Its Aftermath." *Library History* 15 (May 1999): 5–12.

Jones, Plummer Alston, Jr. "The History and Development of Libraries in American Higher Education." *College and Research Libraries News* (July/August 1989): 561–565.

Luyt, Brendan. "Regulating Readers: The Social Origins of the Readers' Advisor in the United States." *Library Quarterly* 71 (2001): 443–466.

Malone, Cheryl Knott. "Books for Black Children: Public Library Collections in Louisville and Nashville, 1915–1925." *Library Quarterly* 70 (April 2000): 179–200.

Mann, Thomas. "The Importance of Books, Free Access, and Libraries as Places—and the Dangerous Inadequacy of the Information Science Paradigm." *Journal of Academic Librarianship* 27 (July 2001): 268–281.

Neill, Sam D. "Why Books?" *Public Library Quarterly* 12 (1992): 19–28.

Nelson, Anne. "How My Hometown Library Failed Me." *Library Journal* 115 (June 15, 1990): 82–85.

Peters, Paul Evan. "Information Age Avatars." *Library Journal* 120 (March 15, 1995): 32–34.

Roehl, Richard, and Hal R. Varian. "Circulating Libraries and Video Rental Stores." *First Monday*. [Online] Available at *http://firstmonday.org/issues/issue6_5/roehl/index.html*. (Accessed on August 28, 2003.)

Sager, Don. "Before the Memory Fades: Public Libraries in the Twentieth Century." *Public Libraries* 39 (March/April 2000): 75–77.

Shearer, Kenneth. "Confusing What Is Most Wanted and What Is Most Used: A Crisis in Public Library Priorities Today." *Public Libraries* 32 (July/August 1993): 193–197.

Summers, F. William. "The Concept of the Indispensable Public Library." *Public Libraries* 32 (July/August 1993): 212–215.

Swan, John C. "Rehumanizing Information: An Alternative Future." *Library Journal* 115 (September 1, 1990): 178–182.

Tisdale, Sallie. "Silence, Please." *Harper's Magazine* 294 (March 1997): 65–74.

Van Slyck, Abigail A. "The Librarian and the Library: Why Place Matters." *Libraries and Culture* 36 (fall 2001): 518–523.

Watson, Paula D. "Founding Mothers: The Contributions of Women's Organizations to Public Library Development in the United States." *Library Quarterly* 64 (1994): 233–269.

Zill, Nicholas, and Marianne Winglee. "Literature Reading in the United States: Data from National Surveys and Their Policy Implications." *Book Research Quarterly* 5 (spring 1989): 24–58.

Appendix A

Major Periodicals, Indexes, Encyclopedias, and Dictionaries in Library and Information Science

Following is a selected list of periodicals, indexes, encyclopedias, and dictionaries that relate directly to the field of library and information science. Emphasis is on U.S. publications. The periodicals are arranged in very general categories that are listed below, with many periodicals having overlapping scope. Keep in mind that periodical titles may vary over time as do publishers of the periodicals. The categories selected are the following:

Academic Libraries
Acquisitions, Selections, Collection Development
Archives
Audiovisual
Automation/Information Technology
Cataloging, Indexing, and Technical Services
Children and Youth Services
Documents
History
Information Science

Interlibrary Loan
International
Libraries—General
Library Education
Management
Preservation
Public Libraries
Reference Services
School Libraries
Special Libraries
State Publications

PERIODICALS

Academic Libraries

> *Choice*. Chicago: ACRL, ALA.
> *College & Research Libraries*. Chicago: ALA.
> *College and Undergraduate Libraries*. Binghamton, N.Y.: Haworth.
> *Journal of Academic Librarianship*. New York: Elsevier.
> *Portal: Libraries and the Academy*. Baltimore, Md.: Johns Hopkins.
> *Rare Books & Manuscripts in Librarianship*. Chicago: ACRL.

Acquisitions, Selections, Collection Development

> *The Acquisitions Librarian*. Binghamton, N.Y.: Haworth.
> *Collection Building*. Bradford, West Yorkshire, England: MCB University Press.
> *Collection Management*. Binghamton, N.Y.: Haworth.
> *Humanities Collections*. Binghamton, N.Y.: Haworth.
> *Library Collections, Acquisitions and Technical Services*. Oxford, England: Elsevier Science.
> *Popular Culture in Libraries*. Binghamton, N.Y.: Haworth.
> *The Serials Librarian*. Binghamton, N.Y.: Haworth.

Archives

> *The American Archivist*. Chicago: Society of American Archivists.
> *Archival Science*. New York: Kluwer Academic/Plenum.
> *Archivaria*. Ottawa: Association of Canadian Archivists.

Archivist. Ottawa, Ont.: Public Archives of Canada.

Audiovisual

> *Audiovisual Librarian*. Aberystwyth, Wales: Aslib, Association for Information Management.
> *Video Librarian*. Brementon, Wash.: Video Librarian.

Information Technology

> *CD-ROM Librarian*. Westport, Conn.: Meckler.
> *CD-ROM Professional*. Wilton, Conn.: Online Inc.
> *Computer and Information Systems Abstract Journal*. Bethesda, Md.: Cambridge Scientific Abstracts.
> *Computers in Libraries*. Medford N.J.: Learned Information Inc.
> *D-Lib Magazine*. Reston, Va.: Corporation for National Research Initiatives.
> *Database: The Magazine of Electronic Database Reviews*. Wilton, Conn.: Online
> *The Electronic Library*. Medford, N.J.: Learned Information.
> *First Monday*. Chicago: University of Illinois
> *Information Development*. London: Mansell.
> *Information Services and Use*. Amsterdam: North Holland.
> *Information Technology and Libraries*. Chicago: Library and Information Technology Association, ALA.
> *Library Hi Tech*. Ann Arbor, Mich.: Pierian Press.
> *Library Hi Tech News*. Ann Arbor, Mich.: Pierian Press.
> *Library Software Review*. Westport, Conn.: Meckler.
> *Library Technology Reports*. Chicago: ALA.
> *Online: The Magazine of Online Information Systems*. Medford, N.J.: Information Today.
> *Online and CD-ROM Review*. Medford, N.J.: Learned Information.
> *Technicalities*. Phoenix, Ariz.:Oryx.

Cataloging, Indexing, and Technical Services

> *Cataloging and Classification Quarterly*. Binghamton, N.Y.: Haworth.
> *Cataloging Service Bulletin*. Washington, D.C.: Library of Congress.
> *The Indexer: Journal of the Society of Indexers and of the Affiliated American, Australian and Canadian Societies*. London: Society of Indexers.

Journal of Internet Cataloging. Binghamton, N.Y.: Haworth.
Knowledge Organization: An International Journal Devoted to Concept Theory, Classification, Indexing, and Knowledge Representation. Wuerzburg, Germany: ERGON-Verlag.
Library Resources and Technical Services. Chicago: ALA.
Technical Services Quarterly. Binghamton, N.Y.: Haworth.

Children and Youth Services

Book Links. Chicago: ALA.
Bulletin of the Center for Children's Books. Chicago: University of Chicago.
Emergency Librarian. Seattle, Wash.: Rockland.
The Horn Book Magazine. Boston: Horn Book.
Journal of Youth Services in Libraries. Chicago: Association for Library Service to Children and Young Adult Library Services Association, ALA.
VOYA: The Voice of Youth Advocates. Metuchen, N.J.: Scarecrow.

Documents

DttP: Documents to the People. College Park, Md.: ALA.
Government Information Quarterly: An International Journal of Policies, Resources, Services and Practices. Greenwich, Conn.: JAI Press.
Journal of Government Information: An International Review of Policy, Issues and Resources. New York: Elsevier Science. (Formerly entitled *Government Publications Review*. Pergamon.)

History

Libraries and Culture: A Journal of Library History. Austin, Tex.: University of Texas Press.
Library History. London: Library History Group of the Library Association.
Library History Roundtable Newsletter. Chicago: ALA.

Information Science

Information Processing & Management: An International Journal. New York: Pergamon.

Journal of the American Society for Information Science and Technology. New York: John Wiley.

Journal of Documentation. London: Aslib, Association for Information Management

Journal of Information Ethics. Jefferson, N.C.: McFarland.

Journal of Information Science. New York: Bowker.

Journal of Librarianship and Information Science. London: Bowker.

Interlibrary Loan

Interlending and Document Supply. West Yorkshire, England: MCB University Press.

Journal of Interlibrary Loan, Document Delivery & Information Supply. Binghamton, N.Y.: Haworth.

International/Publications Focusing on Other Countries

Aslib Proceedings. London, Aslib.

Australian Library Journal. Sydney, Australia: Australian Library and Information Association.

Canadian Journal of Information and Library Science. Downsview, Ont.: Canadian Association for Information Science.

Electronic British Library Journal. London: British Library Board.

Focus on International and Comparative Librarianship. Birmingham, England: International Group of the Library Association.

IFLA Journal. Munich: Verlag Documentation.

International Forum on Information and Documentation. The Hague: International Federation for Documentation.

The International Information and Library Review (IILR). London, San Diego: Academic Press.

International Review of Children's Literature and Librarianship. London: Taylor Graham.

Library Association Record. London: Library Association.

Libri: An International Library Review. Copenhagen: Munksgaard International.

Libraries—General

American Libraries. Chicago: ALA.

Booklist. Chicago: ALA.

Catholic Library World. Haverford, Pa.: Catholic Library Association.
Herald of Library Science. Jodhpur, Rajasthan, India: Scientific
    Publishers.
Library & Information Science Research. New York: Elsevier.
Library Hotline. New York: Bowker.
Library Journal. New York: Bowker.
Library Quarterly. Chicago: University of Chicago.
Library Trends. Urbana-Champaign, Ill.: University of Illinois Press.
Research Strategies. New York: Elsevier.
The Unabashed Librarian. New York: Marvin H. Scilken.

Library Education

*Education for Information: The International Review of Education and
    Training in Library and Information Science.* Amsterdam: North
    Holland.
Journal of Education for Library and Information Science. State College,
    Pa.: Association for Library and Information Science Education.

Management

The Bottom Line. New York: Neal-Schuman.
Journal of Library Administration. Binghamton, N.Y.: Haworth.
Library Administration and Management. Chicago: Library Adminis-
    tration and Management Association, ALA.
Library Mosaics: The Magazine for Support Staff. Culver City, Calif.:
    Yenor.
Library Personnel News. Chicago: Office for Library Personnel
    Resources, ALA.

Preservation

Abby Newsletter. Ann Arbor, Mich.: Academy Book Bindery.
Conservation Online. Stanford, Calif.: Stanford University Preserva-
    tion Department.
DigiNews. Mountain View, Calif.: Research Libraries Group.
Microform Review. West Sussex, England: Bowker-Saur.
PAC Newsletter. Ottawa, Canada: National Library of Canada.

Public Libraries

Library Futures Quarterly. Lakewood, Ohio: L.F.I.
Public Libraries. Chicago: Public Library Association, ALA.
Public Library Quarterly. Binghamton, N.Y.: Haworth.
REFORMA Newsletter. Anaheim, Calif.: National Association to Promote Library Services to the Spanish Speaking.

Reference Services

Internet Reference Services Quarterly. Binghamton, N.Y.: Haworth.
The Reference Librarian. Binghamton, N.Y.: Haworth.
Reference & User Services Quarterly. Chicago: Reference and User Services Association, ALA.
RSR: Reference Services Review. Ann Arbor, Mich.: Pierian Press.

School Libraries

Library Media Connection. Columbus, Ohio: Linworth.
Multimedia Schools. Wilton, Conn.: Online.
The School Librarian's Workshop. Berkeley Heights, N.J.: Library Learning Resources.
School Library Journal: The Magazine of Children's, Young Adult, and School Librarians. New York: Bowker.
School Library Media Activities Monthly. Baltimore: LMS Associates.
School Library Media Quarterly. Chicago: American Association of School Libraries, ALA.
Technology Connection. Worthington, Ohio: Linworth.

Special Libraries

Art Documentation. Tucson, Ariz.: Art Libraries Society of North America.
Art Libraries Journal. Preston, England: ARLIS.
Art Reference Services Quarterly. Binghamton, N.Y.: Haworth.
Asian Libraries. Hong Kong: Library Marking Services.
Behavioral and Social Sciences Librarian. Binghamton, N.Y.: Haworth.
Business Library Review. New York: Gordon & Breach Science.
Church and Synagogue Libraries. Bryn Mawr, Pa.: Church and Synagogue Libraries Association.

Information Outlook. Washington, D.C.: Special Libraries Association.

INSPEL: International Journal of Special Libraries. Berlin: International Federation of Library Associations.

Journal of Business and Finance Librarianship. Binghamton, N.Y.: Haworth.

Journal of the Medical Library Association. Chicago: Medical Library Association. (Formerly entitled *The Bulletin of the Medical Library Association.*)

Judaica Librarianship. New Hyde Park, N.Y.: Association of Jewish Libraries.

Law Library Journal. Chicago: American Association of Law Librarians.

Legal Reference Services Quarterly. Binghamton, N.Y.: Haworth.

Medical Reference Services Quarterly. Binghamton, N.Y.: Haworth.

Music Reference Services Quarterly. Binghamton, N.Y.: Haworth.

Notes. Middleton, Wis.: Music Library Association.

The One-Person Library. New York: OPL Resources.

Science and Technology Libraries. Binghamton, N.Y.: Haworth.

Special Libraries. New York: Special Libraries Association.

STATE/REGIONAL PUBLICATIONS

Georgia Librarian. Tucker, Ga.: Georgia Library Association.

Illinois Libraries. Springfield, Ill: Illinois State Libraries.

New Jersey Libraries. Montclair, N.J.: New Jersey Library Association.

North Carolina Libraries. Greensboro, N.C.: North Carolina Library Association.

Ohio Media Spectrum. Columbus, Ohio: Ohio Educational Library Media Association.

PLA Bulletin. Pittsburgh, Pa.: Pennsylvania Library Association.

Show-Me Libraries. Jefferson City, Mo.: State Library.

Southeastern Librarian. Atlanta, Ga.: Southeastern Library Association.

DICTIONARIES

The ALA Glossary of Library and Information Science. Edited by Young Hartsill. Chicago: ALA, 1983.

Harrod's Librarians' Glossary and Reference Book. Edited by Raymond John Prytherch. 9th edition. Aldershot, England: Gower, 2000.

ENCYCLOPEDIAS

Encyclopedia of Library and Information Science. 2nd edition. New York: Marcel Dekker, 2003.

Encyclopedia of Library History. Edited by Wayne A. Wiegand and Donald G. Davis Jr. New York: Garland, 1994.

World Encyclopedia of Library and Information Science. Edited by Robert Wedgworth. 3rd ed. Chicago: ALA, 1993.

INDEXES

Information Management Index. Washington, D.C.: U.S. Army Corps of Engineers.

Information Science and Technology Abstracts. Medford, N.J.: Information Today.

Library Information Science Abstracts. London: Library Association.

Library Literature. New York: H.W. Wilson.

Appendix B

Summary of Major Library and Information Science Associations and List of Additional Associations

AMERICAN LIBRARY ASSOCIATION (ALA)

The American Library Association is the oldest and largest library association in the world. Founded in 1876, any individual, or organization, who has an interest in libraries can join. A wide variety of types of libraries participate in ALA membership and activities. These include state, public, school, and academic libraries, as well as libraries in government, commerce, the arts, the armed services, hospitals, and prisons. As of July 2003 the organization had 3,973 organizational members, 249 corporate members, and 59,571 personal members for a total of 63,793. The stated mission of the organization is "to provide leadership for the development, promotion, and improvement of library and information services and the profession of librarianship in order to enhance learning and ensure access to information for all" (ALA. *ALA Handbook of Organization 2003–2004*. [Online] Available at *www.ala.org*. Accessed January 22, 2004).

The association has identified five key "action areas" to which it is devoting substantial energies. These are (1) *Diversity*: encouraging the recruitment and retention of people of color as well as people with disabilities, and promoting collections and services that serve all people; (2) *Education and Continuous Learning*: supporting professional develop-

537

ment for all library staff and trustees, and encouraging life-long learn-ing among the citizenry; (3) *Equity of Access*: advocating for resources and policies that support library service to all people; (4) *Intellectual Free-dom*: ensuring the First Amendment rights of all citizens to read and view materials and to seek information without restrictions; and (5) *21st Century Literacy*: promoting information literacy skills for all young people and adults so that they can be effective locators and users of information.

ALA is an impressive bureaucracy with 17 round tables, 11 divi-sions, 57 state and regional chapters, 24 affiliated organizations, and a headquarters staff exceeding 270 employees. ALA is operated by an ex-ecutive director and executive board. There is also a large number of committees comprised primarily of ALA members that play a critical role in reflecting the professional and political interests of the associa-tion. Round tables focus on such areas as continuing library education, armed forces libraries, ethnic materials, library history, and government documents. Among the divisions are those focusing on children's and adult services, public libraries, and academic libraries. Standing com-mittees of the association and of the ALA Council include those for ac-creditation of programs of library and information studies, literacy and outreach, pay equity, diversity, development and recruitment, research and statistics, the status of women in librarianship, and membership. The primary political lobbying is effected by the Washington office of the American Library Association, which monitors political legislation and other activities that could affect the well-being of libraries and at-tempts to influence legislation so that it conforms to the goals of the ALA.

The association authors many publications, including books and journals focusing on a variety of aspects of the profession. These include *Reference & User Services Quarterly*, a publication of the Reference and User Services Association (RUSA); *Public Libraries*, a publication of the Public Library Association (PLA); *Library Administration and Management*, a publication of the Library Administration and Management Division (LAMA); *Journal of Youth Services in Libraries*, a publication of the Asso-ciation for Library Service to Children (ALSC) and the Young Adult Li-brary Services Association (YALSA); *College and Research Libraries*, a pub-lication of the Association of College and Research Libraries (ACRL); and *American Libraries*, the official organ of the American Library Asso-ciation. Such publications not only provide news and information on library activities, but also serve as sources for published research, analysis, and continuing education in professional practice. The association also holds two major conferences a year: the Midwinter Meeting, which is primarily devoted to committee activities, and the Annual Conference, where there are major program presentations.

AMERICAN SOCIETY FOR INFORMATION SCIENCE AND TECHNOLOGY (ASIST)

The American Society for Information Science and Technology was originally known as the American Documentation Institute. In 1968 its name was changed to the American Society for Information Science. In 2000 the name was again altered to its current one. ASIST was founded in 1937 by the Science Service and the microfilm services of the Bibliofilm Service of the U.S. Department of Agriculture. The money to finance the institute originally came from a grant from the Chemical Foundations, and the purpose of the institute was to produce scientific bibliographies, develop microphotography devices, and generally explore other mechanisms for improving the communication of recorded knowledge. Originally only institutional members were permitted, but in 1952 changes were made to the bylaws of the organization to permit individual membership. Membership exceeds 4,000 individuals and more than 100 institutional members. ASIST has 24 special interest groups (SIGs) which are designed to bring together members with common interests. For example, there are SIGs on digital libraries, bioinformatics, medical informatics, human-computer interaction, information architecture, knowledge management, and visualization, images, and sound.

Today, the focus of ASIST is on all aspects of the information transfer process, including organization, storage, retrieval, evaluation, and dissemination of information. Its stated mission is "to advance the information sciences and related applications of information technology by providing focus, opportunity, and support to information professionals and organizations" (ASIST. [Online] Available at *www.asis.org*. Accessed January 20, 2004). Its membership includes, but is not limited to, computer scientists, linguists, librarians, engineers, medical practitioners, chemists, and educators. The society also functions as an instrument of professional development through conferences, continuing education programs, professional development workshops, and publications. Among its major publications are *Journal of the American Society for Information Science and Technology* and *Annual Review of Information*

Science and Technology. ASIST also publishes its conference proceedings and is cosponsor of *Information Science Abstracts*.

ASSOCIATION OF RESEARCH LIBRARIES (ARL)

The Association of Research Libraries (ARL) was founded in December 1932 as a not-for-profit organization. It is governed by a board of directors, executive director, and a small headquarters staff. Unlike most other library organizations, membership is restricted to North American institutions; many of these are university libraries, although some are major public libraries, special libraries, and national libraries. There are approximately 120 members.

The mission of ARL is as follows: "To shape and influence forces affecting the future of research libraries in the process of scholarly communication. The Association articulates the concerns of research libraries and their institutions, forges coalitions, influences information policy development, and supports innovation, and improvement in research library operations" (ARL. [Online] Available at *www.arl.org*. Accessed January 21, 2004). ARL conferences provide a useful opportunity to exchange information on topics related to research libraries' survival. Among the current priorities of ARL are the following: providing educational and political advocacy for research libraries, promoting cost-effective methods and policies that integrate research materials from around the world, supporting access to institution-based repositories for the work of academics, finding cost-effective models for managing scholarly communications, developing effective strategies for the recruitment and retention of staff, and developing new models for measuring the effectiveness of library services. In 2003 ARL was very active in a variety of areas, especially in the policy areas of intellectual property, copyright, and privacy (ARL. [Online] Available at *www.arl.org*. Accessed January 21, 2004).

In 1970 ARL created the Office of Management Services (OMS), now known as the Office of Leadership and Management Services (OLMS), which is intended to improve the leadership and the management of human resources and the collections of research and academic libraries. This office collects statistics, prepares reports, and provides training and staff development in a variety of areas of management. Among the major publications of ARL are the *ARL Annual Salary Survey*, and their annual *Academic Library Statistics*.

INTERNATIONAL FEDERATION OF LIBRARY ASSOCIATIONS AND INSTITUTIONS (IFLA)

The International Federation of Library Associations and Institutions was founded in 1927, primarily to create a place for the leading librarians of Europe and America to meet and discuss contemporary issues of mutual interest. Today, IFLA is "an independent, international, non-governmental, not-for-profit organization" (IFLA. [Online] Available at *www.ifla.org*. Accessed January 21, 2004). Its international scope is broad, with more than 1,700 members from 155 countries. It is headquartered in The Hague.

Among the stated objectives of IFLA are to promote international understanding, cooperation, discussion, research, and development in all fields of library and information service activity; to promote continuing education of library personnel; to serve as an organization through which librarianship can be represented in international matters; and to develop and maintain guidelines for different types of library activities, such as compilation of statistics and preservation.

Many of the major American library associations are members, including ALA, the Association of Research Libraries (ARL), and the American Association of Law Libraries (AALL). IFLA is organized into eight divisions: General Research Libraries, Special Libraries, Libraries Serving the General Public, Bibliographic Control, Collections and Services, Management and Technology, Education and Research, and Regional Activities. These divisions contain 45 different sections.

IFLA has a variety of programs that represent the main interests of the association. These interests include programs to develop international standard bibliographic descriptions through its Universal Bibliographic Control and International MARC program. IFLA also has a program to encourage countries to supply their own publications by loan or photocopy to other requesting countries through the Universal Availability of Publications program. Other programs involve promoting preservation and conservation of library materials, promoting electronic transfer of data (Universal Data Flow and Telecommunication program), and promoting the improvement of library and information services in developing countries (Advancement of Librarianship in the Third World program).

IFLA issues a variety of monographs, professional reports, newsletters, and periodicals including *Libri*, *IFLA Journal*, and the *IFLA Directory*.

THE MEDICAL LIBRARY ASSOCIATION (MLA)

The Medical Library Association was founded in 1898 as the Association of Medical Librarians. It is the second oldest national library association in the United States and serves as the primary professional association for health sciences librarians in the United States and Canada. The purpose of the MLA is to promote the growth and development of medical libraries, to serve as an advocate for health information professionals, and to support the exchange of medical literature among its members. MLA also attempts to promote educational and professional growth among health sciences librarians and provides a considerable number of continuing education programs to meet this purpose.

There are more than 3,800 individual members, 1,200 institutional members, and a growing corporate membership. As of 2004 MLA had 14 geographic regional chapters and 23 special interest groups (SIGs) including those for mental health, clinical librarians, assessment and benchmarking, molecular biology and genomics, pediatric librarians, and primary care librarians.

In contrast to most other forms of librarianship, medical librarians can be certified, and MLA adopted its first formal certification program in 1949. The credentialing criteria established by MLA stress educational qualifications, knowledge in core areas of medical information, and different levels of professional development. Recognition is provided by MLA's Academy of Health Information Professionals (AHIP). The association also produces monographic and periodical publications, including the *Journal of the Medical Library Association* (JMLA), *MLA News,* and *Handbook of Medical Library Practice.*

SPECIAL LIBRARIES ASSOCIATION (SLA)

The Special Libraries Association is a not-for-profit corporation founded in 1909 as a response to a growing number of special libraries. It is an international association of librarians who work in special libraries serving such areas as business, research, government, and universities. There are more than 14,000 members from more than 70 countries. SLA has 57 regional chapters and 24 divisions representing various subject fields and interests, and numerous "caucuses," which are information groups that foster discussion and interaction among members with common interests. In 2003 SLA identified five core values for the association. They are leadership, service, innovation and continuous learning, results and accountability, and collaboration and partnering.

The association provides a variety of services, including consulting services to organizations that want to create or expand their information services and continuing education courses to advance the role of the professional librarian. Its Professional Development Center offers both distance learning and on-site learning experiences to assist in the management of special libraries.

SLA has become more politically active since the 1980s to deal with governmental policy areas that have direct effect on special libraries, such as copyright implementation and compliance, networking legislation, government information policies, and telecommunications. The monthly professional magazine of SLA is *Information Outlook*, which serves as a major professional continuing education tool for special librarians. The Web site is available at *www.sla.org*.

LIST OF ADDITIONAL LIBRARY ASSOCIATIONS OR CLOSELY-RELATED ORGANIZATIONS

General

   American Indian Library Association
   Canadian Library Association
   Council on Library Resources
   Friends of Libraries USA
   Information Industry Association
   National Information Standards Organization
   National Librarians Association

Archives/Bibliographical

   Bibliographical Society of America
   Society of American Archivists

Arts

   American Film and Video Association (formerly the Educational
      Film Library Association)
   Art Libraries Society of North America
   Music Library Association

Theatre Library Association

Asian-American

Asian/Pacific American Librarians Association
Chinese-American Library Association

Government/Federal

Association for Federal Information Resources Management
Chief Officers of State Library Agencies
Federal Library and Information Center Committee
National Association of Government Archives and Records Admin-
istrators

Law

American Association of Law Libraries

Library Education

Association for Library and Information Science Education

Religion

American Theological Library Association
Association of Christian Librarians
Association of Jewish Libraries
Catholic Library Association
Church and Synagogue Library Association
Lutheran Church Library Association

Business/Science

Association of Academic Health Sciences Library Directors
Patent and Trademark Depository Library Association
Society for Competitive Intelligence Professionals

Visual Images

Association for Information and Image Management
Association of Visual Science Librarians

Appendix C

Accredited Master's Programs in Library and Information Science in the United States and Canada

Alabama: University of Alabama. School of Library & Information Studies. Tuscaloosa, AL.
www.slis.ua.edu

Arizona: University of Arizona. School of Information Resources and Library Science. Tucson, AZ.
www.sir.arizona.edu

California: San Jose State University. School of Library and Information Science. San Jose, CA.
slisweb.sjsu.edu

University of California at Los Angeles. Graduate School of Education and Information Science. Department of Information Studies. Los Angeles, CA.
is.gseis.ucla.edu

Colorado: University of Denver. College of Education. Library and Information Science Program. Denver, CO.
www.du.edu/lis

Connecticut: Southern Connecticut State University. School of

Communications, Information and Library Science. Department of Information and Library Science. New Haven, CT.
www.southernct.edu/departments/ils

Florida: Florida State University. School of Information Studies. Tallahassee, FL.
www.lis.fsu.edu

University of South Florida. School of Library and Information Science. Tampa, FL.
www.cas.usf.edu/lis

Georgia: Clark Atlanta University. School of Library and Information Studies. Atlanta, GA.
www.cau.edu/acad_prog/library_info_stu/lib_main.html

Hawaii: University of Hawaii at Manoa. School of Library and Information Studies. Honolulu, HI.
www.hawaii.edu/slis

Illinois: Dominican University. Graduate School of Library and Information Science. River Forest, IL
www.dom.edu/gslis

University of Illinois. Graduate School of Library and Information Science. Champaign, IL.
alexia.lis.uiuc.edu

Indiana: Indiana University. School of Library and Information Science. Bloomington, IN.
www.slis.indiana.edu

Iowa: University of Iowa. School of Library and Information Science. Iowa City, IA.
www.uiowa.edu/~libsci

Kansas: Emporia State University. School of Library and Information Management. Emporia, KS.
slim.emporia.edu

Kentucky: University of Kentucky. School of Library and Information Science. Lexington, KY.
www.uky.edu/CommInfoStudies/SLIS

Louisiana:	Louisiana State University. School of Library and Information Science. Baton Rouge, LA. *slis.lsu.edu*
Maryland:	University of Maryland. College of Library and Information Studies. College Park, MD. *www.clis.umd.edu*
Massachusetts:	Simmons College. Graduate School of Library and Information Science. Boston, MA. *www.simmons.edu/programs/gslis*
Michigan:	University of Michigan. School of Information. Ann Arbor, MI. *www.si.umich.edu*
	Wayne State University. Library and Information Science Program. Detroit, MI. *www.lisp.wayne.edu*
Mississippi:	University of Southern Mississippi. School of Library and Information Science. Hattiesburg, MS. *www.usm.edu/~slis*
Missouri:	University of Missouri. School of Information Science and Learning Technologies. Columbia, MO. *sislt.missouri.edu*
New Jersey:	Rutgers University. School of Communication, Information and Library Studies. New Brunswick, NJ. *www.scils.rutgers.edu*
New York:	Long Island University. Palmer School of Library and Information Science. Brookville, NY. *palmer.cwpost.liu.edu*
	Pratt Institute. School of Information and Library Science. New York, NY. *www.pratt.edu/sils*
	Queens College. City University of New York. Graduate School of Library and Information Studies. Flushing, NY. *qcpages.qc.edu/GSLIS*

Saint John's University. Division of Library and Information Science. Jamaica, NY.
www.stjohns.edu

University at Albany, State University of New York. School of Information Science and Policy. Albany, NY.
www.albany.edu/sisp

University at Buffalo, State University of New York. School of Informatics. Department of Information and Library Studies. Buffalo, NY.
www.informatics.buffalo.edu/lis

Syracuse University. School of Information Studies. Syracuse, NY.
istweb.syr.edu

North Carolina: North Carolina Central University. School of Library and Information Sciences. Durham, NC.
www.nccuslis.org

University of North Carolina. School of Information and Library Science. Chapel Hill, NC.
www.ils.unc.edu

University of North Carolina at Greensboro. Department of Library and Information Studies. Greensboro, NC.
www.uncg.edu/lis

Ohio: Kent State University. School of Library and Information Science. Kent, OH.
www.slis.kent.edu

Oklahoma: University of Oklahoma. School of Library and Information Studies. Norman, OK.
www.ou.edu/cas/slis

Pennsylvania: Clarion University of Pennsylvania. Computer Information Science, and Library Science. Department of Library Science. Clarion, PA.
www.clarion.edu/libsci

Drexel University. College of Information Science and Technology. Philadelphia, PA.

www.cis.drexel.edu

University of Pittsburgh. School of Information Sciences. Pittsburgh, PA.
www.sis.pitt.edu

Puerto Rico: University of Puerto Rico. Escuela Graduada de Ciencia y Tecnologias de la Informacion. San Juan, PR.
egcti.upr.edu

Rhode Island: University of Rhode Island. Graduate School of Library and Information Studies. Kingston, RI.
www.uri.edu/artsci/lsc

South Carolina: University of South Carolina. College of Library and Information Science. Columbia, SC.
www.libsci.sc.edu

Tennessee: University of Tennessee. School of Information Sciences. Knoxville, TN.
www.sis.utk.edu

Texas: Texas Woman's University. School of Library and Information Studies. Denton, TX.
www.twu.edu/cope/slis

University of North Texas. School of Library and Information Sciences. Denton, TX.
www.unt.edu/slis

University of Texas at Austin. Graduate School of Library and Information Science. Austin, TX.
www.gslis.utexas.edu

Washington: University of Washington. Information School. Seattle, WA.
www.ischool.washington.edu

Washington, D.C.   Catholic University. School of Library and Information Science. Washington, DC.
slis.cua.edu

Wisconsin: University of Wisconsin—Madison. School of Library

and Information Science. Madison, WI.
www.slis.wisc.edu

University of Wisconsin—Milwaukee. School of Information Studies. Milwaukee, WI.
www.uwm.edu/Dept/SOIS

Canada: Dalhousie University. School of Library and Information Studies. Halifax, N.S.
www.mgmt.dal.ca/slis

McGill University. Graduate School of Library and Information Studies. Montreal, Que.
www.gslis.mcgill.ca

University of Alberta. Faculty of Library Science. Edmonton, Alta.
www.slis.ualberta.ca

University of British Columbia. School of Library, Archival, and Information Studies. Vancouver, B.C.
www.slais.ubc.ca

University of Montreal, Ecole de Bibliothéconomie et des Sciences de l'Information. Montreal, Que.
www.ebsi.umontreal.ca

University of Toronto. Faculty of Library and Information Studies. Toronto, Ont.
www.fis.utoronto.ca/index_MSIE.htm

University of Western Ontario. Master of Library and Information Science Program. London, Ont.
www.fims.uwo.ca/mlis/index.htm

Appendix D

ACM Code of Ethics and Professional Conduct

Adopted by ACM Council 10/16/92.

PREAMBLE

Commitment to ethical professional conduct is expected of every member (voting members, associate members, and student members) of the Association for Computing Machinery (ACM).

This Code, consisting of 24 imperatives formulated as statements of personal responsibility, identifies the elements of such a commitment. It contains many, but not all, issues professionals are likely to face. Section 1 outlines fundamental ethical considerations, while Section 2 addresses additional, more specific considerations of professional conduct. Statements in Section 3 pertain more specifically to individuals who have a leadership role, whether in the workplace or in a volunteer capacity such as with organizations like ACM. Principles involving compliance with this Code are given in Section 4.

The Code shall be supplemented by a set of Guidelines, which provide explanation to assist members in dealing with the various issues contained in the Code. It is expected that the Guidelines will be changed more frequently than the Code.

The Code and its supplemented Guidelines are intended to serve as a basis for ethical decision making in the conduct of professional work. Secondarily, they may serve as a basis for judging the merit of a formal complaint pertaining to violation of professional ethical standards.

It should be noted that although computing is not mentioned in the imperatives of Section 1, the Code is concerned with how these fundamental imperatives apply to one's conduct as a computing professional. These imperatives are expressed in a general form to emphasize that ethical principles which apply to computer ethics are derived from more general ethical principles.

It is understood that some words and phrases in a code of ethics are subject to varying interpretations, and that any ethical principle may conflict with other ethical principles in specific situations. Questions related to ethical conflicts can best be answered by thoughtful consideration of fundamental principles, rather than reliance on detailed regulations.

1. GENERAL MORAL IMPERATIVES.

As an ACM member I will ....

1.1 Contribute to society and human well-being.

This principle concerning the quality of life of all people affirms an obligation to protect fundamental human rights and to respect the diversity of all cultures. An essential aim of computing professionals is to minimize negative consequences of computing systems, including threats to health and safety. When designing or implementing systems, computing professionals must attempt to ensure that the products of their efforts will be used in socially responsible ways, will meet social needs, and will avoid harmful effects to health and welfare.

In addition to a safe social environment, human well-being includes a safe natural environment. Therefore, computing professionals who design and develop systems must be alert to, and make others aware of, any potential damage to the local or global environment.

1.2 Avoid harm to others.

"Harm" means injury or negative consequences, such as undesirable loss of information, loss of property, property damage, or unwanted environmental impacts. This principle prohibits use of computing technology in ways that result in harm to any of the following: users, the general public, employees, employers. Harmful actions include intentional destruction or modification of files and programs leading to serious loss of resources or unnecessary expenditure of human resources such as the time and effort required to purge systems of "computer viruses."

Well-intended actions, including those that accomplish assigned duties, may lead to harm unexpectedly. In such an event the responsible person or persons are obligated to undo or mitigate the negative consequences as much as possible. One way to avoid unintentional harm is to carefully consider potential impacts on all those affected by decisions made during design and implementation.

To minimize the possibility of indirectly harming others, computing professionals must minimize malfunctions by following generally accepted standards for system design and testing. Furthermore, it is often necessary to assess the social consequences of systems to project the likelihood of any serious harm to others. If system features are misrepresented to users, coworkers, or supervisors, the individual computing professional is responsible for any resulting injury.

In the work environment the computing professional has the additional obligation to report any signs of system dangers that might result in serious personal or social damage. If one's superiors do not act to curtail or mitigate such dangers, it may be necessary to "blow the whistle" to help correct the problem or reduce the risk. However, capricious or misguided reporting of violations can, itself, be harmful. Before reporting violations, all relevant aspects of the incident must be thoroughly assessed. In particular, the assessment of risk and responsibility must be credible. It is suggested that advice be sought from other computing professionals. See principle 2.5 regarding thorough evaluations.

1.3 Be honest and trustworthy.

Honesty is an essential component of trust. Without trust an organization cannot function effectively. The honest computing professional will not make deliberately false or deceptive claims about a system or system design, but will instead provide full disclosure of all pertinent system limitations and problems.

A computer professional has a duty to be honest about his or her own qualifications, and about any circumstances that might lead to conflicts of interest.

Membership in volunteer organizations such as ACM may at times place individuals in situations where their statements or actions could be interpreted as carrying the "weight" of a larger group of professionals. An ACM member will exercise care to not misrepresent ACM or positions and policies of ACM or any ACM units.

1.4 Be fair and take action not to discriminate.

The values of equality, tolerance, respect for others, and the principles of equal justice govern this imperative. Discrimination on the basis of race, sex, religion, age, disability, national origin, or other such factors is an explicit violation of ACM policy and will not be tolerated.

Inequities between different groups of people may result from the use or misuse of information and technology. In a fair society, all individuals would have equal opportunity to participate in, or benefit from, the use of computer resources regardless of race, sex, religion, age, disability, national origin or other such similar factors. However, these ideals do not justify unauthorized use of computer resources nor do they provide an adequate basis for violation of any other ethical imperatives of this code.

1.5 Honor property rights including copyrights and patent.

Violation of copyrights, patents, trade secrets and the terms of license agreements is prohibited by law in most circumstances. Even when software is not so protected, such violations are contrary to professional behavior. Copies of software should be made only with proper authorization. Unauthorized duplication of materials must not be condoned.

1.6 Give proper credit for intellectual property.

Computing professionals are obligated to protect the integrity of intellectual property. Specifically, one must not take credit for others' ideas or work, even in cases where the work has not been explicitly protected by copyright, patent, etc.

1.7 Respect the privacy of others.

Computing and communication technology enables the collection and exchange of personal information on a scale unprecedented in the history of civilization. Thus there is increased potential for violating the privacy of individuals and groups. It is the responsibility of professionals to maintain the privacy and integrity of data describing individuals. This includes taking precautions to ensure the accuracy of data, as well as protecting it from unauthorized access or accidental disclosure to inappropriate individuals. Furthermore, procedures must be established to allow individuals to review their records and correct inaccuracies.

This imperative implies that only the necessary amount of personal information be collected in a system, that retention and disposal periods for that information be clearly defined and enforced, and that personal information gathered for a specific purpose not be used for other purposes without consent of the individual(s). These principles apply to electronic communications, including electronic mail, and prohibit procedures that capture or monitor electronic user data, including messages,without the permission of users or bona fide authorization related to system operation and maintenance. User data observed during the normal duties of system operation and maintenance must be treated with strictest confidentiality, except in cases where it is evidence for the violation of law, organizational regulations, or this Code. In these cases, the nature or contents of that information must be disclosed only to proper authorities.

1.8 Honor confidentiality.

The principle of honesty extends to issues of confidentiality of information whenever one has made an explicit promise to honor confidentiality or, implicitly, when private information not directly related to the performance of one's duties becomes available. The ethical concern is to respect all obligations of confidentiality to employers, clients, and users unless discharged from such obligations by requirements of the law or other principles of this Code.

2. MORE SPECIFIC PROFESSIONAL RESPONSIBILITIES.

As an ACM computing professional I will ....

2.1 Strive to achieve the highest quality, effectiveness and dignity in both the process and products of professional work.

Excellence is perhaps the most important obligation of a professional. The computing professional must strive to achieve quality and to be cognizant of the serious negative consequences that may result from poor quality in a system.

2.2 Acquire and maintain professional competence.

Excellence depends on individuals who take responsibility for acquiring and maintaining professional competence. A professional must participate in setting standards for appropriate levels of competence, and strive to achieve those standards. Upgrading technical knowledge and competence can be achieved in several ways: doing independent study; attending seminars, conferences, or courses; and being involved in professional organizations.

2.3 Know and respect existing laws pertaining to professional work.

ACM members must obey existing local, state, province, national, and international laws unless there is a compelling ethical basis not to do so. Policies and procedures of the organizations in which one participates must also be obeyed. But compliance must be balanced with the recognition that sometimes existing laws and rules may be immoral or inappropriate and, therefore, must be challenged. Violation of a law or regulation may be ethical when that law or rule has inadequate moral basis or when it conflicts with another law judged to be more important. If one decides to violate a law or rule because it is viewed as unethical, or for any other reason, one must fully accept responsibility for one's actions and for the consequences.

2.4 Accept and provide appropriate professional review.

Quality professional work, especially in the computing profession, depends on professional reviewing and critiquing. Whenever appropriate, individual members should seek and utilize peer review as well as provide critical review of the work of others.

2.5 Give comprehensive and thorough evaluations of computer systems and their impacts, including analysis of possible risks.

Computer professionals must strive to be perceptive, thorough, and objective when evaluating, recommending, and presenting system descriptions and alternatives. Computer professionals are in a position of special trust, and therefore have a special responsibility to provide objective, credible evaluations to employers, clients, users, and the public. When providing evaluations the professional must also identify any relevant conflicts of interest, as stated in imperative 1.3.

As noted in the discussion of principle 1.2 on avoiding harm, any signs of danger from systems must be reported to those who have opportunity and/or responsibility to resolve them. See the guidelines for imperative 1.2 for more details concerning harm, including the reporting of professional violations.

2.6 Honor contracts, agreements, and assigned responsibilities.

Honoring one's commitments is a matter of integrity and honesty. For the computer professional this includes ensuring that system elements perform as intended. Also, when one contracts for work with another party, one has an obligation to keep that party properly informed about progress toward completing that work.

A computing professional has a responsibility to request a change in any assignment that he or she feels cannot be completed as defined. Only after serious consideration and with full disclosure of risks and concerns to the employer or client, should one accept the assignment. The major underlying principle here is the obligation to accept personal accountability for professional work. On some occasions other ethical principles may take greater priority.

A judgment that a specific assignment should not be performed may not be accepted. Having clearly identified one's concerns and reasons for that judgment, but failing to procure a change in that assignment, one may yet be obligated, by contract or by law, to proceed as directed. The computing professional's ethical judgment should be the final guide in deciding whether or not to proceed. Regardless of the decision, one must accept the responsibility for the consequences.

However, performing assignments "against one's own judgment" does not relieve the professional of responsibility for any negative consequences.

2.7 Improve public understanding of computing and its consequences.

Computing professionals have a responsibility to share technical knowledge with the public by encouraging understanding of computing, including the impacts of computer systems and their limitations. This imperative implies an obligation to counter any false views related to computing.

2.8 Access computing and communication resources only when authorized to do so.

Theft or destruction of tangible and electronic property is prohibited by imperative 1.2 - "Avoid harm to others." Trespassing and unauthorized use of a computer or communication system is addressed by this imperative. Trespassing includes accessing communication networks and computer systems, or accounts and/or files associated with those systems, without explicit authorization to do so. Individuals and organizations have the right to restrict access to their systems so long as they do not violate the discrimination principle (see 1.4). No one should enter or use another's computer system, software, or data files without permission. One must always have appropriate approval before using system resources, including communication ports, file space, other system peripherals, and computer time.

3. ORGANIZATIONAL LEADERSHIP IMPERATIVES.

As an ACM member and an organizational leader, I will ....

BACKGROUND NOTE: This section draws extensively from the draft IFIP Code of Ethics, especially its sections on organizational ethics and international concerns. The ethical obligations of organizations tend to be neglected in most codes of professional conduct, perhaps because these codes are written from the perspective of the individual member. This dilemma is addressed by stating these imperatives from the perspective of the organizational leader. In this context "leader" is viewed as any organizational member who has leadership or educational responsibilities. These imperatives generally may apply to organizations as well as their leaders. In this context "organizations" are corporations, government agencies, and other "employers," as well as volunteer professional organizations.

3.1 Articulate social responsibilities of members of an organizational unit and encourage full acceptance of those responsibilities.

Because organizations of all kinds have impacts on the public, they must accept responsibilities to society. Organizational procedures and attitudes oriented toward quality and the welfare of society will reduce harm to members of the public, thereby serving public interest and fulfilling social responsibility. Therefore, organizational leaders must encourage full participation in meeting social responsibilities as well as quality performance.

3.2 Manage personnel and resources to design and build information systems that enhance the quality of working life.

Organizational leaders are responsible for ensuring that computer systems enhance, not degrade, the quality of working life. When implementing a computer system, organizations must consider the personal and professional development, physical safety, and human dignity of all workers. Appropriate human-computer ergonomic standards should be considered in system design and in the workplace.

3.3 Acknowledge and support proper and authorized uses of an organization's computing and communication resources.

Because computer systems can become tools to harm as well as to benefit an organization, the leadership has the responsibility to clearly define appropriate and inappropriate uses of organizational computing resources. While the number and scope of such rules should be minimal, they should be fully enforced when established.

3.4 Ensure that users and those who will be affected by a system have their needs clearly articulated during the assessment and design of requirements; later the system must be validated to meet requirements.

Current system users, potential users and other persons whose lives may be affected by a system must have their needs assessed and incorporated in the statement of requirements. System validation should ensure compliance with those requirements.

3.5 Articulate and support policies that protect the dignity of users and others affected by a computing system.

Designing or implementing systems that deliberately or inadvertently demean individuals or groups is ethically unacceptable. Computer professionals who are in decision making positions should verify that systems are designed and implemented to protect personal privacy and enhance personal dignity.

3.6 Create opportunities for members of the organization to learn the principles and limitations of computer systems.

This complements the imperative on public understanding (2.7). Educational opportunities are essential to facilitate optimal participation of all organizational members. Opportunities must be available to all members to help them improve their knowledge and skills in computing, including courses that familiarize them with the consequences and limitations of particular types of systems. In particular, professionals must be made aware of the dangers of building systems around oversimplified models, the improbability of anticipating and designing for every possible operating condition, and other issues related to the complexity of this profession.

4. COMPLIANCE WITH THE CODE.

As an ACM member I will ....

4.1 Uphold and promote the principles of this Code.

The future of the computing profession depends on both technical and ethical excellence. Not only is it important for ACM computing professionals to adhere to the principles expressed in this Code, each member should encourage and support adherence by other members.

4.2 Treat violations of this code as inconsistent with membership in the ACM.

Adherence of professionals to a code of ethics is largely a voluntary matter. However, if a member does not follow this code by engaging in gross misconduct, membership in ACM may be terminated.

This Code and the supplemental Guidelines were developed by the Task Force for the Revision of the ACM Code of Ethics and Professional Conduct: Ronald E. Anderson, Chair, Gerald Engel, Donald Gotterbarn, Grace C. Hertlein, Alex Hoffman, Bruce Jawer, Deborah G. Johnson, Doris K. Lidtke, Joyce Currie Little, Dianne Martin, Donn B. Parker, Judith A. Perrolle, and Richard S. Rosenberg. The Task Force was organized by ACM/SIGCAS and funding was provided by the ACM SIG Discretionary Fund. This Code and the supplemental Guidelines were adopted by the ACM Council on October 16, 1992.

Appendix E

SCIP Code of Ethics for CI Professionals

To continually strive to increase the recognition and respect of the profession.

To comply with all applicable laws, domestic and international.

To accurately disclose all relevant information, including one's identity and organization, prior to all interviews.

To fully respect all requests for confidentiality of information.

To avoid conflicts of interest in fulfilling one's duties.

To provide honest and realistic recommendations and conclusions in the execution of one's duties.

To promote this code of ethics within one's company, with third-party contractors and within the entire profession.

To faithfully adhere to and abide by one's company policies, objectives, and guidelines.

—Copyright 2003 Society of Competitive Intelligence Professionals. Reprinted with permission.

Index